Business Policy

A Canadian Casebook

Third Edition

Business Policy

A Canadian Casebook

▷ Joseph N. Fry
▷ J. Peter Killing
▷ J. Michael Geringer
▷ Roderick E. White
The University of Western Ontario

Prentice Hall Canada Inc., Scarborough, Ontario

Canadian Cataloguing in Publication Data

Main entry under title:

Business policy. 3rd ed.

ISBN 0-13-105685-9

1. Corporate planning - Canada - Case studies.
2. Corporate planning - Case studies.
3. Industrial management - Canada - Case studies.
4. Industrial management - Case studies.
I. Fry, Joseph N., 1936-

HF5351.B87   1992   658.4'01'0971   C91-095569-7

Prentice Hall, Inc., Englewood Cliffs, New Jersey
Prentice-Hall International, Inc., London
Prentice-Hall of Australia, Pty., Ltd., Sydney
Prentice-Hall of India Pvt., Ltd., New Delhi
Prentice-Hall of Japan, Inc., Tokyo
Prentice-Hall of Southeast Asia (Pte.) Ltd., Singapore
Editora Prentice-Hall do Brasil Ltda., Rio de Janeiro
Prentice-Hall Hispanoamericana, S.A., Mexico

ISBN: 0-13-105685-9

Acquisitions Editor: Yolanda de Rooy
Developmental Editor: David Jolliffe
Production Editor: Amy Lui-Ma
Production Coordinator: Florence Rousseau
Cover Design: Monica Kompter
Page Layout: Anita Macklin

1 2 3 4 5   RRD   96 95 94 93 92

Printed and bound in the U.S.A. by R.R. Donnelley

Dedication

To our wives, Cherie Lind, Rebecca, Colette, and Sharon

Contents

PART FOUR INCORPORATING MANAGEMENT PREFERENCES 301

Preface

This is the third edition of *Business Policy: A Canadian Casebook* over a ten-year span. It is being published at a time of unprecedented change for Canadian businesses and Canadian executives. Canada, torn from her relative insularity and her reliance on natural resources for trade, is being pressed into a tougher competitive world of falling trade barriers and globalizing industries.

Think of the differences that are reflected in the evolution, over the various editions, of our Ontario Wine Industry material. In 1982 our attention was focused on Inniskillin Wineries and the prospects for success as a niche business in the highly protected and regulated provincial industry of the late 1970s. Later, in the 1989 edition, we dealt with the strategic initiatives of Hillebrand Wineries as it sought to adapt to an erosion of government support and the prospect of increasing foreign competitive pressure. Now, in 1992, we deal with questions about the very existence of the industry, and the possible sustaining or end-game strategies of T.G. Bright.

We have worked to develop cases that reflect these changing realities. For example, The Note on The Global Airline Industry and the PWA Corporation cases explore the causes and consequences of a globalizing industry; the Molson and IPL cases deal with the impact of the Free Trade Agreement with the United States; Cambridge Products and Japanese-American Seating examine the issues of working with and in other cultures; and Hiram Walker-Gooderham & Worts and Nestlé-Rowntree present the challenges of achieving strategic change on an international scale. In total, 24 of the 37 cases in the book are completely new, and 13 are revised from the second edition.

As always, the underlying theme of the cases is that of a general manager facing issues of strategy formulation and implementation, and strategic change. The cases are complex and intended for students with a basic command of the functional areas of business. All have been classroom tested at Western, and many are used at other schools.

The cases in this book were prepared with the generous cooperation and assistance of a large number of executives. One of the continuing delights of the casewriting process is the opportunity for us to meet and to learn from these individuals. We owe them a great, collective vote of thanks.

There has been a notable change in the roster of authors for this edition. Don Thain has shifted his attention to a major research project on corporate governance; we thank him for his help in the past and wish him success in his very important undertaking. His place is being taken by Mike Geringer, who has taught Business Policy at Western for four years, and has contributed important ideas and materials to the development of the course.

Casewriting is an expensive process. It would not be possible without continued support from the general coffers of The Fund for Excellence at the School of Business Administration, The University of Western Ontario. Some of the businesses that we were studying also helped us indirectly by contributing to the Fund, and others, directly, by picking up expenses ranging from airline tickets to the proverbial free lunch. Thank you all. We would also like to thank the International Institute for Management Development (IMD) in Lausanne, Switzerland, and Queen's University for permission to use their cases.

The encouragement that is essential in sustaining a case development program comes from a supportive administrative context at Western, and from the help of our immediate colleagues. Jim Hatch, Chairman of Research, has been a consistent supporter, as have Dean Bud Johnston, Acting Dean Al Mikalachki, Dean Adrian Ryans, and Associate Dean Terry Deutscher. We have been greatly assisted by our teaching colleagues who have contributed cases, as noted below, and who have been an essential part of the work of testing, refining and, indeed, figuring out how to teach the cases: Paul Beamish (IKEA, Victoria Heavy Equipment, Wayside Industries), the late Harold Crookell, Mary Crossan, Gerald Higgins, and Allen Morrison (Diaper Wars). We have also had the opportunity of working with a cooperative and skilled group of Ph.D. candidates and research assistants, whose names and individual contributions are acknowledged in the cases on which they worked. Finally, we would like to thank Peter Richardson of Queen's who participated in the Noranda-Andacollo case, and Tom Poynter, now a management consultant, who did most of the background work on the Victoria Heavy Equipment case.

We are indebted at our publisher Prentice Hall Canada to Yolanda de Rooy, David Jolliffe, and Amy Lui-Ma, for their help, respectively, in promoting, producing, and editing this book. At Western we are, in particular, obliged to Karen Scrivens who has maintained her cheerfulness as she managed us through her second edition of this casebook.

Joseph N. Fry
J. Peter Killing
J. Michael Geringer
Roderick E. White

London, Ontario
January 1992

Introduction

All of the cases in this book deal with problems facing general managers. Although some are disguised, all are based on real situations and raise issues which are in some way related to a firm's strategy. We have presented the cases in a logical and orderly progression—from analysis (what are the key elements in this firm's situation?) through desired action (what should be done?) to detailed implementation (how should it be done?). However, we do not recommend that the casebook be used alone. It should be employed in conjunction with either a policy textbook or an organized set of readings that present the basic concepts of strategy formulation and implementation, and the management of strategic change.

Our preferred text is *Strategic Analysis and Action,* second edition,[1] and the Diamond E model on which it is based. This model links the firm's strategy with its environment, its resources, the preferences of its managers, and its organization. We have used it for a number of years, and have found that it permits useful insights not only into the cases presented in this book but also into a wide variety of other general management situations.

The key to using the Diamond E model is to begin by identifying the firm's existing or proposed strategy. In *Strategic Analysis and Action,* second edition, we suggest that a description of a firm's strategy should include its goals, product-market strategy and competitive strategy. The model can then be used to assess methodically the new or existing strategy by means of the following questions:

1. Is the strategy internally consistent?
2. Is the strategy consistent with the environment?
3. Is the strategy consistent with present or obtainable resources?
4. Is the strategy consistent with the personal preferences and beliefs of top management?
5. Is the strategy consistent with the firm's organizational attributes?
6. Is the strategy consistent over time with anticipated internal or external change?
7. Is consistency being demonstrated by results (that is, by performance over time)?

---

[1]J.N. Fry and J.P. Killing, *Strategic Analysis and Action,* second edition (Scarborough, Ontario: Prentice Hall Canada Inc., 1989).

The Diamond-E Framework

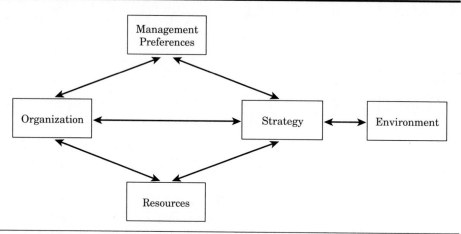

SOURCE: J.N. Fry and J.P. Killing, *Strategic Analysis and Action,* second edition (Scarborough, Ontario: Prentice Hall Canada Inc., 1989).

We have grouped the cases according to the strategy relationships in the Diamond-E model that they emphasize. This is a rough cut as strategic issues do not come in neat packages, but it does provide for a flow of emphasis over the progression of a course. The cases which link strategy with organizational attributes are treated in Part Six because they represent complex situations requiring a good preliminary understanding of the other strategy relationships.

The three cases which comprise Part Seven: Managing Strategic Change are the most difficult in the book. In these, the questions of *what* must be done and *how* it should be done need to be addressed simultaneously. The section in *Strategic Analysis and Action* dealing with this topic introduces three new variables for consideration: the *pace* at which the general manager should attempt to effect change, the *targets* to focus efforts on, and the *tactics* which should be employed. Each issue deserves close examination in the three cases.

We hope that you find these cases enjoyable as well as instructive. We have lived with most of them for several years now, yet they still give us a great deal of satisfaction, provoke argument among us, and give us new insights.

PART

1 INTRODUCTION TO STRATEGIC MANAGEMENT

MEDTRON LIMITED

Joseph N. Fry
with Lawrence Ferguson
and Richard Smith

In early 1983, Dean Nichols, president of Medtron Limited, a fast growing Canadian manufacturer of wheelchairs, was preparing for a strategic planning session with his management group. In recent years Medtron had met its sales growth and dealer expansion objectives and earned healthy profits. Nichols saw tremendous potential for further growth. He was concerned, nevertheless, that growth might outpace the company's financial and manufacturing capabilities and that a larger scale operation would create inflexibility. "Our planning job," said Nichols, "is to identify any constraints and develop a strategy that maintains our reputation for quality products and fast, personalized service."

COMPANY HISTORY

In 1962, National Medical Canada, a wholly owned subsidiary of National Medical Inc. of the United States, opened the first wheelchair manufacturing facility in Canada at a site near Toronto. The plant was built largely as a result of Canadian tariffs and the low level of the Canadian dollar. National Medical built its market share to over 90% of the Canadian market by capitalizing on a blend of Canadian manufactured goods and selected imported items.[1]

In 1967 Lorne Thomas, a National Medical Canada vice president, left the company to start a competitive firm, Medtron Limited, in Markham, Ontario. Medtron was only marginally successful, however, because it was so difficult to break National Medical's hold on wheelchair marketing channels. Faced with continuing mediocre performance, Thomas decided in 1974 to put the company up for sale.

Dean Nichols and James Dixon purchased Medtron from Thomas. Nichols, 33, had previously been working as the manager of a printing equipment plant.

---

[1] The names of the industry participants and certain company and industry data have been disguised. Accordingly, the data in the case should not be used for research purposes.

His partner, Dixon, 47, was entering this business from the presidency of a construction materials firm. Under the new owners, the problem of dealing with the marketing channels assumed top priority. They concentrated on improving product quality, retail prices and dealer margins. They were successful, and by 1978 Medtron sales had doubled and the company was represented in 30 out of the approximately 110 outlets in Canada.

With this new growth, Nichols and Dixon started to add to their management team. Mark Dixon (James' son) joined Medtron in 1978 to assist with finance and marketing. He brought to the company several years of solid marketing and administrative experience with a wholesale travel tour operator. In April 1979, with the untimely death of James Dixon, Dean Nichols became president and Mark Dixon assumed the role of vice president responsible for finance and sales.

Anticipating further growth, Medtron hired two new executives in the fall of 1979. Curtis Dixon (Mark Dixon's brother) became vice president of sales and Gord Jackson (Mark Dixon's brother-in-law) vice president of production. Before joining Medtron, Curtis Dixon had been the top salesperson at a chemicals company, while Gord Jackson had been a high school teacher.

The new management team maintained the record of the original Nichols/ Dixon partnership. By the end of 1982, sales were $2.37 million, the company was represented in over 100 dealer outlets, and profits were a healthy 6% of sales (Exhibits 1 and 2). Furthermore, management was forecasting that sales for 1983 would top $3 million and that profit rates would stay in line with recent experience.

THE CANADIAN WHEELCHAIR INDUSTRY

Total wheelchair unit sales in Canada in 1982 were estimated at between 19 000 and 23 000 units. This generated about $18 to $22 million in sales at the manufacturer level, including between $3 and $5 million in accessory products. The corresponding estimates for the U.S. market were about 230 000 units and revenues of U.S.$ 190 million. Both markets were growing at about 10% per year.

A rough breakdown of the Canadian market is given in Table 1. Standard chairs provided basic transportation and were virtually all manually driven. Specialty chairs were offered in an array of sizes and weights, and with several optional features, including power drive. Custom chairs involved fitting a unique chair for individual needs and preferences. Factory prices ranged across a spectrum from about $250 for standard chairs, to around $800 and $1 500 for manual and powered specialty chairs respectively, and to over $2 000 for custom models. Imports were a significant factor in the market, particularly in the specialty and custom chair categories.

TABLE 1 Primary Classification of the Canadian Wheelchair Market, 1981

Product	Total Market Units (000)	Total Market ($000 000)	Imports ($000 000)
Standard	4–6	1–2	Minimal
Specialty			
Manual	12.5–13.5	9.5–10.5	
Powered	2.5–3.5	4–5	8
Custom	Small volumes		
Accessories	—	3.5–4.5	2.5
Total	19–23	18–22	10.5

For three decades, up to the mid-1970s, there had been little innovation in the wheelchair market. Industry sources attributed the sluggish product and market development to the dominant position of National Medical, the passive nature of the mobility impaired population, and the entanglements rising from government and third-party involvement in the industry. Since the mid-1970s, however, more sympathetic public attitudes had generated an increasingly sensitive and liberalized government approach to the mobility impaired. From this changing environment a more competitive and dynamic industry was emerging.

About 75% of injury-related wheelchair use was temporary, lasting less than six months, and the incidence of need was spread throughout the population. Such temporary requirements were usually met by rental. Disease-related usage was concentrated among the elderly, with arthritis as a major cause. In total there were about 90 000 continuing users in Canada, of which about 60–70% were elderly.

Buyer Segments

The wheelchair market was divided into institutional and individual-user buying segments. Institutional buyers, such as governments and non-profit and private organizations, typically purchased standard chairs in multi-unit orders for use by hospitals, old-age facilities, transportation services and so on. The purchasing process usually involved occupational therapists, social workers and purchasing agents. Supplier offers were assessed in terms of price and product flexibility, operating simplicity and efficiency. Depending on local practices, institutional buyers purchased either directly from a manufacturer or through a dealer.

The process of initial purchase or rental by an individual user was heavily influenced by occupational therapists employed by any of a variety of health service agencies. The therapists helped individual patients determine their specific needs. Various product characteristics, such as weight, size, comfort, reliability, service, price and portability, would affect the decision. The user was typically rather passive, as described by the following comments of a first-time purchaser:

> I didn't choose my chair in the beginning; I just sat in the hallway of the rehab hospital as the O.T. and the wheelchair salesman sized me up. The result was a pressed-steel 55 pound NM as wide as the Texas Panhandle, with arm rests and . . . rests like trusses on the Golden Gate Bridge. And because I had it (i.e., was given it) I felt I needed it.
>
> I didn't question the chair. The first order of business was . . . to make the way smooth again, get back to doing things naturally . . . which meant incorporating a wheelchair into my body image until I could use it as unconsciously as a pencil . . . .

The product life for wheelchairs was estimated to range from four to eight years. Repeat purchases were less likely to be so influenced by occupational therapists, but users, having adapted to a particular make and model of chair, were often resistant to change.

Third-party funding by government agencies, insurance companies and so forth paid for roughly 90% of a user's purchase. Funding arrangements were being progressively consolidated into simplified government programs, but the situation from a marketing standpoint remained complex because of provincial jurisdiction over the funding. There was no consistency in Canada from province to province regarding the user funding, or the criteria for eligible wheelchairs and wheelchair manufacturers. Medtron, for example, was an authorized manufacturer in all provinces except Saskatchewan, Manitoba, Prince Edward Island and Quebec—about one third of the total market. In 1980, Medtron had lost a substantial amount of regular sales in Quebec when the provincial government applied a "Buy Quebec" policy to wheelchair funding programs. National Medical responded to the policy by establishing an assembly operation in Quebec. In Saskatchewan, Quebec and Manitoba, the provincial governments were the primary customers for all wheelchairs, buying either direct from the manufacturer or from suitable provincial dealers.

Channels of Distribution

Roughly 90% of manufacturer sales in Canada flowed through dealers and thence to institutions (15%) and individual users (75%). The balance of sales was mostly standard models sold directly by manufacturers to institutions.

The 55 dealers who operated approximately 125 outlets in Canada were independently owned and carried a diverse line of medical equipment and supplies. Wheelchairs typically provided dealers with 20–30% of their sales volume, at initial markups of 30–50%. Under certain government programs, dealer margins were limited to a fixed percentage. Discounts of up to 20% were common for large purchases. Dealers normally maintained the chairs they sold and most provided a rental service.

Dealers attempted to represent several wheelchair manufacturers, but carried limited inventories—particularly in the case of specialty chairs. Dealer sales personnel were generally well versed in product specifications; some were occupational therapists. A tendency toward multi-unit dealerships was developing in the industry, led by the John Young Ltd. firm in Ontario which now consisted of 18 units.

Few Canadian dealers gave preference to one brand over another because margins were similar and there was a concern for customer and manufacturer alienation. One dealer explained, "Look, what am I going to do? Fifty percent of the people who come in the door ask for a National Medical chair. For those people who don't have a particular product in mind, all I do is show them my stock, explain the features of the chairs, and then let them choose. I don't push Medtron over any other company because there is no real difference in the chairs and I don't want National Medical to get mad at me and withdraw their products."

Many dealers in the United States carried private label as well as manufacturer brands. This practice appeared to be creeping into the Canadian market as well, although the absence of large dealerships restricted this activity to some degree. Medtron was currently providing John Young with private-label specialty chairs. Medtron attempted to offset the lower margins on the private-label chairs with minimum purchase requirements and annual volume commitments.

Competition

The Canadian wheelchair industry consisted of five firms with domestic production capacity. Three of these firms, National Medical Canada Ltd., Medtron Ltd., and Universal Mobile Aids Ltd., had full manufacturing capabilities, while the other two firms, LeClair Ltd. and Franklin Wheelchair Canada Ltd. were assemblers of semi-finished wheelchairs. In addition, there was import competition from a large number of specialized firms in the high tech, high price end of the market.

National Medical Canada

In 1982, National Medical Canada's American parent had corporate sales of over $150 million and had facilities in both North America and Europe. The parent firm's performance had been faltering in recent years. Industry observers suggested that the causes included a lack of innovation, the advent of aggressive competition and a poorly implemented program to consolidate U.S. production in a single facility.

In Canada, National Medical was the market leader, with about 60 to 70% of the total Canadian wheelchair market. This was a drop from the virtual monopoly the company enjoyed throughout the 1960s and 1970s. National Medical's competitive advantage was rooted in its established name and distribution, its full product line and its large and efficient assembly-line production facility. In recent years, however, market demand for more individualized specialty wheelchairs had offset some of the efficiency benefits of the company's assembly-line process. Even loyal dealers were reported to be growing impatient with National Medical's long delivery times on specialty chair orders. The Canadian firm was also said to be suffering from product and part delays due to the problems in the American operations.

Franklin Wheelchair Canada Ltd.

Franklin Canada was the subsidiary of Ohio-based Franklin Wheelchair Inc. In the past five years Franklin Inc. had achieved significant growth in sales and profits in the United States and had become the second largest international wheelchair producer. In the battle to increase share, Franklin had provided quality and innovative products and had undercut National Medical prices.

In 1980 Franklin Canada was formed and a small distribution centre was built in Brantford, Ontario. Franklin had taken this step only after searching without success for a joint venture partner in Canada. Medtron, in particular, had turned down overtures from Franklin. Subsequently, in order to market their products, Franklin had signed a five-year exclusive contract with a regional Canadian dealer. This arrangement had proved unwise, because the dealers' own volume was limited and other Canadian dealers were unwilling to purchase through a competing intermediary. Thus, until 1985 at least, Franklin was not expected to be much of a factor in the Canadian market.

Universal Mobile Aids

Universal was established in 1980 to research, develop, manufacture and market innovative health care products. The principal owners of this private company were four wealthy Toronto businessmen. In September 1981, the company brought out a state-of-the-art power wheelchair. The product was well received in both domestic and export markets, although high retail prices ($4 000 to $5 000 in Canada) and high maintenance costs seemed a barrier to major sales volumes. Although this was currently the only wheelchair produced by the company, several new products were in the development stage, including a wheelchair with an advanced transmitter for remote control of lights, appliances and the telephone. Universal Mobile Aids appeared to be well positioned to become a major force in power wheelchairs, especially in the higher priced end of the market. They had an excellent product development group, a skilled labour force, a flexible manufacturing facility and very substantial indirect financial backing. Medtron had been benefiting from Universal's growth, since Medtron was a major upholstery supplier to Universal.

LeClair Ltd

In the spring of 1982, the Quebec government awarded a $500 000 grant to Charboneau & Carson, a Quebec based bicycle manufacturer, located in the riding of a provincial minister. Concurrently, the federal government awarded an undisclosed amount to the same company through a regional industrial grant. These awards were given with the understanding that Charboneau & Carson would purchase and revitalize LeClair Ltd., a small wheelchair manufacturing firm in Drummondville, Quebec. LeClair's position had improved and the company was now a significant purchaser of Medtron supplied parts and assemblies. LeClair was actively lobbying the Quebec government, which purchased most of the wheelchairs used in the province, for a contract to supply all the government's requirements. It was too early to say whether they would be successful.

Import Competition

Aside from specialty wheelchairs imported and resold by National Medical and Franklin, import competition in Canada was confined largely to the ultralight sports wheelchair and power-chair market segments.

Ultralight sports chairs were imported from the U.S., where firms such as Motech and Modern Wheels Inc. specialized in chairs that were fast, manoeuvrable and strong enough to withstand the rigours of competitive sports. Special designs and materials were required and the chairs retailed at prices more than 50% higher than those of ordinary specialty chairs. The volume of sales had not yet reached the point where domestic manufacturers felt that the entry costs (from $500 000 to $750 000 for special fabricating equipment alone) were justified.

Power wheelchairs were another area where foreign firms, such as Berlin GmbH of West Germany, dominated the market. Even National Medical imported the bulk of its power wheelchair requirements from its parent company. Although the power wheelchair market was a growth segment, the required manufacturing investment posed a significant barrier to entry. For Medtron, for example, it would require at least $1.5 million to add power capability. The initial success of Universal Mobile Aids, however, was being carefully watched by domestic manufacturers.

Government Policy

In recent years, most provincial governments had increased the financial support available to individual wheelchair purchasers. The improved funding arrangements had played a part in the growth of specialty chair demand and, some argued, increased the turnover rate for chairs. Government health-care budgets, however, were coming under severe pressure. There was some concern that more stringent policies might be adopted with respect to user support and industry pricing. It was fully expected that the rationalization of support programs now under way would continue in most provinces, making the relevant government agency a significant force in qualifying manufacturers, establishing product standards, and influencing prices.

The federal government imposed a tariff of 10% on imported wheelchair models that were being simultaneously manufactured domestically. It was expected that even this level of protection would be reduced over time, as the result of general international liberalization under the General Agreement on Tariffs and Trade. Both the federal and Ontario governments offered programs of assistance to manufacturers seeking to export wheelchairs.

Most specific government programs to support research and development in health care were aimed at industry segments with higher profiles than wheelchairs. Nevertheless support was available to firms such as Medtron under general programs for industrial research assistance.

MEDTRON OPERATIONS

Medtron operations were characterized by hands-on management. Dean Nichols tried to divide his time equally between product-line development on the one hand and his presidential duties on the other hand. Gord Jackson was responsible for day-to-day operations in the areas of production, purchasing, shipping and receiving. Curtis Dixon was responsible for marketing and sales and Mark Dixon's primary responsibilities were in accounting, financial management and administration.

The Medtron management group worked informally with a minimum of structured reports and controls. The functional vice presidents helped each other out when workloads were off balance. All of the managers were pressed by the requirements of everyday business. Attention to immediate issues had led to delays in the development of new systems for accounting and production control and at times to tension over jobs that remained undone. The overall view however, was, as one manager put it, "I'm beleaguered . . . but I like feeling beleaguered."

Marketing

In the Canadian market, Medtron considered itself a full-line manufacturer of manual wheelchairs capable of serving all demand segments. The company had also capitalized on recent opportunities for part and assembly sales to other manufacturers.

Medtron's wheelchair line consisted of one standard and seven specialty models, including a sports model. Each specialty model was available in several versions, based on optional features and accessories. A breakdown of sales trends by model category is given in Table 2. Medtron intended to increase its emphasis on specialty chairs to take advantage of their higher profit margins and the company's technical capability and production flexibility.

TABLE 2 Medtron Sales Mix, 1979–82

	1982	*1981*	*1980*	*1979*
Total Revenues ($000)	$2 365	1 968	1 504	1 090
Wheelchairs	1 665	1 463	1 329	1 040
Parts	700	505	175	50
Unit Sales	4 434	3 910	3 304	2 704
Percent Unit Sales by Class				
Standard	37	39	35	39
Low price specialty	35	25	17	18
Premium specialty	28	36	48	43

To build a position in the face of National Medical's historic dominance, Medtron had emphasized a quality product, rapid delivery and personalized dealer service. Medtron's prices ranged from par to a 15% discount relative to comparable National Medical items.

By early 1983, Medtron had achieved representation in about 80% of Canadian outlets. Curtis Dixon had recently hired two representatives to help him service the Canadian dealers—one that worked out of Vancouver, the other out of Toronto. In doing so, he hoped to increase Medtron's sales per outlet by improving dealer product knowledge and providing even more personal, effective response to problems and inquiries. The new salespeople were also to prospect for new dealers and eventually, Dixon hoped, do missionary selling with occupational therapists and government agencies. Both of the new representatives were paid a straight salary.

In the marketplace, dealers reported that Medtron's product quality had improved over the years to a level of equivalence with National Medical and that Medtron's delivery times were substantially better (three weeks compared to eight weeks or more). In the premium specialty segment, however, Medtron did not match the competition in product variety and features.

In foreign markets, Medtron had just engaged its first sales representative in the United States. The intention here was to sell premium-priced private-label models to northeastern U.S. dealers.

Dean Nichols and Curtis Dixon were also starting to investigate the potential for technology transfer and export to developing countries with the assistance of government agencies. The general idea being pursued was to provide technical assistance to start up companies in different countries, to be followed by the export of parts and assemblies and continuing consultation in design and manufacturing.

Curtis Dixon has initiated Medtron's recent move into the U.S. He believed that the company's best growth prospects were in wider market and dealer coverage and was interested in further expansion of this nature.

Manufacturing

Medtron had significantly increased its plant capacity in 1980 and was anticipating further expansion in 1984. The company leased its plant facilities and much of its equipment to preserve capital for operating requirements. This policy resulted, however, in annual lease payment obligations which exceeded $125 000. Dean Nichols had a major hand in plant layout, tooling and equipment acquisition.

A schematic diagram of the manufacturing process is given in Exhibit 3. There were four major production areas: machining, brazing, upholstering, and assembly. In the machine shop area, standard carbon steel tubing and plate was cut, punched, drilled, and bent into parts required by downstream processes. Some of these parts were transferred to the brazing area, where skilled brazers sub-assembled the pieces on jigs and welded them together. The brazing area produced many of the wheelchair frame components, such as side frames and cross pieces, as well as smaller parts such as footrest brackets and brake mounts. All metal parts, including parts not requiring brazing, were sent out for electroplating with chrome and nickel. In parallel to the above operations, wheelchair seats, backs and arm pads were fabricated in the upholstery shop. In the final step of the process all parts, including those purchased, were brought together for assembly. Each chair was assembled by one person.

Production scheduling was based on confirmed sales orders. The combination of sales growth, increasing product variety and the desire to maintain fast and flexible delivery had led to more complicated operations. Almost continuous adjustments to schedules were required to maintain an orderly transfer of parts through the system. Medtron relied heavily on Gord Jackson's experience and that of his three shop supervisors to balance priorities and keep inventories, costs and delivery times under control.

Jackson spent almost half his time on purchasing—which he saw as essential since almost two thirds of Medtron's cost of goods sold was made up of purchased items. There was very little systems support available for inventory control and product costing, but development work was underway in both areas. The working relationships and morale among shop supervisors and personnel were very good, as indicated, for example, by the very low turnover rate.

In product development, Medtron was pursuing a general market preference for lighter chairs by exploring the possibility of building a wheelchair frame from lightweight composite materials. Pacific Hydro had approached Medtron to jointly pursue research into the development of a state-of-the-art, battery powered, lightweight wheelchair for Expo '86 in Vancouver. Medtron accepted Pacific Hydro's offer and was currently seeking funding from the National Research Council. Transport Canada had already approved funding for 75% of the $650 000 project. Dean Nichols was combining his engineering expertise with an outside consultant to do the wheelchair design work. Medtron retained the right to patent any wheelchair-related outcome of the project. Although they were enthusiastic about the project, Medtron's management were also concerned about the implications of such large scale commitment for their financial resources and manufacturing operations.

Finance and Administration

Mark Dixon was responsible for a host of day-to-day accounting and administrative matters including order-invoice processing, cash management, receivables, payroll and trade payables administration, preparation of statements, and so on. He was assisted by a small bookkeeping staff.

Medtron had recently purchased a microcomputer and Mark Dixon was in the process of computerizing these department operations. As the strictly accounting tasks were mastered, Dixon intended to push further and automate inventory control and production scheduling. The conversion to the computer was taking longer than anticipated, however, because it had been necessary to reorganize the company's procedures and because Dixon himself was very busy with on-going tasks.

Mark Dixon was also responsible for forecasting and budgeting and, in his administrative role, with maintaining relationships with outside parties such as the bank and government agencies. He hoped to spend more time on all of these developmental activities when the computer transition was completed. For the moment, that was his priority: "We have to get that computer on stream so that we can improve our control of operations."

The Future

The Medtron management team was anxious for the company to grow and increase its significance, first in domestic and then in international markets. Dean Nichol's attitude toward the next few years was clear-cut, "It's easy for us to grow quickly. I can also understand how easy it is to become bulky, bureaucratic and to forget about our customers. That certainly won't happen as long as I'm around."

EXHIBIT 1   Medtron Income Statements, 1978–82

	1982	1981	1980	1979	1978
Sales	$2 365 662	$1 968 286	$1 504 419	$1 080 048	$924 118
Materials	986 875	785 307	641 446	404 978	379 985
Wages	575 635	465 689	382 123	299 684	262 337
Cost of goods sold	1 562 510	1 250 996	1 023 569	704 664	642 322
Gross profit	803 152	717 290	480 851	375 385	281 797
Expenses:					
Factory overhead	221 654	189 257	154 203	90 440	73 268
Selling and					
administration	424 852	366 629	281 989	226 836	201 543
Total expenses	646 505	555 885	436 192	317 276	274 811
Profit before taxes	156 647	161 405	44 659	58 109	6 986
Less income taxes	13 101	10 491	2 721	7 835	0
Profit after taxes	$ 143 546	$ 150 914	$ 41 938	$ 50 273	$ 6 986

EXHIBIT 2   Medtron Balance Sheet, 1978–82

	1982	1981	1980	1979	1978
Assets					
Cash	$ 300	$ 300	$ 300	$ 300	$ 300
Accounts receivable	421 937	312 932	321 193	198 617	136 134
Inventory	357 003	312 625	244 967	194 710	137 813
Other current assets	24 806	16 192	26 130	32 607	14 123
Total current assets	804 046	642 049	592 590	426 234	288 370
Fixed assets	110 630	79 123	56 102	26 640	25 584
Other assets	8 363	8 363	8 363	8 363	8 363
Total assets	$ 923 039	$ 729 535	$ 657 055	$ 461 237	$ 322 317
Liabilities					
Bank operating loan	$170 849	$139 890	$240 543	$125 374	$ 85 252
Accounts payable	245 744	196 786	207 504	149 228	110 227
Term loans payable	49 500	43 650	12 600	13 538	10 203
Other current liabilities	33 236	29 990	2 729	7 835	0
Total current liabilities	499 329	410 316	463 376	295 975	205 682
Long-term debt	118 371	103 093	81 374	62 957	64 601
Preferred shares	30 000	30 000	30 000	30 000	30 000
Common shares	7 500	7 500	7 500	7 500	7 500
Retained earnings	267 839	178 627	74 805	64 805	14 532
Total equity	305 339	216 127	112 305	102 305	52 032
Total liabilities	$ 923 039	$ 729 535	$ 657 055	$ 461 237	$ 322 317

EXHIBIT 3 Medtron Manufacturing Process Flow

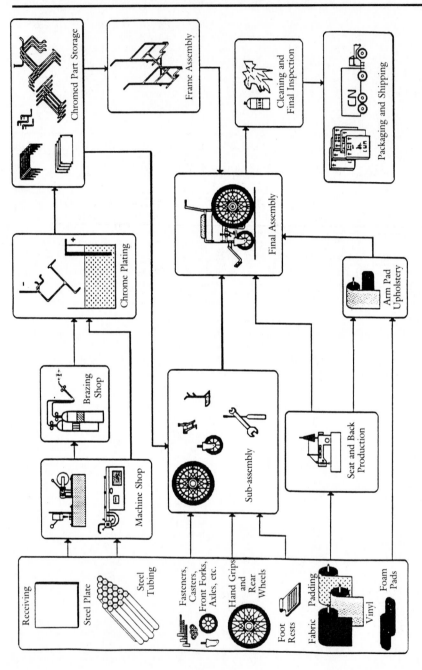

PART

2 ANALYZING THE COMPETITIVE ENVIRONMENT

NOTE ON THE ONTARIO WINE INDUSTRY — 1991

Joseph N. Fry and Honorio Todino

Commercial wine-making began in Ontario in 1811. By the turn of the century over 4 000 acres of grapes were under cultivation, and by 1916 Ontario had ten wine companies. Following World War I, the number of companies grew rapidly, swept along by the contrary political currents of the prohibition movement. Due to pressure from grape growers, wine escaped the clutches of the Ontario Temperance Act and became the only alcoholic beverage legally sold in Ontario. By 1926, there were forty-three companies and by 1927, fifty-seven.

As the only legal supplier of alcohol in Ontario with a large—if illegal—export market in the United States, the industry had to struggle hard to meet demand. With considerable effort and by adding formaldehyde, coal tar, and dyes to provide flavour, body, and colour to the wines, some companies managed to "stretch" a ton of grapes from a normal yield of 700 litres of wine to as much as 2 700 litres.

Unfortunately, what the government gave, it could also take away. In 1927, the Ontario Temperance Act was repealed, giving way to legal but controlled sale of all alcoholic beverages. The Liquor Authority and Control Board, later the Liquor Control Board of Ontario (LCBO), was established to provide government supervision of the quality, distribution and pricing of wine and spirit products. The combination of legal competition from spirits and beer and higher costs due to government quality standards devastated the wine industry. By the early 1940s there were only eight wineries left in operation.

There was little development in the industry until the late 1960s when increases in the demand for table wines presented new opportunities. Domestic producers moved to adapt their product lines and production capacity, and in 1974, Inniskillin Wines became the first new winery to open in decades. Inniskillin was a "boutique" winery—small compared to the established wineries, but focused on the production of quality table wines. By 1991, a dozen more boutique wineries were opened. In the meantime, however, a General Agreement on Tariffs and Trade (GATT) ruling and the Free Trade Agreement with the U.S.

reinforced the traditional foreign producer position of dominance in table wines. Competition was intense, and, in spite of various forms of government support, the domestic producers found their industry a challenging operation.

THE ONTARIO WINE MARKET

In Canada, the regulation of alcoholic beverages was in the hands of the provinces. Each had adopted its own policies to control consumption, generate revenue from the sale of wine, beer and spirits, and, where relevant, protect and support in-province producers. One result was that the Canadian wine market was fragmented by province—"free trade" within the country's borders did not exist. The federal government wanted to reduce or eliminate provincial trade barriers, the wine industry having been specifically mentioned as one of the industries most in need of liberalization. However, the provincial governments were reluctant to change. Ontario wine producers, therefore, had to look first and foremost at the Ontario market, and could not yet count on significant "export" opportunities to other provinces.

Demand Patterns

In 1990, the total demand for wine in Ontario was 76 million litres. For the LCBO's fiscal year ending March 31, 1990, total wine sales in Ontario were $585 million at retail, compared with $1 920 million for beer and $1 250 million for spirits.

Traditionally, the popular wine products in Ontario were the high-alcohol dessert or appetizer wines—those with 14–20% alcohol, and particularly the inexpensive ones. As one industry wag put it some time ago: "People buy wines on the basis of the biggest bang for the buck." In recent years, however, there had been a pronounced shift in demand toward table wines—those with an alcohol content of 10–14%. By 1990, table wines accounted for more than 84% of wine consumed, compared with about 50% in 1973. Wine cooler products, made by combining wine with fruit juice, were a fad in the mid-1980s, with a sales peak of 7 million litres in 1987, before demand rapidly dropped.

An amazing surge in white wine was largely responsible for the vitality of the table wine sector. In the 1970s, white wines became popular as aperitifs and as substitutes for cocktails. Consumption increased at a rate of over 20% per annum from 1973 to 1984 before stabilizing at around 71% of total table wines. With white wines leading the way, table wines of all types broke away from their customary place as meal complements to attain a new position as all-occasion drinks.

The shift in market preference to table wines caught the Ontario wine industry unprepared. The grapes customarily used for winemaking were derived from the native labrusca grape. These grapes were hardy enough to survive the Canadian winter, but imparted a distinctively sharp "foxy" taste to wine. This taste could be disguised in fortified and sparkling wines, but it made the labrusca grape quite unsuitable for quality table wine and, particularly, the more delicately flavoured white wines. While market tastes centered on fortified wines, no serious problem was apparent. As tastes changed, however, the industry was able to shift only very slowly to more suitable grapes. By the time better grapes became available in commercial quantities, the Ontario winery share of the table wine market had fallen from over 50% to 39% in 1977. Better grapes and the assistance of the Ontario government helped Ontario wineries to reverse the share trend and build their position in the table wine market back to 50% by 1982. In 1984, the situation was reversed again as wine surpluses in other producing countries, and a strong Canadian dollar combined to encourage the export of wines to Canada. Exports from France to Ontario, for example, increased from 9.3 million litres in 1982 to 17.4 million litres in 1984, and the Ontario producers share of the table wine market dropped to 45%. The Ontario share fell further to 42% in 1985, and to 40% in 1986. Sales problems for local wineries were compounded in 1986 by adverse publicity which resulted from the presence of ethyl carbamate—a possible carcinogen—in a few dessert wines.

The issue of import competition was complicated by longstanding consumer preferences for European table wines. Domestic wines carried a stigma of low perceived quality that, with its roots in the prohibition days, had been sustained by ineffective attempts to make decent table wines from the labrusca grape, and reinforced by the marketing of "pop" wines such as Baby Duck, Gimli Goose, and Pussy Cat. With the availability of better grapes, and the development efforts of the wineries, the objective quality of Ontario wines was improving significantly. In the marketplace, however, local wine marketers thought that a price advantage of $1 or more was necessary to equate a Canadian wine with a similarly positioned European product. As a consequence of consumer preferences and the structure of government support, domestic table wines were largely confined to the low and lower-medium price segments of the market.

In May, 1986, the Niagara Accord was implemented by the provincial government to help the industry. This mandated the LCBO to apply a 66% markup to imported wines compared to a 1% markup on Canadian wines, which allowed Ontario table wines to enjoy an average retail price differential of $1.25. As a result, Ontario wineries were able to slightly improve to a 41% market share in table wines in 1987.

The Ontario wine and grape growing industry vehemently opposed the Canada-U.S. Free Trade Agreement signed in October, 1987. The brewery industry, which was nine times larger, managed to win exemption from the agreement, but the wine industry was unable to do so. The agreement provided that the markup differential between American and Canadian wines was to be reduced 50% by Jan.1, 1990, and completely eliminated by 1994. There was an immediate impact as American red and white table wine imports in Ontario rose from 433 thousand litres in 1986 to 2.4 million litres in 1990.

Meanwhile, the European Community (EC) complained to a GATT panel about the discriminatory markup, listing and marketing policies being applied to imported wines, beers and spirits by provincial liquor boards. The GATT Council ruled in favour of the EC. After negotiations between Ottawa and the GATT, an agreement was reached in 1988, to phase out the preferential markup for blended wines over the next seven years and for 100% Canadian wines over ten years. Faced with increased foreign competition, the market share of Ontario wine producers in table wines declined to 40% in 1988, 35% in 1989, and 36% in 1990 (Exhibit 1).

The overall demand for table wine had peaked in 1984. By 1990, sales volumes were down to 1981 levels. Several reasons were given by industry observers. There was a trend towards moderation in the consumption of alcohol beverages in general as people became more health- and fitness- conscious and felt the effectiveness of campaigns against drinking and driving. An aging population also contributed to the declining consumption, and so did the recession that began in 1990. In addition, prices had continued to rise as governments focused on the alcoholic beverage industry as a source of tax revenue.

The prime purchase criteria for a particular wine were price, country of origin, sweetness, producer, and brand. Price was widely used as an index of quality. Trial and consumption of table wine was highest in above-average income and education groups. Experience and lifestyle were important factors affecting preference.

THE PRODUCTION AND DISTRIBUTION OF WINE IN ONTARIO

In Canada, only Ontario and British Columbia had sizeable fully integrated wine industries ranging from grape growing to wine production and packaging. In both cases the existence and prosperity of the industry was highly dependent on government policy. From a strictly economic standpoint, it would be substantially less expensive to import grapes, concentrates, or finished wines than to rely on domestic supplies. The primary reasons for government support appeared to be to (1) maintain high value land in agricultural use, (2) provide employment in a concentrated geographic area, and (3) respond to the accumulated political influence of the growers and wineries.

Grape Supply

Grape quality was the most important factor in making wine. In 1990, the majority of Ontario's grapes were grown in the Niagara region, although in recent years parts of Essex and Kent counties as well as Pelee Island had also developed as grape-growing areas. The advantages of the Niagara region included soil conditions and a latitude similar to southern Europe, the moderating effects of Lake Ontario, and the protection of the Niagara Escarpment. However, wine grapes were among the most sensitive of all crops to climatic conditions, and possible extremes in both winter and summer weather made grape growing a challenge and a risk.

There were two primary families of wine-making grapes: the *vinifera* from which almost all European wines were produced and the *labrusca* native varieties. *Hybrids* were sometimes a cross between these two families, but more often between two types of vinifera grapes. In the 1970s, wine producers required an increasing supply of vinifera and hybrid grapes to match the increasing demand for table wines. However, growers were reluctant to convert their vineyards from labrusca production, because this would cost upwards of $17,000 per hectare, the yield of vinifera or hybrid would be 20% less, the risks of a more fragile crop were significant, and full production would take three to five years. Thus, in spite of their willingness to pay much higher prices per ton, Ontario wineries found themselves short of suitable grapes. Nor could they resort to imports because the province's 1976 Wine Content Act limited the use of imported grapes, juice or concentrate to 15% of a winery's Ontario grape purchases.

The supply shortages were reversed by an Ontario government program of interest free conversion loans started in 1975. By 1984, there were 15 million grape vines in Ontario, of which nearly half were vinifera or hybrid. There was also a significant surplus of grapes. Supply had overtaken the relatively static demand of the wineries. The federal and provincial governments stepped in and purchased the excess tonnage (at a cost of $11.5 million), and converted it to concentrate for future sale. This practice continued as the grape surplus peaked in 1984 at 30 000 tons, but declined to 600 tons by 1990 with the assistance of further government support in the form of the Grape Acreage Reduction Program.

In 1988, a new Wine Content Act became law. This was in direct response to the realities of free trade and liberalization. The Act allowed wineries to use a maximum of 70% imported grapes or grape product of the total content in each brand, but required the wineries to purchase at least 25 000 tons of Ontario grapes annually, of which at least 20 000 was to be vinifera or French hybrids for the next 12 years. To ensure quality, the Act reduced the maximum allowable yield per ton of grapes from 1 127 litres to 900 litres, and banned the use of labrusca grapes in table wines. Bulk wine imported for blending, mainly from California, subsequently went up from 2.5 million litres in 1987 to 6.4 million litres in 1990. In June 1991, the provincial government put a further twist on this regulation. Henceforth, Ontario wineries could use up to a maximum of 75% imported grape and grape product in a new brand, and designate it as an import—to be displayed on the imported wine shelves by the LCBO. However, the Federal Department of Consumer and Corporate Affairs quickly scotched the plan, deciding that labels would have to indicate that 25% of grape content was of Ontario origin and the wines would have to be sold in the stores' Canadian section.

The Ontario Grape Growers' Marketing Board (OGGMB) represented around 800 grape growers in Ontario, who cultivated about 9 700 hectares for grape wine production. OGGMB was empowered by provincial legislation to negotiate prices with the wineries. Each year representatives of the OGGMB and the Ontario Wine Council (representing the wineries) negotiated a price per ton for each of the 18 grape classifications grown in Ontario. The OGGMB also acted as a political lobby proposing programs and legislation in favour of the growers. It was OGGMB lobbying, for example, that promoted the passage of the Wine Content Act of 1971, effectively limiting the ability of the wineries to import grape supplies. The main point of the growers case then and now was that the vineyards stood on prime land that would otherwise be put to industrial use, and that the industry employed up to 16 000 workers, the majority of whom were seasonal and part-time help.

The influence of the OGGMB over time had benefitted the growers and the wineries. In 1975, for example, the OGGMB had been a significant supporter of the Ontario Wine Assistance Program, under which the wineries were virtually guaranteed distribution in LCBO stores and allowed to expand winery operated stores. Most observers felt that the wineries, by themselves, would be unable to yield such power. The implementation of free trade, however, created pressures that pulled the interests of growers and wine makers in opposite directions. The wineries favoured increased importation and usage of less expensive foreign grapes and the adoption of market prices for local grapes, which the growers predictably opposed.

The Grape and Wine Adjustment Program of 1988, which the federal and provincial governments created to assist transition to free trade tried to enable wineries to buy Ontario grapes competitively priced with the landed cost of imported grapes based on the U.S. final grape crush report. In practice, the wineries were in a poor bargaining position due to the quota. The weighted average price of all types of vinifera grapes in the 1990 California harvest was $388 per ton plus a freight cost of $220. In comparison, Ontario vinifera cost from $785 to $1 495 per ton and hybrids cost from $408 to $528 depending on the type of grape. Furthermore, a winery operator pointed out that prices of Napa valley grapes for example carried an "appelation value" that did not exist in Niagara grapes. The growers insisted that the freight cost of fresh grapes from California should serve as the basis. On the other hand, the wineries held that the freight cost of bulk wine was more appropriate since that is what they used for blending. The freight cost for the equivalent amount of bulk wine produced from a ton of grapes was $137.50, plus $24.05 in customs duties and $4.10 in brokerage fees.[1] The negotiations between the two groups went into arbitration in 1989. The next year, they were able to arrive at a compromise themselves. Ontario grape production purchased by wineries, costs to wineries and returns to growers are shown in Table 1.

TABLE 1 Winery Purchases of Ontario Grapes

	1987	1988	1989	1990
Ontario grapes purchased (tons)	34 567	26 269	24 756	27 540
Cost to wineries ($000)	17 916	10 455	12 372	13 372
Average cost per ton ($)	518.30	398.00	499.76	485.53
Max. allowable yield (litre)	1 127	900	900	900*
Cost per litre ($)	.46	.44	.55	.54
Grower Revenues				
Gov't price subsidy ($000)	0	4 910	4 125	3 618
Tot. grower revenues ($000)	17 916	15 365	16 497	16 989
Ave. revenue per ton ($)	518.30	584.93	666.37	616.89

* The yield for quality wines would be 700 litres or less per ton.

Wine-Making

The basics of the wine-making process had been the same for centuries. Grapes were harvested from September through October by hand or by machine, and shipped as soon as possible to the winery. After weighing and testing, they were crushed; the juice was then fermented alone (for white wine) or with the skins (for red wine). Once the fermentation was complete, the wine is separated from the sediment and aged before bottling. Special wines such as champagne, sparkling wines and dessert wines required additional steps that, depending on the wine, included pressurizing with carbon dioxide and fortifying with alcohol.

---

[1] Fresh grapes were not charged customs duties or brokerage fees. Duties on American bulk wine would be eliminated by 1994 due to the Free Trade Agreement.

A start-up winery required basic batch processing equipment for crushing, storage, transfer and bottling. Thereafter various levels of sophistication were possible in instrumentation for process and quality control, and in transfer and bottling automation. The investment required for land and capital equipment for a boutique winery of 500 000 to 1 000 000 litres annual capacity ranged upwards from $1.0 million, depending on discretionary factors such as the size and attractiveness of the winery site and buildings, and the degree of process sophistication. The working capital requirements for table wines were substantial since there was a processing and aging period of at least nine to twelve months between the purchase of grapes and the first sale of wine. Holding periods of up to two or three years were typical for dessert wines and, at the discretion of the wine-maker, for higher quality table wines. Contribution margins for table wines in 1990 were on the order of 50–60% of winery selling prices. The primary variable cost elements were grapes, wine-making supplies and packaging (Table 2). Significant savings in packaging costs were possible through the use of four-litre "wine-in-a-box" packages, but a large part of these savings were often passed on to consumers in the form of lower prices. Specialty products like champagne typically gave somewhat higher contributions. The cooler products were a problem for the industry since aggressive pricing and high ingredient and packaging costs had resulted in current contribution margins of only 5%.

For a boutique winery operating in a volume range of from 500 000 to 1 000 000 litres, manufacturing overheads before depreciation charges might range from $.25 to $.35 per litre. Below the line costs for interest, management and marketing were subject to financial structure, and management efficiency and discretion.

TABLE 2 **Estimated Unit Contribution Structure
Litre Bottle of Ontario Table Wine, 1990**

L.C.B.O. retail selling price*		6.75	
Deductions for mark-ups, taxes, etc.		<u>4.04</u>	
Winery revenue		2.71	100%
Grape costs and wine supplies	.65		
Packaging	.60	<u>1.25</u>	
Contribution per litre		1.46	54%

* A common price point for high volume Ontario table wines.

SOURCE: Industry sources and authors' estimates.

Wine Packaging

Wine was traditionally packed in glass bottles and sold in 750 ml., 1.0 litre and 1.5 litre sizes. The introduction in the late 1970s of box packaging, such as bag-in-a-box (a foil bag supported and protected by a cardboard box), presented new opportunities to the Ontario wineries. Box packaging in sizes over 1.5 litres was less expensive, unbreakable, easily disposable and useable for sizes up to at least 4 litres. What was more, the LCBO, in the name of quality assurance and handling ease, restricted the use of non-glass packaging and package sizes over 1.5 litres to Ontario wines. By 1990, approximately 51% of Ontario-produced table wines were sold in 1.5 to 4 litre containers, with about 20% of the total sold in some form of box packaging.

Wine Distribution

The LCBO, by government mandate, was the primary distributor of wine in Ontario. Around 85% of the LCBO's wine sales were made through its system of 623 retail stores; the balance was sold through licensed bars and restaurants. The system included six Vintages stores, which specialized in rare, unusual, and usually expensive wines. Around 100 regular LCBO stores also had small Vintages corners. The LCBO licensed Ontario wineries to sell directly to the public from their own premises and through winery owned shops. Allowing the sale of wines in grocery stores, following Quebec's example, had been discussed for years but had never been realized, and the NDP government of Ontario in 1990 was not inclined to support the idea. The LCBO, after all, was a major revenue source for the province. Wine sales through the LCBO and winery channels are summarized in Table 3.

TABLE 3 Wine Sales through LCBO and Winery Outlets ($000 000)

For LCBO fiscal year ending March 31	*1988*	*1989*	*1990*
LCBO sales			
Ontario wines	$161.6	$160.3	$149.0
Other Canadian	1.2	1.5	1.1
Imported	345.3	367.7	385.0
	508.1	529.5	535.1
Winery sales	48.2	49.1	49.7
Total wine sales	556.3	578.6	584.8

SOURCE: LCBO annual reports.

The wine listings for regular stores in March 1990 covered 1 545 wine products, with 922 imported, 583 Ontario (including 21 coolers), and 7 other Canadian selections. In comparison, listings in the previous year had 904 imported, 692 Ontario (including 60 coolers), and 1 other Canadian selections. Each wine product was sold at the same fixed price in all LCBO outlets. Wines to be stocked and sold in each store were selected by the store manager with a view to maximizing sales volume from the space available. Previously, the LCBO was required by the Ontario Wine Assistance Program of 1975 to stock all new Ontario wine products that met technical quality and packaging standards, and list on an ongoing basis all Ontario wines produced in excess of 1 500 cases. The terms of the Free Trade Agreement and the GATT ruling, however, were putting an end to the preferential listing policies.

To phase in the equalization of markups demanded by the Free Trade Agreement and the GATT ruling, the LCBO increased its markups on Ontario wines in 1991 (Table 4). It was expected that the LCBO would continue to reduce the differential between Ontario and imported wines in the future by raising the Ontario markup levels rather than by reducing the import markups. The impact of the markup changes are also illustrated in Table 4. The markups for the new 75% blended wine category was not yet announced, but it was expected to be around 44%.

TABLE 4 LCBO Markups for Table Wines with Different Origins

Table Wine Type	1985	1986	1990	1991
100% Ontario	58.0	1.0	12.8	27.0
Up to 70% Ontario blend	–	–	23.4	39.0
U.S. import	125.0	66.0	52.8	61.9
Other Canadian	105.0	66.0	52.8	61.9
Non-U.S. import	125.0	66.0	66.0	74.3

SOURCE: WCO.

Wineries were traditionally permitted to sell directly at the winery site and through licensed stand-alone, winery-owned retail stores. Industry lobbying had gained on-site winery stores exemption from Ontario's prohibition on Sunday shopping due to their tourism-oriented aspect. The number of winery outlets grew from 120 in 1982 to 243 in 1990. The 1990 total encompassed 182 conventional stores and 61 mini stores. Mini stores were small stand-alone concessions inside supermarkets and department stores. However, under the terms of the Free Trade agreement a moratorium was in effect in granting new licenses for wine retail stores. A total of 348 licenses for stores had been approved before the moratorium took effect, with 105 not yet in operation. Existing licenses could be purchased from current holders under government approval.

Winery-owned stores were limited to selling their own wines, although it was not a necessity that these wines be distributed as well through the LCBO retail system. Imported wines, even if produced by a wholly owned subsidiary, could not be sold on winery store shelves. The new category of blended wines bottled in Ontario, which could use up to 75% imported grape content, could be sold in winery-owned stores. LCBO list prices governed wines sold through both systems, but the wineries had price flexibility on their exclusive winery store products. The LCBO waived its markup margin on winery store sales and charged instead a licence fee of 2% on sales. The fee used to be 5%, but the LCBO lowered it in 1988 to help the wineries cope with free trade. This gave winery stores higher unit revenues for captive distribution as illustrated in the markup structures in Table 5. This could make the economics of winery owned retail stores even more attractive unless the LCBO also started raising its license fees.

TABLE 5   Comparison of Markup Structures for Sale of One Litre Standard Product through LCBO vs. Winery Store*

	LCBO	*Winery Store*
Price FOB winery	2.71	2.71
Federal excise duty ($.45/litre)	.45	.45
Federal sales tax (19%)	.60	.60
LCBO landed cost	3.76	3.76
LCBO markup (12.8%)	.48	
LCBO flat tax ($1.50/litre)	1.50	
LCBO licence fee (2% of retail price)		.14
Derived winery store markup		1.84
Levy ($.18/750 ml)	.24	.24
Environmental tax (2%)	.05	.05
	6.03	6.03
Provincial sales tax (12%)	.72	.72
Retail price	6.75	6.75

* The incremental revenue to the winery of selling through its own store as compared to the LCBO. No provision is made for store operating costs.

Government Support

Over the years there had been a variety of federal and provincial support programs for the Ontario grape growers and wineries. Specific measures included the purchase of surplus grapes, preferential listing and stocking procedures, discriminatory markup policies, and, more recently, adjustment loans, credits, grants, and price supports.

In 1986 and 1987, government assistance to wineries consisted of three measures: the preferential 65% differential on LCBO markups through the 1986 Niagara Accord, preferential LCBO listing under the 1975 Ontario Wine Assistance Program, and monopoly control of distribution through the LCBO and winery retail outlets. It was estimated that the 65% markup differential on Ontario wines had an opportunity cost to the government of around $130 million annually. Government support to growers hinged on the 1976 Wine Content Act which limited the use of imported grapes and the annual purchase of surplus production by the Agricultural Products Board of Agriculture Canada.

Government assistance was by no means unique to the Ontario industry. In Europe, European Community Common Agricultural Policy (CAP) direct subsidies to the wine industry for storage, marketing and modernization amounted to an estimated $1.8 billion in 1985, and even greater amounts in following years. National and regional programs available within the various countries provided even more support. The predictable result was an enormous accumulating surplus—"lakes of wine"—with pressures to export at almost any price. The wine producing countries were caught in a political trap of subsidy escalation. The absurdity of the situation was marked by attempts in several countries to use wine as a source of industrial alcohol.

Agricultural subsidies and barriers such as the EC's CAP and Japanese exclusion of imported rice were the focus of international trade talks in 1990. GATT was started in 1947 as a multilateral, rules-based system intended to liberalize international trade. Through the years there were efforts to improve the GATT through negotiations (called "rounds"). In 1986, Canada played an instrumental role when GATT members agreed to launch the Uruguay round. The critical talks broke off in December 1990 due to disagreements about agricultural issues between the EC and Japan on one side, and the U.S. and Canada on the other.

In Ontario, the nature and level of government support changed dramatically from 1986 to 1990, as the provincial government, in particular, had to perform a political balancing act between its own contrary objectives of raising revenues while controlling the sale of alcoholic beverages, the competing claims of provincial brewers, spirits producers and wine importers, and pressures for "even-handed" trade from the wine exporting countries.

Preferential markups and listings ended through the Free Trade Agreement and the GATT ruling. In response, the provincial government enacted the 1988 Wine Content Act which allowed higher import content and tried to institute California reference pricing to placate the wineries. At the same time, it tried to appease the growers by imposing a required quota of Ontario grape purchases by wineries, maintaining a limit (albeit higher) on allowable import content of Ontario wines, and doling out subsidy payments to growers to make up for the lower grape prices. This created a dilemma for some wineries since they had to purchase their share of the grape quota, determined by previous year sales, even though they wanted to increase the imported content of their wines. The Act noted that the quota could be revised by the provincial government if demand for Ontario wines went down more than 5% since 1987, which it had, but so far the Ministry of Consumer and Commercial Relations had not moved to change it.

The Federal/Provincial Grape and Wine Adjustment Program was announced in 1988. This was a $100 million assistance package to the industry of which $50 million went to growers as payments under the Grape Acreage Reduction Program to remove a targetted 3 300 hectares of surplus grape vines, more than a third of total acreage. Around $27 million of the package was allocated to finance the price subsidy to growers over twelve years. The program also provided $15 million to wineries for promotion and market development.

Separately, the 12-year $45 million Ontario Winery Adjustment Program was announced in 1989 by the provincial government. These were forgivable loans to wineries tied to their volume of Ontario grape purchases and, to a lesser degree, their sales of the previous year. Loans could be used for productivity improvements, quality programs, product positioning, image building, viticulture and research, but not for direct brand advertising, vineyard expansion, refinancing debts or covering operating losses. Clifford Hatch Sr. of Brights Wines described the situation: "They're giving the wineries money to encourage them to continue to support these 800 farmers."[2]

THE ONTARIO WINERIES

The 19 wineries in Ontario were commonly grouped into three categories: the majors (Andres, Brights, and Cartier), the intermediates (Colio, Hillebrand, Inniskillin, London), and the boutiques (Cave Springs, Chateau des Charmes, Culotta, Henry of Pelham, Konzelmann, Marynissen, Montravin, Pelee Island, Reif, Stonechurch, Stoney Ridge, and Vineland Estates).[3]

The Ontario wineries were all members of the Wine Council of Ontario (WCO). The WCO was a vehicle for the wineries to communicate and act on a common front. It conducted grape pricing negotiations, coordinated industry-wide promotional activities, and lobbied governments on behalf of the industry. In mid-1990, the WCO launched a very aggressive $4-million, provincial government-funded marketing campaign using television and print ads, taste

---

[2] Report on *Business Magazine*, February 1991, p.57.

[3] Ontario also had a sizeable home made wine making industry, attributed to ethnic traditions and a way to avoid taxes. One winery operator claimed that it could amount to more than 27 million litres a year. Imported grapes were mainly used.

testings, contests, and winery tours, and featuring the Vintner's Quality Alliance (VQA) system. This was intended to raise public awareness of Ontario wines and convince consumers that the quality of local wines was comparable to imports.

Some Ontario table wines were reaching world standard due to the conversion to premium grape varieties in the vineyards, and the dramatic increase in the technical competence of wine makers. In 1990, Ontario wineries introduced the VQA system—an "appelation of origin" system patterned after the French "Appellation d'Origine Controlée" system. Only wines meeting very stringent standards of quality, and using authorized grape type and origin, were eligible for the label. Even though only 5–10% of Ontario wines were expected to meet the standards, it was hoped that the system would improve the perceived quality of Ontario wines in general.

The Majors

The majors' aggregate Ontario market share in 1990 was 28.3% (Exhibit 2), down almost six points from 1987. The relative market shares of the three producers in the last four years remained fairly stable, however, reflecting somewhat of a standoff in competitive activities within the group.

The major wineries focused on the low and low-medium price segments. Within these segments, each winery offered a variety of brand/package size combinations. The primary distinction between the brands was in their sweetness rating—from 0 (very dry) to over 7 (sweet). Most brands were sold in two- or three-package sizes.

All of the major wineries employed conventional sales organizations to secure and maintain listings with the LCBO, sell to the bar and restaurant trade, and do public relations work. Similarly, they all engaged in advertising with budgets ranging from $100 000 to $500 000 for each key brand. It was difficult, given the limited range of competitive variables available, for any one producer to achieve a dominant position in the market. If product, packaging or promotional initiatives showed promise, they were quickly duplicated by rival wineries. The relative positions of the majors' key brands and imported brands is illustrated in Exhibit 3.

T.G. Bright & Co. Limited

Brights was founded in Toronto in 1874 and was the traditional pillar of the Ontario industry. A summary of Brights' five-year financial results follow in Table 6.

Brights acquired Jordan and Ste. Michelle Cellars from the Carling O'Keefe brewing company in 1986 for almost $30 million. Jordan was almost the size of Brights and used to be considered a major player in their own right. The acqui-

TABLE 6 Brights' Summary of Results ($000 000)

Fiscal year ending March 31	1987	1988	1989	1990	1991
Sales	75.4	84.8	82.1	74.4	70.2
Working capital	20.0	22.6	23.2	23.5	19.9
Net fixed assets	26.8	26.3	21.8	13.8	14.5
Total assets	74.7	76.5	71.8	63.1	58.1
Profits after tax	3.6	2.6	2.5	(1.1)	1.2
Shareholders' equity	25.9	28.0	30.0	28.4	29.1

sition brought the strong selling Maria Christina red and white table wine and Spumante Bambino labels of Jordan into the array of Brights offerings. Brights already had market leading positions in Ontario table wines with their Entre Lacs, House Wine and President champagne labels. Brights operated 68 retail outlets in Ontario. In 1990, Brights cut its wholesale prices, drawing criticism from other Ontario competitors who felt they had to match the move.

tactical planning

Cartier Wines and Beverages

Cartier was formerly the Chateau-Gai subsidiary of the John Labatt Ltd. brewery. In 1988, it acquired Barnes wines, one of the intermediates in the Ontario wine industry. In 1989, it became a privately held company through a management buyout. Industry insiders thought the firm had become profitable after being a money losing stepchild in the Labatt organization. Cartier had the strongest market position by far in the wine coolers segment. Its L'Ambiance label was in the top five in table wines. The firm had 44 winery retail outlets in Ontario.

Andres Wines Ltd.

Andres was the industry leader in manufacturing and marketing innovation. Other wineries often hired Andres veterans to fill executive posts. Andres was started in British Columbia in 1961 by the Peller family. Now it was based in Ontario and was a publicly traded corporation. It was the largest Ontario winery before the acquisitions made by Brights and Cartier and still the most profitable. A five-year summary of Andres' national results is presented in Table 7.

Andres was the first winery to locate wineries by provincial jurisdictions rather than by raw material source. The company had six wineries in Canada, which were among the most efficient in the industry. Andres only had a token position in grape growing.

TABLE 7 **Andres' Summary of Results** ($000 000)

Fiscal year ending March 31	1987	1988	1989	1990	1991
Sales	56.7	57.0	56.0	53.3	52.6
Working capital	30.9	31.7	32.9	35.3	37.4
Net fixed assets	11.4	11.9	12.1	11.5	10.9
Total assets	48.2	48.1	50.1	51.5	54.2
Profits after tax	4.8	4.0	4.0	4.6	4.5
Shareholders' equity	38.3	39.7	41.1	43.0	44.9

Andres was renowned for its marketing savvy. In the early 1970s, it introduced the idea of a proprietary brand/consumer packaged goods approach to the industry with the launch of Baby Duck, a sweet, sparkling, low-alcohol wine. Other wineries adopted similar products but found it difficult to change their traditional attitudes toward wine marketing. They were accustomed to spending little more than the label costs for a new product, and found it difficult to accept the risks of front end promotional brand investments. By the mid-1970s, Andres was spending more on advertising than the rest of the industry combined, and Baby Duck was the country's largest selling brand. Baby Duck faded in the 1980s as conventional table wines increased in popularity, but Andres had moved into Cellar Cask bag-in-a-box wines in 1975 and into heavily promoted table wine brands.

In 1990, its Hochtaler brand was the leading non-imported table wine brand in Canada. Andres was an importer of French, German and Italian wines and had a small operation in California. Andres was once again quick to capitalize on industry changes, this time brought by free trade, in producing California blends and exporting to the U.S. and Japan. It also had a subsidiary in Bordeaux which sold five wine brands in Canada under the G.M. Dumons label. It had 45 retail outlets.

The Intermediates

Inniskillin Wines

Inniskillin was the first Ontario boutique winery. Its success had pushed it into the ranks of the intermediates in size, but it still considered itself a boutique winery because of its traditional emphasis on premium wines. Inniskillin was founded in 1974 at Niagara-on-the-Lake by Don Ziraldo and his winemaker-partner Karl Kaiser. Inniskillin's original mission was to

1. produce a high-quality Canadian wine from a "cottage" or chateau winery;
2. make wine in the Old World tradition with 100% grape juice (no water amelioration), cold pressing, barrel aging and bottle aging;

3. use only hybrid and pure vinifera grapes; and

4. market through pre-specified channels so as to maintain direct contact with customers whose comments would assist in improving quality.

Ziraldo, a charismatic individual, did a superb job of promoting Inniskillin: he secured listings in prestigious reataurants, favourable media attention and extensive word-of-mouth recommendation. Kaiser produced fine wines from hybrid and vinifera grapes, and Inniskillin fought its way into being.

Following an aggressive expansion in 1978, Inniskillin's market share grew to 1.2% in 1982, and the company was quite profitable. In 1984, after some internal wrangling, it moved towards the "house" wine market, introducing the Braeburn House red and white table wines. The brand was priced between the volume table wines of the Ontario majors and the popular import blends. Ziraldo had hoped the favourable reputation of its varietal wines (wines made at least 80% from one type of grapes and taking the grapes' name such as Pinot Noir or Riesling) would spill over into a volume blended product.

Inniskillin and other boutique wineries helped convince consumers that a good wine could actually be produced in Ontario. But the finer wine market was both limited in total volume and fragmented by a multiplicity of taste, image and price preferences. It was difficult to sustain a business on fine wine alone, which meant that the boutiques also had to look to ordinary wines for volume and contribution.

In 1987, Inniskillin bought 10 hectares in Napa Valley. Ziraldo had Carlos Ott, the Canadian architect of the controversial Paris Opera House, design the label for Inniskillin Napa. Arrangements were made with the Rombauer winery in Napa Valley for production while Ziraldo looked into the possibility of constructing a new winery. By 1991, Inniskillin was selling three of its own California labels in LCBO outlets. Two versions of Chardonnay cost $16 and $18 a 750 ml. bottle, and the Merlot cost $25 a bottle. However, it could not sell these in its four wine stores due to LCBO policy. Inniskillin also had an import division which acted as a distributor for limited quantities of premium wine from small wineries in Australia, France, Italy and the U.S. These wines started at $10 a bottle, and commissions were 10–15% of the wholesale price.

Ziraldo had resisted the trend started by the major wineries in importing bulk wine for blending, and Inniskillin continued to use purely Ontario grapes for its blended house wines. It owned 30 acres of vineyards in Niagara, which provided about 30% of its grape needs, and spent a lot of effort cultivating relationships with independent growers in the area. Ziraldo wanted the growers to stop thinking of themselves as "grape growers" and start thinking like "winegrowers". Production capacity at the Niagara winery was 1.5 million litres.

Inniskillin had developed an international reputation for its ice wines, made from frozen grapes in the middle of Niagara's winter. The 1989 ice wine won a Citadelles d'Or Grands Prix d'Honneur, one of the world's most prestigious wine prizes, at the 1991 Vinexpo in Bordeaux, the world's largest wine fair. It was probably the most significant Canadian ice wine honour to date. Ice wine was sold for $40 a 375 ml bottle, and production was very limited.

The product assortment of Andres, Inniskillin, Hillebrand, two of the boutiques and three major foreign competitors is given in Exhibit 4. Sales volume and prices of major Inniskillin wine brands are shown in Exhibit 5.

Hillebrand Estates Winery Limited

Hillebrand was owned by Underberg AG, a family-owned German wine and spirits company best known for its Underberg natural herb bitters. The operation started out as a boutique winery called Newark in 1968 before being bought by the European firm in 1982. It became the success story of the Ontario wine industry in the 1980s through its aggressive, unconventional retail store program.

The conventional marketing approach of the boutique and medium-sized wineries was to rely heavily on the distribution services and retail exposure provided by the LCBO, and to supplement this with modest media, personal selling and publicity budgets. Most of these wineries operated winery retail stores, but none had expanded in any significant way into additional retail outlets. Even the major wineries, who backed up their LCBO distribution with heavy advertising and personal selling budgets, treated their retail operations more or less passively as supplemental distribution.

Hillebrand opened its first store in downtown Toronto in 1984, bought 12 stores from Barnes in 1988, and by 1990 had 41 retail outlets. Sales grew from 6 000 cases in 1984 to 200 000 cases in 1988. Hillebrand used the sales force of a prominent wine importer, Peter Mielzynski Agencies, to aggressively secure listings in LCBO stores. Peter Mielzynski was the chairman of the board of Hillebrand and represented the Underbergs. Its market share in LCBO store sales multiplied ten times since 1982. In 1988, Hillebrand received a certificate of merit in the Canada Awards for Business Excellence. The same year, it also exported 8 000 cases of wine to Japan and the U.S.

Hillebrand's former general manager John Swan was an Englishman with British wine marketing experience. He saw the profit opportunity in the retailing side of the business. Swan had bet that government and trade pressures would eventually put the brakes on unlimited store expansion, so he had proceeded at a very rapid pace. He was sanguine about the free trade agreement and hoped to be able to offer American wines in his outlets.[4]

---

[4] For example, the British Columbia government was already licensing privately owned wineshops to sell any brand of wine, import or Canadian.

The Boutiques

The Ontario wine industry had 12 boutique wineries which concentrated on premium table wines produced from Ontario-grown French hybrid or classic Vinifera grapes. Some were marginal producers and others were hoping to be the next Inniskillin or Hillebrand. However, under the increased competitive environment, their best hope seemed to be in developing a niche for their products and a loyal following among wine lovers. For participants in the boutique winery business, more than just economic interest was involved; it was for them a way of life.

To survive in the new environment, Pelee Island winery signed an agreement with the William Hill Wine Co. in Napa Valley, California to supply premium wine in bulk for blending with premium Ontario wine and bottling at Kingsville, Ontario. In 1990, Vineland Estates, another boutique winery, opened Ontario's first winery restaurant and bed and breakfast. It also hoped to capitalize on the picturesque setting of its Niagara Bench location to increase sales at the on-site winery store.

Winery Closings

Several wineries had closed shop in the last few years. The most notable failure was the closely watched venture of Seagram. Canadian-based Seagram Co. Ltd. was the world's largest producer of distilled spirits and wines, and became the second largest wine producer in the U.S. with the purchase of several California wineries from Coca-Cola in 1982. In June 1985, Seagram invested $4 million in a greenfield winery operation with a 150 000 case capacity in Niagara to produce wines under its Paul Masson brand. The winery was closed in January, 1989 as Seagram sought to rationalize its world-wide business operations in the face of the declining demand for alcohol beverages.

Two boutique wineries failed in 1989 as well—Willowbanks and Charal. In addition, the wineries of Jordan and Barnes were closed after the companies were acquired as the buyers had excess production capacity and were primarily after the brands. As wine production and consumption in Ontario declined and import barriers fell, it was expected that further consolidations and restructuring in the industry would occur.

EXHIBIT 1   Wines Sales in Ontario by Channel, Origin, Type
(000 litres)

	1982	1987	1988	1989	1990
Aggregate					
All wines	78 000	87 100	83 200	80 100	76 000
By channel					
LCBO	70 000	76 600	73 800	72 000	67 800
Winery stores	8 000	10 500	9 400	8 100	8 200
% LCBO	89.7	87.9	88.7	89.9	89.2
By origin					
Imported	35 000	43 600	43 400	46 500	43 700
Ontario	40 800	43 500	39 800	32 600	31 300
Other Canadian	2 200	1 000	1 000	1 000	1 000
% Ontario	52.3	49.9	47.8	40.7	41.2
By type					
Table	60 600	67 700	66 500	67 000	63 800
Other wines	17 400	12 400	11 300	10 000	9 600
Wine coolers	0	7 000	5 400	3 100	2 600
% Table	77.7	77.7	79.9	83.7	84.0
Table wine—by type					
% White	65.6	70.8	71.4	71.6	71.4
% Red	28.6	21.1	21.6	21.2	20.7
% Other	5.8	8.1	7.0	7.2	7.9
Table wine—by origin					
% Ontario	50.0	41.0	40.0	35.0	36.0

SOURCE: Canadian Wine Institute, LCBO, and authors' estimates.

EXHIBIT 2 Wine Producer Market Shares through Ontario LCBO

Winery	1987	1988	1989	1990
Majors				
T.G. Bright	14.1	12.9	11.7	11.6
Cartier	11.6	11.4	9.6	10.0
Andres	8.4	8.0	7.1	6.7
Total majors	<u>34.1</u>	<u>32.2</u>	<u>28.5</u>	<u>28.3</u>
Intermediate				
London	2.2	2.3	2.3	2.2
Hillebrand	0.8	1.1	1.1	1.0
Inniskillin	1.0	1.0	1.1	.9
Colio	1.4	1.2	.9	.8
Total intermediates	<u>5.4</u>	<u>5.6</u>	<u>5.3</u>	<u>4.9</u>
Selected boutiques				
Pelee Island	.3	.4	.6	.7
Chateau des Charmes	.4	.4	.4	.3
Montravin	.1	.1	.1	.1
Culotta	n.s.	n.s.	.1	.1
Reif	n.s.	.1	.1	.1
Selected imports				
Barton & Guestier (France)	8.4	9.3	9.3	8.7
Piat (France)	4.1	4.5	5.7	6.0
Kressman (France)	5.2	4.5	4.1	4.5
Roux (France)	1.9	2.2	3.1	2.5
Gallo (U.S.)	0.5	0.7	1.2	1.4
Colli Albani (Italy)	1.4	1.4	1.4	1.2
Momessin (France)	1.3	1.4	1.3	1.2
Total—all imports	<u>56.9</u>	<u>56.7</u>	<u>63.9</u>	<u>64.7</u>

SOURCE: Canadian Wine Institute. Based on volumetric sales through the LCBO.

EXHIBIT 3 Top Selling Brands of Wine in Ontario in Selected Categories*

	Litres	Price per litre
French red table wine		
Le Piat d'Or	713 169	8.50
Barton & Guestier Partager Rouge	558 657	7.95
Kressman Selectionne	437 220	7.45
Barton & Guestier Cuvee Speciale	412 218	8.25
Italian red table wine		
Folonari Valpolicella Classico	491 193	8.20
Canadian Red Table Wine		
Brights Entre Lacs Red	244 008	6.30
Cartier L'Ambiance Red	193 995	6.60
Brights House Wine	187 407	6.30
Brights Maria Christina	176 355	6.30
American red table wine		
Gallo Hearty Burgundy	173 772	7.30
French white table wine		
Le Piat D'Or	3 333 510	8.50
Barton & Guestier Partager Blanc	2 646 828	7.70
Kressman Selectionne	2 573 595	7.45
Barton & Guestier Cuvee Speciale	1 757 592	8.25
L'Epayrie Blanc de Blancs	1 388 358	8.25
Italian white table wine		
Colli Albani	602 019	7.40
Canadian white table wine		
Brights Entre Lacs	1 082 709	6.30
Andres Hochtaler	900 585	6.30
Brights House Wine	817 947	6.30
Brights Maria Christina	789 507	6.30
Cartier L'Ambiance	722 124	6.65
American white table wine		
Carlo Rossi Chablis	205 461	7.00
French champagne		
Mumm Extra Dry	48 105	21.00
Canadian champagne		
Brights President Extra Dry	289 665	11.70
Canadian 7% sparkling wine ("pop wines")		
Brights Spumante Bambino White	874 179	6.60
Andres Baby Duck Red	245 727	6.60

* Sales are fiscal year to date and prices are as of March 31, 1991 in LCBO outlets. Prices and packaging sizes have been converted to litres for comparison purposes.

SOURCE: LCBO, Canadian Wine Institute.

EXHIBIT 4 Table Wine Brand/Package Assortment Summary for Selected Ontario Wineries*

Item Count by Price Segment (Price/Litre)

	Low Under $6.95	Low/Medium $6.95–$7.95	High/Medium $7.95–$12.95	High Over $12.95
Andres				
White	30	6	1	0
Red	14	0	0	0
Inniskillin				
White	1	3	8	2
Red	0	3	3	1
Hillebrand				
White	0	13	3	0
Red	0	3	1	0
Pelee Island				
White	4	0	9	0
Red	2	0	3	0
Chateau des Charmes				
White	0	4	5	1
Red	0	4	3	0
Barton & Guestier				
White	0	3	12	1
Red	0	3	7	1
Piat				
White	0	0	3	0
Red	0	0	3	0
Gallo				
White	2	2	2	0
Red	0	3	2	0

* Each brand/package combination counts as one item.

SOURCE: LCBO price list, March 31, 1991.

EXHIBIT 5   Inniskillin Listings, Prices and Volumes, Calendar Years 1989 and 1990*

	Sugar	Package Sizes (ml)	Volume (litres) 1989	1990	Price per Litre
White table wines					
Brae Blanc	(0)	375,750,1000,1500	219 483	208 395	$7.55
Braeburn	(1)	1000	92 574	53 919	6.95
Chardonnay (VQA)	(0)	375,750	53 505	45 468	13.20
Riesling (VQA)	(2)	750	46 107	42 633	10.25
Seyval Blanc (VQA)	(0)	200 750	46 980	25 614	9.20
Gewurztraminer	(0)	750	5 931	14 220	9.65
Riesling/Chardonnay					
Proprietor's Reserve	(0)	750	18 459	13 176	10.00
Vidal (VQA)	(1)	750	6 309	11 547	7.90
Gamay Blanc (VQA)	(0)	750	18 891	8 928	11.00
Other varietals			38 079	32 301	
Total white table wines			546 318	456 201	
Red table wines					
Brae Rouge	(0)	200,375,750, 1000 1 500	106 488	84 717	7.55
Marechal Foch (VQA)	(0)	750	57 033	37 602	8.65
Cabernet Sauvignon/					
Zweigeltrebe					
Proprietor's Reserve	(0)	750	19 737	15 714	10.00
Gamay Noir (VQA)	(0)	750	7 632	9 774	10.53
Millot-Chambourcin	(0)	750	11 448	9 558	8.35
Other varietals			2 493	3 060	
Total red table wines			204 831	160 425	

* LCBO Sales Only.

  (VQA)—wines meeting the Vintner's Quality Alliance appellation.

  Brae Blanc, Brae Rouge and Braeburn were blended house wines. The rest were varietals.

BRIGHTS WINES—1991

Joseph N. Fry and Honorio Todino

In March, 1991, T.G. Bright & Company Limited (Brights) of Niagara Falls, the oldest Canadian winery (in operation for 117 years), was for sale. It was the largest winery in sales and storage capacity in Canada, and the sixth largest in North America. It sold wines in all 12 provinces and territories. Now the Hatch family of Windsor, Ontario, which had owned a controlling interest of Brights since 1933, was looking for a buyer.

The environment, however, was a difficult one in which to sell a wine company. The Canadian economy was in the middle of a recession. Declining alcohol and liquor consumption in Canada, the General Agreement on Tariff and Trade (GATT) settlement, and the Free Trade Agreement had resulted in industry overcapacity and intensified competition from European and American wines. Two different buyers had made and withdrawn offers within the last year, and other industry participants were rumoured to be interested.

HISTORY

Brights Wines was founded in Toronto in 1874 by Thomas Bright and F.A. Sheriff. In 1885, the plant and cellars were moved to its present Niagara site to be closer to the vineyards. By 1933, Brights had a storage capacity of 18 000 000 litres, and ranked as one of the largest privately owned wineries in the world. Prohibition in the United States ended that year, making life difficult for Canadian wineries which, one way or another, had done a brisk business south of the border. In the same year, the late Harry C. Hatch, head of the distillery Hiram Walker and Sons Limited, and his associates purchased control of Brights. They initiated the establishment of wholly owned subsidiaries in Quebec and Saskatchewan, purchased 474 hectares of vineyards in the Niagara area to plant native Niagara and Concord grapes, and started a research program to improve grape and wine quality.

Brights became a leader in Canadian viticulture. It was at the forefront in the development of hybrid and vinifera vines that were suitable for the Ontario climate in the 1930s and 1940s. The company was a pioneer in product development, having been the first in Ontario to produce fermented sparkling wine (1949), non-labrusca table wine (1950), 7% sparkling wine (1953), and vinifera (1956). However, the company was somewhat slow in capitalizing on its product firsts.

The Saskatchewan operation ceased in 1945. However, two smaller Ontario wineries were purchased in the 1950s and Brights grew slowly but steadily. In 1972, Brights built a new winery in St. Hyacinthe, Quebec, and formed a wholly owned subsidiary, Le Vins La Salle Inc, to operate it. The original Quebec subsidiary was renamed Le Vins Brights Ltee in 1981. It operated the original plant in Lachine, plus a new winery at St. Joseph du Lac purchased the previous year. Quebec allowed grocery stores to start selling wines in 1979, and Brights wanted to meet the expected increase in demand. Only wines bottled in the province were eligible for this distribution channel.

In September 1976, Edward S. Arnold was hired as Executive Vice-President to revitalize the company's marketing. There had been no changes in senior management for the prior ten years. Arnold came from Andres Wines, where he had been involved in the launching of the highly successful Baby Duck sparkling wine. In 1977, he managed the company's introduction of Brights House Wine, which became an immediate success in the growing white table wine market. By 1980, he had become President and Chief Executive Officer of Brights.

Brights made an unsuccessful offer to purchase a winery in Kelowna, British Columbia in 1978. However, an agreement with the Inkameep Indian Band in 1981 enabled the company to start operations in a new winery at Oliver, B.C. In early 1984 a small winery was established in Winnipeg, Manitoba. This was later followed by the establishment of another small operation in Dartmouth, Nova Scotia in 1985. These geographic expansion moves were the company's response to interprovincial trade barriers that gave preference to the selling of wines bottled in the same province. Moreover, Ontario wineries and, to a lesser extent, British Columbia's, were restricted to using mostly local grapes, whereas other provinces allowed unlimited use of less expensive imported bulk wine or grape concentrate.

A high Canadian dollar and subsidized European wines resulted in large market share gains for imports and a weak market for Ontario wines in 1984. Brights started importing wines and spirits in a limited fashion that year under the name of Wines of the Globe. It also spent $4 million modernizing the wine cellars at Niagara Falls.

THE ACQUISITION OF JORDAN & ST. MICHELLE

The Niagara Accord, signed in May 1986, seemed to promise relief to Ontario wineries with preferential pricing and distribution policies. In June, Brights made the biggest acquisition of its history, effectively doubling its size. It bought Jordan & St. Michelle Cellars Ltd. from the brewery Carling O'Keefe for $18 million in cash and $11 million in a non-interest bearing note. Industry observers thought Carling O'Keefe had been dissatisfied with the performance of its wine subsidiary. Jordan had lost $2.3 million in fiscal 1986 after a profit of $3.2 million in 1985. Jordan's wineries in St. Catharines, Ontario and Surrey, B.C. were acquired in the purchase. There was some rationalization of staff but the number of employees almost doubled. The acquisition also added 30 wine retail stores in Ontario, bringing the total stores operated by Brights in the province to over 60.

In British Columbia, Brights Entre-Lacs wines were designated the official wines of Expo '86 and the publicity contributed to a huge growth of sales in the province. Policy changes which allowed the opening of retail wine stores prompted the company with two other wineries to open an outlet in Vancouver's Granville market. It was highly successful. The company was also involved in retailing wine through the Woodwards department store chain in B.C. on a test basis.

In Quebec, Brights completed a $1.6 million expansion of facilities, including the expansion of the cooperage at St. Hyacinthe and St. Joseph du Lac and an additional 7 000 square feet for laboratories, offices and a bulk wine receiving area. The old Lachine facility was closed. At this point Brights had two wineries in Ontario, two wineries in Quebec, two wineries in B.C., and one winery each in Manitoba and Nova Scotia. It was now the largest wine company in Canada.

Brights had dominated the Ontario wine industry for many years. However, in the 1970s Andres came up with Baby Duck, a low-alcohol sparkling "pop" wine made from inexpensive native grapes. Supported by advertising and promotion, Baby Duck became the best selling wine in Canada, and Andres became the market share leader overshadowing Brights. Andres relied on innovation, aggressive marketing and product development, and modern production facilities. Brights was generally more conservative in both marketing and production, and typically relied on its having the most extensive product line and thus obtaining the most numerous shelf facings. Arnold thought that rather than coming up with one "big hit" from time to time, Brights could fill most of the wine market's fragmented consumer segments with consistently supported brands. The Jordan acquisition enabled Brights to regain the top market share spot in Ontario and the rest of the country.

BRIGHTS' NEW STRATEGY

The protection from imports provided by the Niagara Accord proved to be short-lived. The whole Canadian wine market was about to lose its barriers to foreign competition. In November 1987, the Free Trade Agreement with the U.S. was signed. In 1988, the federal government negotiated a settlement with the GATT. Both developments resulted in the phase out of import barriers in all provinces over a period of years. For instance, in Ontario and B.C., preferential markups by the liquor control boards would be eliminated in stages within seven to ten years starting January 1, 1989.

Faced with the inevitable onslaught of foreign wines, Brights announced a new seven- point strategy in its 1988 annual report:

1. Develop a global program for alternate sources of raw materials.

2. Continue to be more cost competitive in production.

3. Create new and different packaging and products.

4. Strengthen research and development in premium table wines.

5. Continue to expand the cider market in Canada and other markets.

6. Enter the export market with new products.

7. Maximize returns on real estate holdings in Canada.

MARKET TRENDS

Overall sales of wine in Canada had been on a downwards trend. Sales by volume decreased almost 5% from 1986 to 1990. All provinces and territories except Quebec declined or stayed flat during the period. Alberta showed the biggest decrease in percentage terms—26%, while Ontario had the biggest decline in volume—3.6 million litres. Quebec increased 5% since 1986, but the 1990 volume was down 1.63 million litres from that of 1988 (Exhibit 1).

Canadian wine in all provinces, except for Ontario and B.C., was mainly made of American or French bulk wine or grape concentrate imports bottled in the provinces. Ontario and B.C., both with sizeable grape growing areas, were the only provinces[1] which used their own grapes. Sales of Canadian wine declined at a higher rate than the market from 1986 to 1990 as foreign wines gained market share in Newfoundland, Ontario, Manitoba, Saskatchewan, Alberta and B.C. (Exhibit 2).

Like Ontario, the Quebec and B.C. liquor boards had markup policies that gave preference to certain wines (Table 1). However, these were scheduled to be phased out as well under the free trade and GATT provisions.

Wines were divided into 13 different categories by the provincial liquor control boards. White wines were the largest category, comprising 55% of total wine sales in 1990, and exhibited a 5% increase in volume from 1986 to 1990. Red wines, the second largest category with 21%, declined 16% in the period. Coolers reached their peak in 1988 but were down 36% by 1990. Pop wines (the 7% alcohol sparkling category) were the rage in the Canadian market in the 1970s. However, as the wine market gained sophistication, their popularity fell rapidly, declining 40% in the five-year period (Exhibit 3).

---

[1] Nova Scotia also had a minor grape growing area.

TABLE 1 **Markup Policies of the Liquor Boards in British Columbia and Quebec**

British Columbia	Percentage Markup (Applied to Landed Cost + Vol. Markup)	Cost of Service Differential ($/ltr)
30–100% B.C. content	83%	–
0–29% B.C. content	88	–
Other Canadian	100	0.56
U.S.	100	0.71
Other imported	106	0.56

Note: In addition there was a volume markup of $0.12/litre for all wines.

Quebec	Bottled in Quebec	Not Bottled in Quebec
Applied to each case of twelve 750 ml bottles		
First $25–40	60%	80%
Next $40–75	80	60
Portion over $75	50	50
Plus a fixed charge per case of	$30.75	$35.75

Foreign wines gained market share in the red, rose, greater than 7% alcohol sparkling, port, sherry, vermouth and cooler categories from 1986 to 1990. Canadian wines made inroads in the crackling, champagne, aperitif and miscellaneous categories, and a very slight improvement in the all important white wine category (Exhibit 4).

BRIGHTS' OPERATIONS

Brights national annual sales by wine category is shown in Exhibit 5. Brights and its wholly owned Quebec subsidiary, La Salle, had a combined 11.9% of the Canadian wine market by volume in 1990, the highest market share. Back in 1986, combined Brights, La Salle and Jordan sales were 13.1% of the market. Brights' total volume of wine sales went down 4.8 million litres in the five-year period. The other top Canadian volume producers such as Andres, Cartier and Calona also lost share during the period. Barton & Guestier (a French company) and Dumont (a Quebec bottler of European bulk wine) made gains in both volume and market share. The top seven wine companies in Canada and their relative shares are shown in Exhibit 6.

In white table wines, Brights was number one, with 10.8% of the market in 1990 compared to 11.8% in 1986. Brights' sales volume in the category decreased by 808 thousand litres in the period. Andres and Cartier lost volume as well.

Barton and Guestier, and Piat, another French company, gained volume and market share. In red table wines, Brights was on top as well with a 9.0% share. In 1986, its market share was 9.9% and volume was 1.2 million litres more. Brights continued to dominate the champagne category during the period as well as staying number two in pop wines.

Nationally, the best selling white and red wine in 1990 was the French brand, Le Piat D'Or, with 4.4% and 3.0% market share respectively. La Salle Notre Vin was seventh in white wines with a 1.8% share, and second in red wines with a 2.3% share. Brights Entre Lacs was ninth in white wines and 13th in red wines, with 1.6% and 1.0% respectively. Brights L'Entre Cote was 13th in white wine and sixth in red wine, with 1.1% and 1.7% respectively. Brights Le Villageois had 0.8% share in white wine and 1.0% share in red wine. The latter three brands had actually gained volume and market share since the previous year (Exhibit 7).

In the Ontario market, Brights had the highest market share in six categories out of thirteen in 1990. It was first in champagne, crackling wine, 7% alcohol sparkling wine, port, sherry and aperitifs, and second in white and red table wines to Barton & Guestier. Brights was number three in market share for total wine sales in both Quebec and B.C., but its market share was actually higher in both provinces than in Ontario. Starting 1988, Brights' Quebec volume passed its Ontario volume (Exhibit 8).

In 1990, Le Villageois, Brights' locally bottled brand made from French bulk wine, became the best selling brand of wine bottled in Quebec. Brights, Quebec, significantly increased its imports of French bulk table wine from 785 000 litres in 1986 to 1.6 million litres in 1990. Brights also imported limited quantities of finished premium vintaged wines and alcoholic products from Europe, the U.S. and Japan.

Price Position

In the important Ontario market, Brights' Ontario bottled brands were mainly in the lower to medium low priced segments (Table 2). Its brands were positioned similarly in other provinces.

TABLE 2   Table Wine Brand Package Assortment Summary for Brights

	Low *Under $6.95*	*Low/Medium* *$6.95–$7.95*	*High/Medium* *$7.95–$12.95*	*Premium* *Over $12.95*
White	41	8	0	0
Red	26	4	0	0

The Case of Champagne

President Champagne had been the market leader in Canadian champagnes for a long time, outsold any French champagne, and was Brights' most profitable product per litre. In 1987, French champagne producers and the French government initiated litigation against Brights and other Canadian wineries to prohibit their use of the word "champagne". The Supreme Court of Ontario decided that Canadian champagne had developed its own reputation as a distinct product, and rejected the plaintiffs' arguments. The company breathed a big sigh of relief.

New Products

In 1988, Brights introduced five fruit flavoured Schnapps style wine beverages under the brand name P.J. Shooters. Brights announced that it would try to attract new consumers by introducing new brands to fit changing lifestyles and trends. By 1990, the products were discontinued due to disappointing sales.

Brights got into the market for sparkling alcoholic (6% by volume) apple ciders in B.C. with the Jordan acquisition. Jordan had sold the Growers brand of sparkling cider. Brights decided to aggressively expand the line in 1988, introducing four new fruit flavoured sparkling ciders, revising packaging, and launching new radio and television advertising campaigns. Despite these efforts, sales declined 25% due to new competitive refreshment entries. In 1989, Brights introduced a "soft" cider entering the non-alcoholic beverage market.

In 1989, B.C. followed the practice of other provinces by allowing the bottling of 100% imported bulk wine or grape concentrate. Only Ontario remained a holdout by restricting import content to 70%. In Brights' Western Division, sales of locally bottled bulk wine from California increased over 50%, while locally bottled French wine increased 35% in fiscal 1991. Several new wine blends using American and French bulk wine were introduced in 1988 and 1989. These included California House, Escarmouche and Leonardo.

Sawmill Creek

In 1989, the Sawmill Creek line was introduced in several provinces, positioned as a modern, dry, affordable family of varietal and dual varietal wines. The wines blended Canadian grapes with bulk wine imports from California, Washington state, Chile and Yugoslavia. They had a contemporary looking label that could easily pass for a Napa Valley product and did not mention the name Brights anywhere on it. Promotional point of purchase displays at the LCBO deemphasized its Canadian origin. Prices were $4.95 a 750 ml. bottle for the Dry White and Dry Red, and $5.95 a 750 ml. bottle for the Chardonnay,

Fume Blanc, Riesling, Merlot-Baco, Sauvignon Chardonnay, Sauvignon-Riesling, Semillon-Chardonnay and Zinfandel-Gamay. Sales for the brand at the Ontario LCBO grew from 18 000 litres in 1989 to 243 000 litres in 1990, and it became the best selling Canadian varietal wine in the country. It also formed the nucleus of Brights 1991 restaurant and licencee business along with President Champagne, Entre-Lacs and Brights House Wine. Brights was planning to launch it in the U. S. in the summer of 1991. Brights had gained approval from the Ontario government to blend and bottle 100% imported bulk wine in Niagara Falls for export.

Pricing Tactics

Faced with increasing Ontario LCBO markups and the need to maintain a retail selling price advantage over foreign wines, Brights decided to cut its wholesale price. In July 1990, it lowered the price on 60 products, from 60 cents to a dollar per bottle in Ontario. Explained Arnold, "One of the reasons is that we have some pretty good *vins ordinaires* that have significantly changed in the past couple of years. The fastest way to get to the consumer is not television, but dropping the price."[2] Competitors were not pleased by the move as they responded with the same tactic. "Everybody had to reduce their prices. That will create financial problems. It will lead to a no-profit situation this year in Ontario's operations. I didn't think their price-cutting was necessary in today's environment. Things are uncertain enough already," said an executive from Andres.[3]

Distribution

Brights tried to tailor marketing to specific regional characteristics and demand preferences. Regional production, marketing and selling were under the control of a vice-president and general manager. The Western division managed B.C. and the Prairies; the Central division had Ontario; and the Eastern division was responsible for Quebec and the Maritimes.

Brights wines were distributed by the liquor control boards of the twelve provinces and territories. In addition, Brights wines were sold in Quebec grocery stores, privately owned wine stores in B.C., and in 68 company wine stores in Ontario. Brights completed a store image enhancement program in 1990 to upgrade the ambiance and consumer appeal of Ontario retail outlets. The company expected 60 000 visitors for tours and tastings at the Niagara Falls winery and store for 1991.

---

[2] Report on *Business Magazine*, February 1991, p.57.
[3] Ibid.

A total of 89 licenses for wine stores in Ontario had been approved before the free trade moratorium, and this gave Brights the option of opening 21 more. Annual operating expenses for a conventional retail store in a good location would cost over $100 000 and initial leasehold improvements would cost a minimum of $30 000.

Production Facilities

Faced with a downturn in sales and tougher competition from imports, Brights sought to rationalize its production facilities. At the end of 1987, Brights stopped packaging operations at the St. Catharines winery which used to be the Ontario production facility of Jordan & St. Michelle Cellars. In 1989, the manufacturing, warehousing and distribution facility was dismantled, and the surplus equipment and property sold. This provided an extraordinary gain in income net of taxes of $592 000.

Preferred markups given to wines bottled in Manitoba were eliminated in 1989. This prompted the closing of the small Winnipeg winery. In 1990, the winery in Surrey, B.C. was closed and put on the market. B.C. operations were consolidated at the Oliver plant. In the same year, the winery at St. Joseph du Lac, Quebec was closed and operations consolidated at St. Hyacinthe. The plant closings resulted in an extraordinary charge of $1.97 million to 1990 results leading to a net loss in annual earnings.

The two largest facilities that Brights had remaining were at Niagara Falls, Ontario and St. Hyacinthe, Quebec. The Quebec plant had a capacity of 2.3 million litres, and had two buildings covering 50 000 sq. ft. The Ontario plant had a capacity of 26.5 million litres, and was the largest winery facility in Canada. The bottling line and warehouse covered 63 000 sq. ft. The automated vintage building covered 23 000 sq. ft., and housed 54 stainless steel storage tanks. A $10 million modernization program for the Niagara Falls facility was scheduled to be finished in time for the 1991 harvest. Brights expected the project, which was substantially funded by the Ontario Winery Adjustment Program (OWAP), to yield production efficiencies.

Government Support

Brights made use of the government support programs designed to assist the wine industry to adjust to foreign competition. It obtained an $8 million grant from the OWAP to modernize the Niagara Falls facility. The OWAP was a 12-year $45 million Ontario government program that provided forgivable loans to wineries, provided they met certain conditions—mainly their annual quota of grapes purchased from Ontario growers. This quota was based on the previous year's purchases of local grapes and total sales. Brights was the largest winery in both categories. In fiscal 1991, Brights received $2.5 million of the loan from the Ontario Development Corporation which administered the program. Brights' competitors had also sought government support. For example, Andres received $2.6 million in the same period.

Earlier, Brights received $1 307 000 (or $919 000 net of income tax) from the Ontario Grape Acreage Reduction Program in fiscal 1989 to pull out some of its vines. The program was part of the $100 million Grape and Wine Adjustment Program of the federal and provincial governments, which sought to reduce the land acreage planted with grapes in Ontario by more than a third.

Offers to Buy Brights

In January 1990, the Hatch family which owned 54.3 % of the outstanding shares announced that negotiations were underway to sell Brights. They also stated that the same offer had to be made to all shareholders. The suitor turned out to be Celliers du Monde Inc. of Montreal. Celliers offered $20 a share, or $41.3 million, for Brights. In 1989, Celliers had bought the Canadian interests of Paul Masson from Seagrams, and also imported Paul Masson wines from the U.S. It had around $30 million in sales that year. It was owned by its president, Jean-Denis Cotes (55%) and the Societe d'Investissement Desjardins (45%). Brights shares hit a trading high of $19.38 in the Toronto Stock Exchange due to the news. The following month, Celliers announced that it was withdrawing its bid without further explanation, reportedly losing a $1 million deposit in the process.

Around the same period, Calgary-based Berenger Acquisitions bid $20.50, but the offer was rejected by the Hatch family. The move was described by Brights director Carr Hatch as "smoke and mirrors." Berenger Acquisitions was thought to be owned by Vancouver real estate entreprenuer Nelson Skalbania. Analysts thought he was mainly after the land owned by Brights in the "Golden Horseshoe" of southwestern Ontario and near Vancouver, B.C.

Real Estate

The company was not new to selling its real estate assets for a profit. In the 1970s it recorded gains of hundreds of thousands of dollars from land sales. In 1984, Brights recorded an extraordinary gain of $1.38 million on its earnings statement from real estate sales in Toronto and Montreal. During fiscal 1990, an office building for rental purposes was constructed on some of its vacant land in Niagara Falls. There was much speculation in the news about the value of Brights' landholdings. Mergers and Acquisitions in Canada thought Brights' real estate was worth around $24 million.[4] Other analysts thought it was worth

---

[4] Mergers and Acquisitions in Canada, February 1990, volume 2 number 2, p.16.

$8 to $10 a share. These estimates were contingent on the rezoning of a great deal of agricultural land for commercial and industrial use. There was substantial uncertainty about whether, when and to what degree this would be achieved by Brights or others.

Financial Performance

Brights had taken a $20 million bank term loan to finance the Jordan acquisition. The effective rate was 11%, and principal repayments were scheduled accordingly: November 1988–$1.5 million; November 1989–$1.5 million; November 1990–$3.0 million; November 1991–$6.0 million; and November 1993–$8.0 million. The loan raised the company's interest expense considerably, putting further pressure on Brights' earnings. In their 1991 annual report, the company revealed that a restructuring of the principal repayment terms was being considered.

The same report noted that the company's gross margins increased to 35.3%, compared to 34.8% the previous year due to cost savings. It also noted that the 1991 figure would have been 37.5% if the previous year's average selling prices had held.

The OWAP forgivable loan received in 1990 was not reflected in the company's financials as a source of funds. Rather, Brights reduced the book value of new assets acquired that year by the amount of the loan funds. The company's five-year income statement, balance sheet, and selected performance indicators are shown in Exhibits 9–11.

EXHIBIT 1 Wine Sales in Canada by Province (000 litres)

Year ending March 31	1986	1987	1988	1989	1990
Newfoundland	1 857	1 699	1 731	1 647	1 607
Prince Edward Is.	556	564	580	556	555
Nova Scotia	5 263	5 502	5 225	5 054	4 867
New Brunswick	3 293	3 315	3 283	3 331	3 308
Quebec	71 772	70 346	76 794	76 519	75 295
Ontario	74 513	75 515	76 776	73 421	71 179
Manitoba	7 780	7 569	7 121	6 280	5 952
Saskatchewan	5 318	5 006	5 003	4 324	4 034
Alberta	24 392	21 326	19 655	19 053	18 037
British Columbia	40 546	40 688	41 018	39 820	39,343
Yukon	309	303	319	307	298
Northwest Terr.	327	302	297	272	260
Total Canada	235 926	232 136	237 801	230 583	224 735

EXHIBIT 2 Market Share of Canadian Wines by Province (%)

Year ending March 31	1986	1990
Newfoundland	50.9%	45.3%
Prince Edward Is.	65.0	67.4
Nova Scotia	63.3	65.3
New Brunswick	64.9	70.3
Quebec	33.1	40.9
Ontario	41.8	35.5
Manitoba	51.2	48.4
Saskatchewan	60.7	60.2
Alberta	54.2	47.2
British Columbia	61.8	55.9
Yukon	55.0	59.5
Northwest Terr.	28.3	40.4
Total Canada	45.5	44.0

EXHIBIT 3 Wine Sales in Canada by Category (000 litres)

Year ending March 31	1986	1987	1988	1989	1990
Red Wine	58 716	52 447	50 822	47 993	47 343
White Wine	117 599	116 384	120 121	121 527	123 408
Rose Wine	2 418	2 100	2 060	1 913	1 729
Crackling Wine	1 881	1 428	1 126	905	734
7% Sparkling Wine	12 848	10 737	9 821	8 942	7 763
>7% Sparkling Wine	5 560	5 467	5 685	5 522	5 626
Champagne	2 541	2 389	2 393	2 309	2 120
Port	1 623	1 545	1 448	1 295	1 252
Sherry	8 078	7 672	7 226	6 827	6 694
Vermouth	4 383	3 900	3 674	3 533	3 302
Aperitif	2 169	1 798	1 672	1 586	1 535
Miscellaneous	7 548	8 176	8 797	8 379	8551
Wine Coolers	12 986	18 095	22 956	19 853	14 675
Total	235 926	232 136	237 801	230 583	224 735

EXHIBIT 4 Market Share of Canadian Wines by Category (000 litres)

Year ending March 31	1986	1990
Red Wine	32.9%	28.4%
White Wine	43.0	43.6
Rose Wine	22.7	11.2
Crackling Wine	39.7	43.3
7% Sparkling Wine	100.0	100.0
>7% Sparkling Wine	12.6	8.5
Champagne	58.0	63.2
Port	75.4	70.6
Sherry	77.9	77.6
Vermouth	10.0	9.2
Aperitif	10.2	12.6
Miscellaneous	11.2	12.6
Wine Coolers	100.0	94.4
Total	45.5	44.0

EXHIBIT 5 **Sales Volumes (000 litres) and Market Shares (%) of Brights in Canada by Category***

	1986	1987	1988	1989	1990
All Wines					
Brights	15 777	17 412	16 629	21 837	21 388
Jordan	11 504	10 155	8 384	–	–
La Salle	3 219	3 926	4 483	5 174	4 351
Total sales	30 500	31 493	29 496	27 011	25 739
% of total market	13.05	13.22	12.71	11.95	11.88
Red Wine					
Brights	2 826	2 954	2 800	3 569	3 466
Jordan	1 554	1 284	1 203	–	–
La Salle	1 251	1 400	1 458	1 285	1 111
Total sales	5 631	5 638	5 461	4 854	4 577
% of total market	10.50	10.93	11.30	10.23	10.12
White Wines					
Brights	6 922	7 671	7 526	10 653	10 562
Jordan	5 076	4 476	4 223	–	–
La Salle	1 752	1 400	1 458	1 285	1 111
Total sales	13 750	13 547	13 207	11 938	11 673
% of total market	11.82	11.99	11.88	10.72	10.77
7% Sparkling Wines					
Brights	890	891	870	1 723	1 568
Jordan	2 324	2 064	1 868	–	–
La Salle	15	36	23	678	596
Total sales	3 229	2 991	2 761	2 401	2 164
% of total market	29.44	30.02	30.45	29.84	29.58
Champagne					
Brights	1 124	1 171	1 073	961	792
% of total market	45.43	48.35	46.15	44.33	42.45
Wine Coolers					
Brights	1 132	1 034	50	248	140
Jordan	657	1 202	1 018	–	–
La Salle	–	–	–	280	117
Total sales	1 789	2 236	1 068	528	257
% of total market	10.13	10.06	5.22	3.55	2.00

* Jordan was acquired by Brights in 1986. La Salle is a wholly owned subsidiary of Brights in Quebec.

EXHIBIT 6 **Sales Volume (000 litres) and Market Share (%) of Top Wine Companies in Canada***

1990 rank	Company	1990 Sales	1990 Market Share	% chg since 1989	1986 Rank	1986 Sales	1986 Market Share
Total Wine Market							
1	Brights	25 738	11.9	−4.2	1	30 500	13.1
2	Andres	20 568	9.5	−4.9	2	25 286	10.8
3	Cartier	16 712	7.7	−6.2	3	20 079	8.6
4	S.A.Q.	10 305	4.8	−9.8	4	14 303	6.1
5	Barton & Guestier	8 702	4.0	−9.4	6	7 911	3.4
6	Dumont Vin	7 909	3.6	−10.0	7	5 436	2.3
7	Calona	6 871	3.2	−13.0	5	10 355	4.4
White Wine Market							
1	Brights	12 943	10.8	−2.6	1	13 750	11.8
2	Andres	12 545	10.4	−1.7	2	11 869	10.2
3	Barton & Guestier	6 807	5.7	−8.5	5	5 691	4.9
4	Cartier	6 526	5.4	−3.9	3	8 834	7.6
5	Piat	5 258	4.4	4.7	9	3 789	3.3
Red Wine Market							
1	Brights	4 057	9.0	−3.4	1	5 297	9.9
2	S.A.Q.	2 005	4.4	−19.3	2	4 682	8.7
3	Barton & Guestier	1 895	4.2	−11.6	4	2 220	4.1
4	Andres	1 679	3.7	−3.4	3	2 483	4.6
7% Sparkling Wine Market							
1	Andres	3 050	41.7	−12.7	1	5 297	48.3
2	Brights	2 164	29.6	−9.0	2	3 214	29.3
Champagne							
1	Brights	792	42.5	−17.6	1	1 058	42.7
2	Andres	251	13.5	−2.0	3	214	8.7

* Results for Brights include sales of La Salle and Jordan.
  S.A.Q. is the Quebec liquor control board. Aside from distributing wines, it also imports and bottles wines under its label.
  Calona is a B.C. winery.

EXHIBIT 7   Sales Volume (000 litres) and Market Shares (%) of Best Selling Wine Brands in Canada

1990 Rank	Brand	1990 Sales	1990 Market Share	% chg since 1989	1986 Volume	1986 Market Share
White Wines						
1	Le Piat D'Or	5 251.5	4.4	4.7	3 234.6	2.8
2	Andres Hochtaler	3 969.0	3.3	−2.8	4 558.5	3.9
3	Kressman Selectione	3 796.2	3.2	4.0	4 917.6	4.2
7	La Salle Notre Vin	2 219.4	1.8	−8.3	1 634.4	1.4
8	Andres Domaine D'Or	1 975.5	1.6	4.2	1 182.6	1.0
9	Brights Entre–Lacs	1 940.4	1.6	27.4	989.1	0.9
10	Calona Schloss	1 866.6	1.6	−15.6	2 736.0	2.4
13	Brights L'Entre Cote	1 378.8	1.1	42.1	855.0	0.7
24	Brights Maria Christina	1 047.6	0.9	3.5	1 486.8	1.3
25	Brights House	1 027.8	0.9	−2.8	1 373.4	1.2
27	Brights Le Villageois	952.0	0.8	20.7	411.3	0.4
Red Wines						
1	Le Piat D'Or	1 347.3	3.0	−2.2	1 140.3	2.1
2	La Salle Notre Vin	1 038.6	2.3	−12.9	1 158.3	2.2
6	Brights L'Entre Cote	774.9	1.7	24.8	776.7	1.4
7	Calona Royal	752.4	1.7	−10.4	1 228.5	2.3
8	Chantecler Du Marchand	689.4	1.5	−18.2	918.9	1.7
13	Brights Entre–Lacs	465.3	1.0	16.6	307.8	0.6
14	Brights Le Villageois	458.6	1.0	6.2	301.5	0.6
22	Brights Toscano	270.9	0.6	−9.7	395.1	0.7
28	Brights House	219.6	0.5	−15.2	352.8	0.7
7% Sparkling Wine Market						
1	Brights Spumante Bambino	1 355.4	18.5	−6.6	1 806.3	16.5
2	Andres Baby Champagne	2 163.6	29.6	−9.0	3 213.9	29.3
Champagne						
1	Brights President	516.6	27.7	−18.8	769.5	31.1
2	Andres Dry	171.9	9.2	4.9	83.7	3.4

EXHIBIT 8 Sales Volume (000 litres) and Market Shares (%) of Brights in the Three Largest Markets

	1986	*1988*	*1989*	*1990*	*1991*
British Columbia					
Brights	2 119	2 466	2 335	4 269	4 219
Jordan	3 499	2 843	2 470	–	–
La Salle	–	–	–	108	972
Total sales	5 618	5 309	4 804	4 377	5 191
% of total market	13.82	13.06	11.99	11.16	13.10
Ontario					
Brights	5 825	6 018	5 492	8 379	7 799
Jordan	4 907	4 770	3 992	–	–
La Salle	–	–	–	122	42
Total sales	10 732	10 788	9 484	8 501	7 842
% of total market	14.41	14.09	12.85	11.69	11.61
Quebec					
Brights	5 696	6 553	6 710	5 771	6 392
Jordan	88	100	58	–	–
La Salle	3 219	3 926	4 483	4 911	4 201
Total sales	9 004	10 579	11 251	10 682	10 593
% of total market	12.44	13.73	14.63	14.23	14.73

EXHIBIT 9 Brights' Five-Year Income Statement ($000)

Year ending March 31	*1987*	*1988*	*1989*	*1990*	*1991*
Sales	75 399	84 827	82 132	74 384	70 214
Cost of goods sold	47 916	54 258	53 611	48 513	45 396
SGA	21 023	23 350	22 498	22 547	21 192
Interest	2 217	3 566	3 466	2 041	1 758
Total expenses	71 156	81 174	79 575	73 101	68 346
Income taxes	1 987	1 644	1 072	(1 616)	689
Income before extraordinary items	2 256	2 009	1 485	2 899	1 179
Extraordinary items*	1 381	866	1 311	(3 965)	0
Net income	3 637	2 875	2 796	(1 066)	1 179

* Extraordinary items in 1987 and 1988 are gains on sale of property. Extraordinary item for 1989 consists of Grape Acreage Reduction Program for $0.9 million and gain on sale of property for $0.4 million. Extraordinary items for 1990 is due to rationalization of production facilities in Quebec and B.C.

EXHIBIT 10 Brights' Five-Year Balance Sheet ($000)

Year ending March 31	1987	1988	1989	1990	1991
Cash	286	298	209	102	114
Accounts receivable	11 459	7 638	10 327	7 819	9 645
Inventories	34 278	39 254	31 866	27 461	24 027
Other current assets*	925	620	384	6 394	2 936
Total current assets	46 930	47 810	42 786	41 776	36 722
Fixed assets	26 751	26 311	21 820	13 733	14 522
Other assets	1 046	2 377	7 236	7 560	6 834
Total assets	74 727	76 498	71 842	63 069	58 078
Current liabilities	26 887	24 642	18 559	18 302	16 787
Term loan	20 000	18 500	17 000	14 000	8 517
Other liabilities	1 895	5 049	5 693	2 366	3 707
Capital stock	3 144	3 147	3 150	3 153	3 157
Retained earnings	22 801	25 160	27 440	25 248	25 910
Total shareholder's equity	25 945	28 307	30 590	28 401	29 067

* Other current assets included assets held for resale of $6.0 million and $2.3 million in 1990 and 1991 respectively, as a result of idled fixed assets from the restructuring of production facilities. OWAP forgivable loan grant of $2.5 million in 1991 is reflected as a reduction in the cost of fixed assets acquired during the year. Other assets included mortgages receivable of $5.2 million in 1989, $5.1 million in 1990, and $4.1 million in 1991.

EXHIBIT 11 Brights' Other Indicators

Year ending March 31	1987	1988	1989	1990	1991
Cash Flow Data ($000)					
Net income	3 637	2 875	2 796	(1 066)	1 179
Depreciation	3 579	2 938	2 841	3 111	2 231
Dividends paid	414	516	516	517	517
Per Share Data ($)					
Net income (loss)	1.76	1.23	1.21	(.52)	.57
Dividends	.20	.25	.25	.25	.25
Book value	12.55	13.54	14.50	13.74	14.06
Share price range—					
high	15.50	17.00	14.75	19.37	17.00
low	9.13	8.63	8.75	11.87	7.25
Number of Outstanding					
Shares (000)	2 066.5	2 066.7	2 067.0	2 067.3	2 067.5
Number of Full-time					
Employees	459	431	379	335	287

IKEA CANADA LTD. —1986 (CONDENSED)

Paul W. Beamish
Condensed by J. Peter Killing

Founded as a mail order business in rural Sweden in 1943, IKEA had grown to more than U.S. $1 billion in sales and 70 retail outlets by 1985, and was considered by many to be one of the best run furniture operations in the world. Although only 14% of IKEA's sales were outside Europe, the company's fastest growth was occurring in North America.

Success, however, brought imitators, and in mid-1986 Bjorn Bayley and Anders Berglund, the senior managers of IKEA's North American operations, were examining a just published Sears Canada catalogue, which contained a new 20-page section called "Elements." This section bore a striking resemblance to the format of an IKEA Canada catalogue (see Exhibits 1 and 2 for sample pages), and the furniture being offered was similar to IKEA's knocked-down, self-assembled line in which different "elements" could be ordered by the customer to create particular designs. Bayley and Berglund wondered how serious Sears was about its new initiative, and what, if anything, IKEA should do in response.

THE CANADIAN FURNITURE MARKET

Canadian consumption of furniture totalled more than $2 billion in 1985, an average of well over $600 per household. Imports accounted for approximately 18% of this total, half of which originated in the United States. The duties on furniture imported into Canada were approximately 15%.

Furniture was sold to Canadian consumers through three types of stores: independents, specialty chains and department stores. Although the independents held a 70% market share, this figure was declining due to their inability to compete with the chains in terms of advertising, purchasing power, management sophistication and sales support. The average sales per square metre in 1985 for furniture stores of all three types was $1 666 (the figure was $2 606 for stores which also sold appliances) and the average cost of goods sold was 64.5%.

While the major department stores such as Eaton's and Sears tended to carry traditional furniture lines close to the middle of the price/quality range, chains and independents operated from one end of the spectrum to the other. At the upper end of the market, specialty stores attempted to differentiate themselves by offering unique product lines, superior service and a specialized shopping atmosphere. The lower end of the market, on the other hand, was dominated by furniture warehouses which spent heavily on advertising, and offered lower price, less service, and less emphasis on a fancy image. The warehouses usually kept a larger inventory of furniture on hand than the department stores, but expected customers to pick up their purchases. Over half the warehouse sales involved promotional financing arrangements, including delayed payments, extended terms, and so on.

The major firms in this group, both of whom sold furniture and appliances, were The Brick and Leon's. The Brick had annual sales of $240 million from 15 Canadian stores, and was rapidly expanding from its western Canada base. With 30 additional stores in California under the Furnishings 2000 name, The Brick intended to become the largest furniture retailing company in the world. Leon's had annual sales of $160 million from 14 stores, and was growing rapidly from its Ontario base. These 14 stores were operated under a variety of names. Leon's also franchised its name in smaller cities in Canada. For part of their merchandise requirements, The Brick and Leon's often negotiated with manufacturers for exclusive products, styles and fabrics and imported from the U.S., Europe and the Far East. Although both firms had had problems earlier with entry to the U.S. market, each intended on expanding there.

Most furniture retailers in Canada purchased their products from Canadian manufacturers after examining new designs and models at trade shows. There were approximately 1 400 Canadian furniture manufacturers, mostly located in Ontario and Quebec. Typically, these firms were small (78% of Canadian furniture plants employed less than 50 people), undercapitalized and minimally automated. One industry executive quipped that one of the most significant technological developments for the industry had been the advent of the staple gun.

Canadian-produced furniture typically followed American and European styling. It was generally of adequate to excellent quality but was often more costly to produce. The reason for high Canadian costs was believed to be a combination of short manufacturing runs and high raw material, labour and distribution costs. In an attempt to reduce costs, a few of the larger manufacturers such as Kroehler had vertically integrated—purchasing sawmills, fabric warehouses, fibreboard and wood frame plants—but such practices were very much the exception in the industry.

THE IKEA FORMULA

IKEA's approach to business was fundamentally different from that of the traditional Canadian retailers. The company focussed exclusively on what it called "quick assembly" furniture, which consumers carried from the store in flat packages and assembled at home. This furniture was primarily pine, had a clean European design look to it, and was priced at 15% below the lowest prices for traditional furniture. Its major appeal appeared to be to young families, singles, and frequent movers, who were looking for well designed items that were economically priced and created instant impact.

According to company executives, IKEA was successful because of its revolutionary approach to the most important aspects of the business: product design, procurement, store operations, marketing, and management philosophy, which stressed flexibility and market orientation rather than long-range strategy. Each of these items is discussed in turn.

Product Design

IKEA's European designers, not the company's suppliers, were responsible for the design of most of the furniture and accessories in IKEA's product line, which totalled 15 000 items. The heart of the company's design capability was a 50-person Swedish workshop, which produced prototypes of new items of furniture and smaller components such as "an ingenious little snap lock for table legs which makes a table stronger and cheaper at the same time" and a "clever little screw attachment which allows for the assembly of a pin back chair in five minutes." IKEA's designers were very cost conscious, and were constantly working to lower costs in ways that were not critical to the consumer. The quality of a work top, for example, would be superior to the quality of the back of a bookshelf, which would never be seen. "Low price with a meaning" was the theme.

Although it was not impossible to copyright a particular design or process, IKEA's philosophy was "if somebody steals a model from us we do not bring a lawsuit, because a lawsuit is always negative. We solve the problem by making a new model that is even better."

Procurement

IKEA's early success in Sweden had so threatened traditional European furniture retailers that they had promised to boycott any major supplier that shipped products to the upstart firm. As a result, IKEA had no choice but to go to the smaller suppliers. Since these suppliers had limited resources, IKEA began assuming responsibility for the purchase of raw materials, packaging materials, storage, specialized equipment and machinery, and engineering. What began as a necessity soon became a cornerstone of IKEA's competitive strategy, and by 1986 the firm had nearly 100 production engineers working as purchasers. Together with IKEA's designers, these engineers assisted suppliers in every way they could to help them lower costs, dealing with everything from the introduction of new technology to the alteration of the dimensions of a shipping carton.

Although IKEA sometimes leased equipment and made loans to its suppliers, the firm was adamant that it would not enter the furniture manufacturing business itself. In fact, to avoid control over (and responsibility for) its suppliers, the company had a policy of limiting its purchases to 50% of a supplier's capacity. Many products were obtained from multiple suppliers, and frequently suppliers produced only a single standardized component or input to the final product. Unfinished pine shelves, for example, were obtained directly from saw mills, cabinet doors were purchased from door factories, and cushions came from textile mills.

In total, IKEA purchased goods from 1500 suppliers located in 40 countries. About 52% of the company's purchases were from Scandinavia, 21% from other countries of western Europe, 20% from eastern Europe, and 7% elsewhere.

Store Operations

IKEA stores were usually large one or two storey buildings situated in relatively inexpensive stand-alone locations, neither in prime downtown sites nor in shopping malls. Most stores were surrounded by a large parking lot, adorned with billboards explaining IKEA's delivery policy, product guarantee, and the existence of a coffee shop and/or restaurant.

On entering a store, the customer was immediately made aware of the children's play area (a room filled with hollow multi-coloured balls), a video room for older children, and a receptionist with copies of IKEA catalogues, a metric conversion guide, index cards for detailing purchases, and a store guide. The latter, supplemented by prominent signs, indicated that the store contained lockers and benches for shoppers, a first aid area, restrooms, strollers and a baby care area, an "as-is" department (no returns permitted), numerous check outs, suggestion boxes and, in many cases, a restaurant. All major credit cards were accepted.

Traffic flow in most IKEA stores was guided so as to pass by almost all of the merchandise in the store, which was displayed as it would look in the home, complete with all accessories. Throughout a store, employees could be identified by their bright red IKEA shirts. Part-time employees wore yellow shirts which read "Temporary Help—Please Don't Ask Me Any Hard Questions." The use of sales floor staff was minimal. The IKEA view was that "salesmen are expensive, and can also be irritating. IKEA leaves you to shop in peace."

While IKEA stores were all characterized by their self-serve, self-wrapping, self-transport, and self-assembly operations, the company's philosophy was that each new store would incorporate the latest ideas in use in any of its existing stores. The most recent trend in some countries was an IKEA Contract Sales section, which provided a delivery, invoicing, and assembly service for commercial customers.

Marketing

IKEA's promotional activities were intended to educate the consumer public on the benefits of the IKEA concept and build traffic by attracting new buyers and encouraging repeat visits from existing customers. The primary promotional vehicle was the annual IKEA catalogue, which was selectively mailed out to prime target customers, which in the Toronto area, for instance, had the following characteristics:

—Income $35 000+

—Own condominium or townhouse

—University degree

—White collar

—Primary age group 35–44

—Secondary age group 25–34

—Husband/wife both work

—Two children

—Movers

With minor variations, this "upscale" profile was typical of IKEA's target customers in Europe and North America. In Canada, IKEA management acknowledged the target market, but felt that in fact the IKEA concept appealed to a much wider group of consumers.

IKEA also spent heavily on magazine advertisements, which were noted for their humorous, slightly off-beat approach. In Canada, IKEA spent $2.5 million to print 3.6 million catalogues, $2 million on magazine advertising, and $1.5 million on other forms of promotion in 1984.

Management Philosophy

The philosophy of Ingvar Kamprad, the founder of IKEA, was "to create a better everyday life for the majority of people." In practice, this creed meant that

IKEA was dedicated to offering, and continuing to offer, the lowest prices possible on good quality furniture, so that IKEA products were available to as many people as possible. Fred Andersson, the head of IKEA's corporate product planning group stated, "Unlike other companies, we are not fascinated with what we produce—we make what our customers want." Generally, IKEA management felt that no other company could match IKEA's combination of quality and price across the full width of the product line.

IKEA also made a concerted effort to stay "close to its customers," and it was not unusual for the general manager of IKEA Canada, for instance, to personally telephone customers who had made complaints or suggestions. Each week an employee newsletter detailed all customer comments, and indicated how management felt they should be dealt with.

Another guiding philosophy of the firm was that growth would be in "small bites." The growth objective in Canada, for instance, had been to increase sales and profits by 20% per year, but care was taken to sequence store openings so that managerial and financial resources would not be strained.

Internally, the company's philosophy was stated as "freedom, with responsibility," which meant that IKEA's managers typically operated with a good deal of autonomy. The Canadian operation, for instance, received little in the way of explicit suggestions from head office, even in the one year when the budget was not met. The Canadian management team travelled to head office as a group only once every several years. As Bjorn Bayley explained, "We are a very informal management team, and try to have everyone who works for us believe that they have the freedom to do their job in the best way possible. It's almost impossible to push the philosophy down to the cashier level, but we try."

IKEA IN CANADA

IKEA's formula had worked well in Canada. Under the direction of a four-person management team, which included two Swedes, the company had grown from a single store in 1976 to nine stores totalling 75 000 square metres and, as shown in Exhibit 3, predicted 1986 sales of more than $140 million. The sales of IKEA Canada had exceeded budget in all but one of the past five years, and usually by a wide margin. Net profits were approximately 5% of sales. Profit and loss statements for 1983 and 1984, the only financial statements available, are presented in Exhibit 4.

IKEA Canada carried just less than half of the company's total product line. Individual items were chosen on the basis of what management thought would sell in Canada, and if IKEA could not beat a competitor's price by 10–15% on a particular item, it was dropped. Most of the goods sold in the Canadian stores were supplied from central warehouses in Sweden. To coordinate this process a five-person stock supply department in Vancouver provided Sweden with a three-year forecast of Canada's needs, and placed major orders twice a year. Actual volumes were expected to be within 10% of the forecast level. As Bayley noted, "you needed a gambler in the stock supply job."

Individual stores were expected to maintain 13.5 weeks of inventory on hand (10.5 weeks in the store and 3 weeks in transit), and could order from the central warehouse in Montreal, or, if a product was not in stock in Montreal, direct from Sweden. Shipments from Sweden took six to eight weeks to arrive, from Montreal two to three weeks. In practice, about 50% of the product arriving at a store arrived via each route.

IKEA's success in Canada meant that the firm was often hard pressed to keep the best selling items in stock. (Twenty percent of the firm's present line constituted 80% of sales volume.) At any given time in Canada IKEA stores might have 300 items out of stock, either because actual sales deviated significantly from forecasts or because suppliers could not meet their delivery promises. While management estimated that 75% of customers were willing to wait for IKEA products in a stockout situation, the company nevertheless began a deliberate policy of developing Canadian suppliers for high demand items, even if this meant paying a slight premium. In 1984, the stock control group purchased $57 million worth of goods on IKEA's behalf, $12 million of which was from 30 Canadian suppliers, up from $7 million the previous year.

As indicated in Exhibit 3, IKEA Canada sold products, rather reluctantly, by mail order to customers who preferred not to visit the stores. A senior manager explained: "To date we have engaged in defensive mail orders—only when the customer really wants it and the order is large enough. The separate handling, breaking down of orders, and repackaging required for mail orders would be too expensive and go against the economies-through-volume approach of IKEA. Profit margins of mail order business tend to be half that of a store operation. There are more sales returns, particularly because of damages—maybe 4%—incurred in shipping. It is difficult to know where to draw the market boundaries for a mail order business. We don't want to be substituting mail order customers for store visitors."

In 1986, the management team which had brought success to IKEA's Canadian operations was breaking up. Bjorn Bayley, who had come to Canada in 1978, was slotted to move to Philadelphia to spearhead IKEA's entry into the U.S. market, which had begun in June 1985 with a single store. With early sales running at a level twice as high as the company had predicted, Bayley expected to be busy, and was taking Mike McDonald, the controller, and Mike McMullen, the personnel director, with him. Anders Berglund, who, like Bayley, was a long time IKEA employee and had been in Canada since 1979, was scheduled to take over the Canadian operation. Berglund would report through Bayley to IKEA's North American sales director, who was located in Europe.

New Competition

IKEA's success in Canada had not gone unnoticed. IDOMO was a well established Toronto based competitor, and Sears Canada was a new entrant.

IDOMO

Like IKEA, IDOMO sold knocked down furniture which customers were required to assemble at home. IDOMO offered a somewhat narrower selection than IKEA but emphasized teak furniture to a much greater extent. With stores in Hamilton, Mississauga (across from IKEA), Toronto and Montreal, IDOMO appeared to have capitalized on excess demand that IKEA had developed but was not able to service.

The products and prices offered in both the 96-page IDOMO and 144-page IKEA catalogues were similar, with IKEA's prices lightly lower. Prices in the IKEA catalogue were in effect for a year. IDOMO reserved the right to make adjustments to prices and specifications. A mail order telephone number in Toronto was provided in the IDOMO catalogue. Of late, IDOMO had begun to employ an increased amount of television advertising. IDOMO purchased goods from around the world and operated a number of their own Canadian factories. Their primary source of goods was Denmark.

Sears

The newest entrant in the Canadian knocked-down furniture segment was Sears Canada, a wholly-owned subsidiary of Sears Roebuck of Chicago and, with $3.8 billion in annual revenues, one of Canada's largest merchandising operations. Sears operated 75 department stores in Canada, selling a wide range (700 merchandise lines comprising 100 000 stock keeping units) of medium price and quality goods. Sears Canada also ran a major catalogue operation, which distributed 12 annual catalogues to approximately 4 million Canadian families. Customers could place catalogue orders by mail, by telephone, or in person through one of the company's 1 500 catalogue sales units, which were spread throughout the country.

A quick check by Bayley and Berglund revealed that Sears' Elements line was being sold only in Canada and only through the major Sears catalogues. Elements products were not for sale, nor could they be viewed, in Sears stores. In the Fall-Winter catalogue that they examined, which was over 700 pages in length, the Elements line was given 20 pages. Although Sears appeared to offer the same "type" of products as IKEA, there was a narrower selection within each category. Prices for Elements' products seemed almost identical to IKEA prices. One distinct difference between the catalogues was the much greater emphasis IKEA placed on presenting a large number of coordinated settings and room designs.

Further checking indicated that at least some of the suppliers of the Elements line were Swedish, although it did not appear that IKEA and Sears had any suppliers in common. The IKEA executives knew that Sears was generally able to exert a great deal of influence over its suppliers, usually obtaining prices at least equal to and often below those of its competitors, because of the huge volumes purchased. Sears also worked closely with its suppliers in marketing, research, design and development, production standards and production planning. Many lines of merchandise were manufactured with features exclusive to Sears and were sold under its private brand names. There was a 75% buying overlap for the catalogue and store and about 90% overlap between regions on store purchases.

Like any Sears' product, Elements furniture could be charged to a Sears charge card. Delivery of catalogue items generally took about two weeks, and for a small extra charge catalogue orders would be delivered right to the consumer's home in a Sears truck. If a catalogue item was out of stock, Sears policy was either to tell the customer if and when the product would be available, or to substitute an item of equal or greater value. If goods proved defective, (10% of Sears Roebuck mail order furniture purchasers had received damaged or broken furniture), Sears provided home pick-up and replacement and was willing, for a fee, to install goods, provide parts, and do repairs as products aged. Sears emphasized "satisfaction guaranteed or money refunded." In its advertising, which included all forms of media, Sears stressed its "hassle-free returns" and asked customers to "take a look at the services we offer ... they'll bring you peace of mind, long after the bill is paid."

In their assessment of Sears Canada, Bayley and Berglund recognized that the company seemed to be going through something of a revival. Using the rallying cry that a "new" Sears was being created, Sears executives (the Canadian firm had ten vice-presidents) had experimented with new store layouts, pruned the product line, and improved customer service for catalogue orders. Richard Sharpe, the chairman of Sears Canada, personally addressed as many as 12 000 employees per year, and the company received 3 000 suggestions from employees annually. Perhaps as a result of these initiatives, and a cut in workforce from 65 000 to 50 000 over a several year period, Sears Canada posted its best ever results in 1985.

CONCLUSION

With the limited data they had on Sears, IKEA management recognized their comparison of the two companies would be incomplete. Nonetheless, a decision regarding the Sears competitive threat was required. Any solution would have to reflect Kamprad's philosophy: "Expensive solutions to problems are often signs of medicocrity. We have no interest in a solution until we know what it costs."

EXHIBIT 1 Sample Page from IKEA Catalogue, 1985

GUTE 126/6

GUTE 126/10

GUTE 87/8

GUTE 87/4

$98
GUTE 49/2

GUTE 49/6

GUTE 49/2

GUTE 126/6

$130
GUTE 87/4

GUTE. EIGHTEEN DIFFERENT CHESTS OF DRAWERS TO FIT IN ALMOST ANYWHERE.

GUTE chests of drawers ●möbelfakta White lacquered or pine veneered particleboard, natural or nutbrown stained. W80 cm, D40 cm. QA.
49/2. 2 drawers. H49 cm. White **$94.** Natural or nutbrown **$98.**
49/6. 6 drawers. H49 cm. White **$115.** Natural or nutbrown **$125.**
87/4. 4 drawers. H87 cm. White **$130.** Natural or nutbrown **$145.**

87/8. 8 drawers. H87 cm. White **$170.** Natural or nutbrown **$185.**
126/6. 6 drawers. H126 cm. White **$175.** Natural or nutbrown **$195.**
126/10. 10 drawers. H126 cm. White **$215.** Natural or nutbrown **$225.**

EXHIBIT 2 Sample Page from Sears Catalogue, 1986

Dressers and chests whose quality and practicality are inherent—
in the colors and sizes you want. Assemble them yourself with ease.

Your choice of clear knot-free pine veneer over non-warp platewood core
or White baked-on European-quality low gloss enamel on a platewood core.

3 Drawer Units. 38 cm deep, 54 cm high (15 x 21¼").
Wide. 75 cm wide (29½").
012 065 012 DLT – *Pine* Each.139.98
012 065 002 DLT – *White* Each.139.98
Narrow. 50 cm wide (19½").
012 065 015 DLT – *Pine* Each.119.98
012 065 005 DLT – *White* Each.119.98

4 Drawer Units. 38 cm deep, 69 cm high (15 x 27¼").
Wide. 75 cm wide (29½").
012 065 011 DLT – *Pine* Each.159.98
012 065 001 DLT – *White* Each.159.98
Narrow. 50 cm wide (19½").
012 065 014 DLT – *Pine* Each.139.98
012 065 004 DLT – *White* Each.139.98

6 Drawer Units. 38 cm deep, 99 cm high (15 x 39").
Wide. 75 cm wide (29½").
012 065 010 DLTJ – *Pine* Each.219.98
012 065 000 DLTJ – *White* Each.219.98
Narrow. 50 cm wide (19½").
012 065 013 DLT – *Pine* Each.189.98
012 065 003 DLT – *White* Each.189.98

EXHIBIT 3 IKEA Canada Sales by Store, Including Mail Order %[1]
(Cdn. $000s)

	1981	1982	1983 Actual	1984	1985	1986 Forecast	Mail Order %
Vancouver	12 122	11 824	12 885	19 636	19 240	25 500	6.8
Calgary	7 379	8 550	7 420	7 848	9 220	11 500	8.6
Ottawa	5 730	6 914	8 352	9 015	10 119	12 500	1.8
Montreal			8 617	12 623	15 109	22 000[2]	2.2
Halifax	3 634	4 257	4 474	6 504	7 351	9 000	22.9
Toronto	11 231	13 191	16 249	18 318	22 673	30 500	1.8
Edmonton	6 506	7 474	8 075	8 743	9 986	16 000	15.4
Quebec City		5 057	8 284	9 027	10 037	12 000	6.1
Victoria					2 808	3 500	
Total	46 602	57 267	74 356	91 714	106 543	142 500	6.7

[1] 1984 most recent data available.
[2] Projected growth due to store size expansion.

EXHIBIT 4   IKEA Canada Statement of Earnings and Retained Earnings Year Ended August 31, 1984, with Comparative Figures for 1983

	1984	*1983*
Sales	$92 185 188	74 185 691
Cost of merchandise sold	49 836 889	38 085 173
Gross profit	42 348 299	36 100 518
General, administrative and selling expenses	28 016 473	23 626 727
Operating profit before the undernoted	14 331 826	12 473 791
Depreciation and amortization	1 113 879	1 066 286
Franchise amortization	257 490	257 490
Franchise fee	2 765 558	2 225 571
	4 136 927	3 549 347
Earnings from operations	10 194 899	8 924 444
Rental income	769 719	815 683
Less rental expense	245 803	258 296
	523 916	557 387
Interest expense	2 453 116	3 042 471
Less other income	438 683	65 757
	2 014 433	2 976 714
Earnings before income taxes	8 704 382	6 505 117
Income taxes		
Current	3 789 773	2 716 645
Deferred	(70 400)	175 500
	3 719 373	2 892 145
Net earnings for the year	4 985 009	3 612 972
Retained earnings, beginning of year	5 501 612	1 888 640
Retained earnings, end of year	$10 486 621	5 501 612

SOURCE: Consumer and Corporate Affairs, Canada.

THE DIAPER WAR: KIMBERLY-CLARK VERSUS PROCTER & GAMBLE

Allen J. Morrison and Kerry S. McLellan

On November 1, 1989, the management of Kimberly-Clark (K-C) watched with great interest and concern as Procter & Gamble (P&G) announced the appointment of a new CEO, Edwin Artzt. Artzt had considerable international experience in the disposable diapers industry and management at K-C wondered if his appointment would signal a new phase of competition within the industry.

Six months earlier, prior to Artzt's appointment, P&G had introduced gender-specific disposables with designer colours. While a significant product improvement, gender-specific disposables were not in the tradition of the technological competitive breakthroughs of the past. K-C had responded with test marketing of a similar product, but a national roll-out would still be several months away.

The decision to proceed with a national roll-out was tempered by concern that such a move would acknowledge P&G's leadership in the marketplace. Furthermore, K-C managers questioned whether a move into gender-specific disposables would distract the company from important research and development efforts aimed at the environmental concerns now confronting the industry. In considering options, K-C management was faced with significant financial constraints and they wondered if greater opportunities would be available outside the increasingly competitive North American industry. International opportunities in Europe and Japan merited greater attention, particularly given recent moves by overseas competitors to enter the North American diaper industry. Also of interest to K-C management was the company's ongoing efforts to build a market position for its adult incontinence products. As K-C faced the 1990s, managers braced for heightened competition and wondered how and when to respond.

THE NORTH AMERICAN DIAPER INDUSTRY

The Development of Disposable Diapers

The disposable diaper, invented in postwar Sweden, was introduced to America by Johnson & Johnson in the late 1940s. Kendall and Parke Davis entered the market a decade later. At that time, marketing efforts were focused on travelling parents with infants. Research and development efforts tried to increase product effectiveness by improving the methods of matting the absorbent tissue.

These early diapers, used with fastening pins and plastic pants, were generally perceived as ineffective in keeping both babies and parents dry. With slow sales, prices for the product remained high (10¢ ea. for disposables versus 3¢–5¢ for cloth diaper services and 1¢–2¢ for home laundered diapers). As a result, most firms remained uninterested in making significant investments in this market segment.

Procter & Gamble's Entry: Pampers

There are several stories surrounding the motivation for P&G's initial interest in disposable diaper products. One version cited the frustration of a senior engineer with the state of disposable diaper technology in the 1950s. The engineer was a new grandfather who felt a strong motivation to develop a better product. The other popularized story involved the complaints of a nun in charge of the nursery at a Cincinnati Catholic Hospital. She complained to company personnel regarding the sanitary problems of cloth diapers. Her comments spurred action at the firm to develop a product that would meet the needs of her nursery.

While P&G's initial interest in disposable diapers was surrounded by stories of chance, the firm's commercialization of the product was clearly motivated by shrewd analysis. By the late 1950s, the firm was beginning to recognize elements of opportunity in this dismally viewed market sector. Although the industry was fragmented and the market undeveloped, the conditions fit well with P&G's strategy of trying to introduce products into markets where there was a reasonable expectation that a premium segment niche could be created by effective marketing and superior product characteristics. In 1957, cellulose fibre research began in earnest, spurred on by P&G's purchase of the Charmin Paper Company.

In 1961, P&G announced its entry into the disposable diapers industry with the introduction of Pampers; test marketing began a year later. Pampers provided a clear technological breakthrough from previous products as it was the first disposable diaper to use a plastic back-sheet coupled with absorbent wadding and a porous rayon sheet facing the baby's skin. Despite these advantages, however, the product did not achieve P&G's sales targets, and thus

Pampers was not distributed nationally. This early market failure was blamed on the product's high price of 10¢ per diaper which was similar to that charged by other firms and reflected the underlying manufacturing cost structure of Pampers. The cost problem reflected P&G's production approach of purchasing partially completed components to be assembled later. This manufacturing process, while the norm in the industry, was both expensive and time-consuming.

Recognizing production inefficiencies, P&G concentrated research efforts on reducing the manufacturing costs of the disposable product. In 1964, the firm's engineers developed a continuous process technology that allowed the manufacture of diapers at speeds of 400 per minute. This process proved many times faster than the previous manufacturing method and allowed the use of minimally processed raw materials. This advance, as well as changes in purchasing, allowed P&G to cut costs significantly. As a result, Pampers was reintroduced into a second test market site at a price of 5.5¢ per diaper. The test was very successful and a national introduction followed in 1966. Full national distribution was achieved by 1969.

Kimberly-Clark's Entry: Kimbies

Diaper research at K-C also began in earnest in the mid-1960s, focusing primarily on new product technology. The firm used its experience with feminine napkins to develop a product that used fluff pulp in place of tissue. The pulp provided cheaper and better absorbency. These advantages, coupled with the introduction of adhesive tabs and an improved shape, were incorporated into a new product, called Kimbies, introduced by K-C in 1968. The use of fluff pulp as the primary absorbent material provided competitive cost savings. Kimbies was parity priced with Pampers but competitive cost savings were not passed through to consumers. Rather, K-C re-invested the excess profit into further product improvements. This strategy fit with industry market research that showed a strong relationship between improved product features and market and sales growth. The cost of product improvements could be passed on, as many consumers seemed to show a high degree of price indifference.

Other competitors active during the late 1960s included Scott Paper, Borden, and International Paper. All three were experimenting with a two-piece disposable diaper system in the mid-1960s. This system, which relied on technology developed in Europe, involved a disposable inner liner and a reusable plastic outer shell. The product also had a distinct advantage over Pampers in that the diapers used snaps instead of pins.

By 1970, a competitive pattern had begun to emerge in the industry. Rivalry was increasingly focused on product innovation. However, these improvements were not always translated into market share gains for reasons that appeared to be two-fold: poor marketing communication of product benefits, and the inability of some firms to reduce manufacturing costs to P&G's level. In spite of what some regarded as an inferior product, Pampers appeared unstoppable. By 1970, P&G peaked with an estimated market share of 92%. Observers began recognizing that technology alone was not enough and that many of the large industrial-focused paper companies might be in an untenable position in the industry.

Industry Shake-out

There was a rapid shake-out of the disposable diaper industry in the early 1970s. The restructuring was hastened by a constant series of modifications undertaken by P&G to further strengthen its Pampers line. For example, the company converted from tissue to fluff pulp in 1972 and to adhesive tabs in 1973. As a result of the heightened competition, Borden exited the industry in 1970, Scott left the U.S. market in 1971, International Paper stopped U.S. production in 1972, and Johnson & Johnson's Chicopee discontinued its brand in 1972. Other competitors retreated slowly as continuous costly improvements upped the ante. P&G's dominant position was maintained until K-C's Kimbies began to gather steam in the 1972–74 period.

In 1971, Darwin Smith was appointed as the new president of K-C. Smith's objective was to reduce K-C's reliance on core newsprint and paper operations and to strengthen its position in consumer products. This transformation took several years to complete and involved the selling off of various mills and woodlands, and the strengthening of the company's market leading Kleenex and Kotex brands. This strategic re-focusing produced a war-chest of $350 million that was to be used for further expansion into consumer products.

K-C's Kimbies was an early benefactor of this shift in strategy. Buoyed by increased marketing expenditures, Kimbies' market share peaked in 1974 at 20%. However, as the decade progressed, management did not pay enough attention to Kimbies' performance and sales began to decline.

In spite of the transformation in the industry, disposable diapers were only used regularly on about 35% of babies in 1976. Total market growth remained flat. To most parents, the benefits of disposables were still not large enough to support their added cost.

THE COMPETITION INCREASES

Procter & Gamble Introduces Luvs

In 1976, P&G announced the test marketing and selected regional introduction of a premium diaper product, Luvs. This diaper offered several improvements over Pampers, including a fitted, elasticized shape and a more effective absorbent structure. Luvs was priced 25–30% above Pampers. This introduction was intended to create a new premium market segment, moving Pampers into a middle segment. P&G continued regional market testing for more than two years but seemed indecisive on a national roll-out decision. Many observers believed that this hesitation was related to test market results indicating a large negative impact on Pampers.

Kimberly-Clark Introduces Huggies

By 1978, K-C's corporate transformation was nearly complete and attention was re-focused on the diaper sector. That year, K-C introduced Huggies to replace Kimbies. The product was superior to both Pampers and Luvs. It was better fitting, more absorbent, and offered an improved tape fastening system. In support of the new product, K-C hired top marketing talent and backed the introduction with large promotional and advertising investments.

At the time of Huggies' introduction, Luvs was still available only on a limited regional basis. P&G's indecision provided K-C with a tremendous opportunity to develop a product with characteristics superior to Luvs. Because of the introduction of Huggies, P&G was forced to complete the national roll-out of Luvs. Luvs, suffering from inferior performance relative to that of Huggies, was unable to gain control of the premium segment. K-C continued to produce Kimbies for the market's middle segment, but concentrated resources on Huggies, allowing Kimbies to die a slow death. National distribution of Kimbies was discontinued in 1983.

Huggies' sales grew rapidly as consumers discovered the diaper's superior characteristics. Sales growth came not only through market share growth, but also as a result of the increased usage of disposable diapers. With Huggies, consumers could now see the benefit of switching from traditional cloth diapers to disposable products. Market penetration of disposables increased rapidly.

Procter & Gamble Responds

P&G initially did little to respond to K-C's new market entry. Part of the reason for the slow response was that K-C had introduced Huggies after upgrading its manufacturing processes and P&G had large investments in older diaper machines. P&G was clearly hesitant to make the huge investments necessary to match K-C production processes. This older technology limited P&G's ability to match K-C's product modifications and put the company at somewhat of a cost disadvantage. To avoid this expense, P&G aggressively promoted Pampers; however, sales continued to slump. Brand market share fluctuated widely during the 1981–89 period, with the early 1980s being the most difficult period for P&G (Exhibit 1).

By 1983, market research began to convince P&G management that the middle sector was disappearing. Consumers either wanted the best products for which they seemed willing to pay a premium price or they wanted low priced—typically private label—products, regardless of performance. Pampers appeared to be stuck in the middle.

It was not until late 1984, when Huggies had captured 30% of the market, that P&G upgraded its products with comparable features and fought to regain market share. There were two elements in the strategy. First, P&G decided to reposition Pampers as a premium product, comparable to Luvs. The re-positioning was accomplished through improvements in Pampers' shape and fastening system, and a major improvement in absorbent structure. Also, to improve cost structure and offer the improved features, P&G made major investments in its production system. The competitive upgrade of P&G's diaper lines was very expensive, costing an estimated $500 million for a new plant and equipment. A further $225 million in additional advertising and promotion support was used to re-launch P&G's slumping brands.

The technological leap-frog competition was on. In the first half of 1986 alone, 7 of P&G's 19 patent searches involved diaper product improvements (Exhibit 2). These searches were the subject of great interest to K-C researchers.

New Technology Results in Super-Thin Diapers

During 1986, the competition entered a new stage of intense technological rivalry with both P&G and K-C introducing super-thin, super-absorbent disposables. The new diapers contained polyacrylate, a powder crystal that absorbed 50 times its weight in liquid. By using polyacrylate, diapers could be manufactured that were 30% thinner. The two firms had to re-educate consumers into not associating absorbency with thickness. The campaign was a success and parents seemed to like the new diaper's sleek profile and improved performance. P&G and K-C were able to achieve transportation cost savings and retailers were pleased with improved shelf utilization.

P&G introduced the new technology into the U.S. early in 1986. K-C's introduction followed nine months later. P&G's competitive leadership in North America, however, did not come from development work in the U.S., but rather from access to technology developed in Japan, where the company had considerable operations. Because K-C lacked a significant presence in the Japanese market, the company had been forced to follow P&G's introduction in North America. Initially, P&G and K-C were dependent on Japanese suppliers for polyacrylate and neither was able to obtain the North American license. After two years, however, Cellanese, a U.S. chemical firm, was given a license to manufacture the product in North America.

The introduction of super-thin technology clearly hastened the demise of the mid-market segment. Super-thin technology was regarded as so unique that its use would automatically position a product at the high end of the market. The re-positioning of Pampers in 1984 and the withdrawal of Kimbies in 1983 represented an effective abandonment of the mid-price segment of the market by the major industry players. During the later half of the 1980s, neither P&G nor K-C attempted to introduce products to fill the now largely unserved mid-price market segment. During the early 1980s, however, P&G and K-C had continued to test products aimed at the low-priced segment. K-C tested Snuggems, and P&G experimented with Simply Pampers. Neither product received national distribution, although regional testing continued until the later part of the 1980s. The inability of P&G and K-C to place products in the low-priced segment was primarily the result of the reluctance of mass merchandisers to give Snuggems or Simply Pampers adequate shelf space. The retailers were able to earn much higher margins from their private label brands, targeted at the same segment.

HEAD-TO-HEAD COMPETITION

By the Fall of 1989, the industry had effectively evolved into a duopoly dominated by K-C with a 32% market share, and P&G with a 49% market share. Both companies sold super-thin diapers exclusively. In 1989, total retail sales of disposable diapers exceeded $4.5 billion in the United States and $400 million in Canada. The disposable diaper market appeared saturated with little growth in total market size expected.

As a duopoly, competition between P&G and K-C was intense. Given the huge fixed costs involved in the production of disposable diapers, it was estimated that each percentage gained in market share resulted in $6–10 million in additional annual profit. As a result, competition extended beyond research and development to marketing and promotion, and to manufacturing.

Marketing and Promotion

The war between P&G and K-C started with ads in the magazines that appealed to expectant mothers. The fight entered a more open, intense phase when the companies fought to get their products into maternity wards and pediatricians' offices, where their use carried an implied endorsement by the medical community. Only a handful of promotional firms were allowed to distribute samples in hospitals and both K-C and P&G paid for their services.

Once the free samples had been used, mothers realized just how expensive disposables would be. In 1989, at a price of 18¢–36¢ each, depending on size, it would cost $1 400–$1 700 to diaper one child for 2.5 years in brand name disposables. It was estimated that the cost of cloth diapers supplied by diaper services was comparable, but could be up to 20% lower depending on the type of service provided. Generic or private label disposables were about 30% cheaper than national brands, but most suffered from distressing performance problems. Cloth diapers washed at home would cost $600 or less.

Increasingly, however, price was being discounted as a purchasing criterion. With up to 75% of new mothers working outside the home, many families often valued time and convenience more than money. Similarly, as family size diminished, parents showed an increased willingness to spend money on outfitting babies. This trend meant that more and more families were prepared to pay for quality disposable diapers.

In North America, P&G and K-C were each estimated to spend a total of more than $110 million annually on diaper promotion. This promotion primarily involved commercials and coupons. Retailers often used diapers as loss leaders and the companies supported these activities through volume rebates based upon the number of tons of diapers sold. Couponing potentially saved a consumer 10–15%, but the unwritten rule was that neither firm would undercut the other.

In addition to traditional means of promotion, both firms had successfully tried other innovative measures. P&G had used Pamper Care Vans, staffed by nurses, visiting malls and fairs. The firm had also sponsored childbirth classes and infant communication literature. K-C had countered with a public relations and advertising campaign showing Huggies as the diaper used by baby Elizabeth in the movie *Baby Boom*. After the firms had found these innovative promotional methods effective, they began diverting increased resources to their use.

Both firms had a record of using extensive test marketing prior to national introduction. In the 1960s and 1970s, it took three to five years from test market to complete national distribution. P&G and K-C had cut this time down to months. Despite the pressures on rapid market launch, both firms had continued to conduct extensive test market research.

Manufacturing

The production of disposable diapers was capital intensive. The process was a continuous flow of assembly using large, complex, high speed machines. The machines were several hundred feet long with a cost range of $2–4 million, depending on speed and features. Usually several machines were grouped at each plant location. As a result of the high capital costs, capacity planning and utilization were essential to profitability. Both P&G and K-C attempted to operate their diaper machines 24 hours a day, seven days a week.

Additions to manufacturing capacity required a lead time of 12–18 months, slowing the national roll-out of new products. In addition, most facilities needed several months to work the bugs out of new equipment. In the past, uncertain market share forecasts and fluctuations had led to capacity surpluses and product shortages for both firms. The competition between P&G and K-C had resulted in a history of wide swings in market share. Ironically, manufacturing costs for both firms would have benefitted from reasonable industry stability.

Despite technological improvements, diapers were still a bulky product and transportation costs were estimated to comprise at least 7% of the retail value. To minimize transportation costs, both K-C and P&G had traditionally built regional plants. Transportation costs had been 50% higher prior to the introduction of super-thin, super-absorbent technology.

THE FUTURE BASIS OF COMPETITION

As the rivalry between P&G and K-C heated up, it was uncertain whether the principal focus of the competitive battle would remain fixed on technological innovation and strong promotional support. Some observers thought that consumers would likely pay for only so much technology. Yet the stakes were high and both companies were very intent on winning the battle. It was estimated that K-C and P&G both enjoyed net profit margins of 15% on diapers, as compared to less than 10% on most of their other consumer paper products. In determining the future basis of competition, both P&G and K-C had different resource bases and corporate interests. These are described in the following two sections.

Procter & Gamble Company

In 1989, P&G was a leading competitor in the U.S. household and personal care products industries with $13.3 billion in U.S. sales. For detailed financials, see Exhibit 3. P&G's products held dominant positions in North America in a variety of sectors including detergents (Tide, Cheer), bar soap (Ivory), toothpaste (Crest), shampoo (Head and Shoulders), coffee (Folgers), bakery mixes (Duncan Hines), shortening (Crisco), and peanut butter (Jiff). Disposable diapers were an important product group that comprised approximately 17% of the firm's total sales in North America.

Historically, most of P&G's annual growth had come from the expansion of existing brands where the company's marketing expertise was well known. In building these brands, P&G typically followed a strategy based on developing a superior consumer product, branding it, positioning it as a premium product, and then developing the brand through advertising and promotion. The strategy was consistent with the company's objectives of having top brands and highest market shares in its class. The company strongly believed that profitability would come from dominant market positions.

P&G's marketing strengths were supported by core competencies in research and development. With shorter product lifecycles for many non-food consumer products, R&D was becoming increasingly important to the company. Much of the company's R&D efforts were focused on upgrading existing products. However, in the late 1980s, the firm was devoting large amounts of R&D resources towards several new products, such as Olestra, a fat substitute. In 1989, total P&G research and development expenditures were $628 million, approximately $100 million of which diapers were estimated to have received. Some industry observers had suggested that the slowdown of innovations in the diaper wars may have been partially a result of P&G channelling R&D resources to new product areas.

In addition to being a dominant competitor in the U.S. household products and personal care products industries, P&G also had a strong position in several key international markets. In 1989, international sales surpassed $8.5 billion and income from international operations soared to $417 million, up almost 37% from the previous year. Sales growth in Europe and Japan was particularly impressive, with European sales up almost 15% and Japanese sales up more than 40% over 1988 figures. Performance in international markets was led by strong showings in diapers and detergents.

Kimberly-Clark

In 1989, K-C was a leading manufacturer and marketer of personal, health care and industrial products made primarily from natural and synthetic fibres. In 1989, the firm had revenues of $5.7 billion with a net income of $424 million. Detailed financials are found in Exhibits 4 and 5. Well-known products manufactured by K-C included Kleenex facial tissues, Kotex and New Freedom feminine care products, Hi-Dri household towels and Depend incontinence products. For product analysis, see Exhibit 6. Huggies disposable diapers were K-C's largest single product, contributing $1.4 billion to 1989 sales and an estimated 37% of net income.

K-C was organized into three divisions. By far the largest of these was the personal, health care and industrial products division. Personal products included disposable diapers, feminine care products, disposable hand towels and various incontinence products. Health care products included primarily surgical gowns, packs and wraps. Industrial products included cleaning wipers made of unwoven materials. Together, the division's products contributed 77% of K-C's 1989 sales and 78% of its net income.

K-C also manufactured newsprint and groundwood printing papers, premium business and correspondence papers, cigarette papers, tobacco products and specialty papers. These operations were part of the firm's second division that represented 19% of corporate sales and net income. The importance of the woodlands-related products to K-C had diminished throughout much of the 1970s and 1980s as the company shifted resources into consumer products. The two divisions were, however, closely linked to the degree that many of K-C's consumer products relied on cellulose fibres supplied by the company's woodlands operations. It was estimated that 65% of the wood pulp needs for consumer products were supplied in-house, a level considered high in the industry. It was thought that vertical control provided the advantage of flexibility and security under rapidly changing competitive conditions.

Observers noted that prices for newsprint and paper products had been highly cyclical during much of the 1980s. In 1989, there was an indication that prices were softening and would likely remain depressed as large amounts of capacity were expected to be added to the industry in the early 1990s.

The company's smallest division (4% of revenues and 3% of net income) operated a business aircraft maintenance and refurbishing subsidiary, and Midwest Express Airlines, a commercial airline based in Milwaukee, Wisconsin.

K-C's international operations provided 29% of company sales and 30% of the operating income in 1989. The company's major markets, on a consolidated basis, were Canada, the United Kingdom, France, the Philippines and Brazil. K-C had several international equity investments; the largest, in Mexico, provided $36 million in net income. In 1989, K-C manufactured disposable diapers in nine countries and had sales in more than 100 countries. Outside North America and Europe, however, sales of disposable diapers were very low, largely because of undeveloped markets. Also, after K-C had abandoned the Japanese market, its potential for expansion into growing Asian markets was weakened.

INTERNATIONAL OPPORTUNITIES AND THREATS

After the introduction of super-thin technology from Japan, it became increasingly apparent that the competitive conditions in North America could not be viewed in isolation. By the late 1980s, competitive conditions in both Europe and Japan were having a significant influence on opportunities and threats facing North American competitors.

Japan

Historically, Japanese consumers had enjoyed better quality cloth diapers than consumers in other countries, thus slowing the acceptance of disposables. After the World War II, the new Japanese government appointed a special commission to examine the national supply of diapers. The commission came up with a unique system involving a cloth diaper liner and a woven, absorbent cotton overpanty. This system received the approval of the Japanese Medical Society, significantly increasing its acceptance in traditional Japanese society. In recent years, however, the consumer benefits provided by disposables have become more apparent. Changing roles of women in Japanese society have also led to a rapid growth in the demand for disposable diapers.

P&G's competitive experiences in Japan's diaper industry were remarkably similar to its experiences in North America. In the early 1970s, P&G enjoyed a market share greater than 90% of the Japanese disposable market. However, as in North America, the product had performance problems and total market penetration was weak. P&G's biggest problem was complacency. In 1982, P&G was making its diapers with old-fashioned wood pulp. In the same year Japan's Uni-Charm Corp. (1989 Sales: $600 million) introduced a highly absorbent, granulated polymer to soak up wetness and hold it in the form of a gel, keeping babies dry longer. In 1984, KAO Corporation, a Japanese soapmaker (1989 Sales: $4 Billion) launched a similar brand of super-thin diapers under the brand name Merries. P&G did not begin selling its polymer-packed Pampers in Japan until January 1985. By that time P&G's share of the Japanese market had fallen below 7%. In 1985, Uni-Charm controlled almost half the market and KAO about 30%.

In recommitting to the Japanese market, P&G recognized that Japanese product technology was years ahead of U.S. levels. Being well positioned in Japan meant that P&G would have greater access to Japanese technology which could be exported back to the U.S to use in its battle with K-C. Because K-C had sold its interest in its Japanese equity company in 1987, it was not a major competitor in this market.

By 1989, the Japanese market had not yet reached the same level of maturity demonstrated in the U.S. While the market was worth over $1 billion in 1989, the penetration estimates varied from 35% to 50%. However, Japanese parents changed their babies twice as often as North American parents and therefore used many more diapers. Industry estimates indicated that the Japanese market, if developed to the same degree as the U.S. (85–90% penetration), would be almost as large as the U.S. This result was despite a population size of less than half. As a result, there was tremendous opportunity for growth in the Japanese market.

Faced with intense domestic competition, Japanese firms historically showed little interest in moving internationally. However, there was growing concern in North America that Japanese preoccupation with domestic competition might not last. When in 1988 KAO acquired Jergens Ltd., the U.S. producer of personal care products, several analysts speculated that this move was the beachhead for a major Japanese thrust into the North American market for personal products, including disposable diapers. There was also speculation in the press that Uni-Charm had begun negotiations with Weyerhauser to set up joint production-distribution operations in the U.S. Weyerhauser was a large, integrated U.S. forest products company that held a 50% share of the low-priced, private label market for disposable diapers. It was known that Weyerhauser had been considering a major move into the mid-priced segment for disposables.

Europe

The development of the disposable diapers industry in Europe was decidedly different from that in North America. Europeans began producing disposable diapers using a two-piece system in the early 1960s. Unlike the North American industry, however, the European industry did not experience a high degree of rationalization. There were two main reasons for this. First, Europe was composed of very different, often protected national markets. As a result, production, marketing, and distribution economies were limited. Second, no large European industry leaders emerged and foreign competitors from North America and Japan were preoccupied with domestic competitive battles. As a result, several strong country-specific firms emerged. Beginning in the mid-1980s, both P&G and K-C began to re-focus attention on Europe, achieving some success. However, by 1989 the market was still fragmented with neither firm enjoying the dominant position experienced in their domestic market. The use of super-thin technology, pioneered in Japan and promoted in North America, was gradually becoming the industry norm in Europe.

Penetration of disposables diapers varied widely across Europe. In Scandinavia, the market had been saturated at least five to ten years prior to the North American market. Consumer demand appeared to be entering a new phase, becoming increasingly preoccupied with environmental concerns. Many consumers were experimenting with a variety of alternatives to disposables. Other countries were undergoing similar experiences. In France, 98 out of 100 diaper changes were done using disposables. However, in southern Europe, penetration levels were much lower and the market less sophisticated. Here, the percentage of women employed outside the home was lower, and many observers felt that these markets offered significant growth opportunities. The development of a unified internal market for Europe promised potential industry rationalization opportunities.

By 1989, P&G had established a strong presence in the fragmented European market with a major plant in Germany. At this time, K-C had not moved aggressively into this market. An issue faced by both companies was whether limited investment capital for expensive market development would be better spent at home or overseas; and if overseas, in which market? Also of concern was the potential reaction of European firms, both overseas and in North America, to the perceived aggressiveness of U.S. firms.

ADDITIONAL ISSUES

The Environment

In 1989, almost 19 billion disposable diapers were sold in North America. This produced an estimated 4–5.5 billion pounds of discarded diapers. In some residential landfills, tests showed that disposable diapers constituted almost 5% of the total volume (industry studies showed a much lower estimate of 1–2%), leading to widespread criticism of the industry for the non-biodegradable nature of the plastics in the product. (It took an estimated 250 years for a plastic disposable diaper to bio-degrade.) Environmental groups had highlighted concerns about potential health risks for sanitation workers and the threat to ground water. As the environmental movement gathered steam, many industry experts feared that unless more environmentally friendly disposable diapers were introduced, consumers would increasingly seek out alternative diapering systems.

Additional regulatory pressures were also appearing because of the perceived environmental problem. By 1989, legislation taxing, regulating or banning the sale of disposable diapers had been introduced in eleven U.S. states. It was expected that most other states would consider similar legislation during the early 1990s. However, the legislation had not yet impacted the diaper industry, as most punitive measures were not scheduled to come into effect until 1992–94.

There were signs that the seriousness of the environmental problem had not fully reached either P&G or K-C. For example, Sue Hale, associate director of P&G's public relations was quoted in 1989 as defending the firm's disposable diapers as being 60–70% bio-degradable. Richard R. Nicolosi, vice-president in charge of P&G's worldwide diaper operations, was quoted as saying, "We don't think mothers are willing to give up one of the greatest new products of the postwar era."

Although K-C had a note in its 1989 annual report citing the potential seriousness of the threat, the company had been reticent about specific plans for dealing with the issue. According to Tina Barry, vice-president of corporate communications at K-C, "We're working with our suppliers to find a reliable plastic that is biodegradable. But we haven't come across any plastic material that breaks down and maintains product performance and reliability."

By 1989, no promising technologies had been introduced to address these rising environmental concerns. This situation was in contrast to the Japanese market where the market leaders had avoided or minimized the use of non-biodegradable plastics. It was also recognized that Japanese firms had considerable technological experience with bio-degradable external retaining fabrics. Both P&G and K-C had yet to adopt such technology.

Both firms were trying to divert criticism by testing small-scale recycling projects. The diapers were washed and the components separated. Then the pulp was sanitized and sold to paper mills. The plastic was recovered for use in flower pots and garbage bags. However, the cost of recycling was much higher than the value of the components recovered. Added to this problem were the difficulties associated with collection of soiled diapers.

It was believed that unless environmentally friendly disposables were introduced, cloth diapers would be the main benefactor of the environmental movement. In the late 1980s, both Fisher-Price and Gerber had begun to re-examine this market and had introduced form-fitting, two-piece diaper systems. Claims that cloth diapers were environmentally friendly were countered by the industry with studies showing that the laundering of cloth diapers used six times the amount of water as was used in the manufacture of disposables and the laundering created ten times as much water pollution.

Product Diversification

As the North American disposable diaper market became saturated, both P&G and K-C sought other market opportunities that might utilize the technological expertise gained from their diaper rivalry. One avenue that seemed particularly attractive was increased development of incontinence products for adults. Incontinence products appeared to be an ideal product extension for the super-thin technology used in disposable diapers. With the improvement in incontinence product performance, sales and market penetration had exploded. Some estimated that sales in the U.S. would be as high as $1 billion in 1990, and that the potential size of this market could eventually exceed that of diapers. Of the 31 million North Americans over 65, it was estimated that about 10% had a problem with incontinence. An aging population would allow total market growth opportunities as well as growth through increased penetration.

The fight for the incontinence market was shaping up to be a replay of the disposable diaper war, with the same players. A difference in this competition was the contrasting strengths possessed by each firm in the distribution network. P&G dominated the institutional distribution channel while K-C was the leader in the commercial-retail channel. K-C had broken important new ground in this market and strengthened its distribution position by successfully developing a television advertising program that tastefully promoted the benefits of its incontinence products.

In May 1989, K-C also began the roll-out of its new Huggies Pull-Up Training Pants. This product would extend the length of time children would use Huggies through months of toilet training. By November, national distribution had not yet been achieved but early market results in Western states were promising. Although P&G was watching the product carefully and had registered trademarks suitable for a similar line, the company had not yet responded with its own introduction.

Recent Events

On November 1, 1989, P&G announced the appointment of Edwin Artzt as the company's new CEO. Artzt, who was chosen for the position over an heir apparent, had directed P&G's international operations since 1984. In that capacity he had been responsible for the company's spectacular recovery in Japan, particularly in diapers, and its' double digit growth in Asia and Europe.

K-C was particularly concerned about the possible impact that Artzt's appointment might have on its intense competition with P&G in the North American diaper industry. Managers at K-C wondered whether the appointment of Artzt signalled a shift in P&G's emphasis away from the U.S. market place. They also speculated whether his appointment was designed to strengthen P&G's access to new Japanese technology that could produce more environmentally friendly diapers. In response to these concerns, K-C managers wondered what sort of action to take, either internationally or in North America.

As a backdrop to the technological challenges that lay ahead, there had been ongoing litigation between P&G and K-C over the use of proprietary technologies. P&G had sued K-C for patent infringement on technology developed for elastic waistbands. K-C countersued, claiming P&G had unlawfully monopolized the market for disposable diapers and was in violation of anti-trust laws. While industry observers did not expect significant damages to be awarded in either suit—indeed, neither firm had noted material reserves on its financial statements—both P&G and K-C remained very interested in and suspicious of the other's research activities.

With external pressures mounting, the nature of the competition in the North American disposable diaper industry showed signs of change in 1989. For the first time, neither of the two competitors had introduced major product improvements; instead, each made style changes. In the summer of 1989, P&G had introduced His and Hers diapers with designer colour patterns and special absorbent pads strategically placed for boy and girl babies. P&G had backed the introduction with a huge advertising and promotional campaign which made it difficult to gauge the true market share impacts of the new products. In response, K-C had introduced mild product line extensions and had developed a similar product which was in the test marketing phase. It was estimated that a similar national product introduction for K-C would cost $50–75 million.

In responding to mounting competitive pressures, both K-C and P&G recognized that balance between short-term and long-term perspectives was essential. The focus of this balance was, however, the basis of considerable uncertainty.

EXHIBIT 1 **Market Share Data** (% of U.S. retail shipments)

Brand	1980	1981	1982	1983	1984	1985	1986	1987	1988	1989
K-C Huggies	7.1	11.7	12.3	18.1	24.0	33.0	31.0	31.3	31.7	32.0
P&G Pampers	55.7	48.0	44.7	40.0	35.0	30.5	34.0	38.0	35.6	31.6
P&G Luvs	9.8	17.2	18.0	17.7	17.5	18.4	20.0	17.0	16.1	17.4
Other	27.4	23.1	25.0	24.2	23.5	18.1	15.0	13.7	17.6	19.0

SOURCE: Various publicly available documents on product shipments.

EXHIBIT 2 **Procter & Gamble U.S. Patent Searches** (first half 1986)

Patent	Title
4 562 930	Easy-Open Laminated Container with Optional Re-closing Means and Method of Making
* 4 563 185	Disposable Diaper Having Elasticized Waistband with Non-Linear Severed Edge
4 564 633	Compositions and Methods Useful for Producing Analgesia
4 566 884	Ether Polycarboxylates
4 568 556	Margarine Product and Process
4 571 391	Chromium Acetylacetonate as a Dietary Supplement and Pharmaceutical Agent
* 4 571 924	Method and Apparatus of Manufacturing Porous Pouches Containing Granular Product
* 4 573 966	Disposable Waste-Containment Garment
* 4 576 962	Prostaglandin Analogues
* 4 578 068	Absorbent Laminate Structure
* 4 578 071	Disposable Absorbent Article Having an Improved Liquid Migration Resistant Perimeter Construction
* 4 578 073	Composite Waste-Containment Garment Having Disposable Elasticized Insert
4 578 200	Fabric Softeners
4 582 216	Easy Open-Reclosable Container with Pouring Lip/Drain Surface
4 584 203	Dough Rolling Process for Laminated Cookies
4 589 676	Sanitary Napkin
4 590 006	Oral Compositions
4 591 533	Coffee Product and Process
4 594 184	Chlorine Bleach Compatible Liquid Detergent Compositions
4 596 714	Process for Making a Baked Filled Snack

* Patents related to Disposable Diaper Research.
SOURCE: First Boston Equity Research, August 1986.

EXHIBIT 3 Proctor & Gamble
Consolidated Statement of Earning (millions of dollars except per share amounts)

	Year Ended June 30		
	1989	*1988*	*1987*
Income			
Net sales	$21 398	$19 336	$17 000
Interest and other income	291	155	163
	21 689	19 491	17 163
Costs and Expenses			
Cost of products sold	13 371	11 880	10 411
Marketing administrative and other expenses	5 988	5 660	4 977
Interest expense	391	321	53
Provision for restructuring	—	—	805
	19 750	17 861	16 546
Earnings Before Income Taxes	1 939	1 630	617
Income Taxes	733	610	290
Net Earnings	1 206	1 020	327

Segment Information (millions of dollars)

Geographic Areas		U.S.	Inter-national	Corporate	Total
Net Sales	1987	$11 805	$5 524	$ (329)	$17 000
	1988	12 423	7 294	(381)	19 336
	1989	13 312	8 529	(443)	21 398
Net Earnings*	1987	329	120	(122)	327
	1988	864	305	(149)	1 020
	1989	927	417	(138)	1 206

* Net earnings have been reduced by $357 million in the U.S. and $102 million in International by the provision for restructuring.

Consolidated Balance Sheet (millions of dollars)

	June 30	
	1989	*1988*
Assets		
Current Assets	6 578	5 593
Property Plant and Equipment	6 793	6 778
Goodwill and Other Intangible Assets	2 305	1 944
Other Assets	675	505
Total	$16 351	$14 820
Liabilities and Shareholders' Equity		
Current Liabilities	4 656	4 224
Long-Term Debt	3 698	2 462
Other Liabilities	447	475
Deferred Income Taxes	1 335	1 322
Shareholders' Equity	6 215	6 337
Total	$16 351	$14 820

SOURCE: Procter & Gamble, *1989 Annual Report.*

EXHIBIT 4 Kimberly-Clark Corporation and Subsidiaries Consolidated Income Statement ($ millions of dollars except per share amounts)

	Year Ended December 31		
	1989	*1988*	*1987*
Net sales	$5 733.6	$5 393.5	$4 884.7
Cost of products sold	3 654.1	3 404.2	3 065.9
Distribution expenses	195.8	185.2	181.2
Gross profit	1 883.7	1 804.1	1 637.6
Advertising promotion and selling expense	813.4	784.1	674.9
Research expense	118.0	110.9	110.5
General expense	278.9	268.5	266.1
Operating profit	673.4	640.6	586.1
Interest income	19.3	11.2	7.2
Other income	24.2	24.2	26.2
Interest expense	(68.2)	(80.6)	(65.6)
Other expense	(17.9)	(11.5)	(19.8)
Income before income taxes	630.8	583.9	534.1
Provision for income taxes	242.4	229.8	230.5
Income before equity interests	388.4	354.1	303.6
Share of net income of equity companies	49.3	46.0	35.3
Minority owners' share of subsidiaries' net income	(13.9)	(21.5)	(13.7)
Net Income	$423.8	$378.6	$325.2

Consolidated Balance Sheet (millions of dollars)

	1989	*1988*
Assets		
Total Current Assets	1 443.2	1 278.3
Net Fixed Assets	3 040.9	2 575.3
Investments in Equity Companies	296.6	291.7
Deferred Charges and Other Assets	142.3	121.8
	$4 923.0	$4 267.6
Liabilities		
Total Current Liabilities	$1 263.2	$ 925.7
Long-term Debt	745.1	743.3
Other Noncurrent Liabilities	79.9	53.7
Deferred Income Taxes	643.5	585.0
Minority Owners' Interests in Subsidiaries	105.5	94.3
Total Stockholders' Equity	2 085.8	1 865.5
	$4 923.0	$4 267.6

SOURCE: Kimberly-Clark, *1989 Annual Report.*

EXHIBIT 5 **Kimberly-Clark Corporation and Subsidiaries**
Analysis of 1989 Consolidated Operating Results
($ in millions)

Geographic Areas	1989	% Change vs. 1988	% of 1989 Consolidated
Sales			
North America	$4 664.0	+ 6.4%	81.3%
Outside North America	1 087.1	+ 6.0	19.0
Adjustments	(17.5)		(.3)
Consolidated	$5 733.6	+ 6.3%	100.0%
Net Income			
North America	$316.7	+ 12.1%	74.8%
Outside North America	107.1	+ 11.3	25.2
Consolidated	$423.8	+ 11.9%	100.0%

SOURCE: Kimberly-Clark , *1989 Annual Report.*

Segment Breakdown 1981–89 ($ in millions)

	1981	1982	1983	1984	1985	1986	1987	1988	1989
Net Sales									
Consumer Products									
Division	$2 103	$2 205	$2 464	$2 734	$3 172	$3 370	$3 809	$4 165	$4 481
Forestry Division	781	742	795	845	856	876	1 001	1 121	1 096
Aviation Division	44	61	75	97	118	99	125	166	211
Subtotal	$2 928	$3 008	$3 334	$3 676	$4 146	$4 345	$4 935	$5 452	$5 788
(Interclass)	(42)	(62)	(60)	(60)	(73)	(42)	(50)	(59)	(54)
Total	$2 886	$2 946	$3 274	$3 616	$4 073	$4 303	$4 885	$5 393	$5 734
Operating Income									
Consumer Products									
Division	$171	$173	$221	$263	361	$363	$434	$435	$535
Forestry Division	120	109	118	139	162	145	177	204	129
Aviation Division	3	7	8	11	2	9	13	23	26
Subtotal	$294	$289	$347	$413	$525	$516	$624	$662	$690
Corporate	(16)	(19)	(31)	(38)	(39)	(32)	(38)	(21)	(17)
Total	$278	$270	$316	$375	$486	$485	$586	$641	$673
Return on Average Assets									
Consumer Products									
Division	11.4%	10.5%	12.0%	12.7%	15.3%	14.0%	15.9%	14.2%	15.0%
Forestry Division	22.5	19.6	20.4	23.9	27.1	22.8	26.0	27.7	15.7
Aviation Division	5.0	10.8	12.3	15.0	2.8	12.3	17.0	17.4	16.5
Subtotal	14%	12.7%	13.9%	15.1%	17.4%	15.7%	17.9%	12.0%	11.9%
Unallocated/Interclass	N.M.	N.M.	N.M.	N.M.	N.M.	N.M.	N.M.	N.M.	N.M.
Total	11.7%	10.6%	11.3%	12.3%	14.6%	13.5%	15.5%	11.9%	11.7%

SOURCE: "Duff & Phelps Research Report," Kimberly-Clark *Annual Report*, November 1988.

EXHIBIT 6 Kimberly-Clark Consumer, Health Care Industrial Products ($ in millions)

Domestic Categories	1987 Est. Sales	1987 Est. Oper. Profit	1988 Est. Mkt. Share	Est. Rank of Brands	Major Competitors / Mkt. Share
Disposable Diapers	1 220	220	32%	2	Pampers 35% Luvs 16% (PG); Private Label 17%
Facial Tissue	450	52	45%	1	Puffs 17% (PG); Scotties 10% (Scott Paper)
Feminine Pads	270	21	26%	2	J&J 37%; Always 20% (PG); Maxithins 5%; Private Label 12%
Tampons	30	2	6%	4	Tambrands 58%; Playtex 26%; J&J 8%
Paper Household Towels	170	10	10%	4	Scott Paper 23%; PG 20%; James River 11%
Bathroom Tissue	35	0	N.M.	N.M.	PG 30%; Scott Paper 19%; James River 13%
Table Napkins	30	2	N.M.	N.M.	Scott Paper 23%; James River 8%
Consumer Incont. Products	60	3	49%	1	Attends 28% (PG); Serenity 8% (J&J); Private Label 15%
Inst./Ind. Tissue Products	170	5			
Inst. Healthcare	180	4			
Other Nonwovens	176	4			
Medical	30	2			
Total Domestic	2 821	325			
Canada	250	20			
Sub-Total North America	3 071	345			
Outside North America	738	89			
Total Consumer Division	3 809	434			

SOURCE: "Duff & Phelps Research Report," Kimberly-Clark *Annual Report*, November 1988.

NOTE ON THE GLOBAL AIRLINE INDUSTRY

Joseph N. Fry and Roderick E. White
with Lisa Davidson

In April 1991, Canada and the United States began negotiations for a new and liberalized air treaty. The existing agreement was struck in 1974 and now regarded by both parties as decidedly out-of-date, unnecessarily restrictive and uncompetitive. Previous attempts at substantial revision, however, had proven unsuccessful.

The outcome of the negotiations would be of critical importance to Canada's two major airlines, Air Canada (AC) and Canadian Airlines International Ltd. (CDN). The two airlines were locked in a struggle for share in the Canadian domestic market, and were facing increasingly competitive conditions in their international markets. Both were losing money in the poor travel markets of the 1990–91 recession, and were pursuing asset sales and cost reduction programs to remain solvent. CDN's president, Kevin Jenkins, stated that te Canadian industry was not viable under its present structure, and that the current situation was not sustainable. Some industry observers went so far as to question AC's and CDN's long-term viability as independent carriers.

The Canada-U.S. negotiations also had implications on a broader scale. Some thought that the talks might provide a framework for future negotiations with the European Economic Community (EEC) and with countries in the Asia-Pacific region.

THE GLOBAL MARKET

In 1990, the world's scheduled airlines carried more than one billion passengers for a total of over two trillion passenger kilometres. Domestic services accounted for about 75% of the passenger count and 50% of the passenger kilometres flown, with international (intra- and inter-regional) flights comprising the balance. Table 1 presents traffic statistics and forecasts for selected countries and regions.

TABLE 1 **World RPK Forecast (billions)**
On-Board[1] Scheduled Service and Annual RPK Growth

Domestic Market	1990 RPK[2]	Forecast Average Annual Growth Rate 1990–2000
U.S.	536.1	5.1
Canada	21.3	4.0
Western Europe[3]	56.9	6.3
Asia-Pacific[4]	75.3	6.32
Total Domestic	689.6 vs World Domestic Total: 1 042.2	

International Market		Forecast Average Annual Growth Rate 1990–1995
Intra-regional[5]		
North America	11.1	2.9
Western Europe	72.6	6.7
Asia-Pacific	87.7	8.4
Total	114.9	
Inter-regional[6]		
North America—Western Europe	178.9	5.8
West Europe—Asia Pacific	39.4	12.5
North America—Asia Pacific	123.4	9.5
Total International	456.6 vs World International Total 1 072.2	

[1] No worldwide origin-destination data is available. Consequently, the passenger and RPK data presented are on-board loads between points, not the passengers' origin-destination load.

[2] RPK = Revenue Passenger kilometre. Scheduled services accounted for approximately 90% of traffic flown.

[3] Western Europe includes Turkey, Azores, Canary Islands, Madeira, Malta and Cyprus and extends from Scandinavia, Finland and Iceland to Spain, Italy and Greece.

[4] Asia-Pacific includes Japan, Taiwan, Hong Kong, Macau, South Korea, Malaysia, Philippines, Indonesia, Brunei, Singapore, Thailand, Vietnam, Laos, Cambodia, Burma, Australia, New Zealand, and South Pacific Islands (excluding Hawaii).

[5] Intra-regional refers to travel between the countries of the geographic area, but excludes domestic travel within each country of the geographic area.

[6] Inter-regional refers to travel between different regions only.

SOURCE: Boeing Commercial Airplane Group.

The U.S. was by far the most significant single market. U.S. traffic amounted to about one-half of world total domestic demand (dwarfing Canada by a factor of 25), and about one-third of world international activity. This enormous market gave U.S. carriers a formidable home base.

The world's top 50 airlines carried about 63% of global traffic. These airlines operated from over 30 home countries, and ranged in scale from giants such as American Airlines, Japan Airlines and British Airways with revenues of over US$7 billion to relatively small national carriers such as Austrian and Malaysian with revenues of less than US$1 billion. Together they were engaged in an increasingly competitive marketplace where route and fleet expansion, acquisitions, and commercial alliances were challenging the strategic creativity and operating skills of management throughout the world. See Exhibit 1 for revenue, profit and traffic data for the top 50 airlines.

COMPETITION IN THE AIRLINE INDUSTRY

By the year 2000, it was predicted that the global industry would be dominated by 12 to 20 very large airlines or airline consortia. How to capitalize on or, in some cases, how to survive this restructuring was a dominating concern in the strategies of most airlines. The drive for size was not motivated so much by potential economies of scale,[1] for once past a threshold, already exceeded by the major international carriers, there were few scale economies, but by the need to offer competitive benefits to customers in the form of destinations, frequencies, price and service conveniences. This situation put the world's airlines into competition on two fronts—for access to new markets, and once access was attained, in a classic battle for patronage.

The fundamental growth opportunity for airlines was through the expansion of their route structures. Here they faced three major external constraints: securing government approvals, obtaining airport access, and acquiring appropriate equipment.

Government Regulation and Approvals

For most of their history the world's airlines had operated in a highly regulated environment. Governments had, among other things, restricted ownership, allocated routes and frequencies, controlled prices, and set operating and safety standards. This situation was changing, however, particularly in domestic markets where governments had been persuaded that the public good was better served by less constrained competition. Full-scale deregulation began in the U.S. in 1978. Canada followed in 1985 with a milder version. And with the thrust toward a single market in 1992, Western Europe was moving step by step in this direction.

---

[1] Tretheway, M.W.; Globalization of the Airline Industry and Implications for Canada, *1990 Proceedings: Canadian Transportation Research Forum.*

In addition to individual governments, a world trade organization of scheduled airlines, the International Air Transport Association (IATA), existed to set standards and international fares and to coordinate systems.

The movement toward deregulation was much slower in the case of international services. Here competition was controlled by bilateral agreements between governments which started with such fundamentals as the right of an airline to overfly or pick up fuel in a country (see the "Six Freedoms of the Air" illustrated in Exhibit 2), and went on to encompass routes, capacity, frequencies, tariffs and the conditions under which passengers may be carried between the two countries involved, or even to a third country. As a consequence, any carrier that wanted to add an international destination had to persuade its government to negotiate a bilateral agreement, and to secure terms that preserved the competitive benefits being sought (e.g., in routes, frequency and fares). This thrust the airlines into domestic and international politics. The award of a Chicago-Tokyo route to United Airlines (UAL) in 1990, for example, came after protracted negotiation between U.S. and Japanese government agencies and a bitter political battle inside the U.S. between AA and UAL.

Three important consequences of the bilateral negotiating structure were that

1. airlines found it difficult to react quickly to changing international market conditions and fully capitalize on their competitive strengths;

2. airlines with strong fifth and sixth freedom traffic had a competitive advantage in a global industry, and could use this traffic to feed other international services; and

3. small carriers without traffic rights to desirable foreign destinations had to form alliances with other carriers via an intermediate point, or completely forego that traffic.

The role of bilaterals was expected to diminish in the 1990s as nations moved to bargain as part of regional economic entities, such as the European Community. Logical as this seemed, it would not be easy to reconcile established national interests, including a long established preference of governments for local control of their flag carriers. Many large carriers were government-owned in whole or part, such as Lufthansa (51%), Air France (100%), and SAS (half owned by the governments of Sweden, Norway and Denmark). And in countries with private carriers, such as the U.S., Canada, and the U.K., there were usually restrictions limiting foreign ownership. The limit in Canada was 25% with added provisos forbidding foreign carriers from acquiring "control" of a domestic airline. In early 1991, the U.S. raised its limit on foreign ownership from 25% to 49% of equity. Although ownership of voting stock was still limited to 25%, there was some hope in the industry for an easing of this restriction to improve access to badly needed capital.

In March 1991, U.S. and British negotiators agreed to a dramatic new agreement. AA and UAL received permission to succeed ailing Pan Am and TWA at London's Heathrow Airport, the world's busiest international travel hub. In exchange, the British extracted concessions from the U.S., including rights to fly into the U.S. from intermediate points in Canada and other countries, and to fly directly from the U.S. to various European cities without stopping in Britain—all of which would have to be approved by the other governments involved. British Airways also won the right to code share behind U.S. gateways so that they could "match" U.S. carriers' online service. (Code-sharing was an agreement under which one carrier's flight schedule was listed under a common code with that of another carrier in the computer reservation system. A flight from London, England to Minneapolis, for example, would show as a British Airways flight although passengers would be transferred to Northwest Airlines in Chicago for the final leg.) This new agreement was expected to have a dramatic impact on competition across the Atlantic.

Airport Access

The growth of the industry had put its infrastructure under pressure, from the provision of airlanes, to air traffic control, to airport operating slots and terminal gates. The capacity to handle air traffic was at the limit at key airports around the world. Saturation was expected to be widespread by the year 2000 unless major investments were made in systems and airports; for example, by adding runways to existing airports and investing in air traffic airport control. The expansion of existing airports was frequently opposed by local interest groups, however, creating political difficulties and delays.

The problems of capacity were best represented by the shortage of take-off and landing slots at major airports. This limited airlines that wanted to initiate service or increase frequencies to accepting off-peak times (if available), moving to secondary airports like Newark (for New York) or Nagoya (for Japan), or acquiring slots through other means. In the U.S., incumbent airlines had been granted "grandfather rights" on landing slots, and were allowed to sell them. In Europe, airlines had similar traditional rights but could not sell them. Airport rights on both continents had become a significant factor in airline acquisitions. On transpacific and transatlantic routes the problem was more complex. Bilateral agreements usually contained "equal opportunity" provisions. As a result, if TWA received poor treatment from the Austrians at Vienna, Austrian Airlines could expect problems from the Americans at New York's busy Kennedy Airport. To help avoid "tit-for-tat" disputes over slots at crowded airports, IATA held regular meetings at which slots at various busy international airports around the world were cleared.

Equipment

New aircraft to meet escalating demands for fuel efficient and quiet operation were in scarce supply. The three main manufacturers of aircraft, Airbus Industrie, Boeing and McDonnell Douglas, had full order books and three to five-year backlogs. Boeing was taking orders for delivery of its new 747-400 model in 2000. Future order positions, options and used aircraft were in high demand, and were traded actively among the airlines as well as aircraft leasing companies. When AA lost their bid for the Chicago-Tokyo route in 1990, CDN also lost a prospective $100 million profit on the sale of two 747-400s to American to service the route.

The market for used aircraft, however, had deteriorated in 1990–91 in the face of the traffic consequences of the recession and the Persian Gulf war. For the first time in almost ten years, planes were readily available at reasonable prices. Airlines could no longer count on selling their used equipment for a capital gain.

BASIC OPERATING ECONOMICS

The economics of airline operations were characterized by high fixed costs. Almost all costs were fixed after an airline determined its operating route structure (the combination of destinations, frequencies, aircraft requirements and utilization). Almost the same amount of fuel was used, whether a plane flew empty or full. And crew size was determined by type of aircraft rather than passenger load. A rule of thumb in the industry was that it required 100 people to support a 737 (narrow body) and 200 to support a 767 (wide body) aircraft. The only true variable costs were travel agency and ticketing fees and meals. It was estimated that after break-even was attained on a flight, over 90% of the incremental revenue contributed to operating profit.

Revenue Management

The industry cost structure put heavy pressure on carriers to increase contribution by filling their planes. Within a given operating structure, contribution could be increased by improving load factors and/or yield. See Table 2 for a formal definition of industry economic variables such as load factor. Load factors were a function of capacity and the number of passenger kilometres flown, and could be influenced in the short run by effective promotion and pricing. However, pricing was complicated by competitive considerations, and by the opportunity to charge different passengers different prices for the same flight, depending on class of service (e.g., first, business, economy, excursion), when the ticket was bought, and certain restrictions, such as on returns or exchanges. Cutting prices reduced yields, expressed as average revenue per passenger kilometre flown.

The skilful handling of the trade-off between load factors and yield was a key to airline profitability. Yield management involved the consideration of many factors including: passenger sensitivity to service; time and price; the optimum seat mix on a given flight; accurate overbooking levels; and demand forecasting. Many airlines used data from their computer reservation services to manage loads and yields on a flight by flight basis.

TABLE 2   Glossary of Common Measurements

The following measurements were commonly used to describe industry performance and activity:

1. *Revenue Passenger Kilometres (RPK)*
    The number of paying passengers flown, multiplied by distance carried. An indicator of traffic and demand.
2. *Available Seat Kilometres (ASK)*
    The total number of seats available to passengers, multiplied by the number of kilometres flown. An indicator of available capacity or available supply.
3. *Passenger Load Factor (PLF)*
    RPK divided by ASK. An indicator of capacity utilization.
4. *Yield or Unit Revenue (UR)*
    Revenue (measured in cents) per RPK.
5. *Unit Costs (UC)*
    Cost (measured in cents) per ASK.
6. *Contribution to Operating Profit*
    (RPK X UR) minus (ASK X UC).

Cost Management

Direct operating costs represented only 45.3% of an airline's costs as demonstrated in Table 3. The control of "indirects" was a crucial part of keeping an airline cost competitive.

Typically, Asian carriers had the lowest costs in the industry, followed in increasing order by the U.S., Canadian and European operators. A comparison of key operating statistics for AC, CDN, and selected U.S. carriers is presented in Exhibit 3. Some of the variance in costs between airlines could be explained by differences in their route structures and type of aircraft. But for most large airlines these differences tended to average out. As a consequence, an airline's comparative costs were heavily influenced by its unit fuel and wage costs, and by the productivity of its support operations.

**TABLE 3 Airline Operating Cost Distribution
International Civil Aviation Organization Airlines–1988**

Direct Costs		Indirect Costs	
Fuel	14.5%	Ticketing, sales promotion	17.6%
Maintenance	11.6	User charges, station expenses	14.1
Flight Operations	11.4	Passenger service	10.4
Depreciation	7.8	General and administrative	8.9
		Landing fees	3.7
	45.3%		54.7%

SOURCE: Boeing Commercial Airplane Group, *Current Market Outlook*, February, 1990.

Building Share and Loyalty

The world's airlines employed a number of strategic tools to exploit the economies of the industry and search for advantage. These included the building of hub dominance, investing in captive connector systems, developing proprietary computer reservation systems, operating frequent flyer plans, and forming wide-ranging international alliances.

Hub Dominance

Generally, airlines have tried to structure their operations into so-called hub and spoke systems. These systems fed passengers from outlying points into a central airport (hub), where they connected to other flights for destinations beyond the hub. This practise was much less costly than equivalent frequency point to point service, since it reduced dramatically the number of flights and ultimately number of aircraft required. It created the inconvenience of a hub transfer for passengers (a complaint among frequent flyers was that "you have to fly through Chicago to go anywhere in the U.S."), but gave them countervailing benefits in frequencies and price.

The competitive advantages of dominating specific hubs was not lost on the airlines, and they worked to focus their operations on unique hub and spoke systems. In the U.S., for example, Delta had developed hubs at Atlanta, where it controlled over 75% of the traffic, and Cincinnati, Dallas/Fort Worth, Orlando and Salt Lake City. Hub dominance strategies concentrated competition at many airports to perhaps two big players and some fringe participants. In Dallas/Fort Worth, for example, AA had a market share of over 60% and Delta accounted for a large part of the remainder; UA and AA dominated Chicago.

Connector Services

The hub and spoke systems of the major carriers concentrated on sizeable cities that could be economically served with large jet aircraft. This left a gap in smaller centres that was filled by a second tier of carriers operating smaller jet and propeller driven aircraft. In effect, the second tier airlines filled out the spoke system and their passengers represented important feed for the major carriers. The majors moved to tie up this business, first by simple commercial (interline) agreements covering such matters as prorated fares, codesharing, schedule integration and baggage handling. Many of these agreements proved unstable, however, for reasons ranging from the ambitions of the secondary carriers to competitive raids, prompting some of the majors to secure their positions by equity investment.

Computer Reservation Systems (CRSs)

Over time the largest airlines developed far-flung proprietary systems to facilitate booking and ticketing in the marketplace, and all kinds of internal management chores from yield management to inventory control. The largest, AA Sabre system, supported 85 000 terminals at travel agencies in 47 countries, provided fares and schedules for 665 airlines, 20 000 hotels and 52 rental car companies, and handled over 60 million transactions a day. A U.S. investment company estimated Sabre attained a 30% pretax margin on nearly $500 million of revenues in 1990. The huge capital investment required to develop such a system led some airlines to cooperate in a joint system, or simply to pay for the use of another airlines' CRS.

The benefits accruing to a CRS-owner were: (a) participation and booking fees from travel agents and other airlines; (b) competitive advantages in travel agent convenience and, more subtly, in control of the screen display (in the U.S., however, there were fairness regulations governing schedule); and (c) as a base for sophisticated marketing and operating management. The airlines of North America had been the leaders in CRS development. The European carriers were following with systems which borrowed existing software, but remained independent in terminal distribution and data bases. In spite of some effort, the Asian carriers had yet to develop their own joint CRS network.

AA had been particularly aggressive in introducing their Sabre system to Canada and abroad, providing it free, for example, to travel agencies that booked over a minimum amount of business with AA. In Canada, AC and CDN had agreed in 1987 to merge their separate systems into a joint service called Gemini, and later linked this system with UAL's Apollo to form Apollo by Gemini. While Apollo by Gemini would ultimately be technically similar to Sabre, in 1991 many aspects of the system were still under development.

Frequent Flyer Plans

Frequent flyer programs rewarded loyal passengers with free trips and other benefits based on kilometres flown. This marketing innovation, first introduced by American Airlines, tended to favour large carriers with extensive route systems, permitting customers more easily to accumulate mileage and select desirable reward destinations. As the success of these plans became apparent, all of the major North American airlines had followed suit. The programs were expensive and had created substantial deferred liabilities, but they were regarded as a competitive necessity. By 1990, most of the big European and Asian carriers who had been reluctant to launch their own programs had become involved, at least partially, by linkages through alliances to North American carrier plans.

Alliances

In the 1980s the formation of alliances had become a significant trend among international carriers. Alliances permitted an airline to build a global network without becoming engaged in an outright merger, or waiting and hoping for the approvals to fly to new international destinations, and attempting to gain access to limited airport facilities.

The most common alliance was a simple marketing agreement between carriers for a preferential exchange of traffic. CDN had a marketing agreement with Lufthansa, for example, under which Canadian traffic to a variety of European destinations was booked onward from Frankfurt on Lufthansa. In return, Lufthansa traffic to Canada was booked to its final destination on CDN. From such simple forms, alliances often went further to include agreements ranging from cooperation on specific routes, to joint marketing, scheduling and sales, and to the actual sharing of aircraft and airport facilities.

A major variable in the formation of alliances was the degree of mutual commitment involved, and thus the stability of the arrangement. Simple marketing alliances were quite volatile; partners and terms often changed. AC, for example, once had arrangements with Qantas, Air New Zealand and Lufthansa who were now associated with CDN.

As the linkages between airlines became more complex, they also became more strategic and harder to reverse. In the most complex agreements, minority equity had been arranged by some airlines to cement the relationship. An alliance between Delta, Swissair and Singapore Airlines, for example, which required the purchase of common aircraft and specialized maintenance, had the ultimate aim of a highly integrated global operation. It involved a 5% exchange of equity among the partners.

Industry sources expected the alliance activity of the 1980s would continue and ultimately result in a small number of "megacarriers" that would dominate the world industry. Their expectation was based on the assumption that airlines would respond to the continued growth in lucrative international business travel with a product that focused on convenient, hassle-free, seamless travel. This product would include all elements of a travel itinerary from flight arrangements, pricing and ticketing through to hotel reservations. There were many potential corporate forms for such carriers, such as single "global" airlines operated by international holding companies, or large alliances of "independent franchisees" maintaining separate ownership and brand names, but tied very tightly to a common system. However, creating a seamless global system that offered hassle-free travel throughout the world would be a daunting task, calling for a complex integration of national political interests, strategic preferences, staff, fleets, and operating systems and practises.

THE UNITED STATES MARKET

The U.S. market was massive. Domestic and international traffic accounted for over a third of all scheduled world traffic. Annual growth rates in the order of 5–6 % were expected to continue through the decade ahead.

The Domestic Shake-Out

There was fierce competition in the U.S. market. Subsequent to the 1978 deregulation of the industry, domestic carriers were free to charge fares and open and close routes. The 1980s was marked by competitive battles and industry consolidation which whittled the nation's major airlines to six, and then with the recessionary impact of 1990–91 to only three clear-cut survivors—AA, Delta and UAL. Together these three airlines shared over 50% of the U.S. market. Two other majors, Northwest and USAir were struggling but expected to survive; as was a third, Continental Airlines, which was operating under Chapter 11 protection. Of the other majors, Eastern had ceased operations, and Pan Am and TWA were the walking wounded, postponing the inevitable by shedding assets to stay alive in the short-run. Table 4 gives a brief description of the top five U.S. airlines. It was unlikely that the larger regional carriers would grow to challenge the majors. Midway was operating under Chapter 11 protection, America West was in serious financial trouble and Southwest Airlines and Alaska Airlines, while healthy, seemed confined to and contented with regional roles.

International Expansion

International traffic represented only about 15% of the revenues of the major U.S. carriers in 1990. But now, having established their domestic positions, these airlines were shifting their priorities to international expansion. AA and UAL, in

TABLE 4 Profile of the Top Five U.S. Airlines

Carrier	1989 World Revenue Ranking	Primary Hubs	Fleet Size (owned or leased)	Comments
American Airlines	1	Dallas/Fort Worth, Chicago, San José Raleigh/Durham, Nashville	500	Strong base of North Atlantic service improved by acquisition of TWA's London routes. Big Latin America and Caribbean presence.
United Airlines	2	Chicago, Denver, San Francisco, Washington	429	Number one in Pacific Market. Acquired Pan Am's London routes.
Delta Airlines	4	Atlanta, Dallas/Fort Worth, Cincinnati	402	Conservative management with good operating record. Developing international opportunities.
NWA	8	Minneapolis/St. Paul, Detroit Memphis, Newark	N/A	UA's biggest U.S. challenger in the Pacific. Domestic and North Atlantic systems need work. Management currently preoccupied with heavy debt resulting from LBO.
US Air Group	9	Dayton, Charlotte, Pittsburgh, Philadelphia, Baltimore/ Washington	454	Recovering from serious problems of merging with Piedmont. Focus on domestic medium-haul traffic.

SOURCE: Authors' compilation; annual reports; *Fortune*, September 24, 1990; *Business Week*, January 21, 1991.

particular, were building their international route structures as fast as the purchase of existing rights, new approvals and aircraft availability would permit. Major investments were involved. AA, for example, had paid TWA $195 million for its Chicago to London route in 1989, and $423 million for Eastern's Latin America route system in 1990.

As part of their international expansion activities, the U.S. carriers were developing widespread alliance networks. For AA, in particular, this marked a change in policy from its previous stand alone approach to expansion. A review of key alliances involving U.S. carriers is given in Table 5.

TABLE 5   Key Alliances Involving U.S. Carriers

U.S. Carrier	International Alliance Partner
American Airlines	Air France, Lufthansa, KLM, Cathay Pacific, Qantas— simple marketing agreements Air New Zealand—7.5% equity
United Airlines	British Airways—close ties, equity attempted but withdrawn in 1989
Delta Airlines	Swissair & Singapore—5% equity swap with aim towards a "seamless" operation; planned purchase of identical long-haul aircraft, specialization of repair facilities, exchange of flight crews.
NWA	Hawaiian Airlines—25% KLM holds 20% equity in NWA—8.6% of voting stock
USAir	Alitalia and Air France marketing partners

SOURCE: Authors' compilation.

The prospect of a unified European market was of particular interest to the U.S. carriers. The Americans were attracted to the possibility of a regional, deregulated European market. They believed themselves better prepared for the rigors of competition than the European carriers who had been sheltered under the umbrella of regulation. As one government official put it, "the prospect of sitting across the table from a negotiating team representing a group of nations with a market comparable in size to our own that could join us in constructing a truly competitive, open regime of transatlantic opportunities, is exciting."

While less ecstatic, the Europeans looked at regional bargaining as an opportunity to argue with some force for better access to the U.S. market, and for rights within the U.S. market. Currently, there was a considerable imbalance in the competitive opportunities available to European airlines as compared to those open to American carriers in Europe. In 1989, the U.S. had traffic rights to 34 destinations in 13 European countries; in five further countries they had unlimited rights to all destinations. On the other hand, the European airlines could serve only a total of 19 destinations in the U.S., and they had no cabotage rights within the U.S.

Cabotage was the right of a foreign airline to carry local traffic in a domestic market. As a general rule, cabotage was strictly prohibited. For example, Lufthansa was unable to carry Atlanta-Dallas traffic on its Frankfurt-Atlanta-Dallas service. Although American carriers could not carry Germans between Munich and Frankfurt, European geography allowed U.S. carriers with fifth freedom rights to serve a number of major European cities on a single flight (such as New York-London-Frankfurt) without worrying about cabotage restrictions. This provided the Americans with the opportunity to protect their domestic market while giving up very little. In bilateral negotiations, for example, they had restricted points of entry in the U.S., maximizing the opportunities for U.S. local carriers and, not incidentally, giving their international carriers the advantage of one airline service to and from the ultimate U.S. destination. European carriers were pressing hard for a liberalization of the rules governing cabotage in the vast U.S. domestic market. By acting as a block, European governments could possibly negotiate a reduction to the number of destinations and fifth and sixth freedom rights enjoyed by the U.S. carriers. Similarly, if after 1992 Europe was declared "one territory", it was felt that intra-Europe carriage by non-European carriers might arguably constitute "cabotage", a fact which would greatly strengthen the European's bargaining position. On the other hand, the U.S. might argue that they have bought and paid for third and fourth freedom rights in Europe, and are not prepared to pay anything more when such rights become European cabotage.

THE EUROPEAN MARKET

In 1990, domestic and intra-regional traffic in Western Europe amounted to about 130 billion passenger kilometres, and was growing at a rate of about 8%. Compared to the U.S., the European air travel market was underdeveloped. Although the member nations of the EEC represented 320 million people, only 15% had ever flown, and per capita air travel was less than 30% of the U.S. levels. The European fleet was half the size of the U.S. fleet.

There were several reasons for the lower penetration of air travel in Europe, including shorter distances between major centres, and the availability of excellent rail transportation. But a further reason was regulation—a jungle of regulation that restricted capacity and kept fares extraordinarily high (by comparison with the U.S.). There were signs of movement, however, toward a more competitive air market in Europe. Some countries, such as the U.K., had started the process and others were following, in part because of the single market initiative for 1992. The precise timetable and outcome for the airline industry was uncertain, but the IATA had welcomed as "significant" recent talks between the 12 EEC nations that moved towards permitting cabotage, implementing double disapproval (new and cheap fares would be blocked only if governments at both ends of the route object), and sweeping away restrictions on third, fourth, fifth and sixth freedom traffic within the community.

The top five European carriers were Lufthansa, British Airways, Air France, Scandinavian Airline Systems, and Alitalia. Given their limited domestic markets, these carriers had been working for years to build their international business, within Europe and around the globe. They had established extensive route systems, and were complementing these networks with alliances. In 1989, British Airways was the largest carrier of international traffic, and five of the other top ten international carriers were European as noted in Table 6. A brief description of these airlines and their strategies is given in Table 7.

TABLE 6 Top Ten Carriers of International Traffic
(millions of scheduled international passengers in 1989)

1	British Airways	18.9
2	Air France	12.7
3	Lufthansa	11.6
4	Pan American	9.4
5	Japan Airlines	8.1
6	SAS	7.6
7	Cathay Pacific	7.1
8	Swissair	6.9
9	American Airlines	6.8
10	SIA	6.7

SOURCE: British Airways' annual report, 1990.

THE ASIA-PACIFIC MARKET

Domestic and intra-regional traffic in the Asia-Pacific market was greater than Western Europe, amounting to about 160 billion passenger kilometres in 1990, and it was growing at an 8% annual rate. International traffic was booming; routes to North America and Europe accounted for about 160 billion revenue passenger kilometres, and were experiencing growth rates in the order of 10–20%. The Asia-Pacific airlines were flying with high load factors, and were straining to overcome constraints in planes, pilots and infrastructure.

The top five carriers in Asia were Japan Airlines, All Nippon Airways, Korean Airlines, Singapore Airlines, and Cathay Pacific. A sketch of each of these airlines is given in Table 8. Beyond the largest firms, there were very wide differences in the sizes, strategies and market strengths of the Asian airlines. The similarity of intra-regional and international routes had discouraged commercial agreements amongst the Asian carriers.

The major Asian carriers and their governments were concerned with the possibility of the European protectionist moves, including the power of regional

TABLE 7 **Profile of the Top Five European Airlines**

Carrier	1989 World Revenue Ranking	Primary Hubs	Fleet Size	Comments
British Airways	5	London's Heathrow and Gatwick	224	Privatized by Thatcher in 1987. Strong reputation for service and marketing. Will bear the brunt of competition from United and American at Heathrow but won rights to expanded U.S. service in return.
Lufthansa	6	Frankfurt	148	Poised to cash in on unification and the opening of Eastern Europe. Government-owned carrier recently bought Pan Am's prized inter-German service and now dominates Berlin as well as Frankfurt and Munich. Loyal business travellers, but tough unions.
Air France	10	Paris—Charles de Gaulle (In't) and Orly (Domestic)	N/A	Aggressive, government-owned carrier will be Europe's biggest after acquisition of UTA and Air Inter. Top-notch service and a new marketing link with USAir will help it compete with U.S. carriers. High costs make it vulnerable to European deregulation.
SAS	12	Stockholm and Copenhagen	119	Chairman Jan Carlzon is a maestro of marketing agreements. Ups and downs with his 16% stake in Continental: Shared Newark hub has boosted traffic, but Continental's Chapter 11 forced a $106 million write-down.
Alitalia	16	Rome	N/A	Formed alliance with USAir and Spain's Iberia. Italian government owns 81.2%.

SOURCE: Authors' compilation; annual reports; *Fortune*, September 24, 1990; *Business Week*, January 21, 1991.

TABLE 8 Profile of the Top Five Asian Pacific Airlines

Carrier	1989 World Revenue Ranking	Primary Hubs	Fleet Size (owned or leased)	Comments
Japan Air Lines	3	Tokyo, Nagoya	85	Dominates Tokyo's Narita Airport. Prime vehicle for nation's obsession with worldwide travel, Huge fleet, sprawling route network. Lusts after greater access to U.S., where it has hotels. Domestic rival All Nippon Airways is turning up heat internationally.
All Nippon Airways	11	Tokyo	N/A	One time domestic carrier rapidly expanding service to the U.S. and Europe.
Hanjin Group (Korean Air)	14	Korea	N/A	Also owns ocean freighters and a large trucking company.
Singapore Airlines	22	Singapore	36	This airline has a golden reputation among business customers. Fat 30% margins despite high costs of expansion, labour. Marketing relationship with Delta and Swissair, solidified by reciprocal 5% equity stakes. 80% of business from international markets.
Cathay Pacific	24	Hong Kong	36	Business people love it. Exceptional service doesn't tarnish hefty profits, but Hong Kong's brain drain is pinching margins. Faces sharp rise in labour costs.

SOURCE: Authors' compilation; annual reports; *Fortune*, September 24, 1990; *Business Week*, January 21, 1991.

bargaining against the individual Asian positions. They had served notice that they were prepared to respond in kind, including the formation of their own trading block. This would be a difficult move, however, because of the enormous differences in the region's cultural, economic and geographic circumstances.

THE CANADIAN MARKET

The domestic market in Canada accounted for approximately 21 billion passenger kilometres in 1990, and was growing at a slow rate, by world standards, of about 4%. International traffic amounted to another 20 to 25 billion passenger kilometres, but it, too, was growing at a slow pace.

Market Structure

The airline industry in Canada had undergone significant change from 1985 to 1990. Liberalized regulation had been introduced by the Canadian government permitting an airline to add or drop domestic routes if it simply met the test of being "fit, willing and able" (i.e., if it had adequate liability insurance, met safety regulations, and was Canadian-owned). The regulation of fares and cargo tariffs was largely eliminated. In 1989, the federal government completed the privatization of AC.

Less regulation had led to a remarkably quick and, compared to the U.S. experience, smooth consolidation of the industry. The seven major carriers of 1985—(AC, Canadian Pacific, Pacific Western, Nordair, Quebecair, EPA, and Wardair—and a clutch of mostly independent connector airlines had been reduced to two prime carriers, AC and CDN, and their affiliated connector networks. Foreign ownership in Canadian airlines was limited to 25%, although both AC and CDN had recently suggested to the government that they favoured following the U.S.'s recent increase to a 49% limit.

Among the majors, Wardair had been the last to go. Through its history it had been a successful charter operator, but in 1987 it launched an aggressive and, in retrospect, foolhardy campaign to become a major scheduled domestic carrier. Wardair triggered a fierce round of price competition which it had neither the financial capacity nor operating abilities to sustain. Nearing bankruptcy, it was acquired by CDN in 1989.

With the industry now relatively uncluttered, AC and CDN in 1990 were joined in direct competition for the domestic market, and for access and approvals to international routes. A sketch of each of these airlines is presented in Table 9.

GOVERNMENT POLICY ON INTERNATIONAL ROUTES

Canada's traditional policy on international routes had been to "divide the skies", favouring AC on U.S., Atlantic and Caribbean routes and Canadian Pacific (a predecessor of CDN) over the Pacific and to South America. In 1987,

TABLE 9   Profile of Air Canada and Canadian Airlines

Air Canada
1990 World Revenue Ranking: 20; 1989 Profit Ranking: 13;
1990 Fleet Size (owned and leased): 115 (including 8 in storage pending disposal);
Primary Hubs: Toronto, Montreal, Vancouver

Performance Data ($000)	*1990*	*1989*	*1988*	*1987*	*1986*
Operating Revenue ($)	3 939	3 650	3 404	3 114	2 872
Operating Income ($)	(11)	103	108	103	113
Net Income ($)	(74)	149	89	43	37
Total Assets ($)	4 579	4 121	3 437	3 084	2 923
RPKs (millions)	26.7	26.2	25.1	23.2	23.3
Load Factor %	71.4	69.7	71.4	71.1	67.7

Canadian Airlines International Ltd.
1989 World Revenue Ranking: 23; Profit Ranking: 40;
1990 Fleet Size (owned and leased): 88;
Primary Hubs: Toronto, Vancouver, Calgary

Performance Data ($000)	*1990*	*1989*	*1988*	*1987*	*1986*
Operating Revenue ($)	2 745.6	2 648.7	2 283.6	1 930.5	361.8
Operating Income ($)	(12)	(10)	78	164	25
Net Income ($)	(15)	(56)	30	28	37
Total Assets ($)	2 964	2 912	2 125	1 989	946
RPKs (millions)	22.3	23.7	19.6	16.9	2.7
Load Factor %	64.8	67.2	68.8	69.6	59.9

SOURCE: Company annual reports.

several changes were made to route allocations resulting in a structure with greater overlap as outlined in Exhibit 5.

While the "division of skies" policy had suited a world of regional markets, it was becoming increasingly dysfunctional for a global marketplace. In Southeast Asia, for example, the policy (AC—Singapore, Korea, Malaysia and the Philippines; CDN—Japan, Hong Kong and Thailand) prevented a Canadian carrier such as CDN from fully exploiting the potential for intra-Orient fifth freedom traffic, such as Hong Kong-Singapore or Tokyo-Singapore. Neither airline was satisfied with the current arrangements. AC wanted in particular to extend its service over the Pacific to Japan, and CDN was frustrated by the historical dominance of AC on U.S. routes.

The Canada-U.S. Air Transport Situation

The Canada-U.S. market was the largest bilateral air relationship in the world. In 1989, 13 million passengers generated approximately $2.3 billion in revenue. It was widely predicted that the market would be much larger under a less restrictive air services agreement.

In 1991, transborder services between Canada and the U.S. were based on a 1974 agreement. In spite of the dramatic changes in the industry in subsequent years, only minor amendments had been agreed between the countries—attempts at thorough revision having floundered in the search for what both sides regarded as a reasonable deal. The U.S. position in various negotiations had, since 1978, been based on an "open skies" philosophy of reducing regulation, and letting competition in the marketplace decide who will be served and who will survive. The Canadian side had consistently been unprepared to adopt this approach. Recently, however, the two governments had agreed to give high priority to renegotiating the agreement. In a joint statement, the U.S. Secretary of Transportation Sam Skinner and Canadian Minister of Transport Doug Lewis said, "We share a common vision of a liberalized North American aviation market. In pursuit of that vision, we intend to take a bold approach in these negotiations. We are giving our negotiators broad latitude to explore the prospect of creating an open regime that would dramatically expand air services in and between our two countries. We want an aviation market in which the flow of goods and passengers would be unimpeded by governmental economic regulation." The Canadian government, in particular, had given considerable prominence to negotiations, saying that the current agreement was "unacceptable for business and tourism interests," and that a new agreement would remedy this and "offer Canadian carriers improved access to the world's most lucrative aviation market...and provide expanded horizons and enhance their global network."

The Current Agreements

The crucial parts of the current agreements dealt with scheduled traffic, charter traffic and customs and immigration preclearance. In 1990, there were 83 transborder city pairs designated for scheduled service, of which the U.S. had exclusive rights to 39 routes, Canada to 26 routes, and both countries to 18 routes. These routes gave U.S. carriers access to 90% of the Canadian population, while Canadian carriers had access to only 30% of the American population. Scheduled services accounted for 82% of the 13.1 million transborder passengers in 1989, and U.S. carriers had a 62% share of this business.

No limit was placed on the number of transborder charter flights operated by Canadian carriers in either direction. However, U.S. carriers could operate no more than 40% of the southbound charter capacity of the Canadian operators. The charter business accounted for 2.3 million passengers in 1989, and was dominated by Canadian carriers with a 96% share.

The preclearance agreement provided for pre-flight customs and immigration passage at certain airports in both countries. To date, however, only southbound (U.S.) preclearance facilities had been established at Montreal, Toronto, Winnipeg, Edmonton, Calgary and Vancouver. The airlines using these facilities were required to pay a portion of their costs, and they had not been aggressive in seeking northbound (Canadian) preclearance at U.S. cities.

Service Inadequacies

The current agreement seriously restricted routes, carrier designation and pricing in the cross-border marketplace. There were, for example, no direct scheduled routes from anywhere in Canada to such cities as Atlanta, St. Louis, Cincinnati, Orlando, Fort Lauderdale, New Orleans, San Diego, and Phoenix. The possibilities for new routes without a bilateral were limited to city pairs (1) not served by negotiated routes, (2) where at least one city has a population of less then 500 000 (Canada) or 1 000 000 (U.S.), (3) that are no more than 400 statute miles apart in central Canada and 600 elsewhere, and (4) using aircraft of 60 seats or less. Where service was available, airlines were often limited by restrictions on the number of carriers and pricing controlled by a mechanism which gave each country a veto over fares filed by the other country's carriers.

Poor service had prompted the development in Canada of The Association of Canadian Airport Communities (ACAC) and in the U.S. a counter-part group called USA-Better International Air Service (USA-BIAS). Both groups were lobbying on behalf of their communities, and arguing that the absence of better air arrangements was cutting off up to 2 million additional passengers and incremental benefits to Canadian and U.S. communities of as much as $9.0 billion.

A second inadequacy in the treaty, at least in the eyes of CDN, was in the historical access advantages enjoyed by AC. Under current arrangements, CDN had access to only three cities in the continental U.S., plus San Juan and Hawaii which essentially excluded it from substantive participation in the market.

Early Positions on the Negotiations

The remedies proposed for treaty revision ranged from a radical "open skies" approach, which would remove most regulations including cabotage restrictions, to a conservative renegotiation of specific limited transborder routes. A variety of interested parties had expressed strong views as the governments entered negotiations.

The Canadian Carriers

Both Canadian carriers believed that a new treaty was necessary to rectify the imbalance, but they had deep concerns about their viability in a more liberalized agreement. They were worried in particular that the U.S. carriers enjoyed structural advantages through their hub and spoke systems and, to a lesser degree, through the preclearance system.

The reality of the Canadian market was that it was strung out on an East-West axis close to the border and comprised of perhaps a dozen interesting city-markets. The U.S. market, in contrast, was comprised of hundreds of interesting cities spread throughout the country. By simply integrating a small set of Canadian cities into their hubs, the U.S. airlines offered coverage of both markets. While the Canadian airlines provided a more complete coverage of Canadian markets beyond the key cities, they could not provide same-airline competitive coverage of the U.S. AA, for example, advertised 200 destinations out of Montreal as compared to AC's half a dozen. A passenger who wanted to use AC on a trip to the "194" destinations that it did not serve directly would have to change airlines at the U.S. gateway city.

In those situations in which the transborder traffic was local, between Canadian and U.S. gateways only, such as Toronto—Los Angeles, the Canadian airlines had proven competitive. Their big problem was the capacity of the U.S. carriers to offer one airline service to cities behind the gateway hub.

The availability of southbound preclearance enhanced the U.S. airlines' use of their gateway hub. Where warranted, they could offer "same plane" services through their hubs without the interruption of customs formalities.

The Canadian airlines were also at a disadvantage in unit costs including: higher fuel taxes, higher leasing charges, higher user fees, higher telecommunication costs, greater tax burden due to lower depreciation rates, higher labour costs, and interest rates and exchange rate disadvantages with regard to the acquisition of equipment denominated in U.S. dollars. CDN estimated that without the tax disadvantage its 1990 fuel bill of $450 million would have been about $150 million lower. In addition, Ottawa's 1989 decision to abolish special tax writeoffs for leased equipment made financing costs for new aircraft about 5% higher in Canada than in the U.S.

Apart from agreeing on the need for change, the two Canadian carriers were advocating different negotiating stances. AC had originally come out in favour of full cabotage, but had toned down its position to one of supporting cabotage "in some form", presumably with limits and phase-in provisions. AC was quite clear that it did not want an agreement which simply "robs Peter to pay Paul" to give CDN greater access.

The CDN position was against cabotage of any form. Rather, CDN proposed a tiering of transborder routes into five categories—"high density", "other business", "leisure", "developmental", and "all cargo". These classifications would be used to differentiate the number of carriers allowed; on high density routes each country would designate two carriers, and on other business routes, one carrier; and on developmental routes, the countries would alternate in selecting a single carrier.

Whatever agreement was struck, the Canadian carriers wanted to be sure that it would be gradually phased in, with strong safeguards and review mechanisms. The government concurred in this saying that it was in the national interest to maintain two major Canadian carriers. In a speech to industry executives in May 1991, Doug Lewis, the Minister of Transport, explained the government's position: "The continuing imperative of our airline policies must be to enhance competitiveness. Merging Canada's biggest airlines would not make the remaining entity more competitive. It would not produce a mega-carrier big enough to dominate markets occupied by giants like United and British Airways. But if the assumed benefits of a merger don't come from a more competitive company which wins its battles in the marketplace, then inevitably these benefits must come directly from the consumer pockets in the form of less competition, higher fares and a guaranteed return for the airline. Higher levels of debt, the destruction of thousands of jobs and re-regulation of the airline sector are three other likely products of a merger between our two major carriers."

The U.S. Carriers

The view in the U.S. was that the current air treaty had limited revenue growth in the past decade to half its potential. What the U.S. carriers wanted, essentially, was the right to link their hubs to several key Canadian cities. Don Carty of AA argued for an "open market" claiming that free trade in aviation would result in an immediate increase of at least 1.5 million transborder passengers. He claimed that Canadians were doing themselves a disservice in fearing an open market. He argued that there was no reason to believe that Canadian carriers would not get their share of new business, that for the long term the global competitiveness of the Canadian carriers rested on their access to the entire North American market, and for that to happen, there had to be one unified North American market.

Carty's point on the broader international implications of a transborder agreement touched on a potential opportunity for the Canadian airlines. By using cities such as Toronto and Vancouver as international hubs, they could attempt to build a significant position in international traffic into and out of the U.S. Here they could take advantage of the U.S. policy of limiting international gateways and of the congestion at key U.S. airports. With access to a range of U.S. cities, they could link to their own international flights or those of alliance partners.

In general, the U.S. industry had taken a very positive and cooperative stance with respect to the negotiations. This puzzled some analysts who felt the U.S. had the best of the current situation.

Other Parties

Two related groups had been quite vocal in their representations about the negotiations—ACAC (the airport community group) and the Canadian airline unions. Their views were at opposite ends of the spectrum. ACAC argued for a liberal agreement including the possibility of cabotage. The unions, on the other hand, felt that domestic deregulation in the U.S. and Canada had been a failure, and that further international deregulation was unwise and unnecessary. In particular, the unions were concerned that an "open sky" regime between the U.S. and Canada would result in severe damage to the Canadian carriers and the ultimate dominance of the business by a small handful of U.S. giants.

Europe and Asia-Pacific

While less visible and dramatic, there were also serious policy issues on the horizon with respect to the European and Asian markets. If regional trading blocks emerged in either case, the existing bilateral arrangements would have to be renegotiated. Issues of access and cabotage would almost certainly arise. In all of this, Canadians were bargaining from a relatively small market base. The results of the Canada-U.S. negotiations would have significant impacts for the further international development of the Canadian industry.

CONCLUSION

The world airline industry faced a bleak outlook in early 1991. The industry had been savaged so fast by the combined effects of the war in the Persian Gulf and widespread economic troubles. The airlines' losses had mounted as they flew half-empty aircraft around the world. Airlines all over were cutting capital and labour costs, deferring aircraft deliveries, reducing flight frequencies, and suspending unprofitable routes. British Airways announced plans to slash its payroll by 4 600 people. Belgium's Sabena said it would cut 2 200 jobs, while USAir was dropping 3585 employees. As preparation for the negotiations continued, AC and CDN were cutting further and further back on flights and employment.

In all of this, the sometimes contrary trends toward globalization and regional trading blocks were creating unprecedented opportunities and challenges for the Canadian airline industry. The Canadian negotiating team had the immediate task of trying to position Canada within the North American market. The results of its negotiation would definitely impact on Canada's status in this global industry. What steps would put the country and its airline industry into the best possible position to profit in the future?

EXHIBIT 1 The Top 50 Airline Companies: Rank by Revenues

RANK BY REVENUES 1989	1988	Airline Company	COUNTRY	1989 REVENUES U.S. $ Millions	% Change from 1988 (U.S.)	PROFITS $ Millions	Rank	TRAFFIC Billions of Passenger Kms.	Rank
1	2	AMR	U.S.	10 589.5	20.0	454.8	3	118.5	1
2	1	UAL	U.S.	9 914.5	10.0	324.2	6	112.3	2
3	4	Japan Airlines[1]	Japan	8 509.0	17.4	157.3	10	54.4	8
4	5	Delta	U.S.	8 089.5	17.0	460.9	2	55.9	3
5	7	British Airways[1]	Britain	7 529.1	12.5	309.5	7	90.2	6
6	6	Lufthansa	W. Germany	6 941.2	3.0	56.8	22	57.9	12
7	3	Texas Air	U.S.	6 768.7	(21.0)	(885.6)	47	81.3	4
8	10	NWA	U.S.	6 553.8	16.0	355.2	5	73.7	5
9	9	USAIR Group	U.S.	6 257.3	9.6	(63.2)	41	54.4	9
10	8	Air France	France	6 216.9	4.4	132.0	12	37.0	11
11	11	All Nippon[1]	Japan	4 858.4	9.7	60.2	19	26.0	16
12	12	Scandinavian Airlines	Sweden	4 567.3	3.5	N/A	—	15.3	26
13	13	Trans World	U.S.	4 507.3	3.4	(298.5)	45	56.4	7
14	15	Hanjin Group	South Korea	4 243.6	13.7	69.6	18	17.9	23

EXHIBIT 1 (continued)

1989	1988	Airline Company	COUNTRY	U.S. $ Millions	% Change from 1988 (U.S.)	$ Millions	Rank	Billions of Passenger Kms.	Rank
	RANK BY REVENUES			1989 REVENUES		PROFITS		TRAFFIC	
15	14	Pan Am	U.S.	3 794.4	(8.9)	(336.6)	46	46.6	10
16	16	Alitalia	Italy	3 734.2	14.6	(168.1)	44	20.8	21
17	17	Swissair	Switzerland	3 174.5	1.7	103.3	16	15.8	25
18	20	Air Canada	Canada	3 104.3	11.8	125.8	13	26.3	15
19	18	Iberia	Spain	3 015.5	4.9	52.5	25	21.1	20
20	19	KLM[1]	Netherlands	2 938.9	4.1	184.2	8	24.0	17
21	21	Qantas[2]	Australia	2 655.1	18.1	144.3	11	26.6	14
22	22	Singapore[1]	Singapore	2 295.8	15.2	494.7	1	28.9	13
23	24	PWA	Canada	2 252.9	27.7	(47.3)	40	23.7	18
24	23	Cathay Pacific	Hong Kong	2 212.6	14.4	425.2	4	22.1	19
25	25	Saudia	Saudi Arabia	1 910.1	12.5	(140.0)	43	16.3	24
26	26	Varig	Brazil	1 862.1	21.6	10.4	39	13.9	28
27	28	Ansett Transport[2]	Australia	1 743.9	32.7	108.0	15	7.7	42
28	27	Thai International[3]	Thailand	1 683.8	17.9	182.1	9	18.7	22
29	29	Japan Air System[1]	Japan	1 418.3	12.7	12.2	36	7.3	43
30	30	Air Inter	France	1 356.5	9.5	18.3	32	8.5	39
31	34	China	Taiwan	1 246.4	20.3	115.6	14	10.5	33
32	31	Garuda	Indonesia	1 232.6	11.6	N/A	—	12.9	29

EXHIBIT 1 (continued)

									Place
33	33	Hudson Investments[4]	Britain	1 211.6	11.6	11.7	37	6.9	45
34	36	Finnair[1]	Finland	1 160.9	13.5	18.3	33	9.2	35
35	32	Sabena	Belgium	1 146.9	4.9	18.0	34	6.8	46
36	37	Air New Zealand[1]	New Zealand	1 108.7	9.0	46.6	26	10.6	31
37	38	LTU	West Germany	1 094.4	13.6	N/A	—	9.8	34
38	35	UTA	France	1 058.1	3.2	38.1	28	5.6	48
39	39	Southwest	U.S.	1 031.7	22.6	71.6	17	15	27
40	43	Australian2	Australia	1 013.8	27.9	57.4	21	6.1	47
41	45	America West	U.S.	1 004.2	29.5	20.0	31	12.7	30
42	40	Alaska Air Group	U.S.	929.2	14.1	42.9	27	7.1	44
43	49	S. African Airways[1]	S. Africa	912.2	(9.3)	55.9	24	9.0	37
44	44	Aer Lingus	Ireland	899.5	14.5	56.2	23	3.4	49
45	—	Austrian	Austria	850.5	9.7	11.6	38	2.4	50
46	42	Olympic Airways	Greece	785.0*	(2.2)*	(123.1)*	42	8.1	40
47	47	Mexicana	Mexico	764.3	2.0	13.7	35	10.5	32
48	48	Air India[1]	India	745.4	1.2	28.1	29	9.0	36
49	—	El Al	Israel	713.6	7.3	24.2	30	7.7	41
50	—	Malaysian[1]	Malaysia	712.8	14.0	59.0	20	9.0	38

* Estimate.

[1] Figures are for fiscal year ended March 31, 1989.

[2] Figures are for fiscal year ended June 30, 1989.

[3] Figures are for fiscal year ended September 30, 1989.

[4] Figures are for fiscal year ended October 31, 1989.

Note: All figures converted to U.S. dollars using the average official exchange rate during each company's fiscal year.

SOURCE: Labich, Kenneth, "American Takes on the World", *Fortune*, September 24, 1990, p.52.

EXHIBIT 2 The Six Freedoms of the Air

Each contracting state in a bilateral air agreement can grant to the other contracting state or states the following Freedoms of the air in respect of scheduled international services:

1. The privilege to fly across the territory of another country without landing. For example, Air Canada flies from Montreal to London, England, over Ireland.

2. The privilege to land in another country for technical and other non-traffic purposes. For example, on Air Canada's route between Toronto and Zurich, Air Canada lands at Shannon, Ireland for a technical stop which basically means taking on fuel and food.

3. The privilege to put down passengers, mail and cargo in another country. For example, on Air Canada's flight from Montreal to London, England, Air Canada lands in Shannon, Ireland and lets people get off and then flies on to London, England.

4. The privilege to take on/board passengers, mail and cargo in another country destined for Canada. For example, Air Canada can pick up people in Ireland and fly them back to Canada.

5. The privilege to take on passengers, mail and cargo in one foreign country for carriage to another foreign country. For example, Air Canada on its Toronto/Zurich route can land in Ireland and pick up Irish passengers and carry them to Zurich and vice versa.

6. The privilege of carrying traffic between two foreign countries via one's own country. For example, an American passenger can board an Air Canada flight in Cleveland and go via Montreal to London, England.

These are the six Freedoms of the Air. The two that are very easy to obtain are #1 and #2. Generally speaking, the basic freedoms that are negotiated in a bilateral agreement are #3 and #4. However, fifth and sixth Freedoms are often very difficult to obtain and the trade-offs are usually substantial in order to get them. What is usually never on the table is the freedom of an airline to carry domestic traffic within a foreign country, which is commonly known as "cabotage". For example, Air Canada flies to Chicago and then on to Los Angeles. If Air Canada had the privilege of picking up U.S. passengers in Chicago and carrying them to Los Angeles, this would be a "right-of-cabotage". It is seldom, if ever, granted by any country.

SOURCE: John Christopher and David Cuthbertson, *Canada-U.S. Air Transport Services: An Overview*, Research Branch, Library of Parliament, Ottawa, 1990.

EXHIBIT 3 1990 Key Airline Operating Statistics
(Canadian dollars)

	CDN	*AC*	*AA*	*UAL*	*DELTA*	*U.S. Average**
Passenger Revenue Yield per RPK (¢)	9.9	10.4	9.2	9.1	10.1	9.5
Passenger Revenue per ASK (¢)	6.5	7.4	5.7	6.1	6.0	5.9
Operating Cost per ASK (¢)	8.0	9.0	6.4	7.0	6.5	6.7
Personnel Cost per ASK (¢)	2.3	3.0	2.3	2.2	2.6	2.4
Fuel Cost per ASK (¢)	1.3	1.6	1.1	1.1	1.1	1.1
Other Expenses per ASK (¢)	4.3	4.5	3.4	3.6	2.7	3.2
Passenger Load Factor (%)	64.8%	71.4%	62.3%	66.2%	59.1%	62.5%
Break Even Load Factor (%)	65.2%	73.0%	61.8%	66.5%	61.1%	63.1%
Operating Margin (%)	(0.4)%	(1.3)%	0.6%	(0.3)%	(2.6)%	N/A

Legend: Canadian Airlines International (CDN); Air Canada (AC); American Airlines (AA), United Airlines (UAL).

* Composed of top three U.S. carriers: AA, UA, and Delta.

SOURCE: CDN.

EXHIBIT 4 Major Computer Reservation Systems

System (Ranked by Size)	Members	Number of Daily Transactions	Associated* Systems	Members
1. Sabre	American Airlines	60 million		
2. Apollo (owned by Covia—a United Airlines subsidiary)	United Airlines USAir	N/A	Galileo (25.6% owned by Covia) Apollo by Gemeni (one third owned by Covia)	Aer Lingus, Air Portugal, Alitalia, Austrian, British Airways, KLM, Olympic, Sabena, Swissair Air Canada, Canadian Airlines
3. Worldspan	Delta Airlines Northwestern TWA	N/A	Abacus	Cathay Pacific, Singapore Airlines
4. System One	Texas Air (Continental Airlines +Eastern Airlines)	20.7 million	Amadeus	Air France, Iberia, Lufthansa, SAS

* The Associated Systems utilized software from the Primary System.

SOURCE: *Air Transport World*, August 1990; and authors' compilation.

EXHIBIT 5   Allocation of International Routes between Air Canada and Canadian Airlines International

Europe

Air Canada is assigned to serve Europe except for the Netherlands, Denmark, Sweden, Norway, Italy, the U.S.S.R., Munich and routes linking Western Canada and Frankfurt.

Canadian Airlines International is also assigned to serve one point in the Federal Republic of Germany other than Frankfurt or Dusseldorf from any point in Canada. (By virtue of the Wardair acquisition, Canadian Airlines also services London, Manchester and Paris.)

Asia

Canadian Airlines International is assigned to serve Asia east of Burma except Singapore, Malaysia, Korea and the Philippines, which are assigned to Air Canada.

Air Canada is assigned to serve Asia west of and including Burma excluding across-the-Pacific services to Delhi or Calcutta, India, which are assigned to Canadian Airlines International.

Middle East

For Air Canada.

Africa

For Air Canada.

Australia, New Zealand and the Pacific island countries

For Canadian Airlines International.

The Caribbean, Mexico, Central and South America

Canadian Airlines International for Mexico, Central and South America except for Venezuela, which is assigned to Air Canada. Air Canada for the Caribbean.

SOURCE: *Transport Canada Information*, no. 248/87, October 5, 1987.

PWA CORPORATION

Roderick E. White and Joseph N. Fry with Lisa Davidson

As Rhys Eyton, President and Chief Executive Officer of PWA Corporation (PWA)—the parent company of Canadian Airlines International Ltd. (CDN), examined the list of the top airlines in the world in 1990, he stated: "In five to ten years there are going to be less than a dozen major airline systems and we want to be among them." There was a lot of speculation both inside and outside of CDN about the path CDN should follow over the next few years. With CDN ranked below the top 20 airlines in the world, Eyton had his work cut out for him. In fact, the larger international carriers dwarfed the entire Canadian airline industry.

EVOLUTION OF CDN

CDN was owned by PWA Corporation, a broadly owned public company with holdings in the airline and related businesses. PWA had changed dramatically from its origins in the late 1940s as Pacific Western Airlines, a small, western Canadian carrier. By the early 1980s, PWA was Canada's most profitable carrier and the country's largest regional airline. Based in western Canada, PWA was allied with Air Canada (AC). Like most regional carriers operating in the regulated environment of the day, PWA had many monopoly routes and offered one class of service with one type of aircraft (Boeing 737s).

During the late 1980s, in response to deregulation, the industry restructured dramatically. Taking an aggressive approach, PWA acquired the much larger trunk carrier Canadian Pacific Air Lines (CPAL) for $300 million. This move put PWA into direct competition with AC. In purchasing CPAL, PWA was really acquiring three airlines, CPAL and the regional airlines it had recently acquired: Nordair and Eastern Provincial Airlines. Subsequently, PWA focused its efforts on merging the four predecessor carriers to form one integrated operation. The airline launched its new name and image in April 1987—Canadian Airlines International Ltd.

PWA continued to grow by acquiring Wardair in 1989. Wardair had been a successful international charter airline, but its attempt to institute regularly scheduled domestic service had put the company in jeopardy. Initially, Canadian

Airlines and Wardair were operated separately but with code-sharing[1] and joint operations on a number of transcontinental flights. However, faced with a slowing economy, rising fuel costs and interest rates, PWA moved to combine the two airlines. The management structure was reorganized and, at the same time, steps were taken to reduce operating costs (including substantial staff reductions). The process of integrating different airlines was very complex; it typically involved route restructuring, job reductions, fleet rationalization, and the merger of different computer reservation systems (CRSs), frequent flyer programs and other operating systems. PWA wrote off a pre-tax provision of $73.8 million for costs associated with integrating Wardair.

Current Situation

By 1990, CDN had become a world-scale airline. It ranked 24th in revenue and 18th in passenger volume. CDN and its regional partners operated scheduled air transportation to 114 destinations in 19 countries on five continents. However, growth had not been without problems. Operating income, cashflow and the capital structure needed to be improved if the company was to be viable in the long run. While CDN was approaching AC (its remaining domestic rival in size), it lagged in profitability.

CDN'S ROUTE STRUCTURE

CDN and AC had a roughly comparable mix of routes. CDN's international routes, representing approximately 20% of passengers carried, accounted for 37% of the almost $2.1 billion in revenue from all services during 1990. Domestic service, cargo and mail, contract services and charter flights made up the remainder. AC's 1990 revenue from passenger service was: 58% from domestic routes, and 42% from international routes. Table 1 lists the number of international and domestic destinations served by CDN and AC including their connectors.

CDN and AC competed most directly domestically with almost identical route structures. Internationally because of government policy they did not, for the most part, serve the same city-pairs. Even though CDN served more domestic destinations, its 1990 passenger market share was approximately 41%, compared to about 52.5% for AC with the remainder split between independents and charters.

CDN's historical base in western Canada was reflected in its route structure and passenger volumes. As shown in Table 2 during 1990, CDN's strongest regional market position was in the Prairies and B.C. However, CDN was

---

[1] When one airline lists the flight of another airline as part of its schedule/route structure.

TABLE 1 AC's and CDN's 1990 Destinations, Including Connectors

Destinations	CDN	AC
Canada	109	74
U.S.	7	19
Total	116	93
Europe	8	10
Asia and South Pacific	9	0
Caribbean/Mexico	2	13
South America	5	2
Total International (including U.S.)	31	44

SOURCE: CDN.

TABLE 2 CDN's 1990 Regional Revenue and Domestic Passenger Data by Origin of Ticket Sale*

Region	Passenger Revenue ($000)	CDN's Share (%)	Passenger Volumes (000)	CDN's Share (%)
Ontario	$ 864 729	31.4	2 003	33.9
Prairies	500 223	45.5	1 147	48.9
British Columbia	217 756	57.5	940	57.2
Quebec	252 430	19.9	689	18.2
Atlantic	169 315	34.3	425	36.1
Total	2 165 581	39.2	5 204	39.5

* Represent 70% of ticket sales; 30% is derived from airlines. Compiled by date of sale. Includes Air Canada, Canadian Airlines International Limited and their affiliates, as well as Intair after October 1989.

SOURCE: Bank settlement plans.

weaker in the country's largest region, Ontario. CDN's overall passenger market share declined from 44.2% in 1989 to 39.5% in 1990. Most noticeably, CDN's passenger market share fell from 38.3% to 18.2% in Quebec, largely because of the loss of CDN's Quebec affiliate. CDN's share of revenues did not decline as rapidly, falling from 41.6% in 1989 to 39.2% in 1990.

CDN's largest city-pair, in terms of revenue and passenger volume, was Vancouver-Toronto. AC had a strong position in the Toronto-Ottawa-Montreal market, heavily travelled by business persons, and at least partly attributable to its frequent Rapidair service between these cities. Frequency and capacity share data for the two airlines on major city-pairs are given in Exhibit 1.

In 1991, CDN continued to develop its focus on the business market. Revenue forecasts had predicted domestic business market share gradually increasing over the first six months in 1991 as follows: in Ontario from 35% to 40%; Quebec from 17% to 30%; in the rest of Canada an increase of 0.5 share point, and an overall increase from 41% to 44%.

Connectors

Connectors made up an important part of domestic network of the major airlines. They flew mostly turboprop aircraft on short-haul flights (generally less than 500 kilometres) between outlying communities and major hub airports. Many of their passengers would connect with the flights of the major carriers. CDN estimated 23% of the passengers carried by their affiliates connected with a CDN flight. AC reported their proportion was 35%. The major airlines competed through their affiliated connectors aggressively for this "feed."

Table 3 outlines the connector airlines of CDN, highlighting ownership, destinations served and fleet composition. CDN's strength in western Canada is attributable, in part, to its connector in that region. Time Air had a network of 40 scheduled destinations from Vancouver to Winnipeg, and including the U.S. northwest. However, in the central and eastern regions, even before the loss of Inter-Canadian, their Quebec-based connector, CDN's network afforded less coverage than AC and its affiliates. By establishing marketing agreements with smaller airlines serving more remote communities (like Voyager Airways of North Bay, Ontario and Bearskin Lake Airways of Thunder Bay, Ontario) Air Canada continued to extend its feeder network.

Immediately following deregulation most arrangements between the trunk carriers and connectors had been simple interline agreements and loose marketing alliances. Occasionally the major carrier would take a minority equity position in the affiliate. Many of these relationships proved to be unstable. Both AC and CDN had increased their equity positions in their affiliated connectors. AC had established a controlling equity position in all its major connecting airlines. CDN had recently created a new subsidiary, Canadian Regional Airlines Ltd. It was designed to play a key role in planning, financing and coordinating the growth of CDN's regional partner carriers. CDN's equity interest had increased to 100% in two of its four regional partners: Ontario Express and Time Air.

CDN's affiliation with Inter-Canadian had disintegrated in late 1989. Inter-Canadian wanted to play a larger role than CDN was willing to provide through their commercial agreement. Inter-Canadian changed its name to Intair and began operating independently. As a result of the loss of Inter-Canadian CDN's

TABLE 3 CDN Connectors, April 1991

Air Carrier	% Ownership	Commuter Scheduled Destinations Served	# Passengers Carried	Earned Revenues
Air Atlantic	45%	19 destinations in Eastern Canada and the U.S.	655 000	$80.5 million
Calm Air	45	21 destinations in Northern Manitoba and the Northwest Territories	N/A	$15.7 million
Ontario Express	100	21 destinations in Ontario and Pittsburg, Pennsylvania	630 000	$88.5 million
Time Air	100	40 destinations in Western Canada and the U.S.	1.3 million	$129.6 million

market share in Quebec fell from 36% to under 20%. Intair's attempts to go it alone failed. In early 1991, Canadian Regional Airlines acquired the turboprop assets from the floundering Intair and reentered the Quebec market, moving quickly to establish its market share.

U.S. Routes

CDN and its connectors operated routes to seven U.S. cities: CDN served Los Angeles, San Francisco, and Honolulu; its connectors serviced Seattle, Minneapolis/St.Paul, Pittsburg and Boston (to Halifax). AC and its connectors operated flights to 22 U.S. destinations. Ten U.S. carriers served Canadian destinations.

Routes between Canada and the U.S. were governed by an "out-of-date" bilateral agreement between the two countries. While neither CDN nor AC were satisfied with the existing arrangements, AC was heavily favoured with 16 U.S.-Canada city-pairs versus the four available to CDN. Rhys Eyton estimated that in 1989, CDN made about $50 million in revenue from the U.S. market, while AC made close to $400 million. Because of this imbalance, CDN was anxiously awaiting the results of the "Open Skies" discussions currently taking place between Canada and the U.S.

Alliances with U.S. carriers was one way to expand CDN's presence in the U.S. In a preliminary effort, CDN had established in 1989, a marketing and interline alliance with Midway Airlines linking Chicago's Midway airport and Toronto. However, after more than a year this arrangement had not produced the hoped for results and was ended. The aircraft were redeployed to service the B.C.-California market. Although short-term losses on new routes were typical,

CDN did not foresee a long-term improvement in this situation. Even so, management believed that a significant U.S. ally was critical, in order to handle cross-border traffic effectively and gain credibility internationally.

CDN had talked with AA, UA and Delta. CDN's V.P. Marketing for North America commented that any of these three top U.S. airlines could make an appropriate partner for CDN in terms of fleet and route structure, but he felt that "chemistry" would dictate a fit. Moreover, CDN still had to gain the serious attention and interest of these huge carriers.

One analyst stated that open skies would eliminate US carriers' interest in forming alliances with Canadian airlines. However, a CDN's manager disagreed, saying that interest would remain because the two Canadian carriers would split the Canadian rights versus the US carriers, which would likely face a division of rights between more airlines.

International Routes

PWA became the parent of a significant international carrier with the acquisitions of Canadian Pacific Airlines and Wardair. Because international routes required approvals by governments, the nature of competition shifted. As a result of the Canadian governments "division of the skies" policy, only in a few instances did both Canadian carriers have rights to serve the same international city-pairs. The acquisition of Wardair routes had caused this overlap. CDN wanted to maintain this division.

The most direct competition to AC and CDN on international routes would appear to be with the flag carrier designated by the other nation. However, cooperative arrangements for sharing the traffic between carriers from different nations often evolved due to levels of demand, capacity constraints or each carriers' desire to offer daily service. Indeed, CDN had this type of cooperative arrangement with eight international carriers.

CDN's European Routes

CDN offered service from Toronto to London, Manchester, Milan, Munich, Paris and Rome, and Copenhagen; from Montreal to Paris and Rome, and from western Canada to Frankfurt, London, Manchester and Munich. In order to better serve the European market, CDN had established alliances with Air France, Lufthansa and SAS. These alliances went beyond simple marketing agreements to include block space arrangements and some operational integration.

European alliances were attractive because the main European international carriers—British Airways (BA), Lufthansa, Air France, and SAS—all had strong domestic bases as well as an international focus. However, some industry observers believed carriers were more interested in the U.S. market, and alliances with European carriers would become significant only if CDN could obtain significant access to the U.S. market.

CDN's Asian-Pacific Routes

CDN was the only Canadian carrier across the Pacific. It served nine destinations in the Asia-Pacific market: Auckland, Bangkok, Hong Kong, Nagoya, Nandi, Sydney, Taipei and Tokyo. There were Asian competitors serving Canada.

AC was continuing to lobby the government to try and gain access into Japan, a market designated to CDN. AC concluded that the market was underserved so Canadians were flying on U.S. carriers. In addition, AC argued that the "division of the skies" policy had been breached because CDN had acquired Wardair's routes into London and Paris, two markets which were AC's under the policy. Consequently, AC wanted access to Japan. CDN's management responded with several counter arguments: CDN was constrained by the capacity levels set out in the bilateral; it had arranged joint service with JAL, out of Toronto, to improve the capacity; adding AC to the route would not increase Canada's capacity; instead AC would receive capacity from CDN; and AC had benefited from Wardair's "withdrawal" from scheduled service in many ways. On the European rights question, CDN management added that Wardair had been designated to the U.K. and France, and the acquisition by CDN did not in any way change the competitive mix faced by AC in these markets. Furthermore, they argued that AC had been designated to Korea and Singapore under the Division of the World, and had chosen not to serve Korea and just withdrawn from Singapore.

Air New Zealand and Qantas, previously allies with Air Canada, had recently joined with CDN. Pacific routes had been very profitable for CDN. However, with increased competition resulting from new bilateral agreements, CDN needed to ally with Qantas and Air New Zealand in order to compete with US airlines. CDN's alliance with China Airlines gained access to Taiwan. CDN's existing Asian ally, Japan Airlines (JAL), was cautious and conservative, and it was unclear if this relationship could be expanded. However, CDN management believed that other Asian carriers might be receptive to more comprehensive partnership discussions.

CDN had opposed a request by Cathay Pacific to change the bilateral agreement governing Cathay Pacific access to Canada. Cathay Pacific wanted the right to code share with AC out of Vancouver to access the Toronto market. CDN argued that it was the official carrier designated to serve the Pacific so AC should not be allowed to infringe through a code sharing agreement.

APPROACH TO ALLIANCES

Alliances were a major way CDN hoped to expand its presence worldwide. Although CDN management had not reached a consensus, individual managers highlighted the following characteristics as important in a potential alliance partner: quality of product, management style and the compatibility of company cultures, and services in the long-term. As well, the potential fit between hubs, feed opportunity, infrastructure—airports/slots/maintenance centres, future equipment orders and options, financial structures and CRSs were important considerations. Management believed that CDN had valuable resources to contribute to an alliance including access to the new Terminal III at Toronto's Pearson Airport and its Pacific routes.

One CDN vice-president believed that in the "mid-term" (18 months) four categories of carriers would exist: (1) ten world mega carriers; (2) ten middle carriers—serving either in an international alliance or a market niche; (3) carriers "on the edge"—either large and failing or small and facing a very tough time; or (4) non-private sector carriers—supported by their government. He did not consider any of CDN's existing alliances to be well enough developed to provide the company with a sustainable position in a long-term global network. The current allies of CDN and AC are listed in Table 4.

TABLE 4 Allies of CDN and AC, 1990

Carrier	International Ally	Type of Alliance
CDN	Air France	marketing and codesharing
	Air New Zealand	" "
	China Airlines	" "
	Japan Airlines	" "
	Lufthansa	" "
	Qantas	" "
	SAS	" "
AC	Air France	cargo only
	Air Jamaica	code sharing
	Cathay Pacific	commercial
	CSA—(Czech)	commercial (offering seats)
	Finnair	" "
	Lot Polish	commercial
	Royal Jordanian	commercial (offering seats)
	Singapore Airlines	commercial
	Viasa	" "

SOURCE: 1990 company annual reports.

In the past, Air Canada had operated with a stand-alone philosophy; an approach which differed from CDN's. However, AC had allied with Singapore Airlines and Cathay Pacific in order to access the Pacific market. According to AC's 1989 annual report, this stand-alone attitude was changing, and AC was seeking alliance partners (with or without equity transfers) in Europe and the Pacific. A CDN executive commenting on the CDN's and AC's differing strategy towards international allies remarked that CDN tended to form alliances on its existing routes, whereas AC primarily formed alliances to access new destinations.

AC's Position

Until recently, AC's management had believed they could grow the company out of its inefficiency and high-cost structure, and gradually begin to earn meaningful profits. As Claude Taylor, Chairman, President and CEO of AC, stated, "We so wanted to extend the airline and see it become more international." But, after the dismal first quarter results in 1990, AC decided upon a different approach. A difference in opinion as to how to handle the situation led to the resignation of Pierre Jeanniot, AC's president, in August 1990. As of early 1991, no successor had yet been found for Jeannoit although rumours about American Airlines's V.P., Don Carty, had surfaced. Carty's background included management positions with the former Canadian Pacific Airlines.

Change followed. As one analyst wrote, "In October, Air Canada finally came to terms with the difficult airline environment. Management decided to drop service to several distant routes in Europe and Asia, to reduce the work force by 10%, to sell the head office building in downtown Montreal, to dispose of several older and some new aircraft and to exit some non-core businesses (i.e., EnRoute)." One of CDN's managers stated that the upheaval of AC resulted in short-term gains for CDN, but it would make AC more competitive in the longer term.

AIRCRAFT FLEET AND GROUND FACILITIES

Both AC and CDN were in the process of updating, rationalizing and expanding their fleets. Most pressing was the need to replace their smaller, aging narrow-body aircraft used primarily on medium-haul domestic and transborder routes. The average age of CDN's fleet was 9.3 years, compared to 14.1 years for AC's fleet. However, as CDN's treasurer noted, achieving this young fleet had significantly weakened CDN's balance sheet.

AC had ordered 40 new aircraft at a cost of $2.1 billion, and had options on a further 35 aircraft over the next five years. However, AC was conducting negotiations to delay or cancel ten of the 31 Airbus A320s on firm order. CDN had ordered 16 new aircraft at a cost of $1 billion, and had options on a further 47 aircraft to be delivered between 1992 and 1997. Both AC and CDN had to replace aging aircraft: AC had 35 DC-9s (average age of over 20 years), and CDN had 58 Boeing 737-200 (average age of over ten years) which it planned to phase out over the next ten years. Exhibit 2 contains AC's and CDN's current fleet status as of December 1990, together with firm orders and options available over the next five years. Over the past two years, CDN had sold eight of its 97 aircraft, and reduced its total seat capacity by 10%.

Over the long-term CDN planned to reduce its fleet to three types of aircraft: Boeing 747-400, Boeing 767-300ER, and the Airbus A320-200. The Boeing 747-400, a long-range, large capacity aircraft, was to be used primarily on the North Pacific routes, i.e., Vancouver-Tokyo. The Boeing 767-300ER, a medium-long haul aircraft, had several applications, including transcontinental, Europe, South Pacific and South America. The Airbus A320-200, a short to medium haul aircraft, was to be used on domestic and transborder routes. The Airbus A320 would replace the company's Boeing 737s.

Proceeds from the sale of aircraft, including the anticipated proceeds from the disposal of five A310-300s and surplus spare parts in 1991, would total approximately $500 million, compared to CDN's planned capital expenditures in 1991 of $460 million. Aircraft and spares would represent approximately 75% of these expenditures.

Facilities

Toronto's Pearson International was the third busiest entry point for international traffic in North America, after New York's JFK airport and the Los Angeles airport.

In February 1991, CDN moved from the old and congested Terminal I to the newly opened Terminal III. CDN had already felt the benefits of its new facility. Domestic market share rose from 41% at December 1990 to 42.5% as of March 31, 1991. Each one percent change represented $20 million. The new facility enhanced CDN's passenger service, providing a comfortable environment for passengers and the latest in technology and automated systems for passenger handling. Retail shopping space, a five-star hotel, improved curb access and ample parking facilities were all part of the package.

In response to CDN's new terminal, AC and Transport Canada were spending $100 million to renovate Pearson's Terminal II, adding moving sidewalks, more check-in counters at gates, and other improvements. Renovations were expected to be completed by the fall of 1991.

Computer Reservation System (CRS)

AC and CDN used the same CRS—Gemini. AC, CDN and Covia (a subsidiary of United Airlines) each owned one-third of Gemini. Gemini had the exclusive rights to use Covia's Apollo CRS software in Canada. There were over 3 700 travel agents using Gemini and over 8 000 installed terminals. CDN and AC utilized Gemini primarily as a distribution system and data base. Gemini provided travel agents with information on schedules, availability of seats, and fares. The flight booking information collected through Gemini was used individually by AC and CDN to assist them in operations including yield management and inventory control.

Frequent Flyer Programs

In North America, frequent flyer programs had become a competitive necessity. Both AC and CDN had successful programs and roughly comparable programs. These programs allowed the airlines to identify their high usage customers, and offer them additional incentives (access to special airport lounges, preferential check-in privileges, etc.).

Operating Performance

As shown in Table 5, CDN's passenger volume, as measured by revenue passenger kilometres (RPK) decreased by 6.2% between 1989 and 1990. In the same period revenue grew by 3.7%.

Over the last three years AC's volume had increased by 6.6%. AC's passenger revenue rose $217 million, or 7% in 1990. This was primarily due to the expansion of AC's subsidiary airlines, strong transatlantic and southern services, and major yield gains on the domestic transcontinental routes.

CDN's yield increased from 9.1 cents in 1989 to 9.9 cents in 1990, representing a gain of over $148 million in operating income. CDN attributed the higher yield to an increased focus on the higher yield passenger, tighter controls on the availability of deep discount fare, and the implementation of fare increases during the year to partially cover rising fuel costs. However, CDN's yield still remained below AC's 10.4 cents. CDN attributed this difference to AC's success at developing and sustaining high yield business class traffic; AC's strength in the lucrative Toronto, Ottawa, Montreal corridor; and AC's greater number of transborder routes.

CDN expected its share of the Toronto, Ottawa, Montreal triangle to improve with Intair's recent exit. CDN was hoping its share would rise to 40—45%, or its national average and corresponding to its 40% share of capacity on those

TABLE 5 **Summary Revenue Data of CDN and AC**

Measure	Carrier	1990	1989	1988
Revenue Passenger Kilometres (millions)	CDN	22 286	23 703	19 596
	AC	26 672	26 191	25 025
Passengers Carried (millions)	CDN	9.0	9.5	9.6
	AC	11.8	12.0	11.9
Yield per RPK*	CDN	9.9¢	9.1¢	9.3¢
	AC	10.4¢	10.1¢	9.8¢
	AA	9.2¢	8.8¢	N/A
	UA	9.1¢	8.9¢	N/A
	Delta	10.1¢	9.9¢	N/A
Passenger Load Factor	CDN	64.8%	67.2%	68.8%
	AC	71.4%	69.7%	71.4%
	AA	62.3%	63.8%	N/A
	UA	66.2%	66.6%	N/A
	Delta	59.1%	63.4%	N/A
Revenue per ASK	CDN	6.5¢	6.1¢	N/A
	AC	7.4¢	7.1¢	N/A
	AA	5.7¢	5.6¢	N/A
	UA	6.1¢	5.9¢	N/A
	Delta	6.0¢	6.3¢	N/A

* Excludes CDN's and AC's connector partners.

SOURCE: CDN and Air Canada annual report, and CDN internal reports.

routes. In order to improve its performance, CDN had produced an all economy class with spaced seats and increased leg room by renovating its aircraft. Improved airport facilities at Terminal III and the renovations underway at Dorval airport in Montreal also offered better customer service.

CDN's passenger load factor also dropped to 64.8% in 1990, down 3.6% from the year earlier. Air Canada load factor recovered to over 70%. However, both CDN and Air Canada still had load factors exceeding these achieved by the three major U.S. carriers—AA, UA, and Delta.

The summary provided of cost and productivity performance in Table 6 shows that CDN's operating expenses per available seat kilometre were lower than AC by a full cent, although higher than the major U.S. carriers. The largest cost for all airlines was wages and benefits. It was 29% of operating expenses for CDN during 1990. This was significantly lower than AC's 33.3% and less than the U.S. average of 36%. This advantage appeared to be a function of both wage differentials and higher employee productivity.

TABLE 6 **1990 Cost and Productivity Data**

Measure	CDN	AC	AA	UA	DELTA
Operating expense per ASK	8.0¢	9.0¢	6.4¢	7.0¢	6.5¢
Personnel cost per ASK	2.3¢	3.0¢	2.3¢	2.2¢	2.6¢
Fuel cost per ASK	1.3¢	1.6¢	1.1¢	1.1¢	1.1¢
Other expenses per ASK	4.3¢	4.5¢	3.4¢	3.6¢	2.7¢
Average passenger journey (km)	2 479	1 405			

SOURCE: CDN.

Like other airlines, CDN's financial results were extremely sensitive to the operating variables discussed. Estimates by the company indicated the following impacts on operating income before tax:

Sensitivity Analysis	(Cdn. $ millions)
Increase of US $1 per barrel of crude	$(11)
Increase in passenger load factor by 1%	28
Domestic market growth of 1%	9
Domestic market share increase of 1%	20
A 1¢ increase in yield per RPK	185

At an airline conference in April 1991, an industry analyst commented on AC's past operating results: "In the ten-year period from 1980 to 1989, Air Canada reported net income before extraordinary items of $234 million. Eighty% of that net income came from gains on sale of assets, clever financing and business changes. The airline made almost no money in its main business: flying people and cargo."

FINANCIAL RESULTS

Exhibit 3 presents the 1990 CDN financial statements. As shown, the company's operating loss in 1990 of $11.7 million was roughly equivalent to the $10.4 million loss recorded in 1989. This loss was primarily attributable to the escalation of fuel prices. The Middle East crisis caused jet fuel prices to more than double during the fourth quarter of 1990 which contributed to a 13% increase in the company's fuel expenses.

Interest expense jumped 37% to $104.4 million in 1990 reflecting the assumption of Wardair debt. This increase, however, was more than offset by gains of over $79 million resulting from the sale of A310-300 and 747-400 aircraft. These gains and the absence of further integration costs associated with acquisitions, helped to reduce the company's net loss to $14.6 million in 1990 from the $56.0 million reported in 1989.

The strengthening of the company's balance sheet continued to be a high priority. See Table 7 for some key ratios. Although progress was made in reducing the working capital deficit, the company's leverage remained high.

TABLE 7 Financial Capacity of CDN and AC

Measure	CDN		AC	
	1990	1989	1990	1989
Cashflow[1] ($000)	(43 000)	(71 166)	41 000	139 000
Cashflow coverage of interest	.59x	.07x	1.36x	2.15x
Cashflow coverage of principal, interest and leases[2]	.60x	.46x	1.01x	1.08x
Current ratio	.74:1	.52:1	1.47:1	1.79:1
Debt[3] to equity	2.47:1	2.34:1	3.63:1	2.87:1
Adjusted debt4 to total capital[5]	79%	75%	77%	74%

[1] Cashflow is pretax income + depreciation + other non-cash items.
[2] Includes operating and capital lease obligations
[3] Interest bearing debt and capital leases
[4] Includes interest bearing debt, capital lease obligations and the present value of operating lease commitments.
[5] Capital includes interest bearing debt, capital leases, shareholders equity and the present values of operating lease commitments.
SOURCE: Casewriter analysis, CDN's and AC's annual reports.

Financial Constraints

CDN's treasurer identified two serious financial constraints plaguing CDN: poor operating results, and the tightening of capital in lending markets. The seriousness of operating results was reflected in the first "Special Report" video produced by CDN's president Kevin Jenkins. In the video, Jenkins told company employees that CDN needed to change the way it did business in order to survive. The senior vice-president of finance told employees, "We will soon be out of assets to sell. Then no one will lend us any more money. Since we don't make enough money to pay our expenses and our interest payments, at that point we will be out of business."

CDN's treasurer's predicted the 1991 income statement would be worse than 1990. Although a decline in passenger revenue (a predicted 10–15% decrease in the domestic market) might be offset by savings in fuel costs, there would be little gain on the sale of assets. Putting further pressure on CDN was the tightening of bank funds. Accessing capital in a tough market would be difficult for CDN because of its operating results.

Airlines were hit especially hard in recessionary times due to the high fixed cost structure of the industry. Furthermore, because of union rules on "bumping", cutting capacity or routes only reduce the least expensive labour costs, and caused dislocation and retraining costs.

AC's response to the bleak economic outlook for 1991 was a planned cut in capacity by 11%, and to decrease staff levels by approximately 12% compared to 1990 levels. In April 1991, AC announced it was eliminating 400 management positions, including eight of 23 vice-presidencies. In addition 1 000 workers representing 5% of unionized labour were expecting layoff notices. An AC spokesperson stated: "This is basically a continuation of the program we launched last October (cuts of 2 900 from the original workforce of 22 000, including 200 management positions). There will be more cuts for employees coming, but we don't know where, when or how yet."

THE FUTURE

Rhys Eyton realized much remained to be done in dealing with current the financial situation. The recession and its impact upon travel was still a concern. During the first half of 1991, load factors had fallen to just over 60% even though capacities had been reduced by 6.5%. However, passenger yields had been improved by over 11%. Overall the airline anticipated an operating loss of over $12 million and net income loss of over $4.7 million. More significantly cashflow from operations was projected to be more than $200 million negative; $130 million of this amount had been covered by a rights offering, but Rhys Eyton knew this cashflow pattern could not continue indefinitely.

One bright spot in the recent results was gains in domestic market share attributed to improved service levels and the opening of Terminal III. Air Canada had responded more slowly to the downturn, and as a result its recent performance was reportedly even worse than CDN's.

Rather than be overwhelmed by the immediate situation, Eyton wanted to think about the longer term possibilities, and how CDN might emerge from the domestic and global restructuring which appeared inevitable. There was a range of views both inside and outside of CDN about the future of the company and the industry. One vice-president felt the Canadian market was too small for a company with global ambitions, and CDN must look internationally for growth. However, how to grow internationally was not clear. Indeed, because Canada had two "flag" carriers and most other countries had only one, it was difficult for either Canadian carrier to build a strong international presence. Other observers saw the consequences of the small Canadian market another way, predicting that there would be only one (international) Canadian carrier within five years, resulting from a pooling of CDN and Air Canada.

EXHIBIT 1 PWA's 1990 Typical Daily Frequencies–Winter

City-Pair (Rank by Revenue)	Carrier	Frequency	Capacity (# of seats)	Capacity Share (%)	Aircraft
Toronto–Vancouver	AC	6	1 074	47	Boeing 767
(1)	**CDN**	**6**	**1 206**	**53**	**Boeing 767 + Airbus A310**
	Total	12	2 280	100	
Toronto–Montreal	AC	20	2 669	52	Boeing 727, Airbus A320, 767, DC9
(2)	**CDN**	**15**	**1 530**	**30**	**Boeing 737, Airbus A310**
	Intair	9	945	18	F100
	Total	44	5 144	100	
Toronto–Calgary	AC	5	895	48	Boeing 767
(3)	**CDN**	**5**	**1 005**	**52**	**Boeing 767 + Airbus A310**
	Total	10	1 900	100	
Toronto–Ottawa	AC	14	1 738	51	Boeing 767, 727, Airbus A320, DC9
(4)	**CDN**	**14**	**1 260**	**37**	**Boeing 737**
	Intair	4	420	12	F100
	Total	32	3 418	100	
Toronto–Edmonton	AC	4	716	57	Boeing 767
(5)	**CDN**	**3**	**540**	**43**	**Airbus A310**
	Total	7	1 256	100	
Toronto–Winnipeg	AC	6	816	60	Boeing 727
(6)	**CDN**	**6**	**540**	**40**	**Boeing 737**
	Total	12	1 356	100	
Toronto–Halifax	AC	6	769	59	Boeing 727 + DC9
(7)	**CDN**	**6**	**540**	**41**	**Boeing 737**
	Total	12	1 309	100	
Vancouver–Calgary	AC	7	808	35.2	DC9 + B727
(10)	**CDN**	**14**	**1 488**	**64.8**	**Boeing 737 + B767 or Airbus A310**
	Total	21	2 296	100	
Vancouver–Edmonton	AC	6	600	48	DC9
(11)	**CDN**	**6**	**660**	**52**	**Boeing 737**
	Total	12	1 260	100	

SOURCE: Canadian Airlines International Ltd.

EXHIBIT 2   AC's and CDN's 1990 Fleet Details

Type of Aircraft	# of Seats	In Fleet		On Order		Options		Planned Disposal	
		CDN	AC	DN	AC	CDN	AC	CDN	AC
Airbus A310-300	180	8						8	
Airbus A320-200	136		7	22	31	34	20		
Boeing 727	136		27						27
Boeing 737-200		58						13	
Boeing 747-200			6		3		3		3
Boeing 747-400	392	1	3	2	3	3			
Boeing 767-200	179		12		6		12		
Boeing 767-300ER	222	10	9	4	6	10			
DC-8	cargo		5						1
DC-9	100		35						
DC-10-30	247	11						3	
Lockheed 1011	212/361		14						10
Total		88	115	28	40	47	35	24	41

SOURCE: AC's and CDN's 1990 annual reports.

EXHIBIT 3   PWA's Five-Year Summary

Years ended December 31	1990	1989	1988	1987	1986
Operating Revenues					
Passenger	$ 2 095.2	$ 1 988.1	$ 1 722.7	$ 1 438.6	$ 249.8
Cargo and mail	221.8	209.8	189.1	158.4	21.9
Charter and tour	327.9	332.0	270.1	232.7	70.9
Contract services and other	100.7	118.8	101.7	100.8	19.3
Total Operating Revenues	$ 2 745.6	$ 2 648.7	$ 2 283.6	$ 1 930.5	$ 361.8
Operating Expenses					
Salaries, wages and benefits	$ 801.7	$ 746.9	$ 629.1	$ 528.5	$ 112.7
Fuel	451.7	399.2	352.8	317.6	65.5
Marketing, sales, and					
passenger service	661.7	644.9	559.8	393.8	54.1
Depreciation and amortization	81.5	95.7	67.5	63.8	9.9
Other	760.7	772.4	596.6	462.5	94.3
Total Operating Expenses	$ 2 757.3	$ 2 659.1	$ 2 205.8	$ 1 766.2	$ 336.5
Operating Income (Loss)	$ (11.7)	$ (10.4)	$ 77.8	$ 164.3	$ 25.3
Operating margin	(0.4)%	(0.4)%	3.4%	8.5%	7.0
Other Expense (Income)					
Net interest expense (income)	$ 104.4	$ 76.2	$ 50.4	$ 63.7	$(1.8)
Gain on sale of property					
and equipment	(51.4)	(18.6)	(3.9)	(4.5)	(11.6)
Airline integration costs	–	73.8	–	43.9	–
Other	(27.9)	(18.0)	(13.2)	(4.2)	1.7
Income taxes (reduction)	(22.2)	(67.8)	14.2	37.0	–
Net Income (Loss)	$ (14.6)	$ (56.0)	$ 30.3	$ 28.4	$ 37.0
Total Assets	$ 2 964.4	$ 2 911.6	$ 2 125.0	$ 1 989.2	$ 945.8
Long-term Debt and Capital					
Lease Obligations	$ 1 068.1	$ 1 097.3	$ 646.4	$ 644.5	$ 251.3
Return on Common Equity	(3.2)%	(11.9)%	5.3%	12.7%	12.8%

EXHIBIT 3 (continued)

December 31	1990	1989
Assets		
Current Assets		
Cash and short-term investments	$ 179.6	$ 74.3
Accounts receivable	247.0	211.6
Materials and supplies	134.8	114.1
Other current assets	117.4	36.5
	678.8	436.5
Investments	130.5	123.8
Property and Equipment, at Cost		
Flight equipment	1 854.7	1 968.1
Land, buildings and ground equipment	413.7	387.6
Deposits on flight equipment	146.7	172.4
	2 415.1	2 528.1
Less accumulated depreciation	371.6	261.5
	2 043.5	2 266.6
Other Assets (Note 3)	111.6	84.7
	$ 2 964.4	$ 2 911.6
Liabilities and Shareholders' Equity		
Current Liabilities		
Short-term debt	$25.9	$ –
Accounts payable and accrued liabilities	576.1	573.8
Advance ticket sales	179.7	164.4
Current portion of long-term debt and		
capital lease obligations	131.9	108.4
	931.6	846.6
Long-term Debt and Capital		
Lease Obligations	1 068.1	1 097.3
Deferred Gain on Sale-leaseback of Aircraft	13.3	21.7
Deferred Income Taxes	37.5	74.4
	2 032.5	2 040.0
Subordinated Perpetual Debt	76.7	–
Convertible Debentures and Shareholders' Equity		
Convertible subordinated debentures	249.8	249.8
Shareholders' equity		
Capital stock (Note 8)		
First preferred shares, series A	43.4	44.5
Common shares	431.1	427.5
Retained earnings	130.9	149.8
	605.4	621.8
	$ 2 964.4	$ 2 911.6

MOLSON BREWERIES OF CANADA

J. Peter Killing and Andrew C. Inkpen

Mickey Cohen, the Chief Executive Officer of The Molson Companies Limited (TMCL) was preparing for the firm's January 1989 Board meeting. The main item on the agenda was a proposed merger between TMCL's Molson Brewing Group (Molson) and Carling O'Keefe Breweries of Canada Limited (Carling), owned by Elders IXL Limited (Elders). The new company would be established as a separate, self-financing entity with both TMCL and Elders having equal ownership. The company would be the largest brewer in Canada with more than 50% of the market.

Cohen thought that the Carling merger offered the best prospects for Molson's future success in the brewing industry, both inside and outside Canada. He was convinced that without the merger, Molson would be vulnerable in an industry which was becoming increasingly international, competitive, concentrated, and efficiency driven. Although Cohen was confident that the business synergies created by a Molson-Carling merger would be attractive to the TMCL Board, he was less sure that the Board would be willing to accept an equal ownership arrangement, an issue that had been at the forefront of the negotiations over the past nine months.

THE CANADIAN BREWING INDUSTRY

The Canadian brewing industry was characterized by comprehensive regulation and declining beer consumption. From 1975 to 1988 Canadian per capita beer consumption fell by 11%. The shift in consumer demand away from beer was prompted by several factors: increased health and safety consciousness, changing age demographics, and greater taxation based price escalation for beer relative to other beverages and consumer products. In 1989, there were no indications of any significant reversal; volume was expected to remain static or to decline slightly over the next five years.

Government Regulation

Canada's framework of liquor laws and policies had its genesis in the period 1900–35. Under pressure from the temperance movement, provincial governments across Canada introduced legislation to restrict the production, distribution, and sale of alcoholic beverages of all types. The aim of the movement was to discourage, if not eliminate, the consumption of alcohol.

Interprovincial trade barriers were a key element in the brewing regulatory structure. Except for the Maritime provinces, beer had to be brewed in the province in which it was sold. In the Maritime provinces, out-of-province beer was sold but subject to higher taxes and markups. The brewed-in-province requirements led to the creation of many small and inefficient plants. As a comparison, the average plant size in Canada was 1.1 million hectolitres (hL) versus 6.3 million hL in the United States. The size of an efficient plant in the U.S. was estimated to have risen to more than 10 million hL by the late 1980s.

The taxation of beer served two purposes: it provided a major government funding source and acted as a social "sin tax", which suited the anti-alcohol movement. The provincial taxes added to beer were the single largest cost component in the price of beer. The federal government also had an impact on the cost of production through both federal commodity taxes and control over malting barley, the most important ingredient in the brewing process. Malting barley could only be purchased from the Canadian Wheat Board, which charged brewers a price 2.5 times that paid by U.S. brewers. The combination of commodity and sales taxes accounted for more than 50% of the average beer retail price, ranking Canadian beer taxes the third highest among beer consuming nations. In the U.S., taxes averaged 16%, ranking the U.S. nineteenth.

Additional areas under the jurisdiction of provincial governments included the distribution, advertising, sale and pricing of beer. Except for Quebec and Newfoundland, beer was sold in government owned or controlled outlets. In Ontario, the Brewers Retail company distributed 95% of Ontario-brewed products; the other 5% was sold through government liquor stores. The Brewers Retail was owned by Ontario brewers and sold only Ontario brewed beer. Imported beer was sold in the government liquor stores.

Beer advertising was slowly being deregulated. For example, in Ontario, billboard advertising of beer became legal in 1987. All provincial legislation provided, either directly or indirectly, that provincial authorities could control beer pricing. In the western provinces, price competition had developed as provincial governments moved toward open pricing. In Ontario, price competition was allowable above a price floor but other than a few premium priced brands, all the beer sold in the Brewer's Retail had the same price. Beer pricing in Quebec was quite competitive because beer was sold through independent grocers and "depanneurs." In Atlantic Canada, beer pricing was tightly controlled.

Over the past two decades, the laws governing the beer industry had been substantially liberalized, resulting in more open pricing, reductions in drinking age limits, easing of advertising restrictions, and reduced product introduction and packaging controls. However, the broad regulatory framework involving different provincial standards for production, promotion, distribution, packaging, sales, and interprovincial shipments continued to influence industry structure. This regulation made it necessary for the three national brewers to shape their operations to ten relatively distinct and small marketing areas.

The Canadian regulatory framework had been good for both the government and the brewers. Until recently, Ontario, for example, was one of the most lucrative beer markets in the world with some of the highest margins and one of the most cost efficient distribution systems. The Ontario government generated huge tax revenues from beer sales and was able to control price, distribution, and advertising. The large U.S. brewers were prevented from capitalizing on their cost efficiencies because there was no price competition and more important, interprovincial barriers largely kept the U.S. beer off the shelves.

However, by the late 1980s, the brewing industry, especially in Ontario, was coming under increasing pressure for deregulation and the removal of barriers to foreign competition.

National and International Pressures for Deregulation

The national pressures for deregulation heightened when the 1987 Conference of First Ministers endorsed in principle a general reduction or elimination of interprovincial trade barriers, including those relating to beer. An Interprovincial Negotiating Panel on liquor board marketing practices was appointed. As of early 1989, the Panel had not reached a consensus on action to be taken.

The international pressures were coming from two sources. First, in 1987, a General Agreement on Tariffs and Trade (GATT) panel sided with the European Community (EC) ruling that Canada's pricing, listing, and marketing practices for alcoholic beverages violated its obligations as a GATT member. The ruling was subsequently confirmed by GATT Council. Intensive negotiations began between the Canadian government and the EC over the alleged Canadian discrimination against imported beer, wine, and spirits. Eventually, an agreement was reached which required Canada to open its market to beer imported from EC member states and to remove discriminatory pricing practices. To date, no action had been taken by the Canadian government for two reasons: one, the government claimed that the interprovincial trade situation had to be settled before the market could be opened to imports and two, the implications of the Canada-U.S. Free Trade Agreement had yet to be resolved.

The Canada-U.S. Free Trade Agreement

When free trade talks between Canada and the United States began in the mid-1980s, the Canadian brewers argued for an exemption. They insisted that their inefficiencies relative to U.S. brewers were a direct result of provincial barriers imposed by the government. In October 1987, the brewers' lobbying efforts paid off. Beer and malt beverages were almost entirely exempt from free trade because both Canadian and U.S. negotiators recognized that the industry needed time to adjust. The exemption was agreed to by the U.S. negotiators because of the Canadian government's expressed commitment to support industry adjustment. The exemption allowed Canada to continue to limit access of U.S. brands to distribution channels and to impose higher taxes on U.S. beer.

THE UNITED STATES BREWING INDUSTRY

The U.S. brewing industry was dominated by a small number of firms. However, compared to Canada, a very different competitive environment existed in the U.S., primarily because of less regulation and a much larger market (see Exhibit 1 for comparative information on the Canadian and U.S. industries). For the major brewers, the entire country represented one market with only minor regulatory differences between the states. Therefore, these brewers concentrated on establishing a limited number of national brands which generated substantial production and marketing efficiencies. Beer was distributed to wholesalers who were then free to distribute to retail selling points, which in most states tended to be grocery stores, convenience stores, and drug stores. Prices were controlled only to the extent of taxation.

The two largest firms were Anheuser-Busch Inc., the U.S. industry leader since 1957, with a 1987 market share of 42.0% and Miller Brewing Company with a share of 21.7%. The next three firms in the top five were The Stroh Brewery Company with a share of 11.9%; G. Heileman Brewing Company with 9.0%; and Adolph Coors Company with 8.6% (see Exhibit 2 for information on the five largest brewers). These five firms competed on a national basis in an industry in which all brewers (both national and regional) except Anheuser-Busch, Coors, and Miller were losing market share. In 1987, media advertising expenditures in US$ by the major brewers were: $304 million by Anheuser-Busch; $171 million by Miller; $46 million by Stroh; $16 million by Heileman; and $85 million by Coors.

In the late 1980s, the top ten brands—four brewed by Anheuser-Busch, three by Miller, two by Coors, and one by Stroh—accounted for over 70% of the market. The leader, Budweiser, had a market share of 27.6%, while the second place brand, Miller Lite, had a share of 10.7%. In place of the flagship brands of the 1960s and 1970s such as Schlitz and Pabst Blue Ribbon, new products including Miller Lite, Budweiser Light, and Coors Light had become dominant. Of the major national brands of the 1970s, Budweiser was an exception with its continued share growth.

Canadian Penetration of the U.S. Market

Canadian penetration in the U.S. had been mainly in the import market, the only segment showing sustained growth. The import segment grew from 2.6% of total consumption in 1980 to 5.0% in 1987. In the overall import market, Canadian brands had a 21% share, which was third behind the Netherlands (27%) and Mexico (26%). The leading Canadian exporter was Molson with over 15% of its total sales going to the U.S. market. Of the other national Canadian brewers, Labatt Breweries of Canada's exports totalled 5% of sales and Carling's were 3.5%.

The United States ran a beer trade deficit with Canada of more than 2 million hL in 1987. Over 10% of Canada's beer production was exported to the U.S. while the United States exported only 1% of its production. However, the U.S. export figures did not include the U.S. beer brewed under license in Canada. These licensed brands, which capitalized on spillover advertising, accounted for about 14% of Canadian consumption.

THE MAJOR CANADIAN BREWERS

The Canadian brewing industry was dominated by three firms: Labatt Breweries of Canada (Labatt) with a share of 41.9%; Molson with 31.6%; and Carling O'Keefe Breweries of Canada Limited (Carling) with 19.6% (see Table 1 for market share trends).

Labatt Breweries of Canada

Labatt's brewing operation was part of John Labatt Ltd., a diversified food and beverage company with businesses in three main sectors: brewing, agricultural products, and packaged foods. Labatt was controlled by Brascan Ltd., a large Canadian holding company (see Exhibit 3 for Labatt financial information).

Labatt's market share leadership can be traced back to several events which occurred over the past decade. By 1979, Labatt and Molson had about equal shares of a stagnating beer market. Realizing that profitability could only be sustained through share improvement and not overall market growth, Labatt made the first move in the so-called brand and packaging "wars" of the 1980s. In 1980, Labatt introduced Budweiser under license, the first Canadian brewer to license a major U.S. brand, and quickly gained a 3–5% share. The other

Table 1 Canadian Market Shares

	1972	73	74	75	76	77	78	79	80	81	82	83	84	85	86	87	88
Labatt	33.9	36.9	35.9	36.6	37.6	38.4	38.6	36.6	36.5	34.9	36.7	36.3	34.6	38.0	39.1	40.3	41.9
Molson	29.9	30.5	31.6	33.5	33.6	33.9	34.1	36.2	35.9	35.1	35.8	34.7	31.5	30.6	29.8	31.5	31.6
Carling	30.6	28.3	26.1	25.3	24.9	24.1	23.2	22.7	23.2	22.8	23.1	24.3	28.2	25.0	22.8	22.0	19.6
Other	5.3	4.0	6.1	4.2	3.3	2.9	3.2	3.5	3.5	3.8	2.9	3.6	4.2	4.8	4.5	4.7	4.7
Imports	0.3	0.3	0.3	0.4	0.6	0.7	0.9	1.0	0.9	3.4	1.5	1.1	1.5	1.6	3.8	1.5	2.2
Total	100.0	100.0	100.0	100.0	100.0	100.0	100.0	100.0	100.0	100.0	100.0	100.0	100.0	100.0	100.0	100.01	100.0

source: TMCL, Brewers Association of Canada, and Statistics Canada.

brewers were forced to follow Labatt's lead with their own "Canam" brands—Carling licensed Miller products and Molson licensed Coors brands.

Labatt's next move was in response to a Carling initiative. Prior to 1983, all bottled Canadian beer produced for the domestic market was packaged in a standard brown compact (stubby) returnable bottle which required a bottle opener (bottles accounted for about 78% of the market). This system facilitated a very simple return system since each brewer used the same bottles. In 1983, Carling broke with tradition and introduced Miller High Life and Miller Lite packaged in tall bottles. Both Labatt and Molson, hoping that the bottles would not be a success, held off introducing the new containers. However, the tall bottles were a tremendous success with Miller brands estimated to have captured up to 9% of the total market four months after introduction. In 1984, Carling's market share was at its highest level in ten years.

Labatt responded to Carling's initiative in 1984 by introducing a tall bottle with a twist-off cap, a new packaging device common in the U.S. Labatt's early leadership in twist-off caps was estimated to have added about 1.5–3.0% to its total market share. The twist-off cap also helped Labatt launch its Blue brand as the first real national brand in a Canadian market that had traditionally been dominated by regional brands. In 1984, Molson converted several of its major brands to tall bottles.

By 1989, bottled beer was packaged in a myriad of returnable tall bottles, most with twist-off caps. The industry standard bottle was part of history. Because of the sorting required for recycling, distribution costs had increased substantially, without a corresponding increase in overall market revenue. In addition, the brewers were forced to make sizeable write-offs for their compact bottles on hand in the mid-1980s.

Labatt in 1989

In 1989, Labatt produced 31 different brands and operated 12 breweries in 9 provinces. Labatt's leading brand, Blue, was sold in all provinces and had an estimated 18% national share. The closest brands in market share were Molson Export, which was not sold in western Canada, with a 9% share; Molson Canadian with 8% and sold nationally; and Labatt's 50 Ale with 8% and sold in all provinces except B.C. Carling's strongest brand was O'Keefe Ale with a 6% share and sold only in Ontario and Quebec. Carling's Miller High Life was sold nationally but had a relatively low share.

Labatt had a capacity utilization rate of 95%, compared with 78% for Molson and 61% for Carling. Labatt's profitability, return on equity, and brewing operating income from assets deployed were the highest in the Canadian industry, comparing favourably with major U.S. brewers. Labatt favoured the maintenance of the regulatory status quo and was fundamentally opposed to the liberalization of interprovincial and international trade barriers.

In 1987, Labatt's estimated advertising expenditure was $36 million while Molson's was $28 million and Carling's $26 million. Labatt had close ties with Anheuser-Busch, and like the American firm, focused its brand development through sports and community events; e.g., Labatt owned 45% of the Toronto Blue Jays, a major league baseball team. Labatt's import sales in the U.S. were increasing at a greater rate than either Molson or Carling with 1987 shipments up by 16%. In 1987, Labatt acquired the U.S. regional brewer, Latrobe Brewing Company. Labatt also had associations with regional brewers in the United Kingdom and had targeted European operations from this U.K. base.

Carling O'Keefe Breweries of Canada Limited

Carling, in operation since 1843, was the third largest brewer in Canada and operated seven breweries (see Exhibits 4 and 5 for Carling financial information). In April 1987, Elders IXL Limited (Elders) acquired Carling from Rothmans of Pall Mall Canada for $450 million. Carling was Elders' first brewing acquisition in North America and was seen by many observers as Elders' beachhead for an assault on the U.S. beer market.

Elders, based in Melbourne, Australia, was one of Australia's leading international companies with 1988 consolidated revenues of AU$ 15.35 billion (in early January, 1989, one Australian dollar was worth CDN $1.02) and 32 000 employees worldwide. Elders consisted of over 400 subsidiary companies with core businesses in brewing, finance, international trading (wool, meat, brewing materials, and grain), and agricultural activities (see Exhibit 6 for Elders financial information).

Since 1981, Elders' Brewing Group had grown rapidly through acquisition in Australia and the United Kingdom. By 1988 the Group was the world's seventh largest brewer with a reputation for both high quality beer and efficient manufacturing. With a focus on its Foster's Lager brand, Elders marketed its products in more than 80 countries.

Elders organizational structure was decentralized with each of the core businesses established as a separate entity headed by a managing director who reported directly to the Chairman and Chief Executive, John Elliott. As the orchestrator of Elders' major acquisitions, Elliott had a reputation as an intense and aggressive negotiator.

Elliott was determined to make Foster's Lager a truly global brand. He developed a clever marketing strategy, putting the Australian flag on the beer can and creating an award-winning series of commercials with Australian actor and comedian, Paul Hogan, promoting Foster's as the "golden throatcharmer."

Foster's was established as Elders' flagship brand and became Australia's leading beer in both domestic and export markets. Prominent neon signs were created for Picadilly Circus, London; Times Square, New York; and Victoria

Harbour, Hong Kong. In Britain, Foster's was able to displace the Danish lager, Carlsberg, and take over third place in the draught lager competition.

Carling produced 23 brands of beer in Canada and owned the promotion rights for the Toronto Argonauts Football Club and the Quebec Nordiques Hockey Club. Carling exported several Canadian brands to the U.S. through a wholly-owned subsidiary which distributed Carling beer to 16 states. In the year subsequent to the takeover of Carling, Elders' reduced Carling's production and marketing costs significantly and completed a $200 million expansion and modernization program started by the previous owners. As a result of the aggressive cost cutting, Carling's June 30, 1988 year end operating profit increased substantially.

In July 1988, Carling suffered a setback when it lost the license to brew Carlsberg, the most successful non-U.S. licensed brand in Canada with a share of about 3%. The brewers of Carlsberg, unhappy that their competitors (Elders) in the U.K. were the Canadian licensees of Carlsberg, transferred the license to Labatt. With the loss of Carlsberg and the failure of Foster's (brewed by Carling) to make up the loss, Carling's downward trend continued in 1988 with share dropping to less than 20% by late 1988.

Molson Breweries of Canada

Molson Breweries of Canada was part of TMCL, a diversified Canadian multinational corporation with more than 11 000 employees and revenues of $2.4 billion for the year ended March 31, 1988 (see Exhibit 8 for TMCL financial information). Besides the Molson Brewing Group, TMCL had major operations in three other business groups: Chemical Specialities, Retail Merchandising, and Sports and Entertainment. The Chemical Specialties Group operated through Diversey Corporation, one of the four largest companies in the specialty chemical industry worldwide. The core of the Retail Merchandising Group was Beaver Lumber Company, Canada's largest supplier of lumber, building materials, and related hard goods. Table 2 presents TMCL business group financial information.

Table 2   TMCL Business Groups, Year Ended March 31, 1988
($000 000)

	Brewing	*Chemical Specialities*	*Retail Merch.*	*Sports Enter.*
Revenues	965.3	685.4	362.5	50.4
Profit before interest and taxes	77.8	44.0	25.4	3.0
Total assets	525.2	396.5	277.6	N/A
Average annual growth in revenue 1984–88	6.9%	11.2%	5.3%	N/A

Molson Breweries was founded by John Molson in 1786, and in 1989, was North America's oldest continuing brewer. For two centuries, the Molson family played a significant role in shaping the firm's strategy. In 1989, the family controlled more than 50% of the voting stock and owned about 20% of the equity. The current chairman of TMCL was Eric Molson, the great-great-great grandson of John Molson. The brewing operation and its 200-year heritage was an important part of the corporate culture of TMCL. The 1986 Annual Report, commemorating the 200th anniversary of TMCL, described the heritage as follows:

> Inheriting the legacy of a giant is a privilege, of course, but also a challenge. In every age, there are those whose achievements live beyond them and become integral parts of society as a whole. Such a man was John Molson.

Until 1955, Molson was primarily a regional brewer serving the Quebec market. By the early 1960s, the company had expanded its brewing business and had plants in most Canadian provinces. In 1967, Molson made its first major diversification move with the acquisition of Vilas Industries Limited, a furniture manufacturer, and a year later acquired Anthes Imperial Limited, an industrial conglomerate producing such products such as business forms, gasoline pumps, metal office furniture, and hot water heaters. Over the next ten years, the company, now called The Molson Companies Limited, sold the Vilas and Anthes operations and acquired Diversey Corporation and Beaver Lumber. In 1988, TMCL's non-brewing operations accounted for 45% of revenue and 49% of operating profit and the various operating groups were managed as independent entities.

Declining Share and Rebuilding

By the late 1970s, Molson had outdistanced Carling as the number two brewer in Canada and had a steadily increasing market share. The strength of the Canadian operation, along with a thriving U.S. export business accounting for 15% of production, contributed to an "aura of invincibility" in the organization. Molson looked to the U.S. market for acquisition targets. The first serious consideration was the Pabst Brewing Company, a company faced with substantial excess capacity after several years of declining market share. In 1980, Molson entered into with negotiations with Pabst and went so far as making an offer, which Pabst rejected. In retrospect, senior management conceded, "we were fortunate not to acquire Pabst—we were likely naive in thinking that we would be able to rejuvenate the ailing firm."

Following the Pabst negotiations, Molson had a series of discussions with other U.S. brewers, without any concrete results. Then, before any further U.S. developments could occur, the "wars" of the 1980s erupted in the Canadian market, forcing Molson to put its U.S. expansion strategy on hold. The result of the wars was a substantial drop in Molson's share and earnings. Market share, over 36% in 1979, dropped below 30% by 1986. Earnings peaked in 1983 at $126.6 million and then fell to $30 million in both 1985 and 1986. Molson's management realized that before resources could be utilized for international expansion, the Canadian position would have to be strengthened.

Launching a Canam brand was the first step in the rebuilding effort. Coors and Coors Light were introduced in November, 1985. By 1989, Coors Light was the most successful Canam brand. In 1985, Molson formed the Master's Brewing Company, a short-lived partnership with the Coors Brewing Company and a German brewer. In 1988, a deal was signed with the Kirin Brewery Company of Japan, the world's fourth largest brewer, to brew Kirin beer under license for export to the U.S.

Projects Columbus and Caesar

Molson argued for the exclusion of beer from the Free Trade Agreement until interprovincial trade barriers were dismantled and the brewers were given time to restructure. The company thought it unlikely that beer would remain an exception from free trade for very long. Suspecting that free trade and the elimination of interprovincial trade barriers would become reality within ten years, Molson was again prompted to look outside Canada for expansion opportunities. In August 1987, Projects Columbus and Caesar were launched to develop a strategy and action plan for the brewing operations.

Project Columbus focused on options for entering the U.S. domestic market. Investment in or a partnership with a U.S. brewer were considered the only feasible entry strategies. The smaller national brewers, Heileman, Stroh, and Pabst, were not considered attractive long-term partners and Anheuser-Busch and Miller had existing license agreements with Labatt and Carling. Although Project Columbus did not achieve its objectives, the project was important in that TMCL and Molson gained some understanding of the reality of doing a major deal with a U.S. brewer.

The second strategic initiative, Project Caesar, sought to expand Molson's international market beyond Canada and the U.S. Project Caesar was driven by a conviction that the brewing industry was going global. According to senior management:

> We are all watching the same television with the same videos and listening to the same hit parade. Everybody is using the same vocabulary and wants to use the same brands. In Europe, people want to drink the same brands of beer as people in North America.

Project Caesar identified the United Kingdom and Japan as prime international markets. Japan was seen as a huge potential market with per capita beer consumption about half that of Canada and still growing. To date, Molson beer had been sold in Japan primarily "in gift packs as a funny beer from a funny place." A decision was made to nurture and develop the Molson brand to the point that a licensing deal could be done with a Japanese brewer.

The U.K. beer market was the second largest in Europe. Foreign brands were playing an increasingly important role as drinking habits changed from traditional ales to lagers. Imports had captured over 6% of the U.K. market and 25% of all beer sales were continental brands, most brewed in the U.K. under license. To establish a long-term share in the U.K. market, management believed that Molson had three options: one, ship more beer and charge premium prices; two, brew on the continent; and three, establish a licensing relationship with a major U.K. brewer. Before making a commitment to one of the options, Molson decided to invest significant amounts in the U.K. market to build up its brands.

Molson in 1989 produced and marketed 22 brands across Canada and had a share of 31.9%. Molson also had a cross-licensing agreement with Moosehead Breweries of New Brunswick to brew and sell Moosehead beer under license outside Atlantic Canada and for Moosehead to brew and sell Molson products in the Maritime provinces, where Molson had no breweries. Molson was actively involved in sponsorships and promotions, including the Montreal Canadiens Hockey Club (owned by TMCL); Hockey Night in Canada; the Molson Indy car race; and various other sport, concert, and community events. Molson's importing agency in the U.S., Martlet, was a wholly-owned company and carried out a full range of business activities including marketing, advertising, brand positioning, distribution, credit and related activities. Martlet distributed Molson products in all 50 states.

MOLSON AND CARLING

Almost immediately after Elder's acquisition of Carling, senior management of TMCL met with John Elliott and Peter Bartels, the Chief Executive of Elders Brewing Group. The meetings were initially nothing more than "getting-to-know-you meetings" and were described as follows:

> The initial meetings with Elders were very positive; Elders brewed good beer and ran a very tight operation. The Elders people showed both openness and a willingness for action. Our perception was that both companies understood the business internationally but Elders had done something about it. . . . Elders saw our strategy in the U.K. as very positive and a potential companion with Foster's which had been there for 18 years.

Several possible deals between the two companies were discussed. Molson suggested combining the two firms' Western Canadian operations because with deregulation and U.S. competition, both brewers were finding it very difficult to operate in the West. However, Carling and Elders management were not interested in a deal that involved only part of their organization.

In April 1988, Elders approached TMCL about a possible merger of their respective Canadian brewing operations. Elders' approach coincided with Molson's realization that nothing was happening with Project Columbus and also that the most important factor in a North American strategy would be a strong and efficient domestic infrastructure. Elders' proposal, subsequently called Project 40 by Molson, called for both TMCL and Elders to have equal ownership in the new organization.

Project 40

From the start, TMCL and Molson saw that the business synergies in Project 40 made sense given the changing nature of the global brewing industry. In the short term, the merger would provide a base for the operational efficiencies needed to combat and survive the threat from partial or total Canadian deregulation. In the longer term, Project 40 would establish a strategic alliance with Elders, a committed and significant player in the international brewing industry. The alliance would improve the potential to build the Molson name in the U.K. and other markets by drawing on Elders' distribution system. The alliance would also enhance the likelihood of making a successful move in the U.S. market either by acquisition or alliance, particularly because of Elders' brewing links and financial capability.

As the discussions continued over the summer, the business elements of the merger were clarified. On August 22, these elements were presented to the TMCL Board. The merger called for a rationalization of 16 plants to 9, leaving one plant in each province and increasing utilization to 90% (see Exhibit 7 for the sizes and locations of Molson and Carling plants). The estimated savings in operating costs would be $25 million in 1990, $95 million in 1991, and $120 million in 1992 (casewriter's estimates). The market share of the new company would be over 50% and marketing emphasis would be on the key Molson brands and Carling's O'Keefe, Foster's, and Miller brands. In the U.S., Carling's import operation would be combined with Molson's importer, Martlet.

Molson anticipated that the merger impact on the marketplace would be substantial, increasing competitive intensity and potentially accelerating deregulation. Labatt was expected to continue its aggressive spending to combat the new share leader and a Labatt/Anheuser-Busch alliance was considered possible. A price-based reaction from Labatt was also considered very likely, although in most provinces it would have to wait until further deregulation.

Stalled Negotiations

By November, the TMCL/Elders negotiations had been under way for over six months and although both sides agreed on the potential synergies in the alliance, no real progress was being made on the structure of the deal. A key reason for the lack of progress was that TMCL and Molson management had serious reservations about 50/50 ownership. In particular, there were concerns about which party would control the following: the governance of the new entity; brand marketing support; CEO appointment; financing of the deal; and selection of Board members. Perhaps the most serious reservation about equal ownership was the loss of control over the Molson name and its associated heritage. According to a TMCL executive, "we were hanging tough because we wanted to retain control." The Molson people involved in the discussions also argued that 50/50 deal did not make sense given that Molson was almost twice the size of Carling.

The idea of giving up control over the Molson heritage was a particularly contentious issue and one that prompted a search for other options besides the Carling merger. Late in the summer, Molson's North American options were reviewed in the hope that another alternative could at least be considered. Once again, however, Molson came to the conclusion that there were no desirable acquisition or partnership candidates in the U.S., and in Canada, a Molson/Labatt merger was considered impossible because of Canadian combines legislation.

At this point, TMCL began to believe that the Carling merger was the only deal possible. However, the two sides were still not close to an agreement. By November, the Elders people were getting very frustrated to the extent that some TMCL executives thought they might walk away from the deal. If they did, TMCL had identified a possible outcome that was not particularly in TMCL's favour: Carling might be broken up and its assets sold, with the Ontario and Quebec operations possibly going to Labatt. It was this situation in early November that faced the new CEO and president of TMCL, Mickey Cohen.

Mickey Cohen

Marshall (Mickey) Cohen, 53, graduated from law school in 1960 and joined a prominent Toronto law firm as a tax and securities lawyer, becoming a partner in 1965. In 1970, he was a member of an advisory group to the House of Commons committee that reviewed the government's 1969 paper on tax reform. This position led Cohen to an advisory position in the Department of Finance, and by 1971, he was assistant deputy minister. In 1978, he was promoted to deputy minister of Energy Mines and Resources, followed by a year as deputy minister of Industry Trade and Commerce and then another stint at Energy. In 1982, Cohen was appointed as deputy minister of Finance where he remained until 1985. He then left the government to take a position as president and chief operating officer of Toronto-based Olympia and York Enterprises Ltd.

While practising law and working in the government, Cohen developed skills as a masterful bargainer and dealmaker. His management style relied heavily on delegation and he was well known as an able and unflappable negotiator. Cohen started as president and chief executive officer of TMCL on November 7, 1988, only the third president in the company's history who was not a brewer. He characterized his role at Molson as an "overseer of their diverse operations." He further added:

> Clearly, I am not a brewmaster. I am not a chemical engineer. I am certainly not an entertainer. I am not there to run the individual businesses . . . What I see are four good businesses, a very strong balance sheet, a company that is coming off a very good year and therefore, an enormous opportunity. . . . We have a new economic world coming at us in the next decade. The game is getting tougher, more competitive. One thing I see is to really take Molson into the next century. . . . I think that what I bring are some people skills, some strategic insights, and a sense of how to get shareholder values (*The Globe and Mail*, October 19, 1988, p. B5).

Cohen and the Alliance

Cohen described the situation he found when he arrived at TMCL:

> The alliance deal was not materializing because the three constituents, the Molson family, the Board, and senior management, had been unable to resolve their uncertainty about several factors: one, the future of the Molson name and tradition; two, the implications of entering a partnership with a much larger and more international partner; and three, the reality of a deal of that magnitude. Everyone agreed that a deal had to be done but there was no champion. The focus was on the structural issues instead of the alliance business synergies.

Cohen was convinced of the advantages of the alliance and the vulnerabilities associated with remaining a central Canadian regional brewer in a global industry. Cohen immediately set about resurrecting the negotiations. Within 48 hours of joining TMCL, he arranged a meeting with Elliott and Peter Bartels in London, England.

Elliott indicated that he still wanted to do the deal but did not want majority ownership. However, it soon became clear that Elliott wanted a very attractive "exit option" for Elders to sell its shares to TMCL, if TMCL insisted on controlling the alliance. As a result, 50/50 ownership seemed like the only realistic option. Cohen indicated that he would start working on the numbers and talk to his Board.

The November 28 TMCL Board Meeting

At the TMCL Board meeting on November 28, Cohen reported, "I think the deal can and should be done." He challenged the TMCL conventional wisdom about partnerships and argued that the merger was not a way of selling the brewery but a vehicle for staying in the business and making the Molson name international. He explained to the Board why he favoured 50/50 ownership:

> Elders wants too high a price if they give up control and besides, 51/49 deals are "the seeds of trouble" because they eliminate the opportunity for forced reconciliation. And, if TMCL is in control, we are really only becoming a larger Canadian brewer, as opposed to becoming an equal partner with a major international firm. A 50/50 deal will allow us to retain a discrete investment in brewing and should generate cash which we can use elsewhere.

The next board meeting was planned for January 12, 1989 when the progress of the deal would be reviewed.

The Deal

Cohen immediately got started with the preliminary legal and financial groundwork necessary to make the deal a reality. He also set up a meeting with Elliott and Bartels for January 15, three days after the next TMCL board meeting. Cohen had John Carroll, the president of Molson, spent a week with Ted Kunkel, Carling's president, to see if they were compatible and to see if they could rough out an organization chart for the new company. Carroll reported back that he thought Molson and Carling could work well together.

The specific deal that Cohen hoped to sell to the TMCL board, and one that he thought would be acceptable to Elders, incorporated the following elements:

1. The Canadian and U.S. operations of Molson and Carling would be managed as a single entity and ownership and control would be on a 50/50 basis.

2. The entity management would report to a jointly controlled supervisory board. Both partners would have veto rights over substantive matters at board level.

3. No exit from the partnership would be permitted for the first five years except by mutual consent.

4. The merged entity would be called Molson Breweries with the stronger Molson products as the core brands, therefore ensuring the preservation of the Molson name.

The plant rationalization would take place over a period of three years. Plants in Newfoundland, Manitoba, Saskatchewan, and Alberta would be closed in year one; plants in British Columbia and Ontario in year two; and a Quebec plant in year three. The remaining facilities would be upgraded and capacity expanded by about 3 – 4 million hL. The projected cost of the rationalization was $220 million, requiring cash outlays of $92 million in year one, $83 million in year two, and $45 million in year three. Of the 7 500 employees in the new company, about 1 000 would be made redundant by the rationalization. Cohen knew that industrial relations issues associated with the redundancies would be a high risk. Therefore, a first class plan for severance, retirement, and termination would have to be a major priority.

A final consideration was the financial structure of the alliance. Cohen proposed a financial structure which would make Molson Breweries a free-standing, self-financing entity and allow TMCL, over time, to withdraw capital from the brewing business.

Although the two partners would have equal ownership, TMCL's asset contribution would be substantially greater than Carling's. It was agreed that Molson's brewing assets were worth about $1 billion and Carling's about $600 million. To even out the $400 million difference, Cohen proposed that the new company borrow $400 million which would be distributed to TMCL. He also proposed borrowing a further $400 million to be distributed equally to the two partners, giving TMCL access to a total of $600 million in cash. The debt financing of Molson Breweries would be a non-recourse to the partners and would be based on a target debt equity ratio of 1:1 based on written-up asset values. Carling's long-term debt of about $400 million would remain an obligation of Elders.

EXHIBIT 1 The Canadian and U.S. Brewing Industries

1987 Data	Canada	U.S.
Per capita beer consumption (litres)	81.9	89.7
Domestic production, including exports (000 000 hl)	23.1	213.0
Total exports (000 000 hl)	2.6	3.9
Total imports (000 000 hl)	0.42	11.1
Canadian exports to the U.S. (000 000 hl)	2.3	
U.S. exports to Canada (000 000 hl)		0.26
Average labour cost per hl (Canadian figure is for Ontario and Quebec) (Cdn$)	$12.00	$6.80
Brewery worker production per hour (hl)	1.30	4.37
Estimated production and marketing costs per hl using a representative mix of cans, bottles and draught (Cdn$)	$85.18–102.21*	$68.14

* Canadian production costs vary considerably by province depending on plant size and capacity utilization. The U.S. costs are for a representative Anheuser-Busch brewery and do not vary significantly in different regions because plant locations are a function of the market and not government regulation.

SOURCE: ERC Statistics 1988, *Beverage Industry Annual Manual, Modern Brewery Age*, TMCL.

EXHIBIT 2 1987 U.S. Brewers Information

	Anheuser-Busch	Miller[1]	Stroh[2]	Heileman[3]	Coors
Net sales ($ millions)	8 258	3 105		1 174	1 351
Operating profit ($ millions)	1 129	107		88	89
Total assets ($ millions)	6 492	1 779[4]		706	1 457
Debt equity	33:67	32:68		3:97	
Brewing return on equity	27%	9%		26%	8%
Number of plants	12	6[5]	7	11	1
Annual capacity (000 000 hls)	100	65	30	20	30
Estimated utilization rate	96%	82%	84%	62%	90%
Maximum plant capacity	13.0	8.5	24.2	10.0	N/A
Minimum plant capacity	1.9	4.5	2.9	0.1	N/A

[1] Complete financial data is not available because Miller is owned by Philip Morris.
[2] The Stroh Brewing Company is privately owned and financial information is not available.
[3] 1986 data.
[4] Identifiable assets.
[5] Does not include a 9.4 million hl. plant in Ohio that was built and not used.

SOURCE: Annual reports, *1987 Modern Brewery Age Blue Book,* Wood Gundy Investment Research, 1988 Beer Industry Update.

EXHIBIT 3 John Labatt Financial Information Year Ended June 30 ($000 000)

	Total		Brewing Group	
	1987	*1988*	*1987*	*1988*
Net sales	3 802.2	4 611.0	1 016.3	1 136.6
Net profit	226.9	294.6	120.9	140.1
Assets employed	1 673.1	1 835.7	428.8	527.3
Capital expenditures	157.1	209.0	56.1	76.5
Average growth in sales 1984–88		20.3%		13.5%
Average growth in earnings before interest and taxes		14.6%		14.5%

SOURCE: John Labatt Ltd. annual reports.

EXHIBIT 4 Carling O'Keefe Income Statements ($000 000)

	1984[1]	*1985*	*1986*	*1987[2]*	*1988*
Revenue (Note)	869.3	833.4	832.9	888.4	953.4
Operating expenses				862.9	876.2
Interest on long term debt				9.1	38.9
Other interest				2.8	1.6
Earnings before unusual items and income taxes				15.5	36.7
Unusual item					5.0
Earnings before income taxes				15.5	41.7
Net earnings	73.0	8.1	6.6	10.8	21.8

Note: Revenue includes brewing excise and sales taxes. Brewing excise and sales taxes are included in operating expenses.

[1] Because the Brewing Group was one of several Carling operating groups prior to 1987, complete Brewing financial data is not available.

[2] The year end for 1984–1987 was March 31. Elders IXL acquired Carling O'Keefe Limited and its subsidiary companies with effect from April 23, 1987. During the 1987 fiscal year, the Carling's non-brewing businesses, which had accounted for about 8–9% of total revenue, were sold. On July 1, 1987, IXL Holdings Canada Inc. and the Carling companies were amalgamated to form Carling O'Keefe Breweries of Canada Ltd. The year end was changed to June 30. The 1988 figures are for the year ended June 30, 1988.

SOURCE: Carling annual reports.

EXHIBIT 5 Carling O'Keefe Consolidated Balance Sheet ($000 000)

	June 30 1988	July 1 1987
Assets		
Current Assets		
Cash	—	0.4
Accounts receivable	70.0	59.5
Inventories	79.3	59.5
Prepaid expenses	13.7	14.5
Deferred income taxes	6.8	17.6
Total current assets	169.9	177.6
Property, plant, and equipment	545.0	523.1
Less accumulated depreciation	25.7	3.8
	519.2	528.3
Other assets (Note 1)	31.9	30.8
	721.0	736.7
Liabilities and Shareholders' Equity		
Current Liabilities		
Bank indebtedness	7.4	13.6
Accounts payable and accrued liabilities	130.0	158.5
Due to customers for returnable containers	19.3	19.9
Excise and sales taxes	34.1	31.8
Dividends payable	0.5	0.5
Total current liabilities	191.3	224.4
Long-term Liabilities (Note 2)	403.7	417.8
Deferred Income Taxes	66.3	53.1
Shareholders' Equity		
Capital stock	40.6	41.0
Retained earnings	20.6	0.7
Cumulative translation adjustments	(1.6)	(0.3)
Total shareholders' equity	59.7	41.4
	721.0	736.7

Note 1: Other assets include investments and receivables, sports franchises, and deferred charges and other assets.

Note 2: The effect of the amalgamation between IXL Holdings Canada Inc. and the Carling O'Keefe companies was that the debt of approximately $396 million, being the purchase price paid by IXL Holdings Canada Inc. for the common shares of Carling O'Keefe Limited, and the principal business operations were in the same company.

SOURCE: Carling annual reports.

EXHIBIT 6 Elders IXL Financial Information Year Ended June 30
(AU$ 000 000)*

	1985	1986	1987	1988
Income Statement				
Revenue	6 995	7 659	10 560	15 350
Profit before interest, tax and				
abnormal items	301.5	347.5	758.5	1 133.7
Net interest expense	163.3	113.0	282.1	315.1
Income tax expense	24.9	27.6	127.7	294.0
Minority interest and				
preference dividends	1.7	27.9	85.3	75.9
Abnormal items			133.8	236.3
Net profit	111.7	179.0	263.4	448.6
Balance Sheet				
Shareholders' equity	588	761	2 094	3 312
Total assets	2 147	4 795	9 795	9 298
Return on equity	19.0%	23.5%	19.0%	20.7%
Debt equity ratio	0.70:1	0.63:1	0.68:1	0.32:1
Brewing Group				
Revenue	1 631	1 586	3 424	4 705
Profit	65	81	353	657
Average capital employed	N/A	N/A	2 395	3 954
Return (earnings before				
interest and taxes) on average				
capital employed	N/A	N/A	14.8%	16.6%

* On June 30, 1988, 1 Australian dollar was worth Cdn$ 0.96.

SOURCE: Elders annual reports.

EXHIBIT 7 Brewing Facilities of Molson and Carling

Molson	Capacity (000s of hls)	Carling	Capacity (000s of hls)
St. John's, Nfld.	260	St. John's, Nfld.	220
Montreal, Que.	2 700	Montreal, Que.	2 336
Toronto, Ont.	2 800	Etobikoke, Ont.	3 097
Barrie, Ont.	1 750	Winnipeg, Man.	397
Winnipeg, Man.	275	Saskatoon, Sask.	262
Edmonton, Alta.	400	Calgary, Alta.	772
Regina, Sask.	325	Vancouver, B.C.	882
Lethbridge, Alta.	400		
Vancouver, B.C.	950		

SOURCE: TMCL and Carling, industry experts.

EXHIBIT 8   TMCL Financial Information Year Ended March 31
($000 000)

	1984	1985	1986	1987	1988
Income Statement					
Revenue	1 800.2	1 871.8	2 011.5	2 250.4	2 434.9
Interest expense	21.2	24.0	23.2	17.7	12.6
Earnings before income taxes	108.0	66.0	66.0	86.9	132.9
Income taxes	38.4	19.9	24.6	33.7	53.2
Minority interest				0.8	1.0
Net earnings	51.3	45.2	35.9	52.3	78.7
Cash provided from operations	109.6	100.5	94.3	106.5	138.0
Balance Sheet					
Working capital	188.0	184.8	199.2	195.8	210.1
Total assets	986.7	1 033.9	1 137.7	1 236.8	1 365.4
Long-term debt	238.0	238.8	251.8	176.6	184.7
Shareholders' equity	382.8	402.2	427.9	533.6	591.2
Return on shareholders' equity	13.9%	11.5%	8.7%	10.9%	14.0%
Net debt equity ratio	0.52:1	0.61:1	0.56:1	0.25:1	0.23:1
Brewing Group					
Sales before brewing excise and sales taxes	1 024.7	1 062.8	1 128.2	1 275.0	1 383.4
Net Sales	726.5	746.6	794.7	882.8	965.3
Operating profit	88.1	30.0	30.0	50.1	77.8
Total assets	423.2	467.4	480.9	489.8	525.2
Capital expenditures	42.6	49.5	31.7	36.3	53.3
Depreciation	19.7	23.0	25.3	29.0	32.6
Return on assets	20.8%	6.4%	6.2%	10.2%	14.8%

SOURCE: TMCL annual reports.

PART

3 EVALUATING COMPANY CAPABILITIES

WAYSIDE INDUSTRIES

Paul W. Beamish and Kerry S. McLellan

Wayside Industries, located in Saint John, New Brunswick, was a producer of non-corrugated boxes for the fisheries industry. In March 1990, Bob Snodgrass, the owner and president of the company, was faced with a crucial decision regarding the firm's future direction. He had just received the results of a major marketing study done by a firm of outside consultants. Their report highlighted many of Bob's concerns, and provided detailed marketing data to supplement his own information.

Bob was assessing several alternatives: to invest in a new plant, thereby increasing productivity; to upgrade production equipment, thereby expanding into new markets; to do both; to wait for another year before reaching a decision; or to investigate divestment opportunities. The facility and equipment expansion projects were of comparable size, and both appeared attractive, but Bob had to be realistic about his firm's available resources. His decision had to be ready for the capital budget meeting in April.

BACKGROUND

The $15 million Atlantic Canadian market for non-corrugated cardboard packaging was almost evenly divided into institutional and consumer segments. The institutional market segment was a low-margin, low-technology commodity business dominated by regional producers. Half of the institutional segment was in the fish industry, with the balance in miscellaneous near markets. The higher-margin, higher-technology consumer market was dominated by non-regional producers, principally from Ontario. The regional institutional market was under pressure, while the non-regional consumer market showed a bright future.

Wayside was a successful company within the institutional market segment, with an account base that was primarily composed of fish processing plants. The company had established itself as the market leader in New Brunswick and Nova Scotia for 5–20 lb. wax-coated non-corrugated institutional fish boxes. However, dependence on this market segment presented some inherent difficulties to Wayside:

- The fish processing business was seasonal. Several profitable months of positive cash flow were followed by several months of negative cash flow.

- The fish processing business was in crisis, with demand expected to decline. Dependence on the small independent processors increased the risk to receivables.

The fish industry had always been cyclical, but the latest downturn appeared to be different. Fish stocks had declined precipitously. There were several reasons for this decline. A dispute between the European Community (EC) and Canada was often cited as the principal cause. In 1989, the Northwest Atlantic Fisheries Organization had recommended an EC quota for outside Canada's fishing zone of 13 000 metric tons. The EC had rejected the recommendations of this organization (of which it was a member), and had unilaterally set a quota of 160 000 metric tons. Declining stocks from previous severe overfishing resulted in the EC landing only 79 000 tons of their "quota" and further hurting a rapidly declining resource. Canada had set a domestic quota in 1989 of 270 000 metric tons. The federal government had implemented a quota reduction of 12% in 1989, and had announced a further reduction of 19% for 1990. Department of Fisheries and Oceans scientists had recommended an immediate domestic quota cut to 125 000 metric tons and a total quota of 190 000 metric tons, including all foreign quotas. At the domestic quota level of 270 000, it was estimated that eastern Canadian fish processing plants were operating at only 55–65% of capacity. It was clear that the required quota cuts would force permanent plant closures, and lead to a radical restructuring and reduction in the size of the industry. Industry observers viewed the problems as critical and long-term. This was not another cyclical adjustment.

Wayside's production facility and equipment seriously limited entry into other packaging market segments. At the peak of the fish season, the production of boxes for the current fish customers required all of the company's existing capacity. Thus, it would not be able to meet the orders of new non-fish customers. In addition, Wayside printing equipment was inadequate to produce the quality graphics required on packaging in the consumer market segment.

ASSESSMENT OF MANUFACTURING CAPABILITIES

Wayside's present facility had evolved through a progression of technological and process upgrades. Coupled with the creative use of low-cost labour, they had transformed an antiquated plant into a viable production business. Wayside had compensated for a lack of technical productivity by improving raw material (paper board) quality, by installing the capability to handle paperboard rolls instead of sheets, and by targeting at quality sensitive rather than price sensitive business. The firm depended on two-colour technology, unsuitable for consumer packaging. The existing machinery was inefficient and labour intensive.

The production plant had expanded from the original building which had been a wartime aircraft hangar to an amalgamation of three separate buildings, connected at different levels, with varying ceiling heights. Because the facility was located in a residential area, further expansion and truck access would be restricted. Material handling was difficult, and there was only a limited amount of improvements that could be made to the process flow.

A new 50 000-sq. ft. building in a well-located industrial park would cost $38 per sq.ft to construct. The present facility, plus associated real estate had a realizable market value of approximately $700 000. The new building would provide a 20% productivity increase as a result of layout and material handling improvements. This saving would be incremental to any other changes. Based upon 1989 figures, these annual productivity gains were estimated at $85 000. Annual operating and maintenance savings of $40 000 could also be achieved. In addition, Bob recognized that the present facility would require $150 000 in repairs, including a new roof, within the next few years. There was a possibility that an associated company, A.T. Snodgrass Co. Ltd. (ATSCO Sales), would locate in the building for a saving of $100 000 for that firm. Bob's preliminary investment analysis for the new facility decision showed the project to be very attractive.

The fish business was seasonal with Wayside's peak demand period running from early spring to late fall. Given the very high uncertainty associated with the fish business and the customized nature of the products, Wayside found it very difficult to smooth production rates using forecasted demand planning. The workforce fluctuated from a low of 20 in January to a peak of 50 or more in the summer. This fluctuation made it difficult to hold on to skilled operators. However, since much of the work required only unskilled labour, this was not as serious a problem as it could have been. During the summer months, the plant operated 21 hours per day, 7 days per week, on a two-shift basis. Most workers put in large amounts of overtime. During 1989, the average was 18 hours overtime per week for each worker during the peak period.

The existing machinery was serviced by a firm in Chicago. Historically, there had been only a couple of service calls required each year as Wayside had been very careful with its preventative maintenance program. The U.S. firm had provided excellent service (24-hour response), and would be able to service any equipment contemplated in a modernization. This assurance was necessary due to the unavailability of local trained service personnel.

The key liability of the current Wayside facility was its lack of ability to produce consumer packaging because of limited productivity and capacity. To exploit the market opportunities outside of the fish industry, Wayside had to improve graphics capabilities, lower the variable cost of production, and increase volume capacity.

ASSESSMENT OF GRAPHICS CAPABILITIES

Addressing new markets required colour graphics capabilities beyond Wayside's current scope. Wayside did "double pass" printing to get limited colour graphics capability. This process had serious quality implications restricting entry into consumer packaging markets. To exploit the consumer market a technological leap would be required in equipment and manpower skills.

ASSESSMENT OF PRODUCTIVITY

Plant layout and workflow, unskilled labour, and specific production equipment represented areas where improvement was needed. Plant improvements would have to incorporate a reorganization of the workflow, specifically the loading and staging area which was inadequate and at the furthest point from the inventory. The best solution for most of the productivity problems would be a new facility.

The die cutter was inefficient and had quality control problems. This problem represented a barrier to competitive entry to specific near markets.

ASSESSMENT OF PLANT CAPACITY

The printing capacity would appear to have been the limiting factor on production capacity. However, two bottlenecks in the manufacturing process—die cutting and gluing—meant that existing printing capacity was not being fully used.

A recently released inter-firm comparison of paperbox manufacturers in Eastern Canada, prepared by Peat Marwick Stevenson & Kellogg for the department of Industry, Science and Technology confirmed Bob's own findings and made several other observations. The report noted that Wayside's location provided it with a relatively inexpensive source of labour, but that the effectiveness of the labour was eroded by a very high level of practical capacity utilization, poor plant layout, difficult material handling and outdated equipment. The consultants recommended that the firm review the impact of any changes in production volume on its product mix and cost structure. Because the manufacture of a more complex product would create new bottlenecks, production scheduling and sequencing would become more costly. Wayside processed more rush orders than most industry participants and used a significant amount of overtime in doing so.

ASSESSMENT OF MANAGEMENT

Guy Richard was Wayside's plant manager, vice-president, and partial owner. At only 29, Guy had worked in the institutional paperboard packaging industry since he was 14. This practical experience was complimented by university exposure to Engineering and Business Administration courses. In 1983, when Bob Snodgrass purchased the company, he appointed Guy as plant manager. By 1990, he was handling most of the day-to-day functions, including production planning, maintenance scheduling, and inventory managing.

Ownership of Wayside was a factor in the expansion decision. Bob Snodgrass owned the industrial distribution firm of ATSCO Sales, several other business concerns, and 80% of Wayside. Guy Richard owned the remaining 20%. Bob considered Guy to be the major strength of the company. Guy viewed his minority ownership position as an important part of his compensation package and felt challenged to make it meaningful through increased profitability. Bob was concerned that Guy might become dissatisfied if the firm's future was threatened by lack of response to the decline in fishing activity. He believed that Wayside's demise would be greatly hastened if Guy should leave the firm to pursue other challenges. He was also aware that Guy was apprehensive about diluting his ownership position. Bob had expressed a willingness to sell further shares in the business, provided his majority ownership position was not threatened. However, Guy had just purchased a new home and had limited additional resources to invest. A $250 000-expansion in Wayside's equity base would reduce Guy's ownership to 7.5% unless an arrangement could be negotiated.

Larry O'Neill, the company controller, was involved in the implementation of a new computer system which would integrate manufacturing and accounting, allowing a 100% increase in business without requiring additional management staff. As the designer of the previous system, Larry, a young graduate of the CMA program, who had been with Wayside for more than five years, was familiar with the industry and the cost information required to manage effectively. Guy had been slowly transferring operating responsibilities to Larry and had found Larry competent.

Dave Short was the Director of Sales for Wayside. He had been in industrial sales with the Snodgrass group for more than twenty years. Largely due to his efforts, Wayside had come to dominate the fisheries market. Dave seemed less than enthusiastic about pursuing market opportunities outside the fishery market, indicating that within that sector more work could be done. Dave's experience was with the industrial and institutional market segments which were very different from the consumer packaging segment. Dave had been a loyal, productive employee, and had a strong personal relationship with Bob Snodgrass.

Hazen Douglas was Plant Superintendent, responsible for production and worker supervision. He had proven skills for achieving productivity from low skilled labour and antiquated machinery. Bob was confident that Hazen would be able to manage in an upgraded environment.

Wayside and the other companies within the Snodgrass group of firms were expected to operate as self-financing units. The small management group of four at Wayside enjoyed complete operating autonomy; however, capital budgeting decisions were usually dealt with at the annual planning meeting.

ASSESSMENT OF MARKETING CAPABILITIES

Wayside relied on its sister distribution company, ATSCO, for its sales and marketing efforts, paying 5% of the gross sales for the services provided. ATSCO's 12 sales representatives provided complete coverage of the Atlantic Canada region. The provinces of New Brunswick, Newfoundland and Prince Edward Island were serviced by the 9 sales representatives based out of the Saint John head office. This territory contained a population base of 1.5 million. The province of Nova Scotia was serviced by 3 sales representatives in a Halifax branch office responsible for a territory containing a population of 800 000. This arrangement was a cost effective solution for Wayside and useful in terms of inter-company revenue allocations.

ATSCO was divided into two specialized groups for packaging and office supplies. New hires into sales were well-educated (Bachelor-level graduates) with good communication skills. An old-style sales approach with an aversion to new marketing direction was still evident, though slowly disappearing as the new hires made an impact.

One of Wayside's concern about the marketing capabilities of ATSCO was the absence of a packaging expert with a good understanding of the consumer packaging market. Helping clients improve design and presentation of their packaging was critical to successful penetration of the consumer market. ATSCO was not fully capable of operating as the sales arm of Wayside in the sophisticated consumer packaging market without this expertise. In consumer packaging, the packaging supplier could contribute considerably in the final design of the package, and packaging represented an important value added component of the product—compared with the institutional market where it was just a box.

Bob was aware that the structure of the sales and marketing firm as well as its relationship to Wayside were becoming of concern to Guy. In the past, Wayside's simple products and market focus, as well as its small size, had lent efficiency arguments to the arrangements between the two firms. However, the rapid growth in the firm's sales and the modernization plans had left Guy with doubts as to whether the arrangement would be appropriate in the future. Since ATSCO Sales was 100% owned by Bob Snodgrass, the relationship with Wayside had been very lucrative for ATSCO.

MARKET ANALYSIS

In order to decide upon his recommendations to the capital budget meeting, Bob has to study the analysis of Wayside Industries which had been recently completed by the firm of outside consultants. Exhibit 1 presents their analysis of the fish market, near market and consumer market segments. The fish segment data had been of no surprise to Bob; however, the extent of the opportunities in the other segments had been a pleasant revelation. Each segment was analyzed in terms of product examples, product requirements, key purchasing criteria, the percentage of Wayside's business contributed by the segment, market outlook, estimated size, and market share potentially available to Wayside.

The *fish market* refers to the fish processors who use 5–20 lb. wax-coated boxes. This has been Wayside's primary market.

The *near markets* consist of other types of business with packaging needs which are within Wayside's existing production capability. Examples of this include garment boxes, dairy packaging, and bakery boxes. This segment represents immediate market opportunities for Wayside which could be addressed with the firm's existing technology.

The difficulty faced by Wayside in the near markets had been inconsistently meeting expected quality standards. The principal cause of this had been the confused and congested nature of the existing production facility. In addition, the seasonal nature of the fish industry combined with capacity constraints in the existing facility had resulted in production planning and delivery problems. Wayside management felt that serious effort in the near market would require production in a new expanded facility.

The *consumer market* refers to the market for consumer-oriented packaging such as six-pack beer cartons, frozen food boxes, and boxes for confectionary items. These were mass produced products requiring a high level graphics capability that was beyond Wayside's current production capabilities.

EQUIPMENT UPGRADE REQUIREMENTS

Offset Lithography—The Ideal Technology

In view of the market opportunities, offset lithography represented the best technological option. The versatility and the ability to do small runs were the real assets of offset litho. Plate making equipment would also be required to implement this technology. A mechanical control system would be adequate to address market needs (no need for CAD/CAM user interface).

As alternatives, Bob and Guy had investigated rotogravure and flexograph processes. These processes had much lower costs of production. However, minimum run sizes were so large that there would be few opportunities to use this potential efficiency in Atlantic Canada.

Debottlenecking—Costly but Necessary

There were two weak links in the production process that had to be addressed in order to take advantage of the offset litho's capacity: die cutting and gluing. A large-capacity die cutter, capable of trimming, would be required to increase the production capacity. However, a new die cutter cost three times as much as the cost of an offset litho. Also, an additional gluing machine would be needed to accommodate growth objectives.

The new production levels would require an efficient and productive plant flow, particularly for materials. A new roll handling system would be needed to improve material handling.

The overall cost required to bring plant production capacity up to that of the desired printing technology (offset litho) would be almost four times that of the printing technology itself. This was not as ironic as it appeared, since the most significant improvements to packaging technology during the past three decades had been in production rates. These productivity gains had come as a result of the application of advanced technology to previously simplified mechanical processes.

Modest Infrastructure Requirement

There would be some modest improvements required in the current plant's infrastructure to accommodate the modernization. These included structural reinforcement of the floor for new production equipment, minor roof modifications, additional electrical and plumbing work, a new loading dock and a modern staff services facility.

CAPITAL EQUIPMENT REQUIREMENTS

Three primary pieces of equipment	
4-colour offset litho	$100 000
Die cutter	300 000
Gluer	100 000
Additional equipment (including plate-making, electric pallet system, roll-handling system)	95 000
Infrastructure (including electrical, floor work, roof repairs, loading dock, washroom facilities)	228 500
Allowance for overruns	76 500
Total estimated expenditures—modernization	$900 000

The installation of the equipment could take place in the existing facility although Bob recognized that many productivity gains would have to be foregone. Construction work and installation of the equipment would take a total of five months to complete. Late spring to fall represented the company's busiest and most profitable months. Movement of the production process to a new facility would cost $150 000 to $200 000.

OPERATING REQUIREMENTS

The major impact of the capital equipment changes would be a shift in the workforce skills required. Although Wayside would not become a "high-tech" producer, manual functions would be automated, with workers responsible for the operation of more sophisticated equipment. To aid worker adjustment, Guy had proposed initially using the new equipment to manufacture only the company's existing product line and products which were close to the existing product line. As time progressed, it would become possible to use the new equipment to expand the product offerings and penetrate more sophisticated markets.

Other workforce changes included the elimination or reduction in seasonal workers and overtime, and the addition of four new full-time positions. As a consequence, labour costs would be reduced by $72 000. The increased productivity of the company's labour force would result in an improved competitive position for the firm. Also, Wayside would probably be able to keep the balance of the staff securely employed on a more year-round basis.

Another operating change would be the firm's need to provide creative graphics services to customers in the consumer packaging sector. This service, expected of packaging suppliers, was an important means of tying customers to the firm. Wayside did not possess this skill in-house. Also, Saint John had no graphics firm with extensive expertise in the areas required by Wayside. There were several good local graphics companies but the nearest firm with the required specific experience was in Halifax, Nova Scotia. At the present time, it was unknown whether a local firm would be interested in acquiring the necessary expertise.

SALES GROWTH FORECAST WITH EQUIPMENT MODERNIZATION

The plant modernization would permit Wayside to expand its annual sales from $2.6 million to $4.3 million or more. The question facing management was whether sales growth of $1.7 million could actually be achieved in the consumer packaging market. An external consultant had prepared a forecast of Wayside's potential sales volume in the consumer packaging market. The consultant had been optimistic that the numbers were attainable but realization was going to take some effort.

Wayside's Five-Year Growth in Sales (dollars)

	Year 1	Year 2	Year 3	Year 4	Year 5
Incremental	497 540	402 460	300 000	200 000	300 000
Cumulative	497 540	900 000	1 200 000	1 400 000	1 700 000

Market opportunities had been identified that would reduce the firm's dependence on the fishing industry. However, realization of these opportunities required radical changes to the company in terms of capital equipment and operations.

FINANCIAL ANALYSIS AND FEASIBILITY

The information in Exhibit 2 was compiled to show an investment analysis of the new equipment and the new facility at Wayside, based on a differential cash flow during the first five years of operation. The analysis highlighted the modernization plan's very strong positive cash flow and significant return on investment because of the potential for large increases in revenue without notable increases in the fixed costs of the company. In other words, after the modernization, virtually all of the incremental gross margin would accrue to the net income of the company. At the same time, annual labour savings of $72 000 per annum ($60 000 in wages and $12 000 benefits and employee related expenses) would be achieved. While the first 13 months of construction and operation would not be as profitable, they would, nevertheless, generate a positive incremental cash flow and a strong return on investment.

NO INVESTMENT—NO FUTURE

After an analysis of the firm's situation, Bob had determined that, without investment, operations would remain marginally profitable for the next three years, after which revenues would decline enough to put the company into a loss position. While it might be possible to mitigate the losses to some extent by reducing staffing levels and taking other cost-cutting measures, the eventual outcome would, nevertheless, be the same: the company would go out of business. There was also possibility that the business might be sold as a viable concern to one of the existing competitors in this oligarchic industry. However, Bob was not certain that there would currently be any interest in the business and what price could be expected. In a wind-up scenario Bob expected that the firm's fixed assets might yield $800 000 to $900 000.

The existing business was in decline and the company required strategic investment in order to survive. The equipment modernization could provide the means to breathe new life into the operations of Wayside by shifting its revenue dependence away from the declining fishing industry towards a more diverse and stable client base.

CAPITAL REQUIREMENTS

The first 6 to 12 months of the modernization project would be the most capital intensive. Once in operation, the business would begin to generate sufficient cash to meet ongoing working capital requirements. The company's incremental cash equity requirements would reach a peak in the first 13 months of about $290 000, an amount in excess of what the operating line of credit would be able to provide. The excess amount of $290 000 would arise from several sources related to the start-up of the newly expanded operations: the residual amount of the $900 000 modernization costs (only $675 000 in financing could likely be expected); interest on the interim construction loan totals over $39 000; other start-up/construction factors contributing to the excess including interest on the interest, reduced production capacity due to construction activities, and start-up related training.

The financing issue concerned Bob, but discussions with local banks had assured him that 75% financing could be expected because Snodgrass companies had a very good record with regards to their financial obligations. This financing would be secured by the new facility/equipment. Bob accepted the likelihood that financing guarantees would have to be provided for Wayside's project by one of his other larger, more established firms. Bob was looking at several other attractive investments outside Wayside, and had determined that the maximum cash investment he could infuse into the firm was $250 000. He was willing to sell additional shares to outside investors but he saw many problems that would have to be overcome if he was to pursue this option.

Bob recognized that the modernization and new facility project were critical to the future of Wayside Industries. The project could yield a return on investment in excess of 36% and provide the strategic redirection that would be needed for the welfare of the company in the long-run. The new facility project, with a return on investment of 23%, would improve the firm's long-term efficiency. A combined project, with an estimated ROI of 32%, offered the benefit of avoiding some investment costs. To Bob, the issue was not whether Wayside should move forward with the proposed projects but whether the firm had the resources to undertake both of them. If not, which one should be chosen, and at what pace should the firm proceed? Should the projects be delayed? Or should Bob begin to investigate the possibility of selling the business? Bob was not certain of the best strategy, but he knew the decision would determine the firm's future.

EXHIBIT 1 Segmentation of Maritime Markets for Non-Corrugated Box Cartons

	Fish Market	*Near Markets*	*Consumer Market*
Product Examples	• Wax-coated boxes (tops and bottoms)	• Wiener and sausage boxes • Creamer trays, novelty boxes for dairy products • Pie boxes, cake boxes • Plain shipping cartons • Salt cartons, sugar cartons • Flower boxes	• Local six-pack beer cartons • National Sea seafood dinner boxes • Frozen food packages • Chocolate boxes • Irving tissue boxes
Product Requirements	• Basic wax-coated carton • At most, two-colour print required • Focal point of Wayside's existing product line	• Basic non-corrugated cardboard carton • Two-colour print required • Pie boxes (windows) and salt boxes (spouts) are only products beyond Wayside's current production capabilities	• Require offset litho capabilities • High-level graphics (four to six colours) • Beyond Wayside's current production capabilities
Key Purchasing Criteria Ranked	• Delivery time • Price • Product quality	• Price • Quality • Delivery time	• Quality • Price • Delivery time
% of Wayside's Existing Business	85%	15%	Nil

EXHIBIT 1 (continued)

Market Competitors	• Wayside (60%)—competes on quality, delivery • Price Wilson (20%)—Montreal; competes on price • Ellis Paperboard (15%)—Maine, U.S.; competes on price • Ling Industries (3%) • Royal Print (2%)—Dartmouth, N.S.; quality, price	• Royal Print (45%)—loyal Nova Scotia base • Ling Industries (30%)—strong price competitor • Price-Wilson (15%)—no obvious competitive advantages • Wayside (10%)—New Brunswick base; some quality problems; emphasizes service	• Royal Print (52%)—focus on small runs; monopoly position in this niche • Ontario Suppliers (48%)—Lawson Marden Ltd.; Somerville Packaging; low-cost producers; only interested in very large volume accounts
Segment Outlook	• Declining volumes • Reduced/margins • Increasingly price competitive	• Potential to displace non-biodegradable packaging • Moderate growth segment	• High growth segment • Free Trade Agreement has resulted in tremendous growth in packaged food processing • Ontario suppliers have poor service record and long delivery times • Potential to displace non-biodegradable packaging • Inadequate service by Royal Print
Total Market Size	$3 500 000	$3 500 000	$8 000 000
Amount Available to Wayside	$2 200 000 (Wayside has reached saturation)	$2 000 000 (primarily N.B. and P.E.I.)	$4 000 000 (primarily N.B. and P.E.I.)

EXHIBIT 2   Wayside Investment Analysis of New Equipment Differential Cash Flow Only ($000s)

	Year 1	*Year 2*	*Year 3*	*Year 4*	*Year 5*
Capital Investment	900				
Init. Working Cap. Req.	65				
Amount of Incr. Equity	290				
Amount to be Financed	675				
Incremental Revenue	497	900 000	1 200 000	1 400 000	1 700 000
Var. Cost of Goods Sold	368	666 000	888 000	1 036 000	1 258 000
Contr. from Incr. Rev.	129	234 000	312 000	364 000	442 000
Labour Savings	36	72 000	72 000	72 000	72 000
Prod. Cost Increases	(5)	(10 000)	(10 000)	(10 000)	(10 000)
Incr. Income Before Fin.	160 360	296 000	374 000	426 000	504 000
Inter. (Incl: Oper. Loan)	98 539	113 574	113 736	111 145	109 410
Incr. Income Before Tax	61 821	182 426	260 264	314 855	394 590
Economic Return					
Return on incr. equity	21.32%	62.90%	89.75%	108.57%	136.18%
Return on investment	16.62%	30.67%	38.76%	44.14%	52.23%
5-year average ROE	83.73%				
5-year average ROI	36.48%				

Note: 1. ROE calculations used incremental income before tax.
     2. ROI calculations used incremental income before interest and tax.
     3. Potential tax liabilities were ignored in calculations. Maximum exposure was estimated to be less than 25%.

EXHIBIT 3 Wayside Investment Analysis of New Facility Differential Investment Only

Investment
    Capital cost   1 900 000
    Less: Value of present facility   (700 000)
    Net capital cost   1 200 000

    Less: Avoidance of major repairs   (150 000)
    Less: Avoidance of required infra-
         structure improvements.   (200 000)
    Net additional capital investment   850 000

    Plus: Moving costs   150 000
    Net investment for new facility   1 000 000

Expected Savings
    Expected annual operating and
         maintenance savings   40 000
    Savings on ATSCO sales office   100 000
    Expected productivity improvement
         (direct labour transportation etc.)   85 000
    Total immediate benefits   225 000

Return on Investment/Incremental Equity
    1. As a stand-alone project the ROI was 22.5% while ROE was 42%.

Assumptions and Additional Considerations
    1. Productivity improvement will increase in proportion to sales.
    2. Interest rate is assumed to be 14%.
    3. 75% project financing is assumed.
    4. ROI calculations used incremental savings before interest and tax.
    5. Potential tax liabilities were ignored in calculations. Maximum exposure was estimated to be less than 25%.

EXHIBIT 4 Wayside Investment Analysis of Upgraded Equipment and New Facility
Differential Cash Flow Only

	Year 1	Year 2	Year 3	Year 4	Year 5
Equipment					
Equip. cap. investment	900 000				
Less: Renovations	250 000				
Net equipment invest.	650 000				
Init. working cap. req.	65 000				
Total	715 000				
Equity	227 500				
Financed	507 500				
Building					
Incr. inv. new build.	850 000				
Moving cost	150 000				
Total	1 000 000				
Equity	250 000				
Financed	750 000				
Incremental Revenue	497 540	900 000	1 200 000	1 400 000	1 700 000
Var. cost of goods sold	368 180	666 000	888 000	1 036 000	1 258 000
Contr. from incr. rev.	129 360	234 000	312 000	364 000	442 000
Labour Savings	36 000	72 000	72 000	72 000	72 000
Prod. cost increases	(5 000)	(10 000)	(10 000)	(10 000)	(10 000)
Prod. inc due to new fac.	94 950	103 000	109 000	113 000	119 000
ATSCO office savings	100 000	100 000	100 000	100 000	100 000
Reduced oper. & maint.	40 000	40 000	40 000	40 000	40 000
Incr. income before fin.	395 310	449 000	523 000	679 000	763 000
Interest (inc: oper. ln.)	203 539	218 574	218 736	216 145	214 410
Incr. income before tax	191 771	230 426	304 264	462 855	548 590
Economic Return					
Return on incr. equity	40.16%	48.26%	63.72%	96.94%	114.89%
Return on investment	22.78%	25.88%	30.14%	39.14%	43.98%
5-year average ROE	72.79%				
5-year average ROI	32.39%				

Note: 1. ROE calculations used incremental income before tax.

2. ROI calculations used incremental income before interest and tax.

3. Potential tax liabilities were ignored in calculations. Maximum exposure was estimated to be less than 25%.

EXHIBIT 5 **Wayside Industries (1983) Ltd.**
Income Statement 1985–89 (000s)

	1989	1988	1987	1986	1985
Gross Sales	2 626	2 259	1 991	1 776	1 624
Cost of Goods Sold					
Materials	1 252	1 065	981	822	788
Direct lab.	283	251	216	199	183
Other	596	517	465	397	387
Total COGS	2 131	1 833	1 662	1 418	1 359
Gross Profit	495	426	329	358	265
Expenses					
Selling	148	126	93	98	89
Admin.	182	156	130	132	107
Financial	109	91	81	72	58
Total Expenses	439	373	304	302	254
Taxes	6	0	0	0	0
Net Income	50	53	25	56	11

Balance Sheets as of Nov. 30, 1989 (000s)

	1989	1988
Assets		
Cash	0	0
Receivables	556	549
Inventory	350	347
Prepaids	25	34
Total current assets	931	930
Sundry	49	21
Land	119	117
Net building, machinery, furniture	366	424
Total fixed assets	534	562
Total assets	1 465	1 492
Liabilities		
Bank	405	315
Payables	184	303
Other	89	79
Total current liabilities	678	697
Long-term bank debt	405	459
Loans from shareholders	225	229
Total liabilities	1 308	1 385
Preferred shares	100	100
Common shares	1	1
Retained earnings	56	6
Total shareholders' equity	157	107
Total liab. and shareholders' equity	1 465	1 492

IPL INC.

J. Michael Geringer and Louis Hébert

In April 1988, Julien Métivier, CEO of IPL Inc., was reassessing his company's policy regarding involvement in custom molded plastic products. A leader in the Canadian injection molded plastics industry, IPL had traditionally relied on proprietary products rather than the manufacturing-on-order of custom products for other firms. However, since 1984, IPL had been supplying custom molded auto parts for the Ford Motor Company, and had recently been offered a contract to manufacture a large volume of additional parts for them. Despite its potential strategic benefits, several of IPL's managers were reluctant to accept the new contract because it threatened to dramatically increase the company's reliance on supplying custom molded products, particularly to a single large customer in a potentially unstable industry environment. Having only one month to respond to Ford's offer, Julien was concerned about how he should proceed.

THE CANADIAN PLASTIC PRODUCTS INDUSTRY

In 1986, the Canadian plastic products industry was composed of approximately 2 500 firms, representing more than 95 000 jobs. In about half of these firms, plastic processing represented the major or exclusive activity. The typical firm was small, with about 50 employees and sales under $4 million. The fragmented industry structure was due to the absence of significant entry barriers or governmental regulations during the industry's early years. A small investment in one or two used machines and some knowledge of mechanics was often a sufficient base for entry. Customers' emphasis on the cost of plastic products rather than on quality also helped constrain the development of larger firms, which could not be competitive with these low-cost competitors.

However, the proportion of firms with less than 10 employees had been decreasing rapidly, dropping from 40% to 35% between 1983 and 1985. Several large corporations specializing in plastic processing and with sales above $100 million had subsequently emerged. This increasing concentration was closely related to consumers' growing emphasis on quality and performance of plastic products. In addition to traditional quality-oriented market niches such as electronics and aerospace, high-volume markets had begun demanding increased precision with regard to uniformity in the appearance, performance and physico-mechanic characteristics of the products.

In the early 1980s, Canadian plastics producers had average costs 5% to 15% greater than their U.S. counterparts. With a domestic plastics market approximately 10 times that of Canada's, U.S. firms were often larger and more focused, and they could dedicate machines to the manufacture of a single product. As the number of products per machine increased, there tended to be an increase in tooling and maintenance costs, a decrease in machine utilization rates, and declining scale and experience curve benefits. Nevertheless, competitiveness of Canadian producers had been enhanced by favourable exchange rates, and a tariff of 13.5% on plastic goods from the U.S. versus 5.3% on goods shipped to the U.S.

Costs of plastic resins accounted for an average of 47% of manufacturers' sales in 1986, compared to 12%, 18%, 5% and 8% for labour, overhead, selling and administration, respectively. Most resins were commodity goods, supplied by a small number of large chemical companies. Production capacity constraints experienced by these North American suppliers had led to price increases up to 80% since 1987. In addition, transportation costs represented an important component of delivered costs, and shipment of products for more than 500 kilometres was often uneconomical.

Plastic products were generally classified as either custom molded or proprietary. Firms involved in custom molding were essentially subcontractors that used molds owned by customers for the molding-on-order of plastic products. Custom molders' superior pre-tax return on sales, estimated for 1985 at 9.3% versus 6.7% for producers of proprietary products, was due to the custom segment's higher risks and instability. In contrast, producers of proprietary products generally required greater financial capacity in order to cover the added costs of product development, mold-making, and sales and distribution. However, since they owned both the mold and the product, they were not dependent on the vagaries of subcontracting and were able to sell each product to more than one customer in order to amortize their investment in products and distribution channels. As a result, proprietary product producers tended to have a higher return on investment than did custom producers. Nevertheless, it was common for producers of proprietary products to also devote a portion of their activities to custom molding in order to increase utilization of production capacity.

In 1986, the packaging market was the largest outlet for plastic products, accounting for 39% of the resins consumed by the Canadian industry, compared to 27% and 11% for construction and automotive goods, respectively. In sales volume, the plastic packaging market was estimated at $1.13 billion in 1985, compared to $809 million in 1982. The remainder of the market for plastic products consisted principally of the furniture and furnishings industry with 6%, and electrical and electronics products, housewares, agriculture and toys, each with less than 5%.

THE PLASTIC AUTO PARTS INDUSTRY

Since 1975, the auto industry had been the fastest growing market for plastic products. Deliveries of plastic auto parts by Canadian producers reached $1.3 billion in 1985, compared to $928 million, $732 million, and $521 million in 1984, 1983 and 1982, respectively. The lower cost and lighter weight of plastic products, their ease of processing, technological advances, and efforts by resin suppliers to develop new automotive applications were the main factors promoting this evolution. Further growth was expected because, in 1986, plastics accounted for only 6% of the 56 million tons of materials used worldwide for the manufacture of autos.

North American auto-makers were the main consumers of auto parts, both plastic and non-plastic, delivered by Canadian producers. However, the major auto-makers varied in the extent to which they relied on external suppliers. Chrysler sourced about 70% of its parts and assemblies from external sources, compared to 50% for Ford and 30% for General Motors. The recent market success of foreign manufacturers, especially the Japanese, had resulted in trends toward lower costs, increased product quality, and a reduction in the number of suppliers. In addition, there was increased use of long-term supply contracts, often involving technological cooperation and joint development of parts and systems. However, in return for long-term contracts, suppliers often had to assume a larger part of the costs of tooling, R&D and warranties. Suppliers were also expected to reduce prices by 2–5% each year. Further rationalization of supplier networks was expected as auto-makers intensified their efforts to reduce the number of parts going into their vehicles, along with increased emphasis on purchase of sub-assemblies and finished components systems. Furthermore, just-in-time delivery systems were rapidly gaining acceptance. These systems demanded stringent quality controls, and imposed contract penalties of up to $1 000 a minute if supplier delivery problems caused the auto-maker's assembly line to be shut down. In response, many large suppliers of plastic parts and resins had invested in facilities close to the auto-makers' operations, and this trend threatened to raise a major barrier to the entry of new suppliers.

According to industry observers, Ford was at the forefront of trends toward rationalization of supplier networks and improvement of overall product quality. In 1986, Ford had expressed an intention to reduce its number of suppliers by 90% within five years and to develop lasting relationships with the remaining firms, especially those which obtained Q-1 or TQE (Total Quality Excellence) accreditations. These accreditations were awarded to suppliers which achieved Ford's requirements in quality control and management, as well as R&D and manufacturing capabilities. Such accreditation allowed a supplier's products to be integrated directly into Ford's assembly line without first undergoing quality control inspections.

The plastic auto parts industry was expected to become increasingly competitive as off-shore suppliers already involved with foreign auto-makers followed their customers into the North American market. Thus, the key challenges facing North American auto parts suppliers were the ability to achieve continued improvements in productivity and quality, and to survive the cyclical demand fluctuations characterizing the auto industry.

IPL'S BACKGROUND

Les Industries Provinciales Limitées was founded in 1939 by Emile Métivier in Saint-Damien, a small village about 80 kilometres southeast of Quebec City. Incorporated in 1945 under the IPL name, the firm was initially involved in the manufacture of wooden housewares like brushes, brooms and mops, and in the assembly of plastic toothbrushes. IPL began production of plastic goods after the 1953 acquisition of its supplier of toothbrush components. Over the years, IPL became involved in the manufacture and sale of a variety of plastic housewares and industrial pails, and abandoned production of wooden housewares.

Emile Métivier involved his four sons in IPL's operations during the company's early years. His eldest and youngest sons, Rémi and Julien, gained experience in the marketing and sales of industrial containers and housewares, respectively. Similarly, Clément managed the sawmill which the firm operated until 1961, and later worked on the development of a maple sap gathering system, while Benoît was involved in issues of production and machinery acquisition.

Upon Emile Métivier's death in 1971, his sons took over management of IPL, with Rémi, then 38, becoming CEO. By 1983, when Rémi became Chairman of the Board and Benoît replaced him as CEO, IPL's operational emphasis was on the development of proprietary lines of pails, containers, and material handling products. In 1985, IPL undertook an ambitious modernization program called "IPL 1990," whose objective was to enable IPL to be among the most technologically advanced firms in the North American plastic products industry. The five-year modernization program was financed in part through a 1985 public stock issue of one million shares at a price of $5.75 each, and resulted in IPL being listed on the Montreal Stock Exchange. In late 1986, Benoît left his position and terminated active participation in the firm's management or board activities, but remained a major shareholder and board member. His 48-year-old brother Julien, for many years IPL's only professionally trained manager, became CEO in February 1987.

IPL'S ORGANIZATION

In April 1988, IPL had a functional organization structure with three vice-presidents, a treasurer and five departmental managers reporting to the CEO (Exhibits 1 and 2). A fourth vice-president position, that of marketing, was abolished after the December 1987 departure of that person in response to growing divergences between him and other executives regarding IPL's future development. In addition, no children or close relatives of the Métivier brothers were involved in the firm's management. This situation was not expected to change in the near future.

The firm's operational and strategic management was under the direct responsibility of IPL's 11-person management committee, which usually met once a month. The vice-president of finance, as IPL's secretary, set the agenda for these meetings after consulting with the Committee's other members, but additional topics could be introduced at the end of the meetings. The same committee, without the vice-president of finance, met for several hours every Monday morning to deal with more day-to-day management issues. According to IPL's executives, this process permitted close control of the firm's production and marketing efforts. IPL also had a nine-member Board of Directors, which included two outside directors and the firm's largest shareholders (Exhibit 3). However, the Board's involvement in IPL's operations was limited to a quarterly review of the firm's performance and to formal ratification of the broad strategic orientations proposed by the management committee.

IPL's organization was characterized by a strong emphasis on informality, collegiality, and consensus decision-making. The firm's executives believed these traits helped preserve IPL's family atmosphere and supported innovativeness, entrepreneurship, and teamwork. According to them, this atmosphere represented one of the major factors in the firm's success.

Strategy and Objectives

IPL specialized in the design, manufacture, printing and marketing of plastic products, mainly intended for industrial uses, and made of thermoplastic resins through injection molding. Except for a very limited amount of extrusion molding, the firm was not involved in any other molding process, like blow molding or thermoforming. Furthermore, IPL's policies had traditionally emphasized proprietary products rather than custom molding.

In addition to product mix, IPL distinguished itself from competitors through its emphasis on better quality and performance products, superior engineering and service, innovativeness and the capacity to meet customers' specific needs. According to François Béchard, IPL's success was based on "its ability to sell differentiated products at higher prices while cutting production costs through automation." IPL's executives also emphasized the importance of profitability rather than merely growth. As noted by Béchard, "we learned from the economic downturn in 1982 that it was prudent to maintain a working capital ratio of 2:1, and to keep our debt-to-equity ratio between 0.3 and 0.6. Although these objectives may slow down our growth somewhat, they allow us to keep our balance sheet very sound." IPL's objectives also included an annual growth in sales of 10%, a gross margin of 30%, a net profit after tax ratio of 6%, and the distribution of 25% of net profits in dividends (Exhibits 4 and 5 contain IPL's financial statements).

Products and Markets

With more than 600 products whose similarities were often limited to their manufacturing process, IPL viewed itself as a diversified producer of injection molded products (Exhibit 6). IPL's principal geographic markets stretched across Eastern Canada, from the Maritimes to Ontario, and into the northeastern U.S. In 1987, the Quebec market represented 47% of sales while the U.S., Ontario and Maritimes markets accounted for 25%, 19% and 9% of sales, respectively.

Pails and containers were IPL's largest and most profitable product line; they also accounted for almost all of the company's non-automotive sales outside Quebec. With capacities ranging from 1.4 to 130 litres, IPL offered a wider line of industrial and institutional pails and containers than any other Canadian producer. IPL also had the equipment and expertise for high quality printing of as many as five colours onto containers, a competence seldom found in the industrial container business but which was becoming an increasingly important criterion for selecting suppliers. Except for a handful of large food industry firms, IPL's customers were small- and medium-sized firms that were dissatisfied with the narrow choice of sizes offered by competitors. The customers were mostly in the food processing, chemical and construction industries, and used IPL's containers for a variety of goods, ranging from fruits and cement to chlorine for swimming pools.

In recent years, IPL continued to expand their product line. In 1985, a new line of pails and containers licensed for the Canadian market from the Danish firm Superfos, was marketed under the Flex-Off brand name. With 1987 sales of $2.5 million, these products appeared to have substantial growth potential. In 1987, IPL acquired the plastics division of Edmunston Paper Box Ltd. (EPB), located in Edmunston, New Brunswick, for $4 million. EPB's line of small-size, thin-wall containers for the food processing industry, including margarine, yogurt and ice-cream containers with capacities under 5 litres, complemented IPL's line of larger pails and containers. EPB's products were expected to achieve considerable sales growth, particularly in Quebec and Ontario, because of increased penetration provided by IPL's larger distribution network.

Due to the firm's capacity to meet specific customer needs, as well as the reliability and quality of its products, IPL's pails and containers were priced an average of 5% above competition. Historically, competition in the Canadian market had been moderate, mainly because it was divided among a small number of regional producers and no national company had yet emerged. With each producer dominating their own immediate market, as was the case for IPL in the Quebec market, there had been little incentive for firms to compete on price. However, this situation had begun to change in recent years, with a wave of acquisitions and the increasing presence of American competitors taking advantage of their larger scale of operations. Indeed, IPL was one of the few independent companies left in the Canadian industrial plastic containers business.

IPL's second largest product line was composed of two main types of material handling products. For the Government of Quebec, IPL manufactured rigid-wall, multi-cavity containers used in forest seedling production. With their supply contract ending in 1988, IPL was looking for new markets for this product. However, increasing concerns regarding the effectiveness of paper pots, the major substitute product, suggested that future market prospects for plastic seedling containers were substantial. On the other hand, IPL's carriers for soft drink bottles and milk containers had confronted increasing competition in recent years. Most users of these products had filled their "pipelines", and only replacement production would be needed in the future. In response, IPL was considering introducing related products into the Quebec market, such as European-designed beverage cases for the brewing industry, mobile bins for automated domestic garbage collection, and a line of material handling boxes.

Like most plastic processors, IPL devoted a portion of its operations to custom molding. Every year, IPL was involved in several small development projects for custom molded products intended for such industries as lobster fishing, furniture, or defense. Most of these projects resulted from unsolicited requests from companies looking for products meeting very particular requirements or applications. Currently, the major portion of these activities was related to automotive products molded for Ford.

IPL also manufactured a wide variety of plastic housewares like chopping boards, mixing bowls, wine racks, garbage cans, and chairs. The housewares line had been declining in relative importance, however, because it was perceived to be inconsistent with IPL's strategic focus. Opportunities in that segment were limited, especially since distribution channels were dominated by large housewares firms like Rubbermaid and Sterilite. IPL also produced a plastic-made system for gathering maple sap, the raw material for maple syrup. Quebec pro-

duced 70% of the world's maple syrup, a crop worth over $50 million annually
to sap producers. IPL dominated the North American market for these systems and no significant competition was perceived to exist.

Marketing and Distribution

For sale and distribution of products to its 2 000 customers, IPL operated
regional sales offices and warehouses in Montreal (Quebec), Toronto (Ontario),
and Moncton (New Brunswick), as well as subsidiaries in Edmundston (New
Brunswick) and Boston (Massachusetts). IPL's Canadian sales force, which
included 12 salespeople and 6 manufacturers' representatives, had traditionally
handled both the industrial containers and the material handling product lines.
However, because of a commission system based on total sales volume, salespeople had tended to place greater emphasis on high turnover items such as
pails. As a result, in 1988 IPL hired 2 representatives exclusively for material
handling products. Eight additional representatives were responsible for sales
of the maple sap gathering systems, while housewares were under the responsibility of 2 distributors and 1 salesperson. Furthermore, the company employed
3 Boston-based representatives to sell pails and containers in the U.S.

IPL's salespeople were under the direct supervision of the sales manager and
they also interacted frequently with the product manager responsible for their
product line. IPL's 3 product managers were responsible for the planning and
development of their product lines and for customer service. They were essentially a communication and coordination link between the customers, the sales
force and the firm's other departments.

In the case of auto parts, sales were made through a Detroit-based manufacturing agent who received a commission on sales. Direct responsibility for this
business had traditionally been delegated to the former vice-president of marketing. However, since elimination of that position, the responsibility had been
assumed by the vice-president of R&D.

Human Resources

As stated in IPL's corporate objectives, human resources were viewed as a
major factor contributing to the firm's reputation for quality and innovativeness.
Thus, the firm placed fundamental importance on both the quality and aspirations of its 500 employees, 80% of whom were unionized production workers
affiliated with the Quebec Federation of Labour. IPL's commitment was evi-
denced by the $300 000 devoted annually to employee training, including the
opportunity to take English lessons at company expense. IPL had also maintained overall employment levels, despite extensive modernization and
automation of company facilities. The firm actively promoted participative management, including incentives for employee shareholding, and the creation of

quality circles and other management-labour committees to ensure effective communication between management and the employees. Due to these efforts, implementation of IPL's modernization program had been accomplished without major resistance to change, and management viewed their relations with labour as excellent.

IPL was one of the few Canadian plastics firms to have established an in-house training centre to overcome chronic shortages of skilled labour in the plastics industry. As one IPL executive said, "This centre permits the training of excellent workers whose qualifications satisfy our needs. Yet, just as important, it also makes the workers more sensitive to IPL's culture and helps to preserve our firm's special, family-like work atmosphere." The firm's atmosphere could indeed be characterized as familial, with many employees being related among themselves or with executives. Traditional Quebec family names such as Chabot or Mercier were common throughout the firm. About 50% of the employees lived in Saint-Damien, with the remainder coming from nearby rural communities.

The firm also maintained strong community involvement. Besides being the largest single employer in an area dominated by small farms, forestry, fishing and hunting, IPL contributed as much as $150 000 annually for local charities, sports facilities and the Métivier arena. Moreover, the Métivier brothers had always tried to concentrate IPL's activities in Saint-Damien in recognition of the local population's continuing support.

Manufacturing and Technology

Industry specialists considered IPL's production facilities in Saint-Damien to be among the most modern in North America. For example, a leading plastics industry journal talked about "IPL's factory of the future" and asserted that "no other manufacturer in Canada has gone further into true CIM (Computer Integrated Manufacturing) than IPL."[1] Visitors were often astonished to find these ultra-modern facilities within a rural village of 2 300 inhabitants.

IPL's position as one of the industry's technological leaders was a direct result of the $24 million invested since 1985 as part of the "IPL 1990" program. Most of that investment had been used for the 1986 construction of new production facilities equipped with the most advanced technologies available, including computer numerical control injection molding machines, robots, automated guided vehicles for moving materials around the plant floor, CAD/CAM systems, and MRP II. This new plant had been built as an extension of IPL's existing facilities, resulting in some disturbance to the firm's operations during construction.

---

[1] "Closing the loop," *Canadian Plastics*, June 1988, p.46, and "CIM pays off for Canadian custom molders," *Canadian Plastics*, May 1987, p.24.

IPL's investment in technology allowed them to considerably reduce the gap between their production costs and those associated with large-scale production, while simultaneously maintaining manufacturing flexibility. Furthermore, IPL's facilities operated on a continuous, 24 hours a day, 7 days a week basis, compared to the single shift, 5 days a week schedule typical in the industry. The company was thus able to achieve higher production volumes, which permitted more rapid amortization of equipment and enhanced the feasibility of continued investment in new technologies. The benefits from IPL's substantial investments in production facilities were readily apparent: in 1987, the first full year of operations within the new facilities, total productivity (the amount, in kilograms, of plastic molded per worker) had increased by 15%, inventories had been reduced by 33%, the average changeover time for a mold was cut from 2–3 hours to 10–15 minutes, the rejection rate for finished goods had fallen from 12% to 3%, and the product return rate had declined to almost zero. IPL's achievements in quality control were recognized in 1988 when the firm received the prestigious Mercure award for Total Quality from the Quebec Board of Trade. However, sales growth had been unable to keep up with IPL's rapid and substantial increases in productivity and production capacity. Consequently, the production capacity utilization rate had declined to 72% in early 1988.

IPL's investment in R&D, at 2% of sales, was more than twice the plastics industry average. The 15-person R&D department was responsible for continued automation of production, development of new products, and joint research with European companies, Ford, and universities and other research centres.

IPL'S INVOLVEMENT IN CUSTOM MOLDING

Due to the fluctuating nature of demand, as well as price sensitivity traditionally associated with custom molding, IPL had historically limited its involvement in this activity to 15% of total sales. However, this percentage had been raised to 25% when Benoît Métivier was CEO. The appearance of high-volume markets for custom molding, particularly in the auto industry, had encouraged this change. Collaboration with Ford represented a unique opportunity to enter a market offering rapid growth and profit potential, while capitalizing on IPL's skills in high-quality injection molding. Business with Ford was facilitated by the rapid accreditation of IPL's St. Damien plant as a Q-1 supplier in 1984, making them the first Canadian injection molder to receive that rating. Within the next year, IPL also expected the St. Damien facility to become the first plastics plant in Canada to receive Ford's TQE accreditation.

IPL's sales to Ford had risen from $300 000 in 1984 to $7 million in 1987, and they were expected to exceed $8 million in 1988. IPL had also become more than a mere custom molder for Ford. Initially, IPL had focused on production of non-visible internal parts, like bushings of car door opening mechanisms or internal dashboard parts. Ford considered these parts to be critical because they could involve, in the case of breakage or wear, repairs many times more expensive than their initial costs. Later, IPL began manufacturing visible parts, like external components of dashboards, in which product appearance was also of critical importance. In 1987, the firm became Ford's North American supplier for several visible parts, including air deflectors and steering wheel shrouds. Nevertheless, IPL had remained very selective about which parts it manufactured, and had limited its activities to a small number of high-volume parts.

FORD'S OFFER

For the last 18 months, IPL had been one of two North American firms developing visible, imitation leather parts for Ford's new world car planned to replace the Escort in 1990. Ford had recently offered IPL a five-year contract, beginning in spring 1989 and worth an estimated $10 million annually, for supply of these parts. As with other Ford contracts, the order volume was not guaranteed, but would depend on the sales volume of Ford's cars. All orders would be shipped F.O.B. to Ford's Detroit assembly plants from IPL's Saint-Damien facility. The contract's terms appeared to allow IPL a level of profitability equivalent to the industry's average, but included clauses permitting Ford to withdraw its business at any time and required price reductions of 5% annually, except for uncontrollable cost increases like resin prices. The contract would be in addition to existing business done with Ford, and could thus raise IPL's annual sales to that company to $18 million by 1990. Furthermore, the contract could be executed with IPL's current production capacity and with new equipment already on order. IPL had to respond to Ford's offer within the next month.

MANAGERS' ATTITUDES TOWARD THE AUTO PARTS BUSINESS

Involvement in the auto parts market had often been a source of disagreement among IPL's managers. In recent months, this issue had assumed renewed importance with the possibility of further growth of sales to Ford and, thus, of increasing IPL's reliance on custom molded products. Many IPL executives felt that the custom molding business was not sufficiently profitable, given the risks it usually involved. Initial indications were that the profitability of the recent Ford offer would be similar to or lower than IPL's earlier business, because of the required 5% annual reduction in prices. In addition, some concerns were voiced regarding IPL's increasing dependence on a single, much larger customer. IPL's managers clearly remembered the firm's previous experiences with custom molding. In the early 1970s, IPL had produced a large volume of custom molded products for another major transportation firm. However, IPL lost 25% of its sales volume overnight when that customer moved manufacturing in-house. These memories had been revived by rumors that auto-makers had recently placed orders for large injection molding machinery.

Julien Métivier felt that the automobile market could represent a lucrative opportunity if IPL was able to maintain a good margin on these products and to expand its customer base. However, he was not ruling out increased emphasis on IPL's other product lines, including rejuvenation of the housewares line with the introduction of new products related to gardening. IPL projected sales of up to $2 million in plant pots and plastic patio furniture within two years of the products' introduction.

Both Clément Métivier and Fernand Mercier, respectively IPL's Treasurer and V.P.–Administration, agreed with their CEO that IPL should expand its auto parts business, but only if expansion could be done in a controlled manner. However, they believed that it would soon become difficult to limit IPL's involvement in custom molding to 25% of sales. For them, as well as for several other managers, IPL appeared to have no choice but to eventually create an independent division to exclusively handle this business. However, it was still uncertain how this change could be implemented, due to production and marketing complexities associated with this move.

"IPL cannot afford *not* to be in the automobile parts market," asserted Jean-Marie Chabot, IPL's V.P.–R&D. According to him, all major advances in knowledge in the plastics industry came from work in the auto and aerospace industries. The auto parts market could thus be a priceless source of know-how if IPL was able to develop lasting relationships with auto-makers. He also felt that the auto firms' increasing emphasis on quality rather than just price was consistent with IPL's capabilities. Moreover, IPL was one of the few Canadian firms experienced in the use of the large machinery required for the molding of many automotive parts.

Without denying the benefits of cooperation with Ford in terms of sales and know-how, other executives were less supportive of an expansion of that business. They instead strongly favoured the development of proprietary products. Rémi Métivier, IPL's Chairman, felt that "IPL should at least stick to its 25% policy or further reduce its activities in custom molding and instead focus on the development of proprietary products, especially material handling products." IPL's sales forecasts for most material handling products were excellent. This was particularly the case for recycling boxes, already introduced in the market and whose sales were projected to reach $16 million within five years. IPL was also considering the development of mobile bins for domestic garbage collection, a product that within ten years could represent a potential $200 million market in Quebec alone. Nevertheless, extensive growth of these markets depended on municipal and provincial governments' willingness to adopt this technology of garbage collection on a large scale. Competition in the recycling box and mobile bins segments was also expected to be intense, as many companies had already entered or were expected to do so in the near future. In addition, with cooperation of a West German firm, IPL was developing beverage cases for the brewing industry to replace the traditional cardboard cases. However, IPL had been experiencing some difficulty selling the concept to the major breweries.

François Béchard, V.P.–Finance, also felt IPL should try to limit its vulnerability in the competitive auto parts business, consistent with the approach taken by large plastics firms like Rubbermaid, Scepter and Shaeffer. According to Béchard, IPL should instead take advantage of the proposed Canada-U.S. Free Trade Agreement, and work on increasing penetration of its proprietary products in the U.S. market, but this time with products adapted to the needs of American customers. In many instances, IPL's products had been judged too expensive, inadequate because of their metric sizes, or overengineered for the highly competitive and price sensitive U.S. market. Such problems helped explain why IPL's American subsidiary had been experiencing chronic deficits that reached $300 000 in 1987. As a result, IPL was currently considering investment of over $300 000 in molds for a five-gallon size pail. At a price of $4, management believed IPL could sell more than one million of these pails in Canada and an additional 750 000 south of the border. Because of lower prices in the U.S. market and competition of larger American firms already producing this type of container, margins in that market were expected to be less than half those of the Canadian market. However, IPL management believed this tradeoff was necessary in order to strengthen its U.S. market position.

Along the same lines, several managers suggested that IPL should have manufacturing facilities rather than merely a sales office in the Boston area. IPL was contemplating acquisition of a small U.S. manufacturer of high-quality industrial containers, or small-scale manufacturing of certain products in its U.S. facilities, in order to reduce tariff and transportation costs.

CONCLUSION

In light of the divergence in opinions among his managers, Julien Métivier knew it would be difficult to build a consensus around a particular alternative. However, within the next month, IPL had to respond to Ford's recent contract offer as well as deciding on several other projects the firm was considering. In making these decisions, Julien wanted to avoid major disagreements among IPL's executives and unnecessary threats to the company's successful strategy. He wondered what direction he should move the company and how he should proceed.

EXHIBIT 1   IPL Organization Chart

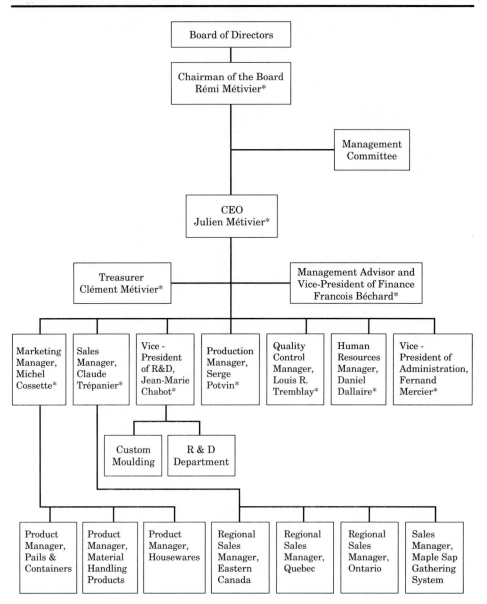

*Members of the management committee.

EXHIBIT 2   Personal Data on IPL's Key Managers as of April 1988

Name	Age	Position	Years with IPL	Background
Rémi Métivier*	54	Chairman of the Board	34	High school education; undergraduate courses in business (Laval University).
Julien Métivier*	50	Chief Executive Officer	28	Master in Commerce (Laval University)
Clément Métivier*	53	Treasurer	32	High School education; involved in costing system issues.
Benoît Métivier	51	Director	31	High school education; resigned as CEO in 1986.
François Béchard*	48	Vice-President of Finance and Secretary	20	MBA (Western); consultant; devoting 4 days/week to IPL from his Quebec City office.
Fernand Mercier*	47	Vice-President of Administration	33	High school education
Jean-Marie Chabot*	43	Vice-President of R&D	20	B. Engineering (Laval University)
Serge Potvin	34	Production Manager	9	B. Engineering (Chicoutimi)
Claude Trépanier	52	Sales Manager	9	High school education; working with plastic companies such as Alibert and Vulcan for 20 years; left IPL between August 1987 and February 1988 to assume general management position at Anchor Plastics Inc.
Louis R. Tremblay	30	Quality Control Manager	6	B. Engineering (Chicourimi)
Daniel Dallaire	33	Human Resources	2	B.B.A. (Sherbrooke); personnel agent and human resources manager with Securities Desjardins between 1981 and 1986.
Michel Cossette	37	Marketing Manager	0.5	B.Sc (UQAM); different sales and marketing positions at IBM for 11 years and LGS Inc. for 3 years.
Paul-Henri Fillion*	60	Director	1	President, Hoblab Inc.; ex-President of the Groupement Québécois d'Enterprises.
Jean-Paul Lortie	60	Director	3	President and CEO, Sico Inc.

*Members of IPL's Board of Directors.

EXHIBIT 3 IPL Major Shareholders

Métivier brothers	76%
IPL vice-presidents	2148
Total[2]	100%

[1] About 60% of IPL's employees were shareholders.

[2] At the end of 1987, IPL announced its intention to repurchase 300 000 shares, or about 4.5% of the outstanding common shares. The main objective of this stock buy-back was to take advantage of the low price of IPL's stock. Following the decline of the stock indexes since October 1987, IPL's stock had dropped to $3, compared to an historic high of $12 in 1986. In April 1988, IPL stock was traded at $3.85.

EXHIBIT 4 IPL Consolidated Income Statement ($000)

	1987	1986	1985	1984	1983	1982	1981	1980
Sales	$48 409	$37 433	$36 719	$30 290	$25 318	$23 803	$23 882	$21 110
Cost of sales	34 808	27 762	25 788	21 646	17 524	17 184	17 593	14 731
Gross margin	13 601	9 671	10 931	8 644	7 794	6 619	6 289	6 379
Expenses								
Selling	5 528	4 595	4 265	3 202	2 790	2 981	3 068	2 594
Administrative	3 823	3 258	2 968	2 730	2 404	2 580	2 487	1 897
Financial	1 192	739	693	407	561	724	513	275
Total expenses	10 543	8 592	7 926	6 339	5 755	6 285	6 068	4 766
Operating profit	3 058	1 079	3 005	2 305	2039	334	221	1 613
Gain (loss on disposal of fixed assets	(41)	418	86					
Amortization of deferred grants	776	491	365					
Other revenue	278	518	258	314	510	132	129	207
Income before income taxes	4 071	2 506	3 714	2 619	2 549	466	350	1 820
Income taxes	1 581	1 014	1 243	977	913	131	218	762
Net income	$2 472	$1 492	$2 471	$1 642	$1 636	$335	$132	$1 058
Earnings per share	$0.37	$0.23	$0.45	$0.30	$0.30	$0.06	$0.02	$0.20
Stock price: High	9.50	12.00	7.625					
Low	3.00	6.00	5.75					

EXHIBIT 5   IPL Consolidated Balance Sheet ($000)

	1987	1986	1985	1984	1983
Assets					
Current assets					
Cash	$1 205	$ —	$ —	$ —	$183
Trade and other debtors	6 759	5 613	5 340	3 780	4 409
Inventories	6 489	5 366	4 532	4 629	3 381
Grant receivable	454	1 215	286	585	68
Income Taxes recoverable	400	1 562	—	—	—
Prepaid expenses	101	35	—	29	59
Total current assets	15 407	13 791	10 158	9 023	8 100
Long-term assets	24 575	20 264	11 357	7 095	5 997
Fixed assets	227	266	218	126	12
Balance of sale price of fixed assets	115	175	—	—	—
Deferred charges	1 049	1 052	684	209	131
Total long-term assets	26 966	21 757	12 259	7 430	6 130
Total assets	$41 662	$35 548	$22 417	$16 453	$14 240
Liabilities					
Current liabilities					
Bank loan and overdraft	—	700	1 182	162	—
Trade and accrued liabilities	4 492	3 864	3 749	2 706	2 501
Income taxes	—	—	186	91	533
Current portion, LT debt	1 605	1 300	400	1 254	912
Total current liabilities	6 097	5 864	5 577	4 213	3 946
Long-term liabilities					
Long-term debt	9 765	7 708	4 133	3 569	3 020
Deferred income taxes	3 377	2 626	1 883	1 649	1 545
Deferred grants	3 787	3 391	1 660	—	—
Total LT liabilities	16 929	13 725	7 676	5 218	4 565
Minority interest					
Equity					
Capital stock	6 828	6 254	323	82	18
Contributed surplus	—	—	—	294	294
Retained earnings	11 578	9 705	8 901	6 646	5 417
Total equity	18 406	15 959	9 224	7 022	5 729
Total liabilities and equity	$41 662	$35 548	$22 417	$16 453	$14 240

EXHIBIT 6 IPL's Product Mix, 1987

Product Lines	Products	Percent of Sales	Contribution Margin
Pails and containers	General-purpose pails	23%	Above the firm's average
	Flex-Off pails and containers	5	
	Margarine and fish containers	10	
	Thin-wall containers	4	
Material handling	Forest seedling containers	15	Equivalent to firm's average
	Beverage cases	8	
Custom molding	Auto parts (Ford)	16	Below the firm's average
	Other	9	
Housewares	Chopping boards, mixing bowls, wine racks, garbage cans, chairs, etc.	5	Equivalent to firm's average
Maple-sap gathering systems	—	5	Above the firm's average

COOPER CANADA LIMITED

Donald H. Thain

In late 1982 CCM Canada, a manufacturer of bicycles, skates and hockey equipment, was put into receivership and the business put up for sale. While CCM's competitors had noted the company's accumulating problems with some satisfaction and relief, they were now faced with new questions: Who would acquire the assets of CCM? What would be the impact on the competitive structure of the industry?

In the meantime, the CCM receiver was pressing for action. John Cooper, vice chairman of Cooper Canada Ltd., one of the interested competitors, described the situation:

> Our people visited the CCM plant and offices last week and they had no sooner returned than the receiver called wanting to know how soon we could make a bid. He said that speed is critical because he expects other bids at any moment and that the creditors want action since CCM's situation worsens every day. We will have to act fast . . . we have a meeting set for next Monday to make an offer if we want to. It is too bad we are under such time pressure but that's the way this deal is.

Cooper was interested only in the skate and hockey equipment part of the CCM business. Here, some elements of the fit between Cooper and CCM's winter goods business were obvious. Cooper could completely outfit a hockey player except for sweaters and skates. CCM's skate line was still one of the most respected in the business. The value of CCM's competing lines of hockey sticks and protective equipment, however, was less clear. The bicycle line was of no interest but Cooper had made arrangements with another prospective buyer to pick up this part of the CCM operation in a joint bid. The question facing Cooper management, under time pressure, was whether they wished to proceed with their side of a bid and, if so, with what price and conditions?

THE SKATE AND HOCKEY EQUIPMENT INDUSTRY

There were four basic product lines in the industry: skates, protective equipment (e.g., helmets, gloves, pads) sticks and apparel. Cooper management estimated the industry's 1981 value of shipments for these lines were as follows:

	($000)
Ice skates	78 000
Hockey equipment	31 500
Hockey sticks	29 000
Apparel	27 000

The overall demand for hockey related products had grown slowly in the 1970s and little or no growth was expected in the 1980s. Population trends in the prime hockey-playing age groups were not favourable and participation rates were under pressure. A major problem with participation was the increasing cost of equipping a player: from $100 to $200 for beginners including used equipment and up to $1500 for a professional.

The rapidly changing technology of hockey equipment was one reason for the high cost of equipment. Product innovation was driving toward lighter, safer and more comfortable gear. As a 1982 article in the Maple Leaf Gardens program described it:

> Space-age hockey equipment is speeding up the game and cutting down on injuries. Technological breakthroughs are sending the NHL where it has never gone before—to lighter, cooler, stronger, tighter-fitting one-piece body protection; aluminum or fibreglass and plastic laminated sticks; and zircon-guarded, carbon-bladed skates encased in ballistic and nylon-wrapped boots.
>
> Leaf trainer Danny Lemelin thinks skates have ``changed most dramatically" in the past few years. He points out that most are four ounces lighter because of the plastic blade holder and nylon boot. This space-age equipment has speeded up the game and cut down on injuries. And, it's made the felt and fibre shin, shoulder, elbow and pant pads, one-piece ash sticks and leather tube skates, so popular only a decade ago, obsolete...
>
> The evolution turned revolution in NHL gear is the by-product of by-products. New foams, plastics, nylon and fibreglass, (many invented in Korea during the fifties to keep fighting forces warm and protected) have made things "lighter and stronger," says one long time equipment manufacturer. All these new inventions have been developed to conform to the game of hockey ...

Canadian brands had established an international reputation for product excellence, and exports of hockey equipment had increased from $20 million in 1971 to $41.5 million in 1980. Skates represented the largest export product. The United States was the largest market, but Scandinavia and western Europe were also strong. Japan and Australia were newly developing markets.

The market shares of the major competitors in the industry by-product line are given in Exhibit 1. The skate business was dominated by three firms, Warrington Industries Ltd. (with three brands—Bauer, Lange and Micron), CCM and Daoust. Cooper was the primary company in hockey equipment. The stick business was shared by half a dozen significant competitors, of which the largest was Sherwood-Drolet. Cooper and Sport Maska were the two most significant competitors in apparel. A brief description of the companies that Cooper considered interested and capable of bidding for CCM is given in Appendix A.

Skates

The demand for skates in Canada had for several years fluctuated between 1 and 1.3 million pairs. There were two basic types of skate boots, sewn and molded. Leather had been the first boot material and was still used in most high quality, high-priced skates. Over 90% of NHL players wore leather skates.

However, in the 1970s molded boots had entered the market and in the low priced market particularly had become competitive with leather booted skates.

Information on the total Canadian hockey-skate market and the shares of major competitors segmented by sewn and molded boots is presented in Exhibit 2. Hockey skates could also be segmented by price point as follows:

Range	Retail Price	1982 Estimated Share (units)
High	More than $200	15%
Medium	$120–$180	20%
Low	Less than $90	65%

Industry observers noted that the high- and low-end market shares were increasing and the medium range decreasing. The breakdown of CCM's total unit skate sales in the high, medium and low price ranges was approximately 60%, 25% and 15% respectively and that of Bauer, the largest brand, was thought to be 20%, 30% and 50% respectively.

Skate blades were another factor in the market. They were available from three sources in Canada. The largest manufacturer, the St. Lawrence company of Montreal, sold mainly to CCM and Daoust. Canpro Ltd., owned by Warrington, sold mainly to Bauer, Micron and Lange. CCM manufactured their own Tuuk blades and sold some to other skate makers. While blade technology had changed significantly in the late 1970s with the introduction of plastic mounts to replace tubes, the major current change was the trend back to carbon steel from the newer stainless steel.

Hockey Equipment

Hockey equipment included all items on the list shown in Table 1, which also shows the range of typical retail prices. Continuous research and development was necessary to ensure that these items provided maximum protection and comfort. Cooper dominated the market with a 69% share.

TABLE 1 Price Ranges for Hockey Equipment

	Typical Retail Price Range	
Item	*Men's*	*Boys'*
Pants	$40–130	$30–60
Gloves	50–140	25–70
Helmet	27–45	27–45
Cooperall	115–125	98
Shin pads	20–75	20–75
Elbow pads	19–50	7–25
Shoulder pads	25–70	14–40

Sticks

The composition of sticks was continually changing. What had started out as a one-piece blade and handle developed into a two-piece solid-wood handle and blade, and later a laminated handle and curved blade with fibreglass reinforcement. The most recent development was an aluminum handle with a replaceable wooden blade. Changes were intended to improve strength and passing and shooting accuracy. Sherwood-Drolet led in this market with a 25% share.

Apparel

Differences in prices of sweaters and socks were due basically to the material used in the product. The most popular sweater materials were polyester and cotton knits because of their strength and lightness. Designs of sweaters were fairly standard, with lettering and cresting done separately. Socks were a standard product with little differentiation. Sport Maska controlled 42% of this market because of its quality product, excellent distribution, and good rapport with dealers.

Distribution

Skates and hockey equipment were sold in a wide range of retail outlets including specialty, independent, department, discount, chain and catalogue stores. Although specific numbers were not available, the split of business between these outlets followed a common retail pattern. The specialty independents and chains dominated in the higher priced items where product knowledge and service were essential. The mass merchandisers were dominant in the lower priced product areas.

In Canada the most common route from manufacturer to retailer was through distributors who used sales agents. Manufacturers wanted agents who would represent their product aggressively, seek out new orders and provide them with market feedback. Usually these agents either were, or had been, actively involved in sports. However, since the agents sold multiple lines, it was difficult to control their activities and level and mix of sales. Most companies used a sales force of 10 to 12 reps to cover most of Canada. A few small companies utilized wholesalers to supplement their sales force.

Retail outlets had experienced little real growth in sales and were finding themselves with increasing inventories. Therefore, retailers started carrying shallower stocks, ordering more frequently and relying on manufacturers or distributors to provide back-up inventories. This trend meant that bargaining power had shifted from the manufacturers to the retailers, who were trying to gain volume discounts and delivery advantages by reducing the number of suppliers.

Promotion

Three types of promotion were used: company and product promotion, media advertising, and trade show participation. Product and image promotion seemed to be the most effective avenue for stimulating sales. Because professional players set industry trends it was important to get popular players to use and endorse products. To recruit these players, professional "detail men" from sports equipment manufacturers were assigned to players to make sure their equipment fit perfectly and that the player was loyal to the brand. It was also important to get as many players as possible wearing the products so that the brand name would enjoy good exposure during televised games. Therefore, the detail men also tried to work through team trainers to supply most of the team with the brand. While some competitors used financial incentives to push a product, Cooper relied on high quality, fast service in fitting and repairs and intensive sales efforts, and was not involved with special deals or endorsement contracts.

Media advertising was primarily confined to the larger firms. Print advertising in the concentrated population areas was the most common approach.

Trade shows significantly influenced retail buyers. Many sales took place at the shows, bookings were made for orders and sales were made on follow-up calls by sales reps. The Canadian Sporting Goods Association organized two shows annually.

COOPER CANADA

In 1946, Jack Cooper left Eaton's to join General Leather Goods Ltd., as its first and, until 1951, only salesperson. Subsequently, Cooper and Cecil Weeks bought out the company's original owner and changed the name to Cooper-

Weeks. In 1954, Cooper acquired Cecil Weeks' interest and the company became the exclusive Canadian manufacturer of Buxton Leather goods. In the following years the company grew through internal development and acquisitions to encompass a wide range of leather and sporting good products. In 1970, the company changed its name to Cooper Canada Ltd. and went public. By 1981, revenues were almost $63 million, but Cooper experienced its first loss in years. Cooper management expected a return to profitability in 1982 in spite of a recession and high interest rates. Financial statements for Cooper Canada from 1977 through 1981 are presented in Exhibits 3 and 4.

In 1982 Cooper was engaged in two major lines of business; sporting goods (hockey equipment, apparel, golf bags, baseball gloves, inflated goods, etc.) and leather goods and finishing (wallets, carrying bags, etc.). The relative scale and performance of these businesses is illustrated in Table 2. Cooper also had a significant sales and distribution operation in the United States as indicated by the geographic segmentation of the business in Table 2.

TABLE 2   Cooper Canada Revenues and Profits by Business Segment, 1981 ($000s)

	Industry Segments		
	Sporting Goods	*Leather Goods & Finishing*	*Consolidated*
Revenue	$46 913	$16 076	62 827
Operating profit	7 434	1 678	8 939
Identifiable assets	28 703	8 001	40 870*
	Geographic Segments		
	Canada	*United States*	*Consolidated*
Revenue	57 122	11 321	62 827
Operating profit	7 823	1 289	8 939
Identifiable assets	30 403	6 301	40 870*

* Includes corporate assets of $4 549.

Management Goals

Jack Cooper, "the chief," and his two sons, John and Don's[1] owned 82% of the company's outstanding common stock. Jack Cooper, who retained voting control, was chairman and chief executive officer and Henry Nolting was president and

---

[1] Don, who had managed the leather goods division for several years, left the company in 1980 and started a women's sportswear retailing company. He remained a director.

chief operating officer. John Cooper was vice chairman and deputy chief executive officer. They worked closely together, meeting for frequent discussions daily. The company's organization is shown in Exhibit 5.

Management's immediate concerns were to increase sales and margins; to implement a badly-needed information system; to strengthen control activities in marketing, production, and finance; to reduce short-term bank debt and high-interest expenses; to bring the leather goods division from a loss to a profit; and to iron out troublesome technical and production problems in J.B. Foam, a manufacturer of plastic foam pads and products that had recently been purchased and moved to Cooper's Toronto plant.

Long-term goals called for further development of sporting goods to increase growth and utilize the great strengths of the Cooper name. Additions to the product line were sought through new product development and/or acquisition. Cooper was also developing more export markets for its sporting goods products.

Performance

Growth had always been foremost among Jack Cooper's goals. Sales had increased continuously since 1969, except in 1975. However, earnings had fluctuated widely over the same period. Earnings dropped in 1979 because of problems in absorbing the purchase of Winnwell Sports. And in 1981, high interest rates, the recession and the disposal of Cooper's unsuccessful production operations in Barbados all hurt the bottom line. However, interim 1982 figures indicated much stronger performance. Although there was little growth in sales, tight inventory and cost controls implemented by Henry Nolting had helped to increase earnings.

Marketing

Cooper products covered a wide range of quality and price points. In hockey equipment, for example, the Cooper line ranged from high end items, used by top professional teams around the world, to medium-low for the beginning player. In baseball equipment and supplies, the quality and price covered a medium-high to low range, appealing to younger and more experienced players, but not professionals.

Hockey equipment was the company's major line and future growth area. To keep its competitive edge, Cooper employed eight people to work full time on product development, with a priority on hockey products. The aim was product leadership, giving athletes the best possible effectiveness and protection. An example of the product development work was Cooper's latest product, the Cooperall, an elasticized body garment which held all the protective pads in place. Cooperalls represented a major innovation and had given Cooper a clear lead on competitors who were currently trying to copy the product.

Distribution of Cooper goods was through its 25-person sales force, which provided the most extensive national coverage of any company in the industry. Sales reps were organized on a geographic basis and were paid on a salary-plus-bonus-minus-expenses system, with no upper limit on bonuses. The total customer base was around 1 600. Because Cooper and CCM had been competitive across a wide product line and Cooper accounts usually sold Bauer skates, significant overlap of Cooper and CCM accounts was not extensive. Sales were distributed equally throughout the East, Ontario, and the West. National coverage by its own sales force gave Cooper an advantage over its competitors, few of whom had such coverage. However, a concern was that 90% of sales were made to 20% of accounts and almost 40% of sales were made to only 20 major customers.

Cliff Gabel, executive vice president, sporting goods reported that the sales force was enthusiastic about adding skates to their line. While no one in the Cooper organization had any in-depth experience in the skate business, Mr. Gabel, who was widely known and highly respected in the industry, had maintained a good relationship with several key marketing managers at CCM, some of whom were now retired. He believed that one man in particular, who had an outstanding reputation as perhaps the "best skate man around," would welcome the opportunity to help Cooper take over and manage CCM should the opportunity arise. A respected and now retired manager from the Bauer Company who was a good friend of John Cooper was also thought to be available.

Cooper was the largest national advertiser in the sporting goods industry and had won awards for the quality of its television and print ads. The latest campaign had featured the Cooperall and was aired during the 1982 Stanley Cup telecasts.

Manufacturing and Distribution

Cooper had two manufacturing facilities. A plant in west Toronto did the bulk of the work but an older woodworking plant in Cambridge produced hockey sticks, baseball bats, and canoe paddles. Each facility manufactured hundreds of separate products that involved thousands of parts, requiring control procedures that were complex and numerous.

There was an excess of relatively expensive manufacturing space in the Toronto plant because it was built larger than necessary in 1976. In addition, several products, previously produced in Canada, had since been contracted to offshore manufacturers at lower costs. These manufacturers were primarily in the Orient and did contract work for most of Cooper's competitors. As a result, Cooper's designs were widely and easily copied by the other companies.

In distribution, Cooper chose to act as a "stockhouse," filling as many customer orders as possible on request. Speedy response was a major factor in maintaining customer loyalty. Cooper had a policy of providing a fill rate of

90% in non-peak seasons and 80% in peak seasons. This required substantial working capital, as Cooper's line encompassed over 12 000 stock-keeping units (SKU's). The sporting goods division carried 65% to 80% of the total company inventory. Sporting goods' finished goods inventory reached as high as $18 million each April for deliveries of fall lines. A company objective was to reduce year-end inventories from $23.7 million in 1981 to a more manageable $18 million by the end of 1982. One manager indicated that a recent reduction in the past company policy of producing 120% of forecast sales to a level of 100% of forecast sales would be a major factor in reducing inventory.

Information Systems

A monthly report of sales and gross profit for each SKU and product line was available to each product manager. Quarterly reports provided by cost accounting attempted to determine actual margins realized by each division on each product line. Product managers were also provided with a report on the inventory of each SKU. Product managers were expected to make decisions on pricing and provide input on production levels based on the information provided by these reports.

Product managers were evaluated on the basis of sales, market share, and product margins. The market share was expected to be maintained or increased to achieve sales growth. Product line margins were compared to the company average. However, a major argument of the department and product managers, particularly for leather goods, was that allocated overheads were not fair or accurate. The cost accounting department had struggled with this problem for years.

Financing

A bank operating loan and other term loans were the company's major sources of financing. Banking services for Canada were provided by the Canadian Imperial Bank of Commerce (CIBC) and for Cooper International by Marine Midland Bank of Buffalo, New York. The CIBC provided an operating loan to a maximum line of $16 million at 0.25% above prime and a term loan at 0.75% above prime to be paid in $1 million per year installments in the first five years and $2 million per year thereafter. The bank prime rate was currently 12% but had been as high as 20% in mid-1982.

A combination of high working capital requirements and high interest rates in the early 1980s had prompted Cooper to seek to minimize capital expenditures without adversely affecting manufacturing or productivity. The payback requirement approval of capital expenditures was 2.5 years or better. Typical annual capital expenditures were additions of new dyes and molds and the purchase of manufacturing equipment.

CCM

Incorporated in 1899 as the Canadian Cycle and Motor Company, CCM was Canada's oldest sporting goods manufacturer. Over its history, CCM had been engaged in three separate businesses; bicycles; automobiles; and skates, hockey sticks and equipment.

The skate business was entered in 1905 to even out the seasonal sales and production of bicycles. Originally CCM manufactured high quality blades and riveted them to the best available boots purchased from George Tackaberry of Brandon, Manitoba to make the skates used by virtually all professional and high-level amateur hockey players. Later, to fill out the line, it purchased lower quality boots from two small shoe companies in Quebec and its hockey equipment from other manufacturers. By 1967, all winter goods were manufactured by the company in what was then a large, modern, efficient plant, in St. Jean, Quebec.

Through industry-leading product innovation, CCM became the world's premier hockey skate manufacturer. For years, customers in Europe equated Canada with hockey and hockey with CCM.

Performance

Starting in 1961 CCM went through an unfortunate series of ownership and management changes. This resulted at various times in serious labour problems, in inadequate attention to marketing and distribution, and in general to a deterioration of the company's reputation for quality and service. Despite sales growth in recent years, profitability had been erratic and in 1982 devastatingly poor, since an operating loss of $4.3 million was expected.

The company's financial position, as at September 30, 1982, was summarized by the interim receiver as follows:

> CCM owes two secured creditors $33 million—the Royal Bank $28 million and the Enterprise Development Board $5 million—while the liquidation value of the company is $11.6 million less than its total debts of $41 million.
>
> Preferred creditors are owed $1.2 million and product liability claims amount to almost $13 million–$12 million of which rests on the resolution of a New York civil suit lodged by a hockey player who suffered an injury while wearing a CCM helmet.

The financial information available to Cooper on CCM's winter goods operation is presented in Exhibits 6 and 7.

Marketing

CCM's world-class strength was in leather skates. Like other leading skate manufacturers, CCM concentrated heavily on supplying skates to professional players because they were the trend setters. Three special pro detail men were employed to sell and service these players, who were often given custom-fitted skates free of charge.

Up to the mid-seventies, when it began to slide, CCM's share of the Canadian and worldwide hockey skate markets had been approximately 60%, 30% and 20% of the high, medium and low priced markets respectively. Because of its domination of the top end of the market, "Supertack," its long-established premium brand name was better known around the world than CCM. Although skate sales were the largest contributor to fixed costs, they declined from 68% of winter goods sales in 1980 to 58% in 1982. At the same time, protective equipment sales roughly doubled from 14% to 26%, with gross margins of 24%. Total gross margin as a percent of sales decreased from 27.8% in 1980 to 26.6% in 1982.

Distribution

From 1945 to 1982 CCM's dealer network had shrunk from 2 500 to 1 500 and its sales force from 21 to 12. All dealers sold the total CCM line but spent most of their time on winter goods. Up to 1970 the ales reps had been paid salary plus car and expenses and had been encouraged to service dealers and customers. However, industry sources reported that by 1982, the sales reps were strictly on a commission basis and, pressured to get orders through as many dealers as possible, spent little time on service.

Although CCM's reputation for service was suffering, its reputation for quality had been maintained fairly well. A quick survey of a few present or past CCM dealers in November 1982 indicated that approximately one third said they would never carry CCM again; one third would consider carrying CCM again if they could be assured of delivery and service; and one third would stick with CCM through thick and thin because they were enthusiastic about the product and the name.

Manufacturing

Early in November Henry Nolting, president, and Jerry Harder, vice president of manufacturing of Cooper Canada Ltd, visited CCM's winter goods plant in St. Jean. Following are excerpts from their reports on the visit:

> The woodworking facility is not modern, looks somewhat like lours as far as equipment and machinery are concerned, and it is not surprising that they do not turn a profit in that part of their operation. The roof in the stick-making facility is leaking and that part of their plant is badly maintained.
>
> The protective equipment manufacturing had nothing in it which we do not know, there is nothing innovative being done and, as far as I am concerned, it is worth very little.

The skate manufacturing operation seems reasonable despite the fact that there are no great innovations. The boot-making part is something which is easily transferable to our location, Jerry feels he would like to have it and can run it. The whole layout seems relatively simple but modern enough and efficient. The equipment is not new but in good repair.

The existing machine shop is old and dirty and there is nothing in it which I would like to buy. They have, at present, approximately 100 people working, but cleaning up work in process. The people are very slow, they seem to be puzzled, unenthusiastic and listless.

There seems to be a lot of old stock in the finished goods warehouse.

The major lasing machines are leased from United Shoe Machinery which is normal in this trade. They say they have 3 000 plus pairs o lasts (many are specials for individual players) at about $25 per pair. The lasts I saw were in very good repair.

The R&D department has two employees. They have had tremendous problems with their Propacs (copies of Cooperall) and are constantly trying to improve the product. They are working very closely with the Quebec Nordiques in perfecting this product. They have never done any helmet-related work at that facility.

We think their sporting goods division lost approximately half a million dollars each year, in '80 and '81, sharing equally in the total company loss of $4.3 million at end of September '82.

The offices are in terrible condition. They are old and in an unbelievable mess.

The president's assessment of the situation is that somebody will buy the assets and he feels that they might go for book value. His opinion is that nobody could pick it up for less.

Not counting raw material storage we would need at least 25 000 sq. ft., which excludes cutting, to accommodate the skate-making operation. This is equal to 42 of our present 600 sq. ft. bays. To give you another perspective, this area would be slightly larger than the whole area now devoted to apparel. Because of the size, we would have to do major relocations of our existing floors (in Toronto plant). Also, we must be careful of the existing electrical supplies— I would make a cautious estimate of a $25 000 rewiring charge.

Organization

As a result of natural attrition and dim prospects, the CCM organization had shrunk to skeleton status. While it was reportedly limping along, many of the best and most experienced managers had either retired or moved on to better opportunities.

DECIDING TO BID

In reviewing a list of possible bidders for CCM (Appendix A), John Cooper felt that the strongest competitive threats would be Warrington and Sport Maska. Both companies had strong management teams, well-established distribution systems and adequate financial strength. In addition, both companies were Canadian-owned and would not face possible delay and veto of their offer by the Foreign Investment Review Agency. Of further concern was the realization that the St. Jean plant represented up to 200 politically sensitive jobs and that the Quebec government might become involved directly or indirectly in the proceedings. Immediate decisions and actions were essential, however, if Cooper wanted to acquire CCM. Two questions puzzled John Cooper: "If we don't buy CCM, who will? And how will it affect our business?"

EXHIBIT 1 Products and Estimated Market Shares of Major Competitors in the Canadian Hockey Equipment Market, 1981

Company	Skates	Hockey Equipment	Sticks	Apparel
Cooper		69	7	31
Canadien		7	12	
CCM	25	7	6	
D & R		7		
Jofa		3		
Koho		2.5	10.5	
Sherwood			25	
Victoriaville			11	
Louisville			6.5	
Titan			11	
Maska				42
Bernard				11
Sandow				10
Bauer*	33			
Lange*	5			
Micron*	13			
Daoust	17			
Orbit	5			
Roos	1			
Ridell	1			
Others		4.5	11	6
	100%	100%	100%	100%
($ 000 000s)	$78	$31.5	$29	$27

* Brands of Warrington Industries Ltd.
SOURCE: Rough estimates by Cooper product managers.

EXHIBIT 2   **Canadian Hockey Skate Production** (000s of pairs)

Year	Sewn	Molded	Total
1977	1050	50	1 100
1978	775	150	925
1979	1050	250	1 300
1980	850	300	1 150
1981	970	400	1 370
1982 (forecast)	750	300	1 050
1983 (forecast)	900	350	1 250

1982 Factory Sales and Market Shares of Leading Competitors (000s of pairs)

	Sewn	%	Molded	%	Total	%	($000)	%	$ Average of Total
Bauer	305	42.9	50	13.7	355	32.9	$20 265	35.4	$57.08
Micron	–	–	185	50.5	185	17.2	8 690	15.2	46.97
Lange	–	–	100	27.3	100	9.3	3 280	5.8	32.80
Daoust	205	28.7	–	–	205	19.0	9 780	17.0	47.70
CCM	147	20.6	6	1.6	153	14.2	12 050	21.0	78.76
Orbit	55	7.8	25	6.8	80	7.4	3 205	5.6	40.06
Totals	712	100	366	100	1 078	100	$52 270	100	$53.13

1982 Hockey Skate Sales by Geographic Market (000s of pairs)

Manufacturer	Canada	U.S.	Europe	Far East	Total
Canadian	785	238	67	15	1 105
Non-Canadian	–	312	233	25	570
Totals	785	550	300	40	1 675

SOURCE: Estimates based on industry information and casewriter's estimates.

EXHIBIT 3   Cooper Consolidated Statement of Income and Retained Earnings Years Ended December 31 ($000s)

	1981	1980	1979	1978	1977
Net Sales	62 827	62 183	55 810	49 429	42 803
Less: Operating costs	57 049	55 901	51 844	44 364	38 538
Net Before Depreciation, etc.	5 778	6 282	3 966	5 064	4 265
Less: Deprec. & amortization	724	746	748	626	609
Long-term debt interest	1 905	934	1 022	929	778
Other interest	2 933	2 866	2 068	1 138	941
Add: Foreign exchange gain	105	369	107	216	173
Earnings, discontinued operation	929	–	–	–	–
Less: Income taxes					
Current	14	176	20	525	518
Deferred	208	48	454	21	58
Net Income, Operations	818	1 977	455	2 039	1 650
Add: Extraordinary item	(1 543)	76	–	–	–
Net Income	725	2 053	455	2 039	1 650
Shares Outstanding					
Common ($000s)	1 486	1 483	1 483	1 404	1 388
Net income per share	(0.49)	1.38	0.31	1.45	1.18

EXHIBIT 4 **Cooper Consolidated Balance Sheet as at December 31** ($000s)

	1981	1980	1979	1978	1977
ASSETS					
Current					
Short-term bank deposit	—	1 790	—	22	95
Accounts receivable	9 726	10 625	10 315	9 185	8 340
Inventories:					
Raw materials	6 177	8 792	13 064	5 675	5 535
Work in progress	1 593	1 758	1 817	1 006	1 379
Finished goods	15 954	11 669	10 530	10 937	10 839
Prepaid expenses, etc.	580	691	545	886	630
	34 030	35 325	39 271	27 714	26 897
Fixed Assets at Cost					
Buildings	6 179	6 145	6 145	6 117	6 078
Machines, equipment, etc.	4 191	4 521	4 171	3 354	3 174
Dies, moulds, etc.	235	567	619	435	284
Land	91	91	91	90	90
Less: Accumulated					
depreciation	5 351	5 104	4 518	4 000	3 712
	5 345	6 220	6 508	5 998	5 914
Investment in non-					
consolidated subsidiaries	1 122	—	—	—	—
Deferred income taxes	373	581	533	—	—
	40 870	42 126	46 312	33 713	32 889
LIABILITIES					
Current					
Bank indebtedness	10 373	15 853	17 423	8 283	6 955
Accts. payable	3 463	3 380	6 380	3 153	3 576
Income & other taxes payable	1 002	695	641	352	314
Long-term debt due	16	233	603	1 134	1 059
	14 854	20 161	25 057	12 924	11 905
Long-Term Debt					
Bank loans	9 000	4 000	5 375	5 875	6 900
10% s.f. debs. due 1990	1 582	1 892	1 920	2 053	2 148
6.5% mortgage, due 1992	248	265	273	291	280
Notes payable to shareholders	—	125	437	504	—
Less: Amount due 1 yr.	16	233	603	1 134	1 059
Deferred Taxes	—	—	—	418	397
SHAREHOLDERS' EQUITY					
Capital Stock					
Common	3 403	3 392	3 392	2 764	2 716
Retained Earnings	11 799	12 524	10 471	10 016	9 600
	40 870	42 126	46 312	33 713	32 889

EXHIBIT 5 Cooper Organization Chart

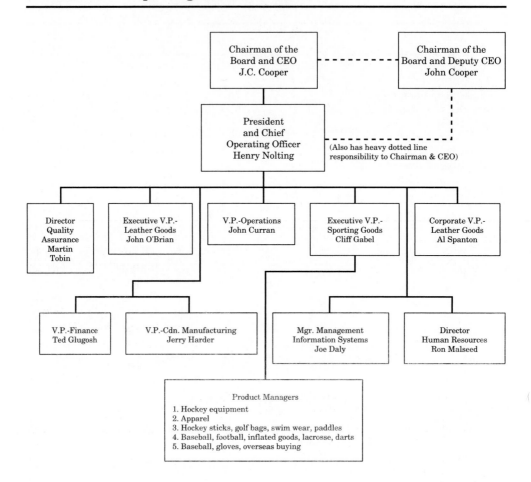

Chairman of the Board and CEO
J.C. Cooper

Chairman of the Board and Deputy CEO
John Cooper

President and Chief Operating Officer
Henry Nolting

(Also has heavy dotted line responsibility to Chairman & CEO)

Director Quality Assurance
Martin Tobin

Executive V.P.- Leather Goods
John O'Brian

V.P.-Operations
John Curran

Executive V.P.- Sporting Goods
Cliff Gabel

Corporate V.P.- Leather Goods
Al Spanton

V.P.-Finance
Ted Glugosh

V.P.-Cdn. Manufacturing
Jerry Harder

Mgr. Management Information Systems
Joe Daly

Director Human Resources
Ron Malseed

Product Managers
1. Hockey equipment
2. Apparel
3. Hockey sticks, golf bags, swim wear, paddles
4. Baseball, football, inflated goods, lacrosse, darts
5. Baseball, gloves, overseas buying

EXHIBIT 6 CCM Inc. Winter Goods Operations ($000s)

	Actual Year Ended				Projected Year Ending			
	Sept. 30/80		Sept. 30/81		Sept. 30/82		Dec. 31/83	
Sales								
Skates	17 148		16 530		14 304		16 500	
Sticks	1 413		2 307		1 445		2 000	
Helmets	1 774		1 814		1 714		2 000	
Protective	3 681		5 047		6 455		6 000	
Sundries	1 250		838		787		1 000	
	25 266		26 536		24 705		27 500	
Gross Margins		%		%		%		%
Skates	5 985	35.0	5 604	34.0	4 577	32.0	5 940	36.0
Sticks	(230)	(16.3)	(30)	(1.3)	(267)	(18.5)	—	—
Helmets	415	23.4	424	23.4	492	28.7	600	30.0
Protective	482	13.1	934	18.5	1 556	24.1	1 350	22.5
Sundries	381	30.5	262	31.3	215	27.3	300	30.0
	7 033	27.8	7 194	27.1	6 573	26.6	8 190	29.8

Expenses

Selling		1 291
Administration		661
Warehouse and distribution (Not Available)		1 086
Financial		618
		3 656
Net before income taxes		4 534

SOURCES: 1980–82 from audited financial statements.
1983 projections estimated by CCM management.

EXHIBIT 7 **Summary of CCM Winter Goods Assets (at Cost)**
October 29, 1982 ($000s)

Inventories
Finished goods

Skates	1 861		
Sticks	407		
Helmets	264		
Protective	1 476		
Sundries	349		
		4 357	

Raw Material

Skates	1 264		
Protective	798		
Blades	1 604		
		3 666	

Work in Process

Skates	216		
Sticks	250		
Protective	234		
Blades	25		
	725		
		8 748	

Fixed Assets

St. Jean	1 200		
Hudson	70		
Nylite	867		
		2 137	

Total 10 885

SOURCE: CCM management estimates.

APPENDIX Competitors in the Skate and Hockey Equipment Industry

There were many manufacturers of hockey equipment, helmets, skates and sticks in Canada. There were seven businesses that Cooper management considered capable and perhaps interested in the CCM winter goods assets.

1. *Canadian Hockey Industries*. CHI was a small company that made high quality hockey sticks. Its use of fibreglass technology and other materials such as graphite, plastics, laminates and aluminum had resulted in the most unique stick line in the market. It also marketed a full line of hockey equipment, including a helmet, but so skates or apparel.

Located in Drummondville, Quebec, it had sales of $10 million in 1981, which had been growing rapidly for the past five years. In the factory it employed approximately 120 workers. It was owned by Amer industries, a Finnish company which also owned Koho.

2. *Koho*. Koho was owned by Amer industries Finland, and shared marketing, distribution and some hockey stick manufacturing with Canadian hockey Industries. It was thought to be the largest hockey stick manufacturer in the world. It also manufactured and marketed hockey equipment and helmets, but no skates or apparel.

Koho had sales of approximately $14 million from about 800 or 900 dealers, serviced by six or seven commission agents who primarily sold Koho and Canadian. Major accounts included large department stores, e.g., Eatons, Simpsons, and Sears, sporting goods chains, e.g., Collegiate Sports, and other stores such as Canadian Tire.

Sticks were manufactured in the Canadian plant in Quebec; sticks and some hockey equipment were manufactured in Finland and some hockey equipment was purchased in the Orient.

Koho's organization in Canada was headed by a sales manager who reported to a president for North America. The United States also had a sales manager who reported to the North American president. This president reported to the head office of Amer, a very large and profitable Finnish corporation that was involved with ship building, steel, food and tobacco.

3. *Jofa*. A Volvo-owned company, Jofa manufactured and marketed hockey equipment, hockey sticks and skates, but not apparel. It had one factory in Sherbrooke, Quebec and others in Sweden. The rest of its products were purchased in the Orient.

Sales of $10 million were achieved through 700 and 800 dealers and approximately seven commissioned sales agents. Major accounts included large department stores and sporting goods stores and Canadian Tire.

The organization of the company was thin, with one director of marketing responsible for all of North America. Supporting him was a sales manager and a small number of commissioned sales agents.

4. *Sherwood-Drolet*. Sherwood-Drolet was a Quebec company, 80% owned by an American firm, ATO Inc. ATO was the world's largest integrated producer of fire protection equipment and also owned Rawlings and Adirondack sporting goods in the United States.

Sherwood, a producer of high quality hockey sticks, had been an industry leader in sales and in the introduction of new materials and production processes. It had one of the most automated plants in the industry, enabling it to produce large volumes of sticks of consistent quality. In 1981 its share of the Canadian market was 25%.

Sales of approximately $15 million came from approximately 600 dealers. The company's direct sales were aided by 10 sales agents who sold to 300 dealers.

5. *Hillerich and Bradsby.* Hillerich and Bradsby's head office and manufacturing facility were located in Wallaceburg, Ontario. The company was a wholly owned subsidiary of H & B, Louisville, Kentucky, the world's to baseball bat manufacturers. Besides producing the Louisville hockey stick and being a market leader in brightly coloured goalie sticks, it was making aggressive inroads into the baseball glove and accessory markets. It had also earned a good name for itself in manufacturing golf clubs that were sold primarily through club professionals. The plant employed 62 people.

Sales in 1981 were about $6 million. H & B distribution system included warehouses in Richmond, B.C., Dorval, Quebec, Winnipeg, Manitoba and Concord, Ontario. The sales were achieved primarily by commission sales agents through approximately 400 dealers. Management was reportedly very strong.

6. *Warrington Industries.* Warrington produced Bauer, Micron, and Lange skates. Bauer had been in the skate business for many years, and was CCM's major competitor. This Canadian owned company was located in Kitchener, Ontario and produced only skates and shoes. It employed 400 in the skate business and 150 in the shoe business.

Sales of approximately $30 million were generated by 12 to 15 agents through a dealership of 1200 stores. Warrington was in turn owned by Cemp Investments, a firm representing the interests of the Bronfman family.

7. *Sport Maska.* Maska was a high quality hockey-jersey manufacturer. Good distribution resulted in Maska being exclusive suppliers to the NHL. Besides hockey jerseys and apparel, its business consisted of spring and summer ball uniforms and apparel, soccer jerseys and leisure wear. The plant in St. Hyacinthe, Quebec employed approximately 175 people.

Sales in Canada were achieved by approximately nine commissioned agents through 120 to 1500 dealers across Canada. The agents did not carry Maska exclusively. It was distributed coast to coast across the United States through the use of commission agents. Recently, Maska had purchased Sandow, another Canadian athletic apparel company, and had consolidated the manufacturing into its own plant.

Sport Maska was a private company that appeared to be profitable and to have a strong equity base. Industry sources felt that the management team, directed by president Denny Coter, was strong and had good depth.

HARLEQUIN ENTERPRISES LIMITED —1979

J. Peter Killing

In 1979 Harlequin Enterprises was the largest publisher of romance novels in the world and was judged by many to be North America's most profitable publishing company. Harlequin's sales and profits had increased every year since 1970 and in 1979 were forecasted at $180 million and $20 million respectively. Harlequin romances were produced in nine languages and sold in more than 90 countries.

As the 1970s drew to a close, the pace of change at Harlequin seemed to be quickening. In 1978, for example, Harlequin had produced its first feature film, based on one of its romance novels, and opened its first retail store, designed to sell educational material produced by the company's "Scholar's Choice" division. In 1979 the company was launching its romance novels in Japan, Scandinavia, Mexico, Venezuela, and Greece, as well as adding new romance series in North America, Germany and Holland. As Larry Heisey, Harlequin's president, looked ahead, he stated:

> Strategies that served us well in the 1970s will be continued into the 1980s. We will work to develop our present resources, to make use of those growth channels that have been established, and to pursue the flexibility that will enable us to react to market opportunities . . . We look to the 1980s as a time of great promise for this company.

THE PUBLISHING INDUSTRY

Apart from educational material, publishing a book is typically a high-risk venture. Each book is a new product with all the risks attendant on any new product introduction. The risks vary with the author's reputation, the subject matter and the predictability of the market's response. Among the numerous decisions facing the publisher are selecting manuscripts out of the thousands submitted each year, deciding how many copies to print and deciding how to promote the book.

Insiders judged that the key to success in hardcover publishing was the creative genius needed to identify good young authors among the hundreds of would-be writers, and then publish and develop them throughout their careers. Sol Stein of Stein and Day Publishers commented that

> Most successful publishers are creative editors at heart, and contribute more than risk capital and marketing expertise to the books they publish. If a publisher does not add value to what he publishes, he's a printer, not a publisher.

Successful hardcover authors and their publishers could profit greatly from the sale of paperback publishing rights and film rights. In the 1970s, prices paid for paperback rights had skyrocketed, as softcover publishers bid astronomical amounts, frequently more than $1 million, for books they judged would sell the numbers necessary for paperback success.

These high prices raised the already high break-even volumes for paperback publishers. Publishers generally received about 50% of the retail price, of which about 13% (15¢ per book) would pay for printing costs, 10% for distribution, 10% for selling expenses, 5–7.5% for advertising and promotion, and the remainder would cover rights and overheads. If the publisher failed to sell enough books, the loss could be substantial. One result was that the mass paperback publishers in the United States earned only about 2% on sales of new releases, whereas Harlequin, using a distinctly different approach to the business, earned in the 15% range. Harlequin's financial results are summarized in Exhibit 1.

HARLEQUIN'S FORMULA: STANDARDIZATION

Harlequin's formula was fundamentally different from that of traditional publishers: content, length, artwork, size, basic formats and print were all standardized. Each book was not a new product, but rather an addition to a clearly defined product line. The consequences of this uniformity were significant. The reader was buying a Harlequin novel, and advertising promoted the Harlequin line, rather than a particular book or author. The standardized size made warehousing and distribution more efficient. A comparison of Harlequin's formula and the operations of traditional "one-off" publishers is presented in Table 1.

Because all its novels were aimed at the same target market—"any and all female readers over the age of 15"—Harlequin could afford to do a significant amount of market research, identifying its customers and their likes and dislikes.

TABLE 1   The Harlequin Formula

	Harlequin	*One-Off Publisher*
Editorial	Emphasis on consistency with extablished guide-lines	Requires separate judgement on potential consumer demand for each manuscript
Rights	Standardized process, usually for established amounts	Can be a complex process, involving subrights, hard/soft cover deals and tying up authors for future books
Author Management	Less dependent of specific authors	Vulnerable to key authors changing publisher
Marketing	Builds the imprint/series	Builds each title/author
Selling	Emphasis on servicing, rack placement and maintaining distribution	Sell on strength of author, cover, critical reviews, special promotional tactics
Production	Consistent format, focus on efficiency	Emphasis on cover design, cost control secondary
Distribution/ order regulation/ information systems	Very sophisticated shipping and returns handling procedures	Traditionally has not received much attention and hence is not as sophisticated

SOURCE: Adapted from a Canada Consulting Group report.

The average Harlequin reader was 35.5 years old, was married, had 2.5 children, was equally likely to be working or a housewife, and had probably finished high school. Harlequin described the relationship between its books and its readers as follows:

> The world of romantic fiction offers the reader delights of a kind which are absent from her everyday life. Identifying herself with the heroine, the romance reader can meet the strong, masterful hero of her dreams and be courted by him. Without stirring from her fireside, she can travel to other countries, learn about other ways of life, and meet new people. After the vicarious enjoyment pro-

vided by such literature, the reader can return to safe reality, where domineering males seldom have to be confronted and trips to exotic parts of the world never happen, so that illusion is always preserved. The romance provides compulsive reading and leaves a feeling of satisfaction and pleasure.

Harlequin's view that its novels could be sold "like other branded consumer products" perhaps explained why employees hired from mass-marketing companies such as Procter and Gamble had skills and aptitudes that led them to do well at Harlequin. The company's 1974 Annual Report documented it mass market focus, its use of sampling techniques, and its entry into television advertising, which in many cities increased sales by as much as 80%.

> We are selling branded literature which can be promoted like other branded consumer products. Sampling techniques, the costs of which are prohibitive to the general publisher because of the variety of books published, are being used by Harlequin to expand its market. For example, several million books were distributed free to the trade in 1973 and 1974 for use in introducing our products to new consumers. Since September 1974, a television advertising campaign has been tested in ten cities in Canada and the United States. Expansion of this advertising will begin in 1975.

Responsibility for the development of Harlequin novels lay with the company's British editorial staff and stable of more than 100 writers, most of whom were also British. Harlequin had acquired this editorial expertise in 1971 when it purchased Mills and Boon, a long established British publisher of romance novels. The genius of the Mills and Boon editors, according to one observer, was that they were able to produce a consistency in the final product, even though many authors were contributing. Readers always knew what they were getting and were satisfied again and again. In addition to the work of its regular writers, Mills and Boon received approximately 5000 unsolicited manuscripts per year. Typically, about 50 of these were accepted.

Harlequin's editorial process did not generate or even encourage best-sellers. "Best-sellers would ruin our system," stated Bill Willson, Harlequin's vice president of finance. "Our objective is steady growth in volume. We have no winners and no losers." All Harlequin books published in any month sold about the same number of copies. Unsold paperback books could be returned to the publisher for credit; a consequence of Harlequin's even and predictable sales was that its rate of return of unsold books was much lower than that of its competitors, 25–30% of sales versus 40–50%.

One industry analyst commented on Harlequin's approach to the industry as follows:

> You've got to realize that these guys at Harlequin revolutionized the North American book industry. They brought professional marketing and business techniques to an industry that seems to publish "for love rather than money." At retail, for instance, they ignored the bookstores. This was a good move

because most people never enter bookstores. Instead they built Harlequin book racks and placed them in supermarkets, mass merchandisers and drug stores where women are. They made each of the books 192 pages by changing the type size. This allowed for standard packaging and six books would fit into each pocket on the rack. Once the books were accepted by the trade they went on a monthly standing order system like magazines. This allowed for uniform print runs, shipping containers, and so on. Everything was done for efficiency, prices were kept low and volumes skyrocketed.

Distribution

In late 1977, Harlequin established a national retail sales organization in Canada, ending a joint venture agreement with another publisher in which a single sales force had represented both companies. By early 1979 Harlequin executives declared themselves well satisfied with the new arrangement, which allowed the sales force to focus solely on Harlequin products.

In the U.S. Harlequin was represented by the Pocket Books Distribution Corporation, a wholly owned subsidiary of Simon and Schuster. Pocket Books' 120-person sales force was responsible for dealing with the 400 or so independent regional distributors who distributed Harlequin's books and the major chains who bought direct, and for ensuring that Harlequin books were properly displayed and managed at the retail level. In addition to handling the Harlequin romance series, the sales force carried Simon and Schuster's own pocket books which were "one-offs" issued monthly.

Harlequin did not print any of its own books. Harlequin novels that were sold in the U.S. were printed by a major American printer of mass market books and distributed through a distribution centre in Buffalo, New York. Harlequins sold in Canada were printed in Canada and distributed through the company's Stratford, Ontario warehouse.

HARLEQUIN'S PRODUCTS AND MARKETS

The Romance Novel

The backbone of Harlequin's business was its two major series, Harlequin Presents and Harlequin Romances, which consistently produced over 90% of the company's sales and earnings. Originally Harlequin had published only the Romances line, consisting of very chaste conservative stories selected from the Mills and Boon line by the wife of one of Harlequin's founders. After a period of time, however, Mills and Boon executives suggested to Harlequin that they were not publishing Mills and Boon's most popular books. Arguing that the British and North American markets were not the same, Harlequin nevertheless tried a blind test—two of its choices and two of the slightly more "racy" Mills and Boon choices—on 500 of its North American customers. To the company's amazement the Mills and Boon selections were very popular and, bowing to its customers' wishes, Harlequin created the Presents line to offer Mills and Boon's less chaste romance stories. In early 1979 the still growing Presents line was increased from four titles per month to six in North America, and sales rose by 50%. At the same time the Romances line was cut back from eight titles per month to six, with the net result that in North America the two lines were selling very similar quantities of books.

Both the Presents and Romances lines were sold at retail and, since 1970, through Harlequin's "Reader Service" book club. This direct mail operation offered heavy Harlequin readers the possibility of purchasing every book the company published, delivered right to the front door. The book club was an important source of profit, as in the U.S. six books were sold through the book club for every ten sold at retail. Furthermore, a book sold through the book club yielded Harlequin the full cover price, whereas a book sold at retail netted the company approximately half the retail price, and required advertising, distribution costs, the acceptance of returns from retailers and so on. As one observer put it "No wonder the company is willing to pay the mailing costs for its book club members!"

Competition

No other publisher concentrated as heavily as Harlequin on the romance novel although, attracted by Harlequin's profit margins, most of the majors had made attempts to penetrate the market. Bantam Books, the largest, and generally considered the best-run conventional paperback publisher in North America, had tried to enter Harlequin's market in the early 1970s with a series titled Red Rose Romances. The line was a failure and had been phased out of existence by 1977. Four or five other major publishers had also attempted to penetrate the romantic novel market in the late 1960s and early 1970s. Consumers were offered Valentine Romances from Curtis Publishing, Rainbow Romances from New American Library, Hamilton House from Fawcett, and Candlelight Romances from Dell. The only one of these series selling in 1979 was Dell's, offering one or two new titles per month. Willson explained that the problem faced by all of these firms was their editorial content. The stories simply weren't good enough. Heisey agreed, adding:

> We are good managers and good marketers, I admit, and those things make us more profitable than we otherwise would be, but the essence of this firm is the editorial department and our group of more than 100 authors. It is these resources which make us unique, and it is precisely these resources which our competition cannot duplicate.

International Markets

Commencing in 1975, Harlequin began to establish foreign language ventures for its romance novels in countries around the world. Typically, a new venture would start with two or four titles per month, translated from the Romances or Presents lines, and then expand as the market allowed. In spite of predictions from many (male) publishers that the Harlequin line would not appeal to the women of their country, virtually all of the new ventures prospered. Entry costs were not high in most countries, and profits came quickly. Harlequin's major international moves are listed in Table 2.

TABLE 2   International Expansion

1975	Harlequin Holland established. Four titles per month. Extremely successful. Second line introduced in 1976. Further expansion in 1977 and 1978. Holland, together with Canada, has Harlequin's highest per capita (women over 15) market penetration rate.
1976	Harlequin paid $2.1 million for a 50% interest in the West German company that had been publishing Mills and Boon novels for several years. The company published five romance titles per month, plus a French detective series. In spite of new competition in the romance area in 1978, the company was performing well.
1977	Harlequin France established. In 1978 a four title per month series was launched, aimed at French, Belgian and Swiss markets. Line expanded in 1979. Company became profitable in 1979.
1978	Mills and Boon's Australian operation (established in 1973) took a major step forward with the introduction of TV advertising and a new line. A successful operation.
1979	New launches in Japan, Scandinavia, Greece, Mexico, and Venezuela.

Harlequin's major new romance novel venture in 1979, representing an investment of $2 million, was its entry into the Japanese market. Despite skepticism from outsiders, initial market research had indicated that the appeal of Harlequin's product would be even stronger in Japan than North America. In early 1979 the company also entered its smallest foreign-language markets to date, those of the Scandinavian countries. A Harlequin executive explained the company's rationale:

> Harlequin's operation in Stockholm is the headquarters for publishing and marketing activities in the Swedish, Finnish and Norwegian languages. We

will begin publishing romance fiction in Sweden and Finland in March, at the rate of four titles per month, and in Norway in April, at two titles per month. Denmark is currently being examined as a potential new market.

The four Scandinavian countries, with populations varying from 4.1 million to 8.3 million, will provide Harlequin with experience in the management of smaller markets. We also believe that, despite their size, they are potentially productive and represent a well-founded investment.

Literary Diversification

Harlequin's heavy dependence on the romance novel had been a source of concern to company executives for a number of years. In 1975 the company had attempted diversification with a line of science fiction novels for the North American market, known as the Laser series. In spite of an intense marketing effort the series was discontinued after 18 months and 58 titles. Heisey indicated that no one factor was responsible, suggesting that the problem was likely part editorial, part distribution, and part pricing (Appendix A).

Subsequent literary diversification attempts were more modest. In 1977, Mills and Boon created a series of romance stories in medical settings focussing on doctors and nurses, and these were introduced at the rate of two titles per month. In 1978 the Masquerade line of historical romances was also introduced at the rate of two titles per month. In Willson's view, these were "the same romance stories, but with long dresses." While both lines showed some initial promise, neither was expected to match the success of Harlequin Presents or Harlequin Romances.

In 1979 Harlequin took the somewhat bolder step of creating a new brand, Worldwide Library, which would act as an umbrella imprint for new products. The first of these was Mystique Books, introduced in March 1979. This romantic suspense series, adapted from a successful line of French novels, was introduced at the rate of four titles per month, with heavy television advertising. It did not carry the Harlequin name.

The importance that Harlequin placed on new series such as these was illustrated in the five-year plan of the North American book division, the company's most important business unit. This division's objective was a 30% annual increase in sales and profits throughout the early 1980s, to be achieved by increasing the U.S. penetration rate of the Presents and Romances lines closer to Canadian levels and at the same time, through the introduction of new "spin off" products, to reduce the overall dependence on those two lines to 65% of sales and profits by 1985. Harlequin's penetration rate in the U.S. (sales per woman over the age of 15) was approximately half that of the Canadian penetration rate.

Scholar's Choice

Scholar's Choice was created in the early 1970s when Harlequin acquired and merged two small Canadian companies involved in the production of educational material for schoolboards and teachers. Dissatisfied with what it described as "mixed results" from "less than buoyant Canadian institutional markets for educator supplies" during the mid-1970s, the company opened a retail store in Toronto in 1977. The success of this store led to a second Toronto store in 1978 and plans for seven more stores across Canada in 1979. All of these stores would sell educational material and would be wholly owned by the company.

Harlequin Films

Harlequin entered the movie-making business in 1977 with the $1.1 million film, "Leopard in the Snow." The movie featured no well-known actors, but it was based on a successful novel by one of Harlequin's established authors. The venture was a first step toward Harlequin's objective of "becoming to women what Walt Disney is to children." Willson elaborated on Harlequin's rationale:

> In the traditional film-making business there are a number of quite separate participants. The screenplay and actual creation of the movie is done by one group, financing by another group, distribution and marketing of the finished product by a variety of people. The people who actually create the product virtually lose control of it by the time it is marketed. Because so many conflicting groups are involved with different objectives and skills, the entire process is extremely inefficient.
>
> Harlequin could manage this process quite differently. We have the books for screen-plays—over 2 000 on our backlist—and we have the finances to make the films. We know how to market and we have far more knowledge about our target market than most movie makers ever do. We could, once we gain confidence, use the distributors only to get the films into the theatres for a flat fee. We would do the promotion ourselves and take the financial risk.
>
> The other advantage to Harlequin is the same one that we have in the publishing business—consistency. For other producers, each film is a new product and new risk and the public has to be educated separately. We could advertise Harlequin films on a pretty intensive scale, and they could reinforce and be reinforced by the book sales. The potential may be tremendous.

The box office results of "Leopard in the Snow" were described by the company as "somewhat inconsistent" and further testing was to be done in 1979 to determine the feasibility of the concept.

Forward Integration

Harlequin's current three-year contract with Pocket Books was going to expire on December 31, 1979 and the company was considering ending the arrangement and establishing its own U.S. sales force. The following factors indicated that such a move might make sense:

1. *Cost.* Harlequin paid Pocket Books a set fee per book sold for the use of its U.S. sales force. As volumes continued to rise, so would Harlequin's total sell-

ing cost, even though Pocket Book's sales force costs were unlikely to increase. Harlequin execuitves estimated that they were already paying "well over half" the total cost of the Pocket Book sales force, even though the volumes of books it handled for Simon and Schuster and Harlequin were approximately equal. In fact, since Simon and Schuster line consisted of "one-offs" which had to be "sold" to the distributors each month and the Harelquin line was all on automatic reorders, there was little doubt that Harlequin received less than half of the sales force's attention. The net result was that Harlequin felt it would get better service at lower cost from its own sales force.

2. *New Products.* As new products like the Mystique line were introduced to the U.S. market with increasing frequency, the attention given to each product line by the sales force would become extremely important. If such new lines were to be a success, Harlequin felt that it would need to be able to directly control the activities of its U.S. sales force.

3. *Returns.* One of the tasks of a Harlequin sales force was known as "order regulation." This job, which was to check with individual retailers to determine their return rate, was necessary because the independent distributors, set up to handle magazines, could not accurately monitor pocket book returns by customer. If the return rate was too high, books were being printed and distributed for no gain. If it was too low, retailers were stocking out and sales were being lost. Larry Heisey commented:

> I ran a check to see what kind of a job Pocket Books was doing for us on order regulation. We had about 400 distributors, each carrying Romances and Presents. That means we could have had up to 800 changes in order positions per month as wholesalers fine-tuned their demands to optimize our return rates. As I recall, there were only about 23 changes per month in the time period we checked. The Pocket Book's sales force simply wasn't managing the situation the way they should have been.

The only concern expressed at Harlequin about dropping Pocket Books was the possible reaction of Dick Snyder, the tough and aggressive president of Simon and Schuster. Snyder had become president of Simon and Schuster in 1975, the same year that the New York-based publisher was acquired by Gulf and Western, a large U.S. conglomerate. Snyder was interested in growth and profits, and was achieving results in both areas. *Newsweek* commented as follows:

> S&S has always been a best-seller house, but Snyder has turned it into the bastion of books-as-product—and the target of derision by other publishers who pride themselves on a commitment to good literature. He expects his editors to bring in twice as many titles per year as are required at other houses...
>
>   The marketing staff is renowned for its aggressiveness—and high turnover rate. "Simon and Schuster runs a sales contest every year," former sales representative Jack O'Leary says only half jokingly. "The winners get to keep their jobs."

The Acquisition Program

In 1977, Heisey and Willson had estimated Harlequin's potential world market for romance novels (all non-communist countries) at $250 million, but as Harlequin's prices and volumes continued to rise, it became apparent that this estimate may have been too low. No matter how big the ultimate market, however neither man felt that the company could penetrate this market any faster than it already was. They also emphasized that Harlequin's romantic fiction business could not profitably absorb all the cash it generated. As a result, Willson, with the aproval of the Torstar Corporation (publisher of the *Toronto Star* newspaper) whch had acquired 59% of Harlequin's shares in the late 1970s, hired several staff analysts and began a search for acquisitions. Early investigation revealed that the major U.S. paperback companies were not for sale, and the minor ones were not attractive.

Willson prepared a list to guide the search process (Exhibit 2), deciding that he was not interested in any company which would add less than 10% to Harlequin's profits. With more than $20 million in cash in 1977 and no debt to speak of, Willson had thought that $40 million would be a reasonable amount to spend on acquisitions; he visualized two major acquisitions, both in the U.S. One would be in the publishing business and the other in a related business.

By 1979, Willson and his group had made several acquisitions, but were still searching for one or two really sizeable takeover candidates. In mid-1977 they had purchased the Ideals Corporation of Milwaukee, a publisher of inspirational magazines and books, as well as greeting cards and a line of cookbooks, for $1.5 million. In 1978 Harlequin acquired a 78% interest in the Laufer Company of Hollywood, California for $10.5 million, approximately $8 million of which represented goodwill. In the nine months ended December 31, 1977 Laufer earned U.S. $814 000 on sales of $10 million. Laufer published eight monthy entertainment magazines including T*iger Beat, Right On!* and *Rona Barrett's Hollywood*, for teenage and adult markets. The Laufer and Ideals businesses were subsequently combined to form the Harlequin Magazine Group. (An organization chart is presented in Exhibit 3.) During the first half of 1979 the magazine group acquired a 50% interest in *ARTnews* ("the most distinguished fine arts magazine in the United States"), a 60% interest in *Antiques World*, which was launched in 1979 as a sister publication to *ARTnews*, and a 57.5% interest in a new Toronto publication titled *Photo Life*.

THE FUTURE

As the financial results for the first six months of 1979 arrived, showing a 45% increase in sales (no doubt in part a result of the 20% and 30% price increases on the Presents and Romances lines in North America—bringing retail prices to $1.50 and $1.25 respectively) and a 23% gain in net income, Larry Heisey looked forward to the 1980s with keen anticipation.

We believe the 1980s will be very important to Harlequin, even more so than the seventies. Our market research indicates substantial growth potential in the English-language markets. The rapid development of markets in Holland and French Canada to per capita levels nearly equivalent to those of English-speaking Canada, our most mature market, suggest the great potential of Mills & Boon romance fiction in other languages.

The goals that we established for ourselves at the beginning of the seventies are being realized, generating an outstanding growth pattern. We have every reason to believe that this pattern will continue in the 1980s, for the company's financial resources are more than adequate to support an active expansion and diversification program.

EXHIBIT 1   Harlequin Summary of Financial Performance

	1978	1977	1976	1975	1974	1973	1972	1971	1970
OPERATING RESULTS ($000 000s)									
Net Revenues									
Publishing	N/A	N/A	44.1	35.1	24.8	16.4	11.0	4.0	3.0
Learning materials*	N/A	N/A	8.3	8.2	6.2	4.0	4.3	4.0	5.1
Total Net Revenues	$125.9	$80.9	$52.4	$43.2	$31.0	$20.4	$15.3	$8.0	$8.0
Net Earnings	$16.8	$12.5	$5.2	$4.4	$3.5	$3.0	$1.6	$.5	$.1
FINANCIAL POSITION ($000 000s)									
Cash and securities	22.5	24.0	9.3	4.2	3.5	3.2	1.1	1.2	
Total current assets	58.4	45.8	23.6	19.2	14.3	10.0	6.1	6.2	4.0
Current liabilities	25.2	21.2	10.5	8.4	7.0	5.0	3.4	4.0	2.1
Working capital	33.2	24.6	13.1	10.8	7.2	5.0	3.0	2.5	2.0
Net fixed assets	2.3	1.7	1.0	.9	.7	.5	.2	.2	.2
Other assets	14.1	6.4	5.8	3.7	3.7	3.7	4.0	4.0	2.2
Shareholders' equity	45.2	30.5	19.4	15.4	11.7	9.1	6.8	4.3	3.9
FINANCIAL RATIOS									
Net earnings on net revenues	13.3%	15.6%	10.2%	10.2%	11.4%	13.4%	10.3%	5.7%	1.4%
Net earnings on equity	37.1%	41.0%	27.5%	28.8%	30.2%	30.0%	23.2%	10.5%	2.8%
Working-capital ratio	2.3:1	2.2:1	2.3:1	2.3:1	2.0:1	2.0:1	1.8:1	1.7:1	1.7:1
Fully diluted earnings per share	$1.06	$.79	$.34	$.29	$.24	$.18	$.12	$.04	$.01
Dividends declared ($000 000s)	2.3	1.4	1.3	1.2	1.0	.4	.1	—	—
OTHER DATA									
Share price —low	7.75	3.83	2.75	1.33	.94	1.30	.44	.23	N/A
—high	16.00	9.00	3.79	3.25	1.72	1.83	1.67	.46	
Number of employees	980	881	584	332	313	240	201	157	188
Number of books sold (000 000s)	125	109	90	72	63	42	29	25	19

* Although exact figures were not available, learning materials were still a relatively low proportion of Harlequin sales in 1978.

EXHIBIT 2   Harlequin's Guide for Acquisitions

Potential Areas to Look for Acquisition in Publishing Business

1. Trade Books
   —paperback fiction and non-fiction
   —hardcover series and partworks
2. Reference Books
   —text books and learned journals
   —professional publishing: legal, medical, accounting
   —reference guides and handbooks
3. Magazines
   —consumer magazines
   —trade and business publications
4. Other publishing
   —greeting cards, stationery
   —sewing patterns
   —diaries and albums
   —music publishing

Areas to Consider for Acquisition in Related Industry

1. Entertainment
   —movies and television films
   —records
   —video tapes
   —music
2. Mass-marketed low-technology consumer products
   —adult games
   —children's games
   —children's toys
3. Handicraft and hobby products

APPENDIX A   Why Harlequin Enterprises Fell Out of Love with Science Fiction by Brian M. Fraser

"It didn't work," says Harlequin Enterprises President W. Lawrence Heisey. "We didn't perceive that it would be profitable in the reasonably short-term future, so we decided to abandon it. Period."

Although noncommittal on the failure, Heisey said no one factor was responsible: "I think it was a lot of problems," he said. "it wasn't any one thing. I don't think the distribution was that bad; it probably begins with editorial and ends with pricing so it was a whole collection of problems. But it didn't work."

Hard-core SF enthusiasts were against the venture from the start, fearing science fiction would be watered down into pap for the masses. And, indeed, this was essentially true: the plots of the Laser books generally took standard ideas in the genre and sketched new adventure stores, but without much depth.

Like its romances, which are mainly sold in supermarkets and drug stores, Harlequin attempted to produce a uniform product in the science fiction category. It also hoped it would prove as addictive to young male readers as the light romances are for some housewives.

Harlequin put all its marketing expertise and resources behind the new SF paperbacks, beginning with six titles plus a free novel (*Seeds of Change* by Thomas F. Monteleone) as incentive to anyone who bought a Laser Book and returned a questionnaire. Like good marketers, they used these names to build a mailing list for promotional material.

An extensive publicity and advertising program was tied to the announcement. Major Canadian media carried articles, focussing on the worldwide financial success of the Harlequin Romances line.

To attract potential readers directly, full-page ads were placed in major science-fiction digest magazines, such as *Analog*, and in amateur fan magazines, such as *Locus*. And, with sage marketing skill, Harlequin also attempted to create a favourable selling environment through ads in *Publisher's Weekly* and the *West Coast Review of Books*, which are read by bookstore managers.

Harlequin even placed trial direct response ads in a girlie magazine, ran radio commercials in Toronto and U.S. test markets, and its ad agency, Compton Advertising of New York, tried out a television commercial.

These innovative merchandising techniques, not part of the repertoire of most Canadian publishers, have been used with some success on the romances.

"The failure can be attributed to a complete misunderstanding of the special appeal of science fiction and the nature of its addictive readers. Nobody "in the know" ever believed this venture would succeed," says veteran U.S. SF editor Donald Woolheim.

The inside-SF consensus is that Harlequin underestimated the intelligence of the science fiction reader who, unlike the devotees of Harlequin romances, looks for non-formula fiction, cerebral material with new and well-developed ideas.

It's conceivable that lack of adequate distribution may have been one of the prime reasons Harlequin pulled out. With the Romances line, Harelequin has been phenomenally successful in penetrating the grocery and drugstore markets, placing racks specifically for their interchangeable 12 titles a month. But no such breakthrough was evident with the Laser line.

SOURCE: Original article appeared in the *Financial Post*, December 17, 1977.

ENGINEERING SOFTWARE LIMITED

J. Michael Geringer

In May 1989, Daniel Markham, the 32-year-old President and CEO of Engineering Software Ltd. (ESL), was pondering the future of his small company. Formed in early 1985, ESL was one of the first firms to successfully develop high density, rapid access digital (HIDRAD) software systems for the computerized storage and retrieval of large and complex engineering documents such as blueprints. Although ESL's products were considered to be among the industry's most innovative and technologically sophisticated, development of this potentially lucrative market had been slower and more expensive than anticipated. ESL's sales had lagged behind projections, and Markham felt that the firm's skills and resources were insufficient to enable it to compete successfully over the long term, particularly since several well-financed competitors had begun to enter the market. As a result, Markham had decided to pursue an alliance with another firm and had identified several prospective partner companies. He knew he had to move quickly in order for the venture to be successful in this rapidly changing market, but was unsure which company would be the best partner.

ENGINEERING DOCUMENT STORAGE SYSTEMS

Engineering document storage systems were the manual, mechanical or electronic systems involved in the storage, retrieval, modification and transfer of non-verbal engineering documents such as blueprints and schematics. These documents were used in virtually all industries. Often proprietary in nature, engineering documents were used for both initial prototypes and final production goods and, even within an individual company, they tended to vary greatly in their size, scale and complexity. For many firms, the number and complexity of engineering documents which had to be managed had been rapidly expanding due to such factors as increasing firm size and product line breadth, geographic dispersion and global integration of manufacturing facilities, and rampant technological change.

Traditional document storage systems, based on manual filing of flat or rolled documents, had proven increasingly inadequate for responding to these trends. Among other problems, these traditional systems were characterized by slow and costly retrieval, difficulties updating documents across multiple manufacturing plants or installations, and competitive disadvantage or potential legal liability from failure to incorporate the most recent technological developments or regulations into new or existing products.

During the 1970s, a number of firms made unsuccessful attempts to overcome limitations of manual engineering document storage systems through computerization. Development in the 1980s of computer hardware and software with increased capacity and speed for data storage and manipulation, along with improved digitization capability, provided the opportunity to overcome many of the problems which had hampered initial computerization efforts. These developments provided the foundation for robust, computer-based systems which would permit storage of documents with increased detail, enhance operators' abilities to manipulate documents (e.g., to select among different levels of detail for a complete document, or take only a small segment of a document and enlarge it for additional detail in design), enable rapid and inexpensive costing of prototypes or product changes, permit quick and accurate updating of documents across multiple sites within a company's operations, reduce costs by permitting re-use or modification of existing designs, and help leverage scarce and expensive design and engineering resources.

Although still in an early stage of development, by 1989 the computerized engineering document storage system industry seemed poised for rapid growth. Competition had been largely restricted to several dozen relatively small start-up firms in North America. However, a number of large corporations had recently purchased stakes in existing firms or had undertaken in-house efforts to design document storage systems, with the implicit intent of engaging in commercial development and sale of such systems within the next few years. Several of these new entrants had existing capabilities in document storage systems for other applications, such as the newspaper or legal industries. Existing installations of computerized engineering document storage systems were primarily within smaller firms or for specialized types of documents. However, several large-scale pilot projects had been initiated in the past year and had achieved promising results. Nevertheless, awareness of potential applications and existing product offerings was still relatively low among prospective users, and there was limited uniformity in terms of product technology or features.

Due to the customized nature of most existing systems, it had been necessary for suppliers to intimately understand the requirements of the users' operations in order to adequately design a workable system. Suppliers had also required a substantial level of specialized computer programming and systems integration expertise. However, once the initial system was de-bugged, the time and skill required for system maintenance or modification within a particular installation site was often reduced substantially. It also appeared that existing systems of certain suppliers could be modified to serve similar applications in a variety of other organizational settings, and at a small fraction of the cost of designing a new system from scratch.

Although a potentially large and profitable business, few industry insiders believed that development of computerized document storage systems solely for smaller firms, with current prices ranging from approximately $10 000 to as much as $250 000 apiece for design and installation, would provide the basis for sustained profitability and growth within the industry. Rather, the most lucrative market appeared to be the design and maintenance of systems for large international firms, such as Boeing, Toyota, Philips, General Motors, IBM, Northern Telecom, and General Electric.

Computerized engineering document storage systems promised substantial strategic benefits for large multinationals because they could enable a firm to efficiently organize large libraries of engineering documents, reinforce links among international operating units and with suppliers and customers, and facilitate rapid incorporation of engineering changes across even widely dispersed operations. These firms required large and complex document storage systems of high reliability, which suggested multi-million dollar contracts for initial system design and installation. The specialized skills, high up-front costs and long lead-time required for in-house development of these systems encouraged use of outside suppliers. In addition, since modifications and maintenance services typically generated 8% to 12% of the initial contract value per annum, these systems could also provide a continuing stream of revenues for suppliers.

However, sales of systems to larger firms had developed more slowly than many of the industry's proponents had envisioned. In a large part, this reflected initial concerns by potential customers about which technology to use, which suppliers would survive and be able to offer adequate service support in case of system malfunctions or modifications, and the high cost and strategic risks associated with design and implementation of such a system. Slow growth was also due to the limited resources which many suppliers had been able to devote to market development activities, and to technical and operational problems encountered by some of the early systems applications. Yet, the substantial operating cost, coordination and other competitive benefits achieved by several existing large-scale pilot projects and the entry of larger firms into the industry suggested that resistance of potential users to adopting these new systems might begin diminishing rapidly. Indeed, although the software market was expected to be between $40 and $50 million in 1989, it was projected to exceed $500 million by 1995 as increased numbers of system installations began generating continuing streams of service-related revenues.

ENGINEERING SOFTWARE LIMITED

Daniel Markham was a brilliant computer programmer and systems integrator who earned a Ph.D. in computer science from M.I.T. at age 25, and then went to work as a computer systems developer within the aerospace industry. Appalled by the inefficiencies of traditional manual engineering document storage systems, Markham and several friends devoted their evenings and weekends to developing a computerized data storage system. Within a year, a simple prototype system based on high density, random access digital (HIDRAD) technology had been developed. Markham convinced his boss to let him test this system within the unit's design department. Over the next 18 months, refinements substantially increased the system's capabilities and reliability. Markham also developed a scaled-down version of the HIDRAD system for a friend who owned an architectural design company. In 1984, Markham and his colleagues designed a successful system for a $150 million manufacturer of custom scientific equipment.

Although convinced that his system offered great benefits, Markham became frustrated when his efforts to expand the system's use into other divisions of the company met with resistance. He discussed formation of a commercial venture with Jerry Blake, a talented but introverted programming specialist with unique skills in critical operating level computer languages who had worked with Markham since 1982. In early 1985, Markham and Blake quit their jobs, moved to Vancouver, and formed ESL with $40 000 of their own money, $250 000 borrowed from family and friends, and a bank loan of $200 000. Markham owned 60% of ESL's shares and Blake owned the remaining 40%.

ESL began operations in 5 000 sq.ft. of warehouse space in a rundown building near Vancouver's downtown. By the end of 1985, ESL had two full-time and eight part-time technical employees, in addition to Markham and Blake and a full-time secretary. Several of Markham's friends and former coworkers also helped the firm on a casual basis, often without pay. This helped conserve the company's limited resources, most of which were tied up in the numerous computers, peripherals and documentation which filled ESL's cluttered facilities.

Markham and Blake had designed the basic structure of ESL's systems so that they could be made compatible with virtually any brand of computer hardware which customers were likely to own. The ability to design systems for a customer's specific circumstances helped broaden ESL's potential customer base, since computer hardware represented over 50% of the initial cost of most document storage systems and users resisted switching hardware systems. In addition, this open architecture permitted more rapid and lower cost modification of an existing system for other sites, as opposed to most competing systems which required that each new application be designed virtually from scratch. This product flexibility also enabled ESL to reduce its reliance on any individual hardware supplier and permitted the firm to incorporate the latest technical developments into its systems. To reinforce their image as an "independent" systems supplier, ESL did not stock or sell any computer hardware itself. However, ESL provided service for most types of hardware, and would also help customers purchase any needed hardware through third-party vendors.

During ESL's first four years, virtually all of its marketing activities were handled by Markham. In addition, because of their steadfast commitment to produce only the highest quality systems available, both Markham and Blake tried to maintain intimate involvement in the design, installation and de-bugging of every document storage system. Their devotion to quality enabled ESL to obtain several small contracts with city and provincial government agencies. ESL had also developed specialized systems for several small- and medium-sized technology and manufacturing firms in British Columbia, Alberta and the northwestern U.S. However, the partners discovered that obtaining larger contracts was a much more time-consuming and costly process. Without other sources of revenue, ESL's limited resources would have been rapidly depleted. Thus, to generate working capital until larger contracts were obtained, ESL began accepting custom computer software design and systems integration business from a variety of firms.

ESL's custom business grew rapidly, accounting for approximately $525 000 in net income on $3.2 million in sales in 1988. In contrast, due to high initial development and service costs, document storage systems generated a loss of nearly $250 000 on revenues of just over $2.4 million. By May 1989, employment had grown to 93 full- and part-time employees. ESL had no time clocks or dress code, and employees, many attired in jeans and wool shirts, filtered in and out of ESL's facilities at all hours of the night and day. Many completed their work at off-site locations. Markham felt that this informal style had been a key factor in ESL's ability to attract and retain some of the brightest talents in the industry.

Despite the growth in ESL's custom business, Markham and Blake emphasized that their goal was to be a major player in the computerized engineering document storage system industry. They felt that this was a reasonable goal, since their product was of such high quality, and ESL had installed more systems than any other firm in the industry. Indeed, in terms of technical sophistication, versatility, efficiency and reliability of its systems, it was clear that ESL was a leader in the industry. This reputation had just recently helped the firm capture a two-year, $1.5-million contract for a pilot system for a major international construction firm based in Southern California. One of the largest document storage system contracts awarded to date, this project represented a particularly important opportunity for promoting the firm's development efforts and visibility. Successful design and implementation of a large system in such a highly visible corporation could further strengthen ESL's leadership position. The partners were determined to take full advantage of this opportunity. They had already assigned eight employees to work full time on the project, in addition to a substantial amount of Markham's and Blake's time, and three additional employees were expected to be hired in the next few months to assist with the project's development.

PROBLEMS CONFRONTING ESL

ESL's new contract also pointed out several glaring problems confronting the firm. First, although ESL had successfully sold a number of systems, Markham knew that the company lacked sufficient marketing expertise. Most of the firm's contracts had been won through his personal skill at communicating with technical people within smaller organizations, or within technical departments of larger firms. However, larger contracts required vastly increased marketing time and other resources, as well as increased contact with non-technical executives. These additional capabilities were simply not present in ESL.

This latter situation raised another concern: the perceived legitimacy of ESL as a viable supplier over the long term. Especially for large, strategically critical systems contracts, a major purchase criterion was the user's perception that ESL would be among the industry's survivors, and that it could muster the human and infrastructural resources necessary to provide adequate support services. Indeed, the ability to provide continued high quality service appeared to be a key to continued growth and profitability in this industry. Before making a multi-million dollar investment in such a system, customers had to be confident that the supplier could quickly and effectively respond to breakdowns, or provide needed modifications as users' needs changed. From a technical standpoint, Markham felt that an effective service system could be established relatively easily. Field service personnel would largely be involved with user training and customer interface, which required relatively limited technical skills. Major technical problems could be dealt with from headquarters. However, ESL's experience suggested there were large economies of scale associated with a service network. ESL's limited service network had been adequate for a large number of small installations which were concentrated in the Pacific Northwest. However, larger contracts involving a number of geographically dispersed sites, though readily handled on a strictly technical level, would overwhelm the firm's limited human and financial resource base.

Markham was also concerned about ESL's weakness in management. He and Blake had been adequately handling many of the firm's administrative tasks, but he recognized that their skills and interests were in the technical rather than managerial arena. Although he had a full-time bookkeeper/accountant who handled most financial matters, and two secretaries who handled much of the administrative detail, Markham was concerned about the potential for increased administrative problems as the firm grew. Markham and Blake were already involved in each of the contracts, and they were beginning to be stretched thin as the number of contracts increased. Requirements for additional administrative tasks would quickly overwhelm them.

OPTIONS FOR ADDRESSING ESL'S PROBLEMS

Markham had considered several different options for overcoming ESL's problems. Although many of the firm's weaknesses could be eliminated by pursuing a strategy of slower or regionally concentrated growth, this could threaten ESL's ability to retain market leadership. Therefore, Markham was unwilling to pursue this path. During the past year, Markham had also been approached by several firms and venture capitalists interested in purchasing all or part of ESL. However, he and Blake were not interested in selling out. They had a strong sense of ownership and pride in their firm, and wanted to see it succeed as an independent entity. In addition, the partners wanted to retain their control over product quality, and feared that this would be hindered if their ownership position was substantially diluted. Instead, Markham decided to seek an alliance with another firm, since that could preserve the partners' control over internal activities while still enabling ESL to access the resources necessary to sustain growth and market leadership.

With the help of a consultant, Markham and Blake had spent the past three months identifying and evaluating prospective partner firms. From an initial list of over thirty companies, they had identified the following four firms which seemed to be the most promising partner candidates.

Johnson Technologies Inc.

Johnson Technologies was a recognized leader in the sales and service of general application computer hardware and software, and related electronic equipment to medium- and large-sized firms in North America and Europe. The company was known for its broad product line; its large, aggressive and technically skilled sales force; and the strength of its worldwide service network. Johnson Technologies' advertisements proclaimed that the company was "dedicated to supplying all of your business technology needs," but its product line did not include any engineering document storage systems. Highly profitable and rapidly growing, the Los Angeles-based company earned over $150 million in 1988 on revenues of $725 million. Although publicly owned, Johnson Technologies was tightly controlled by its founder, Robert Johnson, a shrewd deal-maker who had designed the company as a reflection of his own personality: intelligent, intensely competitive, and dedicated to being number one in its business. Johnson Technologies had recently acquired several subsidiaries, including a software development firm, but had never been involved in joint ventures.

VBF Inc.

VBF was a large, highly diversified multinational firm with interests in retailing, consumer goods, real estate and financial services. Based in New York and with its Canadian operations headquartered in Montreal, VBF had consolidated worldwide sales of over $7 billion in 1988. VBF's current CEO had publicly expressed his commitment toward strengthening the competitive position of the company's smallest unit, the Technical Systems Division. This division, with 1988 sales of $250 million, was involved primarily in the aerospace and electronics industries. Over the past year and a half, the division had committed over $100 million to new acquisitions and joint ventures, and it was expected to continue this strategy for the next several years. Reflecting the diversity among its many businesses, this division was managed in a very decentralized manner. Industry insiders reported that the Technical Systems Division was particularly interested in computer hardware and software businesses in which it could develop a sustainable leadership position, and that it was prepared to invest heavily in order to achieve this objective.

Silcor Inc.

Based in Palo Alto, California, Silcor was a vertically integrated firm involved in the design, manufacture and sale of computer hardware, including microcomputers, minicomputers and monitors. Premium priced to reflect their additional quality and features, Silcor's products were well regarded in the industry, and ESL had incorporated them within a number of its document storage system installations. The bulk of Silcor's nearly $900 million in sales came from a well-trained U.S. and Canadian sales force. Despite a very bureaucratic corporate mentality, Silcor had consistently outperformed the industry during the past five years. To maintain its rapid growth rate and help counteract a recent slump in the hardware industry's sales, Silcor had established a subsidiary which provided computer hardware and software consulting and maintenance services to larger businesses, and was considering expanding this operation to all of the major urban areas in North America. In addition, Silcor had negotiated exclusive licenses for marketing several lines of specialized, premium-priced business software. Silcor had also invested over $50 million in in-house software development efforts, including an attempt to produce a computerized engineering document storage system designed for use with its own computer hardware. However, Silcor had encountered difficulties in developing commercially viable software and was currently considering acquisition of or joint venture with one or more software firm.

Computer Solutions Inc.

Computer Solutions Inc. (CSI), a firm based in San Jose, California, was involved in the design, installation and servicing of a variety of customized computer systems for corporations, including computerized engineering document storage systems. CSI was owned by Nathan Greenberg, a 48-year-old software programmer who had been a well-known participant in the Silicon Valley computer subculture since the mid-1960s. Widely touted as a visionary and charismatic leader, Greenberg had been involved in a number of large and small computer firms during his career, although he had devoted the last dozen years to creating two other start-ups which were subsequently sold to large corporations. CSI was formed in 1986, and was estimated to have achieved over $10 million in revenues and $1.5 million in earnings in 1988. Although its technology differed somewhat from ESL's, CSI's document storage systems were regarded as extremely reliable and utilized compatible hardware. Despite CSI's smaller number of installed systems, Greenberg's reputation had enabled the company to achieve a greater degree of success in selling to large firms, and Markham estimated the combined market share of the two firms would be approximately 20%.

CONCLUSION

Markham was unsure which of the potential partners would be best to pursue, or what criteria he should use in making his decision. However, with the recent entry of several large competitors and the pressure to respond to the rapid growth and changes in the market, it was clear that ESL would have to move quickly in order for the venture to be successful.

DAYTUN INC.

J. Michael Geringer and Lorrie Kope

Seated in his office in Daytun Inc.'s spacious new headquarters in London, Ontario in June 1990, president and majority shareholder Doug Bell was reevaluating his ten-year old company's strategy. Specializing principally in the sales and service of Konica photocopiers, Daytun's reputation for excellent service and high-quality products had helped them achieve the leading market share position in London. Wanting to maintain this performance, Doug had set a goal of increasing Daytun's revenues from the existing $6 million to $10 million within the next two years. However, the copier market was maturing rapidly, and, with an economic recession approaching and indications of increasing competition from such giant multinational firms as Xerox and Canon, significant increases in Konica copier sales and service revenues in the London market seemed unlikely. To achieve their growth objective, Daytun would have to expand their product line in the London area, and/or broaden their scope to new geographic markets. To pursue either option, Doug would have to decide whether to acquire an existing company or establish the venture from scratch.

THE LONDON PHOTOCOPIER MARKET

As the 1990s began, the London photocopier market, like the overall North American market for serviced copiers, was maturing rapidly as most potential customers had satisfied their needs for copier equipment. The use of copiers had become commonplace, and, except for changes associated with increased population, further growth would largely be restricted to identifying remaining unserved niche sites, upgrading existing installations, or changing behaviour patterns of existing users (e.g., encouraging increased consumption at existing sites). Harvey Schilke, Daytun's vice-president and minority shareholder, was projecting zero growth in the London copier market for the next two to three years due, in part, to an economic recession that was expected to grip the region in the coming months.

Competition

Products of four manufacturers — Konica, Xerox, Sharp, and Canon — accounted for 84% of the installed base of copiers in London. Doug estimated that Daytun's base of over 1 700 installed machines provided them with a 30% market share. Exhibit 1 provides estimated U.S. and London market shares by brand name.

Xerox

Xerox and their wholly-owned Xerox Canada subsidiary, were leaders in the U.S. and Canadian copier industry due to strengths in equipment quality, national marketing, and strong branch support and customer service. Other than Kodak, they were the only firm to exclusively use a company-owned branch system rather than dealers to market and service their copiers. Xerox's market position was particularly strong among large accounts, which were their main focus. Although traditionally offering copiers in all market segments, Xerox's product positioning had shifted almost exclusively toward premium priced machines in the mid-1980s. Industry experts reasoned that this change resulted from increasing competition in lower priced copiers and corporate level financial problems which emerged during this time. Xerox also confronted pressure to fund high overhead expenses associated with their extensive research and development expenditures, and national sales and service network. In recent years, several observers had criticized Xerox for lacking depth and flexibility in their technical and commercial service in many local markets, including the London area. Nevertheless, Xerox had placed about 1 400 machines in the London market, including several of the largest accounts.

Canon

Canon enjoyed a reputation similar to Xerox, including a high-quality product line, national advertising and promotion, a high degree of technical innovation, and expertise in marketing and sales. Canon had been successful across a broad product line, including low-priced, personal and full colour copiers. OE Canada, the exclusive distributor for Canon's copiers and other business machines in Ontario and Quebec, had revenues of $250 million in 1989, or 50–60% of total Canon Canada revenues.

Although historically pricing 5–10% below Xerox, Canon's London dealer had failed to successfully leverage Canon's extensive national advertising and high product quality into a strong market position. They had approximately 700 machine placements, mainly with accounts requiring only one or two copiers, and minimal presence in the major London accounts segment. They controlled the limited London colour copying market, as Canon did in the overall North

American market. They devoted minimal investment toward the marketing and service functions. Both the financial situation and market placements had deteriorated as customer satisfaction, especially with respect to service, dwindled. Recently, however, changes had been occurring. Canon U.S. had announced doubled production output in 1989, suggesting pressure to increase placement numbers. In the fall of 1989, OE Canada claimed the assets of Canon's London dealer in settlement of their accounts payable. Concurrently, Canon Canada bought OE Canada and their Toronto and Montreal dealerships, and they began to restructure the London dealership and increase market share through more aggressive pricing.

Sharp

Sharp maintained a presence in all segments, although they primarily competed in low- to mid-volume machines. They were a leader in the facsimile market, and their total 1989 Canadian business machine revenues were $140 million. Sharp's London dealership was formed in 1975, and had nearly 1 000 placements, including a well-established major accounts customer base. Although Sharp's London dealer followed an aggressive pricing strategy, their marketing and service areas had not been regarded as strong, with only two sales representatives, essentially zero local advertising, and limited training and development on the service dimension. Focused on maintaining their existing customer base and foregoing additional growth opportunities, this dealership had recently experienced base erosion as customers switched suppliers.

Copier market shares of the remaining 13 London area dealers were relatively small. The newest competitor was a Ricoh dealership established in October 1989 and spearheaded by two ex-Xerox sales managers. Ricoh's copier placements had grown at an average annual rate of 7.2% in the U.S., and they had recently entered the high-volume copier segments. It was not yet clear what type of support Ricoh might provide for their new London dealer. Nevertheless, with Xerox and Daytun controlling over 90% of London's major accounts, and with Daytun and Canon beginning to more aggressively target smaller accounts, rationalization was expected to occur as smaller dealers were squeezed out of the market.

Buyers

London, with a population of 280 000 had a variety of manufacturing, service, and government organizations, including the headquarters of several national and international businesses. Most of the larger organizations required centralized, high-volume copying stations with decentralized mid-volume copiers positioned for departmental ease of access. Thus, securing a contract for a high-end machine often resulted in the placement of a number of other lower volume copiers. Although small to medium-sized businesses also desired up-to-date copier features to suit their particular needs, they typically needed only one to two copiers, and at a single location.

The London market differed somewhat from the overall North American copier market, in that local businesses' purchase decisions tended to be more extensively influenced by dealer reputation and credibility, established through word-of-mouth and personal relationships. The selling cycle was also longer in London, and it was not uncommon for a dealer to wait two to three years to secure a new contract. London businesses would often give local dealers a chance to bid on a contract, whereas many businesses in larger cities such as Toronto would only consider the dominant share names such as Xerox and Canon.

A recent survey conducted by Daytun revealed that most London businesses were satisfied with their existing suppliers, and that a trend toward longer term supplier relationships was developing. Most Daytun customers based their purchase decision on service, dealer reputation, and price, and would change dealers due to unsatisfactory service, first, or equipment, second. Of those surveyed, 80% who had expressed an equipment or service concern, and had received a satisfactory response had indicated stronger loyalty to their dealer.

THE COMPANY

When Daytun was formed in 1980, Xerox dominated the London market. Doug had recently sold his Savin dealership in Thunder Bay, Ontario, and Harvey was an ex-Xerox employee. These partners saw an opportunity to position Daytun through a strategy of high-quality service at a medium price. They implemented London's first cost-per-copy product packaging approach, which factored the unit cost of the machine and the cost of supplies, toner and service into one price quoted to the customer on a per copy basis. This approach had three advantages: (1) it made it very easy for the customer to acquire a total copying package with uncomplicated cost calculations, and the convenience of one-stop shopping; (2) it focused on the actual users of the equipment in allowing the company to buy copies, not copiers; and (3) it established the basis for a long-term service relationship between Daytun and the client. This strategy could only be successful if backed by an extremely strong service system, which Daytun focused their efforts on developing.

Daytun's costing concept was not used by any other London dealers, who instead used the traditional approach of selling the copier but not necessarily the service contract. Thus competitors' local service systems were not as highly developed as Daytun's. As a result, Daytun's growth averaged of 30–40% annually since 1985, and they were the highest volume distributor of Konica products in Canada over the prior three years (see Exhibit 2 for financial statements).

Daytun's success was based on a strategy of differentiation through exemplary customer, commercial and technical service, and providing a high-quality copier at prices 10% below comparable Xerox copiers. Because Xerox needed high margins to support their overhead and R&D expenses, Doug believed that Xerox posed a limited pricing threat. Recently, Xerox had taken a large University of Western Ontario account from Daytun by offering a price which several industry experts felt would be below Xerox's costs. However, this radical price cutting had not been repeated, suggesting that the action may have been a whim on the part of Xerox.

Daytun's success was also embedded in their customer-focused philosophy, including: their ability to provide quick response to customer problems; technical strength to solve copier problems the first time; customer support for user-training and problem solving; and maintaining a philosophy that if a machine could not be fixed it would be replaced immediately. These conditions held whether the unit had been purchased outright or was maintained under a rental agreement, and Daytun ensured replacement of obsolete or malfunctioning rental copiers. The majority of the rental fleet copiers had been replaced in 1989, enabling Daytun to offer some of the most modern equipment available in the market.

Wanting to maintain Daytun's high growth, Doug had set the following goals: increase revenue to $10 million by 1992 while increasing or at least maintaining profit margins; reduce supplier influence; decrease inventory to approximately $600 000; and build both strength and depth in middle management. Although setting ambitious goals for Daytun over the next two years, Doug and Harvey were particularly concerned about meeting their personal objectives. They wished to maintain their personal base of operations in London; maintain or decrease their present workload, including limiting the time spent at Daytun to 40 hours per week; and generally focus on an improved lifestyle with more time for their families.

Product/Market Focus

Daytun's geographic territory included London and the surrounding counties of Elgin, Perth, Middlesex and Oxford, with over 85% of their business in London. Within these areas, copier sales and service constituted 85% of total revenue, mainly for machines in mid- to high-volume segments. Several low end machines were also carried, because Harvey felt they provided good training for salespeople, enabled Daytun to offer a complete copier package to their customers, and maintained cash flow. More focus was placed on helping customers trade-up to larger, more productive, service-intensive machines, where Daytun could better apply their skills.

Daytun's mid- to high-end copiers offered the latest technological features and advancements. Daytun stayed away from full-colour capabilities as demand was limited, Canon already had a dominant market position, and the technology's extremely high service-intensity dictated a very expensive running cost. Digital copier technology was still in the developmental stage, and Harvey suspected that, when fully developed, the technology would be used by very centralized operations and could be marketed by large, multinational firms such as Xerox or IBM. Daytun's traditional focus of providing a product that belonged in every company made it unlikely that digital technology would be a major element of their future product line. However, Harvey forecast that technological developments would reduce the need for maintenance and repair service on copiers, and he planned to gradually move Daytun toward software support to meet these changing needs.

Facsimiles and typewriters/word processors represented 10% and 5% respectively of Daytun's revenues. Service applications were limited for facsimile machines as they seldom broke down and were generally user-friendly, requiring minimal formal training. Thus, the facsimile distributor market and margins were declining, although Konica facsimiles were still being sold. Typewriter placements were declining rapidly, and the majority of Daytun's business was with one account. Doug did not foresee growth opportunities in either the facsimile or typewriter markets.

Overall, equipment sales, rental and service constituted 50%, 30% and 20% respectively of Daytun's revenues. However, most of Daytun's recent growth in sales and profits had been in the service area, where service contract revenue had been increasing at 20–30% each year. Doug saw this as a sign of increased user preference for service expertise, and that Daytun's competitive strategy in the London market was succeeding.

Suppliers

Daytun currently distributed copier and facsimile equipment for Konica, and typewriters from Panasonic. Daytun had not always distributed Konica copiers. In 1984, they discontinued their Savin copier distributorship due to equipment quality problems. They then carried only Panasonic copiers for 18 months, until Konica approached Daytun in 1985. Dissatisfied with both Savin and Panasonic, they gradually built a base of Konica copiers, and subsequently switched completely to a full Konica line. Attributing Daytun's explosive growth to the Konica line, Doug stated, "If we were still representing only Savin and Panasonic, we wouldn't be where we are today." However, Doug was considering renewing

Daytun's relationship with Savin, since he felt that several recent changes had solved Savin's quality problems and that their mid-priced copiers would complement Konica's line.

Daytun maintained excellent supplier relations, as this was critical to their strategy of pricing 10% below Xerox, and Konica assured Daytun that they would maintain their lower relative price. However, one of Doug's goals was to reduce supplier influence over Daytun's operations. Many dealers became financially bound to their suppliers through excessive accounts payable. Subsequently, the supplier exerted more control over product positioning, marketing and general operations. To maintain autonomy and uphold their strategy of promoting the Daytun name as opposed to the Konica name, Doug aimed to eliminate essentially all debt with Konica. He also intended to add or drop suppliers in order to provide the product mix that would best meet customer needs. The difficulty in adding another supplier was Konica's extensive product line, which left few gaps, and the already established manufacturer/dealer network in London. As many dealers sold on an exclusive basis, acquiring another copier line would likely require the purchase of a competing dealership. Switching suppliers completely was difficult, given the large investment required in equipment, inventory and personnel training. Daytun currently held $1 million in inventory, including a showroom display inventory of $100 000.

Customers

Daytun emphasized larger accounts, where the value of commercial and technical service was appreciated, and pursued a strategy of becoming the preferred major or sole copier supplier for such accounts. Daytun also provided local service for Savin's national accounts. Recently, with saturation of the large accounts segment, Daytun had placed more emphasis on obtaining smaller accounts, particularly those with high-service needs. According to London customer survey results, Daytun had achieved a 90% service satisfaction rating, and an 85% copier reliability satisfaction rating. Believing the quickest way to lose a client was through poor service. Doug wanted to maintain or improve these percentages. As for availability of features, only 5% of customers expressed concerns with the features currently available on Konica copiers.

Structure

As shown in Exhibit 3, the 55-person Daytun organization was headed by Doug and Harvey, and divided functionally into three departments: finance and administration, sales, and service. Their overall structure and culture were based on a model of total excellence, and Daytun's professional atmosphere and culture was described by some as a "mini-Xerox" competing in the London market. They hired the best people in all aspects of the organization, and emphasized continual development of personal and job skills, with outside consultants brought in to provide training in such topics as time management, goal setting and customer relations. Compensation packages were excellent, including many fringe benefits and a gain-sharing plan which paid $30 000 per year to employees. Three of Daytun's nine salespeople earned more than $100 000 per year, earnings uncommon among copier salespeople.

Doug and Harvey encouraged a culture of open communication and total participation which fit well with Daytun's small size. Willing to listen to and experiment with new ideas, Doug encouraged Daytun employees to take responsibility for decisions within the company, stating, "You've got to make the system work, I'm not going to make it work for you." A real sense of purpose was displayed by all areas, stemming from the belief that Daytun's success was dependent upon the team spirit among each and every individual and department. Doug and Harvey did not take credit for the unique Daytun spirit that existed, noting, "We didn't create it, we just allowed it to happen." Yet, because of their extensive knowledge about the industry and the company, the partners were consulted frequently by all levels of the organization. In general, morale was high, turnover was low, and promotions occurred from within when possible.

Doug was responsible for Daytun's strategic direction and long-term planning. He also oversaw the finance, administration and personnel areas. With his visionary optimism and energetic enthusiasm, he had a unique ability to empower others to his excitement to make things happen. He could be described as a charismatic leader representing the heart and soul of Daytun.

Harvey's market driven approach to the sales organization was another key to Daytun's success, helping them land contracts with clients for which other London dealers would be passed over. Harvey's extensive personal involvement had resulted in a very skilled salesforce capable of presenting the appropriate package to meet the client's individual needs. Their highly successful presentation strategies, including the cost per copy concept, allowed Daytun to establish solid contracts from the outset. Although Harvey maintained a few of the largest accounts, he primarily focused on developing Daytun's positioning strategy. Since the fall of 1989, when he assumed responsibility for overseeing the service area as well as sales, day-to-day cooperative decision making between Harvey and the field service managers had consumed most of his time. Although necessary to overcome poor integration which had existed between the two areas — one providing hardware solutions and the other providing software solutions, Harvey wanted to reduce these demands on his time by improving the level of management skills within both areas.

Daytun's salespeople received a straight 40% of gross margin commission. Managers received no extra compensation for managing, and worked 80 hours per week to keep up with their job demands. Salespeople were assigned to territories divided geographically by postal code. They spent 85–95% of their time with existing accounts ensuring that customers were satisfied with service and equipment, adding and upgrading equipment, and renegotiating service contracts. This permitted only limited time for pursuing new accounts or business that currently belonged to competitors. Yet, Harvey emphasized that his salespeople pursue each and every account, stating, "You can't afford to pass by a door and say that you won't call on that particular firm. People talk to everyone here." Harvey wanted Daytun to be talked about.

Another key to Daytun's success was their tremendous service network. Service technicians were encouraged to look and behave as professionals, and all had taken customer relations and time management courses. To promote superior performance, the field service managers used 30/60/90 day goals related to cost cutting, time management, motivation, and customer relations. Technicians were expected to think about and make decisions for themselves as much as possible. They were responsible for their own specific set of machines and yearly performance reviews were, in part, determined through customer satisfaction ratings.

The dispatch area was Daytun's lifeline, as the dispatcher was the first contact a concerned customer would have with Daytun. The dispatcher needed to be knowledgeable of the workings of the business, the parts lingo, and how to relate effectively with both service technicians and customers. Dispatcher training covered an eight-month time span and excellent customer service and telephone techniques, embodied in the philosophy of doing whatever it takes to help the customer. Before moving to the new building, turnover was high in the dispatch area due to poor working conditions, low pay, and a high-stress position. Doug believed that the weak link between sales and service had also contributed to dispatch employee dissatisfaction. Since the move, the dispatchers had seemed quite content.

The controller was responsible for finance and administration. She described the current operations as "chaotic at times," due to the company's fast paced growth. Daytun's prior facilities became severely overcrowded as more clerks were hired to keep up with growth, and increasing amounts of time were required to train new clerks. She believed that more people were still necessary in the administration area to ensure smooth flowing operations.

DECIDING ON A FUTURE STRATEGY FOR THE COMPANY

Recent changes in the competitive environment, including actions by Xerox, Canon, and Ricoh in the London market, had prompted Doug to reexamine Daytun's current strategy. Not wanting to relinquish growth objectives, but realizing that additional growth in the mature London copier market would be difficult, Doug knew that consideration would have to be given to expanding product areas and/or geographical presence.

Growth in the Photocopier Market

Konica, impressed with Daytun's success in London, had been encouraging them to expand into new markets. In the past, opportunities to expand geographically had been turned down because they would have required one of the partners to move to another city. Recently, Konica had proposed two metropolitan areas, one with a population of roughly 350 000, the other with a population of roughly 125 000. The business community structures were similar to London and included several large firms. Since both areas were within 200 kilometres of London, Daytun might be able to leverage its existing reputation and copier sales and service expertise to establish a business in one or both of these areas. While a Konica dealership currently existed in the larger metropolitan area, it had achieved a market share of less than 5% and Konica had suggested that Daytun purchase the dealership. The other option was to establish a new dealership in the smaller community, where Konica did not currently have a dealer.

Doug felt that demands on management time and money would be higher if establishing a new dealership. Duplication of the Daytun philosophy, culture and operations would be challenging within an area unfamiliar to Daytun and where the Konica and Daytun names had not developed the strong reputation achieved in London. Furthermore, in a mature copier industry, it would be difficult to gain market share from established competitors whose efforts were also focused on maintaining existing customers.

Doug was also concerned that purchasing the poorly performing dealer in the larger metropolitan area could put the existing Daytun business at risk, particularly if the two companies were fully integrated. Daytun could be faced with employees and a company culture that did not match Daytun's philosophy. The basis for success in London was a philosophy and culture developed and strengthened over the years through the partners' leadership. Neither partner had been faced with a company turnaround, where existing systems had to be taken apart before rebuilding a new and better system.

Doug had also considered the option of expanding Daytun's business in the London area by purchasing another competitor. The London Sharp dealership was a possibility, given the owner's lack of interest in pursuing a growth strategy. As Daytun focused on the mid- to high-volume copier segments, this option might yield increased market penetration within low-volume copier segments, while also introducing opportunities for upgrading these low-volume accounts. However, Daytun had built its reputation based on exemplary customer service in high-volume segments. These attributes were not as critical in the low-volume segments, where copiers were designed to be maintenance free or user-serviced as much as possible. Daytun would also forego the potential scale benefits achieved by establishing another Konica dealer, including reduced costs, improved margins, and/or continuation of the current strategy of pricing 10% below Xerox.

An opportunity to expand business on a national scale had recently been pre-sented to Doug by a large bank and trust company headquartered in London. This was an option Doug had not previously considered, but one which now held his interest. Although currently supplied by Xerox and Canon, this company had recently announced that their supply contracts were open for outside bids, and they had solicited Daytun's participation. Becoming the preferred national supplier for such a successful, large company could not only generate increased revenues but also enhance the reputation of both Daytun and Konica across Canada. The London base of operations could be maintained, while Daytun arranged for service technicians to be available across Canada on a contract basis with other dealers. As service quality was of utmost importance, tight control on such an arrangement would be necessary. One threat to such an expansion was the potential response from Xerox or Canon.

Growth Into Non-Copier Markets

Diversification into new product markets had also been contemplated. Over the past couple of years, Doug and Harvey had considered—and rejected—a number of different product additions, including microcomputers, electronic data filing systems, and mailing machines. For example, Daytun was approached by two overseas manufacturers to distribute mailing machines in the London market, a business dominated by Pitney Bowes. However, Daytun did not see an opportunity to add value. Both the product and pricing were governmen-tally controlled, hindering Daytun's ability to achieve a product, service or pricing advantage.

One alternative which Doug was currently examining was the acquisition of a dealership for an office products and point-of-sale (POS) systems company which was for sale in London. The POS line was comprised of products ranging from cash registers to fully integrated scanning systems providing inventory management and other analytical functions. Total company sales were approx-imately $800 000, with the POS line contributing over $250 000. The remainder of the firm's revenue came from calculators, typewriters, dictation machines, and lower-end sundry items such as typewriter ribbons. Doug did not foresee sub-stantial growth potential for these latter products. The company was very service-oriented to the point where taking care of the customer superseded making any profit. The resulting break-even financial management approach had not allowed the business to sustain itself and grow over the long term. The company currently employed 11 people: the owner and his wife, four service people, one direct salesperson, and four people in administration. Doug described that company as "stable but stuck in a rut."

This product diversification might complement Daytun's existing business in that the product required regular and ongoing service support by an experienced technician, and it would allow Daytun to add value in the areas of corporate culture and philosophy, customer service and support, financial resources, and the leadership skills of their upper management. Significant near-term growth was forecast in the London market for POS systems, particularly for scanning systems in supermarkets, drug stores and related outlets. Doug believed that competition within the market for POS machines was relatively weak, with a high degree of fragmentation and relatively unknown brand names, allowing Daytun the opportunity to develop a significant market share. Harvey saw an opportunity to position Daytun within the POS systems and software side of the business, as most firms had concentrated on the cash register business. However, this was a product area in which Daytun lacked proven skills or expertise, thus requiring the acquisition of such needed talents. Doug was not convinced that an unhealthy company requiring turnaround management was the best fit with Daytun strengths. Thus, taking over this company, with a well-developed customer base and the ability to provide immediate cash flow, could be a wise option. As with geographical expansion, the acquisition opportunity could place financial pressure on Daytun, and could jeopardize the existing business since Doug expected the current owners to ask in the neighbourhood of $200 000–300 000 for their company.

THE DECISION

The future of Daytun could not be decided upon without keeping in mind the strong preferences of the partners, Daytun's corporate culture and resources, and their specific areas of strength and expertise. The impact of growth was already being questioned by some of the long-term Daytun employees. There was concern that Daytun's culture was changing and everyone had to work much harder at communicating. What would be the impact of an even larger Daytun? How readily transferable were Daytun's copier sales and service expertise to other products or markets? Was Daytun prepared for either strategic direction? These were all considerations which Doug needed to examine thoroughly before a final decision could be made. However, time was of the essence, given the approaching economic recession and rapidly maturing copier market. Doug wondered what direction he should lead Daytun in order to position it for a successful future.

EXHIBIT 1 Estimated Photocopier Market Shares, 1989*

	US (%)	*London (%)*
Xerox	18	25
Canon	14	12
Sharp	13	17
Mita	10	N/A
Konica	7	30
Minolta	6	N/A
Ricoh	6	N/A
Lanier	5	N/A
Toshiba	4	N/A
Savin	4	N/A
Others	12	16

* Figures exclude personal copier replacements. N/A is used when accurate estimates are not available.

SOURCE: Dataquest reports, Daytun Inc. surveys, and casewriter estimates.

EXHIBIT 2 Daytun's Financial Statements[1]

Income Statement		
	1989 (000s)	*1988* (000s)
Revenue		
Equipment Sales	$2 962	$3 146
Equipment Rental	1 749	1 504
Sales of Supplies	297	200
Maintenance Contracts	1 018	789
Miscellaneous Revenues	14	11
Total Revenue	$6 040	$5 650
Expenses		
Cost of Product Sold	2 885	2 645
Installation & Service	832	765
Occupancy Costs	57	51
Selling & Administration[2]	1 366	1 622
Depreciation & Amortization	295	274
Interest on Long Term Debt	140	106
Total Expenses	$5 575	$5 463
Earnings from Operations	465	187
Income Taxes	198	78
Net Earnings	267	109
Shareholder Payouts	127	92
Retained Earnings	$140	$17

[1] Some figures in the text and in the exhibits are disguised, while others represent casewriter estimates.

[2] Includes salaries to owners.

Balance Sheet

	1989 (000s)	1988 (000s)
Current Assets		
Cash	$ 2	$ 2
Accounts Receivable	591	503
Inventory	990	840
Prepaid Expenses	15	11
Total Current Assets	$1 598	$1 356
Revenue Earning Equipment	1 911	1 747
Less: Accumulated Depreciation	(784)	(731)
Fixed Assets	780	560
Less: Accumulated Depreciation	(182)	(213)
Total Assets	$3 323	$2 719
Current Liabilities		
Bank Indebtedness	390	245
Accounts Payable[3]	775	755
Taxes Due	51	44
Deferred Revenue[4]	485	430
Current Portion of Long Term Debt	310	285
Total Current Liabilities	$2 011	$1 759
Long Term Debt[5]	643	431
Shareholder Equity	188	188
Retained Earnings	481	341
Total Liabilities and Shareholder Equity	$3 323	$2 719

[3] Includes accounts payable to Konica Business Machines, Limited of $534 000 in 1989 and $383 000 in 1988.

[4] Under lease agreements involving rental equipment, income is recognized as it is earned. On maintenance contracts, income is recognized on a straight line basis over the term of the contract.

[5] Includes mortgage on headquarters building and land. Bank indebtedness is secured by a general security agreement, a registered security agreement covering specific equipment and/or real property, personal guarantees of the shareholders, and an assignment of fire insurance.

EXHIBIT 3   Daytun's Organization Chart

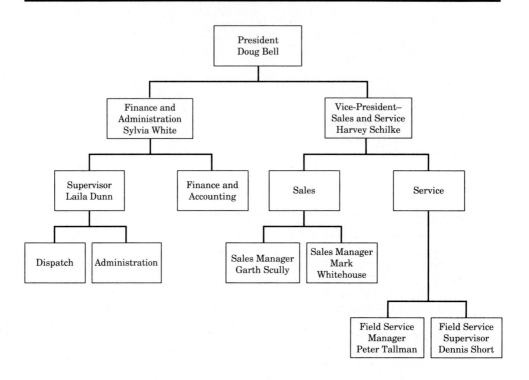

POLYSAR LIMITED AND TORNAC RUBBER

J. Michael Geringer
and William A. Pursell

As he strode his customary three kilometres to his Toronto office on November 8, 1988, Doug Henderson, the recently appointed Group Vice-President of Polysar Limited's Global Rubber business, knew that he would be facing a divided and emotionally charged rubber management team at the meeting he had scheduled for that day. The previous week he had presented the team members with a proposal outlining two alternative strategies for commercializing TORNAC, a hydrogenated nitrile rubber (H-NBR) which Polysar had developed for the emerging high-heat and oil-resistant segment of the rubber business. One of the proposed strategies was to continue the traditional Polysar approach of complete independence, and compete directly with the other two contenders in this segment: Bayer A.G. of Germany and Nippon Zeon of Japan. This option, supported by several of the team members, would require that Polysar assume all of the risk—but reap all of the potential rewards—associated with such independence. The alternative strategy, which also had several supporters on the team, was to forge a strategic alliance with Bayer, and thus share the risk and potential rewards arising from such an alliance. Doug was still uncertain about which alternative he should support, as well as how he should go about making and implementing such a decision without creating serious conflict, and possibly long-term divisions, among the team members. However, because of pressure from Bayer, and because the Polysar 1989 budget data had to be finalized imminently, he knew he would have to reach a decision on this issue within the next two weeks. He needed the rubber management team to explore each option thoroughly, and assist him in making the best decision.

THE SYNTHETIC RUBBER INDUSTRY

Synthetic rubber is a polymer synthesized from derivates of oil and natural gas. Rubber polymers based on petroleum were first developed in the 1930s, and many different kinds of such polymers had been commercialized globally since that time. Wide-spread innovation in both processes and polymer products was normal for the industry. By 1988, nearly 70% of the rubber used globally was of the synthetic type.

Manufacturers of synthetic rubber polymers fell basically into three categories: oil and gas producers that had integrated forward through the intermediate raw materials into the final polymers; end-use polymer consumers (e.g., tire companies) who had integrated backwards into synthetic rubber to secure their supply source; and chemical companies which produced synthetic rubber polymers and the intermediate raw materials as a main-line business. Polysar fell into the third category, as did companies such as Dupont, Bayer, Enichem, and Nippon Zeon.

The capital costs associated with building synthetic rubber plants, providing facilities for the intermediate raw materials, and "cracking" oil and natural gas into usable petrochemical components, were large. A world-scale synthetic rubber plant normally cost in excess of $100 million, an intermediate raw material plant in the $200–300 million range, and a basic oil/gas "cracker" between $500–1 000 million.

The major producers of synthetic rubber polymers and their consumers were concentrated in the industrialized nations of the world, with the value of production in 1988 in the $15–20 billion range. The major end-uses for synthetic rubber arose from such industries as automotive, construction, general manufacturing, oil drilling and production, packaging and textiles.

Synthetic rubber polymers were produced globally in a wide variety of types. These ranged from so-called commodity or general purpose products (such as SBR rubber for tires), through products with some special performance feature, to highly sophisticated products with a combination of special features such as abrasion resistance, flexibility, oil resistance, high temperature resistance, impermeability to gases, design capability, and so on. With rapid advances in end-use and consumer technology, increasingly high standards of performance were being demanded, particularly in the high-end specialty performance segment. This accelerating trend toward replacing general purpose products with higher performance specialty products was expected to continue well into the future.

The Specialty Performance Segment

The synthetic rubber polymer business worldwide comprised approximately 80% general purpose products and 20% specialty products. The high-performance niche, represented by products such as Polysar's TORNAC RUBBER, fell within the specialty category. Global volumes sharply contrasted between categories:

General purpose: 8 million tons
Specialty: 2 million tons
TORNAC type niche: 1–2 thousand tons

Prices also contrasted sharply depending upon product segment. General purpose products were normally sold for less than $1/lb, specialty products in the $1–$5/lb range, and the TORNAC RUBBER niche in the $10–$15/lb range.

Within the Specialty category, one of the major requirements was for synthetic rubber polymers with good heat, ozone (sunlight) and oil resistance. These properties were required for automotive, oil-well, aerospace and industrial component industries. The performance standards for these properties had risen steadily over the previous few decades, with technical requirements becoming increasingly difficult to meet. The main synthetic rubber which had historically been used for these special conditions was nitrile rubber (NBR). Product variations of NBR included many dozens of types for different end-uses and operating conditions. The major international producers of NBR in 1988 were as follows:

Company	Capacity (000 tons)	Plant Location
Nippon Zeon*	65	Japan, U.S., U.K.
Polysar	55	Canada, France
Bayer*	35	Germany
Enichem	35	Italy
Goodyear	34	France, U.S.
JSR	30	Japan
Uniroyal	20	U.S.

* Exhibits 1 and 2 have background information on Nippon Zeon and Bayer respectively.

SOURCE: International Institute of Synthetic Rubber Producers, 1988 statistical data.

The importance of nitrile rubber, and the companies' relative competitive positions globally, arose from the widely held assumption that the top 10% (the high-performance segment) of the NBR business was open to replacement by the superior heat, oil and abrasion resistant products represented by TORNAC rubber and its competitors: Bayer's THERBAN and Nippon Zeon's ZETPOL. Nitrile producers who did not possess a hydrogenated NBR product were vulnerable to the loss of the high growth, premium end of their specialty business, and the premium profit margins expected therefrom.[1]

---

[1] According to industry experts, average return on sales for the rubber industry as a whole was approximately 7–8%.

Hydrogenated NBR Market (H-NBR)

H-NBR was a classic example of a product conceived, and developed in response to market pull from automotive and oil well industries. The increasing technical demands of these industries (spurred by such factors as smaller, hot-running car engines; pressure for fewer auto warranty claims in the face of Japanese competition; and the higher temperatures from deeper oil-well drilling) were not being satisfied by existing products. Regular nitrile rubber was being pushed beyond its performance limits, and more exotic products such as fluorelastomers lacked a proper balance of properties and required very high prices. What was needed was a product with a superior balance of oil, heat and ozone resistance, along with design capability, at an economic cost. H-NBR products were significantly better at satisfying these requirements than were regular NBR products.

In terms of market demand globally for H-NBR products, Polysar's market research study in 1986 (to support its production facility investment proposal early in 1987) included data in Table 1.

TABLE 1 H-NBR Market Forecast (tons)

	1986	1991		1996	
	Actual	*Base*	*Upside*	*Base*	*Upside*
U.S.	60	1 590	2 950	2 640	4 520
Europe	50	1 225	1 890	1 780	2 650
Japan	380	1 440	1 930	1 925	2 555
Other	—	—	300	—	700
Total	490	4 225	7 070	6 345	10 425

At that time, existing Bayer and Polysar facilities were pilot plants, as were 100 tons of the Nippon Zeon 600-ton capacity in Japan. In addition, Zeon had announced an expansion to 1 000 tons in 1987 as well as "evaluation of the feasibility of overseas production." Even with expansion by Nippon Zeon and possible commercialization of a new plant by Bayer in Germany, it was concluded by Polysar management in early 1987 that, based on the market research report, additional global production capacity would be required in the 1990s and, in particular, in the U.S. where the largest and fastest growing market was foreseen.

BACKGROUND ON POLYSAR

Polysar started out in 1943 as a Canadian producer of synthetic rubber to support the war effort; by 1988 it had become a major participant in the world's rubber, plastics and petrochemicals business. Its sales had grown to $2.5 billion, comprising 40% from synthetic rubber, 40% from petrochemicals, and 20% from plastics and diversified products. In synthetic rubber, Polysar was among the world's top three producers, and had been the global leader prior to closings of uneconomic facilities and the sale of non-strategic businesses in the 1987–88 period. Its range of rubber product types was still the broadest in the world, as was the geographic span of its production facilities.

Polysar's competitive strength had arisen from the scope of its international facilities and the comparable international experience of its people; from the technological orientation of its activities and the increasing breadth of its technology; and from its organizational emphasis on identifying and serving customer needs in the various geographic regions. It was particularly strong in the specialty rubber segment. In nitrile rubber, where H-NBR was expected to find its markets, Polysar held approximately 20% of both North American and European markets, and some 10% of the Japanese market.

Polysar's shareholder for most of the 1970s and 1980s had been Canada Development Corporation (CDC), but a fierce takeover battle in 1987, between Nova Corporation of Alberta and CDC, resulted in Polysar Ltd. becoming part of Nova in September 1988. Nova was a regionally oriented petrochemical, gas pipeline and energy company with operations located largely in Alberta. Historically, Nova's pipelines had transported more than 80% of marketed Canadian natural gas production. Its heavy involvement in this capital intensive industry was expected to continue, due to projections of strong growth of demand for gas in the U.S. and Canada through the mid-1990s. As shown in Exhibit 3, the Polysar acquisition substantially increased Nova's debt load, to a total of $4.3 billion. In addition, the Polysar rubber group had encountered difficult business conditions in 1988 and, by 1988's fourth quarter, was recording financial results some 20% below the level of operating income budgeted for that year.[2] According to Doug Henderson, however, "there was no particular financial pressure by Nova to consider an external TORNAC rubber alliance, although the senior management of Nova was kept constantly informed of the situation and the strategic alternatives being examined."

---

[2] Nova Corporation's annual report noted that, for the last 6 months of 1988, the Rubber Division had assets of $1.4 billion, revenues of $417 million and operating income of $37 million.

POLYSAR'S TORNAC RUBBER BUSINESS

As noted above, by the late 1970s and early 1980s, it had become clear to the management of Polysar's rubber division that the automotive industry's need for heat, oil and ozone resistant rubber polymers was not being met adequately by existing products. Not only were warranty claims from failed components becoming excessive, but North American cars were under increasing pressure from what were perceived to be higher quality Japanese vehicles.

Following extensive auto industry contacts, Polysar's R & D personnel had defined the required product parameters in 1981 to meet the above conditions. There followed a number of brain-storming sessions, involving R & D marketing and business managers, to examine the options for achieving such a product at economic cost, and to select a preferred route. More than 150 ideas were examined, and in early 1982, it had been decided to pursue a route of major chemical modification of nitrile rubber, a product in which Polysar was a world leader.

In making this decision, Polysar's management realized that Bayer in Germany had previously developed a nitrile-modified product in 1975, believed to have been R & D as opposed to market-driven. The process had been viewed by Polysar as inefficient and high cost, and Bayer was in fact trying to develop the European market from what was believed to be an uneconomic, semi-commercial 200-ton pilot plant facility. Polysar, therefore, decided in 1982 to develop its own product, based on R & D work it had already carried out on the "hydrogenation" of nitrile rubber.

It had been learned by Polysar that Dr. Gary Remple of the University of Waterloo was interested in, and involved with, "hydrogenation" of polymers to try to improve their performance. A contract was subsequently signed with Dr. Remple to develop a catalyst system to meet the defined product requirements, working with Polysar's technology personnel. A new system was rapidly developed and patent applications were filed late in 1982.

Over the following three years, a number of steps had been taken to develop a satisfactory commercial product, including the installation of a "bench-scale" reactor initially, a "pilot plant" as an intermediate step, and the design and engineering for a full-scale production plant. As Dr. John Dunn, senior scientist at Polysar, said, "It was a high-risk situation—we had to choose the right product route; we had many millions of R & D and future facility investment dollars at stake; we had to get the technology right; we had to move fast and we needed to get lucky. With Gary Remple, we got lucky!"

Polysar's efforts with Dr. Remple were so successful that the new TORNAC rubber technology had been awarded a gold medal for invention in 1987 under the Canadian government's Business Excellence program. The final product was judged by Polysar's technical people to be markedly superior to the Bayer product on both cost and process technology.

Nippon Zeon also had developed its own approach to H-NBR in the early 1980s. A Japanese pilot plant with 100 ton/annum capacity had been built initially, followed by a commercial plant of 500 tons by 1985. Zeon had avoided contravening Bayer's patents by utilizing a different catalyst to accomplish the required chemical modification of nitrile rubber. Initially, the Zeon product had been thought by Polysar to be inferior to TORNAC, but ongoing development work by Zeon produced a fully competitive product by 1987.

POLYSAR'S RUBBER STRATEGY

In April 1987, a full-scale capital investment proposal by Polysar's management for a TORNAC H-NBR production facility in Orange, Texas, was approved by the Polysar board of directors. This site was selected primarily because, with potential customers expected to be aerospace, military, oil well and automotive related, strategic location within the U.S. was critical. In addition, much lower capital and plant installation costs prevailed in Texas relative to possible northern locations. Included in the management justification for the project were the following observations:

TORNAC's Fit With Strategic Plan

The mission of the Global Rubber Business is to be a leading global supplier of elastomers with emphasis on those market sectors offering superior quality of earnings. One of the five Corporate Strategic Directives to the Rubber Business dictates that the Rubber Business "shift technology emphasis with priority to new, high performance products and applications, including externally sourced innovation." The proposed entry into the TORNAC Rubber Business is the first major project which has been successfully advanced towards this goal. Moreover, TORNAC Rubbers are expected to complement and enhance Polysar's strategic global nitrile business in terms of long-term profitability and competitive advantage as a supplier of oil resistant elastomers.

It was apparent, therefore, that the TORNAC rubber thrust was not only an integral part of the 1987 global rubber business strategy, but was also part of a corporate strategy to move increasingly to higher value-added products. This was confirmed in the Polysar rubber business plan issued internally by rubber management in the last quarter of 1988 (Table 2).

TABLE 2   Specialty Component of Rubber Business (% by volume)

	Forecast 1977	*1988*	*1992*
Specialty	45	64	67
Commodity	55	36	33

The definition of specialty rubbers was given as:
- Unit margins exceeded 50% of net selling price.
- Based on proprietary process or product technology.
- Required high level of technical/marketing support.

TORNAC rubber was well within the definition of the type of business in which Polysar wanted to focus its resources.

Competitive Positioning

The April 1987, TORNAC rubber investment project for production facilities in Texas included the following observations by Polysar's rubber management:

> A very significant feature of the feedback on the H-NBR rubber market survey has been the prime importance of the U.S. area in demand forecasts. We believe that Nippon Zeon, the current leader for hydrogenated NBR, will be discouraged from a decision to invest in North American production (1) by a definitive announcement of Polysar's decision to build and operate a global scale TORNAC rubber plant in the U.S., and (2) by the recent announcement by Bayer to build and operate a THERBAN rubber plant in Germany. It is more likely that Nippon Zeon will further expand its ZETPOL Rubber plant in Japan as market demand warrants.
>
> Thus, it is our view that each of the three producers of H-NBR will dominate in a specific major geographic region and have influential positions in the others, (1) Nippon Zeon in the Asia Pacific region, (2) Bayer in Europe, and (3) Polysar in North and South America.
>
> Thus, there is every reason to believe that Polysar will gain ground rapidly with a North American TORNAC rubber facility and superior process technology.

These management observations were followed by their assumptions on market size and the share which could be anticipated by Polysar in a base case situation. Thus, they stated in the 1987 project justification:

> Assuming that the TORNAC rubber plant comes on stream in the fourth quarter of 1988, Polysar should be able to gain a significant market share globally by 1991 and develop a strong leadership position by 1996—including a dominant position in the U.S. (Table 3).

TABLE 3 Polysar Market Share Projection: H-NBR (%)

	U.S.	*Europe*	*Japan*	*Global*
1991	45	20	10	26
1996	65	35	18	43

It was clear, therefore, that the global leadership aspirations of the Polysar rubber management for this market niche depended upon strong demand growth in the U.S., in particular, and also in Europe, and on Polysar securing significant market shares in these two regions. Transportation costs were a negligible factor in inter-regional competition.

POLYSAR'S ORGANIZATION

Over several decades, it had been Polysar's experience that the most effective way to organize for major new projects or businesses was to establish a special team or group separate from the day-to-day organization. Such groups usually reported to a senior member of Polysar's management.

TORNAC rubber was no exception. An original product/process development team was established in 1983 reporting directly to the manager of technical development division. When the product was judged ready for commercialization in 1986, a separate business management organization was established under Keith Ascroft as TORNAC rubber business manager. He had line responsibility for a market development manager, a manufacturing manager, a technical/R&D manager and an engineering (plant construction) manager. Sales were channelled through the regular rubber sales organization.

What happened as a result of this type of organization was immense focus on and dedication to success on the part of the specially selected groups of people. Another result was the development of strong emotional attachments to such projects, and increasingly strong feelings of proprietorship as the business or project unfolded and started to grow. In 1988, the TORNAC rubber business group appeared to fit this pattern of dedication and ownership. They reported directly to Doug Henderson, the Group Vice-President–Rubber.[3]

Financial Data

As part of the Polysar 1987 TORNAC rubber investment project, the following financial information was provided by Polysar's rubber management. In the five years prior to the facility investment proposal in early 1987, TORNAC rubber development costs (including a small pilot plant) were approximately $4 million, partially offset by a Canadian Government grant of $1 million. The investment project is shown in Table 4.

---

[3] See Exhibit 4, Polysar organization charts for 1985, 1987, 1988.

TABLE 4 **Polysar 1987 TORNAC Rubber Investment Project—Spending Profile** (US$ million)

	1986	1987	1988	1991	Total
Phase I (1 500 ton facility)	0.3	6.5	19.0	–	25.8
Phase II (3 000 ton facility)	–	–	–	5.2	5.2
					31.0

The anticipated discounted cash flow return (Base Case assumptions) on this investment was 22.8% for Phase I, and 26.5% for Phase I + II.[4] Polysar's hurdle rate in early 1987 was a minimum 20% discounted cash flow, with a 25% minimum rate for "high-risk" projects.

The 1987–88 Period

In the 18 months prior to the decision faced by Doug Henderson and his management in November 1988, several events had occurred which would have an impact on their deliberations.

Following Board approval in April 1987, the TORNAC rubber production facility investment in Orange, Texas, had gone ahead as planned under the direction of Keith Ascroft, the TORNAC rubber business manager. Towards the end of 1988, it was evident that the plant would come on stream at the turn of the year, as forecast, and its projected costs would be within the approval capital budget of U.S.$25.8 million.

Nippon Zeon not only had proceeded with the announced expansion of its Japanese H-NBR capacity in 1987 from 600 tons to 1 000 tons, but in fact had installed a total capacity of 1 800 tons by late 1988. A large proportion of Zeon's production had been directed toward auto industry applications such as engine drive belts, an $8–10 part whose failure could result in up to $1 000 in replacement costs. Moreover, in the third quarter of 1988, Zeon had announced its intention to construct a production plant in Clear Lake, Texas, with planned capacity of 1 500 tons. Bayer had announced a European production facility of 1 200 tons at the end of 1986, but by late 1988 had not yet proceeded with construction. It was believed by the Polysar management in 1988 that Bayer had neither the environmental clearance to build such a plant, nor a satisfactory production process for H-NBR at economic cost.

---

[4] For sensitivities around the Base Case and for projected cash flow and net income, see Exhibits 5 and 6.

The overall global market growth for the Polysar 1989–93 operating plan, as projected at the end of 1988, was reasonably in line with the 1986 market research report on which the Polysar TORNAC rubber facility was based (Table 5).

TABLE 5 H-NBR Market Demand (tons)

	1986 Actual	*1986 Market Research Base Case Forecast for 1990*	*1988 Revised Forecast for 1990*
U.S.	60	1 410	200
Europe	50	400	500
Japan	380	900	2 000
Total	490	2 710	2 700

The key reason for the deviations between the 1986 and the 1988 geographic forecasts was the behaviour of the respective auto industries of the three geographic regions. The automotive engines developed by the Japanese companies, together with their incessant drive for quality, demanded the higher product performance offered by H-NBR, even at relatively high prices. The European auto manufacturers, spurred by Japanese competition and probably by Japanese-transplant production in Europe, also required higher performance products such as H-NBR. In North America, however, the automobile manufacturers had been extremely slow to adopt Japanese-type engine technology and did not appear to be ready to do the necessary development work, nor to pay higher short-term prices for longer-term quality assurance and reduced post-sale service levels on their automobiles.

The impact of these geographic disparities was immense on the actual and anticipated competitive and market share positions of the three competitors in the H-NBR business. Nippon Zeon was the big winner with essentially 100% of the Japanese market and a significant share of the other much smaller markets, with the help of its already proven commercial product. Bayer, from its semi-commercial pilot plant, benefited somewhat from European growth (although it was judged by Polysar management to be losing a great deal of money from its inefficient production process). Polysar, at the end of 1988, was faced with its own new plant of 1 500 tons in North America, an announced U.S. plant of Zeon of similar capacity, and a market in North America estimated at a mere 200 tons by 1990. Faced with such projections of overcapacity, discussion had begun regarding the attractiveness of exploring formation of an alliance in H-NBR with one of Polysar's competitors.

THE OPPOSING VIEWS

When he faced his management team that morning, Doug had determined that he would play the role of "devil's advocate" to both the "independence" and "alliance" sides of the question, although he was aware that he was in a difficult position to do so. As he stated to the team, "As V.P.–Europe, I had been opposed to the original TORNAC rubber pilot plant investment decision in 1985, and the major production investment which was likely to follow. I had felt that it was too risky and speculative relative to other investment opportunities at that time. Since I just took over the global rubber group in the spring of this year, and have continued to express concern about future TORNAC rubber market forecasts, I know that my own impartiality is open to question by this management team. I am also aware that I have a reputation of being driven by shorter term results! I will try, nevertheless, to take a balanced position during the team's discussions."

As expected, the rubber management team had indeed become sharply divided on the strategic choice facing the TORNAC rubber business. Some members of the team felt that an alliance made good sense in terms of short-term financial benefit, especially since Polysar itself had just changed hands and was now part of Nova Corporation. It was expected that the servicing of Nova's high debt level, and its desire to expand its petrochemical and pipeline businesses (the latter business alone was anticipated to involve expenditures approaching $500 million annually during the early 1990s), would lead to pressure on its cash flow and create severe competition for scarce investment capital. They believed that the credibility of the rubber group as a whole would be in question for future investments if the TORNAC rubber project did not meet its short-term financial projections. This could represent a serious concern, since the rubber group was considering investment in several major projects during the next few years.

From a different perspective, the alliance choice was also supported by Dr. John Beaton, the rubber group's European vice-president, the geographic region where Bayer was particularly strong. He commented, "I support a TORNAC rubber alliance, not for short-term bottom line reasons, but because I believe that there could be real strategic benefits from working more closely with a company of Bayer's technological depth—and marrying this with Polysar's acknowledged skill in the marketplace." This kind of thinking also prevailed with Piere Choquette, President, Polysar Polymers, to whom Doug Henderson reported. Although he did not participate in the rubber management team's H-NBR alliance debate, nor try to influence its outcome, Choquette's willingness to contemplate an alliance option was well-known. He had felt for some time that there could be real benefit from Bayer and Polysar working more closely together because the (polymer) customers of both companies were fairly similar, and they had common and aggressive competition from Japan. In contrast to this sentiment, Pierre's predecessor at Polysar (Bob Dudley, President, Polysar Ltd.), had been fundamentally opposed to any alliance which did not give majority ownership or control to Polysar.

The pro-alliance members of the team also felt that other advantages would accrue to Polysar from a Polysar/Bayer arrangement, e.g., joint production and R & D would help reduce potential experience curve benefits gained by Zeon, because it would lead to better products and lower costs faster than an independent approach; Polysar would gain an opportunity to participate in a joint European production facility expected to be needed in the late 1990s; joint use of the Texas facility would avoid the further supply/demand imbalance which would arise if Bayer proceeded with its announced European plant; and, finally, the two companies would be expected to work well together due to similar corporate cultures with strong technology emphasis. As a pro-alliance team member summed up: "In a sense, I see such a Polysar/Bayer partnership on H-NBR to be a kind of insurance policy against a financial blood-bath which could arise if our forecast market and price numbers prove to be optimistic."

In sharp contrast, other team members were adamantly opposed to an alliance, stating that Polysar had a major competitive advantage over Bayer with a world-scale plant about to come on stream in the U.S. They felt that an alliance would sell Polysar's "birthright" on H-NBR technology and market positioning to a major global competitor, and that much greater benefits would accrue eventually to the TORNAC rubber business it remained as an independent competitor against Bayer and Nippon Zeon. Particularly strong in this view was Dr. Ron Britton, the rubber group's vice-president for North and South America, where Bayer's position was much weaker than in Europe. As Britton noted:

> I feel strongly that we would be giving away the opportunity of a lifetime in the specialty rubber area, without even giving it a chance. We have excellent technology, the only North American production facility about to come on stream, a European competitor whose uneconomic 200-ton pilot plant is sold out, and a U.S. market which looks extremely promising. With customer approvals already in hand from its European pilot plant, we will allow Bayer to move from its current weak position to one of strength in a major market with access to a local production facility. With all the promotion of TORNAC rubber which has been done in anticipation of the new Texas facility, the potential U.S. customers will be very confused indeed if we make an announcement of an alliance with one of our two competitors.

This view was supported vigorously by the TORNAC rubber technology management team. It was also echoed by the European sales director, who presided over perhaps the strongest of Polysar's regional marketing forces. He believed that Polysar's European Rubber sales force, which sold only rubber products, might have an advantage over Bayer in penetrating TORNAC-type markets. This was because Bayer's sales force was responsible for a much broader line of polymer products, and thus might not be able to devote as much time to this particular product.

There was also a strong feeling by these same members of the team that, without a production-sharing deal with Polysar, Bayer would exit this segment of the specialty rubber business, leaving the world market to Polysar and Zeon alone. They were convinced that, with its existing high-pressure process technology, Bayer's production facility would be very high cost, would reflect two to three years' (10–15%) inflation in construction costs relative to the cost of building the earlier Polysar plant, and would have an intrinsic cost disadvantage of 25–30% by being built in Europe rather than the U.S. Gulf Coast.[5] They saw a total Bayer facility cost, with its particular process, being twice the level incurred by Polysar.

Supporting this anti-alliance view was the fact that Bayer had finally come to Polysar looking urgently for an arrangement which would give them economic supply within the anticipated major U.S. market. Moreover, the very fact that Zeon had recently announced the construction of a major U.S. H-NBR facility implied that they, in turn, saw a future U.S. market of significant size— in contrast to some views within Polysar that the U.S. market forecasts were wildly optimistic and uncertain. They justified their optimism by pointing to announcements by Japanese auto manufacturers of at least eight new assembly plants in North America, with a combined annual capacity of nearly two million vehicles by 1991. Also in support of this view was the belief that an alliance with Bayer would, after years of independent effort and progress by Polysar, cause a negative impact on morale and enthusiasm internally at Polysar, and damage the image and reputation of the company externally with customers. While Polysar had traditionally been recognized for their success in commercially adapting others' technologies, rather than for inventing technology themselves, Tornac represented an opportunity to help change this perspective both within and outside the company.

The advantages of an alliance for Bayer were, of course, seen clearly by all members of the rubber management team: the avoidance of a major, very high-risk, European facility investment by payment of an entry fee to the Polysar facility; production presence in the forecast major geographic growth market;

---

[5] For the petrochemical industry, comparative all-in construction cost indices (called "Lang Factors") were available for different geographic regions of the world. For 1988–89 these indices were:

U.S. Gulf Coast:	100
Canada (Ontario):	110–115
Europe (Belgium, Germany):	125–130

access to an efficient production process and higher quality product technology for both U.S. and European customers; combined strength against a formidable Japanese competitor who had already established an initial specialty rubber production presence in Europe as well as the U.S.; and an opportunity to catch up in the marketplace and in technology with two competitors who had jumped well ahead of the product's original developer. As one team member said, "It would be a bit like letting the fox back into the chicken coop!"

John Mills, Global Marketing Manager–Specialty Rubbers, who was attending the management team meeting as an observer, noted: "It will not be an easy decision to make; in essence, the situation comes down to this—for Polysar, it appears that an alliance would mean short-term financial gain for long-term strategic pain; for Bayer, it would mean short-term financial pain for long-term strategic gain."

Difficult as it was, Doug Henderson knew that an immediate decision had to be made because, after lengthy exploratory discussions between Polysar and Bayer (initiated originally by Polysar in 1986, but revived by Bayer in 1988), a fundamental decision point had been reached of a "go" or "no-go" nature.[6] Bayer executives had informed Doug that a decision must be made within the next two weeks. Moreover, Doug was about to submit his 1989 budget and five-year operating plan for final approval, and needed urgent resolution of this issue because of the potential major impact on the financial projections of the rubber group for the ensuing five years. Doug knew that, although the issues would be discussed at length among the rubber management team's members, ultimate responsibility for the alliance "go/no-go" decision would be his. He knew that a decision to pursue an independent approach for TORNAC would need to be carefully presented and supported in the budget. On the other hand, if he decided to pursue an alliance with Bayer, he would have to determine the minimum requirement for such a venture to be acceptable to his own management as well as his superiors. Moreover, he was aware that an alliance could take a number of different forms, and each of these would have to be explored from Polysar's viewpoint. While shared marketing of H-NBR might well be challenged for anti-trust reasons in the U.S. and Europe, Polysar's lawyers had assured him that no such worries would result from a joint production alliance. It was also necessary to examine such issues as degree of facility sharing, technology exchange, management fees, future facility expansion, future R & D innovations, possible European facilities, and initial and ongoing financial contributions. He decided to try to work these alliance choices through his rubber management team before reaching his final decision.

---

[6] Informal contacts and Polysar's prior experience with Nippon Zeon resulted in essentially no support for the formation of an alliance with that firm for H-NBR products.

EXHIBIT 1 Nippon Zeon Profile

Nippon Zeon Co. Ltd. was established in Japan in 1950, and deals in the manufacture and sale of synthetic rubber and latices, as well as various plastics, chemicals and biochemicals. Nearly half of the company's net sales comes from synthetic rubbers and latices, a division that mainly produces oil resistant and general purpose rubber used in the automotive industry. The company's production is conducted at four plants in Japan, one in the United Kingdom, and three in the United States. Nippon Zeon has completed the purchase of three of B.F. Goodrich's businesses related to the production and sale of nitrile rubber (NBR), acrylic rubber, and epichlorohydrin rubber, respectively. In addition, a new plant in Houston, Texas, for the production of hydrogenated nitrile rubber (H-NBR) had been proposed, with completion scheduled for 1990.

Nippon Zeon Group Sales/Financial Data, 1989
(year ending March 31)

		US$ million
Net sales		830.3
Net income after tax		23.7
Total assets		1 080.9
Shareholders' equity		238.0
Number of employees		2 831.0
Sales breakdown	Synthetic Rubber	48%
	Plastics	25%
	Other	27%

EXHIBIT 2 Bayer Profile

Bayer AG was established in 1863 in Germany to produce aniline dyestuffs. Today, the Bayer Group worldwide is comprised of some 460 affiliated companies manufacturing more than 10 000 different products with 170 000 employees.

In addition to being one of the largest and most diversified chemical manufacturers in the world, Bayer is ranked by sales as the third largest producer of photographic and imaging materials, and sixth largest in pharmaceuticals and other healthcare products.

Bayer has a long history of technical innovation, ranging from the discovery of aspirin in the late 19th century and the world's first synthetic rubber, to polyurethane technology and some of today's most innovative chemical and health-related research. More than 12 000 employees are currently engaged in research and development worldwide, and Bayer holds 151 763 patents, a number virtually unequalled in the industries in which the company competes.

Bayer Group Sales, 1988

By Market	US$	%	*By Sector*	%
Europe	13.5	59	Polymers	17
N. America	4.6	20	Organic prods.	14
Latin America	1.4	6	Industrial prods.	21
Asia	2.4	11	Health care	18
Africa	1.0	4	Agrochemicals	13
			Imaging techs	17
Total	22.9	100		100

EXHIBIT 3 Nova Corporation's Five-Year Financial Review
(millions of dollars, except for common share amounts)

	1988	1987	1986[1]	1985	1984
Operating Results					
Revenue	$ 3 941	2 322	2 681	3 347	3 793
Operating income	978	528	573	674	677
Net income (loss)	424	179	100	(82)	203
Total Assets	$ 8 242	4 686	4 763	6 218	6 343
Capitalization					
Long-term debt	$ 4 304	2 434	2 461	2 704	2 901
Preferred shares	216	329	827	862	780
Common equity[2]	1 974	1 303	649	563	743
Total capitalization	6 494	4 067	3 937	4 129	4 424
Cash Flow Data					
From operations	$ 863	478	547	609	658
Spending on plant property and equipment	439	200	326	387	624
Capital issued					
—long-term debt	1 646	218	100	124	411
—common and preferred equity	534[2]	31	982	125	24
Ratios					
Common shareholder					
Return on average common equity	% 24.5	13.3	2.73	*	18.1
Capital					
Long-term debt to common equity	2.2:1	1.9:1	3.8:1	4.8:1	3.9:1
Interest coverage	2.9x	2.1x	2.1x	2.1x	1.7x

[1] Ownership in Husky Oil Ltd. was reduced to below 50%, and the investment was deconsolidated.
[2] Includes convertible debentures and warrants.
* Not comparable.

EXHIBIT 4   Polysar Organizations: 1985, 1987, 1988 Rubber Business Focus

A. 1985 TORNAC Rubber Pilot Plant Investment Decision

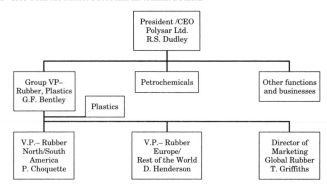

B. 1987 TORNAC Rubber Production Plant Investment Decision

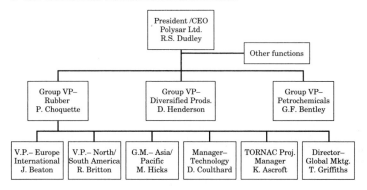

C. End 1988 Bayer H - NBR Alliance Issue

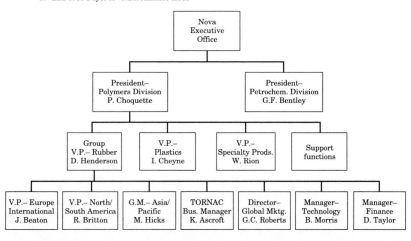

**EXHIBIT 5   TORNAC Rubber Project Investment
Discounted Cash Flow Sensitivities
Base Case, 1991 (Phase I)**

Sensitivities of different TORNAC rubber sales volumes, unit profit margins and capital investment costs, from those assumed for the 1991 Base Case, are shown below. These figures were contained in the 1987 Tornac rubber facilities investment proposal.

Differences from Base Case	*Impact on Base Case DCF Outlook*
If 1991 sales volume is:	
+30%	+3.4%
−10%	−1.4%
If 1991 unit profit margins are:	
+10%	+3.4%
−30%	−9.9%
If project capital investment costs are:	
+10%	−1.2%
−10%	+1.4%

EXHIBIT 6   TORNAC Rubber Project
Financial Projections, 1987–99

The following graphs illustrate the anticipated cumulative cash-flow-after-tax and the net income-after-tax for the TORNAC rubber project to the end of its assumed life in 1999. These figures were contained in the 1987 Tornac rubber facilities investment proposal. Phase I (1 500 ton capacity) and Phase I + II (3 000 ton capacity) are displayed:

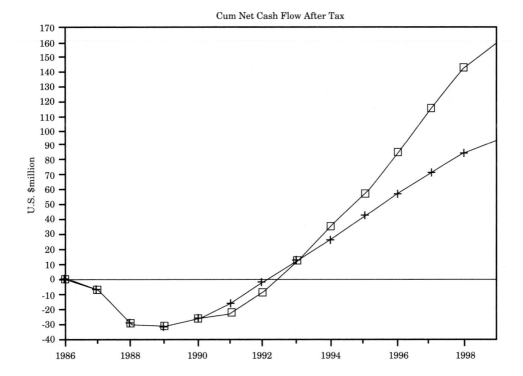

Cum Net Cash Flow After Tax

EXHIBIT 6 (continued)

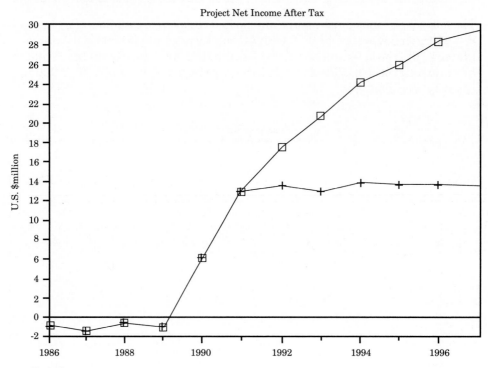

Legend:

☐ Total Project

+ Phase 1

PART
4 INCORPORATING MANAGEMENT PREFERENCES

DESIGNER CLASSICS CARPET MANUFACTURING LTD.

Roderick E. White

Jim Dunlop, a self-admitted entrepreneur and the principal owner of Designer Classics Carpet (DCC), had just received the financial results for 1986. Dunlop, age 39, had gotten into the custom wool carpet business four years earlier by acquiring the assets of Conestoga Carpet, a failed company located in Waterloo, Ontario. Using over $300 000 of his own capital, he had modernized and added some production equipment, moved the plant to a nearby location, added new products, and perhaps most importantly, expanded the firm's market scope greatly through his own efforts.

In mid-January 1987, as Dunlop reflected on the four-year financial summary (Exhibit 1), he was proud of the large increases in sales. However, this growth had resulted in scheduling problems and bottlenecks in the plant. Additional sales from the Waterloo plant would require alleviating these problems. Dunlop, always on the lookout for opportunities to expand and strengthen the business, had recently acquired a wool yarn spinning mill in Waterford, about 75 kilometres from Waterloo. This purchase would allow DCC to set specific standards for its yarn and secure a source of supply for this major raw material. Several other growth opportunities could be pursued. Preliminary negotiations were underway for the acquisition of Elite Carpet, a woven carpet manufacturer in Quebec with $5.1 million in sales and significant unused capacity. Dunlop was also considering the establishment of an importing/distribution company in Seattle, Washington to bring in custom wool carpets from Thailand. In addition, one of DCC's major dealers in the U. S. had expressed an interest in selling a minority interest to DCC.

Picking up on new initiatives would have to be done by Jim Dunlop. There was no one else available. Since he also had to deal with many of the day-to-day demands of the business, establishing priorities and timing were critical.

THE BUSINESS

All of DCC's current products were custom ordered for residential and commercial buyers. Each was unique in size, colour, pattern and texture. Sales were made through sales agents and dealers, with only a very few direct transactions with customers. In 1986, residential customers accounted for about 20% of annual sales. Of the remaining 80% for commercial applications, half were used as carpet murals for subdividing passenger aircraft, and the remainder were sold as floor covering in offices and hotels.

Products and Markets

Costing between $50 per square metre for broadloom and up to $500 per square metre for a hand tufted product, custom carpets appealed to small, specialized segments of the carpet market. The *custom* wool carpet market in North America was estimated to be approximately $300 million and growing at 15% annually (Table 1). In all except the aircraft segment, DCC's share was not large. Currently, commercial sales outside North America were small, less than 10% of the total; Canada accounted for about 20% of DCC's sales; and the U.S., about 70%.

TABLE 1 North American Custom Wool Carpet Market

Market Segment	Size	DCC's Share	Sales
Residential	18%	2.0%	20%
Commercial:			40%
Hotel	50%	1.5%	
Office	30%	2.0%	
Aircraft	2%	60%	40%
	$ 300m		

SOURCE: Estimates by Jim Dunlop and selected carpet dealers.

Residential Segment

Custom wool carpet appealed to upscale home-owners. The home-owner would either deal directly with a dealer having in-house design expertise, or through an interior decorator/designer who would ultimately source through a dealer. Many dealers served both the residential and commercial market. Some dealers competed with manufacturers for part of the value added by doing not only the design work but also their own in-house "cutting and pasting" of the carpet. However, this was the exception and most dealers preferred to have the carpet completed by the manufacturer. No really close substitutes existed for wool carpets. High-end synthetics did not have the same "feel" or snob appeal. Oriental rugs could be viewed as an alternative to the customer, but generally had somewhat different applications, and appealed to different customer tastes than custom wool area carpets.

Quality was important in all DCC's markets, as was on-time delivery performance. Order lead times for the residential segment were typically three to five months; rapid response to orders was not usually critical, since customers generally ordered well in advance. Customers did not tend to comparison shop for price.

This segment was believed to be growing at 10–15% percent annually.

Commercial Segment

This segment was composed of two different customer groups: office and hotel. Office applications were limited to lobbies, board rooms and executive suites. Recently the U.S. office market appeared to be growing, but the Canadian market was in decline. The other group, luxury hotels, used this product in high visibility areas like lobbies. *Woven* wool carpets were typically used in rooms. Luxury hotels were increasing their penetration of the North American market.

Delivery time was important, especially for most office applications, as was price. Some hotel chains had inhouse designers, but many hotels and most office customers used an outside design house or carpet consultant to develop specifications and aid in product selection. Roughly 80% of the business was tendered directly to carpet manufacturers, and the remainder was placed through dealers.

Aircraft Segment

Carpet murals were used for decorative purposes on bulkhead walls in some commercial passenger and corporate aircraft. Currently carpet murals were not used by air carriers outside North America. Approximately 50% of the North American fleet had these murals. However, recent proposed changes in FAA regulations governing material content of aircraft cabin interiors had put this market in jeopardy. Although Dunlop believed the likelihood of a permanent ban on wool bulkhead murals was unlikely, sales could be disrupted during negotiations between the FAA and aircraft manufacturers.

Customers in this segment were somewhat price sensitive, but tended to buy on reputation for quality. Airlines working with a design house and/or the firm finishing the aircraft's interior would develop carpet specifications. Orders were placed by the finisher, either the aircraft manufacturer (e.g., Boeing) or a specialized interior finisher (e.g., Innotech Aviation), with an aircraft supply house or directly with the manufacturer. In the U.S., one supply house handled a large part of the aircraft interiors market, including floor and wall coverings, seats, etc. as well as bulkhead murals. DCC was this firm's exclusive supplier of carpet murals. Eighty-five percent of sales in this segment were made in the U.S.; and 15% in Canada primarily to Canadian Pacific Airlines.

DCC's Position

DCC faced three major competitors (Table 2). The remaining competition was fragmented, although some were significant in small niches (e.g., Carter and Carousel).

TABLE 2 Competitive Position

	Market Share—Excluding Aircraft	Market Share—Aircraft
Hong Kong Carpet	65%	—
Edward Fields	5	10%
V'Soske	4	9
Designer Classics	2	60
Carousel	0.5	14
Carter	0.5	8
Other	24	

SOURCE: Industry estimates.

Hong Kong Carpet (HKC) was a large, apparently well-financed corporation with manufacturing facilities scattered around the Far East. It produced under several different labels. HKC was believed to be the low-cost producer and typically offered the lowest price, but also had a reputation for somewhat lower quality and had 12- to 24-week delivery times. HKC had extensive dealer representation in North America and advertised exclusively to dealers.

Fields and V'Soske were similar in many respects. Both were high-priced and high-quality with long delivery times: about 21 weeks for Fields and, partly because of its Puerto Rican production facilities, 23 weeks for V'Soske. V'Soske utilized exclusive dealers and had strong representatives in most markets. Fields, headquartered in New York City, had company showrooms in major metropolitan centers. Like V'Soske, Fields branded its product and had high awareness.

DCC, by way of comparison, was medium to high quality and price. DCC had the ability to deliver a small sample of the desired colour, pattern and texture, within ten days to two weeks; compared to four weeks for most of the competition. The finished order would follow in about six weeks. According to Dunlop, DCC was able to offer faster sample turnaround because of their proximity to major customers and the capabilities of the sample making department. To the extent economically feasible, sample making had separate facilities. However, some equipment, tufting and dying, was shared with regular manufacturing and inevitable conflicts arose. While still good compared to other manufacturers, this turnaround time, because of capacity constraints and labour turnover, had been increasing. DCC did not have a strong brand identity, and in certain markets, the prior association with Conestoga was a hindrance. All four major manufacturers, including DCC, had in-house dye facilities.

THE COMPANY

DCC's product range was all wool and made to order. It included completely hand tufted carpets and murals, machine tufted and overtufted carpets (machine tufted but finished by hand), both for broadloom (wall-to-wall) and area applications. As shown in Table 3, gross profit margins differed amongst product categories.

TABLE 3 DCC Cost and Gross Profit by Major Custom Tufted Product Group (percent of selling price)

	Hand Tufted	Hand + Machine			Machine Tufted	
	Area	Broadloom	Area	Aircraft	Broadloom	Area
Materials	34%	44%	30%	20%	49%	29%
Labour	52	34	43	31	22	37
Gross Profit	14	22	27	49	29	34

SOURCE: Sales records August through October, 1986.

Marketing and Distribution

In total, DCC had about 200 customers. However, the top ten accounted for 61% of sales during 1986, and the top two for 53%. One of these was an aircraft supply house representing DCC's carpet murals, and the other was a residential and commercial dealer in the southwestern U.S. The old Conestoga

Carpet had focused almost exclusively on the Toronto residential and commercial market. Over the last four years, Jim Dunlop, with his real flair for sales and marketing, had expanded distribution and sales into the U.S. market, and the airline carpet mural business in particular.

Designer Classics had two salespersons covering the U.S. They serviced the dealer network as well as direct sales to major hotel customers. The company had one European sales representative with responsibility for direct sales to hotel clients, and an agent network in six countries that sold to local dealers. Two sales agents, one in Europe and the other in the U.S., covered the aircraft market. The company's general sales manager, with an in-house staff of three, handled Canadian sales, both through the dealer network and direct to hotels and aircraft finishers. Jim Dunlop maintained contact with key customers, and was involved in developing most new dealer or agent relationships. His salesmanship and interpersonal abilities were important strengths in this area.

Once access to the customer was established, the selling task involved producing a suitable sample. The ability to match the colour, texture and pattern needs of the customer with this sample was critical to making the sale. Delivery of a finished product consistent with the sample was important to a firm's reputation. Accomplishing this required close coordination with the production department. The importance of delivery and price varied by segment.

Manufacturing

The production process was a custom job shop. Basic steps for a tufted carpet are outlined in Exhibit 2. The mix of skills varied; dyeing was a complicated operation—part art, part science, requiring a high level of skill and experience. Finishing was semi-skilled; an operator could be trained in one to two months. However, because this step was the last in the chain, mistakes were costly. Tufting skill requirements varied with the complexity of the pattern.

DCC had trouble retaining production employees. The Kitchener-Waterloo area was in the midst of an economic boom. Unemployment was 4%, and an Employment Canada official reported that unskilled labourers were changing jobs for as little as 10¢ to 15¢ per hour wage differentials. DCC currently paid $6.20 for unskilled labour (after a three-month probationary period). The factory workforce of 101 people, many of them recent immigrants to Canada, turned over by 34% in 1986.

The labour situation was further complicated by the company's recent unionization. The union and the company were negotiating their second contract, and management's goal was to achieve a "no wage increase" settlement. Historically, DCC had not laid off plant workers, even when sales volumes were low. Dunlop had taken the unionization as a personal affront, and was determined not to lend legitimacy by conceding a wage increase in the upcoming contract negotiations. He felt most employees did not want a union, and he was anxious to return his firm to non union status.

Union problems aside, labour availability was limiting output in certain areas. In hand tufting, it was difficult to get reliable, low-cost labour. In addition to the availability of labour, variability in skill requirements on a job-by-job, pattern-by-pattern basis complicated breaking this bottleneck. Capital requirements for expanding hand tufting capacity were small. However, bottlenecks existed in other areas. There were quality and capacity problems in the dye shop. Waterloo had very hard water, which required softening before use in dyeing operations. The addition of storage tanks for softened water, an investment of about $12 000, would hopefully solve this problem, reducing delays and rework. The quality of wool yarn had also been affecting the dyeing process, causing delays and rework. It was hoped the acquisition of Waterford Spinning Mills would alleviate this problem.

In order to meet demand, DCC's key manufacturing operations were operating three shifts of 8 hours each on weekdays, and two 12-hour shifts on weekends. The business was somewhat seasonal, increasing during the last quarter of the year. During the October to December 1986 period, over 70% of orders were late, averaging 15 days; 90% were labelled RUSH. In addition, quality as measured by remakes had been deteriorating (Exhibit 3). Adding more capacity would be expensive and, Dunlop suspected, unnecessary. He felt the real problem lay with manufacturing management:

> The growth in sales has overtaxed our current manufacturing management. We have gone from 14 to 130 employees over the last four years. The ability to manage a schedule in a complex job shop is now very important. It has been complicated by quality and availability problems for wool yarn.
>
> We need someone with experience managing a complicated job shop. The specifics of the carpet business can be picked up quickly.

And while Jim Dunlop understood the importance of manufacturing to his business, he had stated:

> Manufacturing frustrates me, it's not something I'm, personally, really interested in or good at. I'm a marketer rather than an administrator.

Two months earlier Dunlop had created and staffed the position of manufacturing manager. This person was to help sort out the problems at the Waterloo-plant and assume overall resposibilities for all of DCC's manufacturing plants, Waterford Spinning Mills, and the Elite plant, if purchased. The individual hired for this position had recently, by way of letter and without explanation, informed Dunlop of his immediate resignation. The position remained unfilled.

Suppliers

In addition to labour, the other key input into the product was wool yarn. Raw wool from Great Britain and New Zealand was most suitable for high-quality carpets. There were numerous suppliers of raw wool. DCC used a broker who bought their wool at auction; and while a "commodity," it varied dramatically in quality and required considerable buying expertise. Spinners were then contracted to process the wool into yarn. In North America, there were seven wool carpet yarn producers. The recently purchased Waterford Spinning Mill, with some equipment modifications and additions, could supply about 95% of DCC's wool yarn requirements and still have considerable additional capacity. The remaining 5% of DCC's requirements were yarn types Waterford could not make.

Waterford Spinning Mills (WSM) had been purchased because of quality and delivery problems with two yarn suppliers. The plant became available when Sunbeam, which had been spinning yarn for its electric blankets, decided to exit this part of the business. Sunbeam had another larger facility in the area, and in order to avoid any bad feelings from a plant, closure was prepared to "give the spinning equipment to DCC." Dunlop Holdings had purchased the old building and equipment for $110 000. However, conversion to spinning wool for carpets required purchasing some additional (used) equipment and building improvements at a cost of $65 000. The deal closed in July 1986, and the plant was producing (at a low level) by August. By year end things were running relatively smoothly, and capacity exceeded demand.

Dunlop knew of no other custom carpet manufacturer with their own spinning mill. WSM was already providing more consistent quality and delivery of this major raw material. This facilitated operations at Waterloo. Failure of an earlier supplier to meet delivery promises had resulted in disruptions to the manufacturing process, and on one occasion a plant shut down. DCC had been partially coping with this supply problem by holding large yarn inventories. When the WSM operation was coordinated with DCC's Waterloo plant, much of the inventory could be held as raw fleece at WSM.

Other materials, like poly backing, were easily available. Production equipment, while specialized, could be obtained from several suppliers.

Financial Capacity

DCC had substantial leverage (Exhibit 1). However, working capital could be financed by customer deposits, normally 50% of sales and government assisted financing for export sales.

After the sale of an earlier venture in the production of turkey breeding stock, Jim Dunlop had emerged with considerable personal wealth. He commented on his willingness to infuse additional capital into the business:

We've been the rounds with venture capitalists. They have a real get-rich-quick mentality and I do not foresee us using them.

Our financial policy is to leverage these operations as much as possible through the use of debt. However, if the right opportunity should come along, Dunlop Holdings[1] would be willing to back it financially. I do attempt to limit our exposure. I have not given personal guarantees for DCC's obligation. In addition, DCC only holds the operating assets. Real estate assets are held by a separate company owned by my wife, and DCC makes lease payments.

Management and Organization

Jim Dunlop and the four key managers described below made up the management group:

Name	Position	Time with DCC	Background
Jim Dunlop	Owner	4 years	International marketing
Larry Weiss	V-P Finance	-~ 2 years	Chartered accountant
Chris Spence	Controller	3 years	Accounting at Electrohome
Wayne Pauli	Sales Manager Manufacturing Mgr	-~ 1 year	Large-scale manufacturing
—			
Rick Hennige	Plant Manager	4 years	Conestoga Carpets

In the pursuit of opportunities, Dunlop spent almost half his time away from the office. As a result, the firm did not have a full-time, resident general manager. Jim Dunlop did most of the missionary marketing, but also felt it was important for him to be involved in key operational decisions. Even when he was away, Dunlop maintained daily contact with the office. However, problems between functions often remained unresolved and decisions unmade during his absence.

Employees received annual bonuses as part of their regular pay cheques. They were set at Jim Dunlop's discretion. All supervisors were required to make an annual performance appraisal of their subordinates.

Personally, Dunlop had some aggressive goals for the company:

Dunlop Holdings, of which DCC is a part, will continue to have rapid growth and some diversification. We plan to stay within architectural and design materials and services, but might add fabric, other kinds of flooring, like hardwood, things like that. Of course any decision will be made when the opportunity knocks.

---

[1] A family holding company which held DCC and several other ventures.

I would like us, in the foreseeable future, to grow to $100 million in sales. We will probably, at some point, have to go public to finance this growth. You might say I want to build a little empire, a significant Canadian, even international, entity in this field.

Of course my role has to change as we grow. I've been very active in the business, heavily involved in marketing. I'll have to get more involved in general management.

STRATEGIC INITIATIVES

Dunlop and DCC were confronting several important decisions. Perhaps the most significant was the acquisition of Elite Carpet in Quebec.

Elite was the only manufacturer of *woven* wool carpets remaining in Canada. The woven product was more equipment, less labour intensive, and more long-run oriented than custom tufted carpets. Woven carpets could have intricate but necessarily repetitive patterns. Unique patterning, overtufting, sculpting and custom borders were only possible with a custom tufted product.

Elite's product was currently sold only in Canada, primarily to hotels. Woven carpets tended to be used in corridors, restaurants and rooms, whereas tufted custom carpets were used in lobbies and suites. Elite's reputation and good sales representation in the Canadian market and the overlap in customer group with DCC, and the potential in the U.S. for Elite's product was what initially had attracted Dunlop's interest.

Dunlop had visited their facility in St. Therese, Quebec in 1984 to explore the possibility of the two companies collaborating on contracts requiring both tufted and woven carpets, but nothing had come of this initial contact. In early 1986 Dunlop had again approached Elite, this time to suggest they manufacture a woven line for DCC to brand and distribute. The proposal had been rejected. However, when they learned of the WSM acquisition, Elite had enquired about sourcing yarn. Dunlop had invited the president of Elite to Waterloo in October. At this time Dunlop had proposed the purchase of an equity interest in Elite. Unexpectedly, Elite's president had asked if Dunlop would like to buy all of Elite.

Jim Dunlop was surprised by the proposal for an outright purchase, and visited Elite in late December 1986. Elite's management had not been prepared to provide detailed financial statements at this time. However, he had learned that since the firm had been sold by its original Scottish owners to the employees in 1978, Elite had declining sales and losses in six and small profits in only two of the subsequent years. For the 11-month fiscal year ended in October, Elite had sales of $5.1 million, gross profits of $1.1 million, and an operating loss of $138 000 with an estimated tax loss carry forward of $750 000. Total current assets were about $1.7 million; total current liabilities, $1.8 million. Fixed assets including the land and building were $1.1 million. Long-term debt was about $500 000 and equity about $600 000 (but this latter amount included a

$1.12 million government "loan"). The current assets were made up of about $1 million in good quality accounts receivables and $700 000 in inventory. Dunlop judged the inventory levels was too high, but based on a quick walk through inspection, it appeared to be current. The building and production equipment appeared well-maintained.

Dunlop also learned that Elite was under pressure from their banker to secure additional financing and turn around their sales and profit performance. Dunlop foresaw several areas for improvement. Elite currently purchased yarn from England and paid a 12% duty. There was no duty on fleece. WSM could provide yarn at less than the price Elite was paying their English supplier before duty and transportation costs. Yarn costs were about 35% of sales. Furthermore, WSM had more than sufficient yarn capacity to supply Elite's needs. By combining product lines, sales effort and expanding the sale of Elite's products beyond Canada, Dunlop felt sales could be increased considerably. The plant had estimated capacity to support over $25 million in sales. Some savings could also be realized by centralizing administration and bookkeeping.

While net book value for the company was negative, Dunlop felt he would have to offer something for its equity. He was informed that about 100 of the employees had each invested $3 000 when they had purchased the company in 1978. In addition, the bank would expect an equity infusion.

On another front, Dunlop had been having discussions with his major U.S. wholesaler/agent about an exchange of ownership. Dunlop explained:

> My major wholesaler in the U.S. accounts for about 35–40% of our sales. Because they're so important to DCC, we've been talking about an exchange of shares. Although we haven't gotten to specifics, they have very few hard assets, basically an office, a few sales people and a phone, we would probably give 4% of DCC for 25% of their operation. It's a small business and the owner takes a large salary, but I'm more interested in cementing the relationship than making a big return on my investment.

Dunlop also wanted to set up an importing company, probably in Seattle, Washington in order to bring in hand tufted carpets from Thailand. DCC already did a small amount of importing of hand tufted carpets. Rather than lose a sale to a price sensitive customer who was willing to accept longer delivery terms, DCC sales representatives would offer the import option. The order would be placed through Dunco International, another company owned by Dunlop Holdings, with a supplier in Thailand.

Geographic growth was also being pursued. DCC had two European agents, and had just hired a full time representative based in England. Much of this off-shore business was for major commercial development projects. For example, through a European dealer DCC had just been asked to bid on a major hotel/commercial complex in the Middle East. DCC's international competitiveness was influenced by strong local competition, the 14% tariff and currency fluctuations. This latter factor was currently in DCC's favour.

EXHIBIT 1 **DCC Financial Summary** ($000)

| | Designer Classics Carpet | | | | WSM |
	1983	1984	1985	1986	1986
Gross Sales	1 140	2 430	3 721	5 200	
Less deductions **		380	595	810	
Net Sales		2050	3126	4390	
Cost of Goods Sold					
Labour	160	435	530	700	
Material	610	677	792	1 142	
Overhead —variable	206	331	507	680	
— fixed		219	408	500	
Gross Margin	164	388	889	1 368	
Selling Expense **	226	150	285	580	
Unusual item				75*	
Administrative Expense	159	346	497	650	
Income before tax	(209)	(108)	108	63	
Excluding unusual item				138	
Assets					
Accounts receivable			769	1 036	51
Inventories			412	707	18
Prepaid expenses			86	117	
Total Current Assets			1 268	1 862	73
Machinery & Equipment (net)			349	363	183†
Trademarks				10	
Total Assets	591	1 380	1 617	2 234	256
Liabilities & Equity					
Bank loans			139	298	39
Accounts payable††			688	801	67
Payable to affiliates				49	
ODC export loans			157	423	
Shareholder loan			11	10	
l-t principal due			51	68	
Total Current Liabilities			1 046	1 648	106
Long-term Debt			310	235	139*†
Equity & Retained Earnings			261	352	10
Total	591	1 380	1 617	2 234	256
Number of employees	45	60	85	130	

* Unusual item: upfront payment to U.S. sales representative who delivered no sales.

** Commissions to agents, duties, freight, etc. included as selling expense in 1983 deducted from sales 1984 onward.

† Includes land (25), buildings (103) and equipment (58) less depreciation (3).

†† Includes Small Business Loan and loan from parent company (48).

EXHIBIT 2 DCC Tufted Carpet: Production Steps

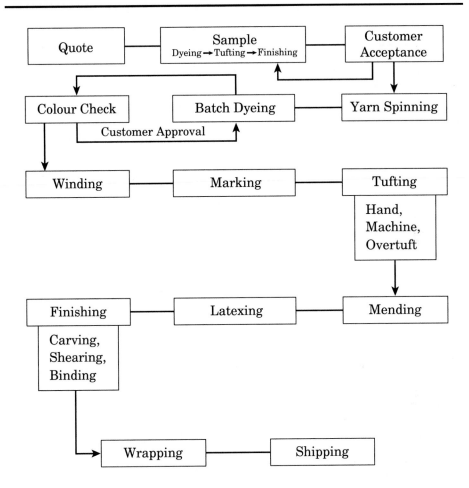

EXHIBIT 3 **DCC Remake Charges as a Percentage of Sales**

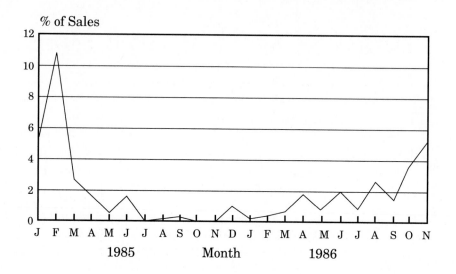

CAMBRIDGE PRODUCTS INC. (A)

Donald J. Lecraw and Ken Coelho

Seated in his Cambridge, Massachusetts office one morning in June 1982, Bill Spencer picked up one of his recently printed business cards. On one side, above his name, address, title (Vice-President, Corporate Relations) and the "Cambridge Products Inc." logo, an American flag stood out prominently against a silver background; on the other side, the same information was printed in Japanese characters. The cards and the company brochures printed in Japanese were just the latest (and relatively minor) expense item in CPI's bid to export its conventional top of the range cookware products to Japan.

A week earlier, in Tokyo, Spencer had met with Jiro Hattori, president of The Kuwahara Co., one of the largest manufacturers of cookware in Japan. Hattori had proposed that Kuwahara would distribute 1 500 sets of CPI cookware a month in the Japanese market starting in October, if CPI could produce an exclusive cookware product, with whistling knobs and specially designed handles. In a few hours' time, Bill would be meeting with Jack Nolin, executive vice president, to discuss whether CPI should begin a crash development program to modify CPI's existing product at an anticipated cost of over $140 000, and place orders for steel and other raw materials worth over $100 000 by the end of the week, to prepare for the expected october delivery. For CPI, with 1981 sales of $6.3 million and net profits of $500 000, this represented a substantial investment.

As he gazed at the Japanese print on his business card, Bill Spencer wondered what he should recommend to Jack Nolin. Should CPI make the investment? There appeared to be considerable potential in the Japanese market but the risks were enormous. Would CPI be better off concentrating on familiar markets in which it was already quite successful, rather than attempting to penetrate that notoriously difficult market in a far corner of the world?

THE COMPANY

CPI's origins can be traced back to 1944, when Brian Wilson, a young entrepreneur, started up a small metal finishing plant that polished "anything in metal." Sales in that first year were $4 000. The company specialized in custom metal-working jobs that included polishing of cookware for other manufacturers. In 1952, Wear Ever, one of CPI's customers, went bankrupt and left CPI holding a substantial quantity of cookware. CPI inadvertently entered the cookware business.

Initially, CPI marketed aluminum cookware manufactured for them by others. By the early 1960s, the company brought in new equipment and began to manufacture their own cookware products. Cookware sales in the early 1960s reached $1 million. CPI, which until then sold only aluminum cookware, began to experiment with stainless steel, and discovered that stainless steel cookware was "a market whose time had come." By 1967, CPI was completely out of aluminum and sold only stainless steel cookware. By the late 1960s, CPI had acquired major department store accounts, and sales had risen to $200 000 a month. Throughout this period the company maintained its original industrial sales business, which provided a fall-back position when problems arose in the cookware industry. In the 1970s, the American market for cookware declined. Competition was strong, and included both foreign and domestic companies such as Supreme Aluminum Ltd., Soren, Paderno, Regal, Culinaire, Westbend, Ekco and Lagostina.

Yet CPI performed well in this market, managing to capture a market share of approximately 20% in the segments in which it competed. It had managed to accomplish this by constant product innovation and efficient, low-cost production. In fact, CPI had, at one time or another, supplied parts directly to its competitors at prices lower than the competitors could produce for themselves, while still making a profit. In 1981, CPI operated an 80 000-square foot manufacturing facility in Cambridge, Mass., where it also conducted its R&D activities, and a sales office in Toronto, Canada.

PRODUCT DEVELOPMENT

In the late 1960s, CPI was the first developer—at a cost of $1 million—of five-ply cookware, which it marketed under the brand name "Ultraware." Five-ply construction bonded a three-layer aluminum core between two layers of stainless steel. Because of aluminum's exceptionally good capacity to store and conduct heat, the multi-layered construction resulted in quick and even heat distribution across the bottom and sides of the utensil, reducing cooking time and saving energy. CPI also experimented and designed specially weighted covers, knobs, and handles—innovations that paid off well in terms of sales.

In the early 1980s, CPI began experimenting with seven-ply cookware and magnetic steel which, in the future, could be used with magnetic stoves then being developed in Japan. The use of magnetic stoves and utensils would result in energy savings of up to 30%, which was of far greater significance in energy-poor Japan than in North America (three-ply cookware sold better in the U.S. and Canada than the five-ply variety, which, although more expensive, was more energy efficient).

EXPORTS

When CPI first started in the cookware business in the early 1950s, it realized that the regional market was not large enough to support an efficient scale operation. CPI found it convenient to do business through Wear Ever distributors in the U.S. and Everglo in eastern Canada. It promoted products through trade shows both in the U.S. and abroad. CPI's industrial sales division also sold its products in Canada.

By 1979, exports constituted $2 million of $4.8 million in total sales. Canadian exports made up 70% of total exports. The other countries to which CPI exported included Italy, Australia, and South Africa. Exports to EEC countries were especially difficult, since the EEC had imposed tariffs of up to 22.5% on cookware. In the 1980s, CPI put sales to Canada "on the back-burner," while it concentrated on markets in Japan, Australia, and Europe.

In 1981, CPI exports were $3.5 million of total company sales of $6.3 million (Exhibit 1). Of the total exports, $2 million were to Canada, $800 000 to Australia, and the remainder ($700 000) to Europe, Hong Kong, Singapore, and Japan. Sales to Japan, however, were very small and sporadic. Every once in a while CPI received an order, but there was little ongoing business.

ENTRY INTO THE JAPANESE MARKET

CPI's entry into the Japanese market was almost accidental. An earlier routine introductory letter to the U.S. embassy in Japan had elicited the reply that the Japanese market was too difficult for CPI to successfully penetrate— they should not even try. CPI did have one customer in Japan prior to 1981, who had seen CPI cookware at a trade show and ordered about 100 sets (worth approximately $16 500) sporadically (every two or three months).

In early 1982, David Taylor, vice-president of CPI's Canadian subsidiary, showed samples of CPI cookware to an acquaintance, Izu Tsukamoto. Tsukamoto, born of Japanese parents in China, had moved to Japan with his parents as a child. Shortly after World War II, the Tsukamotos migrated to Canada. Izu spoke Japanese, and was familiar with Japanese customs. In 1982, Izu Tsukamoto worked as a Vancouver-based distributor of cookware on a 5% commission basis. Tsukamoto felt that CPI's product would sell well in Japan, and sent samples by Federal Express to distributors in Japan.

Tsukamoto's first contact was Jiro Hattori, President of Kuwahara Co., a Japanese import-export firm specializing in cookware and related items such as china and cutlery. Kuwahara was 50% owned by Hattori, and 50% by Ohto Overseas Corp., one of the largest pen manufacturers in the world, with assets of over two billion yen (U.S. $100 million). Kuwahara in 1981 distributed approximately 100 000 sets of Regal and Westbend cookware (imported from the U. S.) and one product line of Japanese make, to six or seven direct sales organizations.

CPI's five-ply cookware, relatively new to Japan, was so well received by Jiro Hattori, that Tsukamoto decided to travel personally to Japan. Thus began a series of trips by Tsukamoto, Taylor, Nolin, and Spencer which culminated in Jiro Hattori's proposal to CPI in June 1982.

HATTORI'S PROPOSAL

Jiro Hattori expressed an interest in distributing three of CPI's 20 styles of cookware. However, he wanted exclusive products and two major modifications—a whistling knob and specially designed wraparound flameguards. These flameguards around the handles were desirable, said Hattori, because most Japanese customers used liquid propane gas (LPG) for cooking (even though the existing cookware did have heat resistant phenolic handles). If CPI could have satisfactory samples of the redesigned cookware ready by the end of August, Hattori would accept deliveries of 1 500 sets a month for four months and more thereafter. The exact price would be negotiated later, but Spencer had tentatively suggested a price of $130 a set, cif.

Bill Spencer gathered all the notes on the Japanese market that he had made during his trips—the useful information provided by the Massachusetts government trade office in Japan (the U.S. government office in Japan, in contrast was useless, Bill felt), and his analysis of the development costs. There were several factors he would have to consider before making his recommendations to Jack Nolin.

THE MARKET

The Japanese purchased more cookware per capita than any other country in the world. The market for cookware in Japan was estimated to be about $100 million. It was (as the market for most consumer goods in Japan appeared to be) very competitive. The high end in which CPI would be competing was approximately $60 million and was dominated by imports (97%).

Regal, which had just introduced five-ply cookware and developed a whistle knob (which was probably the reason for Hattori's haste, Bill thought), Westbend, and Ekco, which produced bonded bottom cookware, were already well entrenched in the market. Two local Japanese manufacturers served the low end of the market.

THE JAPANESE CONSUMER

The cliches about a Japanese consumer—"very knowledgeable, extremely quality conscious, and willing to pay high prices for exclusive, prestigious products"—appeared to be quite true, Bill Spencer reflected. He recalled conversations with the CPI and other executives doing business in Japan:

> The Japanese market is the toughest in the world. I would prefer to deal in Taiwan or South Korea.
>
> The Japanese customer is very knowledgeable, very demanding, and the market is extremely competitive. Understanding Japanese customs and preferences is a necessary prerequisite for doing business in Japan.
>
> The Japanese are very thrifty—as individuals they are among the highest savers in the world. They are willing to spend money only on high-quality goods. In the U.S. there are three criteria by which consumers select cookware: (1) Price, (2) Quality, and (3) Appearance. In Japan they are: (1) Quality, (2) Quality, and (3) Quality! The Japanese are so quality conscious, it is almost revolting; there are customers who check cookware handles using a screwdriver! It is not unusual to see a car buyer *underneath* a car in a showroom, checking it out.
>
> Japanese consumers are very knowledgeable. They read every word in a brochure (you must have literature in Japanese), and ask pointed questions. The distributors are also extremely knowledgeable—the typical distributor knows as much about a product's characteristics as a manufacturer in North America.
>
> The Japanese are also very fond of exclusivity—and designer names; this appears to be the only exception to the Quality rule. We know this from experience. A line of cheap yellow-coloured pans sold a million sets in a very short time because they bore the designer name—Pierre Cardin!
>
> It is important to understand Japanese customs. Because the islands are so crowded and houses are so small, it is common for a family of four to occupy a one-bedroom apartment. Cookware is hung on the wall so it is important for the cookware to look good (and to be exclusive).
>
> Understanding Japanese customs is also important when negotiating. They use a lot of euphemisms—if they say they will "think about it" more than three times, most likely they are politely saying no. If they do say no, directly, you had better leave quickly.
>
> They may take very long to make decisions. When negotiating with a team, it is difficult to identify the decision-maker—he is usually silent. The person you do most of your talking to is not usually the decision-maker. When negotiating with the Japanese, you have to be very well prepared—know precisely what your costs are, and what potential modifications will cost you.

METHOD OF ENTRY

Given the potential in the Japanese market, there were other possible means of entry besides sales through the Kuwahara company. CPI had ruled out a wholly owned subsidiary or a joint venture in Japan, since CPI did not have the necessary resources. Even a sales office would be too expensive to maintain for a company with sales of $6 million and net profits of $500 000. Bill estimated that it would cost $50 000 in salary and $150 000 in expenses for a one-man operation. Licensing was a poor option; patents were, for all practical purposes, ineffective in protecting cookware design and, in addition, the prestige associated with "imported" goods was an important buying criterion for the Japanese customer.

The choice of the appropriate distribution system in Japan often posed a serious problem to many companies trying to penetrate the Japanese market. There were three broad patterns of distribution for consumer goods (Exhibit 2). Distribution varied depending on the type of product. (The distinction between the three routes are for illustrative purposes only. In actual fact, the distribution routes could be very complex.)

The Open Distribution Route

The open distribution route was used for distributing merchandise over extremely broad areas, and involved many intermediate distributors, such as primary and secondary wholesalers. Manufacturers who sold products through this route usually entrusted ensuing sales to the wholesaler, not knowing clearly where or how their merchandise would be sold from then on. They had little direct contact with the secondary wholesalers or retailers. This form of distribution was adopted primarily for basic essential products with a wide demand, such as fresh and processed foods.

The Restricted Distribution Route

The restricted distribution route was restricted to certain licenses retail stores with the products going through specialized distribution channels. This form of distribution was common for specialty items such as pharmaceutical and cosmetics.

The Direct Distribution Route

The direct distribution route involved direct transactions between the producer and retailer, or the producer and consumers via door-to-door sales-persons. The Kuwahara Company employed a form of this method of direct sales, common for imported products in the cookware category where the originality and specific features of the foreign merchandise had to be directly conveyed to consumers. While in Japan, the CPI executives had contacted several distributors besides Kuwahara: Basic Japan, Silverware, Noah, Zeny, Prima, Magry Systems, Royal Cookware, and Sunware. These were operations similar to the Kuwahara

Company, one of the largest and better established firms distributing 8 000 cookware sets a month as well as other kitchenware products.

The direct sales organizations that Kuwahara had connections with comprised several hundred door-to-door salespersons who underwent a six to eight weeks' training program organized by Kuwahara. Each sales organization serviced a certain region, such as Osaka. The selling techniques emphasized getting in the door—once that was accomplished, there was usually an 80% chance of getting a sale. Part of the selling job included lessons on how to use the cookware. Some distributors had even set up test kitchens to teach women how to cook and to display cookware. This tactic proved very effective. It was estimated that approximately 80% of Japanese women learned to cook outside their homes. The average salesperson sold two to three cookware sets a week, in addition to related items such as china and cutlery.

PRICING

The tentative sales price that CPI and Hattori agreed on—$125 per set—would enable CPI to earn a margin of 15%, which was normal for a volume of 1 500 to 2 000 sets a month. CPI would charge up to 35% for smaller columns. Izu Tsukamoto would earn a 5% commission and David Taylor would get 5% after Tsukamoto's commission. The cookware would be subjected to a 20% tariff, and Juwahara would usually sell at a 30% markup over landed costs. The door-to-door salesperson would sell at a 75% markup over the Kuwahara price. Payment would be made by Letters of Credit. An illustration of the margins involved is shown in Exhibit 3.

DEVELOPMENT COSTS

The modifications that Jiro Hattori requested would, under normal circumstances, take CPI about five months to develop; but Hattori wanted samples by the end of August, and that left CPI only ten weeks in which to redesign the handles and knobs. Bill was confident it could be done. The costs involved would be as follows:

Whistle knob development	$100 000
Two molds for new handles @ $20 000 each	40 000
Total	$140 000

In addition, at $5 000 per trip to Japan for travel and the traditional Japanese after-hours business entertainment, CPI had already spent $25 000 on exploring the market; and travel costs could be expected to total at least $50 000 more if the decision to begin product development was made.

CAPACITY

The cookware industry enjoyed boom years in 1980–81. Manufacturers in the industry were usually affected by downturns in the economy with a six-month lag, being cushioned by retailers' preplanned orders. In late 1981, however, the U.S. and Canadian economies had turned sharply downward, and demand for cookware was expected to decrease in the second half of 1982. CPI was working at full normal capacity which involved 10-hour shifts, 4 days a week, producing approximately 4 125 sets a month. The machines could be worked up to 18 hours a day (one 8-hour shift 5 days per week and one 10-hour shift 4 days per week), or the work week extended to accommodate extra sales to Japan if necessary, but such a pace could not be maintained in the long run (over one year) without adversely affecting machine maintenance. Also, CIP's planned a four-year, $2-million machine-upgrading program might have to be speeded up should capacity utilization be increased.

CPI currently employed approximately 60 production workers, and an increase in capacity utilization would necessitate hiring about 30–40 new employees. To begin deliveries in October, CPI would have to begin hiring and training workers by July. In addition, because of the long lead times involved, steel and other raw materials worth over $100 000 would have to be ordered by the end of the week. By the end of August, orders for a further $200 000 in steel (which constituted 50% of the direct costs of sales) would have to be placed, for a total investment of $300 000 in raw materials, $140 000 in product development, and $75 000 in travel costs before a firm order could be obtained. Because of CPI's good relationship with its banks, Bill foresaw no problem in obtaining an extension in its line of credit to cover the increased working capital.

As he reviewed his notes, Bill Spencer wondered what recommendations he should make to Jack. Could CPI compete in the Japanese market? The risks were enormous. As yet, CPI had no written contract with Jiro Hattori, and once product development was started and the steel was ordered, these costs were sunk. The decision that the CPI managers would make that day would indeed be critical to CPI's future operations.

EXHIBIT 1 CPI 1981 Financial Summary

Total sales	$6.3 million
Total exports	$3.5 million
Profit before taxes	$800 000
Net profit	$500 000

Assets (as of 1982)	*Net Book Value*	*Realizable Value*
Inventory	$3 million	$3 million
Building	$500 000	$2 million
Machinery and equipment (10% straight-line depreciation)	$800 000	$2.5 million
Dyes, tools	0	$500 000
Equity and retained earnings	$1.4 million	

EXHIBIT 2 Examples of Distribution Routes for Consumer Goods in Japan

1. Open Distribution Route

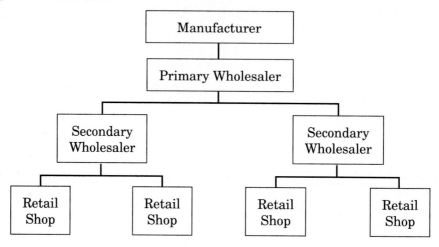

b. Restricted Distribution Route

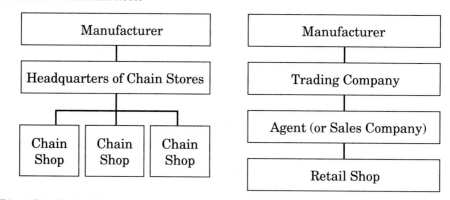

c. Direct Distribution Route

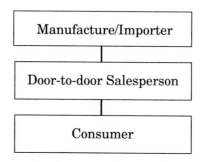

EXHIBIT 3 CPI Margins

CPI direct cost	$ 70.00
CPI cost	100.00
CPI price (ex factory)	115.00
Freight and insurance	15.00
	$130.00
Tsukamoto's commission	5.75
Taylor's commission	5.45
CPI's price to Kuwahara (C.I.F.)	141.20
Tariffs	28.44
Kuwahara's landed costs	169.44
Kuwahara's price to sales organization	220.27
Price to final customer	$385.50

AER LINGUS – ATS (A)

J. Peter Killing

On July 15, 1985, Denis Hanrahan was flying from Dublin to Toronto, as he had many times over the past 11 months, to meet with Klaus Woerner, the owner and president of Automation Tooling Systems (ATS), a robotics firm based in Kitchener, Ontario. Mr. Hanrahan's job was to expand the "non airline" activities of Aer Lingus, and ATS was a company in which he wanted to acquire an equity position.

The negotiations between Denis and Klaus had been friendly but protracted, and it appeared that they were finally nearing an end. The deal, which both sides had agreed to orally, was that Aer Lingus would purchase 75% of the shares of ATS, and that Klaus would stay on and manage the company. The price that he would receive for his shares would depend on the earnings of ATS in the years ending September 30, 1985 and 1986. If ATS met the profit forecast that Klaus had prepared for it, he would receive a total of $4.6 million in cash, and retain a 25% interest in the company.

AER LINGUS

Aer Lingus was the Irish international airline, wholly owned by the Irish government. Aer Lingus, like many airlines, had difficulty producing a consistently high level of earnings (Table 1). The early 1980s in particular were not good years for the airline (nor for any other), and only the consistent profitability of the group's hotels, airline related businesses (maintenance and overhaul of the other firm's aircraft, training of flight crews and so on), and financial and commercial businesses kept the company's overall losses in check.

A small group of managers under the leadership of Gerry Dempsey were responsible for managing and expanding Aer Lingus's non airline activities. Denis Hanrahan, second in command, commented:

> We all recognize that the airline business is a cyclical one, and our goal is to create a stable base of earnings which will see the airline safely through the bottom of the cycles. We have been successful so far so we don't know if the government would bail us out if we did make continued heavy losses, and we don't want to have to find out! The mission of our "ancillary activities" is to increase the Group's reported earnings and to strengthen its balance sheet.

**TABLE 1 Aer Lingus Financial Results[1]
Years Ending March 31**
(millions of Irish pounds)[2]

	1985		1984		1983		1982		1981	
	Revenue	*Profit*	*Revenue*	*Profit*	*Revenue*	*Profit*	*Revenue*	*Profit*	*Revenue*	*Profit*
Air Transport	281	.5	270	1.4	244	(2.7)	218	(11.2)	164	(15.9)
Ancillary Operations										
Airline Related	110	12.7	82	11.1	66	9.0	62	8.6	47	7.5
Hotel & Leisure	79	11.7	82	7.7	82	6.0	71	7.8	54	7.7
Financial & Commerical	33	5.4	24	4.5	11	3.6	8	2.0	6	1.3
Net Profit After Head Office Expenses, Interest, Tax[3]	11.6		4.9		(2.5)		(9.2)		(13.6)	

[1] In 1985 the group total assets stood at £285 million. A breakdown of assets employed in each business area was not publicly reported.
[2] Canadian dollars per Irish pound:
1981—1.90
1982—1.75
1983—1.54
1984—1.41
1985—1.44
[3] The company earned a positive net profit in each of the four years preceding 1981.

The "financial and commercial" results in Figure 1 include a data processing firm, an insurance company, a helicopter company, a hospital management firm, a land development company, and a 25% interest in GPA, formerly Guiness Peat Aviation. Many of these firms, with the exception of the hotels, were founded by former Aer Lingus employees. Although most of the companies were performing well, the undoubted star was GPA. A manager explained:

> In 1975 or so, Tony Ryan, our New York station maanger, was transferred back to Ireland and asked to lease out a 747 which we did not need for the winter. In looking at the leasing market, he thought he saw a very good business opportunity, and he convinced us and a related British company to each put up 45% of the capital required to start an aircraft leasing company. He kept the remaining 10%. As things have developed, he was certainly right about the opportunity. In the ten intervening years, we have received almost 20 million Irish pounds from that business, and our initial investment was only 2.2 million! We still own 25% of the compamy, and now have firms like Air Canada and the General Electric Credit Corporation as partners. GPA is one of the Irish success stories of the past decade.

THE MOVE INTO ROBOTICS

In 1983, Denis Hanrahan began an informal search for a new area of investment which could provide healthy financial returns to Aer Lingus for at least the next decade. By January 1984, he had concluded that robotics was an extremely interesting field. Robots had been used in Japan since the 1960s but were not adopted in Europe and the U.S. until the late 1970s. Many analysts expected a robotics boom, with growth rates as high as 30% per annum, as Western firms strove to catch up.

Although robot manufacturing appeared to Denis to be an overcrowded field, he was excited about the possibility of becoming a developer of the ancillary technology and components that were required by firms wanting to install robot-based flexible manufacturing assembly lines. His figures suggested that the market value of ancillary systems was at least equal to the value of the robots themselves. Although the volume of business being done in this new area was impossible to quantify with any degree of precision, it appeared to be growing quickly and offer high margins. There were as yet no major companies in the business. Denis described Aer Lingus' initial entry into the field:

> The first company we looked at was in the U.K. We quickly decided that it was too big, too sexy, and considering its size, depended too heavily on a single supplier of robots. One thing you have to watch out for in this business is guys in very classy suits who know more about doing deals and driving for the initial public

offering which is going to make them rich than they do about robotics. It turned out that we were right about that company, as it went bankrupt afterwards.

The company we did buy was Airstead Industrial Systems of the U.K. This is a very small company, much smaller that ATS, but it has the rights to distribute Seiko robots in England. Seiko, in addition to producing products such as watches and Epson computer printers, is a prominent robot manufacturer and doing very well in some fast growing niches.

After the acquisition of Airstead, Aer Lingus dispatched an analyst to North America to examine six companies that Seiko had identified as the most promising North American robotics systems firms. On August 15th, Denis received a telex containing a thumbnail sketch of ATS, indicating that it was the best of the three firms the analyst had seen to date, and was worth a closer look. On August 28, Denis was in Kitchener for his first meeting with Klaus Woerner.

KLAUS WOERNER AND ATS

Born in Germany in 1940, Klaus Woerner emigrated to Canada at age 20 after serving an apprenticeship in the tool and die business. He subsequently worked for a variety of manufacturing firms in Canada but, tired of the "hierarchies and rigidities of large corporations", founded ATS in 1978. The new company was not successful, however, until Klaus turned it away from manufacturing and into systems work. The move into robotics was made in late 1981.

By the summer of 1984 ATS had grown to employ 44 perople, including 26 tool makers, 15 hardware and software designers, and 3 in sales and administration. Denis was encouraged to see that Klaus was a technically oriented hands-on manager whose elegant and creative solutions to systems problems played a major role in the company's success. Klaus, Denis observed, was more at home on the shop floor than talking to accountants, bankers or lawyers. In his summary of their first meeting, Denis made the following points:

1. Woerner was an easy individual to get along with, though I would anticipate that he is used to getting his own way. He is the key decision-maker in the company, although he does solicit the opinions of his senior colleagues.

2. The company currently turns over approximately $3.5 million per year, and expects to double its sales this year on last year, after a number of years of relatively slow growth. Woerner reports a current backlog of $3 million.

3. The major financial problem with the business is that there is a significant working capital requirement. I have heared a rule of thumb that suggests 40% of turnover is required in this business, but Klaus thought that was far too high. The practical problem is that the final payment of 30% of systems costs tends to be delayed for several months after completion of the work while fine tuning is being performed.

4. Woerner recently came very close to selling ATS to Berton Industries,[1] a major Canadian corporation in the automotive components business. One hundred percent of ATS was to be acquired and, depending on results, it would have been valued at $3–4 million. Woerner got very concerned, however, at what he perceived to be the inordinate length of time being taken in detailed negotiations, and at the aggressive attitude of the other party's attorneys. In addition, Berton would not give him any assurances about future investment in ATS, and apparently Woerner learned that plans had been made to move ATS to another location without any consultation with him. When the president of Berton then ignored Woerner's request that a number of written commitments be made within one week, the deal was off.

5. Woerner's proposal was that Aer Lingus would take 50% of the company for an undetermined amount, 50% of which would be left in the company, and that he would take 50% out. I indicated to him that 50% would probably be the minimum share that we would require, and it could be that we would want considerably more. However, any deal that we would do would be structured in such a way that he and his key people would be committed to staying with the company. He had no difficulty with this point, and conceded that he was not wedded to the 50:50 formula, which was clearly an ideal going in position from his point of view.

6. On balance, I found ATS to be very impressive. Though operating in cramped facilities, it does appear to have a real technical depth, and undoubtedly has an established customer base. The company appears to be an appropriate size to take over since it is neither so small as to be extraordinarily risky nor so big as to be extraordinarily expensive.

The meeting ended with the two men agreeing to continue discussions, and to try to reach a gentlemen's agreement reasonably quickly rather than getting bogged down in protracted technical or legal discussions. Woerner promised to send some financial information as soon as he could get it together, although he warned that his business plan should not be taken too literally as "these things are more exercises than necessarily forecasts of reality."

SUBSEQUENT MEETINGS

Over the next six months, Denis Hanrahan held a number of meetings with Klaus Woerner, bringing with him on occasion Gerry Dempsey and Larry Stanley, two of Aer Lingus's ancillary business managers. Both men subsequently supported Denis's view that ATS would be a good acquisition. This positive feedback was also strengthened by comments from Seiko's North

---

[1] Disguised name.

American sales manager, who stated that in ten years ATS would be "one of the top three robot systems integrator firms in North America" if it grew to its potential. The meetings with Klaus also yielded more information about his expectations and the operations of ATS. The following excerpts are taken from Denis Hanrahan's notes and comments on various meetings, all of which were held in either Kitchener or Toronto.

Meeting of November 6

Present: G.P. Dempsey, Denis Hanrahan, Klaus Woerner, and Peter Jones[2], who was Klaus Woerner's personal financial advisor and company accountant.

1. Woerner outlined his expectations for growth of the automation and robotics industry and for ATS. It seems clear that they have not done very much forward planning. Woerner quoted Laura Conigliaro of Prudential-Bache as suggesting growth from $250 million in 1984 to $1 billion by 1987, but these figures were not very convincing since they related to the total industry rather than to the sub segment in which ATS is involved.

2. Woerner stated that he expected ATS revenues to total $4 million for the year ending September 1984, $6 million for 1985 (rather than the $5 million he had earlier been projecting), and to reach $10 million in three years' time. He believed that growth to $10 million could be financed through a combination of retained earnings and bank debt.

3. Northern Telecom, a major Canadian multinational firm, apparently accounts for approximately 40% of ATS revenues. Woerner indicated that this proportion would fall to one-third in 1985 due to the growth of ATS. He stated strongly that in spite of the company's high dependence on Northern Telecom he could, if necessary, survive a total loss of Northern's business by falling back on traditional non flexible production line work ("hard" automation). However, he expressed the view that Northern Telecom could not break the relationship with him since they were dependent on ATS for maintenance and software updates.

4. There was an extensive discussion on the subject of control. Woerner's recent negotiations with Berton have left him very uneasy about the behaviour of large corporations, and he again expressed his strong preference for a 50-50 partnership. Dempsey responded that our whole approach to subsidiares was to work in partnership with the management of them, and that this approach was not altered whether the shareholding was 2%, 50%, or 99%. Woerner appeared to implicitly accept that we might go to 75% or higher of the equity as long as we were concerned only with issues such as overall earnings and growth rather than the detailed operating practices involved. Dempsey suggested that Woerner should write to us in simple non legal terms outlining those issues upon which he believed he would require assurance from us. Woerner accepted this suggestion.

---

[2] Disguised name.

5. Woerner also expressed concern that his was a small company in danger of being "trampled on" by Aer Lingus. While he was happy enough with the people he currently knew in Aer Lingus, he felt that these individuals could change and he could thus find himself exposed to changes of policy or personality. Dempsey responded that we could not fully reassure him on this issue. We had now had a wide range of relationships with subsidiaries over a long period of time; this had not occurred historically, and he saw no reason why it should happen in the future.

6. There were no specific discussions on the matter of price. Dempsey stated on a number of occasions that it was purposeless to discuss price until the financials were available and had been reviewed. Woerner concurred.

7. The meeting ended on a positive and progressive note. It was agreed that we would appoint Peat Marwick to review the affairs of ATS, and they would contact Jones as necessary. Also Jones would shortly produce a three-year forecast for ATS.

Meeting of January 10

The next meeting between Klaus and Denis included Bill Harcourt[3] of Peat Marwick Mitchell. During this meeting the ATS financial statements and projections (Exhibits 1 and 2) were given to Denis. These were to have been sent to Ireland several weeks earlier.

Denis learned during this meeting that Klaus had not written the promised letter concerning his specific issues of concern because he preferred to discuss them face to face. Further discussion ensued during which Klaus reiterated his general unease at the prospect of being controlled, and repeated his desire for a 50-50 deal. While still not raising any specific concerns, Klaus repeatedly referred to the Berton deal and how lucky he was to have avoided it. Denis commented after the meeting:

> All of this was territory that we had covered several times previously with him, and we essentially just covered it again. It was clear that, as the discussion progressed, Klaus began to get more comfortable, and his fears began to recede. I have no doubt that after I depart from Canada he begins to get uneasy again at the unknown. He reiterated that he was quite comfortable working with Mr. Dempsey or myself, but that the could naturally have no assurance that we would be around forever.
>
> In the earlier part of the meeting when Klaus was appearing very reluctant, Bill Harcourt asked him directly if he, in fact, wanted to sell ATS. Klaus replied that he didn't really want to—he had devoted all of his time in the last few years in building up the company, and wished to continue to do so in the future—but because ATS would not be producing large amounts of cash in the short term he had no choice. He believes that ATS can and must grow very rapidly to

---

[3] Disguised name.

forestall the competition—the opportunities are there, and if ATS does not take advantage of them, someone else will. In this vein he mentioned that he had just revised his estimate of the current year's sales from $6 million to $9 million.

The other reason that Klaus feels that he has to sell ATS is that important customers like Northern Telecom are nervous of becoming too dependent on him, as long as he does not have a major corporate backer. Klaus told us in the meeting that Northern had in fact deliberately cut back their orders to him for this reason, and we independently checked that this was indeed the case.

The meeting ended on a very friendly note with Denis again encouraging Klaus to make up a list of his specific concerns so that they could be addressed, and Klaus inviting Bill Harcourt to visit the ATS plant before the next meeting so that he could develop a better understanding of what they were doing.

Meetings of January 24 and February 20

The meetings of January 24 and February 20 were devoted to discussions of a deal whereby Aer Lingus would acquire 75% of ATS' stock, with Klaus Woerner holding the remaining 25%. At the January 24 meeting, Klaus appeared to accept the idea that he would sell the 75% of the company, but apparently as a result of his earlier negotiations with Berton, was adamant that ATS was worth at least $6 million. In the February 20th meeting, Denis finally agreed that ATS could be worth $6 million if the company met Klaus's new projections for it, but at that moment it was not. As a consequence, Denis proposed that the amount paid to Klaus should depend on the company's performance in 1985 and 1986. The details, spelled out in a letter from Denis to Klaus following the February meeting, were as follows:

1. We propose that a valuation be established for ATS as of September 30, 1986. This valuation will be calculated by taking 3.5 times the pre-tax income for the fiscal year ended September 30, 1985, and adding to it 3.5 times the incremental pre-tax income earned in the fiscal year ending September, 1986. By incremental income here, I mean the excess of pre-tax income in fiscal 1986 over that earned in fiscal 1985.

2. In determining pre-tax income, research and development costs shall be charged at the rate contained in your financial projections or at a higher rate if so incurred. Profit sharing to employees shall be charged at 10% of pre-tax income before profit sharing or such higher rate as may be incurred. In addition, we would require the company to maintain a key-man insurance policy on yourself in the amount of $5 000 000, and the cost of such coverage would be borne as a charge before striking pre-tax income.

3. On the basis of the pre-tax income figures outlined above, the company would have a total value of $6 835 000 as of September 30, 1986.

4. Under the above formula, the maximum value that we would be prepared to put on ATS would be $7 000 000, even if the results are better than projected.

5. It is our view that the company is in need of significant additional funds to allow it to develop to the sales and income levels in your projections. Accordingly, we are willing to inject $2 000 000 into ATS for agreed working capital and investment use in the form of a secured debt with a 10% interest rate. It would be our intention to make available $750 000 at time of closing, $750 000 at time of completion of the 1985 audit, and the remaining $500 000 as needed by the company on an agreed basis during 1986.

6. It would be our intention that this loan would be used to purchase treasury stock from ATS at the end of 1986, using the valuation for the company as established by the formula outlined above. In other words, if the company was valued at $6 835 000, the $2 000 000 loan would convert to give us 22.6% of the enlarged equity in the company. The attraction of this arrangement from your point-of-view is that it provides you with the money now to grow, but that the shares are ultimately purchased in ATS at the valuation achieved in 1986 rather than at a current valuation. Depending upon the ulimate valuation of the company, the percentage of its enlarged equity that would be bought by the $2 000 000 referred to above would vary. It would then be our intention to purchase directly from you existing shares held by you in ATS such as would give us 75% of the then enlarged equity of the company. In the example quoted above, we would need to purchase 67% of your shareholding to give us a total of 75% of the enlarged equity. Using the value above, this would cost $4 600 000. In other words, what you would receive would be $4 600 000 in cash plus 25% interest in the $2 000 000 injected by us: for a total of $5 100 000, which is 75% of $6 835 000.

7. We propose that you would be paid for these shares as follows: on closing, $500 000; in March 1986 and March 1987, further payments of $500 000; in March 1988 and March 1989, further payments of $1 000 000 each; the balance, payable on March 1990. To the degree that the final value of the company is larger or smaller than the $6 835 000 figure, the above payments would be pro-rated.

MOVING FORWARD

On March 16, Bill Harcourt phoned Denis to report that the had met with Klaus, subsequent to the February 22 meeting. Denis recalled the discussion:

> Apparently Klaus was initially very unhappy with the limit of $7 million that we put on the company, although he is now willing to live with it, and in fact has become very positive about doing a deal with Aer Lingus. He appears to have overcome his hesitance and concern at another party becoming the majority

shareholder of ATS. This may be due to the fact that he has taken advice from a friend name Bob Tivey, who is retired president of Monarch Canada.[4] Some minor improvements are required, however.

One of these is that Klaus wants us to increase the $500 000 coming to him on closing so that he can pay employee bonuses—these will come out of his own pocket—and have more for himself. He also wants us to pay interest on the portion of the purchase price which remains unpaid until the earn-out is completed. Finally, he would like a personal contract which will last five years, and include a good salary, plus a bonus that is 2% of pre-tax earnings, and a car.

Other news included the fact that Klaus is in the process of hiring a financial person, and is considering a second-year registered industrial accountancy student. Bill suggested that he discuss this matter in some detail with us, as it might be advisable to opt for a more high-powered person. Bill also told me that Klaus was facing an immediate decision with respect to new premises for ATS—the major question being whether the company should rent or buy. Purchase cost will be close to $1 million.

Shortly after his phone call, Denis received a letter from Klaus, which began, "I wish to advise you that as I am prepared to accept the proposal as outlined ... subject to the following changes." As expected, the most important of the requested changes were an increased initial payment, the payment of interest on the unpaid portion of the purchase price, and a five-year employment contract.

After some negotiation, Aer Lingus agreed to increase its initial payment to allow Klaus to pay employee bonuses, and to increase the initial funds going to his own pocket by appproximately 50%, which was less than he had requested, but was deemed satisfactory.

In early April, Klaus travelled to Ireland for a meeting with the Chief Executive of Aer Lingus, and later that month the Aer Lingus board approved the purchase of a 75% shareholding of ATS on the terms which had been agreed with Klaus.

At the end of April, Denis was once again in Kitchener, where he and Klaus held a most amicable meeting. Denis learned that Klaus and Bob Tivey had prepared a new business plan which they had used to obtain an increase in the ATS credit line. Also, Klaus had decided to proceed with the acquisition, his only objection being that eight board meetings a year was too many. Denis concluded his notes on the meeting with the following:

> We discussed at length the need for ATS management to develop credibility with me, and for me to develop credibility on ATS subjects in Dublin, which he seemed to accept. All in all, the discussions were satisfactory and straightforward, and have put to rest a significant number of my fears concerning Mr.

---

[4] Disguised name.

Woerner's independence and his unwillingness to accommodate the requirements of a major corporate shareholder. In my view, he will accept direction, provided that the direction is fast-paced and is seen by him as being responsive to ATS's needed.

Due to some apparent foot-dragging on the part of Klaus's lawyers and intervening vacations, it was July before Denis arrived in Kitchener to review the drafts of the sale contracts, and bring the deal to a conclusion.

THE MEETING OF JULY 16

Klaus attended this meeting with Ron Jutras, his new financial controller, who had been hired without consultation with Aer Lingus, and Bob Tivey, who was acting as a consultant to Klaus. Denis recalled the meeting as follows:

> They opened the meeting by tabling a number of requirements which they said were critical to the deal going ahead. These were:
>
> 1. A reluctance to hand over control to us before the valuation date of September 1986.
> 2. A five-year guaranteed contract for Klaus, with a ten-year period before we can force him out of share ownership.
> 3. A degree of protection against the possibility that one off costs may depress 1986 earnings—specifically a *minimum* buy-out price of $6 million!
>
> I was very distressed to find such a total about-face on something that we had agreed three months earlier, and when faced with this, Klaus acknowledged that he was changing his mind, but said that he could not afford the possibility of one bad year depressing his buy-out price. As for the contract length, Klaus was very emotional when the possibility of anything shorter than a five-year contract was raised.
>
> The question facing me as I sat in that meeting was how to react. Was it time to give up on this long and apparently fruitless process, or should I continue—and if so, how?

EXHIBIT 1 ATS Financial Statements (Cdn $000)

	1980	1981	1982	1983	1984
Sales	332	765	1 210	1 753	4 168
Cost of Sales	187	491	902	1 450	3 197
Gross Margin	145	274	308	303	971
Overheads	58	127	188	243	451
Operating Profit	87	147	120	60	520
Interest	2	10	20	26	71
Tax	11	22	4	0	18
Net Profit	74	115	96	34	431

Balance Sheets

	1980	1981	1982	1983	1984
Fixed Assets	106	211	308	390	517
Current Assets	113	282	384	457	1 300
Current Liabilities	(35)	(129)	(209)	(252)	(390)
Working Capital	78	153	175	205	910
	184	364	483	595	1 427

Funded by:

	1980	1981	1982	1983	1984
Share Capital	1	6	5	3	3
Revenue Reserves	79	114	177	(160)	164
Shareholder's Funds	80	120	182	(157)	167
Loan Capital	104	244	301	752	1 260
	184	364	483	595	1 427

EXHIBIT 2 Projected ATS Financial Statements* (Cdn $000)

	1985	1986	1987	1988
Sales	8 000	11 000	14 000	17 000
Cost of Sales	5 920	8 360	10 920	13 260
Gross Margin	2 080	2 640	3 080	3 740
Overheads	1 040	1 430	1 750	2 210
Operating Profit	1 040	1 210	1 330	1 530
Interest	70	120	200	300
Tax	427	480	497	541
Net Profit	543	610	633	689
Dividends (Projected)	0	0	250	300

Projected Balance Sheets	1984	1985	1986	1987	1988
Fixed Assets	517	680	1 030	1 310	1 860
Development				1 000	1 000
Current Assets	1 300	2 417	4 904	5 740	6 580
Current Liabilities	(390)	(760)	(1 720)	(1 886)	(2 260)
Working Capital	910	1 657	3 184	3 854	4 320
	1 427	2 337	4 214	6 164	7 180
Funded by:					
Share Capital	3	750	2 000	2 300	2 700
Revenue Reserves	164	707	1 317	1 701	2 090
Shareholder's Funds	167	1 457	3 317	4 001	3 790
Loan Capital	1 260	880	897	2 163	3 390
	1 427	2 337	4 214	6 164	7 180

* These projections were prepared by Klaus Woerner and Peter Jones.

EXHIBIT 3 Revised ATS Income Projections* (Cdn $000)

	1985	1986	1987	1988
Sales	8 000	14 000	20 000	30 000
Gross Margin	2 080	3 360	4 400	6 000
	(26%)	(24%)	(22%)	(20%)
General & Admin.	862	1 190	1 578	2 159
Income	1 218	2 170	2 822	3 841
Profit Sharing	120	217	282	384
Pre-Tax Income	1 098	1 953	2 540	3 457
Tax at 45%	494	879	1 143	1 556
After Tax Income	604	1 074	1 397	1 901

* These revisions were dated February 20, 1985. They were prepared by Klaus Woerner, working
with Bill Harcourt.

NORANDA-ANDACOLLO

J. Peter Killing and Peter R. Richardson

> *Our ultimate decision on this project must obviously be governed by economic and commercial considerations. Nevertheless, we remain convinced that we are on the right moral side of this particular question.*
>
> – Alf Powis
> Noranda Mines Ltd.
> Annual Meeting, April 1977

In July 1980 Mr. Powis, chairman and chief executive officer of Noranda, had to decide whether or not the Andacollo (pronounced Andacoya) project should be submitted to the board of directors for final approval. The $390 million mining project had been under consideration within Noranda for five years, but with feasibility studies now complete, the financing in place and equipment about to be ordered, this was his last chance to withdraw Noranda from the project before it really got started. He commented:

> We might have dropped this venture three years ago when we were in tough financial shape and cutting back on non-essential projects, if it hadn't been for the campaign mounted against us by the Taskforce on the Churches and Corporate Responsibility. We found their presumption in telling us not to invest in Chile very annoying, and were particularly upset with the protests they organized at our annual meetings and at the occupation of our Montreal office.
>
> Our annoyance kept this project alive during those years when the copper price didn't justify it. The irony about our dispute with the churches is that even in a strict moral sense the investment *should* be made, as we have been told repeatedly by Chilean church leaders that they want our investment and the jobs it can provide in a region of poverty.

NORANDA: A VERY CANADIAN COMPANY

Noranda Mines Limited was a large, diversified natural resource company with its head offices in Toronto and operations throughout Canada. Its businesses included mining, smelting and refining, forest products, manufacturing and oil and gas. The company's distribution of revenues and earnings for 1977–79 is shown in Exhibit 1. Although part of the company's recent growth had taken place abroad (particularly in the U.S.), Noranda consciously cultivated a Canadian identity. Internal statements of goals and objectives stressed the intent of its executives to remain primarily an operating company in Canada.

Originally established to work the rich Horne copper-gold mine in Noranda, Quebec, the firm subsequently integrated forward into smelting, refining and metal manufacturing. In the early 1960s, however, new lead-zinc mines were opened in addition to the copper mines. Later in the 1960s and through the 1970s the scope of diversification broadened and quickened to include activities as diverse as aluminum and fibre optics as well as a major position in the Canadian forest products industry. Late in the 1970s, Canadian Hunter, a subsidiary, discovered a major gas field in Western Canada. Capital requirements for the development of this field were expected to be significant until the mid-1980s when it would become a major cash contributor.

Copper still remained an important company business in 1980. Revenues from copper mining, smelting and refining accounted for 20% of net revenues and almost 40% of pre-tax profits. These high earnings, however, followed a period from 1975 to 1977 when the copper industry had endured a prolonged, disastrous slump.

In addition to the mines listed in Exhibit 1, Noranda had interests in other large copper mines through its investments in associated companies such as Placer Development. These companies, however, operated relatively autonomously and Noranda had no direct influence over the disposition of these mines' concentrate output. Noranda used concentrates to feed its two large smelter operations in Quebec at Rouyn-Noranda and Murdochville. These smelters in turn provided metal for Noranda's refinery in Montreal.

While the copper business had been depressed in recent years, Noranda remained committed to this part of its business. Executives viewed the slump as typical of the cyclical fluctuations that characterized the copper industry (see price graph, Exhibit 2). Accordingly, when profits rebounded in 1978 and 1979, the company moved rapidly to activate a number of new mining projects. Early in 1980 there were 13 underway (Exhibit 3). Most of these were relatively small operations, however, and company executives felt that a large new copper mine was needed if Noranda was to remain in the leading ranks of world copper producers. Unfortunately, while Noranda concentrated most of its exploration in Canada, there was considered to be little chance of discovering a major new deposit there.

Thus, major new copper mining ventures were likely to take place abroad. Chile, being the world's largest producer of copper outside the U.S., was the most attractive place, geologically, to seek new sources of concentrate and metal. Producing approximately 1 million short tons of copper per year, Chile's output constituted 12–14% of total world production in the late 1970s, down from as much as 20% in the 1940s.

ANDACOLLO: THE EARLY YEARS

In 1974 Noranda was asked by the World Bank to carry out an evaluation of the Chilean copper industry. World Bank officials were concerned that forecasts of copper production they had received from the new government of Chile, headed by General Pinochet and a military junta, would prove to be hopelessly optimistic because of the chaos following the "particularly bloody" military coup which ousted the Marxist government of Salvador Allende in September 1973. Although the involvement of the United States' Central Intelligence Agency in the coup may not have proved decisive (a 1980 observer commented, "The anger of the middle classes in Chile against Allende had become so intense by 1973 that the coup would have occurred with or without a few words and dollars of encouragement from Mr. Kissinger"), it was apparently sufficiently publicized that the World Bank concluded it would be wiser to send non-American copper executives to carry out the Chilean investigation. While making the survey in Chile, the three Noranda executives had a good look at the Andacollo deposit. They judged it to be one of the largest available copper deposits in the free world, although of rather low grade. After reporting to the World Bank that the Chileans would meet their output forecasts (which they did), and discussing the Andacollo situation within Noranda, the executives wrote to the government of Chile indicating that Noranda would be interested in investigating the possible development of the Andacollo deposit in partnership with one of the Chilean state-owned mining companies.

The Chileans replied that they would be interested in having the deposit developed, but intended to invite a number of companies to bid on the project. Three or four other mining companies competed with Noranda in the bidding but in April 1975 it was announced that Noranda had been selected. A company executive indicated that Noranda won the bid because of (1) its acknowledged copper mining expertise, (2) a proposal having the shortest time schedule for developing the deposit, (3) a plan to investigate the construction of a smelter in Chile as well as a mine (an extra $100 million investment), and (4) its favourable cost projections. Noranda proposed that a joint mining company be formed, owned 50% by a state mining company and 50% by Noranda. Acceptance of the bid did not obligate Noranda to carry out the whole project, merely to proceed with a detailed feasibility study that would cost several million dollars and take two or three years to complete.

At this point Gary German, a Spanish- and Portuguese-speaking Noranda manager who had been negotiating to establish a smelter in Brazil, was called in to work out a detailed agreement with the Chileans. Negotiations dealing with such issues as royalties, taxes, ownership and bank guarantees were originally to take no longer than 120 days according to the preliminary agreement, but actually took 19 months and a final contract was not signed until July 1977. German was credited by many people within Noranda for keeping the project alive during this period when copper prices were low (Exhibit 2), protest groups were active and fresh difficulties, such as the fact that the copper deposit was contaminated with mercury, were discovered. He explained:

> I never asked any of our managers to devote a major portion of his budget to the project. I just requested say $50 000 here and $20 000 there, enough to keep it moving but with a low profile. No one really had to ask "Do we want to continue with this?" because the amounts I was asking for were so low.
>
> One thing I did find disconcerting during the negotiations were the fluctuations in copper price. One month I would be negotiating with copper at 50¢ a pound, which meant the project made no sense, and two months later it was 70¢ per pound, which was getting close. (Early estimates were that a copper price of 90¢ per pound would be needed for the project to be economic.)

RISING OPPOSITION

The Canadian Taskforce on the Churches and Corporate Responsibility was formed in 1975. This group, consisting of representatives of the Anglican, Baptist, Catholic, Lutheran, Presbyterian and United Churches, was created to examine a "central issue in present day society . . . the role of major corporations in terms of social responsibility." The particular attention of the group was to be focussed on "the continued abuses of human rights and social justice in Southern Africa, and in Chile." Chile was a target after the 1973 coup because that country's record on human rights was one of the worst in South America. From the perspective of 1980, the *Economist* described the mid-1970s in Chile as follows:

> Until recently, any democratic pressure in Chile was answered by repression. Not on the bloodthirsty, Hitlerian scale depicted by some outsiders. But repression of the bad, old-fashioned, Latin American military kind. It began with a blood-bath in 1973, when some 3 000 people were killed in the fighting during the overthrow, and probable murder, of Allende. After most of those held in mass round-ups during the early days had been released, some 4 000 political prisoners lingered on in detention, while some 2 000 were held for "criminal" activities. Four prison camps were set up and there were reported to be other, secret ones. Torture was common.

Noranda, because of its prominence and the size of the Andacollo project, was among the first corporations to feel the presence of the new group. During meetings with Noranda executives in May 1975 and March 1976 the Taskforce explained its position to Noranda; that the company should not proceed with its proposed investment in Chile until human rights and democracy were restored in that country. Taskforce members also argued that the copper industry had been democratically nationalized and private investment was being encouraged by the junta against the wishes of the Chilean majority.

> . . . in 1971, the Chilean government, supported unanimously by all parties, nationalized the copper industry. The Chilean government of the day was thus able to direct the surplus from its main industry into vital social services and other development programs . . . The policy of the junta to return Chile's copper production to the private sector reversed a decision made by the Chilean people when it was still able to express its will freely and democratically.

Noranda executives were not moved by this logic and the two sides met again in April 1976 at the company's annual shareholders' meeting, in the first of what were to become annual confrontations. Taskforce members presented their position at the meeting, but a motion that the company delay its investment in Chile pending the restoration of human rights and democracy was defeated. A Chilean refugee recently arrived in Canada made a personal statement concerning her imprisonment and torture at the hands of the Chilean police. At the meeting a prepared statement by Mr. Powis was distributed which included the following comments.

> Naturally, we deplore the suppression of basic freedoms wherever it may occur. We have no way of knowing with certainty whether what is alleged to be happening in Chile is accurate or exaggerated. If it is accurate, we do not know whether this is unique to the present regime.
>
> Positions relating to trade and international investment are matters of foreign policy to be decided upon by the Canadian government. It would be wrong for individual private enterprises to substitute their judgement for that of the government in terms of which countries are good and can be dealt with, and which ones are bad and are to be boycotted.
>
> It has been suggested that Noranda use its influence with the government of Chile to change its policies. In the first place, such suggestions seriously exaggerate Noranda's influence. Also, it would be completely unacceptable for Noranda, as a foreign company, to interfere in the internal political affairs of another country.

Prior to the next annual meeting a number of developments took place. Orlando Letelier, the former Chilean ambassador to the United States, was assassinated in Washington, allegedly by the Chilean secret police. Frustrated by Pinochet's unwillingness to cooperate in the investigation, the U.S. withdrew its ambassador from Chile. Britain had already recalled its ambassador after a 1975 incident in which a British female doctor who had tended to a guerilla leader on the run was tortured to reveal his whereabouts. In December 1976 the United Nations voted for a second time, with Canada's support, to condemn the junta's violations of human rights. Amnesty International noted in its 1975–76 report that Chilean government officials did "not attempt to deny that torture is used but put forward arguments in justification." In late 1976 three Canadian parliamentarians visited Latin America (travelling as private citizens) to investigate conditions first hand, but at the last moment were denied entry to Chile for no stated reason. David MacDonald, a Conservative M.P., stated "I just don't see, if Canadian parliamentarians can't visit there, how we can have a Canadian investment there." Also during this period, the Northwestern Quebec chapter of the United Steelworkers based in Rouyn-Noranda, came out in support of the church group claiming that the proposed investment would "rob the workers of Canada" and "consolidate the regime of Pinochet." Finally, a Dutch firm decided not to make a planned investment in Chile, apparently on moral grounds.

Noranda countered the growing momentum of the church group by pointing out that few Canadian church leaders had ever been to Chile, and suggested that they were being misled by political radicals who were upset with the overthrow of the Marxist Allende. The Canadian church leaders, Noranda executives argued, were out of touch with reality in Chile. In fact Chilean church leaders *wanted* the investment to be made. The following is part of a statement by the president of the Episcopal Conference, the Archbishop of La Serena, printed in Santiago's major newspaper on April 27, 1977, the day before Noranda's annual meeting.

> I must tell you frankly that as a shepherd I feel the duty to fervently pray to God to allow this project (Andacollo) to become a reality in the short term among us. And may the Lord not permit that vested interests obstruct the carrying out of this project, inasmuch as this would mean taking away the bread from the mouths of over three thousand children in basic education in that municipality, of thousands of children under age, of old men and women, and of sick or disabled people.

However, leaders of the Catholic church, the major church of Chile, were largely silent on the issue.

The 1977 annual meeting was preceded by a protest walk made from Trinity Church to the Royal York Hotel (covered by the CBC) and Noranda's Montreal offices were peacefully "occupied." Speaking in favour of the Taskforce's position at the meeting itself were representatives of the Ontario and Quebec Federations of Labour, Local 76 of the Canadian Union of Public Employees, the National Board of the YWCA, the Ontario English Catholic Teacher's Association and

Toronto Alderman Dan Heap, who informed the meeting that the Toronto City Council had passed motions condemning the proposed investment. Powis allowed each of these groups as much time as they wished to make their statements. Excerpts from his reply are given below.

> I should explain to shareholders that, for the past several months, Noranda has been the target of a well-organized and well-financed campaign, coordinated by the Taskforce on the Churches and Corporate Responsibility . . .
>
> Tactics planned for this campaign included pressure on the Canadian government, a press campaign, public demonstrations, picketing of our offices in various parts of the country, and occupation today of your Montreal office, a canvass of certain institutional holders of Noranda shares, pressure on the management through a nationwide campaign of petitions and letters of protest (of which we have received a couple of hundred, mostly form letters) and of course today's appearance at our shareholders' meeting.
>
> Noranda's position on this matter has not changed since our shareholders' meeting last year, and there is little to be gained by repeating the statement made at that time. . . .

During 1977 and 1978 several church leaders did visit Chile, and found that conditions were improving in the country, particularly in comparison to the final years under Allende and the early years of the junta. Canon S.D. Abraham reported on his trip in the *Toronto Sun*. He stated the Anglican Bishop of Chile, Colin Bazley, felt that the "human rights situation has now improved to the extent that investment should take place" and Abraham's own conclusion was that the Canadian churches should recognize the changing conditions and "review their strategy of opposition to the investment." The Reverend Rooke of Clarkson, Mississauga, reported on his trip to Chile in a public letter in which he concluded "the present government . . . merits the support of all people of goodwill throughout the world." The *Economist* described the changes in its 1980 survey. Other portions of this review are included in Appendix A.

> Today, Chile's regime is less harsh than the governments of Argentina, Uruguay, Cuba, and Guatemala and a great deal less so than many governments in Africa and Asia . . . Most of the political prisoners have been freed . . . The regime shows its nastier side in having 15–20 people picked up on the quiet every month. They are interrogated and tortured, then freed, usually at dead of night . . . Yet the repression has eased, and opposition groups are taking the opportunity of making themselves heard. On the streets demonstrations, once unthinkable, are more and more frequent these days. Although they are usually broken up and the protestors arrested, the courts now almost invariably set free any peaceful demonstrators brought before them. Labour leaders at unofficial union meetings—and even sometimes on the Christian Democratic radio station—get away with shredding the government's social and economic policies.

Another favourable development for Noranda was the creation of the Confederation of Church and Business People, a group formed by several hundred businessmen and a few church leaders exasperated with what they saw as one-sided and heavily-distorted views of business being put forward by church people in general, and the Taskforce in particular. Mr. Bradfield, former chairman of Noranda Mines and one of the two founders of the new group, explained that its objectives were very long-term in nature and were to "get the people in the pews to elect knowledgeable, responsible people to represent them at Synod meetings." He explained, "We are trying to get people away from this attitude that all businessmen are crooks." The Confederation published a series of articles presenting their views on various issues, including investment in Chile, one of which was a statement by Canon Abraham, similar to that quoted earlier.

In March 1978 Pinochet replaced the "state of siege" which had been in force in Chile since 1973 with a "state of emergency," although whether or not this made any practical difference was a matter of some debate. In any case, in September 1978 the state of siege was reinstituted in El Loa province in response to a peaceful protest in support of wage claims by the workers of the Chuquicamota copper mine. Amnesty International described the protest and its aftermath:

> The protest included a boycott by workers of the company canteen. About 70 people, mostly workers, were arrested and taken to remote areas. The health of many of these people was affected because of the harsh climate. Other workers were forced to leave the province and forbidden to return for the six months that the state of siege was in force.

Developments such as these kept the protest activity alive, although there were occasional lulls in the action. In 1980 the board of trustees of Queen's University agreed, at the urging of their students, to send a representative to Noranda's annual meeting to say that Queen's students did not want the firm to invest in Chile because of that country's human rights record. Queen's students had been hoping to get the University itself, which had over $1 million worth of Noranda stock, to oppose the investment. As it was they generated considerable publicity for their position. A lengthy article on the Taskforce on the Churches and Corporate Responsibility appeared in the *Globe and Mail* in the fall of 1980. Some excerpts follow:

> Businessmen and businesses have their own standards of conduct, of course, but a cynical public often dismisses these as having evolved more out of expediency than any real sense of social responsibility. By definition, a businessman is someone whose purpose is economic advancement. It stands to reason that anything interfering with generating profits makes bad business.

However, despite popular books on Machiavellian office politics, most businessmen, according to a Harvard study on the subject, don't consider themselves manipulative, underhanded or especially immoral. In fact, most of those surveyed described themselves as more ethical than average.

Noranda Mines spokesman Gary German says it is "presumptuous" to think a company can negotiate anything but economic matters, adding that we should have a little more faith in our businessmen who, he suggests, may function almost as merchant missionaries.

"There are no 'companies' as such; there are only people," German says. "The churches and businesses don't belong to two mutually exclusive groups. Businessmen, too, can be good Christians or Jews, or whatever, and they aren't hypocrites, and they'll represent their churches themselves. If you trust people, if you trust Canadians, you can count on them to behave in a socially responsible manner. If we don't see a foreign investment as both socially responsible and economically sound, we won't invest."

"It's often a case of the forest and the trees," Davis (Treasurer of the United Church of Canada) counters. "It seems possible for a group of people, all with the best of intentions, to get together and become involved in something that isn't acceptable to any of them individually."

Renate Pratt, the Taskforce chairman, was quoted:

"Businessmen can be extraordinarily divorced from real life. They ride up and down on their elevators, they all wear the same sort of suits, and none of them have anything to do with the lives of the people they're affecting."

As an example, she described how the president of one of Canada's largest banks reacted during a meeting with the TCCR to discuss loans to Brazil. "We told them how priests were being killed, and bishops stripped and tortured by the military for their political opinions. His response was, `Whoever these people are, I'd be more than happy to meet them for a drink and discuss things with them.' How do you begin to explain that we're not talking about the sort of people you invite over for cocktails?"

In March 1980 the Toronto Dominion Bank announced, after the TCCR had negotiated with its president, Richard Thompson, for four and a half years, that it will neither renew existing loans nor "make new loans to the government of South Africa or its agencies under present conditions."

THE ANDACOLLO INVESTMENT

Andacollo was possibly the largest known undeveloped copper deposit in Chile. Copper had been mined in the locality for many years, but operations had been small and limited to areas of high grade mineralization. Noranda's exploration indicated proven reserves of 193 million tons of ore grading 0.646% copper and

0.008 ounces per ton of gold. A further 192 million tons of lower grade material might prove economic at higher copper prices. Noranda planned a 30 000 ton per day open-pit mine with a minimum expected life of 16 years commencing operation in January 1983. The ore would be treated on-site in a concentrator that would produce 263 500 tons of copper concentrate annually containing between 26–27% copper, and about .13 ounces of gold per ton of concentrate. This concentrate would then be shipped to smelters (probably not owned by Noranda) for conversion to metal.

In early 1980 the project was expected to have a total capital cost of $378.7 million in 1983 dollars.[1] This figure included allowance for inflation at 10%, 15% for contingencies and interest expense on debt to 1983. Funding for the project would be 80/20% debt-equity. By the summer of 1980 Noranda had arranged for a group of financial institutions to underwrite the debt portion of the capital requirements. This debt would be secured by the assets of the project, not by the parent companies. Any overruns, however, would have to be borne by the equity partners in the venture. This provision caused some concern to Noranda executives because of the rate of inflation in Chile, and the fact that the country's government had recently "pegged" the peso at a fixed exchange rate to the dollar.

In 1983 dollars, operating costs would amount to approximately $5.00 per ton of ore mined. The costs were broken down as follows:

Mining cost per ton of ore	$0.70
Shipping cost per ton of overburden	0.70
Milling costs	2.50
Plant and service costs	0.53
General and administration costs	0.57
Total	$5.00

Government taxes would amount to approximately a further $3.50 per ton of ore mined. Smelting charges were estimated to be approximately $0.26 per pound of copper. Thus, if the copper price was in the region of $0.95 per pound, the return to the mine and net of smelting costs would be approximately $0.69 per pound of copper.

By the summer of 1980 a mining plan had been established for the open-pit operation. This plan was affected by several recent developments, however, which caused some concern to Noranda executives. First, the presence of mercury as a contaminant in the ore might lead to slightly higher smelter charges of one or two cents per pound for its removal. Second, wage rates in Chile were escalating at a rate in excess of 2% per month. Since labour costs amounted to roughly 20% of operating costs, increased rates could seriously affect cash flow projections five and ten years in the future. Some latitude did exist, however,

---

[1] All figures are in U.S. dollars.

to increase cash flows early in the life of the project by mining higher grade ores first. Current plans called for an average ore grade of 0.684% copper during the first three years of operations. This figure could possibly be raised to .695–.70% if required.

The decision to proceed had to be taken formally by the end of September 1980 at the latest. By that time the company would have committed in excess of $5 million to the project, and additional cancellation charges would be incurred after that date on equipment already ordered. In July 1980 Noranda's cash flow model indicated that a copper price of U.S. $1.20 per pound would be required in 1983 for a 20% discounted cash flow return on Noranda's equity. A copper price of U.S. $1.00 per pound would be required just to fund operations and service the debt. As Exhibit 2 might suggest, copper prices are difficult to forecast with any accuracy. During 1980 one analyst changed his estimate of 1981 prices from $1.30 to $1.10 per pound. Another was predicting $.90–$1.00 per pound. No analysts were willing to publish or even privately predict 1983 prices. Noranda's management estimated that the cost of copper produced from the Andacollo Mine would be lower than the costs of at least 50% of the copper mines currently in production.

ANNOUNCING THE DECISION

Gary German:

> If we announce a decision to proceed with the mine, there will be a few protests and some negative publicity, but we feel this issue has generally blown over. The churches are reconsidering their position, as in some cases the opinions being expressed by the Taskforce are not those of a majority of the church members. They are becoming aware of the fact that they are being led astray by a few vocal radicals. Churchmen who have actually visited Chile are becoming much more moderate. Of course the political groups, many of whom do not even acknowledge Noranda's right to exist as a corporation, will make as much noise as possible. Their problem is that a Marxist government was thrown out of power.

Alf Powis:

> I believe that there is a cost to incurring the bad will of certain segments of society, but it is an impossible thing to quantify. The churches can put pressure on institutions to sell their Noranda stock. Individual shareholders may choose to sell, but in my clubs I would incur more disfavour by acceding to the churches' demands than by making the investment. I do not believe our stock price will move in either direction because of this decision. Of course the unions could affect us. Any kind of pressure from customers is extremely unlikely, as we do not sell consumer products.
>
> Our overall position is this: we won't do anything we regard as morally wrong, but subject to that constraint, we would invest in any country, if the economics were right.

EXHIBIT 1 Noranda Mines Limited Financial Summary ($000 000s)

	1979	1978	1977
Revenue[1]			
Copper mining, smelting and refining	$ 490	$ 359	$ 310
Other mining and metallurgical	990	501	429
Total mining and metallurgical	1480	860	739
Manufacturing	155	810	704
Forest products	800	707	552
Gross revenue	3 436	2369	1 995
Less: Sales between divisions	170	110	127
Less: Sales by associated companies	791	568	472
Revenue as reported	$2 475	$1 691	$1 396
Earnings			
Copper mining, smelting and refining operations	$176	$ 52	$ 35
Other mining and metallurgical operations	150	53	29
Earnings from mining investments	7	1	4
Gross mining and metallurgical earnings	334	107	68
Less: Exploration written off	28	13	17
Net mining and metallurgical earnings	305	94	52
Manufacturing operations and investments	68	22	33
Forest products operations	63	61	30
Earnings before borrowing cost	437	178	115
Less: Cost of borrowing (net of tax)	43	43	43
Return on Net Assets[2]			
Net mining and metallurgical earnings	20.0%	9.8%	5.1%
Manufacturing operations	11.1%	3.9%	6.6%
Forest products operations	16.6%	22.0%	13.2%
Earnings before borrowing cost	17.2%	9.8%	6.6%
Balance Sheet Items			
Shareholders' equity	$1 463	$ 884	$ 759
Long-term debt	602	604	589
Total assets	2 518	1 773	1 569

[1] Gross revenues and earnings include Noranda's share of the revenues and earnings of associated companies accounted for on an equity basis.

[2] Earnings before borrowing cost expressed as a percentage of net assets employed (operating working capital, fixed assets at cost less accumulated depreciation, investments and other assets at book value).

Mining Summary
Copper Group—Existing Operations

Mineral Inventory

Division (mine)	Ore Reserves (000 tons)	Grade			1979 Ore Treated (000 tons)
		% Cu	% Zn	Ag o.p.t.	
GECO	22 438	1.86	3.8	1.53	1 627[2]
BELL	44 525	.52		.011	5 475
GRANISLE[1]	41 943	.41			394
GASPÉ (a)	7 334	1.21			629[2]
(b) (i)	101 784	.40			
(ii)	25 194	.44			5 583

[1] The Granisle mine was purchased on November 30, 1979.

[2] Geco and Gaspé (a) are underground mines, the others are open-pit.

EXHIBIT 2 World Copper Price Trends

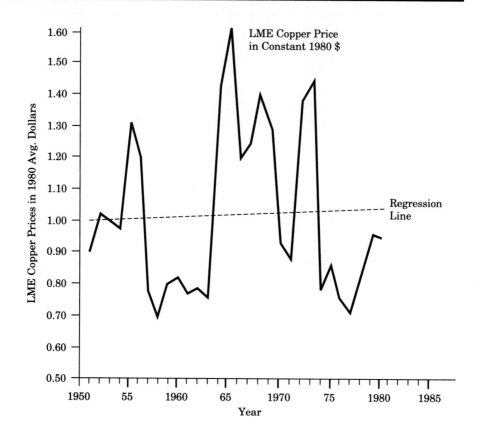

EXHIBIT 3 Noranda-Andacollo New Mining Projects

Location	Noranda Interest (%)	Inventory (million tons)	Mineral Grade	Date of Start of Production	Production Rate (tons/day)	Capital Cost ($000 000s)
Ontario	100	4	6.5% Zn; 1.2% Cu: 3.4 o.p.t. Ag; 0.6% Pb	July '80	1 000	$ 27
N.W.T.	52	0.04	0.88 o.p.t. Au	July '80	150	4
Arizona	77.5	22 Oxide	1.2% Cu:	July '80	6 000	US 40
		50 Sulfide	0.7% Cu:	July '82	10 000	US 42
Utah	33	0.5	4.7% o.p.t. Ag; 8.4% Zn, 5.9% Pb	July '80	440	US 12
Ontario	100	0.6	0.5% Pbl 1.8 o.p.t. Ag	Jan. '81	400	$ 7
N.W. Quebec	51	1.8	5.4% Zn	July '81	1 000	5
Florida	100	10	72% Bon Phosphate Lime	Dec. '81	1 400	US 90
N.W. Quebec	60–85	1.7	1.1% Cu; 4.9% Zn	Jan. '82	500	$ 6
California	100	.1	0.16 o.p.t. Au; 0.48 o.p.t. Ag	June '82	700	US 10
N.W. Quebec	100	0.6	2.6% Cu	'82	500	5
B.C.	50–85	0.4	3.7% Cu; 2.7%Zn; 0.56 o.p.t. Ag	Dec. '82	1 360	62
Chile*	51	210	0.6% Cu	Jan. '83	30 000	US 390
Idaho	75	4	0.76% Co; 1.2% Cu	Apr. '84	2 000	US 78

* Andacollo.
Legend: Cu—Copper, Zn—Zinc, Pb—Lead, Ag—Silver, Au—Gold, Co—Cobalt, o.p.t.—ounces per ton.

APPENDIX A   Noranda-Andacollo: Chile's Economic Experiment*

President Pinochet, who has now ruled Chile for longer than any president this century, was very nearly one of the shortest-lived. In March 1975, as Chile was supposed to be on its way to economic recovery, his economists told him that the collapse in world copper prices would cost Chile $1 billion a year in lost export earnings; that the increase in world oil prices would cost Chile some $300 million a year in higher imports; that these increases would cut Chile's GNP by 13%; that if he tried to spend his way out of trouble he would end up with higher inflation than Allende; that no one was going to lend Chile the money needed to stay out of trouble . . . and that "shock treatment" was the only answer. Pinochet then appointed a new finance minister to head a team of austerity-minded economists. Some of them had been to the University of Chicago, though few had actually been taught by Professor Milton Friedman. Never mind: to Chileans, they became the "Chicago boys."

Price controls were abolished in 1973. Under Allende, prices of many goods had been frozen; as a result, many of them could only be bought on the black market. With the ending of controls, prices soared, adding mightily in the short term to inflation. The government claims that, in the long term, competition will regulate prices much more effectively than the government ever did.

Interest rates were freed in mid-1975, in order to stimulate personal savings, which had been almost non-existent in a country with negative real interest rates under Allende. . . .

Chile's clandestine capital market has been allowed out into the open. The banks are being freed of central bank controls. Foreign banks are being allowed into the country. Minimum reserve requirements are being relaxed.

Tariff barriers have been brought steadily down. In 1973 many foreign goods were effectively barred from the country by tariffs of up to 600%. The average tariff was 100%. Today, average tariffs are only 10%, where they will stay. . . .

After four years of such treatment, the government proudly claims that the Chilean economy is on its feet again. Inflation is down from 600% under Allende to some 30% last year. The GNP, which shrank some 12% in 1974, has grown at an average rate of nearly 8% over the past three years. Chile's exports—particularly its non-traditional ones—rose from $1.8 billion in 1975 to $2.8 billion in 1978. And, at the same time, the Chicago boys point out that Chile has sharply reduced its dependence on copper, which amounted to only 47% of Chile's exports in 1978, compared with 80% in 1975.

But the switch toward a much freer market created more pain than the government admits. An independent survey reckons that about 70 000 Chileans lost their jobs as a direct result of the liberalization of trade. Chile's sugar beet industry went bust as soon as cheaper cane sugar started flowing into the country. Chile's bevy of small, competing electronics firms had to merge into one to survive. Some small mines closed, unable to compete with low-priced minerals from abroad. . . .

Pain or no pain, the creation of a freer economy would not have been complete (or successful) had not the doors been opened to foreign investment. A foreign investment statute of quite astonishing brevity

---

* These excerpts and those mentioned in the text have been taken from "Chile's Counter-Revolution," a survey written by Robert Harvey, and are reprinted with permission from the *Economist*, February 2, 1980. Copyright © 1980 by The Economist Newspaper Limited. All rights reserved.

by Latin American standards was drawn up in 1977. As a result Chile had to withdraw from the Andean Pact, a Latin American grouping of countries with firm ideas about what foreigners can go and do with their money. Under the new Chilean law, foreign companies just have to fill in a short, three-page description of their project, in which they have to satisfy the foreign investment committee that it is not simply a dodge to allow them to write off tax in their own countries.

Then, the foreign companies can step right on in. From the outset, they can send all their profits back home. After three years, they can repatriate as much of their invested capital as they want. The Chicago boys disapprove of any restrictions on foreign investment. They say that foreign firms, like domestic firms, employ Chilean labour; pay half of what they make in taxes; and are a source of much-needed development capital. What if they are taking advantage of a cheap labour force to produce goods for an outside market and are creaming off large profits which they spend back home? They still bring jobs and earnings to Chile. What if they do gobble up raw materials? The country has plenty.

After a slow start, money from abroad is starting to come in fast. In the first six months of last year alone, more than $1.6 billion in proposed foreign investment was approved, compared with $1.3 billion in 1968, $900 million in 1977 and just $24 million in 1974. Of the more than $4 billion invested or proposed since the present government took over, 77% comes from the United States and 15% from Canada. Significantly, of the total 346 projects proposed since 1974, 14 mining projects will tie up no less than $3.7 billion, or nearly 90% of total investment. . . . The transition from state direction toward a liberal economy was far from painless. Indeed, the depression of 1975-76 hit Chile as hard as the slump in the 1930s hit Britain. At

first, the rate of unemployment just climbed and climbed. It peaked in 1975 at 16.5% in greater Santiago as men lost their jobs, and more women went to work, particularly in domestic service, to make up their family's earnings.

The fifth of Chileans who live in third-world poverty were not spared the squeeze. Diets became poorer: national consumption of calories fell by 12% between 1970 and 1978; protein consumption fell by 18%. This contributed to more frequent outbreaks of diseases like typhoid whose incidence per 1 000 inhabitants tripled to more than 100 cases between 1973 and 1977. Only small children have benefited from the grandfather in President Pinochet: infant mortality has fallen sharply, from 65 deaths to under 50 per 1 000 live births. The number of children suffering from malnutrition also fell by 4% between 1970 and 1978.

The cuts have hit hard, however, at education. The number of children completing primary education fell by about 40 000 between 1973 and 1978, as poorer families kept their children away from school to work. The government has halved the number of school meals it pays for. Housing has been another target: public sector housing starts were cut back from an average of 28 000 a year in 1965–73 to some 9000 a year in 1974–78. Chile is short of about 600 000 houses—and as many as 60 000 new dwellings every year are needed to meet the needs of the expanding population and to replace the decaying, jerry-built shacks in Santiago's callampas—mushrooming shanty towns . . .
The economists will now be judged by whether they can improve the lot of the ordinary Chilean in the 1980s after the lost decade of the 1970s. If they fail, Chileans will brush aside the present economic policies as soon as they regain a say in governing themselves—as eventually they surely will.

PART
5 SUSTAINING STRATEGIC BALANCE

YORK RIVER PAPER COMPANY

J. Peter Killing

On January 10, 1990, John Morgan, president of the York River Paper Company ("York") was startled and angered to learn that Rubin Paper Products had made a $46-million takeover offer for Paper Box Limited, one of York's major customers. If the acquisition were completed and Rubin replaced York as Paper Box's supplier of container materials (there was no doubt in Morgan's mind that this was the rationale for the takeover offer), York would lose a customer which accounted for more than 25% of its sales of container materials. The offer was a generous one, representing approximately 15 times Paper Box's predicted 1989 earnings of $3 million, a premium of $30 million above book value, and more than double the current market price of the stock.

York and Rubin were the only Canadian producers of linerboards and corrugating materials—items required in quantity by firms such as Paper Box, which produced cardboard boxes. Rubin Paper had been nibbling away at York's dominant Canadian market position for 20 years, but this was Harry Rubin's first frontal attack on his much larger competitor. Morgan felt that maybe, finally, it was time to declare all out war on Rubin's family-owned firm, which had grown from nothing in the 1960s to capture almost a 20% market share in recent years. Morgan's intention was to make a counter offer, at a higher price, for the shares of Paper Box, and a quick poll of his board members suggested that the majority would support him in such a move. Morgan believed that York could afford to outbid Rubin for Paper Box, in spite of the considerable wealth of the Rubin family, which was invested in such diverse businesses as mining, fishing, and a mini steel mill. However, the situation was complicated by the fact that any bid by York for Paper Box would probably be challenged in court by the Restrictive Trade Practices Commission, since York already owned 35% of Chapel Containers, a competitor of Paper Box. The experience of other firms in the same situation suggested that the court case could be protracted, and York's lawyers estimated that the firm's chances of winning the case (and thus of being allowed to bid for Paper Box) might be no better than 50-50.

YORK RIVER

The York River Paper Company was formed in Montreal in the late 1940s to provide coarse paper for the Canadian market. Coarse paper is brown paper, used to manufacture bags of the type used by supermarkets, corrugated cardboard boxes, and cartonboard containers such as those used for cereal packages and milk containers. The firm had no competition in its early years, and enjoyed tariff protection which tended to keep imports from Europe and the U.S. out of the local market. The challenge for the company in those years was to expand production quickly enough to serve the growing packaging market, and supplies to customers were often allocated as the firm worked to install new and larger paper machines.

York's inability to fully supply the domestic market attracted several competitors, the most durable of whom turned out to be Harry Rubin. Starting with a small paper making machine in the late 1960s in Vancouver, which he fed with a mixture of purchased pulp, wastepaper, and scrap from York's local mill, Rubin began to offer a low-quality linerboard and corrugating material to Canadian container manufacturers. His pricing policy, continued to the 1990s, was to price $10 per ton below York's prices, which were high by world standards. In spite of Rubin's unpredictable and generally low levels of quality, and his firm's almost total lack of technical service, customers supported him because they were eager to develop a second source of supply. Rubin's volume rose steadily but not spectacularly, breaking 120 000 tons in 1983, and peaking in 1987 at 185 000 tons (Exhibit 1).

York executives found competing with Rubin Paper difficult. The Rubin family managed their company in a deliberately low-cost manner. They preferred, for instance, to copy York's new product developments rather than do their own; to meet environmental regulations only at the last moment and by the smallest of margins; and to supply limited range of products to customers in a limited geographic market. York, on the other hand, produced a wide range of product, and sold it to customers anywhere in the country. As a result, York managers believed Rubin's overheads were significantly lower than their own, although it was felt that his variable costs per ton might be higher because his machines were less efficient. (Variable costs in the industry averaged approximately 50% of sales, and could be substantially lower for firms fully served by their own pulp mills.) In spite of Rubin's steady growth, York was reluctant to engage in a price war, reasoning that they had more to lose than Rubin did because of their much larger volumes. Eventually, Rubin built a small pulp mill of his own, although he had no access to trees in Canada, and integrated forward with a 50% interest in a small paper box manufacturer named Court Packaging.

By the late 1980s, York found that its growth had levelled off, and that it had more than enough paper making capacity to serve its local markets. In 1989, a poor year for the company, the mills ran at just over 70% of capacity. In addition, the company was just completing a $200 million pulp mill expansion which would make the company self-sufficient in pulp for the first time, and in fact York would now have pulp available for export or sale to other Canadian users. Unfortunately, selling this pulp could prove difficult, as export markets were depressed, and a substantial capital investment would be required to process the pulp into a form useful for Canadian customers. The company had access to sufficient wood to run the pulp mill at capacity on a continuing basis, and in addition operated a wastepaper collection service in Toronto and Montreal, blending the wastepaper with pulp to lower its raw material costs. Financial statements are summarized in Exhibit 2.

PRODUCTS AND MARKETS

York Paper produced three major categories of coarse paper products. These were container materials, papers, and cartonboard. As can be seen in Exhibit 1, virtually all of the company's growth between 1983 and 1988 came from increased sales of container materials, resulting in fact that 62% of corporate sales consisted of container materials in 1989. It was a source of considerable concern to York's senior managers that the company's aggregate share of the markets it served had fallen from 82% in 1983 to 72% in 1988. An analysis prepared by one of York's managers (Table 1), showed that both the rate of market growth, and York's growth rate were falling.

TABLE 1 York River's Annual Growth Rates
        (percentages based on tonnage figures)

	Domestic Market	
	York Type Products	York Sales
1976–79	6.2%	5.3%
1980–81	Erratic	Erratic
1982–88	2.7%	0.4%

A more detailed comparison (Exhibit 1) reveals that between 1982 and 1988 York had been losing market share in the container materials business to Rubin Paper and, in the paper and cartonboard businesses, had been losing to imports. Even though York was the sole Canadian producer of brown paper and cartonboards, this did not mean that the domestic market was not competitive. A substantial proportion of the company's papers were used to produce check-out bags for supermarkets, a market that in the 1980s was under severe attack from plastic bags. Some major chains had already converted to plastic, and more were expected to follow. York had offered one large chain a substantial financial inducement to stay with paper, but to no avail. York market analysts predicted that by 1995 the company might lose 10 000 tons per year (t.p.y.) to plastic bags of this type. Other problems in the paper bag business were the growing use of tear-off plastic bags by fruit sellers, plastic covered polystyrene trays used by supermarkets for meat and fruit, and polyethylene/light paper combinations used for confectionery. Plastics had virtually eliminated the use of waxed paper. These applications, in total, were expected to erode paper sales by a further 10 000 t.p.y. in three or four years' time.

In the cartonboard business the outlook was for steady sales. Cartonboards were used to make containers for such products as food, milk, other beverages, and cigarettes. Because of the nature of its product line, which was not easily altered, York only marginally participated in the fast food and beverage businesses, which were the only areas of the market demonstrating any growth. Over the last three years, the company had lost share in the fast food business to imports. The trend in this market and other cartonboard applications seemed to be toward a type of high-quality cartonboard, which York was not capable of producing. Although York had over 300 cartonboard customers, three (one of whom was Thorne Industries, of which more later) accounted for 41% of 1989 cartonboard sales.

York's third major product area, container materials, is discussed in more detail.

CONTAINER MATERIALS

Container materials consisted of various grades of linerboard (the smooth outer and inner walls of a cardboard box), and corrugating medium—the middle of the sandwich. These products were sold by the ton to "converters", who used them to manufacture boxes which were in turn sold to end-users. Roughly half of the boxes sold in Canada were used to contain and transport food products, and another 15–20% were used for beverages. Little growth was predicted for the container market in the 1990s, and it was expected that the market would become increasingly competitive as the manufacturers of rival materials tried to displace the cardboard box from its historically dominant position. Pre-eminent among these newcomers was shrinkwrap, which was 15–20% less expensive than cartons, offering water resistance and a clear view of the materials contained. Shrinkwrap was expected to displace perhaps 20 000 tons of container materials in the Canadian market, but the rate and extent of displacement would depend, to a significant extent, on the pricing policies of paper manufacturers and converters.

York River executives believed that the market was evolving into three distinct segments, based on price and quality:

1. Low Cost Lightweight Boxes: These boxes were becoming a commodity product for packaging high-volume, low-margin goods. The battle in this market was expected to be between shrinkwrap and boxes made from 100% wastepaper. Within five years this segment could account for 20–25% of the total market.

2. Medium Weight Boxes: In this segment, the structural characteristics of the box were important because the enclosed products could not support their own weight. Boxes were expected to retain their dominance in this segment, as products like shrinkwrap were not useful for packaging such products. There was expected to be an increasing need for boxes which could cope with high humidity conditions. The segment was believed to be approximately 60% of the total market.

3. High Performance Boxes: Approximately 20% of the market was expected to be for carefully designed and constructed boxes offering perhaps a high level of graphics for high-value added, low-volume goods.

There were three major converters in Canada, and a variety of smaller ones. The majors were Paper Box Ltd., Thorne Industries, and Chapel Converters. These converters were faced with a choice of buying their supplies from York River or Rubin Paper, or importing. The price that each converter paid for its linerboard and corrugating medium was a critical factor in its success, as these purchases comprised 70—75% of a converter's total costs. Importing often looked attractive to these firms in the face of the high domestic prices changed by York River and Rubin Paper. Converters sometimes found that they could source product in the United States, pay freight and duty, and still land material in Canada for less than domestic prices. However, import prices were volatile, as U.S. mills served their domestic markets first, and Canadian converters were reluctant to enter any long-term contracts with their customers if they had to depend on an import price not rising for, say, twelve months in order for the deal to be profitable. In addition, there were some very real advantages to dealing with the local firms, particularly York, in terms of quick delivery (which allowed the converter to carry less inventory), technical service assistance, and a less demanding payment schedule. York managers calculated that these advantages were worth $30–50 per ton to their customers.

One recent move by Thorne Industries to lower the cost of raw material was the installation of a paper machine which made corrugating paper using the scrap generated by Thorne's own converting equipment. In 1989 the company installed a second, larger machine, which could allow it to process as much as 30 000 tons by 1995. Other converters were not yet following such a practice, although the economics of the move appeared to be very attractive.

As part of their planning process, and prior to Rubin's bid for Paper Box, marketing executives at York had put together estimates of the 1990 container material market (Table 2).

TABLE 2 **York River's 1990 Market Estimates of Container Materials** (000s tons)

	Thorne Industries	Chapel Containers	Paper Box	Court Packaging	Other	Total
York River	145	110	110	—	49	414
Rubin Paper	24	34	8	36	35	137
Thorne Industries	21	—	—	—	—	21
Imports	27	—	—	—	3	30
	217	144	118	36	87	602

These relationships are shown in Exhibit 4. Brief descriptions of the three major Canadian converters follow.

THORNE INDUSTRIES

Thorne Industries was an extremely aggressive private company, owned and managed by Jack Thorne. Like Harry Rubin, Dick Thorne was a self-made millionaire, who prided himself on being an outstanding entrepreneur. His company had steadily gained market share at the expense of its competitors, and a minor acquisition in 1989 had brought Thorne to the point that it was almost as large in the container market as its two largest rivals combined. Throne pushed its suppliers almost as hard as it did its competitors, constantly threatening to import if York didn't lower its prices (and carrying through with this threat with increasing frequency), playing off Rubin and York against one another, and infuriating both companies by installing its own paper making machine to reprocess scrap paper. An outsider, listening to the antagonistic, competitive terms in which York's vice-president of marketing described Dick Thorne and his company, could be forgiven for thinking he was hearing a description of a competitor, rather than York's largest customer.

CHAPEL CONTAINERS

Chapel Containers was a less aggressive firm than Thorne Industries, and market confrontations between the two firms were often won by Thorne, with the result that Thorne was gaining market share at Chapel's expense. One of Chapel's problems was that its plants were relatively old and inefficient, making it difficult for the firm to match Thorne's prices. Industry opinion was that Chapel needed to close several of its old plants, replacing them with a single up-to-date facility.

Chapel was owned 65% by Chapel Holdings of Great Britain and 35% by York River Paper. However, York's ownership position did not give it much influence over Chapel's management decisions, as historically Chapel had bought a lower proportion of its supplies from York than either Thorne or Paper Box—a source of considerable frustration to York executives.

PAPER BOX

Paper Box was considered to be a well managed company, not as aggressive as Thorne Industries, but holding its market share in spite of the onslaught of Dick Thorne. The company was of particular interest because it was the only Canadian converter whose shares were publicly traded, and whose financial results were public knowledge. In recent years, profit after tax had been in the 5–7% of sales range, and 7–9% of assets, although 1989 results were expected to be substantially below these averages. With its head office in Toronto, Paper Box had plants in Vancouver, Calgary, Toronto, Montreal, and Halifax.

Paper Box was 70% owned by Api, a large French conglomerate, with the remainder of the shares widely distributed among local shareholders. Api also owned a variety of other companies in Canada, all of whom purchased their containers from paper Box. These "house accounts" accounted for approximately 15% of Paper Box's sales. York executives judged that if Paper Box changed hands, at least half of these house accounts would be lost to Thorne and/or Chapel, and prices on the business which Paper Box retained would be lowered.

THE TAKEOVER BID

The night after the takeover bid was made, John Morgan held a late night session with his senior managers to work out why Rubin had made the bid, and what York's response should be. They concluded that three unrelated factors had pushed Rubin, out of desperation, to make the bid. A fourth factor was the legal advice that one York manager believed Rubin had received, namely, that York would be prohibited from entering the bidding because of restraint of trade considerations, and that had made it seem an easy step to take. John Morgan explained:

> One cause of Rubin's action was surely the 1989 recession. In recent weeks we have come to believe that, while we have all been hurt in the recession, Rubin has lost share as imports of container material doubled, but we held our share. Our previous estimate of his volume of 140 000 tons may be 20 000 tons too high. Rubin has a capacity of 180 000 tons per year, and in fact can cheaply expand that to 230 000 tons per year. He certainly is not happy at 120 000.
>
> The second factor was probably an action that we took to try and stem our losses to shrinkwrap. We introduced a new low priced product made from 100%

wastepaper to allow the converters to sell a product close to shrinkwrap in price. Rubin had no choice but to meet our price with his existing product in this area, and it hurt him greatly because this low-quality area is precisely where he does most of his business. So not only is he losing business to us (and shrinkwrap) in his major market, but he also has had a substantial cut in his profit margin.

At approximately the same time as this was happening, Thorne engineered a confrontation with Rubin to try and get him to lower prices on a certain grade of product. We think that Thorne's real target was us, reasoning that if he could get Rubin to lower prices on this product, we would be forced to follow suit. However, it didn't work. An emotional battle developed during which Rubin refused to lower his prices. Thorne responded by totally cutting him off, and he has bought absolutely nothing from Rubin in recent months.

With all of this, we believe Rubin was looking at a pretty grim 1990, and his bid for Paper Box was to guarantee himself a market of 120 000 t.p.y. Combined with this guaranteed business from Court Container, he will need to pick up very little on the open market.

As the meeting continued, York's management team plunged heavily into the "what if" questions. If York bought Paper Box, what would Thorne do? If Rubin bought Paper Box, what would Chapel Containers do? The list of questions was longer than the list of answers, but some of the group's major guesstimates were as follows:

- If Rubin bought Paper Box, Chapel would cut back its purchases from Rubin dramatically, switching these purchases to York. Thorne Industries would continue to buy little or nothing from Rubin, but might be willing to purchase minor volumes if offered a very good price. Both Chapel and Thorne would be torn between punishing Rubin for moving into direct competition, and giving Rubin some business to keep some pressure on York.

- If York bought Paper Box, both Thorne and Chapel would shift as much as possible of their business to Rubin and international sources. Both companies would feel extremely threatened by the fact that their major supplier was also a major competitor. It was estimated that Thorne's purchases from York might fall to as little as 80 000 t.p.y., and Chapel's might fall to 70 000 t.p.y.

Neither of these scenarios left John Morgan feeling very comfortable, and as he rose, somewhat tired, the next morning, he still faced the question of what action he should take. As a delaying tactic, Morgan thought that perhaps he could make a bid for Paper Box, which would in all likelihood be challenged by the Restrictive Trade Practices Commission. While the court case was proceeding, which could be as long as six to nine months, Rubin would be prevented from making the takeover. The disadvantage of such a plan was that lawyers' fees would probably cost York $20 000 a week, and a huge amount of management time would be required to prepare the arguments explaining why York should be allowed to bid for Paper Box.

EXHIBIT 1 York Rivers' Market History (000s tons)

Year	York River Sales					Exports	Local Competition		Imports				
	Total Domestic	Container Materials	Papers	Carton Boards	Misc.		Rubin	Others	Total	Container Materials	Paper	Carton Board	Misc.
1965	315	130	87	76	22	1	14	23	45	12	12	17	4
1970	421	212	104	79	26	8	37	54	45	6	11	20	3
1975	584	300	115	128	41	22	85	14	48	4	15	25	7
1983	683	375	128	116	64	19	120	—	57	2	13	36	6
1989	685	392	118	118	57	24	135	—	59	6	13	32	8
1985	650	360	125	118	47	35	160	—	80	8	19	44	8
1986	695	411	126	106	52	83	165	—	79	6	16	47	10
1987	703	431	125	103	44	81	185	—	76	9	15	40	11
1988	702	421	128	104	49	64	170	—	90	14	18	46	11
1989	654	398	105	99	43	45	140	—	96	28	15	41	12

SOURCE: These estimates were made by York River's marketing department.

EXHIBIT 2 York River's Financial Summary ($ millions)

	1989	1988	1987	1986	1985
Profit and Loss Statements					
Sales	440	462	440	382	320
Gross Earnings	76	101	104	88	72
Depreciation	25	25	24	22	20
Interest	15	12	10	11	10
Tax	6	23	26	19	14
Net Earnings	30	41	44	36	28
Dividends Paid	18	18	18	16	14
Capital Expenditures*	15	40	40	30	20
Balance Sheet Items					
Shareholders Equity	231	219	196	170	150
Bank Debt	100	124	128	132	136
Net Fixed Assets	239	249	234	218	210
Working Capital	48	50	46	40	32

* The new pulp mill was being financed off the balance sheet. Lease payments of $22 million per year would commence in 1990, when the mill commenced operations.

EXHIBIT 3 York River's 1982–88 Market Share Changes

	1982					1988				
	Domestic Market (000s tons)	York Share	Rubin Share	Imports		Domestic Market (000s tons)	York Share	Rubin Share	Imports	Self-Manufactured
Container Material	485	78%	22%	1%		601	70%	26%	2%	2%[1]
Papers	142	90%	Nil	10%[2]		146	87%	Nil	13%[2]	Nil
Carton Board	146	83%	Nil	17%		150	69%	Nil	31%	Nil
Other	62	94%	Nil	6%		106	68%	17%	15%	Nil

[1] Thorne Industries, see text.
[2] These figures are somewhat deceptive, as approximately half of the 1982 paper imports were imported by York itself, and 45% of the 1975 imports were made by York.

EXHIBIT 4 York River's Anticipated 1990 Product Flows Prior to Announcement of Takeover Bid (000s tons)

Total	York	Rubin	Source	
			Imports	Self-Manufacture
(000s tons)				
217	67%	11%	12%	10%
118	93%	7%		
144	76%	24%		
36	100%			

York → Thorne: 145 (35%)
York → Paper Box: 110 (27%)
York → Paper Box: 110 (27%)
York → Chapel: 8K (6%)
Rubin → Chapel: 34K (25%)
Rubin → Court: 36K (26%)

Boxes: York, Rubin, Thorne, Paper Box, Chapel, Court

THE POMERLEAU GROUP

J. Michael Geringer and Louis Hébert

On March 13, 1989, Hervé Pomerleau, CEO and sole owner of the Pomerleau Group, was assessing his company's recent financial performance. The largest construction company in Quebec and the ninth largest in Canada, the Pomerleau Group had been following a vertical integration strategy that had enabled the company to double in size since 1984 and its 1988 sales to reach $212 million. However, results from Hyalin International Inc., the Group's largest manufacturing subsidiary with sales of $29 million, were less encouraging. Since its acquisition in 1985, this subsidiary specializing in the manufacturing of insulated glass and the installation of glazing and curtain walls had experienced continuous financial problems. In 1988, Hyalin was showing its third loss in a row of over $1 million. On his desk, Hervé Pomerleau had a report from consultants hired to propose a strategy for Hyalin. Hervé Pomerleau wondered about what decision he should make regarding the consultants' report and Hyalin's future within the Group.

THE CANADIAN CONSTRUCTION INDUSTRY

The Canadian construction industry was composed of the firms engaged in the building, renovation, repair and demolition of immobile structures, and in the alteration of natural topography. In 1988, the industry consisted of approximately 130 000 firms, represented more than 680 000 jobs, and accounted for about 51% of the $87 billion of construction undertaken in Canada that year. Governments, utility companies and other firms not primarily involved in construction accounted for the remaining 49%. The industry was composed primarily of firms of small size; only 5% of the firms had billings of $1 million or more and accounted for 59% of the work. The small firms tended to operate at the local level, while larger firms had a regional or provincial focus. Less than 20 firms had operations in all provinces and outside Canada, primarily in the U.S. and in developing countries. Entry into the industry was perceived as easy since it did not require extensive investments in plant and equipment.

Construction companies were classified as either general contractors, engineering contractors, or trade contractors. General contractors were engaged in the construction of buildings for residential, industrial, commercial, and institutional purposes. Engineering contractors were involved in non-building construction such as marine construction, roads and highways, waterworks, dams, electric power plants, railways and oil and gas facilities. Trade contractors were essentially subcontractors performing specialized services for both engineering and general contractors. Such services included electrical and mechanical works, construction of walls and ceilings, roofing and sheet metal, excavation and foundation, steel erection, concrete, glazing and curtain walls, demolition and painting. Trade contractors accounted for 83% of the industry's firms, compared to 14% and 3% for general and engineering contractors, respectively. They were also of smaller size, with average 1986 revenues estimated at $550 000 versus $2.4 million for engineering contractors and $1 million for general contractors. Nevertheless, their pre-tax return on sales, at 4.3%, was above the overall industry average of 3.6%.

Construction contracts were awarded to general and engineering contractors through an open bid process. It was then their responsibility to divide the projects into specific tasks and to distribute them to subcontractors, either through an open bid process or not. Contracts and subcontracts were mostly awarded on the basis of price. However, reputation as a reliable and quality-conscious builder could also heavily influence decisions. Technology, engineering and project management capabilities were also critical in engineering construction.

Contractors varied in their relative reliance on subcontractors. Many were composed of only a small nucleus of people that assumed supervision of the construction site, while all remaining work was subcontracted, and the work force was hired on a project-by-project basis. Some other firms relied on internal resources for major parts of a contract, and resorted to subcontractors only for specific tasks. All participants to a project were responsible for the on-time completion of their task and their work's quality. Generally, 10–15% of their individual contract's value was withheld either by the general contractor or the project's owners. That guarantee was returned to contractors and subcontractors if their task had been completed on time and with good workmanship, 90 days after completion of the job.

With variations greater than those of the GDP, construction activity was volatile and cyclical in nature, in addition to being vulnerable to business cycle fluctuations. Pressures to bid competitively during periods of reduced economic activity, and labour and material shortages during boom times, constrained profitability. Canadian contractors also had to cope with sharp seasonal fluctuations due to Canadian climatic conditions. Furthermore, because construction was a labour-intensive industry, labour represented approximately 30% of total costs. As a result, labour-management relations had a significant influence on firms' performance.

Since 1984, construction output increased by more than 50%. Building construction, fueled by a boom in housing, had been the fastest growing construction market in Canada, especially in Ontario and, to a smaller extent, in Quebec (Exhibits 1 & 2). However, having reached its peak in 1988, the construction market was forecasted to stabilize at around $80 billion until 1992. Furthermore, industry observers were concerned by Canadian firms' limited competitiveness in international markets. The common explanations of this situation were the absence of firms with diversified technological capabilities and integration of engineering and general construction, productivity problems, insufficient or non-existent R&D, and shortage of skilled labour. Moreover, Canadian construction performed abroad was estimated at only $900 million in a market evaluated at over $1 600 billion. Canada was among the few industrialized countries without integrated construction companies having the size and resources required to compete effectively with international firms such as Bechtel (USA), Fluor (USA), Bourguyes (France), Holzman (FRG) or Shimizu (Japan). This was happening at the same time that the construction industry was becoming increasingly global, and that giant Japanese construction companies were moving in force into the North American market.

GLASS AND THE CONSTRUCTION INDUSTRY

The construction industry was the largest user of flat glass, with 50% of the Canadian consumption, compared to 33% for the transportation industry. Used mainly for windows, doors and glazings, percentage of material costs for flat glass in building construction had risen from 2% to 15% in the last 25 years, and had thus become one of the main materials used in this type of construction. Flat glass was used for single-glazed applications as well as for the manufacture of processed glass, such as insulated, tempered and laminated glass.

Insulated glass was made by bonding two or three layers of glass separated by a spacer and sealed around their perimeters. This process was of limited technological complexity and could be done manually. However, automation of facilities was becoming necessary for insulated glass manufacturers wanting to reduce labour costs in the face of intensifying price competition, and to meet the increasingly stringent delivery and quality requirements of insulated glass users. Typically, automation of insulated glass manufacturing represented investments of $2 million and required an annual production volume of about four million square feet of insulated glass to be cost effective.

Tempering and laminating of glass were technologically complex processes. In tempering, glass was toughened by heating above its strain point and then quickly cooled. In laminating, two or more layers of glass were bonded together with an elastomer interlayer. Laminated and tempered glass were used for insulated or non-insulated windows and glazing designed principally for non-residential usage. Compared to tempered glass, laminated glass was less resistant to failure, did not implode and could be transformed, cut or machined once laminated. Both processes required investments of at least $1.5 million and a production volume greater than three million square feet.

In Canada, unprocessed and processed flat glass was marketed directly from flat glass producers to large glaziers and window and door manufacturers. In this segment, demand consisted mostly of large volumes of standard sizes of glass used for mass production of windows. Customers were highly price sensitive and requested rapid delivery. Some glazing/curtain wall contractors were also supplied directly from the glass-making plants. These contractors specialized in the installation of glass, windows and curtain wall systems on construction sites. Curtain wall systems were a lightweight exterior cladding, hung on a building structure, and used for almost all office and non-residential buildings. These systems were an economic and time-saving construction technique, and could provide a variety of finished exterior appearances with glass as well as metal. Flat glass producers also provided their large customers with glazing/curtain wall contracting services.

Unprocessed and processed glass was also marketed through distributors to small glaziers, glazing/curtain wall contractors and window manufacturers, whose demand was usually too small to be supplied directly from flat glass producers. Some distributors were involved in the manufacture of insulated, tempered and laminated glass for the same clientele. Typically, they served a segment requiring custom sizes of glass, and emphasized quality and service in addition to price. However, these firms were often competing directly with flat glass producers for larger supply contracts, and resorted to price cuts to obtain them. In 1986, 35 firms were manufacturing insulated glass in Canada, compared to 18 and 7 for tempered and laminated glass, respectively. In these numbers were included PPG Industries and AFG Inc., both U.S. companies' subsidiaries with facilities in the Toronto area, and Canada's only flat glass producers. These large firms also produced other processed glass such as coloured, coated and stained glass. The typical insulated glass manufacturer had less than 20 employees and production below three million square feet annually. Furthermore, over 1 800 glazing contractors were in operation, but only the 20 largest were involved in curtain walls.

Demand for glass was directly related to the construction market. As a result of the construction boom, demand had risen sharply since 1982. Consumption of insulated glass reached $108 million in 1986, compared to $57 million in 1983, while demand for tempered glass increased from $29 million to $57 million. However, the market for laminated glass grew from $20 million in 1983 to $30 million in 1985, before dropping to $20 million in 1986. Imports of flat glass were evaluated at $150 million in 1986, and consisted mainly of specialty glass, such as reflecting or wired glass, which was uneconomical to produce in Canada's small market. With the exception of tempered glass where imports accounted for roughly 20% of the Canadian market, imports and exports were negligible in the laminated and insulated glass segments, mainly because of transportation costs.

Transportation costs for glass could account for 25% of total costs and consequently, shipment for more than 500–700 kilometres was often uneconomical. These costs as well as users' requirements for rapid delivery explained why the Canadian insulated glass market was divided among a small number of regional producers. With many large users switching to "Just-In-Time" procurement systems requiring more responsiveness, proximity and service, the regionalization of the industry was expected to further increase in the near future.

With construction plateauing until 1992, industry observers anticipated some difficult years, especially for producers of insulated glass, since this type of glass was now present in close to 80% of residential and non-residential buildings. However, demand for tempered and laminated glass was expected to grow with the increasing use of skylights, solariums, greenhouses, sloped glazings, bent glass and other applications which required these types of glass; indeed regulations enforcing their use in most non-residential applications were soon expected.

Low-emissivity (Low-E) and heat-mirror glass were also major emerging products in North America. With a coating or a polymer layer that reduced heat loss in winter and heat gain in summer, these types of glass had the potential to conserve more energy than traditional insulated glass, a characteristic considered ideal for the Canadian market. In 1988, they were used in less than 10% of insulated windows in Canada, but this percentage was forecasted to reach at least 30% by 1995.

Because of the renovation market's growth, insulated glass, like many construction materials, was increasingly perceived as a consumer product rather than a mere industrial one. This trend was expected to transform the business strategies of many construction material suppliers. As the industry became more marketing intensive, producers had to give more emphasis to branding, product recognition and pull marketing, as well as to the quality and image of the product.

THE POMERLEAU GROUP

In 1964, when the construction company employing him went bankrupt and could not finish a project in Saint-Georges-de-Beauce, Hervé Pomerleau went to see the owner and proposed that he complete the project. At age 32, with more than ten years' experience as a construction worker and no high school degree, and speaking no English, he had decided to start his own construction company in this small town located 100 kilometres southeast of Quebec City and 350 kilometres northeast of Montreal. Hervé Pomerleau cited self-confidence and ambition resulting from Quebec's "Quiet Revolution", as well as the necessity to contribute to his native region's development to explain his decision. Twenty-five years later, Hervé Pomerleau was CEO, and still sole owner of the Pomerleau Group, the largest construction company in Quebec (Exhibits 3 & 4). With 1988 revenues of $212 million, almost totally from Quebec, the Group ranked fourth largest among Canada's largest builders, and ninth largest among contractors (Exhibits 5 & 6). Its profitability was also well above the industry's average. Hervé Pomerleau and his company had become one of the main success stories of Beauce, a remote region of Quebec, historically dominated by farming and forestry, that had produced "more free-enterprisers than any other region of the country".[1]

Management often refered to tenacity and perseverance to explain the company's achievements. These characteristics permeated the entire organization and were reflected in the company's policies. For instance, hiring and promotion policies emphasized determination and unremitting efforts, in addition to superior abilities in the evaluation of potential or existing employees. The company and its management had the reputation of being hard negotiators, and if they required significant concessions from subcontractors, they also allowed them fair returns. As a result, the company was well known for succeeding in projects in which others would have been doomed for failure, or for executing projects within specifications and deadlines that other contractors would avoid or refuse.

The Group's goal was straightforward: to provide jobs to workers and ensure the pride of a whole population by becoming the leading construction company first in Quebec and then in Canada. In addition, the Group took great pride in its entrepreneurship and its capacity to seize opportunities when they occurred. Despite its size, the firm wanted to preserve a familial atmosphere and the respect of the community in which it had grown.

The Structure of the Company

Among the Pomerleau Group's six business units, the construction subsidiary, Hervé Pomerleau Inc., was the core of the company and accounted for 65% of the Group's revenues. At the beginning, Hervé Pomerleau was especially good at obtaining contracts for government buildings, and his company built over 150 public buildings such as schools, prisons, and office blocks in Quebec. Later, the company gradually specialized in commercial, industrial and institutional construction, particularly in larger and more complex projects. This led to the construction of many office buildings, shopping malls, large manufacturing

---

[1] Fraser, M., 1987. *Quebec Inc.* Toronto: Key Porter Books, p.43.

plants, dams and electricity stations. In periods of slowdown, the company pursued smaller projects that would not be considered at other times, but that enabled it to maintain the volume of its activities. In fact, the company was even profitable throughout the 1978–82 recession, when the company was forced to take possession of many buildings and shopping malls because their owners were unable to continue making payments. During the same period, the company became involved in a couple of small construction projects in Algeria. Nevertheless, for the future, the company wanted to maintain its focus on large scale projects, and to expand its geographical scope, mainly toward Ontario and the U.S. It also sought to increase its penetration of the industrial construction market, and to participate actively in the second phase of the James Bay hydroelectric projects.

Since the 1970s, the firm had been following a vertical integration strategy designed to achieve greater control over those activities critical to the quality of appearance and on-time completion of construction projects. This vertical integration strategy had resulted in the internalization of many activities usually distributed to specialty trade contractors. Compared to its competitors, the Pomerleau Group relied to a significantly smaller extent on subcontractors for critical sections of construction projects. Through the years, the company also developed skills considered unique in Quebec in excavation/foundation and concrete work. In areas requiring extensive specialization, such as electrical and mechanical work, the Group had built lasting relationships with specific subcontractors. The Group had helped to create electrical and mechanical contractors, sometimes even guaranteeing the first bank loans, and had ensured their development by continuously providing them with contracts. In return, these subcontractors provided the Group with better prices and conditions for their services.

More importantly, however, the Group's vertical integration strategy led to the creation and acquisition of four subsidiaries, whose operations were directly related to the visible parts of buildings and the critical path of construction projects. In 1988, these subsidiaries accounted for 25% of the Group's sales. Ciments et Tuiles de Beauce (CTB), was created in 1970, and specialized in the finishing of concrete floors and the covering of floors, walls and fronts of buildings with different materials such as ceramics, granite, marble and terrazo. Seven years later, Hervé Pomerleau founded Ebénisterie Beaubois (EB), a carpentry and architectural millwork firm. This subsidiary manufactured customized and built-in furniture for offices and public buildings, and offered finishing services for malls, stores, restaurants and offices. After a substantial deficit in 1986, changes in management, and implementation of a costing system and a bonus system for employees based on productivity increases, quickly returned the subsidiary to profitability. In 1982, the Group bought a majority position in Béton Bolduc Inc., which produced different concrete products such as plain and decorative blocks, bricks, paving, and prefabricated concrete architectural elements for exterior facings. The company was on the verge of bankruptcy when the owners came to the Group for help. Financial and management support from the Group enabled the firm to show its highest profits ever in 1988.

Hyalin International Inc., a manufacturer of insulated glass and a glazing/curtain wall subcontractor, had been the last firm to become part of the Pomerleau Group. The largest of the Group's manufacturing subsidiaries, it was also the only one located outside Beauce. For some years, this firm had been experiencing serious financial problems. Since its acquisition by the Group in 1985, turnaround attempts had been unsuccessful, and the subsidiary had failed to show any profits yet.

In 1974, the Group became involved in real estate through HLP Inc. This subsidiary owned and managed numerous shopping malls, office buildings, warehouses and hotels throughout Quebec, Ontario and the Maritimes. It helped the Group to capitalize, as sole owner or with partners, on its knowledge of the construction industry. Among the $500 million in projects already in the Group's order book for the next two years, $60 million were for HLP's projects. Accounting for 10% of the Group's revenues in 1988, HLP's importance within the company was expected to increase significantly in the future.

The real estate subsidiary, the manufacturing and construction companies, and in-house engineering and architecture resources enabled the Group to provide its customers with a wide range of products and services. With 27 engineers and its own team of architects, the Group offered turnkey projects, a capability seldom found among Quebec contractors. Such projects included everything from selection of sites and preparation of drawings to suggestion of potential tenants and advice on the management of the buildings, rather than the mere construction of buildings based on drawings and specifications done by another firm. The Group also had sometimes obtained contracts because it could rely on internal sources of construction products through its manufacturing subsidiaries. In turn, these subsidiaries participated in the Group's projects as often as was possible and economic. In this way, more than 50% of CTB's and EB's sales were directly related to the Group's projects. Béton Bolduc and Hyalin were much more autonomous, and depended on the Group for only 15% and 25% of their sales, respectively.

The Organization

The Group was directed by a seven-member executive committee composed of Hervé Pomerleau, three vice-presidents for construction, and the VPs for finance, administration and real estate development. Since the 1987 departure of the VP for the subsidiaries, this position's responsibilities were assumed by the CEO. The executive committee usually met every second Saturday morning for two to four hours. The responsibility for setting the meetings' agenda was rotated among participants at each meeting.

Construction VPs and the CEO devoted a large portion of their time to the research and negotiation of contracts. Construction VPs also supervised the preparation of tender offers and the work of project managers and supervisors. Project managers and supervisors were key elements in the profitability and on-time completion of projects as they assumed direct responsibility for each project's execution. These positions had similar functions. Both oversaw construction site superintendents, although managers were more experienced and enjoyed significantly more autonomy. Good project managers and supervisors were difficult to find, and their training, under a construction VP or a senior project manager, lasted up to five years. Sometimes, a construction VP assumed direct responsibility for especially large and important projects.

Although the basic functioning of the construction subsidiary was similar to the industry norm, its organization differed in three very significant ways. First, the typical construction VP in the industry was more than 50 years old and, while gaining experience, had passed through the positions of manager and supervisor, after having started as superintendent at 25 years old. Consequently, managers and supervisors were generally around 40 years old. However, at Hervé Pomerleau Inc., this "pyramid" was somewhat inverted: while superintendents were over 40 years old, supervisors were less than 28, managers less than 35, and VPs less than 40. According to management, this structure allowed the company to benefit from the aggressiveness and dynamism of younger individuals within its organization, while drawing from the experience of older superintendents at individual sites.

Second, in contrast to competitors who typically hired all construction workers on the basis of contracts or individual projects, and whose only permanent employees were project managers, Hervé Pomerleau Inc. offered permanency to a large number of employees. In fact, all construction site supervisors and foremen, about 300 individuals, as well as a core of more than 400 skilled construction workers were assured of work for 12 months a year. The remaining labour was hired according to the size and type of projects the Group was executing.

Thirdly, these permanent employees were eligible for a company-wide profit sharing system based on the employee's position in the organization, the profitability of the projects he or she had been directly involved with, and the company's overall results. As employees moved up in the company's hierarchy, bonuses were increasingly based on the company's overall results. The vice-presidents' bonuses depended solely on the Group's profits. The manufacturing subsidiaries also had profit-sharing systems, but these bonuses were based strictly on the units' performance. As a result, total remuneration for any position in the Group was superior to the industry's average, even though basic wages were below those offered by competitors. Coexistence of permanency and profit-sharing was identified as an important factor in the company's exceptional performance. One vice-president affirmed:

> This permanency allows us to offer profit-sharing that stimulates our employees and makes them feel more involved in the company. However, it creates substantial pressure on us [the managers] to have so many permanent employees. We have to keep them on the job and always find more projects to keep them working. We don't want to lose people we have trained.

HYALIN INTERNATIONAL INC.

In 1988, Hyalin International Inc. had sales of $29 million and 200 employees, compared to $12 million and 180 employees in 1986 (Exhibit 7). Despite this growth and continuous efforts to cut costs at all levels of the organization, the firm's deficit was in the range of $1 million for the third consecutive year. The Pomerleau Group had acquired Hyalin, then called Cayouette-Superseal, after that firm went bankrupt in August 1985. Hyalin was then supplying glazing and curtain walls for three of the Group's projects, and especially for the construction of the Laurentian Group's 32-story, class A office building in downtown Montréal. This was not only the Group's largest project ever, but also its first major office tower project in Montreal, a market segment the company had tried to enter decisively for many years. Hyalin's bankruptcy jeopardized the on-time completion of the project. It also threatened the Group's reputation as a reliable builder, and possibly caused this to be its first and last major project in Montreal. The acquisition was completed when Hyalin's suppliers accepted the Group's proposal to receive 25% of the $4 million Hyalin owed them.

Problems of the Cayouette Group, a manufacturer of wood windows, kitchen cabinets, and steel and patio doors as well as a glazing/curtain walls contractor, had begun with the 1983 acquisition of Superseal, a major supplier of glass and windows. Following this merger, sales plummeted as Superseal customers that also competed with Cayouette began sourcing from other firms. When the Pomerleau Group took over management of the firm, it was in terrible shape. In the previous two years, the firm's headquarters had been moved three times with the result that most files were still in boxes. The firm was also still in the middle of a troublesome implementation of a new computer system and, consequently, no accurate cost estimates or financial data were available. Furthermore, most young and skilled personnel had deserted the company. Finally, there were concerns among the local community, the personnel, and particularly suppliers and customers, that the Pomerleau Group would operate Hyalin until the Laurentian building was finished and then would close down the company. In an assembly of Hyalin's personnel, Hervé Pomerleau made the personal commitment to keep Hyalin in operation. Concerned with the social costs of layoffs, he also promised to protect existing jobs, and even to create some more.

With the temporary assistance of the Group's VP–finance and an accountant, the VP for subsidiaries took over as Hyalin's general manager, although with some reluctance. Within a few months, Cayouette's window and cabinet businesses and their related plants were sold. Equipment and personnel involved in the door and curtain wall/glazing businesses were concentrated in Superseal's insulated glass facilities in Saint-Hyacinthe. This was accomplished with some difficulties, since it required relocation into a single site of personnel from different plants, businesses and organizationl cultures. Nevertheless, the VP for subsidiaries left both Hyalin and the Group shortly after an expected $200 000 profit for 1987 was transformed into a $1 million loss by the discovery of an accounting error. Hyalin's marketing manager, hired in April 1987, replaced him as general manager of the troublesome subsidiary.

Hyalin's Operations

Hyalin specialized in the distribution of glass and the manufacture of insulated glass destined for manufacturers and distributors of windows and doors, and for small- and medium-sized glaziers. Despite intense competition, aggressive pricing and rapid delivery (three days rather than the industry's five-day average) resulted in sales of insulated glass reaching $8.5 million in 1988, compared to $3.5 million in 1986. With a 1988 production of 2 million square feet of insulated glass, Hyalin's share of the Quebec market was estimated at 20%. This growth had been fueled particularly by sales of standard size insulated glass to residential window manufacturers. Hyalin's strategy of territorial expansion also led the firm to enter the Ontario and Maritimes markets.

In the Quebec insulated glass market, Hyalin was competing against single-product firms whose size and scope were similar to or smaller than its insulated glass business. Price competition had traditionally been intense in this market. It had reached new heights in recent months since one competitor, Cover, had automated its facilities, and had reduced its debt and interest load by going public. Hyalin and the other producers, with their labour-intensive and manual production lines, had encountered difficulties competing effectively in a market where insulated glass prices were lower in 1988 than in 1985. In fact, rumours were that Hyalin's two other competitors had financial difficulties despite their close relationships with large window manufacturers. PPG Industries had even exited the market, but Cover was still showing strong and growing profits.

Hyalin's steel and patio doors were sold to manufacturers and distributors of doors and windows, as well as to manufacturers of prefabricated houses. A steel door was made from two steel sheets, bought from large steel companies, and mounted on a wood frame that was injected with foam for insulation. Patio doors were made of tempered glass mounted on a wood and vinyl frame. This product line, after extensive modifications to make it more competitive, had seen its sales grow from $3.5 million to $6.5 million between 1986 and 1988. With 50 000 steel doors worth about $4.5 million, Hyalin was still a small player in this market compared to Stanley, the leader with more than 300 000 doors. Further expansion in this market was perceived as difficult, since it would require investment in expensive new equipment. In the patio door market, Hyalin was in direct competition with its supplier of vinyl moulding, a firm that was also one of Quebec's major manufacturers of patio doors. In both cases, competition was intense and essentially price-based.

Finally, Hyalin was a glazing/curtain wall contractor for the construction industry. This had been Hyalin's fastest growing business with sales rising from $5 million in 1986 to $13 million in 1988. Part of this performance was attributed to contracts with the Pomerleau Group, which accounted for 50% of glazing and curtain wall contracts. In spite of reluctance by other contractors to do business with one of Pomerleau's subsidiaries, Hyalin had been able to establish good relationships with many of them, while others worked only with Hyalin's two competitors.

One of these competitors, LBL, was a publicly owned company that focused on the installation of glazing and curtain walls, and outsourced all materials. Having doubled in size in the last two years, this firm's sales had reached $30 million in 1988. In contrast, the other competitor, Zimmcor, was a private company more than three times Hyalin's size. It fabricated the metal structure, and had the equipment for painting and anodization, but outsourced its glass. Hyalin was somewhat in the middle, buying the metallic structure but using its own insulated glass. However, half the contracts used tempered glass that had to be outsourced. To improve its market position, Hyalin recently hired an individual who had 30 years of experience with one of its competitors. Hyalin's management believed this individual would substantially improve the firm's credibility and technological knowledge in the curtain wall market.

Nevertheless, management believed Hyalin's competitiveness was also undermined by high raw materials costs. According to them, suppliers were charging Hyalin a 5–7% premium on their products to recover the losses encountered at Hyalin's acquisition. A supplier of steel even required the Pomerleau Group to pay a guarantee on behalf of Hyalin in order to deliver the goods ordered by the subsidiary. Moreover, despite efforts in this direction, and because of the complexities associated with the number of products and the different sizes and types of glass related products, Hyalin did not yet have reliable data on its product lines' profitability. Finally, years of deficits and attempts to reduce costs were perceived as limiting Hyalin's potential for long term development. Indeed, for many years, the firm had made few investments in R&D, new product development and new equipment.

THE CONSULTANTS' REPORT

In an attempt to find solutions to Hyalin's problems, Hervé Pomerleau asked a group of consultants to propose a turnaround strategy for Hyalin. The report was presented to the Group and Hyalin management in March of 1989. A section of the report's executive summary follows:

> We recommend that Hyalin implement the following strategies for its three product lines:
>
> 1. For the insulated glass line: Hyalin should try to further increase its penetration in the Quebec "non-standard" segment with a product and customer service of superior quality. Furthermore, Hyalin should stop trying to expand the geographical market of its standard insulated glass, at least until accurate profitability data is available.
>
> 2. For the steel and patio doors line: Hyalin should expand its penetration in the fast-growing segment of renovation. Hyalin should also offer a differentiated product, at higher price and to a larger array of customers.
>
> 3. For the glazing/curtain wall contracting business: Hyalin should emphasize the development of that business which represents an unique opportunity to build on that market's profitability, as well as on the synergies resulting from Hyalin's association with the Pomerleau Group. Hyalin should also continue trying to diversify its customer base in this business.

In their report, the consultants also stressed that Hyalin lacked the elements required to compete effectively on low price. Furthermore, they did not recommend any major changes in the firm's basic product/market focus. According to them, in the absence of a reliable costing system and, thus, of accurate profitability estimates, they could not suggest dropping any of the existing product lines.

The consultants' report was received by the Group's managers with mixed reactions. They did not fundamentally disagree with its recommendations. However, it did not provide the short-term solutions to Hyalin's problems that they were looking for. In fact, Hyalin's successive operating deficits had cost the senior managers more than $200 000 in bonuses in the last three years. A decision had to be made regarding Hyalin in order to stop the hemorrhaging. Furthermore, options offered to the Group were limited. Attempts to sell the subsidiary as a whole or in part had been unsuccessful, while closing Hyalin was simply out of the question. According to one manager:

> This company's culture stresses tenacity. We never abandon, and we particularly hate seeing our competitors doing better than ourselves. Moreover, too much pride and personal commitment are involved in this situation for us to quit.

Corporate management believed that implementing the consultants' report would be difficult. Automation of insulated glass production appeared necessary for Hyalin to be competitive, but because of recent losses, management showed little interest in investing more millions in the subsidiary for automation or for tempering or laminating. However, corporate management was dismayed by Hyalin's problems. Being essentially "construction people", they knew little about manufacturing, and especially about the insulated glass and door business. According to one of the managers: "This business is a sales and marketing one, involving advertising, public relations and R&D, about which we know little". Indeed, Hyalin was the Group's only manufacturing subsidiary whose operations were not totally related to the commercial and industrial construction industries.

For these reasons, many managers believed Hyalin had to focus on glazing and curtain wall contracting. This business and construction shared many similar traits. Indeed, preparing and presenting projects, negotiating with owners, suppliers and subcontractors, and supervising construction sites were activities involved in this business for which the Group had the required resources and competences to support Hyalin. Because glazing and curtain walls were omnipresent in non-residential building construction, remaining in this business was consistent with the Group's objective to be a major player in this segment. However, turmoil was expected for glazing/curtain wall contractors. Already in the U.S., many firms, including PPG, had exited because of their inability to cope with this business' high risk and volatility. According to one contractor, the business had become very complex as developers "asked for Mercedes design and then tried to build at Chevrolet prices". Furthermore, as a result of well publicized unreliability and leakage problems for many curtain wall systems, project owners required long-term liability from curtain wall contractors, and often pressured them to make good on broken glass and other defects for up to 20 years after the job's completion.

Hyalin's general manager did not like the idea of dropping product lines, and she was a little annoyed by corporate managers' reactions and comments. She believed that Hyalin first needed some time to allow the organization to adjust to its rapid growth of the last two years. Almost half of Hyalin's personnel were new employees that had required training, since little skilled labour was available. They now needed to gain experience. The new computer system also required a breaking-in period before it could provide the financial information everybody had been awaiting for years. Furthermore, focusing on glazing/curtain wall contracting involved some risks since insulated glass and doors provided the firm with some stability. It also meant laying off close to 50% of Hyalin's personnel. Manufacturing of insulated glass also increased Hyalin's purchase volume of flat glass, enabling it to benefit from better prices from suppliers. In brief, according to its general manager, Hyalin needed more time as well as more support and attention from corporate management:

Everyone has to recognize that we have come a long way since 1986, and that we did and changed a lot of things. However, we have not yet shown any profits. This situation is rather difficult to handle in a company as successful as the Pomerleau Group.

CONCLUSION

A few days after that meeting, Hervé Pomerleau was re-examining the consultants' report. He understood his managers' concerns regarding Hyalin and the report. However, he also remembered his commitment regarding Hyalin, and his decision had to take that into account. Furthermore, he knew that Hyalin's general manager had been upset by his managers' reactions, and that she was thinking about resigning. He wondered what he should do regarding Hyalin.

EXHIBIT 1 **Value of Construction Work Performed in Canada, 1976–88 and Forecast to 1991** (in millions of current dollars)

| | Building Construction | | Engineering Construction | | | | | |
	Residential	Non-Residential	Roads, Highways, Runways	Marine, Dam, Sewage	Elec.Power Railway, Phone	Oil & Gas Facilities	Other Engineering	Total
Actual								
1976	12 669	7 803	2 394	1 756	4 176	2 154	2 178	33 131
1977	13 126	8 181	2 691	2 065	4 757	2 724	2 259	35 803
1978	13 780	8 454	3 035	2 175	5 298	3 336	2 113	38 190
1979	14 267	10 439	3 380	2 272	5 900	4 643	2 122	43 023
1980	13 762	12 668	3 731	2 467	6 148	6 709	2 731	48 327
1981	16 365	15 173	4 092	2 829	6 943	8 780	2 704	56 884
1982	13 581	15 262	4 310	3 038	7 255	9 706	2 912	56 065
1983	16 851	13 901	4 326	2 946	6 866	8 128	2 930	55 948
1984	16 647	14 765	4 276	2 916	6 387	8 552	3 031	56 574
1985	24 145	17 314	5 179	3 143	6 101	9 207	2 893	67 983
1986	28 885	18 542	5 193	2 955	6 123	6 728	3 275	71 701
1987 [1]	36 003	21 225	5 065	2 903	6 579	5 917	3 164	80 856
1988 [2]	35 651	22 626	5 284	3 329	7 467	7 490	3 432	85 279
Forecasts[3]								
1989	33 000	21 000	5 900	3 400	7 800	8 100	3 500	82 700
1990	31 000	19 000	6 400	3 700	8 000	8 700	3 600	80 400
1991	30 000	19 000	6 600	3 800	8 900	8 800	3 700	80 800

[1] Preliminary.

[2] Intentions.

[3] MacLean Hunter Research Bureau estimates in association with Construction Forecast Company.

SOURCE: MacLean Hunter Research Bureau, 1988. *Construction Canada*.

EXHIBIT 2 **Value of Construction Performed, by Region, 1984–88**
(in % of the construction performed in Canada)

	1984	*1985*	*1986*	*1987*	*1988*
Atlantic Provinces	9.0	8.5	8.0	7.3	7.2
Quebec	20.8	21.2	21.7	22.4	21.9
Ontario	29.6	31.1	35.3	37.4	36.7
Manitoba	3.3	3.6	3.9	3.6	3.7
Saskatchewan	4.6	4.8	4.1	4.1	4.1
Alberta	16.8	16.6	14.4	12.9	14.0
British Columbia	15.7	14.3	12.5	12.3	12.4
Canada, total	100.0	100.0	100.0	100.0	100.0
Canada, total ($ billion)	56.5	67.9	71.7	80.8	85.2

SOURCE: Maclean Hunter Research Bureau.

EXHIBIT 3 **Quebec's Ten Largest Contractors, 1988** ($ million)

Rank			*Sales*		*Assets*		*Employees*	
1988	*1987*	*Company*	*1988*	*1987*	*1988*	*1987*	*1988*	*1897*
1	1	Groupe Pomerleau	212.3	181.9	299.2	223.9	1235	1390
2	2	Sintra	152.4	145.4	59.8	64.7	1055	1177
3	3	BG Checo Int.	113.2	98.8	57.8	42.9	1170	1137
4	5	Simard-Beaudry	97.1	89.0	48.6	39.3	550	300
5	4	Groupe Vibec	90.8	90.0	70.0	45.0	660	650
6	—	Laurent Gagnon	80.0	30.0	125.0	75.0	1000	325
7	7	Pavage Beaver	69.0	62.0	36.0	34.0	600	800
8	8	C. de Const. Nat.	56.0	52.0	3.0	2.5	700	600
9	9	Lambert Somec	43.3	46.5	24.9	28.1	980	940
10	—	Plibrico	42.0	38.5	10.0	10.0	625	625

SOURCE: *Les Affaires*, June 11, 1988 and June 17, 1989.

EXHIBIT 4   Selected Data on the Pomerleau Group, 1979–88

Year	Sales ($ million)	Assets ($ million)	Number of Employees
1979	53.4	42.0	675
1980	60.6	54.2	714
1981	66.4	45.8	737
1982	64.0	68.8	887
1983	89.8	85.4	1 028
1984	122.8	140.9	1 647
1985	166.4	192.3	1 283
1986	184.2	176.4	1 283
1987	181.9	223.9	1 390
1988	212.9	299.2	1 235

EXHIBIT 5   Canada's Ten Largest Contractors, 1988 ($ million)

Rank 1988	Rank 1987	Company	Location	Sales 1988	Sales 1987	Main Activities*
1	1	PCL Const. Group	Edmonton, AB	1 184.5	1 259.9	b,r,i,hc
2	2	Ellis-Don	London, ON	811.0	756.0	b,e
3	6	Banister Continental	Edmonton, AB	365.8	204.4	hc,b,e,s
4	3	Georges Wimpey Canada	Toronto, ON	349.0	351.0	r,hb,e,s
5	—	Fluor Daniel Canada	Calgary, AB	314.1	—	i
6	8	Commonwealth Const.	Burnaby, BC	290.4	183.0	h,i
7	4	Dominion Bridge	Rexdale, ON	260.0	260.0	b,str
8	5	Comstock	Scarborough,ON	232.0	218.8	me,u
9	9	Pomerleau Group	St-Georges, QC	212.9	181.9	b,e
10	11	Eastern Construction	Toronto, ON	201.0	173.9	b

* b: building construction
r: roadbuilding
i: industrial construction
hc: heavy civil engineering
e: excavation & foundation
s: sewer
h: heavy construction
str: structural work
me: mechanical & electrical work
u: utilities

SOURCE: *Canadian Construction Record*, June 1989.

EXHIBIT 6 **Canada's Ten Largest Builders, 1988** ($ million)

Rank				Sales	
1988	*1987*	*Company*	*Location*	*1988*	*1987*
1	1	PCL Const. Group	Edmonton, AB	1 184.5	1 259.9
2	2	Ellis-Don	London, ON	811.0	756.0
3	3	Dominion-Bridge-AMCA	Rexdale, ON	260.0	260.0
4	5	Pomerleau Group	St-Georges, QC	212.9	181.9
5	7	Eastern Const. Co.	Toronto, ON	201.0	173.9
6	—	Menkes Developments	North York, ON	200.0	N/A
7	10	Dilligham Const.	Vancouver, BC	199.6	161.0
8	4	Canron Inc.	Toronto, ON	181.5	195.2
9	6	Stuart Olson Const.	Edmonton, AB	180.9	175.1
10	—	CANA Ltd.	Calgary, AB	168.7	142.7

SOURCE: *Canadian Construction Record*, June 1989.

EXHIBIT 7 **Selected Data on Hyalin International, 1985–88**

	1985	*1986*	*1987*	*1988*
Sales ($ million)	15.7	12.9	17.9	27.7
Gross margin (%)	11.6	13.4	7.7	10.3
Assets ($ million)	7.1	10.6	12.9	17.6

MR. JAX FASHION INC.

J. Michael Geringer
and Patrick C. Woodcock

It was 6:30 a.m., Monday, January 16, 1989. Dawn had not yet broken on the Vancouver skyline, and Louis Eisman, President of Mr. Jax Fashion Inc., was sitting at his desk pondering opportunities for future growth. Growth had been an important objective for Eisman and the other principle shareholder, Joseph Segal. Initially the company had focused on the professional/career women's dresses, suits and coordinates market, but by 1986 it had virtually saturated its ability to grow within this market segment in Canada. Growth was then sought through the acquisition of four companies: a woolen textile mill and three apparel manufacturing companies. The result of this decade-long expansion was a company that had become the sixth largest apparel manufacturer in Canada.

In the future, Eisman felt continued growth would require a different approach. A good option appeared to be expansion into the U.S. market. Strong growth was forecast in the women's career/professional market, Mr. Jax's principle market segment, and the recently ratified Free Trade Agreement (FTA) provided an excellent low tariff environment for expansion into the U.S. Yet, Eisman wanted to ensure the appropriate growth strategy was selected. He was confident that, if the right approach was taken, Mr. Jax could become a major international apparel company by the end of the next decade.

THE INDUSTRY

The apparel industry was divided into a variety of market segments based upon gender, type of garment and price points. Based on price points, the women's segments ranged from low-priced unexceptional to runway fashion segments. Low-priced segments competed on a low-cost manufacturing capability, while the higher quality segments tended to compete on design and marketing capabilities. Companies in the higher priced segments often subcontracted out manufacturing.

The professional/career women's segment ranged from the medium to medium-high price points. During the late 1970s and early 1980s, this segment had experienced strong growth due to the demographic growth in career-oriented, professional women. In the U.S., it had grown by 50% annually during the first half of the 1980s, but had slowed to about 20% in 1988. Experts predicted that by the mid-1990s, growth would drop to the rate of GNP growth. The U.S. professional/career women's segment was estimated to be $2 billion in 1988. The Canadian market was estimated to be one tenth this size and growth was expected to emulate the U.S. market. Yet, the exact timing of the slowing of growth was difficult to predict because of extreme cyclicality in the fashion industry. During difficult economic times, women tended to delay purchases, particularly in the mid-priced, fashionable market sectors. Then during times of economic prosperity, women who would not otherwise be able to afford fashionable items tended to have more resources to devote to these items.

Competition

Some of the more prominent Canada-based companies competing in the professional/career women's segment included the following.

Jones New York of Canada

Jones New York of Canada, a marketing subsidiary of a U.S.-based fashion company, was thought to share the leadership position with Mr. Jax in the Canadian professional/career women's market. The company focused exclusively on marketing clothes to this market segment. Manufacturing was contracted out to Asian companies.

The Monaco Group

The Monaco Group had become a major Canadian designer and retailer of men's and women's fashions during the 1980s. By 1988, the company had sales of $21 million and a rate of return on capital of over 20%. The company designed their own fashion lines, which were merchandised through their own retail outlets as well as major department stores. Manufacturing was contracted out to Asian companies. Recently, the company had been purchased by Dylex Inc., a large Canada-based retail conglomerate with 2 000 retail apparel stores located in both Canada and the U.S.

Nygard International Ltd.

Nygard International Ltd., with revenues of over $200 million, was Canada's largest apparel manufacturer. Approximately one-third of their sales and production were located in the U.S. This company had historically focused on lower priced clothing, but they had hired away Mr. Jax's former designer to create the

Peter Nygard Signature Collection, a fashion line aimed at the professional/career women's market. This new line had been out for only six months, and sales were rumored to be moderate.

Additional competition in this Canadian segment included a wide variety of U.S. and European imports. These companies generally manufactured garments in Asia and marketed them in Canada through independent Canadian sales agents. Historically, most had concentrated their marketing resources on the rapidly growing U.S. market, yet many had captured a significant share of the Canadian market based upon strong international brand recognition. Prominent U.S.- based competition included the following companies.

Liz Claiborne

Liz Claiborne, as the originator of the professional/career women's fashion look, had utilized their first-mover advantage to build a dominant position in this segment. This company, started in 1976, grew tremendously during the late 1970s and early 1980s, and by 1988 they had sales in excess of $1.2 billion (U.S.), or nearly two-thirds of the market. Claiborne generally competed on price and brand recognition, a strategy copied by many of the larger companies which had begun to compete in this segment. To keep prices low, Claiborne contracted out manufacturing to low-cost manufacturers, 85% of which were Asian. The company's large size allowed them to wield considerable influence over these manufacturing relationships. Recently, the company had diversified into retailing.

J.H. Collectibles

J.H. Collectibles, a Milwaukee-based company with sales of $200 million (U.S.), had one of the more unique strategies in this segment. They produced slightly upscale products which emphasized an English country-sporting look. Using facilities in Wisconsin and Missouri, they were the only company to both manufacture all of their products in-house and to produce all of them in the U.S. In addition to providing stronger quality control, this strategy enabled J.H. Collectibles to provide very fast delivery service in the U.S. Limiting distribution of their product to strong market regions and retailers also enabled them to maintain production at levels estimated to be at or near their plants' capacities.

Jones of New York

Jones of New York, the parent company of Jones New York of Canada, was a major competitor in the U.S. market. In fact, the majority of their U.S.$200 million in sales was derived from this market.

Evan-Picone

Evan-Picone was a U.S.-based apparel designer and marketer which had become very successful in the slightly older professional/career women's market. This company also contracted out their manufacturing function, and had annual sales in excess of U.S.$200 million.

In addition, there were a myriad of other apparel designers, marketers and manufacturers competing in this segment. They included such companies as Christian Dior, Kasper, Pendleton, Carole Little, Susan Bristol, J.G. Hooke, Ellen Tracy, Anne Klein II, Perry Ellis, Adrienne Vittadini, Tahari, Harve Bernard, Norma Kamali, Philippe Adec, Gianni Sport, Regina Porter, and Herman Geist.

Profitability in this segment had been excellent. According to data from annual reports and financial analyst reports, Liz Claiborne led profitability in the apparel industry with a five-year average return on equity of 56% and a 12-month return of 45%, and J.H. Collectibles had averaged over 40% return on equity during the last five years. This compared to an average return on equity in the overall apparel industry of 12.5% in the U.S., and 16% in Canada during the past five years.

Distribution

The selection and maintenance of retail distribution channels had become a very important consideration for apparel manufacturers in the 1980s. The retail industry had gone through a particularly bad year in 1988, although the professional/career women's segment had been relatively profitable. Overall demand had declined, and retail analysts were predicting revenue increases of only 1–2% in 1989, which paled beside the 6–7% growth experienced in the mid-1980s. The consensus was that high interest rates and inflation, as well as somewhat stagnant demand levels, were suppressing overall profitability.

Although initially considered a mild downturn, recent market indicators suggested that this downward trend was relatively stable and long lasting. Industry analysts had begun to suspect that permanent market changes might be occurring. With baby boomers reaching their childbearing years, further constraints on disposable income might result as this group's consumption patterns reflected increasing emphasis on purchases of homes, or the decision by many women to permanently or temporarily leave the workforce to raise their children. In addition, the effects of rampant growth in the number of retail outlets during the 1980s were beginning to take their toll. Vicious competition had been eroding margins at the retailer level, and the industry appeared to be moving into a period of consolidation. As a result of these developments, a shift in power from the designers to the retailers appeared to be underway.

To counter the retailers' increasing power, some apparel designers had been vertically integrating into retailing. The attractiveness of this option was based on controlling the downstream distribution channel activities, and thus enabling an apparel company to aggressively pursue increased market share. The principal components for success in the retail apparel industry were location, brand awareness and superior purchasing skills. The apparel companies which had integrated successfully into retailing were the more market-oriented firms such as Benetton and Esprit.

The Free Trade Agreement

Historically, developed nations had protected their textile and clothing industries through the imposition of relatively high tariffs and import quotas. Tariffs for apparel imported into Canada averaged 24.5%, and 22.5% into the U.S. Tariffs for worsted woolen fabrics, one of the principal ingredients for Mr. Jax's products, were 40% into Canada, and 22.5% into the U.S. Import quotas were used to further limit the ability of developing country manufacturers to import into either country. Despite these obstacles, Canadian apparel imports had grown from 20% to 30% of total shipments during the 1980s; most of which came from developing countries. Shipments into Canada from the U.S. represented an estimated $200 million in 1988, while Canadian manufacturers exported approximately $70 million to the U.S.

The FTA would alter trade restrictions in North America considerably. Over the next ten years, all clothing and textile tariffs between the two countries would be eliminated, but stringent "rules of origin" would apply. To qualify, goods not only had to be manufactured in North America, but they also had to utilize raw materials (i.e., yarn, in the case of textiles, and fabric, in the case of apparel) manufactured in North America. Unfortunately, these "rules of origin" favoured U.S. apparel manufacturers as 85% of the textiles they used were sourced in the U.S., while Canadian manufacturers utilized mostly imported textiles. To ameliorate this disadvantage, a clause was appended to the agreement which allowed Canadians to export $500 million worth of apparel annually into the U.S. that was exempt from the "rules of origin" but would have a 50% Canadian value-added content. There was much speculation as to how this exemption would be allocated when, in approximately five years, exports were projected to exceed the exemption limit. Experts expected the companies successfully demonstrating their ability to export into the U.S. would have first rights to these exceptions.

Many industry experts had contemplated the consequences of the FTA. There was some agreement that in the short-term, the FTA would most severely impact the lower priced apparel segments in Canada because of the economies

of scale which existed in the U.S. market (i.e., the average U.S. apparel manufacturer was ten times larger than its Canadian counterpart). Yet, long-term
prospects for all segments were restrained because the industry was slowly
being pressured by the Canadian government to become internationally competitive. The question was when international negotiations would eliminate
more of the protection afforded to the industry. It was with this concern in
mind that Eisman had been continuously pushing the company to become a
major international fashion designer and manufacturer.

Overall, Eisman considered the FTA a mixed blessing. Competition in
Canada would increase moderately over time, but he felt that the lower tariff
rates and the company's high-quality, in-house woolen mill presented a won-
derful opportunity for potential expansion into the U.S. market.

MR. JAX FASHIONS

In 1979, a venture capital company owned by Joseph Segal acquired a sleepy
Vancouver-based apparel manufacturer having $3 million in sales, 70% of which
was in men's wear. Segal immediately recruited Louis Eisman, a well-known
women's fashion executive, who proceeded to drop the men's clothing line, and
aggressively refocus the company on the career/professional women's market segment.

Eisman appreciated the importance of fashion, and for the first three years
he designed all of the new lines. In 1982, he recruited an up-and-coming young
Canadian fashion designer, yet he continued to influence the direction of designs
considerably. He travelled to Europe for approximately two months annually to
review European trends and procure quality fabrics appropriate for the upcoming season. He personally reviewed all designs. The combined women's fashion
knowledge and designing abilities provided Mr. Jax with a high-quality, clas-
sically designed product which differentiated it from most other Canadian
competition. In 1989, the designer resigned, and Eisman recruited a New York-
based fashion designer, Ron Leal. Leal had excellent experience in several large
U.S. design houses and, unlike the previous designer, he brought considerable
U.S. market experience and presence.

Eisman's energy and drive were also critical in establishing the merchandising and distribution network. He personally developed relationships with
many of the major retailers. He hired and developed sales agents, in-house
sales staff, and in 1983, recruited Jackie Clabon who subsequently became
Vice-President–Marketing and Sales. The sales staff were considered to be
some of the best in the industry. Clabon's extensive Canadian sales and merchandising experience, combined with Eisman's design and marketing strength,
provided Mr. Jax with considerable ability in these critical activities.

Initially, acceptance by Eastern fashion buyers was cool. The fashion "establishment" was highly skeptical of this new Vancouver-based apparel designer

and manufacturer. Thus, Eisman focused on smaller independent retail stores, which were more easily swayed in their purchasing decisions. As Mr. Jax gained a reputation for high quality, classical design and excellent service, larger retail chains started to place orders. By 1988, Mr. Jax's products were sold in over 400 department and specialty stores across Canada. Major customers included The Bay, Eaton's, Holt Renfrew and Simpson's, and, although initial marketing efforts had been aimed at the smaller retailer, the majority of Mr. Jax's sales were now to the larger retail chains. The apparel lines were sold through a combination of sales agents and in-house salespersons. Ontario and Quebec accounted for 72% of sales. In addition, two retail stores had recently been established in Vancouver and Seattle; the Vancouver store was very profitable, but the Seattle store was very unprofitable. Industry observers had suggested a number of factors to explain the two stores' performance differences. These factors included increased competition in U.S. metropolitan areas due to increased market density, lower levels of regulation and other entry barriers, greater product selection, and more timely fashion trend shifts compared to the Canadian market, which often exhibited lags in fashion developments of six months or more. Mr. Jax also had a local presence in Vancouver, which was believed to have helped their store by way of reputation, ancillary promotions, and easier access to skilled resources.

Many industry experts felt that Mr. Jax's product line success could be attributed directly to Eisman. He was known for his energy and brashness, as well as his creativity and knowledge of the women's fashion market. In his prior merchandising and marketing experience, he had developed an intuitive skill for the capricious women's apparel market. This industry was often considered to be one of instinct rather than rationality. Eisman was particularly good at design, merchandising and marketing (Exhibit 1). He worked very closely with these departments, often getting involved in the smallest details. As Eisman said, "It is the details that make the difference in our business." Although Eisman concentrated a great deal of his effort and time on these functions, he also attempted to provide guidance to production. The production function had been important in providing the service advantage, particularly in terms of delivery time, which Mr. Jax held over imports. By 1988, Mr. Jax's professional/career women's fashion lines accounted for $25 million in revenues and $3 million in net income (Exhibit 2).

Diversification through Acquisitions

In 1986, Segal and Eisman took Mr. Jax public, raising in excess of $17 million although they both retained one-third of equity ownership. The newly raised capital was used to diversify growth through the acquisition of four semi-related companies.

Surrey Classics Manufacturing Ltd.

Surrey Classics Manufacturing Ltd., a family-owned, Vancouver-based firm, was purchased for $2 million in 1986. This company was principally a manufacturer of lower priced women's apparel and coats. The acquisition was initially made with the objective of keeping the company an autonomous unit. However, the previous owner and his management team adapted poorly to their position within the Mr. Jax organization, and, upon expiration of their non-competition clauses, they resigned and started a competing company. Unfortunately, sales began to decline rapidly because of this new competition and the absence of managerial talent. To stem the losses, a variety of designers were hired under contract. However, Surrey's poor cash flow could not support the required promotional campaigns and the new fashion lines faired poorly, resulting in mounting operating losses.

In late 1988, Eisman reassigned Mr. Jax's Vice-President–Finance as interim manager of Surrey Classics. As Eisman stated, "The company needed a manager who knew the financial priorities in the industry and could maximize the effectiveness of the company's productive capacity." Several administrative functions were transferred to Mr. Jax, including design, pattern making, sizing and scaling operations. Marketing and production continued to be independent operations housed in a leased facility just outside of Vancouver. Surrey Classics now produced a diversified product line which included Highland Queen, a licensed older women's line of woolen apparel, and Jaki Petite, a Mr. Jax fashion line patterned for smaller women. During this turnaround, Eisman himself provided the required industry specific management skills, which demanded a considerable amount of his time and attention. Eisman kept in daily contact and was involved in most major decisions. During this time Surrey's revenues had declined from $12 million in 1986 to $10.8 million in 1988, and net income had dropped from $100 000 in 1986 to a loss of approximately $2 million in 1988. Eisman felt that in the next two years Surrey's operations would have to be further rationalized into Mr. Jax's to save on overhead costs.

West Coast Woolen Mills Ltd.

West Coast Woolen Mills Ltd. was a 40-year-old family-owned, Vancouver-based worsted woolen mill. Mr. Jax acquired the company for $2.2 million in 1987. Eisman was able to retain most of the previous management, all of whom had skills quite unique to the industry. West Coast marketed fabric to customers across Canada. In 1986, its sales were $5 million, profits were nil, and its estimated capacity was $10 million annually. The company was the smallest of three worsted woolen mills in Canada, and in the U.S. there were about 18 worsted woolen manufacturers, several being divisions of the world's largest textile manufacturing companies.

Both Mr. Jax and West Coast had mutually benefitted from this acquisition. The affiliation allowed Mr. Jax to obtain control of fabric production scheduling, design and quality. In particular, Mr. Jax had been able to significantly reduce order lead times for fabric produced at this subsidiary, although the effects of this on West Coast had not been studied. West Coast benefitted from increased capital funding which allowed it to invest in new equipment and technology, both important attributes in such a capital intensive industry. These investments supported the company's long-term strategic objective of becoming the highest quality, most design-conscious worsted woolen mill in North America. This objective had already been reached in Canada.

Mr. Jax was presently fulfilling 30% to 40% of its textile demands through West Coast. The remainder was being sourced in Europe. By 1988, West Coast's revenues were $6.5 million and profitability was at the break-even point.

Olympic Pant and Sportswear Co. Ltd. and Canadian Sportswear Co. Ltd.

Mr. Jax acquired Olympic Pant and Sportswear Co. Ltd. and Canadian Sportswear Co. Ltd., both privately owned companies, in 1987 for $18.3 million. The former management, excluding owners, was retained in both of these Winnipeg-based companies.

Olympic manufactured lower priced men's and boys' pants and outerwear as well as some women's sportswear. Canadian Sportswear manufactured low-priced women's and girls' outerwear and coats. Canadian Sportswear was also a certified apparel supplier to the Canadian Armed Forces, and, although these types of sales made up a minority of their revenue base, such a certification provided the company with a small but protected market niche. The disparity in target markets and locations between these companies, and Mr. Jax dictated that they operate largely independently. The expected synergies were limited to a few corporate administrative functions such as finance and systems management.

Combined revenues for these companies had declined from $35 million in 1986 to $30 million in 1988. Both of these companies had remained profitable during this period, although profits had declined. In 1988, combined net income was $1.2 million. Management blamed declining revenues on increased competition and a shortage of management because of the previous owners' retirement.

The Corporation's Present Situation

Diversification had provided the company with excellent growth, but it had also created problems. The most serious was the lack of management control over the now diversified structure (Exhibit 3). By 1988, it had become quite clear that without the entrepreneurial control and drive of the previous owners, the companies were not as successful as they had been prior to their acquisition. Therefore in late 1988, Eisman recruited a new CFO, Judith Madill, to coordinate a corporate control consolidation program. Madill had extensive accounting and corporate reorganization experience, but had limited operating experience in an entrepreneurial environment such as the fashion industry. Madill suggested that corporate personnel, financial, and systems management departments be established to integrate and aid in the management of the subsidiaries. Eisman was not completely convinced this was the right approach. He had always maintained that one of Mr. Jax's competitive strengths was its flexibility and rapid response time. He thought increased administrative overhead would restrict this entrepreneurial ability, and that extra costs would severely restrict future expansion opportunities. Thus, he had limited the administrative expansion to two industrial accountants for the next year.

Consolidation was also occurring in the existing organization. Eisman was trying to recruit a vice-president of production. Mr. Jax had never officially had such a position, and, unfortunately, recruiting a suitable candidate was proving to be difficult. There were relatively few experienced apparel manufacturing executives in North America. Furthermore, Vancouver was not an attractive place for fashion executives because it, not being a fashion centre, would isolate him or her from future employment opportunities. Higher salaries as well as lower taxes tended to keep qualified individuals in the U.S. Yet, a manager of production was badly needed to coordinate the internal production consolidation program.

Originally, production had been located in an old 22 000-square foot facility. By 1986, it had grown to 48 000 square feet located in four buildings throughout Vancouver. Production flow encompassed the typical apparel industry operational tasks (Exhibit 4). However, the division of tasks between buildings made production planning and scheduling very difficult. Production problems slowly accumulated between 1986 and 1988. The problems not only restricted capacity, but also caused customer service to deteriorate from an excellent shipment rate of approximately 95% of orders to recently being sometimes below the industry average of 75%. Mr. Jax's ability to ship had been a key to their growth strategy in Canada. Normally, apparel manufacturers met between 70% and 80% of their orders, but Mr. Jax had built a reputation for shipping more than 90% of orders.

Consolidation had begun in the latter part of 1987. An old building in downtown Vancouver was acquired and renovated. The facility incorporated some of the most modern production equipment available. In total, the company had spent approximately $3.5 million on upgrading production technology. Equipment in the new facility included a $220 000 Gerber automatic cloth cutting machine to improve efficiency and reduce waste; $300 000 of modern sewing equipment to improve productivity and production capacity; a $200 000 Gerber production moving system to automatically move work to appropriate work stations as required; and a computerized design assistance system to integrate the above equipment (i.e., tracking in-process inventory, scheduling, planning and arranging and sizing cloth patterns for cutting). The objectives of these investments were to lower labour content, improve production capacity, and reduce the time required to produce a garment.

In the last quarter of 1988, Mr. Jax had moved into this new head office facility. The building, which was renovated by one of Italy's leading architects, represented a design marvel with its skylights and soaring atriums. The production department had just recently settled into its expansive space. However, the move had not gone without incident. The equipment operators had difficulties adapting to the new machines. Most of the workers had become accustomed to the repetitive tasks required of the old technology. The new equipment was forcing them to retrain themselves and required additional effort; something that was not appreciated by many of the workers. In addition, the largely Asian work force had difficulty understanding retraining instructions because English was their second language.

To further facilitate the implementation of the consolidation program, an apparel production consultant had been hired. The consultant was using time-motion studies to reorganize and improve task efficiency and effectiveness. An example of a problem which had resulted from the move was the need for integration between overall production planning, task assignment, worker remuneration, and the new Gerber production moving system. If these elements were not integrated, the new system would in fact slow production. Unfortunately, this integration had not been considered until after the move, and the machine subsequently had to be removed until adjustments were made. The adjustments required converting workers from a salary base to a piece rate pay scale. The consultants were training all the workers to convert to piece rate work, and to operate the necessary equipment in the most efficient manner. Three workers were being trained per week. The conversion was expected to take two years.

Despite these ongoing problems, production appeared to be improving, and operational activities were now organized and coordinated with some degree of efficiency. Eisman was hopeful that production would gain the upper hand in the fight to remedy scheduling problems within the next six months.

Opportunities for Future Growth

Despite problems such as those detailed above, Mr. Jax's revenues and profits had grown by 1 500% and 500% respectively over the past eight years.

Furthermore, Eisman was extremely positive about further growth opportunities in the U.S. market. During the past two years, Eisman had tested the Dallas and New York markets. Local sales agents had carried the Mr. Jax fashion line, and 1988 revenues had grown to U.S. $1 million, the majority of which had come from Dallas. Follow-up research revealed that retail purchasers liked the "classical European styling combined with the North American flair."

This initial success had been inspiring, but it had also exposed Eisman to the difficulties of entering the highly competitive U.S. market. In particular, attaining good sales representation and excellent service, both of which were demanded by U.S. retailers, would be difficult. Securing first-class sales representation required having either a strong market presence or a promising promotional program. In addition, Mr. Jax had found U.S. retailers to be extremely onerous in their service demands. These demands were generally a result of the more competitive retail environment. Demands were particularly stringent for smaller apparel suppliers because of their nominal selling power. These demands ranged from very low wholesale prices to extremely fast order-filling and re-stocking requirements. Eisman recognized that Mr. Jax would have to establish a focused, coordinated and aggressive marketing campaign to achieve its desired objectives in this market.

Eisman had studied two alternate approaches to entering the U.S. market. One approach involved establishing a retailing chain, while the other involved starting a U.S.-based wholesale distribution subsidiary responsible for managing the aggressive promotional and sales campaign required.

Establishing a retail chain would require both new capital and skills. Capital costs, including leasehold improvements and inventory, would be initially very high, and an administrative infrastructure as well as a distribution and product inventorying system would have to be developed. Yet, starting a retail chain did have benefits. The retail approach would provide controllability, visibility and rapid market penetration. It was the approach taken by many of the aggressive apparel companies in the women's professional/career market segment, such as Liz Claiborne, Benetton, and Esprit. Furthermore, Mr. Jax's marketing strength fit well with this approach. It was estimated that the initial capital required would be about $10 million to open the first 30 stores, and then cost $300 000 per outlet thereafter. Sales revenues would grow to between $300 000 and $750 000 per outlet, depending upon the location, after two to five years. Operating margins on apparel stores averaged slightly less than 10%. Experts felt that within five years the company could possibly open 45 outlets; five the first year, and ten each year thereafter. In summary, this option would entail the greatest financial risk, but it would also have the greatest potential return.

The alternative approach was to establish a U.S. distribution subsidiary. This alternative would require capital and more of the same skills the company had developed in Canada. In general, the company would have to set up one or more showrooms throughout the U.S. The location of the showrooms would be critical to the approach eventually implemented. Exhibit 5 illustrates regional apparel buying patterns in North America.

A wholesale distribution approach could be carried out in one of two ways: either on a regional or national basis. A regional approach would involve focusing on the smaller regional retail stores. These stores tended to attract less competitive attention because of the higher sales expense-to-revenue ratio inherent in servicing these accounts. The approach required the new distributor to provide good-quality fashion lines, and service the accounts in a better manner than established suppliers. An advantage to this approach was that regional retailers demanded fewer and smaller price concessions compared to the larger national chains. The obstacles to this approach included the large sales force required and the superior service capability. Even though Mr. Jax had utilized this strategy successfully in Canada, success was not assured in the U.S. because of the very competitive environment. These factors made this approach both difficult to implement and slow relative to other approaches. Experts estimated fixed costs to average $1 million annually per region, of which 75% would be advertising and 25% other promotional costs. Additional operating costs would consist of sales commissions (7% of sales) and administrative overhead costs (see below). Revenues would be dependent upon many factors, but an initial annual growth rate of $1 million annually within each region was considered attainable over the next five years. In summary, this approach would minimize Mr. Jax's risk exposure, but it would also minimize the short term opportunities.

The national approach was also a viable option. The greatest challenge in a national strategy would be the difficulty in penetrating well established buyer/seller relationships. Floor space was expensive, and national chains and department stores tended to buy conservatively, sticking with the more reputable suppliers who they knew could produce a saleable product and service large orders. They also tended to demand low prices and rapid reorder terms. In summary, the national approach provided significant entry barriers, but it also provided the greatest potential for market share growth. Clearly, if economies of scale and competitive advantage in the larger North American context was the desired goal, this had to be the eventual strategy.

The principal costs of this approach would be the advertising and promotional expenses. National apparel companies had advertising expenditures of many millions of dollars. In discussions with Eisman, industry advertising executives had recommended an advertising expenditure of between $3 and $5 million annually in the first three years and then, if successful, increasing it by $1 million annually in the next two successive years. Additional operating costs would be required for sales commissions (7% of sales) and administrative overhead (see below). The results of this approach were very uncertain and two outcomes were possible. If the approach was successful, Eisman expected that one or two accounts grossing $1 to $2 million annually could be captured in the first two years. Eisman then felt the sales would expand to about $5 million in the third year, and increase by $5 million annually for the next two successive years. However, if the expected quality, design or service requirements were not sustained, sales would probably decline in the third year to that of the first year and then virtually disappear thereafter.

Both the national and regional approaches would require an infrastructure. Depending upon the approach taken, the head office could be located in a number of places. If a national approach was taken, Mr. Jax would have to locate in one of the major U.S. apparel centres (e.g., New York or California). Eisman estimated that the national approach would require a full-time Director of U.S. Operations immediately, while the regional approach could delay this hiring until required. Such a managing director would require extensive previous experience in the industry, and be both capable and compatible with Mr. Jax's marketing, operating and strategic approach. To ensure top-quality candidates, Eisman felt that a signing bonus of at least $100 000 would have to be offered. The remuneration would be tied to sales growth and volume, but a continued minimum salary guarantee might be necessary until the sales reached some minimum volume. In addition, a full-time sales manager would be required. Eisman estimated that the subsidiary's administrative overhead expense would be $500 000 if a regional approach was taken, versus $1 million for a national approach in both cases. These overhead costs would then escalate by approximately $0.5 million annually for the first five years.

Eisman had now studied the U.S. growth options for over six months. He felt a decision had to be made very soon, otherwise the company would forgo the window of opportunity which existed. The new FTA environment and the growth in the professional/career women's market segment were strong incentives, and delaying a decision would only increase the costs as well as the possibility of failure. Eisman realized the decision was critical to the company's evolution toward its ultimate goal of becoming a major international fashion company. The challenge was deciding which approach to take, as well as the sequencing and timing of the subsequent actions.

EXHIBIT 1   Mr. Jax Fashion's President Helping in a Promotional Photo Session

EXHIBIT 2 Mr. Jax Fashion Inc. Financial Statements

Income Statement (000s)

	1981	1982	1983	1984	1985	1986	1987 9 months	1988
Sales	4 592	4 315	5 472	7 666	13 018	24 705	53 391	72 027
Cost of sales	2 875	2 803	3 404	4 797	7 885	14 667	38 165	49 558
Gross profit	1 717	1 512	2 068	2 869	5 133	10 038	15 226	22 469
Selling & gen. admin.	1 172	1 117	1 458	1 898	2 434	4 530	9 071	18 175
Income from operations	545	395	610	971	2 699	5 508	6 155	4 294
Other income	22	25	25	10	16	564	418	117
Loss from discontinued operation								(554)
Income before taxes	567	420	635	981	2 715	6 072	6 573	3 857
Income taxes–								
Current	150	194	285	432	1 251	2 874	2 746	1 825
Deferred	47	2	(5)	28	24	57	245	(195)
Net income	370	224	355	521	1 440	3 141	3 582	2 227
Share price range						$7.5–$11	$8–$18	$7.5–$14

Note: In 1987, the accounting year end was changed from February 1988 to November 1987. This made the 1987 accounting year nine months in duration.

Balance Sheet (000s)

	1981	1982	1983	1984	1985	1986	1987	1988
Assets								
Current Assets								
Short-term investments	–	–	–	–	–	5 027	1 794	495
Accounts receivable	709	874	961	1 697	2 974	6 430	16 133	14 923
Inventories	464	474	684	736	1 431	3 026	15 431	16 914
Prepaid expenses	11	15	20	22	201	398	404	293
Income taxes recoverable	–	–	–	–	–	–	–	1 074
Prop., Plant & Equip.	318	349	424	572	795	4 042	7 789	13 645
Other Assets	–	–	–	–	–	273	526	513
Total Assets	1 502	1 712	2 089	3 027	5 401	22 196	42 077	47 857
Liabilities								
Current Liabilities								
Bank indebtness	129	356	114	351	579	575	1788	4 729
Accounts payable	490	435	678	963	1 494	3 100	4 893	6 934
Income taxes payable	126	58	86	153	809	1 047	546	
Deferred Taxes	84	86	81	109	133	217	462	267
Shareholder Equity								
Share equity	127	7	13	5	4	12 252	26 577	26 577
Retained earnings	546	770	1 125	1 446	2 347	5 005	7 811	9 350
Total Liabilities	1 502	1 712	2 097	3 027	5 401	22 196	42 077	47 857

Note: Years 1981–84 were estimated from change in financial position statements.

EXHIBIT 3 Mr. Jax Fashion's Organization Chart

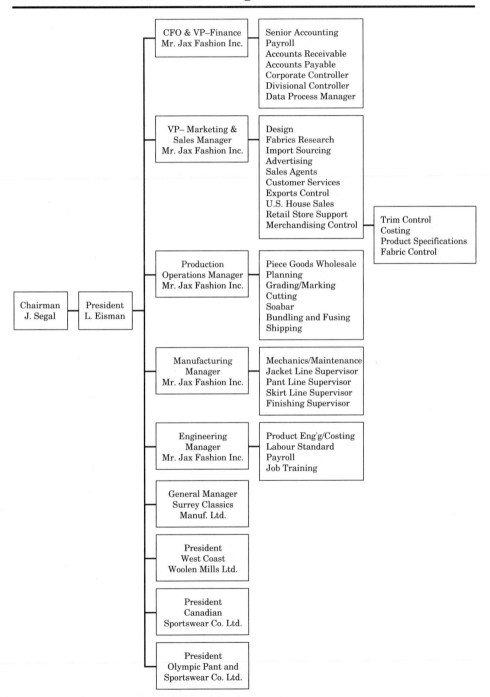

EXHIBIT 4 Mr. Jax Fashion's Production Flow Chart

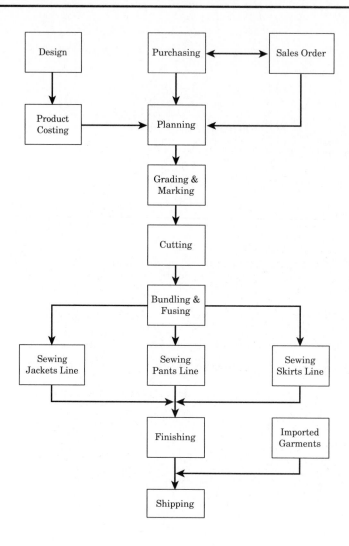

EXHIBIT 5   North American Apparel Consumption by Region

SOURCE: U.S. and Canadian governments.

IMASCO LIMITED: THE ROY ROGERS ACQUISITION

Joseph N. Fry and Kent E. Neupert

In January 1990, Purdy Crawford, the chairman, president and CEO of Imasco Limited, was reviewing an acquisition proposal from one of Imasco's operating companies, Hardee's Food Systems, Inc. (Hardee's) to purchase the Roy Rogers restaurant chain. Bill Prather, Hardee's CEO, was coming to Montreal the following day to present the proposal to the Imasco board. Prather thought the acquisition would permit Hardee's to expand rapidly into markets where they had very little presence. While Crawford was inclined to support Prather's proposal, he wanted to carefully weigh its broader impact for Imasco as a whole. The probable price of more than $390 million represented a substantial commitment of funds, at a time when growth in the U.S. fast food business was slowing.

IMASCO BACKGROUND

Imasco was a diversified Canadian public corporation with consolidated revenues of $5.7 billion in 1989 and net profits of $366 million. Imasco's founding and largest shareholder was B.A.T Industries (B.A.T), which had maintained a relatively constant 40% equity ownership over the years. B.A.T was a very large diversified British company with roots, like Imasco, in the tobacco business. The balance of Imasco shares were widely held.

In 1990, Imasco's operations were focused on four major operating companies, "the four legs of the table," as Crawford referred to them. The companies were: Imperial Tobacco, Canada's largest manufacturer and distributor of cigarettes; CT Financial, the holding company for Canada Trust, a major Canadian retail financial services business; Imasco Drug Retailing Group, made up of Shoppers Drug Mart in Canada and Peoples Drug Stores in the U.S.; and Hardee's Food Systems, Inc. in the U.S. A fifth, smaller company was The UCS Group, Canada's leading small space specialty retailer. Highlights of Imasco's operations for the years 1985–89 are shown in Table 1.

TABLE 1 **Imasco Operating Highlights** ($ million unless otherwise noted)

	1989	1988	1987	1986	1985
System-wide Sales	14 715.6	13 836.5	12 951.5	11 132.2	8 371.8
Revenues	5 724.7	6 000.6	5 924.4	5 596.6	5 110.2
Operating Earnings	692.0	636.7	578.4	455.6	464.1
Total Assets	5 378.0	5 310.2	5 656.6	5 505.5	2 905.7
Earnings before					
Extraordinary Items	366.1	314.3	282.7	226.4	261.6
EPS before					
Extraordinary Items	2.87	2.51	2.24	1.92	2.40
DVDS/Share	1.12	1.04	0.96	0.84	0.72

IMASCO DIVERSIFICATION ACTIVITIES

Imasco Limited was created in 1969 as a corporate entity to encompass and oversee the tobacco, food and distribution businesses of Imperial Tobacco Limited, and to manage a program of further diversification. The aim was to build a broadly based corporation that would rely less on the tobacco business and be better received in the stock market.

Paul Paré was the first president, chairman and CEO of Imasco, and the person with prime responsibility for its diversification program up to his retirement from the chairmanship in 1987. Paré's 38-year career began in the legal department of Imperial Tobacco and led to senior positions in the marketing areas. He became President and CEO in 1969 and Chairman in 1979. Except for a two-year stint with the Department of National Defence, his career was always in the tobacco industry. Paré's approach to diversification in the early years had been a conservative one. He preferred to make a number of relatively small investments, and build or divest the positions as experience dictated.

Crawford, Paré's successor, pictured the first ten years of diversification as a process of experimentation and learning. He described the evolution of thought and action: "Imperial's first attempt at diversification had been through vertical integration." Crawford explained: "Although it appeared logical that if Imperial bought a tinfoil company and made foil wrap themselves there were economies to be realized, we quickly learned that making cigarettes and making tinfoil are two different things." Imperial knew little about the highly specialized tinfoil business, and also discovered that "the competition didn't like the idea of buying tinfoil from us."

Upon reflection, management determined that they were "in the business of converting and marketing agricultural products." Crawford recounted: "It made sense then that the next acquisition was a winery. Unfortunately, we failed to take into consideration provincial liquor regulations which made it impossible to operate at a sufficient scale to be profitable."

Management then broadened its perspective and decided that they were best at marketing. This led to acquisitions that "embodied exciting new marketing concepts," such as two sporting goods companies, Collegiate and Arlington, and a discount bottler and retailer of soft drinks called PoP Shoppes. These investments were held for several years, but they failed to live up to their promise and were subsequently sold off. Other acquisitions, in food processing and distribution, for example, were quite successful, but not on a scale of importance to Imasco. These were later divested when Imasco refocussed its efforts.

For the most part, these early diversification moves involved the acquisition of several small companies, and subsequent restructuring of them into a larger enterprise. Most of these acquisitions were then later divested. For example, Imasco's three food companies, which were sold in the late 1970s and early 1980s, were originally ten different companies. Amco Vending, sold in 1977, was built up from eight separate vending companies across Canada. Other businesses which were grown and later sold included wines, drycleaning, and video tape services.

With time, Paré's team built an understanding of its capabilities, sharpened its sense of mission, and focused its acquisition criteria. The mission was to "create shareholder value as a leading North American consumer products and services company." Based on their learning, the criteria for acquisitions were formalized. Imasco would acquire companies that (1) were well positioned in the consumer goods and services sector of the economy; (2) had a capable management team in place, or were able to be smoothly integrated into an existing operating division; (3) had above average growth potential, and were capable of making a meaningful and immediate contribution to profits; and (4) were North American based, preferably in Canada. Crawford noted that "perhaps the most important end result of approximately ten years of experimentation was that we developed a clear vision of what the company was and was not."

As Imasco became more focused and confident of its skills, the acquisitions became less frequent and larger in size, and the diversification from tobacco more significant. Imasco's acquisitions and net investments are given in Exhibit 1. The most significant events of the 1980s are described below in the review of the present-day Imasco operating companies. The net result of 20 years of diversification was that Imasco increased its revenues tenfold and its earnings twentyfold. Moreover, its reliance on tobacco for corporate earnings went from 100% in 1970 to 48% in 1989. A twenty year review of Imasco performance is given in Exhibit 2.

Corporate Management

While Imasco's diversification policy was directed from the central office, its operations were not centralized. The corporate management structure was decentralized and rather flat. Only 50 people staffed the head office in Montreal.

The various companies, with operations across Canada and most of the U.S., were encouraged to aggressively pursue the development of their businesses and related trademarks. Management believed that "combining the experience and expertise that flow from the individual operating companies creates a unique opportunity to add value to all of its (Imasco's) operations and assets." Accordingly, Imasco saw its greatest strengths as the high degree of autonomy, and clear lines of authority and responsibility, which existed between Imasco's head office (the Imasco Centre) and the operating companies. While each company's CEO operated with the widest possible autonomy, they also contributed to the development of the annual and five-year plans, and "to furthering Imasco's overall growth objectives." The role of the Imasco Centre was to guide Imasco's overall growth without interfering with the operating companies. The 1988 business plan stipulated that "the role of the Imasco Centre is to be a source of excellence in management dedicated to achieving overall corporate objectives, and supporting Imasco's operating companies in the fulfilment of their respective missions and objectives."

It was very important to Imasco that any acquisition be friendly. While it was not formally stipulated in the acquisition criteria, it was evident in Imasco's actions, such as the aborted acquisition of Canadian Tire in 1983.

In June of that year, Imasco initiated an acquisition attempt of Canadian Tire, but later withdrew the offer. Imasco had outlined a proposal to the members of the Billes family, majority shareholders in Canadian Tire, and the management of Canadian Tire in which Imasco would purchase as many of Canadian Tire's outstanding common and Class "A" shares as would be tendered. Imasco stipulated the offer was conditional on family and management support. Imasco expected the cost of the acquisition to be about $1.13 billion.

Several days later, Paré issued a press release in which he stated:

> We at Imasco are obviously disappointed with the reaction of the senior management group at Canadian Tire to purchase all of the outstanding shares of the company. We stated at the outset that we were seeking both the support of the major voting shareholders and the endorsement of management. It now appears that such support and endorsement are not forthcoming. In light of this and in view of the announcement made ... by the trustees of the John W. Billes estate, we have concluded that one or more of the conditions to our offer will not be satisfied. Therefore, we do not propose to proceed with our previously announced offer.

In explaining Imasco's rationale for withdrawing the offer, Paré continued:

> Throughout the negotiations, we have been keenly aware of the essential ingredients that have made Canadian Tire one of the retail success stories in Canada. These ingredients include the able leadership of the management group, the unique relationship between management and the associate-dealers, and the employee profit-sharing and share-ownership plans. As we have mentioned on

several occasions, it was our intention to preserve these relationships and the formulas that have so obviously contributed to the success of the Canadian Tire organization.

OPERATING COMPANIES

Imperial Tobacco

Imperial Tobacco was the largest tobacco enterprise in Canada, with operations ranging from leaf tobacco buying and processing, to the manufacture and distribution of a broad range of tobacco products. The manufacture and sale of cigarettes constituted the largest segment of its business, representing 89.4% of Imperial Tobacco's revenues in 1989. Highlights of Imperial Tobacco's operations for the years 1985–89 are shown in Table 2.

TABLE 2 Imperial Tobacco Operating Summary ($ million unless otherwise noted)

	1989	1988	1987	1986	1985
Revenues	2 385.6	2 018.1	1 926.0	1 754.6	1 701.8
Revenues, Net of Sales and Excise Taxes	896.2	862.0	816.2	712.0	757.5
Operating Earnings	334.0	308.0	279.1	208.1	243.7
Operating Margins (%)	37.3	35.7	34.2	29.2	32.2
Market Share–Domestic	57.9	56.2	54.4	51.5	52.6
Capital Employed*	558.1	496.4	513.9	594.6†	587.0†

* Capital employed of each consolidated segment consists of directly identifiable assets at net book value, less current liabilities, excluding income taxes payable and bank and other debt. Corporate assets and corporate current liabilities are also excluded.
† Reflects fiscal year ending March 31.

Over the years, Imperial had concentrated on building its market share in Canada from a low of 36% in 1970 to 57.9% in 1989. Revenues in 1989 reached an all time high of almost $2.4 billion, in spite of a 4% decline in unit sales to 27.5 billion cigarettes. The market share gains had been achieved by focusing on the strength of Imperial Tobacco's trademarks, particularly the continued growth of its two leading Canadian brands, Player's and du Maurier. Together these two brands held 47.4% of the market in 1989.

Imperial Tobacco had production and packaging facilities in Montreal and Joliette, Quebec, and Guelph, Ontario, and leaf processing facilities in Joliette and LaSalle, Quebec, and Aylmer, Ontario. Imperial continually modernized its production facilities to the point that management claimed them to be "the most technologically advanced in the tobacco industry in Canada." The distribution and promotion of Imperial Tobacco's products to wholesalers and retailers was carried out through a nationwide sales staff operating out of the sales offices and distribution centres in St. Johns, Moncton, Montreal, Toronto, Winnipeg, Calgary and Vancouver.

Imasco Enterprises (Including Canada Trust)

Imasco Enterprises Inc. (IEI) was wholly owned through Imasco Limited and three of its other companies, making it an indirect wholly owned subsidiary. In 1986, Imasco announced its intention to acquire all of the outstanding common shares of Genstar Corporation (Genstar) through IEI. At the time, Imasco's primary objective was to gain entry into the financial services sector by assuming Genstar's 98% ownership position in Canada Trust. Genstar had purchased Canada Trust in 1985 for $1.2 billion dollars and merged it with Canada Permanent Mortgage Corporation, which Genstar had purchased in 1981. This merger created Canada's seventh largest financial institution with $50 billion in assets under administration.

Once acquired, Imasco intended to sell off all of Genstar's non-financial assets. Within the year, all of the shares were acquired at a cost of approximately $2.6 billion. This was the first acquisition orchestrated by Crawford.

In addition to Canada Trust, Genstar had holdings in an assortment of other businesses. Most of these, such as the cement and related operations, Genstar Container Corporation, and Seaspan International, were sold off. The cost of those assets retained, including Canada Trust, was about $2.4 billion, of which all but $150 million was attributed to the Canada Trust holding. The balance of the amount was accounted for by a variety of assets which included Genstar Development Company, Genstar Mortgage Corporation, a one-third limited partnership in Sutter Hill Ventures, a portfolio of other venture capital investments, and certain other assets and liabilities. Genstar Development Company was involved in land development in primary Canadian metropolitan areas, such as Vancouver, Calgary, Edmonton, Winnipeg, Toronto and Ottawa. U.S.-based Sutter Hill Ventures had capital investments in over 43 different companies. Most of these investments were in the areas of medical research, biotechnology, communications and computer hardware and software. Highlights of investments in IEI are shown in Table 3.

TABLE 3 Investments in Imasco Enterprises, Inc. ($ million)

	1989	*1988*	*1987**
Equity in Net Earnings of Imasco Enterprises	152.5	142.1	126.5
Investment in Imasco Enterprises	2 700.2	2 655.4	2 613.5

* Financial information is shown beginning with 1987 to reflect the acquisition of Canada Trust in 1986.

CT Financial was the holding company for the Canada Trust group of companies. In 1989, Canada Trust was Canada's second largest trust and loan company, and a major residential real estate broker. The principal businesses of Canada Trust were financial intermediary services, such as deposit services, credit card services, mortgage lending, consumer lending, corporate and commercial lending, and investments. It also offered trust services, real estate services and real estate development. Canada Trust operated 331 financial services branches, 22 personal and pension trust services offices, and 275 company operated and franchised real estate offices. Total assets under the administration of Canada Trust at the end of 1989 were $74.1 billion, comprised of $32.7 billion in corporate assets, and $41.4 billion in assets administered for estate, trust and agency accounts. Total personal deposits were estimated to be the fourth largest among Canadian financial institutions. The return of common shareholders' average equity was 17.3% compared with an average of 7.7% for Canada's six largest banks. Highlights of CT Financial operations are shown in Table 4.

TABLE 4 Operating Performance Data for CT Financial ($ million unless otherwise noted)

	1989	*1988*	*1987**
Assets under Administration	74 096.0	67 401.0	60 626.0
Corporate Assets	32 666.0	29 219.2	25 514.8
Deposits	30 403.0	27 319.5	23 859.0
Loans	24 201.1	22 661.7	19 679.3
Net Earnings Attributed to Common Shares	240.2	232.0	201.0
Return on Common Shareholders Average Equity (%)	17.3	19.0	19.4

* Financial information is shown beginning with 1987 to reflect the acquisition of Canada Trust in 1986.

Imasco Drug Retailing

Shoppers Drug Mart

Shoppers Drug Mart provided a wide range of marketing and management services to a group of 633 associated retail drug stores located throughout Canada, operating under the trademarks Shoppers Drug Mart (585 stores), and Pharmaprix in Quebec (48 stores). The Shoppers Drug Mart stores also included the extended concepts of Shoppers Drug Mart Food Baskets and Shoppers Drug Mart Home Health Care Centres.

In 1989, Shoppers Drug Mart was the largest drug store group in Canada with about 33% of the retail drug store market. In system wide sales, it ranked first and fifth among all drug store groups in Canada and North America, respectively. In the past, competition had come primarily from regional chains and independent drug stores, but food stores with drug departments represented a growing challenge. During 1989, management had emphasized strengthening the productivity and profitability of existing stores, particularly the former Super X Drugs and Howie's stores, recently converted to Shoppers Drug Mart stores.

The Shoppers Drug Mart operating division utilized licensing and franchise agreements. Under the licensing arrangement, each Shoppers Drug Mart was owned and operated by a licensed pharmacist, called an Associate. In Quebec, Pharmaprix stores used a franchise system. In return for an annual fee, each Associate of a Shoppers Drug Mart store and Franchisee of a Pharmaprix store had access to a variety of services, such as store design, merchandising techniques, financial analysis, training, advertising and marketing. Highlights of Shoppers Drug Mart operations are shown in Table 5.

TABLE 5 **Shoppers Drug Mart Operating Summary** ($ million unless otherwise noted)

	1989	*1988*	*1987*	*1986*	*1985*
System-wide Sales	2 597.7	2 355.6	2 073.4	1 775.0	1 522.3
Revenues	136.2	114.9	95.7	86.6	73.4
Operating Earnings	70.6	57.1	51.3	48.9	42.5
Operating Margins (%)	51.8	49.7	53.6	56.5	57.9
Average Sales per Store	4.1	4.2	4.1	3.9	3.6
Number of Stores	633	613	586	543	431
Capital Expenditures	24.0	28.0	27.6	23.3	16.4
Capital Employed*	204.1	209.8	194.2	117.9†	106.8†
Depreciation	26.6	20.6	17.9	13.0	11.8

* Capital employed of each consolidated segment consists of directly identifiable assets at net book value, less current liabilities, excluding income taxes payable and bank and other debt. Corporate assets and corporate current liabilities are also excluded.

† Reflects fiscal year ending March 31.

Peoples Drug Stores

Peoples Drug Stores, Incorporated (Peoples) operated 490 company owned drug stores in the U.S.during 1989. The stores were primarily operated from leased premises under the trade names Peoples Drug Stores, Health Mart, and Rea and Derick. Imasco had built the Peoples operating division from several acquired drug store chains in six eastern U.S. states and the District of Columbia.

After a disappointing performance in 1986, Peoples began a comprehensive plan to revitalise the chain and focus on areas of market strength. Earnings steadily improved, with operating earnings of $8.0 million in 1989, compared with operating losses of $8.3 million in 1988 and $22.5 million in 1987. The turnaround involved restructuring, including the divestment of Peoples' Reed, Lane, Midwest, Bud's Deep Discount, and other smaller divisions. During 1989, a total of 326 drug stores were sold, 21 were closed, and 13 opened for a net decrease of 334 stores. At the beginning of 1990, only five Bud's stores remained to be sold. The result was a concentration on People's strongest markets, primarily, the District of Columbia, Maryland, Virginia, West Virginia and Pennsylvania. The highlights of Peoples operations are shown in Table 6.

TABLE 6 Peoples Drug Stores Operating Summary ($ million unless otherwise noted)

	1989	1988	1987	1986	1985
Revenues	1 207.2	1 841.6	1 850.2	1 922.5	1 737.3
Operating Earnings	8.0	(8.3)	(22.5)	0.1	52.5
Operating Margins (%)	0.7	(0.5)	(1.2)	—	3.0
Average Sales per Store (US $)	2.1	1.8	1.7	1.7	1.5
Number of Stores	490	829	819	830	824
Capital Expenditures	12.4	41.9	29.1	32.7	58.5
Capital Employed*	369.4	523.5	703.6	819.5†	653.5†

* Capital employed of each consolidated segment consists of directly identifiable assets at net book value, less current liabilities, excluding income taxes payable and bank and other debt. Corporate assets and corporate current liabilities are also excluded.
† Reflects fiscal year ending March 31.

The UCS Group

In 1989, The UCS Group operated 531 stores in Canada from leased premises. The stores carried a wide variety of everyday convenience items, including newspapers and magazines, cigarettes and smokers accessories, confectionary, snack foods, gifts and souvenir selections. The retail outlets were all company-operated, and included UCS newsstands in shopping centres, commercial office towers, airports, hotels, and other high consumer traffic locations. The UCS group operated 531 stores in five divisions: Woolco/Woolworth, Specialty Stores, Hotel/Airport, Den for Men/AuMasculin, and Tax and Duty Free. Highlights of The UCS Group operations are shown in Table 7.

TABLE 7 The UCS Group Operating Summary ($ million unless otherwise noted)

	1989	1988	1987	1986	1985
Revenues	286.1	256.6	235.3	206.0	187.8
Operating Earnings	8.3	7.5	6.7	6.6	5.5
Operating Margins (%)	2.9	2.9	2.9	3.2	2.9
Average Sales per Stores ($000)	543	489	461	432	410
Average Sales per Sq.Ft. ($)	790	718	675	651	629
Number of Stores	531	525	524	494	460
Capital Employed (Est.)*	41.4	45.6	40.7	37.6†	57.2†

* Capital employed of each consolidated segment consists of directly identifiable assets at net book value, less current liabilities, excluding income taxes payable and bank and other debt. Corporate assets and corporate current liabilities are also excluded.
† Reflects fiscal year ending March 31.

Hardee's Food Systems

Imasco's move to make a major investment in a U.S.-based company arose in part from the greater opportunity offered by the U.S. economy for potential acquisitions of an interesting nature and scale, and in part from the constraints on Canadian acquisitions posed by the Foreign Investment Review Act (FIRA). The purpose of FIRA was to review certain forms of foreign investment in Canada, particularly controlling acquisitions of Canadian business enterprises, and diversifications of existing foreign controlled firms into unrelated businesses. For several years, Imasco came under the control of FIRA due to B.A.T's 40% ownership of Imasco. In later years, however, Imasco was re-classified as a Canadian owned enterprise.

Imasco's involvement with Hardee's and the U.S. restaurant business developed slowly. Imasco first became acquainted with Hardee's in 1969 when its pension fund manager was on holiday in South Carolina. The manager and his family were so fond of the Hardee's hamburgers that upon returning to Montreal, he investigated Hardee's as a possible pension fund investment. The following year, Imasco made a relatively small investment in Hardee's.

Later, when Hardee's was looking for expansion capital, it approached Imasco. In March 1977, Imasco invested $18.2 million in convertible preferred shares which, if converted, would give Imasco a 25% position in Hardee's. Between March 1980 and January 1981, Imasco converted their preferred shares and purchased the outstanding common shares at a cost of $114.1 million. At this time, Hardee's was the seventh largest hamburger restaurant chain in the U.S. Later, Imasco made additional investments in Hardee's to facilitate growth and acquisition.

By 1989, Hardee's Food Systems, Inc. (Hardee's) was the third largest hamburger restaurant chain in the U.S., as measured by system wide sales and average unit sales volume. In number of outlets, it ranked fourth. With its head office in Rocky Mount, North Carolina, Hardee's restaurant operations consisted of 3 298 restaurants, of which 1 086 were company-operated and 2 212 were licensed. Of these restaurants, 3 257 were located in 39 states and the District of Columbia in the U.S., and 41 were located in nine other countries in the Middle East, Central America, and Southeast Asia. Average annual unit sales for 1989 were $1 060 300, compared with $1 058 000 in 1988. Highlights of Hardee's operations are shown in Table 8.

TABLE 8 Hardee's Operating Summary ($ million unless otherwise noted)

	1989	*1988*	*1987*	*1986*	*1985*
System-wide Sales	4 146.7	4 058.9*	4 059.1	3 721.6	3 248.4
Revenues	1 786.5	1 756.9	1 801.7	1 642.0	1 457.0
Operating Earnings	118.6	130.3	137.3	129.0	117.1
Operating Margins (%)	6.6	7.4	7.6	7.9	8.0
Average Sales per Restaurant (US $)	922	920	877	837	801
Capital Expenditures	155.3	209.9	217.0	135.6	99.9
Depreciation	78.9	78.0	75.5	63.0	53.4
Restaurants Company Owned	1 086	1 070	995	893	876
Restaurants Franchised	2 212	2 081	1 962	1 818	1 662
Total Restaurants	3 298	3 151	2 957	2 711	2 538
Capital Employed**	618.3	587.7*	777.5	668.1†	555.4†

*   Includes sale and leaseback of properties.
**   Capital employed of each consolidated segment consists of directly identifiable assets at net book value, less current liabilities, excluding income taxes payable and bank and other debt. Corporate assets and corporate current liabilities are also excluded.
†   Reflects fiscal year ending March 31.

Hardee's had encouraged multi-unit development by licensees. In some cases, Hardee's granted exclusive territorial development rights to licensees on the condition that minimum numbers of new licensed restaurants in the area be opened within specific periods of time. As of December 31, 1989, Hardee's had license agreements with 234 licensee groups operating 2 205 restaurants. The ten largest of these licensees operated 1 213 restaurants, representing 55% of the licensed restaurants in the chain, and the two largest operated 738 licensed restaurants, or approximately 33% of the licensed restaurants.

Hardee's restaurants were limited-menu, quick-service family restaurants, and featured moderately priced items for all meals. These products were principally hamburgers, roast beef, chicken, turkey club, ham and cheese and fish sandwiches, breakfast biscuits, frankfurters, french fries, salads, turnovers, cookies, ice cream, and assorted beverages for both take-out and on-premise consumption. Recent additions to the Hardee's menu included a grilled chicken sandwich, Crispy Curl fries, and pancakes. These new products followed a series of initiatives taken in 1988, which included being the first hamburger chain to switch to all vegetable cooking oil in order to lower fat and cholesterol levels in fried products. Hardee's also introduced more salads and more desserts to the menu.

Fast Food Merchandisers, Inc. (FFM) was an operating division of Hardee's that furnished restaurants with food and paper products through its food processing and distribution operations. All company-operated Hardee's restaurants purchased their food and paper products from FFM. Although licensees were not obligated to purchase from FFM, approximately 75% of Hardee's licensees purchased some or all of their requirements from FFM. FFM operated three food processing plants and eleven distribution centres. FFM also sold products to other food service and supermarket accounts.

THE PROPOSED ROY ROGERS ACQUISITION

The U.S. Food Service Industry[1]

Over the past twenty years, Americans spent a rising portion of their food dollars at restaurants. More two-income families, fewer women as full-time homemakers and a decline in the number of children to feed made dining out increasingly popular. In 1989, U.S. consumers spent $167 billion at 400 000 restaurants. This excluded an estimated $61 billion spent at other food and beverage outlets, such as employee cafeterias, hospitals, ice-cream stands and

---

[1] Industry figures in U.S. dollars.

taverns. Although sales growth for the restaurant industry outpaced the economy in recent years, industry analysts noted indications of outlet saturation. In 1989, franchise restaurant chains expected to have U.S sales of $70.4 billion, up 7.4% from the year before. However, on a per unit basis, 1989 sales for franchise chain units averaged $737 000, up only 4.3% from the previous year. Analysts pointed out that this rise corresponded to increases in menu prices.

Quick service or "fast food" restaurants had led industry growth for several decades, and were expected to do so over the near term. However, industry analysts cautioned that, as the average age of the American consumers increased, a shift away from fast food restaurants toward mid-scale restaurants might occur. Increased emphasis on take-out service and home delivery would help to maintain momentum, but analysts expected that fast food sales and new unit growth would not be up to the 6.6% compound annual rate from 1985 to 1989. McDonald's 8 000 U.S. outlets had sales of $12 billion, or about 7% of total U.S. restaurant spending. Chains that emphasized hamburgers, hot dogs, or roast beef were the largest part of the U.S. franchise restaurant industry, with 1989 sales of $33.8 billion from 36 206 outlets. McDonald's U.S. market share in the segment was about 36.1%, followed by Burger King (19.2%), Hardee's (9.9%), and Wendy's (8.5%).

Nature of Operations

The large hamburger chains generated revenues from three sources: (1) the operation of company owned restaurants; (2) franchising, which encompassed royalties and initial fees from licensees operating under the trade name; and (3) commissary, consisting of food processing and the distribution of food, restaurant supplies and equipment essential to the operation of the company and franchised outlets. Profitable operation of company-owned restaurant operations called for high unit sales volume and tight control of operating margins.

Franchising had been the major chains' initial growth strategy. This enabled them to increase revenues, establish a competitive position, and achieve the scale necessary for efficient commissary and marketing operations. In 1989, there were 90 000 franchise operations accounting for 40% of U.S.restaurant operations. In 1989, McDonald's operating profit from franchising ($1.2 billion) substantially exceeded its profit from company operated restaurants ($822 million).

It was often the case that in a franchising relationship, the cost of the land, building and equipment were the responsibility of the franchisee. The franchisee also paid a royalty, typically 3–6% of sales, and were charged 1–5% of sales for common advertising expenses. In return, the franchisee got brand name recognition, training and marketing support. However, some of the larger chains had taken an alternate approach by owning the land and the building. Not only did such an approach provide lease revenue but it also allowed the company to maintain some control over the franchisee's facilities.

Competition

Fast food restaurants competed with at-home eating, other restaurant types, and each other. To build and maintain unit volumes, top chains developed strategies to differentiate themselves by target market, style of operation, menu and promotional approach, among other methods.

McDonald's

McDonald's was the leader of the fast food restaurant business. The chain began in the early 1950s in California. The McDonald brothers discovered that a combination of assembly line procedures, product standardization and high volume made it possible to offer exceptional value, providing consistent quality food at a reasonable price. The potential of their concept was recognized by Ray Kroc, a paper cup and milkshake mixer salesman. He acquired the operations, and provided the leadership for the formation and subsequent growth of the McDonald's corporation.

McDonald's had traditionally targeted children, teens and young families, and focused its menu of products around hamburgers and french fries. Scale, experience and simplified operating procedures permitted McDonald's to operate at significantly lower costs than its competitors. In the late 1970s, the company broadened its target market to follow demographic shifts and increase unit volumes. The menu was expanded to include breakfast line and chicken items, and the hours of operation were increased. The emphasis on simplicity and efficiency was maintained, and the company continued its rigorous dedication to quality, service and cleanliness. This strategy was supported by the largest promotional budget in the industry. McDonald's typical arrangement with franchisees was that it owned the property, which the franchisee then leased. Highlights of McDonald's operations are shown in Table 9.

Burger King

Burger King had been a subsidiary of Pillsbury until December 1988, when Grand Metropolitan PLC acquired Pillsbury and its holdings, which included Burger King. Burger King's traditional market target market had been the 25–39 age group, but it was trying to improve its appeal to the family trade. The key element of Burger King's competitive strategy had been to offer more product choice than McDonald's. Burger King's food preparation system was centred

TABLE 9 McDonald's Operating Summary (US $ million unless otherwise noted)

	1989	1988	1987
Revenues	6 142.0	5 566.3	4 893.5
Depreciation	364.0	324.0	278.9
Operating Income	1 459.0	1 283.7	1 161.9
Operating Profit Margin (%)	23.7	23.1	23.7
Interest Expense	332.0	266.8	224.8
Pretax Income	1 157.0	1 046.5	958.8
Net Income	727.0	645.9	596.5
Net Income Margin (%)	11.8	11.6	12.2
Earnings Per Share	1.95	1.72	1.45
Dividend Per Share	.30	.27	.24
Market Price Year End	34.50	24.06	22.00
Price/Earnings Ratio	17.7	14.0	15.2
Shareholders Equity	3 549.0	3 412.8	2 916.7
Total Common Shares Outstanding (million)	362	375	378

SOURCE: *Worldscope 1990.*

around a hamburger that could be dressed to customer specifications, with onions, lettuce, tomato, etc. Burger King had been the first hamburger chain to diversify significantly into additional hot sandwich items, but this had resulted in somewhat longer service times and higher food preparation costs.

In 1989, Burger King's profits were $48.2 million, down 49% from the previous two years. Its market share was 19.2%, down from 19.9% in 1987. Average unit sales in 1989 were $1.05 million. Burger King had four different CEOs during the past ten years, and was having problems with its marketing program, changing advertising campaigns five times in two years. Additionally, Burger King had experienced problems with their franchisees prior to the acquisition by Grand Metropolitan, but these were beginning to subside with the ownership change.

Wendy's

Wendy's also targeted the young adult market. Like Burger King, it provided food prepared to specification, and had broadened its initial emphasis on hamburgers to cover a variety of items, including chili and a self-service buffet and salad bar. In 1989, Wendy's 3,490 restaurants' had average unit sales of $.79 million. This was an increase from $.76 million and $.74 million in 1988 and 1987, respectively. Highlights of Wendy's operations are shown in Table 10.

TABLE 10 Wendy's Operating Summary ($ US million unless other-
wise noted)

	1989	1988	1987
Revenues	1 069.7	1 045.9	1 051.1
Depreciation	56.4	57.3	55.4
Operating Income	51.3	44.0	0.1
Operating Profit Margin (%)	4.8	4.2	NIL
Interest Expense	22.3	16.9	24.2
Pretax Income	36.9	43.8	(12.8)
Net Income	30.4	28.5	4.5
Net Income Margin %	2.8	2.7	0.4
Earnings Per Share ($)	.25	.30	.04
Dividend Per Share ($)	.24	.24	.24
Market Price Year End ($)	4.63	5.75	5.63
Price/Earnings Ratio	18.5	19.2	140.6
Shareholder Equity	428.9	419.6	412.2
Total Common Shares Outstanding (million)	96	96	96

SOURCE: *Worldscope 1990.*

Hardee's

Hardee's was the third largest hamburger-based fast food chain in the U.S., in terms of total sales and unit sales volume; and fourth in outlets. Approximately 30% of Hardee's sales were at breakfast, and it was a leader in the breakfast trade. The other major sales category was hamburgers, with 34% of sales.

The demographic profile of Hardee's customers was skewed slightly to males. Children and 25- to 34-year-olds were two groups that had been targeted for higher penetration. The introduction of ice cream in 1987 had spurred a 98% increase in visits by children under 13. Packaged salads and the broadening of menu selections were expected to help attract 25– to 34-year-olds.

Hardee's management was highly regarded in the food service industry for taking a very shaky firm in 1972–73 and turning it into a good performer. In 1979, Hardee's was cited by Restaurant Business magazine as a prime example of a corporate turnaround. In 1981, Jack Laughery, Hardee's CEO through the turnaround period, was awarded the Food Manufacturer's Association gold plate award for exemplary involvement in the food service industry. In 1990, Laughery was Hardee's Chairman, and Bill Prather was the President and CEO.

Hardee's Acquisition of Burger Chef

In 1981, Hardee's was relatively small in the industry, and decided it had to expand quickly just to keep pace with its larger competitors. Competition had intensified, and the ability to support heavy fixed promotional costs became increasingly critical. Hardee's viewed an acquisition as a way to build a stronger market share base to support an increased television campaign.

Burger Chef, acquired by General Foods in 1968, had 1981 sales of $391 million. General Foods had nurtured it into a profitable regional chain. However, due to management changes at General Foods and the acquisition of the Oscar Meyer company, Burger Chef was no longer important to General Food future plans.

Imasco and Hardee's saw this as an opportunity. The Burger Chef chain was made up of about 250 company units and 450 franchised units, located primarily in the states of Michigan, Ohio, Indiana, Iowa and Kentucky. Most of the locations complemented Hardee's markets. Imasco purchased Burger Chef in 1981 for $51.8 million. During the next three years, they converted the sites to Hardee's at a cost of about $80 000 per unit. The acquisition of Burger Chef created two more market areas for Hardee's overnight. By 1986, the stores in these areas were, and still are, the most profitable in the entire Hardee's system. Similarly, in 1972, Hardee's had expanded their market base by acquiring Sandy's Systems, a fast food chain of about 200 restaurants for $5.7 million.

The Roy Rogers Opportunity

The Roy Rogers restaurant chain was owned by the Marriott Corporation (Marriott), and was located in the northeastern U.S. In Baltimore, Washington, DC., Philadelphia and New York, it was second only to McDonald's in number of locations. Roy Rogers restaurants were well known for fresh fried chicken and roast beef sandwiches. In 1989, Roy Rogers system-wide sales[2] were $713 million, up from the previous year's $661 million. In 1988, revenues were $431 million, up from $399 million in 1987. Operating earnings in 1988 were $43.7 million, up from $38 million the year before. The chain had 660 units, up from 610 the previous year, with average annual unit sales of $1 081 000.

Marriott was a leader in the hotel lodging industry and had extensive restaurant holdings. In 1988, Marriott began to refocus on lodging. As a result, it had reevaluated its other holdings, among these the Roy Rogers chain. In 1988, Marriott had talked to Hardee's about the possible sale of Roy Rogers. However, Marriott was not yet committed to selling the chain and the two companies were unable to agree on a sale price. In late 1989, Marriott announced it was again interested in selling Roy Rogers.

Prather contacted Marriott about the details. Marriott was offering to sell 648 of its Roy Rogers units, of which 363 were company owned and 285 were franchised. These units were in attractive market locations that would not otherwise be available. However, Marriott wanted to retain several sites located on

---

[2] System-wide sales reflect retail sales figures of both company-owned and franchisee stores. Revenues reflect retail sales of only company-owned stores, in addition to royalties received from franchisees.

various turnpikes and interstate highways. Additionally, Marriott had a 14-point contract to which any purchaser had to agree. The contract addressed such things as Marriott's concern for Roy Rogers franchisees and indemnification against future litigation.

Prather saw this as the opportunity he had been waiting for and began putting together an acquisition proposal. Before he could make a serious offer to Marriott, he had to first get the approval of Crawford and the Imasco board. While preparing the proposal, Prather had reflected on what it was like to work in the Imasco organization. He had built his career in the food service industry, coming up through the ranks, starting as an assistant store manager. Until 1986, he had been the Number Three man at Burger King, Vice President in charge of World Operations. Prather had spent 14 years with the company, when it was owned by Pillsbury. Pillsbury, a highly centralized company, had required that any expenditures over $1 million had to be authorized by the head office. He thought how much this contrasted with Imasco. For him, Imasco was "like a breath of fresh air," a decentralized organization in the best sense. He had a great working relationship with Crawford and the others at the Centre, in contact by phone every couple weeks or as required. There was easy and open access with no surprises.

Prather had received preliminary approval from Crawford to proceed with the negotiations. Marriott had structured the Roy Rogers sale in two rounds. In the first round, all those parties who were interested in the chain were interviewed, "much like a job interview," Prather recalled. It was during this first round that Marriott expressed their concerns for their franchisees, and assessed the capabilities and sincerity of those interested in buying the chain. To Prather, "the first round was a screening process just to get into the game."

Prather made it through the first round, but there were three or four other interested groups still in the running. During the next round, the terms of the sale would be negotiated. Although the rumoured price had initially been $390 million, Prather thought that it might be more. Prather felt he could convince Marriott that Hardee's offered the best means of exit, given Marriott's concern for the franchisees, and that a solid offer of $420 million would convince them to sell Roy Rogers to Hardee's.

Prather figured conversion to Hardee's outlets would cost $80 000 to $115 000 per unit, depending on local conditions. He weighed this against the average "from scratch" start-up cost of $1.2 million per site. Additionally, Roy Rogers' menu, which included their popular fresh fried chicken, would complement Hardee's current menu. However, he was not sure it would be an "easy sell" in Montreal. Imasco's 40%-shareholder, B.A.T, was in the midst of fighting off a takeover bid from Sir James Goldsmith (see Appendix). Prather knew that Crawford and the board would be concerned about Goldsmith's run at B.A.T, but the Roy Rogers deal was just what he needed to solidify Hardee's number three industry position.

EXHIBIT 1 Imasco Acquisitions: Distinguishable Eras in Acquisition Size

1963–77
Canada Foils
Growers Wine
Simtel and Editel
S&W Foods: $18.4 million (Canadian)
Uddo & Taormina (Progresso): $32.5 million (Canadian)
Pasquale Brothers (Unico): $4 million (Canadian)
Grissol: $12.2 million (Canadian)
Collegiate: $1.4 million (Canadian)
Arlington Sports
Top Drug Mart and Top Value Discount
Tinderbox: $1.4 million (US)
PoP Shoppes investment: $10.5 million (Canadian)
Canada Northwest Land Ltd. investment
Hardee's Food Systems investment: $15 million (US)
— Includes Imperial Tobacco Limited acquisitions

1978–86
Shoppers Drug Mart (Koffler's): $66.6 million (Canadian)
Further Hardee's investment: $15 million (Canadian)
Hardee's totally acquired: $76 million (US)
Burger Chef: $44 million (US)
Peoples Drug Stores: $398 million (Canadian)
Rea & Derick Drug Stores: $114 million (Canadian)
Genstar: $2.4 billion (Canadian)

EXHIBIT 2 **20-Year Financials: Imasco Ltd. and Tobacco Business** ($ million unless noted)

	Imasco Ltd.				Tobacco Business			Imasco Ltd.		
Year	Total Revenues	Operating Earnings	Net Earnings Before Extraordinary Items	Earnings Per Common Share[4,5]	Tobacco Operating Earnings/Total Operating Earnings (%)	Tobacco Revenue	Tobacco Operating Earnings	Stock Price High[6]	Stock Price Low[6]	Annual Dividend[5] Per Common Share
1970[1]	582.2	37.3	15.7	.20	.88	435.2	32.7	16.13	12.00	0.10
1971[1]	569.6	40.6	17.7	.22	.88	418.0	35.9	20.50	15.25	0.125
1972[1]	625.6	48.1	22.2	.28	.84	430.4	40.4	28.38	19.00	0.1375
1973[1]	717.1	56.0	28.0	.36	.81	446.9	45.4	34.75	25.75	0.15
1975[3]	1030.3	78.5	36.8	.47	.79	610.5	62.0	33.25	18.75	0.19375
1976[2]	941.2	74.9	36.5	.47	.81	560.1	60.7	32.00	26.00	0.1625
1977[2]	1031.6	74.7	34.9	.45	.81	605.4	60.9	27.25	20.63	0.169
1978[2]	1049.4	84.2	43.1	.55	.81	655.0	68.3	31.63	24.00	0.18
1979[2]	1161.5	114.8	56.4	.70	.69	741.4	78.8	40.75	29.75	0.205
1980[2]	1150.5	132.1	68.2	.83	.75	826.7	99.1	47.25	38.25	0.25
1981[2]	1423.7	168.8	89.6	1.07	.73	952.9	123.2	38.25	21.25	0.30
1982[2]	2190.7	247.0	124.2	1.39	.63	1120.2	156.0	44.50	29.50	0.35
1983[2]	2713.9	300.3	156.8	1.73	.61	1242.9	182.3	37.50	18.00	0.40
1984[2]	2873.2	339.6	194.2	2.03	.60	1358.9	205.2	36.25	29.88	0.50
1985[2]	4353.2	432.0	234.1	2.25	.52	1451.1	224.0	28.25	17.38	0.645
1986[2]	5325.1	465.9	261.7	2.40	.53	1769.8	246.0	35.00	22.63	0.75
1987[1]	5924.4	578.4	282.7	2.24	.48	1926.0	279.1	46.00	24.25	0.96
1988[1]	6000.6	636.7	314.3	2.51	.48	2018.1	308.0	29.50	23.75	1.04
1989[1]	5724.7	692.0	366.1	2.87	.48	2385.6	334.0	40.50	27.63	1.12

[1] January – December Fiscal Year.
[2] April – March Fiscal Year.
[3] Reflects 15-month period from January 1974 to March 1975.
[4] Before extraordinary items.
[5] Prior to 1980, adjusted to reflect three stock splits; after 1980, 2 for 1 stock splits July 1980, November 1982, and March 1985.
[6] Not adjusted for stock splits.

SOURCE: Imasco Limited.

APPENDIX   IMASCO Limited, 1990

In the summer of 1989, Sir James Goldsmith formed a syndicate of investors under the name of Hoylake Investments Limited to mount a takeover attempt on B.A.T, Imasco's largest shareholder. Goldsmith's argument was that B.A.T was being valued by the market at less than the sum of its parts, and that the true value would only be realized by the "unbundling" of B.A.T. The stakes in the bid were enormous—it was estimated that Hoylake and its partners would have to put up over $25 billion to carry through on the transaction. Hoylake's intentions with respect to the block of Imasco's shares that B.A.T owned were unknown. Imasco's position was that, while it was an "interested observer", it was not directly involved in the proceedings and would only monitor developments related to the offer. While the specifics of Goldsmith's case are not pertinent here, the general arguments are. These are given below as excerpts from Goldsmith's letter to B.A.T shareholders dated August 8, 1989.

The Key Questions

The case for this bid must rest on the answer to simple questions. Has the existing management placed B.A.T in a position to compete successfully? Are the subsidiaries growing healthily, or are they failing relative to their competitors? Have shareholders' funds been invested in a wise and progressive way which adds value to the shares of the company? Is the conglomerate structure able to provide strength and innovation over the longer term to its diversified subsidiaries? In short, is B.A.T in a state to compete in the modern world and to face the future with confidence? Or has it been managed in a way which could lead to progressive senescence and decay? That is the crux of the argument.

Conglomeration — B.A.T's Failure

It is our case that B.A.T's management has sought size rather than quality or value; it has used shareholders' funds to acquire totally unconnected businesses, about which it knew little, and which are being damaged by having been brought under the control of B.A.T's bureaucratic yoke.

The Cause of Failure

Before presenting the case in factual detail, I would like to explain why such a state of affairs can occur. It is not that the men in charge are malevolent. Not at all. No doubt they are serious administrators. The problem originates from their belief that tobacco was a declining business, and that the company should diversify into other industries. This logic sounded compelling. The flaw was that B.A.T's management knew something about tobacco, but little about the businesses of the companies that it was acquiring. Also there exists a very natural conflict of interest between management and shareholders. Management wishes its company to be big. The bigger it is, the greater the respect, power and honours that flow to management. Shareholders, on the other hand, want value. They do not seek size for the sake of size. They want growth to be the result of excellence, and thereby to improve the short- and long-term value of their investment. Some conglomerates have performed well under the leadership of their founders. But that ceases when the flame of the founder is replaced by the dead hand of the corporate bureaucrat. That is why great conglomerates often have been well advised to de-conglomerate before they retire.

Purpose of the Offer

1. We intend to reverse B.A.T's strategy. Instead of accumulating miscellaneous companies within B.A.T, we intend to release them and, as described below, return the proceeds to you.
2. We would concentrate B.A.T's attention on running its core business, tobacco. That is the process which we have described as "unbundling."

Consequences

Of course, you will be concerned to know the consequences for the companies being released, and for those who work within them. Will those companies suffer? Will jobs be sacrificed? Would their future be jeopardised, for example, by a reduction in the level of investment in research, development and capital equipment? That is what you may have been led to believe. The reality is the opposite. Instead of vegetating within B.A.T, those companies would either return to independence, or they would join more homogeneous companies. Such companies have the skills which would contribute to future development, and a true mutuality of interest would result. This would lead to increased opportunity for employees, greater long-term investment, productivity and growth. The real danger to employees is that they should remain trapped within B.A.T, and condemned to slow but progressive relative decline. Ultimately that would lead to employee hardship, despite the benevolent intentions of existing management.

Conclusion

To summarize, the flawed architecture of the tobacco-based conglomerates was exposed, first with the acquisition of Imperial Group by Hanson in 1986, and late last year when the management and directors of RJR/Nabisco recognized that shareholder values could only be properly realized by a sale of the company.

Size is often a protection against change, but these same basic structural defects have now been revealed, and the logic of unbundling B.A.T has become inescapable.

PART

6 STRATEGY AND ORGANIZATION

CONTINENTAL REALITY

Joseph N. Fry and Randy A. Pepper

"This company has been immensely successful," said John Morrison, president of Continental Realty Ltd., as he looked west from his Vancouver office window, "and we intend to continue that way." His view of the skyline was punctuated by construction cranes rising above the foundations of new office towers. The west was booming and the company was growing apace. "The challenge," he said, "will be in finding the best people and keeping them with us."

BACKGROUND

Continental Realty was among the largest commercial and industrial real estate agencies in Canada. In its most recent fiscal year the company had acted in lease and sales transactions totalling more than $200 million. The first office and present headquarters of the company was in Vancouver. Branches operated in Calgary, Edmonton, Toronto, Houston and Phoenix. Continental currently employed over 40 agents; but its early days were very much the story of one man, Gordon Nelson, owner and chairman.

Nelson grew up in small-town Alberta, where he caught a sense of the coming promise of the west. He went east to obtain an Honours Business Administration degree from the University of Western Ontario, and then spent a year travelling and studying in Europe. On his return, he entered the real estate business. In three years he moved from Toronto to Winnipeg to Vancouver.

Nelson derived his approach to operating a real estate agency from his experience during these early years. His employers and colleagues were secretive—unwilling or unprepared to teach him the business. Information, even technical and background data, was treated as a resource to be rationed. Nelson persisted and eventually met a senior industry executive who was prepared to share his knowledge and who helped Nelson develop the technical expertise needed to move ahead in the business.

Nelson sold over $7 million worth of property in his first year with J.B. Hobbs & Co. in Vancouver. Shortly after, with two partners, he bought out the Hobbs agency and changed its name to Continental Realty.

Continental prospered, but the deal that established Nelson's reputation was Burrard Square. While examining an aerial photograph of Vancouver, Nelson became intrigued with a spread of property between the railway main-line and Burrard Inlet immediately west of the city's downtown core. The property, owned by Construction Aggregates Ltd., was the first fully assembled yet undeveloped parcel in the area. Through his investment contacts, Nelson determined that a British-financial firm, Tate Development Corp., was seeking attractive investment opportunities in North America. He evaluated Construction Aggregates' willingness to sell, convinced Tate of the property's investment potential, and the concept of Burrard Square was born. The steps from concept to reality were protracted, and marked by continuous negotiation as designs, approvals, financing and tenants were brought together. But five years later, in what was then a landmark deal for Vancouver, arrangements were completed and construction started on the multi-million integrated apartment, commercial and retail complex.

After Burrard Square, Continental grew in volume and geographic coverage, and Nelson crystallized a strategy and set of operating policies that made the company unique in the industry.

THE BUSINESS

Continental confined its operations to the commercial and industrial realty markets, where it aimed to operate as one of the few true "agency" businesses, as compared to the hundreds of "brokerage" operations across the country. According to Bob McLaren, Continental's general manager, the distinction lay in the degree of professionalism in the operator's methods.

To draw a clear contrast, McLaren compared residential selling to Continental's approach. He explained, in his usual hyperbolic style:

> The residential business is largely a clearing-house operation. That's what the Multiple Listing Service (MLS) is all about. All the houses for sale are in a big pot with an index card and they are picked out of a hat and fed to the prospects. The residential realtor aims at completing a sales transaction. He derives his commission not from counselling his client but from moving the property.

It was not surprising, according to another industry source, that the popular image of a real estate broker was "a guy with a bright yellow jacket who leads housewives through endless kitchens and comments on the abundance of closet space."

Commercial and industrial negotiators, particularly Continental's, operated in a different world, with business clients and high-value properties. But the broker approach was also prevalent here. One of Canada's largest firms, a competitor of Continental, advertised a national computerized system that could quickly supply a list of potential properties to fit a client's space, location and cost requirements. To Continental, this shotgun approach served a client's interests poorly.

Continental negotiators operated on an exclusive basis, as the only agent attempting to sell or lease a client's property. Like a lawyer, a Continental negotiator would act for only one party in a transaction, the client, and in this relationship acted as much as an advisor as a salesperson. For example, he or she might advise a client not to accept an offer to purchase or lease if the agent established that it was not to the client's advantage. In this way, Continental sought to position itself as a true agency, more consistent with European than North American practice, under a single basic policy: "Treat the property as if it were your own."

If the cornerstone of Continental's agency concept was the exclusive concentration on client interest, the building blocks were formed from the creative pursuit of realty opportunities. The Burrard Square deal demonstrated this: through imagination, knowledge, and contacts, Nelson was well positioned to conceive a project. Continental aimed to do more than represent other people's ideas or projects for clients, and in so doing add value to its agency role and, for that matter, to the economy as a whole.

In developing this approach, Continental pioneered a transformation in procedures for selling commercial and industrial real estate. For generations, the realty industry had been an old man's game, where commercial transactions took place among well-acquainted, senior colleagues. In such an environment, the building of social links was paramount in the operation of a successful realty business. Continental outflanked these industry norms by emphasizing technical and analytical skills. Gradually, the industry became a young man's field, where business relationships based on trust and skill became the basis of successful client-negotiator interaction.

Creating and negotiating a deal was the essence of the agency business. The following examples illustrate the frequently circuitous, sometimes protracted, and often frustrating aspects of a transaction.

A Land Assembly

A Canadian chartered bank approached Continental and R.E. Lang and Co., a significant Continental competitor, asking them to work together to assemble a major site in Edmonton's downtown core. Continental refused to collaborate, suggesting as an alternative that each agent propose six potential properties that the bank could then review. The bank agreed.

A senior Continental negotiator, through whom the initial contact had been made, took responsibility for the project. His activities included identifying potential rentable sites; judging the willingness of the site owners to sell and estimating prices; consulting with architects and planning consultants on the suitability of each site; checking out the necessary approvals and establishing a time frame for the regulatory process. He had to do all this discreetly and confidentially. Continental was first to propose sites to the bank and ultimately the bank chose a property on Continental's list.

The site selected was owned by an international utility company that had a policy of never selling its investment properties. The first step was to determine what amount to offer the company—an amount that would at least induce the utility to counter with an asking price. The situation was complicated by the bank's unwillingness to disclose its identity. This made the utility company even more nervous. It was not interested in selling to a speculator and giving that person the opportunity to flip the property at a later date.

After lengthy talks the utility sold, but on the condition that development would begin on the site within 18 months. The transaction had taken countless meetings over approximately six months. The Continental negotiator walked away with a handsome commission, however, and a good chance of becoming the leasing agent of the future bank tower.

Developing an Office Tower

Hugh Thorburn, a veteran Continental negotiator, first saw this potential opportunity while trying to lease space in a new office tower. Thorburn had attended a board meeting of the subsidiary of a large American mining firm to propose that an above-ground walkway be built between its building and an adjoining tower that he was trying to lease. At this meeting he learned that a committee was looking into the expansion of office space.

Conscious of its U.S. headquarters' attitudes, the subsidiary wanted to be very thorough in its examination of relocation space. It sent out an extremely detailed call for tender to 18 different office buildings in Vancouver. Meanwhile, Continental's general manager, Bob McLaren, who had been briefed by Thorburn on the mining company's search for space and who was the agent for a medium-sized Vancouver developer, decided that his client had the most suitable site for the mining company. The site was essentially raw land—a group of derelict buildings—but advantageously located for the mining firm. McLaren did not submit a proposal, but sent Thorburn a letter with a copy to the mining company outlining his client's plan to build on the site. The developer, inexperienced in the commercial market, was unwilling to begin construction unless the mining company was secured as lead tenant. Within two months McLaren obtained a letter of commitment from the mining subsidiary.

The mechanics of the process were as follows. As with most major development projects, McLaren's client had formed a team composed of an architect, a space planner, a contractor and a realty agent, to study the project's feasibility. Public relations and advertising people later helped to put presentations together. Proposal costs were shared between Continental Realty and the negotiator. In a deal such as this, McLaren was the "lister" of the property. His responsibilities include searching the property's title, preparing and distributing promotional material, advising the landowner on the project's marketability and negotiating with major tenants.

The amount of client/developer involvement usually depended on the client's size and experience in the negotiation process. In this deal, McLaren's nervous developer was constantly trying to involve himself in direct negotiations despite his inexperience in commercial dealing. It therefore became important for McLaren, a hard-nosed, number-oriented salesman, to maintain firm control over his client. Meanwhile, the more affable Thorburn was continually assuring the mining company of the project's wisdom. As Thorburn observed, the different personalities of the two negotiators were very well suited to the job requirements.

"In a major leasing agreement," explained Thorburn, "the resolution of several common negotiating points determines the deal's success." Rent was not in dispute in this deal; however, the prospective tenant wanted to alter the building's design. The mining subsidiary was also determined to extend the lease period from 10–20 years, and to obtain a guaranteed lease rate should it require more space on additional floors. After all these points had been satisfactorily resolved, the mining company's Los Angeles head office decided that it wanted either 50% or 100% ownership of the building. McLaren's client agreed to a 50% equity participation by the mining firm. A further catch arose here, for Continental assessed the building's replacement value at $29.4 million, but the mining company's head office had authorized a capital expenditure of only $13 million. After several trips to the U.S. and hard negotiation, much of it aimed at avoiding having to re-submit a capital expenditure proposal and risk a turndown by the U.S. parent, the deal was concluded.

THE CONTINENTAL FORMULA

Providing genuine agency services had helped Continental grow, and charge full commission rates in the process. (The specific rates varied by the size, nature and location of the project, but were generally in the range of 3–5% of the dollar value of a transaction.) Gordon Nelson's ability to impose discipline on the activities of the high-flying, performance-oriented individuals who made up his negotiator team was a crucial ingredient in Continental's success. His company was known throughout the industry for its rigorous operating policies.

To remain with the firm, Continental negotiators (after a period of training) were required to generate a minimum of $90 000 in commissions annually. The average production in the past year for negotiators with greater than one year's experience was $234 000. Negotiator compensation was based on a sliding scale starting at 20% of commission generated, to 60% for commission earned over $100 000. The $15 000 salary was tied to the sliding scale, so that when a negotiator achieved the $90 000 minimum his total income would be $45 000. Negotiators were required to pay their own expenses, and they were not paid their share of commissions billed until Continental was in full receipt of the invoiced amounts.

Continental encouraged an open flow of information concerning client activity. Negotiators were required to submit a weekly applicant report, which identified their clients and outlined the probability of success of current deals. If clients were not so listed, they were regarded as fair game for other negotiators. This report allowed the branch manager to monitor negotiator progress (and discourage over-registration, if necessary) and informed other negotiators of development activities in various sectors of the city. "There is no fear of being scooped," as one negotiator put it. In contrast, negotiators with most Canadian brokerage houses tended to be secretive with details of their potential deals.

There were no sales territories, but most deals were transacted within the negotiator's city base. Management encouraged negotiators to focus their activities, to limit their client list, and to concentrate on big deals. Continental, in Nelson's words, was "not after all the business available, but all the big business." Deals completed by a negotiator outside of this branch were credited to the negotiator as usual, but for credit to the branch territory in which the deal occurred.

Continental procedures required all offices to hold sales meetings commencing no later than 8 a.m. on Monday, Wednesday and Friday of each week. These meetings were the primary forum for announcements of new development activities, for the collection of information on prospective buyers or sellers, and for discussion of proposed or current projects' sale or lease potential. The first item on the agenda of a Calgary meeting attended by the casewriter, for example, was a presentation by branch manager Steve Jannock. It began with a discussion of the marketing feasibility of a new condominium office building and whether or not the concept would sell in south-west Calgary. One negotiator noted that a rival developer was planning a similar project at the opposite end of the block. The discussion then moved to potential customers and a price estimate for such a project. Jannock pointed out that the proposal was complicated by the developer's desire for a short-term investor before proceeding. An architect's layout was then examined and suggestions were offered regarding the amount of glass space, the number and speed of elevators, and other improvements to increase the project's salability. Finally, the total credibility of the project was examined; two points of concern were that it was the developer's first effort in the condominium market, and that the architect was from out of town.

An important part of Continental's application of the agency concept was a strict investment policy. All Continental personnel were forbidden to purchase speculative real estate in Canada or any state in the U.S. in which the company maintained an active office. Infringement of the rule was grounds for immediate dismissal. McLaren explained that the logic of the policy was easy to understand: the time spent investing and developing one's own real estate holdings should be spent representing one's clients. Moreover, sophisticated clients came to respect their negotiator's advice because the latter was not plucking out the good properties for himself. Continental was one of very few real estate agencies in Canada operating with such a policy.

Continental maintained a high level of internal competition. Each negotiator's performance was charted on a graph, which was reviewed monthly before a panel of his or her peers. At the annual meeting of all Continental personnel, each negotiator's graphs were projected on a screen, and his or her performance was reviewed. Another meeting, held in the late summer or early fall, is further illustration of Continental's approach: with the chairman, president, general manager, and all branch managers present, negotiators who had not yet reached $50 000 in annual production had to account for their performance, and were offered advice for improvement by this executive team. A past Xerox salesperson who had risen quickly within Continental saw these practices as straightforward and reasonable: "One has to play on these guys' egos. It's the only way to motivate such achievement-oriented people."

Working trips were another ingredient in the Continental recipe for success. These trips were described in the company procedure manual as an incentive program to encourage negotiators to broaden their concept of commercial real estate. The manual noted that a good negotiator was expected to make many trips on his or her own, but the company would help to defray the cost of specific trips. During a negotiator's first year, western negotiators were to fly to eastern Canada and the U.S., while eastern negotiators were to fly west. In the third year, the destination was Europe; in the fourth, it was southeast Asia; and in the fifth year, the negotiator was to visit the Caribbean or Hawaii. In the course of these trips, while the negotiators were acquainting themselves with the dynamics of a new market, they were also required to update and expand the company's Buyer's Book. This book was a listing of international investors who had expressed interest in North American real estate. It included details on the clients' buying behaviour, investment criteria and history.

CORPORATE AND BRANCH MANAGEMENT

Continental operated with a lean management structure (Exhibit 1). Senior managers, including the president, general manager and branch managers, all acted as negotiators as well as administrators, and had their production charted. It was argued that few services were necessary for the effective operation of the company. The primary organizational function was the supply to negotiators of current information—applicant listings, sales data, office-space surveys, Buyer's Book—and each branch was responsible for its own surveys and record updating.

In recent years, Gordon Nelson had removed himself from management of Continental's day-to-day activities in order to spend more time as a property developer. As chairman, he remained involved in policy matters and in quite close touch with the business, informally and through quarterly board meetings.

Nelson's first replacement as president was Larry Newman, at the time branch manager in Calgary. Newman remained in Calgary after taking on his new responsibilities. He grew restless in his dual role, however, and left Continental after two years to start his own agency firm. Nelson filled the gap for a time, and then asked John Morrison to join the firm as president.

John Morrison was senior vice-president of a large insurance company at the time. He had received his B.A. from the University of Western Ontario, M.B.A. from Harvard Business School, and was a Chartered Life Underwriter. He had known Nelson for some time because of his insurance company's participation in several financing deals. Morrison was attracted by Continental's prospects, and moved to Vancouver to become president.

A few months after John Morrison's appointment, Stan Jameson, the general manager, left Continental. Jameson had been an exception in the Continental ranks. His background was as a developer rather than an agent, and he did not himself get involved in transactions. Rather, most of his time was spent travelling from branch to branch reviewing progress with individual negotiators and offering counsel and advice. He was, several negotiators mentioned, very respected in this role, and his branch visits were welcomed.

Bob McLaren, Jameson's successor, was cut from different cloth, not unlike that of his mentor, Gordon Nelson. McLaren had joined Continental after completing his M.B.A. at the University of Western Ontario. He had recently been promoted from Vancouver branch manager to executive vice-president.

McLaren was an aggressive and knowledgeable negotiator whose advice was highly valued by fellow negotiators. He continued his selling activities and was a consistently high producer, travelling about 160 000 km a year and working 70–75 hours a week. Administratively, McLaren saw his prime function as that of recruiting and training branch managers, although he could not avoid involvement in many spot problems, ranging from difficulties with deals to personnel issues. McLaren turned the monthly performance-review task over to the branch managers. On the demands of his job, McLaren commented:

> You don't enjoy success without paying the price. And you don't do it unless you want do. You have to enjoy it. You can't dedicate such physical and mental energy and sacrifice unless you get a lot of enjoyment out of what you are doing. A person who says he doesn't is a person who's not going to be successful at it.

Morrison and McLaren both felt that sales involvement and a proven sales record were important for a leadership position in Continental. The rationale was basically that of credibility, plus a latent feeling that perhaps the worst thing that could happen to Continental would be the building of "non-productive" overheads and becoming "over-administered." In this context, Morrison and McLaren had assumed a largely implicit division of management tasks. Morrison dealt with the general tasks of corporate administration and representation, McLaren with the more immediate problems of branch supervision and production.

Planning and budgeting in Continental were relatively simple procedures. Revenue by branch was estimated annually on the basis of branch input and forecasts of market activity. By far the largest cost item was negotiator commission expense and it was directly variable with revenue. Branch-office and head-office expense budgets were also prepared, and these tended to reflect a no-frills approach to operations. Only a limited amount of savings could be squeezed out of the administrative process, however, since the costs were already pared to the bone.

THE BIG BRANCHES

Vancouver

Continental's lead market, Vancouver, was beginning to emerge from a slump in office development. With 25 million square feet of existing space, compared to Calgary's 14 million square feet, Vancouver was often viewed by developers as more stable than the overheated Calgary market. Continental's Vancouver branch had maintained a relatively stable production level with a fluctuating rate of sales to leasing. The branch employed ten negotiators whose average age was 37 years.

The Vancouver branch manager, Per Ek, had less than two years with Continental when he succeeded McLaren as branch manager. Born in Sweden, Ek was raised in Switzerland and had obtained a Ph.D. in Economics from the University of Geneva. After work with a major Swiss bank, Ek moved to Montreal where he assembled properties for a consortium of European banks. Ek was brought into Continental as a European representative to supplement Gordon Nelson, who had reduced his global travelling. Ek did not see himself as a high-powered salesperson, but as a professional who specialized in large sales projects. His production graph, which bounded upward in large steps, attested to his ability. Ek believed that it was important to lead by example and, though he had hired an administrator to handle office affairs, he still found only Sunday afternoons free. With his three hats—branch manager, agent, and international representative—Ek was unable to devote much time to work with individual agents.

Edmonton

The Edmonton branch consisted of eight agents, and represented an increasing proportion of Continental's total production. A year before, a group of four senior agents had left the branch, led by the previous manager, John Thompson. Those left were young, of average age 32, and were managed by Cliff Baetz, who maintained a relatively relaxed atmosphere. In spite of the defections, production was only 10% below the levels of the year before, an accomplishment that was cause for a great deal of pride among the Edmonton negotiators.

At 36, Cliff Baetz was the old man of the Edmonton office. C.B., as his fellow negotiators called him, held a B. Comm. from the University of Alberta and had joined Continental in Edmonton as an assistant to the branch manager. Baetz's responsibilities included making the branch productive and setting the office's pace, but he maintained a casual, sociable atmosphere. As a point of comparison, negotiators in Edmonton sometimes wandered into the 8:00 a.m. sales meeting ten minutes late; in Vancouver, the door was locked at 8:00. Baetz noted that Edmonton's productivity per negotiator was higher than that of any other Continental office.

The Edmonton manager's laid-back nature was deceptive. His typical day began at 7:00 a.m. and stretched to 6:30 p.m.; on the two days that the casewriter was present, his lunch was two hot dogs swallowed while dialing the phone. Baetz was currently Continental's top producer. He described his job as "a pressure cooker," but he enjoyed the autonomy of his work. He liked to give his negotiators similar freedom. While Baetz admitted that he had little motivation to train his employees, he believed that few negotiators required or would tolerate direct supervision.

Calgary

The Calgary commercial-development business was in the midst of unprecedented growth and Continental had just enjoyed a superb year. Production was substantially improved over the relatively poor record of two years earlier when several key personnel had left the Calgary office, some to expand the company into Houston, others to strike out on their own. Production had dropped by over 50%. The branch had rebuilt, however, from 9 negotiators to 17, with an average age of 38.

The Calgary branch manager, Steve Jannock, had ten years of experience with Continental. A former Xerox salesman, Jannock, 44, believed that more effort had to be put into retaining Continental's leading producers. "Calgary was seriously injured by Newman's departure, and Edmonton may still feel the effects of Thompson's exit," he cautioned. Talking with the commitment of a man who understood the high producers' predicament, Jannock explained,

"When the investment policy removes a successful negotiator's most obvious tax shelter and participation is not offered, at some point it is no longer economical for an individual to remain in the company." The investment policy was too important a selling tool to sacrifice, according to Jannock, but something had to be done to retain Continental's "shooters." Another veteran negotiator quipped, "Gordon Nelson created a monster; he produces wealthy prima donnas that the tax system forces out of the company!"

NEGOTIATOR MANAGEMENT

Recruiting, training and retaining negotiators were the acknowledged keys to Continental's future growth.

Recruiting

Continental recruited from the universities and from the ranks of experienced salespeople. In recent years, university recruiting had been confined to the Universities of British Columbia, Reading (near London, England) and Western Ontario. British Columbia and Reading had courses specifically related to the real estate field, and Reading offered a Master's degree in urban land appraisal.

Recently, Xerox and IBM sales managers had been recruited into the company as junior negotiators. As well-trained, professional salespeople, these recruits brought a new style to the negotiation task. Their concentration on selling technique, combined with Continental's traditional stress on product knowledge, had produced some very satisfactory results. Negotiators with a Xerox background thought that individual negotiator productivity could be substantially improved at Continental. They identified in particular a need for instruction in more effective selling methods. As one successful, ex-Xerox negotiator put it, "Everybody here works hard, but only a handful work smart."

There was no shortage of potential recruits to Continental. As Steve Jannock noted, "I have more people phoning me for jobs than I know what to do with." The question was one of quality, of being able to succeed in the Continental milieu.

Training

An assistantship program was Continental's primary training vehicle. With the permission of the company, a negotiator could hire an assistant if he had achieved $100 000 production for two consecutive years. A second assistant could be hired if the negotiator had achieved $200 000 production over the past two years, or if he had obtained a new major office or industrial listing (over 150 000 square feet). A new assistant was paid $700 per month for the first six months, $750 per month after six months, and could be eligible for a salary of $800 per month if he or she had experience. No production bonus was allowed during the assistant's first year. One recent Western M.B.A. recruit described his initial reluctance to join Continental at $700 per month: "Hell, that was less than I was making during my summers at school!"

An assistant was hired by a single negotiator who became responsible for the assistant's training. The quality of training provided by the negotiator varied, and this factor contributed, at times, to assistant turnover. In the Calgary branch, for example, approximately five assistants had moved in and out of the office in the past two years.

For most trainees, the apprenticeship period lasted 12 months. At the end of that time, the negotiator in charge and the assistant determined a future course. On occasion, the assistants would stay on in a trainee capacity, with increased responsibilities and a cut into the bonus system. Otherwise they became full negotiators subject to the performance requirements.

Some prospective recruits were unwilling or financially unable to accept the reduction in earnings involved in an assistant position. In particular cases, if past sales experience justified it, certain recruits were permitted to enter the negotiation field directly. Their training period was typically three months, after which they became regular negotiators with $15 000 salary and a more lucrative commission rate. The junior negotiators were usually "blinkered"— assigned to a specific project or area to improve their understanding of a particular aspect of real estate development.

Apart from the assistantship program, Continental had no formal training procedures or materials. However, one senior negotiator, Brad Connelly, was assembling an extensive and detailed manual of procedures and techniques. Connelly planned to enter the consulting field eventually, providing advice on realty matters to major developers, and the manual tied in with these plans. Negotiators and branch managers alike felt that Connelly's efforts would substantially fill the present training gap in the company. One branch manager, who felt that training was critical to the company's continued success, praised Connelly's activities; he was relieved to have the responsibility off his desk.

Retraining

High turnover was characteristic of Continental's operation. Two-thirds of Continental's present negotiator group had been with the company in that capacity for less than two years. Over past years, there was an 84% probability that a negotiator would leave before his fifth year with the company. Part of the turnover, of course, was due to recruits who found they did not fit, or who could not produce the required $90 000 in annual commissions. Another part of the turnover, more consequential for the firm, was made up of successful negotiators who, for reasons varying from economics to personal autonomy, chose to leave.

Whether it was possible or desirable to lengthen the stay of negotiators was somewhat of a moot point at Continental. The company had implemented incentive programs aimed at stimulating continuity (Exhibit 2) and had developed a pension plan that would allow a negotiator to collect $60 000 per year on retirement and vested in ten years. These did not, however, seem to have had a major tangible impact. McLaren took a pretty hard-nosed view of the situation: "After a person has made $200 000 to $300 000 for three or four years, you can't expect him to stay." Shortly after having said this, McLaren met the casewriter at another Continental office; he had just received a message that the Toronto branch manager had resigned.

FUTURE GROWTH

There were, in the view of senior Continental personnel, two broad avenues of future growth. The first was through opening additional branches, and the second through expansion of branch volume by entry into new product areas.

Branching

New branches were generally seen as the prime growth vehicle, although it was by no means clear, on the record, that the Continental approach could be easily transferred out of the Vancouver-Calgary-Edmonton triangle. The performance of the Toronto branch had been erratic, and was attributed variously to market conditions, well-established competition, and poor management and recruiting. In spite of the difficulties, there was a general opinion in the west that an effective and energetic manager could put the operation on its feet. In the U.S., the two branches in Houston and Phoenix had been open for only a short time. Houston was, nevertheless, regarded as somewhat of a disappointment, due perhaps to the timing (relatively late in Houston's development boom) and narrow initial contact base (Continental had entered the market to work with one Canadian developer who was also entering the market). There was greater enthusiasm for the Phoenix office, which had just been opened by an aggressive negotiator. The Phoenix market was growing rapidly and had become an attractive expansion point for Canadian developers moving south.

In Bob McLaren's view, Continental should have offices established in 15 key cities within seven to ten years. The major constraints, he explained, were the availability of suitable people and his own time.

It will take from four to seven years to build a base in a new city. By the time the lead producer peaks out in a new area, the base for effective dealing has been established. My job is to identify when a young negotiator has ripened sufficiently, place him in the new market, and help him get going. We must do this with our own people. Bringing in negotiators from outside the firm or acquiring an existing firm would bring us the worst of both worlds.

On this program, branch growth was limited by McLaren's capacity to train and supervise new managers, which amounted, in his view, to having no more than two junior branches at any one time.

New Products

An area of immediate growth potential lay in the further expansion of Continental's activities in the industrial and property-management markets.

In both Calgary and Edmonton, industrial opportunities were being pursued, but no particular priority had been given to them. Development and decision-making in the industrial market were different, Continental personnel pointed out, involving different customers and different criteria. "They are an earthy lot," one negotiator explained, "but I get along better with the tire-kickers than the oil executives." Most of the negotiators concentrating on the Calgary industrial market had not selected their placements; they had been assigned to the market. Another industrial negotiator explained, "The deals are small, you work twice as hard and make half as much." Edmonton had always had its finger in the industrial area, but, historically, only one negotiator in that office specialized in such deals.

Continental's property-management operations were headquartered in Vancouver under Ted Foster, a public accountant who had joined the company in its early years. The essential function provided was coverage of the on-going tasks of operating an office; property-tenant relations, physical maintenance, insurance, security, etc. The major competitor was the owner himself, who was always tempted to perform the management function. Management contracts were sought by negotiators and turned over to Foster when a deal was made. In the coming year the property-management operation was expected to gross about $1 million, with Vancouver contributing about 50%, Calgary 25% and the balance from Edmonton and Toronto. The business was profitable and was growing at about 15% per year.

Another, quite different, view of growth objectives and methods was presented by a veteran representative, Dick Thorson, reflecting in some degree the thoughts of some other senior agents. His concern was that dynamic growth might cause the company to trade off quality for quantity and slip toward becoming a "brokerage" house. Using Calgary as an example, Thorson suggested that there should be only five to seven negotiators, rather than the current 17. Only these negotiators would attend the morning meetings, ensuring a free flow of information and counsel. Each negotiator however, would have two executive assistants and would be held accountable for the production and profit of his three-person group. To retain the senior negotiators, Thorson proposed a change in the investment policy: negotiators would still be prohibited from dealing in city-core or raw land, but a sector of land would be opened for investment. All Continental clients would be informed of the nature and extent of the investment area. Finally, Thorson would limit branch expansion to the high-growth markets in western Canada and to a few dynamic American cities.

Thorson's proposal thus preserved the firm's strategy, but recommended a fundamental change in operating method. Few negotiators were so presumptuous. Most felt that Gordon Nelson had developed a wondrous formula for success which should not be tampered with. Asked why others had not been able to duplicate Continental's methods, one negotiator replied, "Nobody else has copied the formula because nobody else has the spunk."

EXHIBIT 1 Continental's Organization Chart

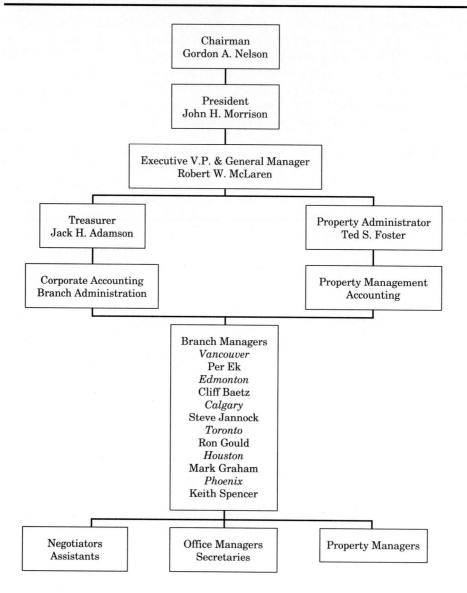

EXHIBIT 2 Continental's Incentive Program

Old System	*Present Schedule*		*Prize*
$ 100 000	2.5 ×	minimum production	Gold watch
$ 300 000	5 ×	minimum production	Colour television
$ 750 000	10 ×	minimum production	Lincoln Continental automobile
$ 1 000 000	20 ×	minimum production	University education for salesperson's children
Proposed 30 × minimum production			Option to purchase 5% interest in $5 million property
Proposed 40 × minimum production			Entitled to exercise option

PETRO-CANADA LIMITED

J. Peter Killing with Gary Neville

In January 1983, Bill West was finalizing his proposal to restructure the Petro-Canada Products Group (PCP), a division of Petro-Canada. Informal discussion of his plan, which proposed the creation of three strong regional business groups, had produced mixed reactions. Bill Hopper, the chairman and chief executive officer of Petro-Canada, made the following comments:

> It appears that the market may be changing and I believe that the guy who's going to be the winner is the scrambler, the guy who pares down his organization to efficiency. I don't want chaos in the organization, but I will accept some chaos with great results. The important thing is that the regions don't get out of control. I don't want any little "tin gods" running around out there. I think it's important to have good people in place. It seems if you have good people then things always work out.

Ed Lakusta, who had joined Petro-Canada in the summer of 1982 as president and CEO, commented on the fact that West's proposed organization was a marked departure from usual practice in the oil industry:

> Here at Petro-Canada we are not steeped in tradition. I like to be able to measure the bottom line easily. If something makes sense, we are willing to try a different approach.

COMPANY BACKGROUND

Petro-Canada commenced operations in January 1976 as a Crown corporation owned by the Canadian government. The company's mandate was to focus on oil and gas exploration as part of the government's drive to make Canada more self-sufficient in oil. Hopper's first major move was the $342 million purchase of Atlantic Richfield Canada Ltd., which was engaged in the exploration and production of oil and gas in western Canada.

This initial focus on exploration soon broadened, however, with the acquisitions of Pacific Petroleum in 1979 (for $1.5 billion, at that time the largest takeover in Canadian history) and Petro Fina in 1981. The Petro Fina purchase cost Petro-Canada $1.6 billion, nearly double Petro Fina's market value six months earlier, and led to a considerable outcry in the press. Hopper explained the rationale for the acquisitions:

> Our initial mandate involved the upstream; we were told to spend money in the frontier regions of Canada as effectively as possible. It was not our intention to get involved in the downstream part of the business. It actually happened more by chance. Pacific Petroleum was 95% an upstream purchase. The marketing and refining portion only represented about 5% of the total value—about 400 retail outlets. We had to decide whether to keep that section of the business or sell it off. However when some of these stations were converted to the Petro-Canada name, to our surprise their sales took off like crazy. So when Fina in Montreal came up as an acquisition candidate it was of interest because one-third of its value was in the downstream.
>
> We were selling gasoline then at a rate I would never have believed. The question became, do we get rid of the downstream or do we retain it as a source of funds for our upstream exploration activities? If we held on to it we needed to increase our strength in the Ontario market where there were 9 million people and we only had 300 or 400 stations. That was why in October 1982 we decided to buy the marketing and refining businesses of BP (British Petroleum) Canada. This will bring us another 1 600 outlets and a couple of refineries.

The acquisition of BP was expected to be completed in early 1983, and Petro-Canada executives hoped that the conversion of BP stations to Petro-Canada stations would result in the same 5–15% volume increase per station that they had experienced with earlier conversions. This "Maple Leaf factor," as it became known, had resulted in a retail sales increase of 4% for Petro-Canada in 1982, a year in which industry sales of gasoline at service stations fell by 7% nationally.

By the end of 1982 Petro-Canada had become the largest oil company in Canada. Details of the acquired companies and Petro-Canada's financial and operating statistics are given in Exhibits 1 and 2.

ORGANIZATION

Due to the rapid pace of acquisition at Petro-Canada, the company's organization had undergone a number of changes. The most recent was in October 1982 when the company was split into upstream and downstream divisions (Exhibit 3) and Bill West was hired. Ed Lakusta explained the rationale for the new structure:

> We realized early that the upstream and the downstream parts of our business were very different. I liked the business unit concept because I liked to be able to measure my bottom line easily. Splitting the company up into two

main business units made a lot of sense. The downstream part should "operate commercially," and, hence, generate cash flow for the upstream exploration costs in the frontiers. Furthermore, the downstream is a very visible part of our business as well as more tangible to the average Canadian, and we had plans to have it run as the best downstream operation in Canada.

Other forces driving the reorganization were growing concerns regarding the company's processes for controlling expenditures, its ability to rank its investment opportunities according to priorities and its ability to generate sufficient cash to meet its investment requirements. Jim Stanford, head of the upstream division, recounted some of the discussions which led to the reorganization:

> Because of the widespread price increases which followed the "oil shocks" of the 1970s, worldwide demand for petroleum products is decreasing, forcing price declines and squeezing margins in the industry as a whole. Domestic sales in Canada have dropped by almost 20% from 1979 to 1982 and will probably drop by close to 10% in 1983. As a result the market is changing. There are 51 refineries in Canada and we think we are going to see seven of them mothballed this year.
>
> A lot of the issues we discussed involved where accountability would lie in the company and how accountability would be measured. There is a lot of pressure on everyone right now to get their organizations up and running.

The October reorganization also resulted in the creation of a five-man executive committee which included Hopper, Lakusta, Stanford, West and O'Brien (the vice president of finance and planning). The group's early meetings focussed on the need for developing a single Petro-Canada operating philosophy and a centralized human resources group which could look at staffing issues, such as the job duplication which had arisen from the acquisitions.

PETRO-CANADA PRODUCTS GROUP

PCP's main business was the refining of crude oil and the marketing of gasoline, diesel and home heating oil to commercial and retail customers. Over 40% of Petro-Canada's employees were in the division, and that figure would rise considerably when the acquisition of BP was completed in early 1983. On the refining side of the business, the challenge was to optimize the proportion of various products to be extracted from a barrel of crude oil, and to maximize the productivity and efficiency of the company's refineries. The supply function of PCP had to decide where to obtain product (product swaps between companies in the oil industry were common) and to arrange the supply of product to distribution terminals and retail outlets. Marketing was responsible for advertising, local promotion, market research, the production of sales forecasts, and so on.

When Bill West arrived at Petro-Canada in October 1982 he discovered that there was no head-office group for his recently created PCP division. The marketing, supply and refining decisions were made in the eastern region by executives formerly of the Fina organization who reported directly to West, and in the western region by former managers of the Pacific Petroleum organization, who reported to West through a central vice-president. These arrangements were clearly leading to some difficulties.

Some of the first concerns to surface were in the marketing area. The eastern region, for example, had designed a black Petro-Canada can to promote 10W30 motor oil. However, the western region was using a red container with a different design. Another issue was the tires, batteries and accessories (TBA) programs. The old Fina organization in the east had an active TBA business with its own brand of "Fina" tires. The marketing group in the east was receptive to the idea of converting to a Petro-Canada tire and continuing in this business. However, the old Pacific company had only a minimal TBA business with no "Pacific" tires and had little interest in introducing a line of Petro-Canada tires. In fact, the manager of marketing in the West did not believe the TBA business to be a profitable one and was not interested in expanding into that area at all.

Also of concern was the authority given to dealer operators in the two regions. It was common in the petroleum industry to use agents to operate bulk plants. In the previous Fina agreement, agents required the company's permission to extend credit to a customer. However, in the Pacific organization the dealer extended credit on his or her own judgement, which had resulted in an unusually high level of bad-debt accounts.

Other concerns regarding the task of integrating the regional companies into a national oil company were arising everywhere. The Pacific company had operated with a Univac computer which was incompatible with Fina's Honeywell computer. The result was chaos and no plans had yet been drawn up to correct the situation. A decision also needed to be made about the role of purchasing[1] Should it be centralized or decentralized by region? Furthermore, there appeared to be a lack of discipline in the downstream portions of the acquired companies. The accounts receivable, bad debts, inventory levels, and refinery safety records were all out of line with industry averages. It was also common, as many motorists could attest, to drive into a Petro-Canada station and be met by an attendant with a Fina badge on his or her coat.

Bill West saw the clear need for organizational change in Petro-Canada as a "grassroots opportunity" to set up a new organization which would "do it right," and avoid some of the organizational problems which plagued other major oil companies. Accordingly, one of his first moves as divisional president was to hire a consultant to assist in designing a new organization structure.

---

[1] Purchasing typically handled all purchases except crude oil for the refineries.

Bill soon learned, however, that the consultant's inclination was to go with a traditional, functionally organized and centrally controlled organization. The consultant commented:

> Structural clarity is required. Growth by acquisition has not resulted in realigned structures, leaving much of the Pacific and Petro Fina organizations intact. This has not encouraged a common strategy and has not integrated the staff into a common culture. Further, the relationships between functional areas in Petro-Canada Products (i.e., refining, distribution, supply, marketing) appear to be poor. There is no single decision-communication process. Integrating BP personnel into the existing Petro-Canada structure will require a major effort.
>
> Another problem is the lack of a central human resource function. Currently there is no inventory of staff skills, nor is there a plan to maximize the use of human resources throughout Petro-Canada Products. The prime focus of the realignment of the business group must be the integration of the various corporate backgrounds into a cohesive culture.

BILL WEST'S PROPOSAL

Prior to joining Petro-Canada, Bill West spent 25 years working in the downstream area of a major U.S. oil company operating in Canada. For the most part, his career was spent in staff groups or executive management in the areas of refining, supply, planning and marketing. The American company had a highly centralized organizational structure, but Bill was not convinced that this was the optimal design. He explained:

> The typical downstream organization in an oil company is structured along functional lines. This usually involves a large head-office staff reporting to functional vice-presidents, and almost all strategic decisions are centralized. I believe there are a number of reasons why this has been the case. First of all, Imperial Oil started out that way and it seems everyone just followed. Second, the person at the top didn't trust the regions to be knowledgeable of all the factors which need to be taken into account when strategic decisions are made. Third, the functional V.P.'s felt that they should have staff around them to have more direct control over any strategic planning studies being conducted.
>
> One of the advantages of a centralized organization is that it is easier to coordinate marketing, refining and supply nationwide—particularly supply. Major strategic changes are handled more smoothly and are usually more consistent. The problem I have is that they also tend to be more incorrect. Often the people making decisions at a centralized level in the organization are too far out of touch with the real situation in the region. They don't know the business on a day-to-day basis.
>
> Furthermore, when decisions are made at the regional level they need to be funnelled up through the system to be reviewed at the top and channelled back

down before action can be taken. This often results in a slow reaction time to local needs and can be very frustrating for the managers involved. This type of structure also entails added expenses because of large staff groups at head office—it's really not very efficient.

In the organization I have in mind there will be less consistency and more confrontation. National co-ordination is essential but what is also needed is more power in the field so that the regions can react quickly to local needs. Confrontation between the regions and head office is likely to occur. But if I do a good job of resolving the differences, I feel that we will end up with a more effective organization.

West's proposed organization, shown in Exhibit 4, was based on the following concepts.

1. *A Regional Focus.* Each region would be a self-sustaining business unit, containing expertise in each of the required functional areas and would be headed by a strong general manager. Any investment decision over $5 million, however, would require the approval of the executive committee. Responsibility for national accounts (i.e., major customers whose operations span the country) will rest with the business unit in which the head office of the account is located.

2. *Head-Office Support.* Head-office support groups would deal directly with regional functional groups to ensure consistent policy application across the company. The business unit heads would cooperate with the Coordination and Development (C&D) support groups so as not to sacrifice the overall good of PCP for independent regional gains. The C&D group would be responsible for setting standards, procedures and policies for all of PCP, and for developing national programs, such as national television advertising.

3. *Integration.* Supporting mechanisms were to be developed to ensure strong integration and a "common culture" between the business units. This would include common systems and procedures.

Bill West offered the following assessment of his proposed organization:

It is unconventional in that it pushes responsibility for the bottom line to a lower level in the organization. Because of the way Petro-Canada has been formed, we have a unique opportunity to take advantage of the competition between the regions and the cultures therein to develop a very effective and efficient organization.

In favour of such an organization I see the advantages of better development of business leaders at lower levels in the organization, the development of a bottom-line motivation throughout the organization and good regional influence on the business. Such an organization should be able to react quickly to local needs in a business environment where competition is keen. I feel this is very important. Because of the leaning toward a fast-acting organization, we might not be able to put together as well-documented a long-range plan as we would with a more centralized organization. However, I think the work that would be done would be of higher quality since it should be more practical. Finally, I think this type of organization with less head-office people should be much more efficient than that used by our competitors.

On the other hand, such an organization may be a little more difficult to control and may require more travelling by the president in order to understand what is going on in each region of the country. By necessity it tends toward more of a matrix organization with functional leaders in the head office providing co-ordination of activities for such things as marketing and refining. With less focus on rapid development in functional areas, it will be up to the staff leaders in the central office to ensure that developments in each functional area are transmitted to the field as necessary.

Bill's main concern was how to staff the new organization. Although the acquisitions had resulted in duplication in some job areas, it was not clear that there was anyone in the company who would be able to perform some of the more senior roles in the proposed organization, as there would be significantly less control from the top than had been the case in either Fina or Pacific. For the positions which would require recruiting from outside the company, such as the head of C&D, Bill and John Lynch decided to try to hire high-calibre individuals who had a good reputation within the industry. John Lynch offered his views on the prospects of attracting such managers:

> Over the years I have often heard the majors talking about decentralizing their organizations, but none of them ever had enough conviction to really go for it. I think there might be a lot of managers out there who are somewhat frustrated with the traditional functional set up. The opportunity to organize it differently might have a lot of attraction for them.

In order to firmly establish the power base of the new senior vice-president of C&D, particularly *vis-à-vis* the regional business unit heads, Bill decided to call a meeting of all the regional heads, and issue a formal statement explaining that the senior vice-president of C&D had the most important job in the organization. This point would be reinforced by the following administrative changes:

1. In the absence of Bill West, the senior V.P. of C&D would chair the twice-monthly management meeting at which each region head would present his or her operating performance. The region with the best performance for the month would present first, second best would present second, and so on.

2. The senior V.P. of C&D would chair all functional committee meetings (i.e., meetings between support functions and regional functional areas), initially to be held bi-weekly and later monthly.

3. Five vice-presidents would report to the senior V.P. of C&D.

FINAL COMMENTS

Prior to taking his proposal to the executive committee, Bill discussed it informally with O'Brien, Stanford, Lynch, Lakusta and Hopper. The comments he received from Hopper and Lakusta are documented at the beginning of the case, the others follow.

David O'Brien—V.P., Finance & Planning

> It seems to me that the existing cultures in each of the acquired companies are too strong. There's a need to make everyone Petro-Canada people. You want them to be acting in the national company's best interests, not as regional strongholds. It's important that Petro-Canada be viewed as a national company. West is the guy with the experience in the downstream. I really don't know that much about it—but if it was up to me, I guess I would set it up functionally like the rest of the oil companies.

Jim Stanford—President, Petro-Canada Resources

> The advantage of going functionally is that you get rapid unification. On the other hand, the disadvantage is that economic assessment can only be done at the top. Then, if something fails, marketing blames supply and vice versa. There's a trade-off to be made.

John Lynch—V.P., Human Resources

> One of the disadvantages of going with a quasi-matrix design is the time required to set it up. It also makes it harder to decrease the individual culture bases to develop a Petro-Canada identity. And you'd have to worry about under-the-table competition between the regions. On the other hand, although it may be harder to set up initially, it may prove to be more profitable and better later on.

EXHIBIT 1   Petro-Canada Summary Data on Acquired Companies

	Atlantic Richfield Canada Ltd.	Pacific Petroleums Ltd.	BP Canada Petro Fina Canada Inc.	Marketing & Refining
Total assets ($000 000s)	132.5	1000	918	?
Former owner	Atlantic Richfield Company, U.S.A. (100%)	Philips Petroleum Company, U.S. (46%)	Petro Fina S.A. Belgium (51%)	British Petroleum Company, England (64%)
Year acquired	1976	1979	1981	(Expected: 1983)
Price	$343.4 million	$1.5 billion	$1.6 billion	(Expected: approx. $400 million)
Principal assets	• Oil and gas producing properties • Undeveloped oil and gas properties —Western Canada —Frontiers • Oil sands leases	• Oil and gas producing properties • Undeveloped oil and gas properties —Western Canada —Frontiers • Oil sands and coal leases • 9% int., Alsands Energy Ltd.	• Oil and gas producing properties • 5% Syncrude Canada Ltd. • 8% Alsands Energy Ltd. • Coal leases	
Refineries (crude)		Taylor, B.C. (2410 m³/d)	Montreal, Quebec (14 300 m³/d) Nfld. (Mothballed '76) (15 900 m³/d)	Oakville, Ontario (12 719 m³/d) Montreal, Quebec* (11 900 m³/d)
Number of retail marketing outlets		426 (West)	953 (East)	1 640 (Central)
Number of employees	400	1 100	3 000	2 200

* Planned closure for May, 1983.

EXHIBIT 2   Petro-Canada Five-Year Financial and Operating Summary

	1982	1981	1980	1979	1978
Summary of earnings ($000 000s)					
Revenue	$3 378	$2 715	$1 035	$ 766	$ 205
Expenses	3 071	2 286	716	513	128
	307	429	319	253	76
Add (deduct):					
Provision for income taxes	(188)	(225)	(155)	(121)	(42)
Gain on sale of subsidiary	7	—	—	—	—
Minority interest	4	—	—	(5)	(7)
Net earnings before preferred share dividends of subsidiary	130	203	163	126	27
Preferred share dividends of subsidiary	120	138	107	95	13
Net earnings after preferred share dividends of subsidiary	$ 10	$ 64	$ 55	$ 30	$ 13
Other financial data ($000 000s)					
Working capital provided from operations	$ 500	$ 526	$ 457	$ 357	$ 113
Capital expenditures	1 046	679	430	367	230
Petroleum Incentives Program grants	299	138	9	—	—
Acquisition of subsidiary companies	7	868	—	749	763
Total assets	7 552	6 612	3 766	3 411	3 348
Working capital	793	685	135	186	82
Long-term debt	330	1 312	283	329	337
Minority interest in subsidiaries	566	787	—	—	279
Preferred shares issued by a subsidiary	1 464	1 464	1 464	1 464	1 464
Shareholders' equity	3 341	1 640	1 114	978	802
Domestic daily production from oil and gas wells (net before royalties)					
—Crude oil and natural gas liquids (thousands of m³)	10.8	11.3	9.9	11.1	10.9
—Natural gas (millions of m³)	10.6	10.7	9.3	11.3	10.7
—Synthetic crude oil (thousands of m³)	2.3	2.1	1.5	1.2	—
Domestic proven reserves* (net before royalties)					
—Crude oil (millions of m³)	47.1	47.0	42.3	44.8	45.7
—Natural gas (billions of m³)	135.8	138.3	115.4	107.8	118.7
Marketing					
Sales volumes (millions of m³)					
—Gasoline and distillates	4.6	4.0	1.4	1.3	0.2
—Liquefied petroleum gases	1.3	1.2	1.2	1.2	0.2
Marketing outlets	1 605	1 504	407	420	426
Employees					
Number at December 31	6 166	5 801	2 823	2 246	2 038

Note: Financial and operating results are included from November 11, 1978, for the former Pacific Petroleums Ltd., for the former PetroFina Canada Inc. operations, and from May 1, 1982, for the operations of Panartic Oils Ltd.

* Excludes the company's share of Syncrude Project.

EXHIBIT 3 Partial Organization Chart of Petro-Canada Showing the "Downstream" as of January, 1983

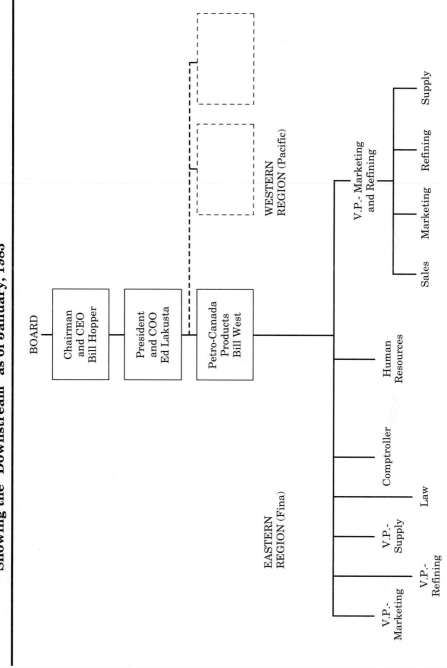

EXHIBIT 4 Proposed Organizational Structure for Petro-Canada Products, January 1983

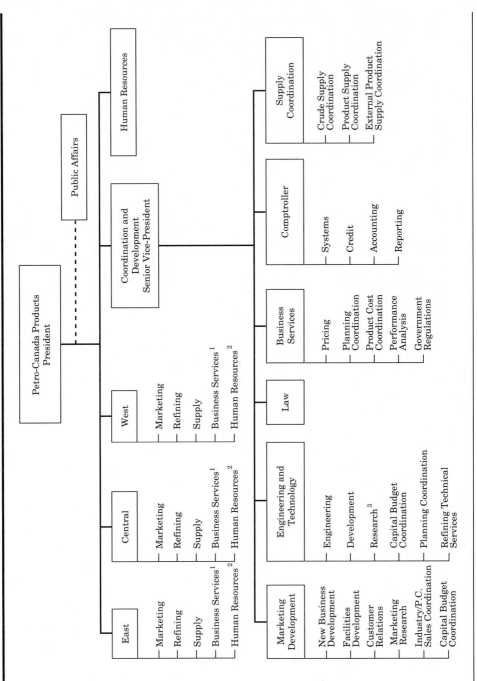

1 To report to C&D's Business Service.
2 To report to Human Resources V.P.
3 To work closely with counterparts in Petro-Canada Resources.

ATLANTIC PAPER COMPANY

J. Peter Killing

In January 1991, Jack Vickers was appointed President of the Atlantic Paper Company, Australia's largest producer of linerboard and brown paper. Atlantic was a wholly owned subsidiary of Cumberland Industries, and provided almost 50% of Cumberland's total sales volume, but its recent financial performance had not been encouraging. In spite of its historically dominant position in its businesses, the company had been losing market share to two smaller competitors since the early 1980s, and had also seen its markets shrink through the introduction of plastic products such as shrinkwrap and plastic check-out bags used in supermarkets. Vicker's predecessor Marcel Ruban had taken early retirement at age 55, having spent his last years in office struggling with unions and local governments in a successful but exhausting battle to close the company's smaller and less efficient paper mills.

Jack Vickers, age 40, had become a part of the Cumberland organization in 1988 when Cumberland acquired the Australian transport company of which he was majority owner and president. Vickers had founded the company in 1979, after completing his MBA in the United States. A series of well executed acquisitions in the early 1980s not only tripled the size of the trucking company, but earned Vickers the reputation of being a very shrewd financial operator whose eye was firmly fixed on the bottom line.

After the 1988 takeover, Vickers continued to manage what was now the transport division of Cumberland Industries, and joined the company's board of directors. The board included, among others, Cumberland's president and chief financial officer, and the presidents of its Atlantic Paper and Diamond Cement subsidiaries. Vickers was widely seen as an "up and comer" in the organization, but as time passed, it became clear that if he were to have a chance of becoming president of Cumberland, he would first have to successfully manage one or the other of Cumberland's two major subsidiaries. In late 1990, when Marcel Ruban's retirement was announced, Vickers was taken aside by the president of Cumberland and asked if he would take over Atlantic and "get the company back on track."

THE COMPANY

In 1988, Atlantic's head office staff moved out of Cumberland's downtown office tower to much more modest offices in Acton, a suburb 20 kilometres away. The instigators of the move were Jim Smythe and John Collins, two of Atlantic's vice-presidents. Jim Smythe explained:

> The distance between Cumberland's head office and ours is not far, but psychologically it's an important gap. Their head office is full of mahogany and plush carpets. Our relatively austere offices in Acton are much more appropriate for a company that has been closing mills and laying people off for the past three years.
>
> Another advantage of the move is that we have gained a little independence from Cumberland's president and financial people, most of whom used to work for Atlantic. They still like to tell us how to run the company. Also, we took the opportunity presented by the move to eliminate about 30 technical staff, who were necessary in our expansion stage, but aren't now.

As shown in Exhibit 1, Atlantic was a functionally organized company, with five vice-presidents reporting to the president. There were currently approximately 65 employees in the Acton head office, 60 in regional sales offices, and 2 500 spread across the company's four remaining mill sites. Within the past 18 months, employment had been reduced by approximately 800 people through mill and machine closings and head office cutbacks. Two hundred of these cuts had come in the last six months.

Each of the company's mill sites is described below.

The Northern Mill

The Northern Mill was Atlantic's largest. Built on a rural site in a timber growing area approximately 200 kilometres from Acton, the Northern Mill housed three pulp mills and three paper machines. Two of the pulp mills were relatively old and small, but the third was new and very large, and due to come on stream in late 1991. With the new mill in place the company's pulp capacity would more than triple. The new pulp mill was being financed "off balance sheet," which meant that Atlantic would make lease payments of approximately $15 million per year to the (related) company that would own the pulp mill. These fixed annual payments, beginning in 1991–92, would not vary with the mill's output.

Atlantic's paper machines were highly specialized, efficient at producing only a specific type of product. Two of the paper machines on the Northern site, N1 and N2, used virgin pulp and recycled wasted paper to produce brown paper, which was sold to paper bag makers. The third machine, N3, was the largest and most efficient machine the company owned. It was used to make linerboard, which was sold to manufacturers of corrugated boxes. The efficient operation of N3 was of such importance to the company that Chris Reid, the senior vice-president to whom the mills reported, was aware of its production on a daily basis, and even Marcel Ruban usually knew if there were any problems on N3.

Because of the complex interrelationships between the pulp mills and the paper machines, and the fact that these pulp mills supplied all of Atlantic's other mill sites, the Northern site was very difficult to run well. There would be, in fact, few sites as complex in the world, once the new pulp mill was operational.

Jim Smythe, who had successfully managed the Northern Mill in the 1980s when N3 was installed, was concerned that with the addition of the new pulp mill the job of managing the Northern Mill would be beyond the capabilities of any of Atlantic's managers. The successful operation of the new pulp mill was a high priority both because of its economic importance, and the fact that the decision to build it had been made by Hector Day, currently the president of Cumberland Industries. Smythe commented, "It was difficult enough managing that site in my day, now I wonder if we have anyone who can do it." Smythe himself was reported to have been one of the two most effective Northern Mill managers in Atlantic's history.

The Senator Mill

The Senator Mill was located about 20 kilometres from Acton on the edge of the city. It was a very old mill with two active paper machines, one of which produced linerboard, and the other brown paper. The Senator Mill was plagued by hostile labour relations, and had been the site of many industrial disputes. The mill seemed to be caught in a vicious circle: its poor industrial relations record had led to even more aggressive union behaviour. Few aspiring managers in Atlantic were eager to run the Senator Mill, and it was widely believed that the current manager had now proved beyond doubt that he could not handle the unions and would soon have to be replaced. Whether a new mill manager would prove any more successful was an open question.

The Lautrec Mill

The Lautrec Mill was furthest from Atlantic's head office, about 800 kilometres, and to some within the company that was sufficient explanation of why it was so well managed. The Lautrec Mill contained one paper machine, Atlantic's only machine that could produce white papers. However, the machine was very old, and was being run constantly at speeds well above its designed capacity levels. As a result, quality was suffering in a market in which quality was becoming ever more important. Ken Mauger, the mill manager, claimed that he was "hanging on by the skin of his teeth." He explained:

White papers is one of Atlantic's few markets that shows any growth at all. But the growth is in higher quality paper than we can make. Even for the low quality end of the market our product is marginal. We are very vulnerable. We clearly need a new paper machine. The cost will be high (about $80 million) but this company has to build a future for itself.

The Johansson Mill

In 1991 the Johansson Mill was also a single machine mill, although as recently as 1989 it had housed three machines. Located in a major urban centre, the mill specialized in the conversion of recycled waste paper (plus a little pulp) into low-grade linerboards. Formerly the site of many industrial relations problems the mill now appeared to be stable and running without major problems.

VICKERS' FIRST WEEKS

Jack Vickers' first two weeks at Acton were devoted to meeting his senior management team, and reviewing the company's past and projected financial performance. One of the first documents he read was the company's five-year plan, dated October 1990, excerpts of which follow. He was not surprised to learn that Atlantic had met Cumberland's target of a 17.5% return on funds employed only once in the past five years, or that the most recent financial year, ended June 30, 1990, had come in at 6.7% (Exhibit 2). He was, however, startled to discover that Atlantic's plan showed that the 17.5% target would not be met in the foreseeable future.

Vickers discovered that the prime author of the five-year plan was Jim Smythe, and that much of its content was the result of a three-man task force which Smythe had headed up over a recent six-month period. Alarmed at the company's apparently bleak future, Smythe had formed the group on his own initiative, involving the market services manager and a senior accountant. The three-man group met widely with customers, suppliers, personnel in Atlantic's mills, and gathered what data they could about the competition. Jim Smythe described the results to Jack Vickers as follows:

> Our conclusion was that there was no reason to be optimistic about the future of this company. Our five-year plan may not look too good to you Jack, as an outsider, but believe me if we sit here and do nothing our future is going to be lot worse than this. Even meeting these projections is going to be a big job.
>
> Let me give you one example of the kinds of problems we face. Fibrebox Ltd. is our largest single customer. It's a well run, aggressive, growing company. They have just bought a new paper machine which will allow them to recycle their own waste. They don't need pulp to make low quality linerboard, and their box plants are now big enough that their own waste, combined with

some purchased scrap paper are sufficient to supply a 40 000 ton per year machine. One of the things our task force did was to calculate Fibrebox's return on investment on that new machine. It's about 45%! There is nothing we can do in terms of pricing or anything else to make that into a bad investment for them. So we're going to lose 35 000–40 000 tons next year.

We have two other big linerboard customers. Are they going to just sit and watch? So far they have done nothing, but how soon will they act?

Excerpts from Atlantic's Five-Year Plan

We have set ourselves a profitability objective of 17.5% earnings before interest and tax on total assets.

This is high compared to earlier achievements. Over the past 11 years our return before interest and taxes on total assets has ranged from 4.4% in 1982 to 18.5% in 1987. Achievement of our aim is made more difficult because of our recent $67 million investment in forest lands that currently does not yield any significant return. Our total forest assets comprise $156 million of the total funds employed in 1990/91 of $541 million, rising to $178 million out of a total of $550 million in 1995.

A 17.5% return is higher than the average return achieved by each of the various industry sectors in this country and would put us in the top 75 performers of all listed companies. This may be ambitious but we consider it an appropriate aim which will highlight the question of idle assets.

The financial projections in the five-year plan (summarized) were as follows:

Earnings Forecast, Years Ending June 30 (millions of dollars)

	1991	1991	1993	1994	1995
Sales	420	425	470	514	585
Profits before interest and tax	55	48[1]	70	73	89
Net profit	38	27	37	40	48
Total assets[2]					
PBIT as a percentage of funds employed	10.2%	8.7	12.8	13.4	16.2
Deliveries Forecast (thousands of tons)					
Base forecast	587	576	577	572	578
Backward integration of Fibrebox Ltd.	–	(39)	(50)	(50)	(50)
"Super Pulp" project	–	(38)	(38)	(38)	(38)
New white paper products	–	–	9	22	41
Exports	45	50	50	50	50
Total	632	549	548	556	581

[1] Profit decline due to start up of a new pulp mill.
[2] Major asset changes were the projected white paper investment and a mill closure due to the super pulp project.

This conversation triggered a series of meetings to discuss the five-year plan which lasted most of Vickers third week in the company. These meetings included Bill Leroy, Vice-President of Finance, and John Collins, Vice-President of Marketing, in addition to Vickers and Smythe. Although invited to the meetings, Chris Reid put in only a minimal appearance, explaining that he had urgent issues that had to be dealt with at the Northern Mill. The meetings touched on a wide variety of topics, and it was clear to Vickers by the end of the week that three major initiatives were being proposed to him, none of which had yet been presented to Cumberland management. These were the white papers project, the super pulp project, and the reorganization of the company. All appeared to have had their origins in Jim Smythe's task force.

THE WHITE PAPERS PROJECT

Jim Smythe explained the origin and rationale of the white papers project:

> Ken Mauger, the manager of the Lautrec Mill, had been telling us for a couple of years that we're missing out on a growth market in copier and computer paper because we can't produce the right qualities of white paper. We haven't paid too much attention because the capital required to produce the necessary quality seemed to be prohibitive.
>
> Several things have prompted us to reconsider. One is that this company can no longer afford to overlook any growing markets in related business. Another is that it looks like we're going to have to reinvest $20 million or so to upgrade Ken's existing machine, just to let him hang on to the market he's got. Maybe we should spend an extra $60 million to increase his capacity and let him produce these other grades.
>
> The task force commissioned a market research study on the white papers market which concluded that there is a market worth going after, and we think we can get 90 000 tons of new business in this area within four or five years of arriving on the market, if we get serious about it. In our geographic area Benson Industries is the only major company in the business, and its customers tell us that they would welcome a second reputable supplier.

Vickers learned that the white papers project had not yet reached the official proposal stage. No one, for instance, had contacted equipment suppliers to get exact prices, developed an in-depth marketing plan or worked out the financial implications of the proposal in other than a fairly rough fashion. Some back of the envelope calculations suggested that the financial return on the project might be in the range of 25–30% before tax. Smythe indicated that he was reluctant to talk to equipment suppliers until Cumberland's board indicated that it was willing to change its long standing policy of not competing directly with Benson Industries. Benson and Atlantic were approximately of equal size. Benson was dominant in white paper markets, and Atlantic in linerboard and brown paper.

THE "SUPER PULP" PROJECT

The super pulp idea was created about eight months before Vicker's arrival by the members of Smythe's task force. The idea, which was to use much more pulp and much less recycled waste paper in the company's linerboards, had been debated by the senior management group ever since. Technical trials carried out in the interim indicated that making super pulp linerboard would not be a problem. The company could do it. The question was whether or not it should.

The attraction of the super pulp project was that it might solve three problems at once.

Firstly, by increasing the company's need for pulp, the project would mean that Atlantic's new pulp mill would be run at capacity. Without the project it would run at 75% of capacity, primarily because the demand projections put together when the mill was planned had been too optimistic. Selling excess pulp to other companies was not a viable option as the market was poor and Atlantic's pulp was wet, which meant it was expensive to transport. Running the pulp mill below capacity would reduce its efficiency, and would mean that the large lease payment might not be offset by increased earnings.

Secondly, if the firm were to switch to super pulp linerboards, it would produce fewer tons of linerboard per year even while producing the same area. This was because the new linerboards would be thinner and lighter than existing ones of the same strength. Thus even though a square metre of linerboard would cost more to produce (as the variable cost of pulp was about 20% higher than that of recycled paper), total costs could be reduced because less machine time would be required to produce the linerboard. In practice this meant that if Atlantic switched to super pulp linerboards the Senator Mill could be closed. The net saving would be approximately $6 million per year, and the continual headaches associated with the mill would be ended.

Finally, the introduction of the super pulp linerboard might slow down the inroads which Atlantic's two smaller competitors had been making into the linerboard market. (Atlantic's market share had fallen from approximately 70% to 50% over the past seven or eight years.) Neither of these companies had access to pulp, and there was no way that either of them could produce a super pulp linerboard in the foreseeable future. If super pulp linerboard became the norm for all but the lowest grades of linerboard, these two firms would be restricted to the bottom end of the market, which was where plastic products such as shrinkwrap were making inroads and margins were the lowest.

John Collins told Vickers that he was not particularly impressed by these arguments. He commented:

> This is a production and finance driven initiative. Our customers, the box-makers, aren't asking for it. Neither are their customers, the end users. Not much of the market really cares about box performance in a major way. Most of the time it's just a question of price. We're talking now about introducing super pulp liners at a 3% cheaper price per square metre than normal linerboard. That's a joke, because as soon as we do our competitors will put their prices 3% below ours, just as they always have.
>
> What this product could do is create a lot of confusion in the market, and we could be the big losers. We're better off to stay away from it.

Bill Leroy countered Collins' final argument by stating that the paper machines of both of Atlantic's linerboard competitors were currently at capacity, and that it would be impossible for them to take advantage of any confusion in the market. He also liked the fact that no capital investment would be required. Leroy supported the initiative, and thought its timing was ideal.

Another argument that Vickers heard concerning the super pulp project was that, by withdrawing from the wastepaper market, Atlantic would lower prices of industrial waste paper and thus help out their competitors, who placed heavy reliance on such waste. On the domestic waste collection side, some managers argued that the large wastepaper collection trucks with "Atlantic" written on the side were a significant source of goodwill for the company, necessary to offset their image in environmental circles as a company primarily interested in cutting down trees, raping the forests, and so on.

REORGANIZATION

Jim Smythe had sent an eight-page handwritten memo to Marcel Ruban shortly before he retired, suggesting that Atlantic be reorganized into four product divisions. Because of Ruban's impending retirement, of which Smythe was unaware, no action had been taken. Smythe explained the proposal to John Vickers.

> One of the conclusions that I came to as a result of our task force investigation was that Atlantic would perform much better if separate groups of people focused on each of our three product areas, and a fourth group concentrated

on making pulp. Right now we all spend a lot of time worrying about liner-board because it has the largest sales volume, but a lot of important issues in the other businesses slip by unnoticed.

The marketing group, for instance, spends all its time thinking about Fibrebox and our other two big linerboard customers, but we know very little, as the market research study revealed, about white papers. I am certain that this is also true of brown papers. Also, we have always used the same salesforce to sell all three product lines, but we could do much better with one for each product.

The biggest improvement, I have no doubt, would come from having a general manager looking after each business. Maybe we could eventually pay bonuses based on product group performance. Right now everyone here is on straight salary.

Smythe's memo contained the proposed organization charts which are shown in Exhibits 3 and 4. It also listed some further advantages and some disadvantages of his proposed reorganization.

Other Advantages

- Each product group would get more individual attention, which in turn should give faster reactions, better digestion of market intelligence, more thought to product performance and profitability, and less complex product development.
- Bringing marketing and manufacturing closer together may reduce some of the present counter productive activity.
- Promising staff members can be more readily exposed to broader business concerns, and be offered general management experience earlier in their careers.
- Reorganization may change the market's view of Atlantic as a slow moving monolith.
- Current head office staff (engineering, technical, industrial relations) can be moved to the Northern Mill where their involvement in mill operations will be useful. Other mills needing technical assistance can seek it from Northern.
- Reorganization will reduce numbers at head office by rationalization and reduction of one level of management.

Disadvantages

- More flexible attitudes will be required at the Northern Mill, Senator Mill, regional sales offices, and head office.

- This is a radical change to the traditional marketing and operations organizations. Change will be neither easy nor pleasant.
- Mill managers at Northern and Senator Mills will become site managers, responsible for managing the site, but not the product mix or output.
- The four groups are not of even size.
- Some additional marketing/sales staff may be required.

After reading Smythe's memo, Vickers asked him to elaborate on the probable reaction of Atlantic's senior employees to such an organizational change. Smythe replied:

> Neither the senior marketing nor the senior operations people will support this move because it means breaking up their big functional groups. The mill managers, for instance, have long been the 'kings' in this organization. With this plan, machine managers would report directly to their own product group. On multimachine sites like Northern and Senator the machine managers would also have a dotted line relationship to the site manager, who would be responsible for insuring that the site was properly run.
>
> Managers without an organizational axe to grind, like Bill Leroy, believe that this is an excellent idea. (Vickers later confirmed that this was indeed the case.)

THE FOURTH WEEK

On the Monday of his fourth week in Acton, Vickers received the financial report for the six months ending December 31, 1990 (Exhibit 5). It did not make good reading. In spite of the fact that sales were as budgeted (which meant that the company had made an 8% price increase stick, its first in several years), profit before tax was only 68% of budget. Even with what looked like some creative tax accounting, earnings after tax would show less than a 10% return on shareholders equity.

In discussing this report with Chris Reid, Vickers learned that the fundamental problem was that N3, the big linerboard machine, had not been operating efficiently. Reid had made some personnel changes, but to no avail. He now wanted to bring in a very experienced "hands-on", American papermaker for two years to get the machine operating well and to raise the skill level of the machine crews. He had found such a man—but he was asking more in salary than any of Atlantic's vice-presidents were earning. This was a result of the fact, Vickers discovered, that when the man's current employer learned he was talking to Atlantic, they gave him an immediate 30% raise. Vickers told Chris Reid he would "think it over and get back to him."

Reid's request, on which he wanted to quick answer, pushed Vickers to the conclusion that it was time to decide what changes he wanted to make at Atlantic, and how he should go about them. He did not want to start making ad hoc decisions on single issues which, when added together, would make little sense.

The problem was where to start and how fast to move. In considering Jim Smythe's reorganization plan, for example, Vickers could not see how he could find four general managers in an organization that had no one with general management experience it. After living with Atlantic's senior managers for a month, he felt he could bet on Jim Smythe and Bill Leroy as good potential general managers, but as for the rest, he wasn't sure.

EXHIBIT 1 Atlantic Paper Company Organization Chart

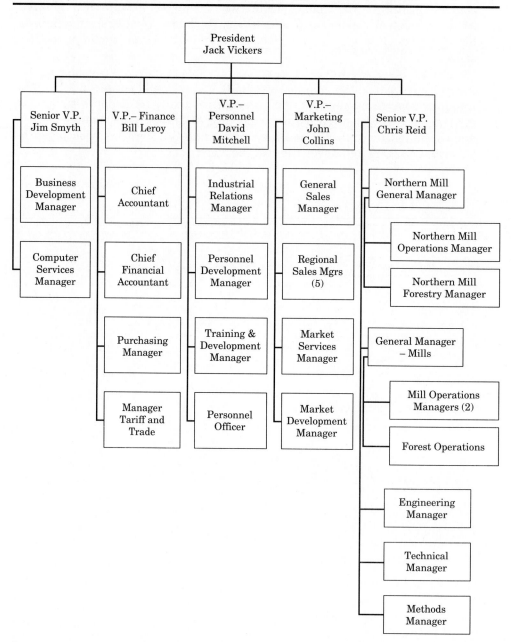

EXHIBIT 2   Atlantic Paper Company Summary Statements

12 months ending June 30		1990		1989
Earnings ($000)	*Budget*	*Actual*		*Actual*
Net sales	$ 445 420	$ 397 630		$ 420 058
Gross earnings before depreciation	94 470	68 840		92 391
Less: Depreciation	22 000	21 550		20 789
Overheads	11 670	10 960		10 514
Earnings before interest and tax	60 800	36 330		61 088
Less: Interest	11 600	7 790		10 304
Earnings before tax	49 200	28 540		50 784
Less: Income tax charge	13 400	7 030		20 759
Net earnings after tax	$ 35 800	$ 21 510		$ 30 025

Other Information

Earnings before interest and tax as a percentage of funds employed	11.2%	6.7%		12.9%
Gross margins (based on earnings before depreciation and overheads)	21.2%	17.3%		22.0%
Deliveries (tons)	685 000	640 296		715 476
Average selling price ($ per ton)	650.2	621.0		587.1
Average cost ($ per ton)	560.9	564.2		501.7

EXHIBIT 3 Atlantic Paper Company
Jim Smythe's Proposed Organization Chart

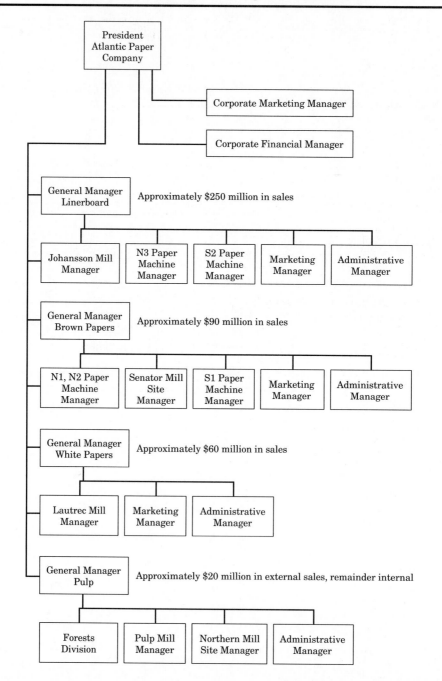

**EXHIBIT 4 Atlantic Paper Company
Jim Smythe's Proposed Corporate Marketing
Organization**

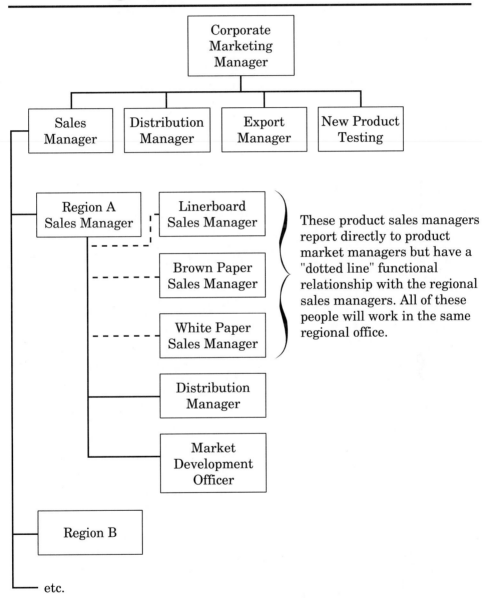

EXHIBIT 5 Atlantic Paper Company Six-Month Financial Results

6 months ending December 31		1990	1989
Earnings ($000)	*Budget*	*Actual*	*Actual*
Net sales	$ 211 550	$ 217 600	$ 214 210
Gross earnings before depreciation	51 120	40 860	39 380
Less: Depreciation	12 950	11 830	11 660
Overheads	5 950	6 190	6 130
Earnings before interest and tax	32 220	22 840	21 590
Less: Interest	4 690	4 090	3 780
Earnings before tax	27 530	18 750	17 810
Less: Income tax charge	4 920	10	3 690
Net earnings after tax	$ 22 610	$ 18 740	$ 14 120

Other Information

Annualized earnings before interest and tax as a percentage of funds employed	11.9%	8.4%	7.9%
Gross margins (based on earnings before depreciation and overheads)	24.2%	18.8%	18.4%
Deliveries (tons)	323 000	326 240	346 680
Average selling price ($ per ton)	654.9	666.9	617.8
Average cost ($ per ton)	555.2	596.9	555.6

KETTLE CREEK CANVAS COMPANY —1985 (A)

Joseph N. Fry and Robert G. Blunden

It was April 1985. Mellanie Stephens was sitting in her natural-pine office, bare feet on a desk she had built from a sewing machine cabinet, gazing out her window to the point where the Kettle Creek emptied into Lake Erie. Once again she had just managed to cover the day's outstanding cheques. Tomorrow she would face the problem again. But this was nothing new; it was the way things always seemed to be at kettle Creek.

"It doesn't make sense," Mellanie mused to herself, "Here I am running a business that is more successful than I ever dreamed and I have more problems than ever. I can't go on like this; it just isn't fun any more. Either I get this business running smoothly so I can spend my time on the important things or I have to get out."

COMPANY BACKGROUND

The Kettle Creek Canvas Company (Kettle Creek) was located in the quiet fishing village of Port Stanley, Ontario on the shores of Lake Erie. Port Stanley had a permanent population of about 1900 which increased to 10 000 in the summer months as city folk moved to their cottages and took advantage of the area's beaches.

Mellanie Stephens was born and brought up on Port Stanley. The youngest of eight children, she dropped out of high school after grade eleven and travelled for a while. Never holding the same job for more than nine months, she tried her hand at truck gardening, cooking in a bush camp and retail sales, among other things. At the age of 26, Mell, as her friends called her, found herself back in Port Stanley without a job, but with the realization that she could make more money working for herself than for someone else. A friend showed her an expensive quilt that she had just bought and Mell realized she could make one at least as well; and at those prices make a good dollar. So she started making quilts for a nearby store. When, having outgrown her apartment, she rented a yacht broker's basement, sailors attracted by the sewing machine noise asked her to make canvas bags for them. Before long she was making as many bags as quilts and decided to open her own store. Six banks turned her down before a friend guaranteed a $15 000 loan to get the business started.

Mellanie had planned to call the business the Kettle Creek Canvas Bag Company after the creek that ran through the town, but the sign painter convinced her to drop the word "Bag." Embarrassed by the many empty shelves as opening day approached, Mellanie made some simple drawstring pants and matching tops to fill the space. By 3 p.m. on that first day in May 1979 everything was sold out; and the clothing had gone first. The Kettle Creek Canvas Company was in business and simple cotton clothing was leading the way.

Initially Mellanie sewed all week, opened the store on the weekends, sold everything produced and started the cycle again on Monday. But she couldn't produce enough to keep up with demand. To expand production while maintaining the homemade appearance, Mellanie turned to home sewers—local women who would sew garments together in their own homes. But real growth required more than capacity expansion; it required an expanded product line. And an expanded product line in turn necessitated professional design skills.

Mellanie found those skills in David MacDonnell, a recent graduate of Fanshawe College. MacDonnell translated Mellanie's concepts into the designs that were to drive the success of Kettle Creek. The theme unifying the product line was a casual look delivered by garments that were classic in style, simple in structure, and easy to wear. Each item was designed with both function and attractiveness in mind and was made of 100% cotton fabric. The line was characterized by the use of bold primary colours. The items, fabrics and colours were designed to facilitate mixing and matching to produce different looks and to appeal to a broad range of buyers and ages. Garments were designed to be loose and easy fitting, adding to their versatility and comfort. All products carried a distinctive and highly visible brand badge with the name "The Kettle Creek Canvas Co." Representative Kettle Creek products are shown in Exhibit 1.

The Kettle Creek products found ready acceptance and the company grew rapidly. By the end of 1979 a second store was opened in London and in 1980 a third store in Toronto. Although demand for the product was clearly evident in each market that Kettle Creek entered, further expansion was limited by the financial resources of the firm. There appeared to be two primary alternatives: sell to mass merchandisers of franchise. The decision was made to go the franchise route; it would bring in immediate cash as franchise rights were sold and allow Kettle Creek more control over the product and its distribution. The first franchise opened in December 1981; by 1985 Kettle Creek had grown to 36 outlets, of which 32 were franchised and 4 were completely or partially company owned. The sales growth was soon followed by substantial profits. Table 1 provides a summary of both sales and profits for the firm.

TABLE 1 Kettle Creek Sales and Profit Summary

	Sales ($000s)	Profit After Tax ($000s)
1979	38	N/A
1980	129	N/A
1981	194	(16)
1982	927	89
1983	2 030	204
1984	3 324	202

KETTLE CREEK'S CUSTOMERS, PRODUCT LINE AND COMPETITION

The industry in which Kettle Creek operated had grown rapidly in the late 1970s and early 1980s. For example, shipments of Canadian-manufactured women's clothing had doubled in value between 1974 and 1982. While only about 5% of the garments were cotton in 1982 cotton garments were growing more rapidly than other fabrics and were becoming an increasingly important segment of the women's clothing industry.

Social trends to smaller, dual-income families with higher disposable incomes had contributed to the growth, as had the apparent desire of buyers to purchase goods that closely reflected their lifestyles. These trends had led to an increased fragmentation of tastes and consumer demand for clothing. Opportunities in these new niche markets fuelled rapid increases in the number of fashion concepts and brand names in the market. Success in this market was heavily dependent upon product positioning; target niches, brand image and distribution strategy were the primary positioning variables.

Customers

The Kettle Creek customer was not easily identified in demographic terms. Kettle Creek products were sold to all age groups. A recently added children's-wear line was selling well. Teenagers made up a significant number of purchasers, primarily buying bags and the traditional Kettle Creek clothing, with its highly visible tags. Middle-class and upper middle-class women, and to a lesser extent men, made most of the purchases. And older retired persons, again primarily women, bought and wore a significant portion of Kettle Creek is so versatile it looks great on everybody. They are the only clothes in my daughter's wardrobe that I can wear without being 'way out' and yet my mother wears some Kettle Creek fashions. You can't say that about many products."

Management and franchises alike believed that Kettle Creek fashions had something to offer each of those groups. For children, Kettle Creek products were thought to offer durability, ease of care and a sizing system that provided lots of room to grow. Kettle Creek products were "in" with some teen groups. For adults the garments were comfortable and of high quality, fashionable without being too trendy and very flexible in how they were worn. The elderly or hard to fit individual was thought to be well served by the comfort of the loose fit in a fashionable garment.

Possibly the best way of describing Kettle Creek customers was by the benefits they sought: comfortable, durable, natural clothing of high quality, sold in a straightforward manner, by a store that cared about them and stood behind their products.

Product Line

The Kettle Creek product line consisted of two major categories; goods manufactured by Kettle Creek and items purchased for resale. The internally manufactured items included tops, blouses, pants, skirts, dresses, coats, jackets, bags and accessories. The externally sourced items included 100% cotton sweaters, leather belts, bags and accessories and jewelry. Table 2 provides forecast sales by major product categories and additional data on the product line for 1985.

TABLE 2   The Kettle Creek Product Line: Forecasts for 1985

Products	Number of Styles	Wholesale Price Range	Units (000s)	Value ($ 000s)	Average Price	% of Sales
Manufactured						
Clothing	45	$12–64	163.3	$4 378	$27	85
Bags	14	3–23	69.5	444	6	8
Purchased for resale						
Sweaters	3	38–55	2.7	122	45	2
Leather	12	3–33	20.5	164	8	3
Jewelry	16	7–33	4.0	57	14	2
All goods		$3–64	260.0	$5 165	$20	100

Kettle Creek's product line had evolved and broadened under David MacDonnell, but remained in keeping with Mellanie's original concept. Table 3 illustrates the overall growth in the line. New items were introduced at either the spring or fall shows, and about 30% of the line changed each year.

TABLE 3 Kettle Creek Product Line Growth, Manufactured Clothing Products, 1979–85

	Styles	Colours	Sizes	SKU's*
1979	7	1	3	21
1980	7	6	6	234
1981	7	6	6	234
1982	7	6	6	234
1983	25	10	6	1 367
1984	35	14	6	2 765
1985 (Forecast)	45	14	6	3 515

* Stock keeping units were not the simple product of styles, colours and sizes because not all items were produced in all colours and sizes.

Mellanie's plans for future additions to the product line included: (1) the expanded use of purchased and internally developed prints to supplement the solid coloured garments, (2) introduction of pre-shrunk fabrics permitting development of a more tailored look in some fashions, (3) a line of "rough wear" described as "kids clothing for adults" and (4) additions of outerwear, footwear and hats.

In all the product decisions quality was a prime consideration. Garments were not designed to meet predetermined price points, but rather to be comfortable and functional as dictated by the Kettle Creek concept. A typical Kettle Creek manufactured clothing garment that retailed for $54 was sold to franchises at a 50% discount for $27. that same garment's direct manufacturing cost was about $16, made up as follows: direct material, 50% and direct labour, 50%. All retail prices were rounded to even dollars. The Kettle Creek guarantee was complete and simple, "If our quality does not measure up to your expectations, return the garment for repair, replacement or refund."

Competition

The retailing of apparel had changed with the market and the industry had become highly segmented at the retail level. The many individual competitors could be grouped into three major classes: (1) specialty chains, (2) traditional department stores and (3) independent local outlets.

Several types of specialty chains existed. Some were controlled by garment manufacturers, others were franchise operations, but most were distinct corporate retail operations. Some corporations operated single chains while others owned many differently positioned retailers. For example, the largest specialty apparel retailer in Canada was Dylex, with more than 1 000 stores. Dylex sold women's clothing through Fairweather, Braemar, L.A. Express, Harry Rosen Women, Town and Country, Petites, Suzy Shier and other stores. Dylex men's wear was sold through Tip Top, Big Steel Man and Harry Rosen.

The traditional department stores, such as Eaton's, Simpsons and The Bay, sold clothing through their concept boutiques and regular departments but had lost market share to the specialty chains and independent specialty retailers in recent years.

At the manufacturers' level, too, the apparel industry was fragmented and competitive. While there were more than 2 300 clothing manufacturers in Canada, many of the garments sold by Canadian retailers came from international sources. Economies of scale were not significant for most garments because retailers or marketing companies often assembled the product line and developed the brand in the marketplace. Fabric was readily available from large, cost-efficient suppliers.

Nevertheless, there were exceptions. Some manufacturers developed their own brands—Levi, Haggar, Arrow and Stanfield for example. And for some types of garments, such as jeans and knitted clothing, economies of scale were significant. The following examples give an idea of the variety of concepts and competitors.

Polo/Ralph Lauren

The Polo/Ralph Lauren line of upscale men's and women's wear was sold in North America through 48 franchised Polo shops, 132 department store boutiques and 16 discount outlets. Although the product line ranged from clothing to fragrances to furniture, men's clothing was its base. The men's-wear line varied from casual blue jeans to elegantly styled suits, all at premium prices. In Lauren's words, the central concept was "originality, but always with integrity and a respect for tradition."

Benetton

The Italian sweater manufacturer sold its line through 2 000 exclusive franchised outlets worldwide. It produced fashionable but casual knitted garments in bright colours. Benetton garments were predominantly made of natural fibres. Agents were given large retail territories and encouraged to develop the areas themselves, or by adding others who shared the "Benetton way of thinking." Franchises did not pay royalties, but agreed to sell Benetton products exclusively, and adhere to suggested markups. Benetton, as the manufacturer, made its money on the supply of merchandise rather than on royalties.

Roots

This company, too, was a specialty retailing success story. Starting with shoes, it had expanded its product line to include a broad range of activewear and sweatwear, targeted primarily at teenagers. In keeping with its faddish image among the high school set, most garments displayed large Roots logos. The Roots cut was best described as "oversize." Roots' prices placed it in the moderate to premium price-range. Their 19 Canadian and 10 U.S. outlets included both company owned stores and franchised outlets.

North by Northwest

North by Northwest was a recent, independent addition to the Canadian specialty apparel business. Its single outlet, located in London, Ontario, sold a mix of moderate to premium priced outdoors wear. Clothing for men, women and children ranged from safari styles to sweatwear to specialized hiking and climbing apparel.

Other speciality apparel brands and retailers active in Canada included Ports, Tabi, Le Château, Lindor, The Frat House, Beaver Canoe, Penningtons, Madame Angelo, Senor Angelo and others, both chains and independent local stores. There were no apparent limits to the number of market segments, or to the imagination of entrepreneurs in sensing and targeting them.

In all of this, Kettle Creek management saw no direct competitors, in part because they thought of the Kettle Creek concept as more than the product itself. In their view, Kettle Creek was unique in its philosophy, its approach to the marketplace and its franchise network.

THE FRANCHISE NETWORK

Franchising had been a key to Kettle Creek's growth. The company's success and high media profile had made it relatively easy to attract franchises. Franchise territories sold for between $20 000 and $25 000; but by 1985 there were few territories remaining in Canada. The scope of the franchise network is illustrated in Exhibit 2. Most future Canadian growth was expected to come from additional stores within existing territories and increased sales per outlet.

In exchange for the franchise fee, Kettle Creek provided the franchisee with a protected geographic territory, and assistance in site selection, store layout and merchandising. An in-house Kettle Creek crew installed leasehold improvements and store fixtures using a common rough-plank and pine-trim decor. Leasehold improvements were billed to the franchisee at Kettle Creek's cost. Outlets ranged in size from 450 to 1 500 square feet with the majority of stores being approximately 800 square feet.

Franchisees were obliged to purchase all merchandise from Kettle Creek and maintain certain operating standards, such as hours of operation, inventory levels, reporting requirements and minimum order size. Kettle Creek also approved the franchisee's local advertising and display.

Kettle Creek franchises were an enthusiastic lot; they were active in the daily operations of their businesses and they believed in the Kettle Creek product and concept. Like many of their customers they identified with Kettle Creek and the lifestyle it represented. They also had good reason to believe in the concept and be enthusiastic; most outlets were profitable and considered successful by their owners. In a few cases the success was extraordinary. However, there were also some outlets experiencing difficulty. Kettle Creek management attributed their poor performance to either inadequate financing or poor locations.

There were some areas of tension between the franchisees and the firm. One potential problem area was the ordering system. Franchisees could only order twice a year, at the spring and fall shows. If they found that a particular colour or item was selling better than anticipated and wanted to order more they could not. In an effort to ease the effect of not being able to draw on Kettle creek inventories, the franchisees cooperated extensively among themselves, selling each other stock when possible. In fact, the transactions were even made via the Kettle Creek accounting system. The Kettle Creek ordering policy had developed in this manner for two reasons: (1) the 12- to 16-week lead times Kettle Creek faced for purchasing fabric necessitated significant advance planning and (2) the success of the Kettle Creek line meant that the franchisees were unwilling to rock the boat as long as they were selling everything they got.

A related and annoying problem for franchisees was that they never knew what was being shipped, when, or in what quantity. Goods were shipped against standing orders as produced and could arrive at less than opportune times. In some stores some items might be in excess while in others they were unavailable.

Advertising was another area of concern. Since local market conditions and franchise target markets varied considerably from outlet to outlet, some franchisees felt that the corporate advertising program did not meet their needs as well as it could.

THE KETTLE CREEK BUSINESS SYSTEM

The business system at Kettle Creek was simple and efficient for the firm, even if it was less flexible in response than some franchisees might have preferred.

A new garment started as a sketch on the designer's pad. Fabric was chosen, samples were made and final design details confirmed. The garment was then presented at either the spring or fall show and orders were taken. At this point sufficient fabric was ordered to produce the required garments. As the fabrics were received the garments were produced and shipped immediately to franchisees for retail sale.

From Kettle Creek's perspective the system was ideal. Major risks in ordering fabric were avoided by having firm orders from the franchisees. Fabric inventories were minimized by shipping and invoicing garments to the franchisees immediately upon the completion. Production efficiencies were maximized and the process kept simple by cutting large quantities of a single garment at one time.

The continued success of Kettle Creek's simple and effective business system depended upon its continued acceptability to the franchisees. In effect it precluded Kettle Creek from selling through department stores or other retail chains which, in general, would not accept such ordering and delivery terms.

Production

Most company operations were housed in a refurbished herring processing plant, the "fish house," in Port Stanley. Its approximately 13 000 square foot area was home to Kettle Creek's factory operations, finished goods and raw materials storage areas, as well as a retail outlet, executive offices and a design centre.

The production process consisted of the following sequential steps: (1) raw material sourcing; (2) pattern and marker making; (3) fabric layout and cutting; (4) garment bundling and invoicing; (5) in-house serging; (6) contract sewing off premises; (7) in-house finishing; (8) quality control inspection; and (9) shipping.

Material was purchased from one of two sources: a Toronto supplier, or manufacturers in the Far East represented locally by a broker. The Canadian manufactured fabrics were sent to Montreal for dyeing after they were ordered. Lead times for delivery from both sources were approximately 12 to 16 weeks.

Fabric was spread out on a 48-foot cutting table, 150 to 225 plies deep, depending on the fabric's weight. A cutting market, containing the garment patterns in all sizes, was fastened to the top of the fabric and then the pile was cut by hand, using electric knives. The cut pieces were bundled into sewing units. Necessary trims (zippers etc.) were included, and a four-part sewer invoice outlining the batch's description, quantity, piece rate and total wholesale value was attached.

In-house serging involved sewing the cut edge to prevent fraying. The home sewers collected their bundles and returned previously sewn garments about once a week. Returned garments were finished in the factory with buttonholes, buttons and any additional final touches required. The finished garments were inspected in quality control and passed goods were invoiced and shipped to the retail outlets daily by an express carrier.

The home sewers were a critical link in the production process. Manufacturing at Kettle Creek had evolved around the home sewers for four reasons. First, management believed that the quality of the home sewn product was superior to that of a garment produced in a traditional factory because they believed that independent sewers assembling a complete garment took greater pride in their work than typical assembly-line workers. Second, home sewing had enabled the firm to avoid the significant investment in plant, equipment, fringe benefits and overhead that would have otherwise been required. Third, home sewing provided additional production flexibility to the firm. Fourth, the home-sewn craftlike nature of the product had become an important part of the Kettle Creek product; factory-produced garments. Luckily, there appeared to be no limit to the availibility of home sewers. Whenever the call for more home sewers went out through the network of existing sewers, as many as were required materialized. The only practical constraint appeared to be Kettle Creek's capacity to manage and organize them.

The home sewers' piece rates were based upon a standard hourly rate of $6, although there was some question as to how precisely they had been determined. Almost all of the home sewers were Asians and recent immigrants to Canada. Many had poor English skills which, together with their home-bound young children, limited their alternative employment prospects. Home sewing permitted caring for the children and a weekly income of approximately $225 to $275, more than they cold make in most other jobs.

The separation of tasks between home sewers and factory workers was based upon the machinery required. Home sewers had industrial sewing machines which they bought at cost from Kettle Creek and performed all tasks suitable to those machines. Tasks such as serging, buttonhole making and attaching buttons required specialized machines and were completed in the factory.

The commitment to home sewing limited garment design and precluded the use of sewing techniques not easily performed on existing home sewing equipment. David MacDonnell wanted to produce a jean-like pant with double stitched seams, for example, but that could not be done on the home sewers' machines.

Layup and cut-time set the pace for production. The average size of a clothing cut was 1000 garments with a wholesale value of $25 000. Operating with two production shifts permitted four cuts per week. An automatic fabric spreader, at a cost of $35 000, could increase this capacity to ten cuts per week. Its purchase was under consideration.

THE ORGANIZATION AND
SENIOR MANAGEMENT TEAM

The key members of Kettle Creek's management team were Mellanie Stephens, 32, president; David MacDonnell, 31, designer; David Smith, 38, comptroller; Karen Crawford, 36, production manager; Paul Lambert, 28, and Walter Hambrock, 33, franchise liaison supervisors, and Susan McConnell, 29, advertising and public relations. With the exception of Hambrock, who had been with Kettle Creek for six months, this group, the core of the "fish house" gang, had been through the trials of start-up. "They are survivors," said Mellanie, "they are a close and optimistic group ... if you are not optimistic you don't last long around here!" Brief biographies of these managers are given in Exhibit 3.

The Kettle Creek management team operated on a very informal basis. Mellanie was the centre of a loose network through which work was prioritized and coordinated. Each manager had primary responsibility for a particular area of operations, but there were no job descriptions or formal performance appraisals. If a job needed to be done, someone just did it without worrying about whether it was part of their responsibility or someone else's.

Co-ordination and control were achieved by high levels of informal discussion and interaction between committed individuals. This informal discussion was most likely to take place over coffee in the staff lounge or when one person wandered into another's work area or simply by hollering across the office; there was rarely a memo used internally. In addition, on every Friday morning, the seven senior managers met to discuss problems and plans and co-ordinate operations.

The management team felt that they and the other employees were members of an extended family. Seniority was a matter of pride at Kettle Creek, not because it equated with security or money but because it meant being a part of Kettle Creek's history and difficult times. Many long-term employees had foregone pay-cheques when money was tight and each had, in their own way, helped to shape the firm over its brief but dynamic history. New employees were quickly assimilated into this culture and "the family."

David MacDonnell was the only member of the management team who had significant experience in the fashion industry before joining Kettle Creek. He was attracted by the opportunity to develop a product line and shape a concept himself, and he like the people. Other managers expressed similar reasons for joining Kettle Creek—the people, the optimism, the informality and the sense of achievement. From their perspective, Kettle Creek consisted of a group of people who liked each other and liked what they were doing. As they saw it, the absence of corporate structures and bureaucracy was a significant plus.

In total, Kettle Creek employed about 80 people of whom about 40 were home sewers. None were unionized. The employees, like the management group, felt themselves to be a part of an exciting organization, not just workers doing a day's work. Everyone from Mell on down was on a first-name basis with everyone else. On the plant floor, Mellanie was as likely to enquire about someone's sick child or pregnant dog as she was to ask about the task at hand. Many of the staff worked flexible hours. It was common to see production staff listening to their favourite music on a walkman while they worked. The plant atmosphere was informal and pleasant; quite unlike the sweatship image common to the garment industry. Employees genuinely appeared to enjoy their work.

The disadvantage of the Kettle Creek management approach was that it was very demanding of Mellanie's time. As sales and the number of franchisees grew, the number of issues with which she had to deal seemed to increase exponentially. Operating problems piled up and frustrated Mellanie, whose real interests were in developing the Kettle Creek concept and product line and taking it to the market.

FINANCE

Financial statements for the years 1982–84 are presented in Exhibit 4. Mellanie commented on the financial situation:

> The root of most of our problems at Kettle Creek has been inadequate financing. Up until May 1983 we ran this business on a $50 000 line of credit with the bank and supplier money whenever possible. Now we have a bank line of $250 000 but that isn't enough either. We've been growing so fast that we just can't finance operations out of current profits and yet we made money every year but one...You know, even with a credit line of $100 000 like we have with our primary fabric supplier it's not enough. We can cut that much cloth in a week.

Mellanie continued:

> I don't fit into the bankers' neat little categories. I don't get dressed up to go see them. When I started I didn't know cash flow from profit; that took a while to figure out. And then because we were operating on such a tight financial position I had enough writs and bounced cheques to paper this office. Here we were making a good profit and growing like mad but no one wanted to lend us enough money to do it right. As a result our banking relations have always been strained, to put it politely.

FUTURE GROWTH AND DIRECTION

Mellanie and her management team were optimistic about the future of Kettle Creek. Their profit and sales forecasts for 1985 greatly exceeded 1984 levels. Profits were forecast at more than double previous earnings over $400 000 in

1985 while sales were forecast to expand by 55% to $5 165 000. Growth potential was viewed as excellent for the foreseeable future. In Mellanie's opinion, Canada could support approximately thirty more Kettle creek outlets and then there was the huge potential of the U.S. market beckoning. A U.S. expansion had been discussed for several years, but Mellanie wanted to work out all the details of the operation in Canada before tackling that market.

In 1983, Kettle Creek tested the U.S. market through a deal with Bamberger's a subsidiary of Macy's department stores. They put Kettle Creek boutiques into 13 Bamberger's stores in new Jersey, Delaware, Maryland and Pennsylvania. The consumer response was described by Mellanie as positive, but the arrangement was discontinued because of complications in exporting to the U.S. and the high prices that resulted when the import duties on men's clothing were applied to Kettle Creek's unisex garments.

Future expansion aside, it was clear to Mellanie at the moment that both she and Kettle Creek had been pushed to the limit. Some significant changes would have to be made to relieve the pressure and open up the future.

EXHIBIT 1 **Typical Kettle Creek Products**

AVAILABLE EXCLUSIVELY AT KETTLE CREEK CANVAS CO.
IN TORONTO: DELISLE COURT-1560 YONGE STREET
                HAZELTON LANES-55 AVENUE ROAD
                QUEENS QUAY TERMINAL, HARBOURFRONT
                AND,
                828 YONGE STREET-YONGE AT CUMBERLAND
IN HAMILTON: JACKSON SQUARE-2 KING STREET WEST
IN BURLINGTON: VILLAGE SQUARE-ELIZABETH STREET

EXHIBIT 2 **Kettle Creek Store Location Summary**

Store Openings	1979	1980	1981	1982	1983	1984	1985
Port Stanley*	S						
London	S						
Toronto		S					
St. Catharines			S				
Kitchener			S				
Sarnia			S				
Burlington				M			
Calgary				M			
Cobourg				S			
Midland				M			
Ottawa				S			
Unionville				S			
Barrie					S		
Guelph					S		
Montreal					S		
Niagara-On-The-Lake					S		
Oakville					S		
Port Carling (seasonal)				S			
Queens Quay (2nd Toronto outlet)*				M			
Saint John					M		
Saskatoon					M		
Thunder Bay					S		
Vancouver					S		
Victoria					S		
Windsor					S		
Bracebridge						S	
Delisle Court (3rd Toronto outlet)*					S		
Edmonton						M	
Halifax						M	
Hamilton						M	
Hazelton Lanes (4th Toronto outlet)*					M		
Kingston						S	
Orillia						S	
Quebec City						M	
Sudbury						M	
Winnipeg						M	
Charlottetown							M
Mahone Bay							M
Regina						S	
Aurora							M
Etobicoke							M
Victoria (2nd outlet)							M

} Proposed 1985

S—storefront location
M—mall location
*Wholly or partly company-owned.

Total   8   13   10

EXHIBIT 3 Kettle Creek Senior Management, Positions and Responsibilities

MELLANIE STEPHENS—*President*
At the age of 32, Mellanie Stephens was the president, founder and majority shareholder of Kettle Creek Canvas Co., as well as the entrepreneurial leader of the business. Born under the astrological sign of Capricorn, she left school after grade eleven and travelled, spending short periods of time at a wide variety of jobs: from truck gardening to cooking in a bush camp to retail sales. She was the very colourful public spokesperson for and symbol of Kettle Creek. Her corporate responsibilities include the strategic direction and daily coordination of the business.

DAVID MACDONNELL—*Designer*
David MacDonnell, a shareholder and the designer responsible for most of Kettle Creek's fashions since 1979, was 31 years old and an Aries. He had completed two years of university and then obtained diplomas from Fanshawe College, London, Ontario in Fine Arts and Fashion Design. His previous experience included a work term for top Canadian designer Linda Lundstrom and time with Kayser Roth. His responsibilities included the design of the product line, new product development, costing, grading and pattern and sample making.

DAVID SMITH—*Comptroller*
David Smith was 38 years old, a chartered accountant, comptroller and secretary of Kettle Creek, and a Scorpio. He was responsible for the preparation of annual budgets, monitoring of operating results, working capital, management information systems and administration.

KAREN CRAWFORD—*Production Manager*
Karen Crawford, was 36 years old, the mother of two and had been Kettle Creek's first home sewer. She was a high-school graduate and prior to sewing for Kettle Creek had spent twelve years at home raising a family. Karen, a Capricorn, was responsible for the administration of sales and cutting orders and production scheduling for both in-house operations and home sewers.

PAUL LAMBERT—*Franchise Liaison Supervisor*
Paul Lambert, at 28 years of age, was Franchise Liaison Supervisor for Kettle Creek in central Ontario and eastern Canada and had been with the firm since 1983. A Gemini, he had completed grade 12 and some university courses in psychology and business. His previous business experience included retail management and financial sales. Paul was responsible for franchise development and operations, including the preparation and monitoring of retail budgets for each franchise, franchisee liaison, marketing support, and maintenance of the retail continuity of Kettle Creek's image and presentation in central Ontario and eastern Canada.

WALTER HAMBROCK—*Franchise Liaison Supervisor*
Walter Hambrock, franchise liaison supervisor for northern Ontario and western Canada, was 33 years old and had joined Kettle Creek six months earlier. Also a Gemini, he was a graduate of Ryerson Polytechnical Institute in retail management and marketing. His prior business experience included retail consulting, retail management with Le Château and Elks and a period with General Motors.

EXHIBIT 3 (continued)

He was responsible for franchise development and operations, including the preparation and monitoring of retail budgets for each franchise, franchisee liaison, marketing support, and maintenance of the retail continuity of Kettle Creek's image and presentation in northern Ontario and western Canada.

SUSAN MCCONNELL—*Public Relations and Advertising Manager*
Susan McConnell, at 29 years of age, was responsible for all public relations and advertising activities of Kettle Creek. An Aries, she had completed the first year of university and gone on to work as a news reporter, the editor of both daily and community newspapers and a public relations consultant. She had joined Kettle Creek in 1980. Susan's management responsibilities included all public relations activities, the administration of artwork production, organization of the spring and fall fashion shows, the franchisee newsletter, advertising program development and the ultimate implementation of the advertising program.

2 - Capricorns
2 - Aries
2 - Geminis
1 - Scorpio

EXHIBIT 4 Kettle Creek Summary of Operations (000s)

	December 31, 1984		December 31, 1983		December 31, 1982	
Sales	$3 324	100.0%	$2 030	100.0%	$ 927	100.0%
Cost of sales	2 023	60.9	1 190	58.6	$ 558	60.2
Gross profit	1 301	39.1	840	41.4	369	39.8
Operating expense	982	29.5	650	32.0	231	24.9
Net operating income	319	9.6	190	9.4	138	14.9
Net franchise income (loss)[1]	(95)	(2.9)	69	3.4	(39)	(4.2)
Net income before tax	224	6.7	259	12.8	99	10.7
Net income after tax	$ 202	6.1%	$ 204	10.0%	$ 89	9.6%
ASSETS						
Current						
Cash	$ 38		$ 19		$ —	
Accounts receivable	814		256		191	
Due from related parties	44		90		60	
Due from shareholders	146		157		—	
Inventory	368		309		110	
Other	23		15		22	
Total Current Assets	1 433		846		383	
Fixed assets (net)	523		390		211	
Long-term investments[2]	166		170		—	
Other	6		5		2	
	$2 128		$1 411		$ 596	
LIABILITIES AND SHAREHOLDERS' EQUITY						
Current						
Bank loan	250		250		87	
Notes payable	101		—		—	
Accounts payable	714		395		231	
Other current liabilities	44		72		19	
Current portion long-term debt	27		16		5	
Total Current Liabilities	1 136		733		342	
Long-term debt	306		241		153	
Deferred revenue	105		108		—	
Deferred taxes	38		36		—	
Shareholders' Equity						
Share capital	60		10		20	
Retained earnings	483		283		81	
	543		293		101	
Total Liabilities and Shareholders' Equity	$2 128		$1 411		$ 596	

[1] Net franchise income (loss) = Franchise fees—Franchise management expense. Franchise management expense excludes the one-time and continuing expenses related to the franchise system such as travel, salaries and benefits, advertising and promotion.

[2] Represents investments in three franchises by way of foregoing certain franchise fees.

SOURCE: Audited financial statements.

KETTLE CREEK CANVAS COMPANY —1985 (B)

Joseph N. Fry and Robert G. Blunden

In April 1985 Mellanie Stevens was considering three particular steps to deal with the financial and operating problems at Kettle Creek (see the Kettle Creek Canvas Company 1985 (A) case). They were to: (1) sell equity, even the whole business if necessary, (2) recruit a board of directors and (3) hire a general manager.

FINANCES

Mellanie knew that Kettle Creek needed additional equity. In her darker moments she even considered selling the business.

> Kettle Creek isn't an ego trip for me; I think of it more as my ticket to freedom or my golden goose. I don't want to kill it, and I would sell it, if I thought that was best for everyone concerned. But what I would prefer to do is sell a piece of it, get more equity into the business and get the bank off my back.

There were 10 000 common shares outstanding of which Mellanie controlled 7 250. The others were owned by five persons in approximately equal amounts.

A BOARD OF DIRECTORS

Mellanie continued,

> You know, I'm really lonely business-wise. Family and friends listen but they don't understand the problems. Over time I've developed a group of business people whom I can share ideas with and whose brains I can pick but I've always been careful not to overdo it. I don't want to be a parasite. Some time ago I heard someone talking about a board of directors as a group making decisions for the good of the company. I've been thinking more about that lately. I like the

idea of having a group of advisors who know more than I do about business to share things with. And for some reason Kettle Creek catches peoples' attention. Several interesting and very successful people from business and government have offered to join a board if I put one together.

A GENERAL MANAGER

In February, Mellanie had instructed her accountants to conduct a limited search for a general manager. Although the accountants would have preferred a more extensive search, they placed an advertisement and screened the responses. The résumés of the three best prospects had been forwarded to Mellanie and now rested on her desk. They are included as Appendix A.

Mellanie commented,

> When I started out with Kettle Creek I didn't know anything about business except that I was a good salesperson. Well, I learned as I went along and made lots of mistakes, but things always turned out OK. I still explain these things by saying, `It's magic, you know.' But for the past year or so I have had the feeling that my limited expertise has been handicapping the business. That's why I've been thinking about hiring a general manager. I want somebody to do the things that I do, only better. Kettle Creek has grown to the point where it needs some systems, and some professional management, and I can't give it those things. I'm disorganized, I can't manage. I'm not good on follow up—when I ask people to do something I assume they will do it. But I can motivate; that's what I've done here.
>
> The general manager would have to run the business on a day-to-day basis. He can make changes in most areas, even to some extent with the Kettle Creek concept, but he can't beat up the people. . . . you know, that is what Kettle Creek is, it's the people.
>
> I want Kettle Creek to move forward but at the same time I'm terrified that the company might move too fast for me or move into areas that I know nothin'g about. If I were to stay involved with Kettle Creek I would have to keep a total veto on how the product gets to the street. And I would want to have lots of input on the speed and direction of the firm.
>
> With the right general manager I could do the things that are fun for me. I'd have more time for the design, fabric and colour selection, advertising, retail presentation and store design. You know—all the creative things that directly impact the customer. The general manager would look after the administration, planning, bank relations, firefighting and development of systems to make things run smoother.

Mellanie's thoughts turned to the résumés of the three candidates for the general manager's position. Should she hire one of them? If so, which one?

APPENDIX A Kettle Creek Canvas Company
Applicants for Position of General Manager

DAVID P. JOHNSTONE
1403 – 1936 Sherington Way, Toronto, Ontario M5J 2H9
(416) 771-5369

Personal Data: Born: November 23, 1933
Married: No dependants
Citizen: Great Britain; Landed Immigrant: Canada
Health: Excellent

Education: Bachelor of Arts (Economics), 1955
University of Manchester, England

Experience: Farmers' Co-Op Dairy
Edmonton, Alberta
May 1982 – April 1985
President of Farmers' Co-Op Dairy, a $40 million co-operative. This
was a three-year contract position. I was hired to built a management team and distribution network and put professional
management systems in place to facilitate ongoing operations. All
three objectives were achieved on schedule.

Traher and Traher Ltd.
Toronto, Ontario
August 1972 – May 1982
As General Manager and Chief Executive Officer of Traher and
Traher, I increased sales from less than $10 million in 1972 to
$83 million in 1981. This was accomplished by adding new lines
to our existing food brokerage business and in large part by
establishing a U.S. distribution system. By 1982, when I left the
firm, U.S. sales represented approximately one half of total sales.

Valleyfield Foods Ltd.
Toronto, Ontario
May 1964 – July 1972
During this period I was General Manager of an $8 million, family-
owned food brokerage operation

International Packaged Goods Inc.
Toronto, Ontario
September 1955 – April 1964
I started with International Packaged Goods as an Assistant
Product Manager and rose through the organization to Product
Manager and Group Product Manager in their Grocery Division.

Activities: Classical music, reading and live theatre.

APPENDIX A (continued)

EDWARD J. KING
386 Duke Street, Ayr, Ontario, N2A 3C7
(416) 339-2715

Personal Data:	Born: June 12, 1952
	Married: Two children
	Citizen: Canada
	Health: Excellent

Education: Certified Management Accountant, 1979
Society of Management Accountants of Ontario
Bachelor of Business Administration, 1975
Wilfrid Laurier University, Waterloo, Ontario
Majored in accounting

Experience: National Hardware Distributors
Mississauga, Ontario

November 1981 – Present
Plant Manager at National's paint manufacturing facility located in Ayr, Ontario. Responsible for all general management activities at the plant level including annual plans and budgets for the paint line, personnel, distribution and production management. All plant production is marketed through the National franchise network of approximately425 outlets nationwide.

April 1978 – November 1981
Traffic Manager for National, located at corporate headquarters in Mississauga. Reported to the Vice President, Distribution and was responsible for the effective and efficient movement of all corporate freight traffic. Oversaw the implementation of new, computerized systems to manage the traffic function.

January 1977 – March 1978
Systems Analyst in the traffic department responsible for the development and installation of new systems and sub-systems to trace and manage National's freight traffic.

May 1975 – December 1976
Junior Accountant, Accounts Payable, reporting to the Accounts Payable Supervisor.

Activities: Interested in most sports, especially team sports and play both hockey and baseball.

APPENDIX A   (continued)

PETER G. WRIGHT

89 Elizabeth Street, Aurora, Ontario

(416) 818-2620

Personal Data: Born: April 7, 1954
Married: Two children
Citizen: Canada
Health: Excellent

Education: Bachelor of Commerce, 1977
McGill University, Montreal, Quebec

Experience: American Sportswear Inc. Canadian Catalogue Division
Toronto, Ontario

October 1982 – Present
General Manager of the Canadian Catalogue Division of American Sportswear located in Toronto, Ontario. Canadian catalogue sales of men's and women's quality casual wear are $4 million annually. Responsible for all aspects of Canadian catalogue operations and divisional profit/loss. Report to the Vice-President, Catalogue Operations in New York. As part of a corporate reorganization the Canadian Catalogue Division is being closed with its activities being assumed by the U.S. catalogue division.

August 1979 – September 1982
Marketing Manager, responsible for all marketing activities of American Sportswear's Canadian Catalogue Division.

A.H. Johnson and Sons Ltd., Montreal, Quebec

June 1977 – July 1979
Assistant Marketing Manager of a $20-million, family-owned men's suit manufacturer.

Activities: Sunday school teacher and youth group leader in the Anglican church, skiing, tennis and golf.

TWILL ENTERPRISES LIMITED

Joseph N. Fry with William R. Killeen

Ken Shelstad leaned forward in his chair, flashed a great smile and said, "Look, I love what I'm doing! I'm at it 70 hours a week—but that's the limit, after that I feel fuzzy and I can't concentrate. I enjoy every minute! Hell, I own half this company and we're making money. Lots of it! Profits, I love 'em!"

Shelstad, 51, was President of Twill Enterprises Limited, a growing and prosperous company in the printing and packaging industry. He was clearly in his element, but he expressed some misgivings about the future as he pushed the company into one of its most aggressive expansion projects. The issues, he thought, were not so much in the market opportunity as in his and his peoples' ability to handle the anticipated growth. "What concerns me," he said, "is that the company may be outgrowing me. I used to know exactly what was going on in every department. Lately, I feel like I've lost some of that control. The consultants have been telling me for years that I should change the way I run things. Maybe they are finally right."

COMPANY BACKGROUND

In 1945, Barry Shelstad, Ken's father, purchased a small Toronto-based producer of business forms and labels, and started Twill Enterprises. Over the next 20 years, Barry Shelstad built the business by internal growth, and by the careful acquisition of similar small companies in Canada and the United States. With time Barry Shelstad brought his sons John and Ken into the business. By 1965 John, the eldest, was the president, and in 1974 he became chairman. Ken began in the company as a salesman, moved up through the ranks to become vice-president of manufacturing, and in 1974 became president. When Barry Shelstad passed away in 1975, he left the ownership of the company in equal shares to the two brothers.

By 1988, Twill revenues were over $150 million, and the company's product range encompassed blister and flexible packaging, labels and business forms. The company operated seven packaging, ten business form and seven label plants at various locations in North America. In recent years, Twill's growth had been somewhat higher than the 5–7% rates experienced by the industry, and profitability had been consistently higher than the 2–3% after tax return on sales and the 4–7% return on average assets of comparable firms.

Twill's new venture was in the rigid plastic container business. Ken Shelstad had acquired the rights to European technology, which promised greater design flexibility and lower cost production in some lines of jars and bottles than was currently in place in North America. His projections showed the new lines would add over $40 million to Twill's revenues within three years of start-up. The capital investment implications of the venture were sizeable, however, and for the first time ever Shelstad had run into difficulty working out financial arrangements with Twill's long-time bank. "They wanted to know who the project manager was going to be," said Shelstad, "and when I told them, first, that it was none of their business, and, second, that it was going to be me, they wanted to have a consultant hired to monitor the operation. Well, there was no way I was going to operate with some jerk looking over my shoulder, so we got financing elsewhere." At the time of this case, Twill had made commitment for land in Toronto, and for the purchase of the major items of equipment.

INDUSTRY CHARACTERISTICS

The markets in which Twill operated were fiercely competitive. Typically, a few large competitors would account for about 70% of the sales in a region, and the balance would be filled by literally hundreds of small companies. Most products were made to customer specifications so operations took on job shop characteristics. Profitability was a reflection of efficient manufacturing operations and local pricing, customer and product mix decisions. Raw materials usually represented over 60% of direct product costs.

Price, delivery, quality and service tended to become equated among local producers. Often a competitive edge was decided by the reputation of the producer for especially good service, and the personal relations between the supplier firm personnel and their customers. The larger suppliers had somewhat more of an advantage with larger accounts because the scope of their operations allowed them to meet the national requirements of their customers.

Twill was fortunate to have focused its operations in Toronto, one of the two largest centres for printing concentration in North America (Chicago being the other). On the downside, this created a fiercely competitive environment, in which suppliers had to offer a high degree of sophistication, technical capability and a range of production options. The challenge was to make more complicated products with faster response times and lower costs.

The outlook for industry demand in Twill's market areas was generally positive. Demand tended to follow the fortunes of the economy as a whole, and in recent years had been outpacing this indicator. Existing competitors had reacted by expanding their capacity, and new entrants had been attracted to the industry. Competition would continue to be intense and there was some concern that an economic downturn would leave suppliers in a state of serious overcapacity.

TWILL'S STRATEGY

Goals

The Shelstad's goals for Twill were for it to continue to operate as a large, successful, growing, family firm. Twill had been owned and run by the Shelstad family for nearly 45 years. Ken had three sons working for the firm, and while they were still in their early 20s, he hoped they would provide for family succession.

The Shelstads were known as prudent, successful businessmen. They had built Twill with a conservative growth strategy. Typically, whether acquisition or internal expansion was involved, Twill started new projects and followed them to completion before progressing to a new venture. Twill's recent plastic container expansion represented a more aggressive step than had been typical for the company.

Product Market Strategy

Twill had always chosen to expand into markets in which it could be profitable by exploiting its competitive strengths—in particular, high-service levels, low-cost production, and in-house capabilities. When a market opportunity was uncovered (usually in the form of a neglected niche with high prices and low customer satisfaction), Twill was quick to respond. Table 1 provides a general review of Twill's market position.

In recent years, Twill had experimented with a variety of plastic container products. Their strategy had been to "test the waters" with product entries based on sub-contracted production. Over time, the company had developed its understanding of the market. In 1989, Twill planned to start up its own production facilities in Toronto. The new facility represented a major step by Twill into a highly competitive market. The Shelstads were confident, however, that their current competitive advantages would transfer readily into the new market.

TABLE 1 Twill Market Position

	Blister and Flexible Packaging	Labels	Business Forms
Expect overall market growth[1]	4–6%	1–3%	3–4%
Industry key	Product development	Personal relationships	
Success factors	Range of technical capabilities Quality and service Cost control	Service reputation Cost control	
Twill share of served market[2]	12%	19%	10%
% Twill revenues	Over 50%	About 15%	About 35%
Plants[3]	7	7	10

[1] Management estimate.

[2] Twill did not compete in all product formats or geographic regions in North America. The market share estimates are based on Twill's sales in its served markets.

[3] Some of Twill's plants occupied the same site and even the same building. They had distinct plant managers, however.

Competitive Strategy

Twill aimed to be competitive in price and distinctive in service. The company had always endeavoured to ensure that customers got the product they wanted, when they wanted it. To this end, Twill offered their own in-house design and typesetting service, and employed a large direct sales organization and delivery fleet.

The Shelstads ran a no-nonsense, low-cost operation. Money was spent where it was necessary—on equipment modernization and maintenance. Otherwise, there were few frills at a Twill plant. Parking lots were not paved, and offices were not carpeted. Salesmen shared spartan office space, which kept costs to a minimum and "forced" them to stay on the road. Expediting and cost control were inbred habits throughout the organization.

Recently Twill had been attempting to supplement its low-cost emphasis with a greater concern for quality. The aim was to eliminate situations in which substandard but usable products would be sent to customers. Under the current program, such a client could be informed of quality problems, given a sample, and asked for their approval prior to shipment.

TWILL'S ORGANIZATION

The practice of management at Twill had remained relatively unchanged for 20 years. Growth had added to the complexity of the business, but to this point had not forced any significant change in basic management structures or systems and style. There were, however, continuing questions about how best to handle the inherently and increasingly complicated operations of the company, as will be illustrated in the following description of the way in which the organization worked.

Management Structure

Twill was managed through a functional structure as outlined in the partial organization chart in Exhibit 1. The senior managers in the structure—John and Ken Shelstad, Larry Dixon, Vice-President of Sales and Marketing, and Doug Burgess, Vice-President of Production—had been in their positions since 1974. Each senior manager, based on his long experience, would step outside of their strict functional responsibilities to handle specific projects, and often, day-to-day activities. Together they nurtured an intense, "hands-on" style of management.

Top-level coordination was handled through a management committee. The committee consisted of six members—the Shelstads, Doug Burgess, Larry Dixon, Tim O'Dowda, and Jeff Bak. The group attempted to meet weekly (schedules limited this number to about 30 meetings annually) for two to four hours. John Shelstad set an agenda but new topics could be informally introduced. No minutes were taken. The group's role was to develop strategy; day-to-day operations were not discussed. Final decisions rested with the Shelstads, but no decisions were made without the assistance and input of the committee.

John and Ken Shelstad's roles in the management structure were vastly different. The older brother, John, had a number of outside interests and limited his involvement to strategic issues. Ken, on the other hand, was highly involved in all of the company's activities—from the management committee to daily decision making. As one manager observed: "Twill gets its pulse from Ken. He commands respect and he gets it. He's very dynamic. He drives this company. But there is a problem—I think people are losing contact with him."

Another added an ominous note: "Ken is going to kill himself. He pushes himself too hard. He recently delegated the monthly cheque signing. Umpteen hundred a month and he used to sign—and check—every one. That's 15 hours minimum right there."

From time to time, Twill had attempted to modify its structure and decentralize its operations through the use of general management positions. These attempts had been unsuccessful, however, for a variety of reasons that ranged from incapable personnel to corporate culture to head office interference. Twill's experience with its Denver plant was a prime example.

Twill had purchased a profitable business in Denver, and had put a "general manager" in charge. Within one year, however, the revenues and profits of the Denver operation had declined to the point where consideration was being given to shutting it down. The cause of the problem was not clear. The manager may not have been competent, head office might have stifled him—or whatever; head office did take over, the manager was fired, and another notch was marked against a general manager concept.

Management Systems

Twill's job shop operations were inherently complex, and worked under the pressure of tight delivery schedules and cost containment. The following description of order processing gives some idea of the manner in which the operating problems were handled by the company.

Order Processing

In 1971 Twill had implemented an on-line electronic data interchange (EDI) system. Orders were either brought, phoned, or mailed in, and then keyed into a terminal at the Order department. By 1987, three separate systems were in use, reflecting the differing information needs of the major product lines—packaging, labels and business forms.

An EDI file was created for each client. After entering an order, a delivery slip was created and sent to shipping. Stock items were shipped immediately. Made-to-order product delivery dates were confirmed by the Order department representative, who acted as an interface between manufacturing and the salesman or client.

Each salesman at Twill (over 100 in all) had a corresponding representative in the Order department. The Order department people served as the vital link between sales and production, and helped to maintain the excellent relations between these two departments. This was a significant accomplishment since the processing of a job was very complex.

When a new product order was received, it passed through some or all of the order, graphics, art, typesetting, scheduling, plant, and shipping departments. There was no set pattern within these departments because of the iterative steps required to process each order. The Graphics people, for example, could theoretically handle one order dozens of times.

Each department at this level of the organization had their own hierarchy. The order and art departments reported to the sales vice-president, while graphics, typesetting, and scheduling reported to the production vice-president. Budget authority did not necessarily follow these lines: the graphics budget, for example, was set by sales, yet that manager reported to production personnel.

The complex nature of Twill's structure was also apparent in the sales organization. It was separated as two distinct entities, but in fact operated as a single sales force. The sales force for the packaging division was arranged geographically, while the labels and forms sales force was arranged along product lines. In both cases, large single accounts were handled by a few national salespeople. In spite of these formal differences, each salesperson tended to be a generalist, selling all products to their individual customers.

Control

Budgets and standards were the way of life at Twill. In production, for example, standard objectives included waste, productivity, safety and cost. These standards were set by discussion with everyone right down to the machine operators who were paid piecework rates related to the standards. Meeting standards was both a corporate goal and an individual goal at Twill. The value system created by the Shelstads dictated that meeting standards would result in a reward and security.

In larger scope, Twill's planning and accounting system was based on 18 separate profit centres, representing individual products, product ranges, or plant/product combinations. Monthly reports were prepared which identified the contribution of each product at each profit centre. Ken Shelstad and Doug Burgess followed these monthly reports very carefully, and were quick to pick up on any problems that they observed.

But the pursuit of control at Twill went much deeper than this. Both Ken and Doug personally reviewed the monthly general ledger, in which every transaction of the company was entered and allocated to the profit centres. By combining this with the ledger overview, they could examine activities down to the level, for example, of specific orders, customers or purchases. It was a common occurrence for either Ken or Doug to question a plant manager, for example, about costs that were only slightly off standard or about a specific purchase transaction.

Ken explained the ledger reviews as a type of policing: "You can cross-check the allocations and make sure costs are being charged against the right profit centre and you can identify potential problems right at the start. Just the other day I picked off a cheque for $300 that had been issued to one of our competitors—I had to go down and ask why the hell we were doing business with them." Doug Burgess was proud of the fact that, as he put it: "We ask more questions and discover more horror stories than any other company. That is what has led to our success." Despite his claims, Burgess, at the time of the interview, had been unable to review his ledger, which was literally hundreds of pages deep, for two months. Time was a problem.

Staffing

Twill had always strived to take care of its employees through internal promotion, job security and profit sharing. Twill encouraged employees to move up through the ranks. In addition, as Doug Burgess explained: "No one has ever been laid off. Jobs have been eliminated but we've always been able to shift people around." Pay was above industry averages, and a pension plan was currently under consideration. Every six months, all staff above, including the supervisory level, received a bonus based on company profits. This system was highly reliant on the Shelstads' credibility since actual profit figures were not revealed.

In 1986, Twill had initiated a Management Assistant Program. "We've got to increase our management team," said Larry Dixon, "our recent management assistant hirees are a step in this direction." In 1987, two young men were hired to assume various roles in the organization, with the goal of assuming management (and ultimately, executive) positions within a few years. Slow development from within was essential. Twill's culture dictated that managers ask questions, be nitpickers, work long hours, and get involved in everything. Only by having moved up through the ranks could one develop the essential experience and attitudes. Initiative was the trait most often looked for in personnel, and the trait which most often led to promotions.

KEY MANAGER VIEWS

The casewriter interviewed ten key Twill employees to secure their views about the issues facing Twill. These managers were cooperative and candid in their remarks.

It is worth noting that these interviews were frequently interrupted. The diversity of roles and the informal nature of management meant that senior people were inextricably involved in the problems of the day. For example, during an interview with Larry Dixon, Ken Shelstad and Jeff Bak dropped into the office, unannounced, seeking pricing information for Denver. Three hours later, Ken interrupted a meeting with Doug Burgess, this time to discuss a firewall at one of the new plants under construction. Within 30 minutes, Ken was back for an answer to a shipping problem—no space was available for a loaded truck in the yard.

Doug Burgess

Doug Burgess had been vice-president of production since 1969. He was an extremely hard worker, a detail-man, and a man with a lot of authority.

I'm very cognizant of my authority, and sure, I like power. I really enjoy it when Ken is away. Don't misunderstand me, because I respect Ken a lot. I think he is Twill's biggest asset. He's also our biggest drawback.

I don't like detail! It's the culture of the company though. Things have to get done and I'm the one who does it. What I like is solving problems and developing people.

I usually work 8 to 8, with a little weekend work. It ends up being a 70-hour week and it's been steady like this for the last ten years. I'm definitely at my limit and I've been actively trying to cut back by delegating a fair bit. I'm tied to my desk too much right now. I get bored with the paperwork.

I see a couple of things occurring within ten years. Personally, I believe that I'll be managing more generalities, rather than specifics. We must manage towards growth. This may require us to also move towards general managers, with much more sales involvement. I realize that our strength has been in production but there has been a shift in recent years towards sales.

Twill has had difficulties with general managers. A real general manager wants autonomy and we haven't provided it. At Excelon, our Canadian poster plant, we tried a general manager and he delegated too much. He basically abdicated his office. I fired him. The new guy starts next week—with much less authority. In our plastic container start-ups, one guy was given a general manager title but he never grabbed all the reins. He still has the title but he certainly doesn't run the area.

It's been difficult to change things because the people have been here for too long. We were here when you could check on everything. Now we can't. Another justification for our structure is our results. Both our space utilization and inventory turnover are excellent. We're making money in areas other companies are not.

I acknowledge that we've done little to develop managers here but we're now at a junction in our history where something has to be done. I believe we'll have to develop from within. Jeff Bak is an exception because he's such a nit-picker that he fit right into the Twill culture.

Larry Dixon

Larry Dixon was vice-president of sales and marketing, and nominally had profit and loss responsibilities for 17 (of 18) profit centres. He worked 60-hour weeks, with the majority of his time spent in meetings. When he started at Twill in 1959, he worked 80- to 90-hour weeks.

> I enjoy what I'm doing so I don't mind the long hours. I get my kicks from the diversity—of the job and the organization. The success of the company has also been an incentive. Many people work hard and don't get the rewards. To use a cliche, at Twill we've seen our hard work bear fruit.

In the early sixties I was general manager of business forms but over the years I've grown from a generalist to a specialist. We all have. Twenty years ago the four of us did everything. We can't anymore. The day-to-day work is diminishing because it has to diminish. Likewise, we've got to increase our management team. The recent management assistant hirees are an admission of this.

Managing is getting things done through people. We're getting more people to get more done. Perhaps general managers will be that way in the future, but we have not been successful with this concept. The main reason is that we're all "hands-on" managers and we can't let go. After thirty years of experience, I've seen situations that allow me to understand things better than others. So I get involved to make things happen right.

We've also discussed creating the positions of senior V.P.'s for sales and production and bringing in more V.P.'s (or some other title). I don't know what will happen. We do recognize that we must pass on authority and give people responsibilities for areas.

Each year the six of us (on the Committee) go down to a management retreat in Florida for four days in September. This year we are each assuming another's role and providing recommendations to achieve given goals. I want to do a bang-up job on my production role, so I'm putting in 40 hours on the task. I'm sure the others will do the same. Sure it's a challenge but it's supposed to give each of us a better base of knowledge at Twill.

Jeff Bak

Jeff Bak, the vice-president of finance, was responsible for all accounting functions including payables, cost accounting, payroll, and credit.

I've only been here for four and a half years. I guess that makes me the new kid on the block. I've had to adjust somewhat to fit in with these guys but it hasn't been difficult.

My role here is mainly administrative. The finance title is really a misnomer. When I arrived here the payables were screwed up so I spent half my time fixing them. Last year, half my time was spent in Denver. I still spend one day a week there. Ken thought this was too much time away but it had to be done. We had purchased this plant and the operations were not in good shape. Doug Burgess was already on another plant project so I was given this one.

I like getting responsibilities for these projects. I get a kick out of finding something that's not right, making it right, and then backing off. Denver is a prime example. It's at a point now where production is all set—all we need are sales. I'm a hired hand here. They gave me Denver, so I turned it around.

Another role of mine at Twill is to sit on the management committee. Ken and John are very good at getting the opinions of other people, so that is the ultimate purpose of the meetings. They end up deciding things, because we can't have decision by committee. After all, it is their company!

John and Ken have proven they are knowledgeable businessmen. Twill has been successful and I don't foresee any problems with the new plastic container expansion. This is what keeps things exciting around here—growth. I don't want to get bored and as long as we keep growing I won't get bored.

As for general managers, well, it seems that all of our attempts with them have been mistakes. I don't foresee a change in our organizational structure for just that reason. I also believe that a reorganization is generally done to wake people up. We don't need to be woken up at Twill.

Tim O'Dowda

Tim O'Dowda, the packaging sales manager, has been with Twill for 16 years. He oversees the sales of packaging products, one of Twill's core product lines, representing one-half of the company's annual sales. Eighty percent of his time is spent in his office, and seven sales managers report directly to him.

Twill has always been a strong manufacturing company. It's been dominated by four individuals for 20 years—John and Ken Shelstad, Larry Dixon and Doug Burgess. I think the major strength of this company is the dominance of these four individuals. I also think it's our major weakness.

Inside the management committee, Ken and Doug are the two major players and they haven't got a sales bone in their bodies! Ken is the autocratic king at Twill in my opinion, but he's on overload now. He's the best internal auditor I've ever seen. He's always reading. It's amazing, I thought he was at his limit ten years ago but he keeps on going. He really isn't a good delegator, either of tasks or authority. If someone makes a decision he'll end up questioning it.

Doug Burgess. I've never met anyone who works harder than Doug. His detail is incredible. He's on overload too. He's got no social life. He's also a real taskmaster—I sure wouldn't want to work for him. This has led to quite a turnover in production. In sales, I've lost one person in ten years, so I know that they don't have the depth of quality that we have.

Twill is unique because of the domination of these two men. They're always involved in new plants and construction. Ken really gets his jollies there. They get involved in all the materials purchasing—and I mean *all*. They are tough buyers. I couldn't sell to them.

We've had growing pains. An example right now is a salary problem we're having with our salesmen. Hay Associates have been in here to try and fix things up. Some of the salesmen are pulling in a lot more than their managers. One 24-year-old made $48 000 last year. That's obscene and he knows it. This is one control system that I've got to get a hold on.

One thing we've done in the last year is install Crosby's QYS culture at Twill. The management committee took Crosby's three-day course in Florida. Doug Burgess actually took it first and got hooked. If someone else had brought it back, say, Larry, I'm sure it wouldn't have caught on. Anyways, it's certainly helped. Errors in the sales department alone have been reduced 75%. We're at the "confrontation stage" as Crosby describes it. We're policing everybody and some people don't like it. This will only last another three months though.

Twill has to expand. There are too many opportunities out there. I want to double my sales force. I also believe that we'll have to go divisional and "general-managerized" within ten years. But we're too people-poor now. There's also a low level of trust. General managers have only stepped on the toes of the vice-presidents, especially Doug's and Larry's, so it's been difficult to change the organizational chart. I started in production and I would love the opportunity to be general manager of packaging and oversee everything in that area. We'll see. I think that Ken's kids are going to end up running the company eventually so they'll probably be the ones forced to change the structure around here.

Bruce Roberts

In 1987, Twill began a new hiring program to enhance their managerial staff. The new so-called management assistants were to complete a rotation with each member of the management committee during their first two years with Twill. Bruce Roberts, 27, was the first of two assistants hired.

I remember going through the interview process last year. There I was, sitting in this boardroom with eight guys that run Twill. That's the way things work around here. Everyone seems to get involved in everything. "Hands-on" is a very appropriate term here, especially when applied to Ken and Doug.

We were hired with the impression that John and Ken Shelstad were looking for people to step into the upper management at Twill within ten years. They're not going to last forever and they're trying to develop people that can assume their roles. Seeing firsthand how hard these guys work makes me question whether that's where I want to end up.

It has been quite a learning experience thus far. At times it gets frustrating though. I'm currently trying to solve a problem we have with our branch dealers. Twill bought them years ago and they represent about $20 million in annual sales. But they are losing money, very little, mind you, but at Twill any loss is a shock. I've been on this now for six months but my project boss, Tim O'Dowda, had been on it for two years. I can't find a solution. It's really a no-win proposition. I've suggested two alternatives, sell or franchise, and boy, was I shot down by Ken! "No way," he said, "find an answer that I want to hear." Ever since he's been checking on me weekly. He's interested but he's really provided no help.

CROSSROADS

Ken Shelstad was quite aware of the pressures and cross-currents in Twill. In fact, some flipcharts in his office summarized his position. One sheet identified the "Corporate Success Factors" as: (1) low-cost production; (2) maintaining account relationships; and (3) broad service. However, in small print at the bottom of the sheet, the following words jumped out: "Get competent people at all levels."

A second sheet, entitled "Power Thinking," provided a laundry list of the major personal concerns facing Ken Shelstad. These included questions about himself, his brother, his family, and the business. These sheets had been on Shelstad's wall for over a year, and he acknowledged their importance. He, and the others, had to give considerable thought to all of these issues. Management could tire, and they would find themselves short of suitable replacements. People could limit the growth. And an economic downturn could severely impact the performance of both the new and existing products. Ken Shelstad and Twill faced an interesting future.

"I know what you are thinking," said Shelstad, smiling again, "I've had smart guys tell me to change our management structure before. And in general I agree—we must free up our time. Why, general managers would allow this simply by taking the phone calls we currently get! But it's not that simple. Our plant and distribution setup makes the general management concept difficult. We have a tough time finding good people—the general management pool is small, and most of the prospects don't even know how to spell profit. And we are smarter than they will ever be. I do have an answer though, when people get pushy. I say, 'Look, let's compare tax returns.'"

EXHIBIT 1 Twill's Simplified Organization Chart

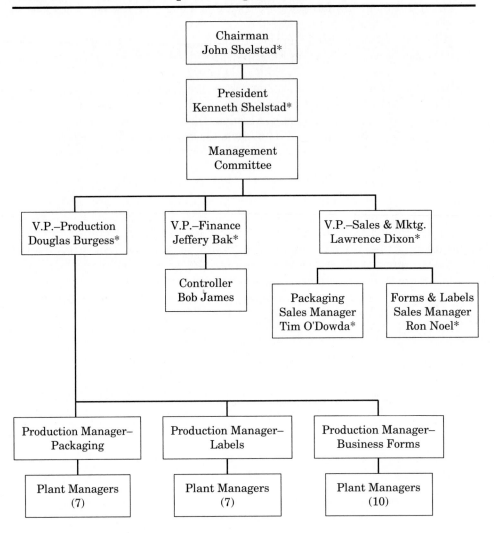

*Member, Management Comittee.

VICTORIA HEAVY EQUIPMENT LIMITED (Revised)

Paul W. Beamish and Thomas A. Poynter

Brian Walters sat back in the seat of his Lear jet as it broke through the clouds en route from Squamish, a small town near Vancouver, British Columbia, to Sacramento, California. As chairman of the board, majority shareholder, and chief executive officer, the 51-year-old Walters had run Victoria Heavy Equipment Limited as a closely held company for years. During this time Victoria had become the second-largest producer of mobile cranes in the world, with 1985 sales of $100 million and exports to more than 70 countries. But in early 1986 the problem of succession was in his thoughts. His son and daughter were not yet ready to run the organization, and he personally wanted to devote more time to other interests. He wondered about the kind of person he should hire to become president. There was also a nagging thought that there might be other problems with Victoria that would have to be worked out before he eased out of his present role.

COMPANY HISTORY

Victoria Heavy Equipment was established in 1902 in Victoria, British Columbia, to produce horse-drawn log skidders for the forest industry. The young firm showed a flair for product innovation, pioneering the development of motorized skidders and later, after diversifying into the crane business, producing the country's first commercially successful hydraulic crane controls. In spite of these innovations, the company was experiencing severe financial difficulties in 1948 when it was purchased by Brian Walters Sr., the father of the current chairman. By installing tight financial controls and paying close attention to productivity, Walters was able to turn the company around, and in the mid-1950s he decided that Victoria would focus its attention exclusively on cranes, and go after the international market.

By the time of Brian Walters Sr.'s retirement in 1968, it was clear that the decision to concentrate on the crane business had been a good one. The company's sales and profits were growing, and Victoria cranes were beginning to do well in export markets. Walters Sr. was succeeded as president by his brother, James, who began to exercise very close personal control over the company's operations. However, as Victoria continued to grow in size and complexity, the load on James became so great that his health began to fail. The solution was to appoint an assistant general manager, John Rivers, through whom tight supervision could be maintained while James Walters' workload was eased. This move was to no avail, however. James Walters suffered a heart attack in 1970, and Rivers became general manager. At the same time, the young Brian Walters, the current chairman and chief executive officer, became head of the U.S. operation.

When Brian Walters took responsibility for Victoria's U.S. business, the firm's American distributor was selling 30–40 cranes per year. Walters thought the company should be selling at least 150. Even worse, the orders that the American firm did get tended to come in large quantities—as many as 50 cranes in a single order—which played havoc with Victoria's production scheduling. Walters commented "We would rather have ten orders of ten cranes each than a single order for 100." In 1975, when the U.S. distributor's agreement expired, Walters offered the company a five-year renewal if it would guarantee sales of 150 units per year. When the firm refused, Walters bought it, and in the first month fired 13 of the 15 employees and cancelled most existing dealerships. He then set to work to rebuild—only accepting orders for 10 cranes or less. His hope was to gain a foothold and a solid reputation in the U.S. market before the big U.S. firms even noticed him.

This strategy quickly showed results, and in 1976 Walters came back to Canada. As Rivers was still general manager, there was not enough to occupy him fully, and he began travelling three or four months a year. While he was still very much a part of the company, it was not a full-time involvement.

VICTORIA IN THE 1980s

Victoria entered the 1980s with sales of approximately $50 million and by 1985, partly as a result of opening the new plant in California, had succeeded in doubling this figure. Profits reached their highest level ever in 1983, but declined somewhat over the next two years as costs rose and the rate of sales growth slowed. Financial statements are presented in Exhibits 1 and 2. The following sections describe the company and its environment in the 1980s.

Product Line

The bulk of Victoria's crane sales in the 1980s came from a single product line, the LTM 1000, which was produced both in the company's Squamish facility (the firm had moved from Victoria to Squamish in the early 1900s) and its smaller plant in California, built in 1979. The LTM 1000 line consisted of mobile cranes of five basic sizes, averaging approximately $500 000 in price. Numerous options were available for these cranes, which could provide uncompromised on-site performance, precision lifting capabilities, fast highway travel, and effortless city driving. Because of the numerous choices available, Victoria preferred not to build them to stock. The company guaranteed 60-day delivery and "tailor-made" cranes to customer specifications. This required a large inventory of both parts and raw material.

The most recent addition to the LTM 1000 line was developed in 1982, when Walters learned that a company trying to move unusually long and heavy logs from a new tract of redwood trees in British Columbia was having serious problems with its existing cranes. A crane with a larger than average height and lifting capacity was required. Up to this point, for technical reasons, it had not been possible to produce a crane with the required specifications. However, Walters vowed that Victoria would develop such a crane, and six months later it had succeeded.

Although the LTM 1000 series provided almost all of Victoria's crane sales, a new crane had been introduced in 1984 after considerable expenditure on design, development and manufacture. The $650 000 A-100 had a 70-tonne capacity and could lift loads to heights of 61 metres, a combination previously unheard of in the industry. Through the use of smooth hydraulics even the heaviest loads could be picked up without jolts. In spite of these features, and an optional ram-operated tilt-back cab designed to alleviate the stiff necks which operators commonly developed from watching high loads, sales of the A-100 were disappointing. As a result, several of the six machines built were leased to customers at unattractive rates. The A-100 had, however, proven to be a very effective crowd attraction device at equipment shows.

Markets

There were two important segments in the crane market—custom-built cranes and standard cranes—and although the world mobile crane market was judged to be $630 million in 1985, no estimates were available as to the size of each segment. Victoria competed primarily in the custom segment, in the medium-and heavy-capacity end of the market. In the medium-capacity custom crane class, Victoria's prices were approximately 75% of those of its two main competitors.

The gap closed as the cranes became heavier, with Victoria holding a 15% advantage over Washington Cranes in the heavy custom crane business. In heavy standard cranes Victoria did not have a price advantage.

Victoria's two most important markets were Canada and the United States. The U.S. market was approximately $240 million in 1985, and Victoria's share was about 15%. Victoria's Sacramento plant, serving both the U.S. market and export sales involving U.S. aid and financing, produced 60 to 70 cranes per year. The Canadian market was much smaller, about $44 million in 1985, but Victoria was the dominant firm in the country, with a 60% share. The Squamish plant, producing 130 to 150 cranes per year, supplied both the Canadian market and all export sales not covered by the U.S. plant. There had been very little real growth in the world market since 1980.

The primary consumers in the mobile crane industry were contractors. Because the amount of equipment downtime could make the difference between showing a profit or loss on a contract, contractors were very sensitive to machine dependability as well as parts and service availability. Price was important, but it was not everything. Independent surveys suggested that Washington Crane, Victoria's most significant competitor, offered somewhat superior service and reliability, and if Victoria attempted to sell similar equipment at prices comparable to Washington's, it would fail. As a result, Victoria tried to reduce its costs through extensive backward integration, manufacturing 85% of its crane components in-house, the highest percentage in the industry. This drive to reduce costs was somewhat offset, however, by the fact that much of the equipment in the Squamish plant was very old. In recent years, some of the slower and less versatile machinery had been replaced, but by 1985 only 15% of the machinery in the plant was new, efficient, numerically controlled equipment.

Victoria divided the world into eight marketing regions. The firm carried out little conventional advertising, but did participate frequently at equipment trade shows. One of the company's most effective selling tools was its ability to fly in prospective customers from all over the world in Walters' executive jet. Victoria believed that the combination of its integrated plant, worker loyalty, and the single-product concentration evident in their Canadian plant produced a convinced customer. There were over 14 such visits to the British Columbia plant in 1985, including delegations from The People's Republic of China, Korea, France and Turkey.

Competition

Victoria, as the world's second largest producer of cranes, faced competition from five major firms, all of whom were much larger and more diversified. The industry leader was the Washington Crane Company with 1985 sales of $400 million and a world market share of 50%. Washington had become a name synonymous around the world with heavy-duty equipment and had been able to maintain a sales growth-rate of over 15% per annum for the past five years. It manufactured in the U.S., Mexico and Australia. Key to its operations were 100 strong dealers worldwide with over 200 outlets. Washington had almost 30% of Canada's crane market.

Next in size after Victoria was Texas Star, another large manufacturer whose cranes were generally smaller than Victoria's and sold through the company's extensive worldwide equipment dealerships. The next two largest competitors were both very large U.S. multinational producers whose crane lines formed a small part of their overall business. With the exception of Washington, industry observers suggested that crane sales for these latter firms had been stable (at best) for quite some time. The exception was the Japanese crane producer Toshio which had been aggressively pursuing sales worldwide and had entered the North American market recently. Sato, another Japanese firm, had started in the North American market as well. Walters commented:

> My father laid the groundwork for the success that this company has enjoyed, but it is clear that we now have some major challenges ahead of us. Washington Cranes is four times our size and I know that we are at the top of their hit list. Our Japanese competitors, Toshio and Sato, are also going to be tough. The key to our success is to remain flexible—we must not develop the same kind of organization as the big U.S. firms.

Organization

In 1979, a number of accumulating problems had ended Brian Walters' semi-retirement and brought him back into the firm full time. Although sales were growing, Walters saw that work was piling up and things were not getting done. He believed that new cranes needed to be developed, and he wanted a profit-sharing plan put in place. One of his most serious concerns was the development of middle managers. Walters commented, "we had to develop middle-level line managers—we had no depth." The root cause of these problems, Walters believed, was that the firm was overly centralized. Most of the functional managers reported to Rivers, and Rivers made most of the decisions. Walters concluded that action was necessary—"We have to change," he said. "If we want to grow further we have to do things."

Between 1979 and 1982 Walters reorganized the firm by setting up separate operating companies and a corporate staff group. In several cases, senior operating executives were placed in staff/advisory positions, while in others, executives held positions in both operating and staff groups. Exhibit 3 illustrates Victoria's organizational chart as of 1983.

By early 1984 Walters was beginning to wonder "if I had made a very bad decision." The staff groups weren't working. Rivers had been unable to accept the redistribution of power and had resigned. There was "civil war in the company." Politics and factional disputes were the rule rather than the exception. Line managers were upset by the intervention of the staff VPs of employee relations, manufacturing, and marketing. Staff personnel, on the other hand, were upset by "poor" line decisions.

As a result, the marketing and manufacturing staff functions were eradicated with the late-1985 organizational restructuring illustrated in Exhibit 4. The services previously supplied by the staff groups were duplicated to varying extents inside each division.

In place of most of the staff groups, an executive committee was established in 1984. Membership in this group included the president and head of all staff groups and presidents (general managers) of the four divisions. Meeting monthly, the executive committee was intended to evaluate the performance of the firm's profit and cost problems, handle mutual problems such as transfer prices, and allocate capital expenditures among the four operating divisions. Subcommittees handled subjects such as R&D and new products.

The new organization contained seven major centres for performance measurement purposes. The cost centres were:

1. Engineering; R&D (reporting to Victco Ltd.).
2. International Marketing (Victoria Marketing Ltd.).
3. Corporate staff.

The major profit centres were:

4. CraneCorp. Inc. (U.S. production and sales).
5. Victco Ltd. (supplying Victoria with components).
6. Craneco (Canadian production and marketing).
7. Victoria-owned Canadian sales outlets (reporting to Victoria Marketing Ltd.).

The major profit centres had considerable autonomy in their day-to-day operations and were motivated to behave as if their division was a separate, independent firm.

By mid-1985, Brian Walters had moved out of his position as president, and Michael Carter—a long-time employee close to retirement—was asked to take the position of president until a new one could be found.

Walters saw his role changing. "If I was anything, I was a bit of an entrepreneur. My job was to supply that thrust but to let people develop on their own accord. I was not concerned about things not working, but I was concerned when nothing was being done about it."

In the new organization Walters did not sit on the executive committee. However, as chairman of the board and chief executive officer, the committee's recommendations came to him and " . . . they tried me on six ways from Sunday." His intention was to monitor the firm's major activities rather than to set them. He did have to sit on the product development subcommittee, however, when " . . . things were not working . . . there was conflict . . . the engineering group (engineering, R&D) had designed a whole new crane and nobody including me knew about it." Mr. McCarthy, the V.P. of engineering and R&D, called only five to six committee meetings. The crane his group developed was not to Walters' liking. (There had been a high turnover rate in this group, with four V.P.s since 1983.) Recognizing these problems, Walters brought in consultants to tackle the problems of the management information system and the definition of staff/line responsibilities.

In spite of these moves, dissatisfaction still existed within the company in 1986. The new organization had resulted in considerable dissension. Some conflict centred around the establishment of appropriately challenging budgets for each operating firm and even more conflict had erupted over transfer pricing and allocation of capital budgets. In 1985–86, even though requested budgets were cut equally, lack of central control over spending resulted in overexpenditures by several of the profit and cost centres.

The views of staff and the operating companies' presidents varied considerably when they discussed Victoria's organizational evolution and the operation of the present structure.

Diane Walters, the president of Victoria International Marketing, liked the autonomous system because it helped to identify the true performance of sections of the company. "We had separate little buckets and could easily identify results." Furthermore, she felt that there was no loss of efficiency (due to the duplication of certain staff functions within the divisions) since there was little duplication of systems between groups, and each group acted as a check and balance on the other groups so that "manufacturing won't make what marketing won't sell." Comments from other executives were as follows:

> The divisionalized system allowed me to get closer to my staff because we were a separate group.
> We ended up with sales and marketing expertise that was much better than if we had stayed under manufacturing.
> If you (run the firm) with a manufacturing-oriented organization, you could forget what people want.
> In a divisionalized system there was bound to be conflict between divisions, but that was not necessarily unhealthy.

Some executives saw the decentralized, semi-autonomous operating company structure as a means of giving each person the opportunity to grow and develop without the hindrance of other functional executives. Most, if not all, of the operating company presidents and staff V.P.s were aware that decentralization brought benefits, especially in terms of the autonomy it gave them to modify existing practices. One senior executive even saw the present structure as an indicator of their basic competitive stance: "Either we centralize the structure and retract, or we stay as we are and fight with the big guys." With minimal direction supplied from Brian Walters, presidents were able to build up their staff, establish priorities and programs, and, essentially, were only held responsible for the bottom line.

Other executives believed that Victoria's structure was inappropriate. As one executive put it, "The semi-independence of the operating companies and the lack of a real leader for the firm has resulted in poor co-ordination of problem solving and difficulty in allocating responsibility." As an example, he noted how engineering's response to manufacturing was often slow and poorly communicated. Even worse, the executive noted, was how the priorities of different units were not synchronized. "When you manufacture just one product line all your activities are interrelated. So when one group puts new products first on a priority list while another is still working out bugs in the existing product, conflict and inefficiencies have to develop."

The opposing group argued that the present organization was more appropriate to a larger, faster growing and more complex company. As one senior executive put it, "We're too small to be as decentralized as we are now. All of this was done to accommodate the `Walters kids' anyway, and it's now going to detract from profitability and growth." Another of these executives stated that rather than being a president of an operating company he would prefer to be a general manager at the head of a functional group, reporting to a group head. "If we had the right Victoria Heavy Equipment president," he said, "we wouldn't need all these divisional presidents." Another continued,

> Right now the players (divisional presidents and staff V.P.s) run the company. Brian Walters gives us a shot of adrenaline four or six times a year but doesn't provide any active leadership. When Brian leaves, things stop. Instead, Brian now wants to monitor the game plan rather than set it up for others to run. As we still only have an interim president (Carter), it is the marketplace that leads us, not any strategic plan or goal.

THE NEW PRESIDENT

Individual views about the appropriate characteristics of a new president were determined by what each executive thought was wrong with Victoria. Everyone realized that the new president would have to accommodate Brian Walters' presence and role in the firm and the existence of his two children in the organization. They all generally saw Brian as wanting to supply ideas and major strategies but little else.

All but one of Victoria's executives agreed that the new president should *not* get involved in day-to-day activities or in major decision making. Instead, he should "arbitrate" among the line general managers (subsidiary presidents) and staff V.P.s and become more of a "bureaucrat-cum-diplomat" than an aggressive leader. As another put it, "The company will drive itself; only once in a while he'll steer a little."

THE 1986 SITUATION

Industry analysts predicted a decline of 10% in world crane sales—which totalled 1200 units in 1985—and as much as a 30% decrease in the North American market in 1986. Victoria's sales and production levels were down. Seventy-five shop floor employees had been laid off at Squamish, bringing total employment there to 850, and similar cuts were expected in Sacramento. Worker morale was suffering as a result, and the profit sharing plan, which had been introduced in early 1985 at Walters' initiative, was not helping matters. In spite of the optimism conveyed to workers when the plan was initiated, management had announced in October that no bonus would be paid for the year. Aggravating the problem was the workforce's observation that while certain groups met their budget, others did not, and hence all were penalized. This problem arose because each bonus was based on overall as well as divisional profits.

Many of the shop-floor workers and the supervisory staff were also disgruntled with the additions to the central and divisional staff groups, which had continued even while the workforce was being reduced. They felt that the paperwork these staff functions created was time-consuming and of little benefit. They noted, for example, that there were four or five times as many people in production control in 1986 as there were in 1980 for the same volume of production. In addition, they pointed out that despite all sorts of efforts on the part of a computer-assisted production control group, inventory levels were still too high.

Brian Walters commented on the 1986 situation and his view of the company's future:

> What we are seeing in 1986 is a temporary decline in the market. This does not pose a serious problem for us, and certainly does not impact on my longer term goals for this company, which are to achieve a 25% share of the world market by 1990, and reach sales of $250 million by 1999. We can reach these goals as long as we don't turn into one of these bureaucratic, grey-suited companies that are so common in North America. There are three keys for success

in this business—a quality product, professional people and the motivation for Victoria to be the standard of excellence in our business. This means that almost everything depends on the competence and motivation of our people. We will grow by being more entrepreneurial, more dedicated, and more flexible than our competitors. With our single product line we are also more focussed than our competitors. They manage only by the numbers—there is no room in those companies for an emotional plea, they won't look at sustaining losses to get into a new area, they'll turn the key on a loser . . . we look at the longer term picture.

"The hazard for Victoria," Walters said as he looked out of his window toward the Sacramento airstrip, "is that we could develop the same kind of bureaucratic, quantitatively oriented, grey-suited managers that slow down the large U.S. competitors." "But that," he said, turning to his audience, "is something I'm going to watch like a hawk. We need the right people."

EXHIBIT 1 Victoria Balance Sheet for the Years 1981–85 ($000s)

	1981	1982	1983	1984	1985
ASSETS					
Current Assets					
Accounts receivable	8 328	7 960	9 776	10 512	10 951
Allowance for doubtful accounts	(293)	(310)	(287)	(297)	(316)
Inventories	21 153	24 425	24 698	25 626	27 045
Prepaid expenses	119	104	156	106	129
Total current assets	29 307	32 179	34 343	35 947	37 809
Advances to shareholders	1 300	1 300	1 300	1 300	1 300
Fixed assets: property plant and equipment	6 840	6 980	6 875	7 353	7 389
Total assets	37 447	40 459	42 518	44 600	46 598
LIABILITIES AND SHAREHOLDERS' EQUITY					
Current Liabilities					
Notes payable to bank	7 733	8 219	9 258	10 161	11 332
Accounts payable	9 712	11 353	10 543	10 465	10 986
Accrued expenses	1 074	1 119	1 742	1 501	1 155
Deferred income tax	419	400	396	408	345
Income tax payable	545	692	612	520	516
Current portion of long-term debt	912	891	867	888	903
Total current liabilities	20 395	22 674	23 418	23 943	25 237
Long-term debt	6 284	6 110	6 020	6 005	6 114
Total liabilities	26 679	28 784	29 438	29 948	31 351
Shareholders' Equity					
Common shares	200	290	295	390	435
Retained earnings	10 568	11 385	12 790	14 262	14 812
Total shareholders' equity	10 768	11 675	13 080	14 652	15 247
Total liabilities and shareholders' equity	37 447	40 459	42 518	44 600	46 598

EXHIBIT 2 Victoria Income Statement for the Years 1981–85 ($000s)

	1981	*1982*	*1983*	*1984*	*1985*
Revenue					
Net sales	63 386	77 711	86 346	94 886	100 943
Costs and Expenses					
Cost of sales	49 238	59 837	63 996	71 818	75 808
Selling expense	7 470	9 234	10 935	11 437	13 104
Administrative expense	2 684	3 867	5 490	5 795	7 038
Engineering expense	1 342	1 689	1 832	1 949	2 109
Gross income	2 652	3 084	4 093	3 887	2 884
Income taxes	1 081	1 281	1 630	1 505	1 254
Net income	$1 571	$1 803	$2 463	$2 382	$1 630

EXHIBIT 3 Victoria Organizational Structure, 1979–83

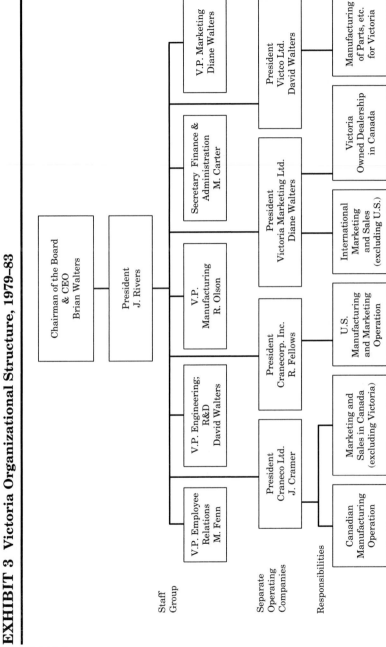

EXHIBIT 4 Victoria Organizational Structure, Late 1985

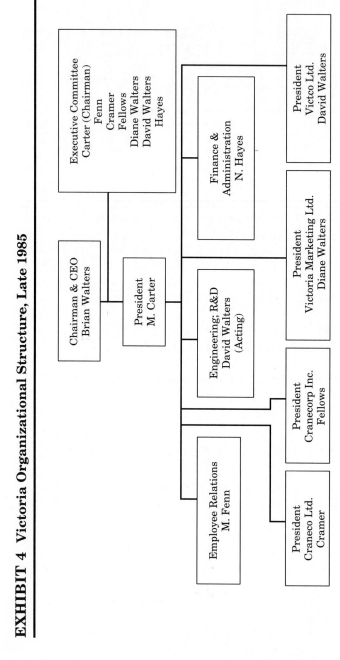

UNIVERSITY HOSPITAL —1987

Roderick E. White and Mary M. Crossan

"Finding a better way."[1]

In the fall of 1987, University Hospital (UH) had just completed, with the assistance of outside consultants, an extensive strategy review culminating in a formal strategic plan. The original stimulus for the plan had been to better understand the growth patterns and potential of the hospital's services in order to forecast the need for and justify a significant expansion of the hospital's facilities. However, the final document had gone beyond this original intention, raising questions about the hospital's "service portfolio" and its future potential.

The strategic plan had seven key recommendations (Exhibit 1), several of which represented significant departures from past practice. As part of the planning process, the hospital's services had been put into different categories, a portfolio approach, with apparent implications for future emphasis and resource allocation. As one UH vice-president commented:

> The plan has forced us to establish some priorities for our different services. Not everything we do is, or will be, world-class, and the plan will help us allocate our increasingly scarce resources, capital and operating funds, towards our premier services.

Further, the plan recommended organizing business units around these "service clusters" (or product lines), and continuing the planning process as an ongoing, in-house activity.

As Pat Blewett, President and C.E.O. of UH, reviewed the report and its recommendations, he was satisfied with both the process and the results. Blewett was widely recognized as a highly positive, entrepreneurial type of administrator willing to try new ideas and promote innovative services. Results had been impressive. New services had contributed substantially to UH's growth and cashflow. However, the facility was straining within its existing physical space. In addition, UH, like other hospitals in the province of Ontario, had to cope with

---

[1] UH's motto; attributed to Thomas Edison.

increasing budgetary pressures from the Ministry of Health, while demand for all services continued to grow. Blewett hoped the recommendations from the strategic plan would allow the hospital to deal with these issues while maintaining the institution's innovative and entrepreneurial spirit.

BACKGROUND

While a separate institution, UH was part of a larger health sciences complex of the University of Western Ontario. UH had been an educational and research, as well as a health care delivery facility since opening in 1972. The newest of the three major acute care hospitals in London, Ontario, a community of about 300 000 in southwestern Ontario, UH was established, owned and operated by the London Health Association (LHA).

Founded in 1909, the LHA's activities had changed dramatically over the years. Originally, it had operated a tuberculosis sanatorium on the outskirts of the city. As the number of tuberculosis patients declined, the LHA made plans to diversify into chest diseases and purchased property adjacent to the University for a new hospital. However, in the decade of the 1960s, the University was growing rapidly, especially in the health sciences, and wanted a full-fledged teaching/research hospital attached to the University. The LHA was persuaded to undertake this more ambitious task, but stipulated that their institution would remain administratively separate from the University.

Planning for the new facility began in 1966. An innovative spirit was evident from the outset. Hospitals tend to be very traditional institutions, but the planning group, in its efforts to create an outstanding medical facility, were willing to deviate from conventional practices. The UH motto, "Finding a better way," was applied to facilities design, organizational practice, as well as patient care and research activities. Using a philosophy of form follows function, the hospital layout was guided by an analysis of function. The result was revolutionary with physicians' offices, research areas, inpatient and outpatient departments, and teaching space all on the same floor. Essentially each of the floors operated as a specialized mini-hospital sharing support services within a larger hospital setting. UH's deviation from accepted hospital practices were wide ranging from the use of noise-deadening carpeted floors, a hospital blasphemy at the time, to the decentralized organizational structure with an unconventional division of tasks.

The Health Care Environment

Canada's health care system was one of the most comprehensive in the world, providing equal access to all Canadians. The publicly funded system was the responsibility of the provincial governments, although a substantial portion of the funding came from the federal level by way of transfer payments. In Ontario, the Ministry of Health (MOH) was the department concerned with hospitals. Health care costs accounted for 32% of the province's $32 billion budget, the single largest category of expenditure with the most rapid growth. As a result, the province was becoming increasingly active in its efforts to contain these costs. Examples included the banning of extra billing by doctors, cuts in the number of medical residency positions and provision for the MOH to take over any hospital in a deficit position.

Health care funding had evolved in a piecemeal fashion into an extremely complex and often ambiguous system. Basically, the MOH contracted with the hospitals to provide services, in an approved plant, at an approved ("global") budget. Further, the Ministry expected each hospital to show an excess of revenue over expenses sufficient to provide for a reasonable accumulation of funds for future capital requirements. Program, service reductions, or bed closures which related directly to patient care required the agreement of the Ministry. However, under pressure to balance budgets, some hospitals were reducing services without the formal agreement of the Ministry. Using a universal formula based largely on history, the Ministry arrived at a hospital's global operating budget. Most MOH revenues were *not* directly tied to actual expenditures or the provision of services. New programs could be initiated by the hospital, but incremental capital and/or operating costs were incorporated into the existing global funding base. Additional funds were forthcoming only if approved by the Ministry.

In the approval of new programs, District Health Councils had a prominent voice. They provided the forum for ensuring that changes met the health care needs of the *local* community. The Thames Valley District Health Council (TVDHC) was responsible for the 18 hospitals in the London area. New program proposals submitted to TVDHC were very diverse, ranging from a $400 000 request from UH for a four-bed epilepsy unit, to Victoria Hospital's $94 million expansion request. Evaluating programs on a regional basis, based on local community need, did not allow much consideration of the type of care provided or the referral base they served. UH frequently went outside this process, appealing directly to the Ministry, or failing that, by funding projects from their own accumulated surplus.

The government's influence upon hospitals extended well beyond the control of global operating budgets and new programs. It also affected the supply of nurses, residents, and physicians by controlling the number of available positions in nursing and medical schools, by influencing the certification of immigrants, and by limiting the number of hospital residency positions funded. The MOH had recently reduced, province-wide, the number of medical residency positions for physicians doing post-graduate specialty training. Essentially, medical residents learned a specialty while providing patient care in a hospital, freeing physicians to do teaching, research and other activities. Reduction in residency positions created a gap in the provision of service in larger, teaching hospitals, and would ultimately lead to a decline in the number of indigenously trained medical specialists and researchers.

Pressures on the health care system were increasing partly because of an aging population. Demand for basic services was expected to increase into the 21st century. Further, increasingly sophisticated and expensive new medical technologies not only improved existing services, but also developed new treatments for previously untreatable illnesses, all at a cost, however. While gross measures of productivity, like patient days in hospital per procedure, had been improving, the increasing sophistication of treatments appeared to be increasing costs at a faster rate than offsetting gains in productivity. Further, most gains in productivity came about by requiring fewer personnel to do the same tasks, rather than reducing the number of tasks. The increasing stresses and turnover that naturally resulted were present in all hospital health care professionals, but especially evident in the exodus from the nursing profession. Although not as severe in the London area, it was estimated 600–800 beds in Toronto hospitals were closed because of lack of nursing staff. Shortages of staff existed in other areas; like occupational and physical therapists, radiologists, and pharmacists.

The province's basic approach to managing demand (and costs) appeared to be by limiting supply. As a result, waiting lists were growing, especially for elective procedures. Certain serious, but not immediately life threatening conditions, had waiting lists for treatment of six months to a year, and were getting longer.

Social and political expectations also put pressures on the system. Universal, free access to a health care system offering equal, high-quality care to all had become a societal expectation and a political sacred cow. Politically acceptable ideas for fundamentally restructuring the industry were not obvious. There was no apparent way to reconcile increasing demand and costs with the governmental funding likely to be available. As a result, many observers felt that the health care system was out of control. And the Ministry was under tremendous pressure to control costs and account for its expenditures, while at the same time providing more, new and enhanced services. Without an overall approach to the health care situation, it was not clear how the Ministry would allocate funds in the future. Choices between high technology, expensive procedures, like heart transplantation and intensive care for premature infants, and basic care for the aged were difficult to make and politically sensitive.

UNIVERSITY HOSPITAL

UH was a well-designed and maintained facility. It was located in north London, Ontario. Rising from a three-floor service podium, each of its seven tower floors was divided into two basic components—one an inpatient area, and the other an outpatient, office, research and teaching area. Each inpatient area, except paediatrics, had a corresponding outpatient department for initial assessment follow-up, and the performance of minor procedures. UH had 463 inpatient beds with an average occupancy rate of over 90%, which effectively meant 100% utilization. The occupancy rate and number of beds had been fairly constant over the past few years. Although space was severely constrained within the hospital, there was a land bank available for future expansion.

In the past, UH had employed some creative solutions to its problem of space constraints. Services had been reviewed to determine whether they could be more effectively provided in one of the other London hospitals, or, as in the case of the Occupational Health Centre, whether they could be better served in an off-site location. Some specialization had already occurred within the city. For example, since another major acute-care hospital specialized in maternity, UH did not duplicate this service. However, UH did have an in-vitro fertilization program (popularly known as test-tube babies).

In a major move during 1986, the Robarts Research Institute (RRI) was opened adjacent to UH. A separate but affiliated institution with its own board, the RRI specialized in heart and stroke research. Moving researchers from UH to this new facility helped to alleviate, at least temporarily, some of the hospital's space pressures. The five-floor, 69 000-square-foot institute housed 35 laboratories. By the end of 1987, it was expected 80 RRI researchers would be active in conducting basic research into stroke and aging, heart and circulation, and immunological disorders relating to transplantations.

UH housed some of the latest medical technology. For example, a magnetic resonance imaging (MRI) machine costing $3 million was added in 1986. One of the most powerful machines in Canada, the MRI provided unparalleled images of all body organs. Interestingly, neither funding for the total capital cost nor the majority of the ongoing operating costs for this advanced technology instrument was assumed by the Ministry. However, this had not deterred Blewett, and UH was considering other high technology equipment like a $3 million gamma knife which would enable neurosurgeons to operate without having to cut the skin surface.

Mission & Strategy

UH's mission involved three core activities: research, teaching, and patient care. And in this way it did not differ from other university affiliated teaching hospitals. What made it more unique was the emphasis on innovative, leading edge research. Clinical and teaching activities were expected to reflect and reinforce this focus. This strategy had implications for UH's product/market scope and its service portfolio.

Product/Market Scope

UH attempted to serve the needs of three related, but different markets: teaching, research, and the health care needs of the community. Local community and basic teaching needs generally required a broad base of standard services. On the other hand, research needs argued for focus and specialization of products offered with a physician's clinical activities related to their research and necessarily drawing from a large patient referral base.

With three different markets service focus was not easy to achieve. The initial design of UH had included only a small emergency service because another hospital in the city specialized in trauma. However, in response to local community pressure, a larger emergency department was incorporated. Balancing the product/service portfolio under increasing space constraints, funding pressure and demand for basic health care services was becoming ever more challenging.

Overall UH's mix of cases had a high proportion of acute cases—very ill patients requiring high levels of care. UH had approximately 1% of the approved hospital beds in Ontario, as well as 1% of discharges and patient days in acute care public hospitals. However, when broken down by the acuity/difficulty of the procedure, UH's tertiary focus was clear (Table 1).

TABLE 1 UH Market Share of Ontario Patients by Acuity*

	UH Share	*Number of Cases*
Level I: Primary	0.7%	8 092
Level II: Secondary	1.4	2 616
Level III: Tertiary	4.2	2 783
Examples:		
heart transplant	66.0	31
liver transplant	30.8	175
kidney transplant	27.0	71
craniotomy (age > 18 yrs)	15.7	388

* As classified by a scheme developed in the U.S. designed to reflect intensity of nursing care required. Higher level indicates more acute.

Geographically, 81% of UH's admitted patients came from the primary service area of Southwestern Ontario, with one-third of all patients originating from the hospital's primary service area of Middlesex County. Fifteen percent of all patients came from the secondary service area, which consisted of all parts of Ontario outside the primary region. The remaining 4% of patients came from outside the province of Ontario. However, because these cases tended to be more acute than the norm they accounted for a disproportionate share of patient days, approximately 6% and an even larger proportion of revenues. Exhibit 2 provides a breakdown of current patient origin by service. For the future the strategic plan had identified:

– transplantation	– in vitro fertilization
– neurosciences	– diabetes
– cardiology/cardiovascular surgery	– epilepsy
– orthopaedics/sport injury	– occupational health care

as services with high, out-of-province potential.

To help manage the service/product portfolio, the strategic plan called for the following designation of products: *Premier Product Lines* were designated on the basis of the world-class, cutting-edge nature of the service; *Intermediate Product Lines* represented those services that were approaching premier status or that stood alone as a service entity; *Service Support Clusters* were services that supported the intermediate and premier product lines; *Ambulatory / Emergency Services* included outpatient clinics, emergency services and regional joint venture arrangements; and *Diversification / Collaboration Ventures* were stand alone services that generated revenue for UH. The services for premier and intermediate categories are listed in Exhibit 3. A more detailed profile of the premier product lines is provided in Appendix A.

Product Innovation

Developing new and improved leading edge treatments for health problems was a key element of UH's mission relating to research and teaching. And while the institution, over its relatively brief history, had participated in a number of medical innovations this success did not appear attributable to formal planning. Rather new programs and services developed at UH in a seemingly ad hoc fashion. As Ken Stuart, Vice-President Medical, observed, "New services happen because of individuals—they just grow. There is some targeted research, but it is not the route of most (activities) because it would stifle people's ideas. They need to fiddle with things and be able to fail." The development of the Epilepsy Unit, outlined in Appendix B, describes an example of this process.

Blewett commented on the development of new programs at UH:

> The fact that the hospital is so small—everyone knows everyone—I can get around. Everyone knows what's going on in the hospital. ... People just drop in to see me. Someone will come down and tell me that they've found a real winner and they just have to have him/her, and so we go out and get them. There's always room for one more; we find a way to say yes.

When it impacts other resources, Diane (Stewart, Executive Vice-President) becomes involved. She says it's easy for me to agree, but her people have to pick up the pieces. In order to better identify the requirements for new physicians and new programs Diane came up with the idea of the Impact Analysis (a study of how new or expanded programs affected hospital staffing, supplies and facilities). But even when the study is done we don't use it as a reason to say no; we use it to find out what we have to do to make it happen.

Diane Stewart, the Executive Vice-President, was sensitive to the need for continued innovation. She had stated, "We like to leave the door open to try new things. We go by the philosophy that to try and fail is at least to learn." A UH vice-president commented:

> People here are well read. When ideas break, anywhere in the world, they want them. There is a lot of compromising. But things get resolved. It just takes some time. We haven't learned the meaning of the word "no." But we're at a juncture where we may have to start saying no. We're just beginning to be (in the tight financial position), where many other hospitals have been for several years.

Revenues and Costs

UH's revenues and costs could not be neatly assigned to its major areas of activity. As shown in Exhibit 4a, in 1983 73% of UH's sources of funds were a "global allocation" from the MOH, and by 1987 this amount had been reduced to 70%. For the most part these funds were not attached to specific activities, acuity of patients or outcomes. Over the past few years, UH, like all other hospitals, had simply been getting an annual increase in its global allocation to off-set inflation. The stipulation attached to MOH funds was that there could be no deficit.

Some small part of MOH funding was tied to activity levels. Increases in out-patient activity did, through a complex formula, eventually result in increased funding to the hospital. Further, the Ministry had established a special "life support fund" to fund volume increases for specified procedures. However, this fund was capped and the number of claims by all hospitals already exceeded funds available, so only partial funding was received. The MOH also funded the clinical education of medical students and interns. This accounted for most of the $5.8 million in revenue from MOH programs (Exhibit 4a).

Approximately 30% of UH's revenues did not come directly from the Ministry of Health through its global funding allocation. A large percentage of these self-generated revenues originated from servicing out-of-province patients. For patients from other provinces the MOH negotiated with the paying provinces, a per diem charge for services provided. Even so, as out-of-province patients generated incremental revenues above and beyond the global allocation, they were a very attractive market. For out-of-country patients, UH could set their own price for services provided, thereby ensuring that the full cost of providing health care was recovered. But, as shown in Table 2, the out-of-province and out-of-country revenue appeared to have reached a plateau at around 14% of total revenue. There was also a sense the mix of this component was shifting away from out-of-country patients towards out-of-province.

TABLE 2 UH Revenue Breakdown

Fiscal Year	MOH Global Base	Other Revenue	Out-of-Province & Out-of-Country
1983	74.6%	25.4%	7.4%
1984	73.7	26.3	8.7
1985	72.1	27.9	11.3
1986	69.3	30.7	13.8
1987	70.5	29.5	13.9

Additional funds also came from the University Hospital Foundation of London and other entrepreneurial activities. The numerous fund-raising appeals by the Foundation included sales of operating room greens in sizes ranging from doll-size through to a small child, and a specially produced record and music video. The Foundation was a separate financial entity and funds flowing to UH appeared as an addition to UH equity (and cash) with no effect on revenues.

Salaries, wages and benefits made up the single largest cost category. (The base salary of medical staff, who were employees of the University, were not directly included in this number.) As a proportion of total revenues these costs had declined marginally over the last five years. Other costs had, however, increased, in particular medical supplies and drugs. Much of this increase was due to the MOH's unwillingness to pay for certain drug therapies. For example, drugs used to prevent rejection of transplanted organs were not paid for by the MOH because the drugs were considered experimental, and therefore the cost of these drugs had to be covered under the hospital's global budget. Similar funding limitations had evolved with other drugs and medical apparatus, e.g., implantable defibrillators. The boundary between clinical research and clinical practice was often difficult to draw. Research funding bodies, like the Medical Research Council, would not pay for medical procedures beyond the purely experimental stage. And often the MOH would not immediately step in, and fund procedures after research grants expired.

On balance UH had never recorded a deficit year. However, its operating surplus had been decreasing (Exhibit 4a). Blewett felt the key to UH's future financial success was reduced reliance on Ministry funding. (UH's reliance on Ministry funding was already less than most hospitals.) UH was actively pursuing opportunities with the potential to generate funds. One recent development was the Occupational Health Centre (OHC), which opened in 1986 as a separate private, for-profit organization to provide occupational health care services to the business community. By the end of 1987, it had 30 companies with 11 000 employees as clients. However, like most startups, the OHC had required an initial infusion of cash, and was not expected to generate net positive cash flow for several years.

Not all of the activity undertaken at UH was reflected in its financial statements and operating statistics. Research grants and many of their associated costs were not included in the hospital's statements, even though they were administered by the University, and much of the activity was conducted at UH. During 1986-87, UH physicians and researchers were involved in over 200 projects with annual funding of $9.5 million. Table 3 lists the services most involved in research. In an effort to capitalize on the revenue potential of the innovations developed at UH, an innovations inventory was being compiled and the potential for licensing explored. It was expected this activity, if it demonstrated potential, would be spun out into a private, for profit corporation.

TABLE 3   UH Clinical Services with Largest Research Budgets

Service	*Amount ($000)*
Transplantation & Nephrology	$1 979
Gynaecology	1 454
Neurology	1 105
Endocrinology	923
Cardiology	678

SOURCE: *Research Annual Compendium*, not including the Robarts Research Institute.

Staffing and Organization

UH was a large and diverse organization employing 2 600 personnel. There were 128 medical clinicians and researchers, 70 residents, 44 interns and research fellows, 875 nursing staff, 140 paramedical, 312 technical, 214 supervisory and specialist, 444 clerical and 379 service staff.

The relationship with UH's medical staff was especially unique. *All* UH physicians held joint appointments with UH and the University, and were technically University employees. As well, they did not have a private practice outside of University Hospital. As a consequence, all patients (except those admitted through the emergency department) were referred to UH by outside physicians. At most other hospitals, physicians were not salaried employees. They had hospital privileges, and spent part of their time at the hospital and the rest at their own clinics/offices, usually separate from the hospital. These physicians billed OHIP directly for all patient care delivered. At UH, the "GFT"[2] relationship with physicians was very different. They were paid a base salary by the University. Physicians negotiated with the Dean of Medicine and Department Chairperson for salaries in excess of this base. This negotiated portion was called the "if earned" portion. UH physicians were expected to make OHIP billings from clinical work inside the hospital at least up to the level of their "if earned" portion. Any additional billings were "donated" to the University, and were placed into a research fund. Although arrangements varied, the physicians who contributed their billings usually had some say in the allocation of these research funds.

Because of this GFT relationship, the medical staff at UH generally developed a stronger identification and affiliation with the institution. Even so, retaining medical staff was not easy. Most could make significantly higher incomes if they gave up their teaching and research activities, and devoted all their efforts to private practice. While the salary of UH physicians was competitive with similar institutions in Canada, many research hospitals in the U.S. were perceived to offer higher compensation and often better support for research. To further complicate matters, the available number of University positions in the medical faculty and the dollar amount of the salary had been frozen for several years. As a result, the base salary for any net new positions or salary increases were funded entirely by UH.

Structure

The physicians were by nature highly autonomous and independent. Nominally at least medical staff were responsible through their clinical service head (e.g., Neurology) or a department head (e.g., Neurosciences) to Ken Stuart, Vice-President Medical. The role of service and department head was a part-time responsibility rotated amongst senior clinicians in the particular specialty. The heads of services and departments in the hospital often, but not always, held parallel appointments in the Faculty of Medicine at the University.

The division of services and departments was in most instances determined by traditional professional practice. However, "product offerings" which crossed

---

[2] Geographic Full-Time.

traditional departmental boundaries were common. At UH, the only one with formal organizational recognition was the multi-organ transplant service (MOTS). It had its own medical head, manager and budget. Other multi-disciplinary units, like the Epilepsy Unit, did not have formal organizational status, even though the strategic plan recommended organizing around product lines (or business units).

In general, the hierarchy could best be described as loose and collegial. Although it varied from individual to individual, most physicians, while they might consult with their service and department heads when confronted with a problem or pursuing an opportunity, felt no requirement to do so. Typically they dealt directly with the persons concerned. Most chiefs of services supported this *laissez-faire* approach, since they wanted to encourage initiative and did not wish to become overly involved in administration, coordination and control.

At an operational level, the primary organizational difference between UH and traditional hospitals was its decentralized approach. Each floor acted as a mini-hospital. A triumvirate of medical, nursing and administrative staff were responsible for the operation of their unit. In many hospitals, nurses spent much of their time doing non-nursing tasks including administrative duties like budget preparation, coordinating maintenance and repairs, etc. At UH, a service coordinator located on each floor handled non-nursing responsibilities for each unit and interfaced with centralized services like purchasing, housekeeping, and engineering. Whenever possible, the allied health professionals, such as psychologists, occupational therapists and physiotherapists, were also located on the floors. In traditional hospitals, hiring, staff development, quality assurance and staff assignment of nurses were done on a centralized basis. At UH, a nursing manager, located in each service, handled the nursing supervision responsibilities. A nursing co-ordinator handled the clinical guidance and supervision of the nurses.

Organizationally service coordinators and allied health professionals reported through their respective managers to the newly created, and as yet unfilled, position of Vice-President Patient Services. Nurses reported through nursing managers to the Vice-President Nursing. In practice, the physicians, nurses and service coordinators on each floor formed a team which managed their floor. Ideally, integration occurred, and operational issues were addressed at the floor level, only rarely referred up for resolution.

Non-medical personnel working in centralized laboratories and services, but not directly involved in patient care reported to the Vice-President Administration. Activities dealing with financial, accounting and information were the responsibility of the Vice-President Finance. While final hiring decisions for non-physician positions were decentralized to the units concerned, job description, posting and initial screening was done in the human resources department. In addition, some employee education and health services were handled through this department. The hiring of physicians, even though technically University employees, was usually initiated within UH. Typically, service or department heads would identify desirable candidates. If the person was being hired for a new position (as opposed to a replacement), then after discussion of the physician's plans, an impact analysis would be prepared identifying the resources required. Generally, Pat Blewett was very involved in the recruitment of physicians.

UH was considered progressive in its staffing and organization, having recorded many firsts among Canadian hospitals. Over the years, they had been one of the first to introduce service coordinators, paid maternity leave, dental benefits, 12-hour shifts, job-sharing, workload measurement and productivity monitoring. The concern for employees was reflected in UH's relatively low turnover, in the 9% range. Exit interviews indicated very few people went to another health care job because they were dissatisfied with UH. Aside from normal attrition, the biggest reason for leaving was lack of upward job mobility, a situation caused by UH's flat structure and low turnover.

Committees at all levels and often crossing departments were a fact of life at UH, and reflected the organization's decentralized and participative approach to decision-making. Diane Stewart, for example, was a member of 48 different hospital and board committees. Medical staff were also expected to be involved, as Ken Stuart explained:

> Committee work is not a physician's favourite activity. But it's important they be involved in the management of the hospital. I balance committee assignments amongst the medical staff and no one can continually refuse to do their part. This is a demand UH makes of its GFT physicians that other hospitals do not.

UH's management group had recently undergone a reorganization, reducing the number of direct reports to Pat Blewett from five to three. Now the Vice-President Human Resources and the Vice-President Administration, along with the Vice-Presidents of Patient Services and Nursing, reported to the Executive Vice-President, Diane Stewart (Exhibit 5). The reorganization centered control of operations around Stewart, allowing Blewett to concentrate on physicians, external relationships and the future direction of UH.

Budgets

There were five groups that submitted budgets to administration: support services, nursing, allied health, diagnostic services, and administrative services. The annual capital and operating budgetary processes involved a lot of meetings, and give-and-take. As one manager described:

... The budget of each department is circulated to the other departments within our service. We have a meeting with ... V.P. Administration and ... V.P. Finance and all the department heads. Although the department heads are physicians, often the department managers will either accompany or represent the department head. In that meeting we review each department's budget, questioning any items which seem out of place. The department will either remain firm on its budget, back down, or decide to postpone the expenditure to the following year. People do back down. If we can't get our collective budgets within the budget for our service, the vice-presidents will either make trade-offs with the other service categories, or speak with the department heads privately to try and obtain further cuts. The majority of cuts are made in the meeting. ... It works because the department heads are fiscally responsible, and there is a lot of trust between the departments and between the departments and administration.

Operating budgets were coordinated by the service coordinator on each floor, but really driven by the plans of the medical staff. Each year physicians were asked about their activity levels for the upcoming year; these were translated into staffing and supplies requirements, in terms of number of hours worked and the physical volume of supplies consumed. Costs were attached and the overall expense budget tabulated later by the finance department. In the last fiscal year, when the overall budget was tabulated, it exceeded the estimated revenues of the hospital by over $10 million, roughly 10%. Ross Chapin, Vice-President–Finance, explained what happened:

> We went back to each of the clinical services and looked at their proposed level of activity. The hospital had already been operating at 100 plus percent of its physical capacity. Most of the services had not taken this into account in preparing their plans. They had assumed more space and more patient beds would be available. Since this just wasn't going to happen, at least in the short term, we asked them to re-do their budgets with more realistic space assumptions. As a result our revenue and expense budgets came more into line.

While the activity of the medical staff drove the operating expenditures of the hospital, physicians were not in the ongoing budgetary loop. If expenditures were exceeding budget, physicians might not even be aware, and if aware, had no incentive to cut expenses and reduce activity levels in order to meet budget. Aside from the number of physicians and the limits of their own time, the major constraint on expenditures was space and the availability of support services. A patient could not be admitted unless a bed was available; an outpatient procedure could not be conducted unless a consultation room was free and the needed support services, e.g., radiology, physical therapy, etc., could be scheduled.

Because of MOH funding and space constraints, the hospital had a set number of inpatient beds. The allocation of beds amongst services was determined by a committee made up of the manager of admitting, several of physicians and chaired by the Vice-President Medical. Since bed availability affected the activity level of the services and their physicians, this allocation was a sensitive area. Services would often lend an unused bed to another, usually adjacent, service. However, the formal reallocation of beds was done infrequently. And when done, was based on waiting lists (by service) and bed utilization rates.

New Programs

While capital and operating budgets for ongoing activities originated with the managers' on the floors, the medical staff usually intitiated requests for new programs and equipment. Money to fund large outlays associated with new or expanded programs would be requested from the MOH, or might be part of a special fund raising campaign. Private charitable foundations had made significant contributions to the Epilepsy Unit, the MOTU and the MRI facility. When proposals for a new program or the addition of a new physician were made, an impact analysis was undertaken. These studies detailed the resource requirement: space, support staff, supplies, etc. of the initiative, and summarized the overall financial impact. The analysis did not, however, identify the availability or source of the required resources should the initiative be pursued. As one vice president explained:

> The impact analysis might show that if we bring on a new orthopaedic surgeon, we'll need two more physical therapists (PTs). But there is no space (and probably no money) for the PTs. Quite often the physician is hired anyway, and the PTs currently on staff have to try and manage the additional work load. We *know* what a new physician will need beforehand, but we don't always ensure it's there before they come on board.

Recently a new physician had arrived after being hired, and office space was not available.

Basis for Success

UH attributed its success to several factors. A primary factor was the GFT status of the medical staff, which cultivated a high degree of loyalty and commitment to the hospital, and supported the integration of excellence in teaching, research and practice. The ability of the medical staff to attract out-of-province patients contributed to the hospital's revenues. The strong entrepreneurial orientation of management, its ability to identify and create additional sources of revenue, and a widely shared understanding of the mission of UH helped to foster commitment to the organization's goals.

Early in its development, UH had attracted physicians/researchers capable of developing major internationally recognized research and clinical programs, like Doctors Drake and Barnett in neurosciences and Dr. Stiller in transplantation. These physicians and their programs had developed international recognition, and generated patient referrals from all over the country and around the world.

UH's product portfolio required a delicate balance. It was natural for products to evolve and mature. As innovative procedures became more commonplace, they tended to diffuse to other hospitals. Indeed, UH contributed to this process by training physicians in these procedures as part of their teaching mission. As a consequence, UH's patient referral base would shrink, and so too would out-of-country, out-of-province revenues from maturing service. UH required a constant inflow of innovative, internationally recognized clinical procedures in order to sustain its out-of-province referral base.

THE STRATEGIC PLAN

UH did not have an internal ongoing strategic planning process. In 1985, a change occurred. UH signed an affiliation agreement with the Hospital Corporation of Canada (HCC), an affiliate of the Hospital Corporation of America (HCA), and a large, publicly owned international health care company, which gave UH access to HCA strategic planning expertise. For UH's existing service portfolio, the consultants assessed underlying demand, UH's share of market, its capability base and abilities relative to other research and teaching hospitals. They did not specifically consider MOH funding policy.

Senior management wanted a process that would enable people to buy into the emerging plan, so they conducted a series of planning sessions. The first information session was conducted in the fall of 1986, when general information about the health care environment was presented to the chiefs of services and administration. In December, a day-long retreat was held to disseminate information, and to provide some education on key strategic concepts such as market share and product life cycle. In January 1987, a second retreat was held. The Chiefs of Services were asked to come prepared to make a presentation on the direction of their department, resource requirements and priorities. Blewett commented on the meeting:

> The chiefs did an outstanding job. They really got into it, using business ideas to look at their services and where they are going. They were talking about market share and product life cycles. I believe it gave them a new way to think about things. Really, the chiefs were presenting to each other and they wanted to do a good job and make their best case. A lot of information sharing occurred.

In late February, the consultants' initial recommendations were presented to administration. One of the recommendations was to adopt a portfolio approach to planning. A preliminary designation of products into portfolios of premier, intermediate and service support clusters was provided. The initial criteria used to determine premier status were:

– geographic "draw"
– consensus as a priority
– "leading edge" service
– future orientation of its people

Subsequent meetings with the medical staff led to some modifications of these designations. Blewett reflected on the process of identifying the product/service portfolio.

> I never thought we would do it. But when it came down to making the hard decisions, it didn't take that long. I give a lot of credit to the planners and to our administrative person, who kept in close contact with everyone, and made sure that concerns were taken care of. ... The GFTs are committed to this institution, therefore it's easier to mobilize these people. ... We also made it clear that services could move between categories, which provides some incentive.

Indeed, Sport Medicine had not initially been categorized as a premier service, but in the final version of the plan was placed in this category.

The final strategic plan, a 150-page document, was approved by both the Medical Advisory Committee of the hospital and by its Board of Directors. As Blewett reflected on the process, he was pleased with the results of the effort which had taken over a year to complete. Blewett knew many of his senior managers had applauded the direction the report had taken in providing a more solid foundation on which to make difficult resource allocation decisions. However, he was concerned the plan not be used as a reason to say "no", to stifle initiative and the emergence of new areas of excellence. He wondered how an ongoing planning process would have affected the evolution of the epilepsy unit described in Appendix B. With this in mind, he was wondering where to go from here: How could the plan, its recommendations and following activities be used to help guide the hospital?

EXHIBIT 1   UH Key Recommendations from the Strategic Plan

1. Pursue a Seruuce Cluster/Product Line Development Approach

Product line management is a system that organizes management accountability and operations around discrete service or product lines. Service clusters are those groups of services that are provided to distinct market segments.

By shifting management focus to product line development, hospitals can increase their market share by improving the efficiency of their services and by tailoring services to specific market needs.

2. Adopt an Appropriate Bed Complement for UH in the 1990s

To facilitate the implementation of a service cluster or product line concept for University Hospital, it will be essential to adopt an appropriate bed complement (for each service).

3. Address Facility Considerations through a Medical Mall Implementation Strategy

The purpose of the medical mall is multifold:

- It compartmentalizes functions and services to allow an optimum level of capital expense by type of service.
- It targets and controls traffic by patient type while ensuring convenience and accessibility.
- It provides a "one-stop" location for multiple levels of inpatient and outpatient support services.

4. Pursue a Networking Strategy as Part of the Role of Tertiary Care

Pursuit of a networking strategy asserts that the role of University Hospital in tertiary care should represent a "hub" within the Canadian and international health care system.

As such, options have been developed to ensure University Hospital is able to accept patients who need to be "stepped-up" from community hospitals and outpatient settings, and also to "step down" patients who no longer require UH's intensity of services.

5. Adopt a Diversification Strategy

To encourage management to investigate which type of integration makes most sense for UH, given its tertiary nature and commitment to research and education. Diversification efforts can be adopted by an institution in basically three ways. Through vertical integration, horizontal integration or geographic dispersion.

EXHIBIT 1 (continued)

6. *Implement an Organizational Enhancement Strategy*

Due to the complexity and dynamic nature of University Hospital, ongoing strategic planning and administrative support and leadership will be essential. The recommended organizational enhancement strategy has, as its focus, to

- Pursue process planning and implementation by adopting an ongoing annual planning cycle.
- Assign responsibility/authority for successful ongoing strategic planning.
- Address management/medical staff succession.
- Exploit the benefits of University Hospital's relationship with HCA.

At the heart of this strategy is the need to formalize and integrate current planning mechanisms into an ongoing process.

7. *Continue an Aggressive Financial Strategy: Preserve/Enhance Financial Resources*

The objectives of this recommendation are twofold:

- To enhance financial resources.
- To preserve financial resources.

EXHIBIT 2   UH Patient Origin by Service—1986 (percent)

Service	Origin			
	Primary	*Secondary*	*Tertiary*	
	(S-W Ont.)	*(Remainder of Ont.)*	*Canada (except Ont.)*	*International*
Cardiology	71.9	22.3	3.9	1.9
Cardiovascular and Thoracic Surgery	61.4	28.8	7.8	2.1
Chest Diseases	88.1	10.8	0.6	0.5
Dentistry	89.1	10.8	0.0	0.1
Endocrinology	83.2	15.4	0.0	1.5
Gastroenterology	80.1	15.7	2.5	1.0
General Surgery	87.5	11.1	0.6	0.8
Gynaecology	70.9	24.4	3.8	1.0
Haematology	92.2	6.8	0.0	1.0
Immunology	90.0	10.0	0.0	0.0
Internal Medicine, Infectious Diseases	85.6	10.1	0.2	2.0
Nephrology	76.8	20.4	0.2	2.5
Neurology	70.0	26.2	2.4	1.4
Neurosurgery	42.6	36.3	2.4	18.6
Ophthalmology	75.9	23.7	0.0	0.4
Orthopaedic Surgery	85.6	13.4	0.3	0.7
Otolaryngology	92.2	7.0	0.4	0.0
Paediatrics	42.6	45.0	0.0	12.4
Plastic Surgery	86.8	12.4	0.2	0.6
Psychiatry	91.0	6.7	0.3	2.0
Rheumatology	91.9	7.7	0.0	0.4
Urology	92.9	7.1	0.0	0.0

SOURCE: UH Strategic Plan.

EXHIBIT 3 UH Services by Strategic Category

Premier Product Lines

Cardiology/Cardiovascular Surgery—
Arrythmia Investigation and Surgery
V.A.D.

Clinical Neurological Sciences (Neurology/Neurosurgery)—
Epilepsy Unit
Stroke Investigation
Multiple Sclerosis
Aneurysm Surgery

Multiple Organ Transplant Centre (Adult and Paediatric)—

Kidney	Pancreas
Liver	Small Bowel
Heart	Bone Marrow
Heart/Lung	Whole Joint and Bone
Other	

Reproductive Biology—
I.V.F. Clinic

Intermediate Product Lines

Chest Diseases	Dentistry
Endocrinology/Metabolism	Gastroenterology
General Internal Medicine	General Surgery
Haematology	Immunology
Nephrology	Ophthalmology
— Dialysis Unit	Otolaryngology
Orthopaedic Surgery	Plastic/Reconstructive Surgery
Paediatrics	Psychiatry
Physical Medicine and Rehabilitation	Urology
Rheumatology	

EXHIBIT 4a UH Statement of Revenues and Expenses for the Year Ended March 31 ($000s)

	1983	1984	1985	1986	1987
Revenue					
MOH allocation	$47 067	$51 527	$56 329	$61 103	$69 502
In-patient services	5 355	7 482	9 986	13 945	14 771
Accommodation differential	1 548	1 624	1 746	2 277	2 537
Out-patient services	1 692	2 069	2 033	2 428	3 135
MOH programs	4 908	5 083	5 405	5 503	5 811
Other revenue	3 626	3 471	4 079	4 510	4 836
	64 196	71 256	79 578	89 766	100 592
Expenses					
Salaries and wages	35 779	39 4804	3 505	47 450	53 581
Employee benefits	3 869	4 4414	711	4 866	5 628
Supplies and other services	10 312	11 751	13 640	15 289	18 960
Ministry of Health programs	4 978	5 376	5 701	5 976	6 099
Medical supplies	3 679	3 915	4 842	5 506	6 547
Drugs	2 226	2 079	2 871	3 846	5 220
Depreciation	2 444	2 818	3 121	3 398	3 843
Bad debts	192	205	165	197	141
Interest	75	137	144	122	420
	63 554	70 202	78 699	86 650	100 439
Excess of revenue over expenses from operations	642	1 054	878	3 116	153
Add (deduct) unusual items:					
debenture issue cost					(154)
gain on asset sale					466
Excess of revenue over exp.	642	1 054	878	3 116	465

Operating Statistics

	1983	1984	1985	1986	1987
Inpatient days (000)	137.5	138.5	139.7	140.4	142.0
Inpatient admissions (000)	11.8	11.9	12.5	12.9	13.1
Average inpatient stay (days)	11.7	11.6	11.2	10.9	10.8
Occupancy (per cent)	89.5%	89.9%	90.3%	91.0%	90.9%
Outpatient visits (000)	96.5	101.9	108.4	113.1	122.4
Total patients seen	N/A	N/A	221 090	233 688	254 001
Equivalent patient days	N/A	N/A	208 932	214 980	222 137
Bookings Ahead:					
urgent				294	584
elective				650	724
UH employees:					
Number of beds:					
approved	421	424	424	428	436
rated	451	451	451	463	463

EXHIBIT 4b UH Balance Sheet as of March 31 ($000)

Assets	1983	1984	1985	1986	1987
Integrated Funds[1]					
Current:					
Cash and securities	$2 795	$1 580	$1562	$1 799	$1 541
Accounts receivable:					
province	3 095	3 341	4 324	6 068	7 508
other	2 299	3 119	3 742	6 394	7 006
Inventories	1 005	1 147	1 130	1 127	1 064
Prepaid expenses	101	109	99	78	100
Total current assets	9 231	9 296	10 857	15 466	17 219
Funds available to purchase plant property and equipment	2 099	3 701	3 086	2 764	6 800
Fixed assets:					
Property plant & equip.	36 884	37 873	38 511	40 325	48 223
Capital leases	173	144	141	40 249	48 114
	37 057	38 017	38 652	40 325	48 223
	48 387	51 014	52 596	58 555	72 242
Special Funds[1]					
Cash and deposits	19	21	35	40	90
Marketable securities (cost)	4 256	5 042	5 948	7 105	7 817
Accrued interest	57	103	108	123	141
Mortgage receivable	59	56	53	49	46
Advance to integrated fund	1 264	1 004	744	734	1 775
	5 655	6 227	6 888	8 051	9 869
	54 042	57 241	59 485	66 606	82 112

[1] Revenue and expenses relating to the day-to-day activities of the Hospital are recorded in the statement of revenue and expenses and the integrated fund statement of assets. Activities relating to funds made available to the LHA under conditions specified by the donor are recorded in the special funds statement. Most of these monies were donated to the LHA prior to the establishment of the Foundation.

EXHIBIT 4b (continued)

Liabilities and Equity	1983	1984	1985	1986	1987
Integrated Funds					
Current:					
Account Payable	2 941	4 490	4 153	5 618	6 987
Accrued Charges	2 401	2 074	2 580	2 988	3 668
Current portion of					
leases and loans	417	401	400	260	307
Total current liabilities	5 759	6 965	7 133	8.866	10 962
Long-term:					
Debentures[2]					5 629
Advances from special funds	1 265	1 004	744	734	1 775
Capital lease	175	141	95	18	12
	1 440	1 145	839	752	7 417
Less principal due	417	401	400	260	307
	1 023	744	439	492	7 109
Integrated equity	41 605	43 305	45 025	49 196	54 170
	$48 387	$51 014	$52 597	$58 554	$72 241
Special Fund[3]					
Equity	5 656	6 227	6 888	8 052	9 870
Total Equity and Liabilities	54 042	57 241	59 485	66 606	82 111

---

[2] In February 1987 the Hospital issued debentures to finance the new parking garage and attached office facility.

[3] The hospital has received the following advances from the Special Fund, repayable with interest:

Year	Amount	Purpose
1983	$1 264 000	New telephone system
1986	$ 250 000	Establishment of Occupational Health Centre
1987	$1 400 000	Finance MRI building.

EXHIBIT 4c UH Statement of Changes in Equity for the Year Ended March 31

Statement of Equity	1983	1984	1985	1986	1987
Integrated Funds					
Balance beginning of year	$40 386	$41 605	$43 305	$45 025	$49 196
Add (deduct) MOH settlements	(1 114)				
	39 272	41 605	43 305	45 025	49 196
Donations & grants	1 692	646	842	1 054	4 509
Excess of revenue over expenses	641	1 054	878	3 117	465
	2 333	1 700	1 720	4 171	4 974
Balance end of year	$41 605	$43 305	$45 025	$49 196	$54 170
Special Funds					
Balance beginning of year	$ 5 044	$ 5 651	$ 6 227	$ 6 888	$ 8 052
Add:					
Donations and bequests	1	1	11	409	835
Net investment income	606	575	650	755	983
Balance end of year	$ 5 651	$6 227	$6 888	$8 052	$9 870
Represented by:					
Non-expendable funds	$492	$492	$492	$492	$492
Expendable funds	5 139	5 734	6 396	7 560	9 378
	$5 651	$6 227	$6 888	$8 052	$9 870

EXHIBIT 5 UH Organization Chart

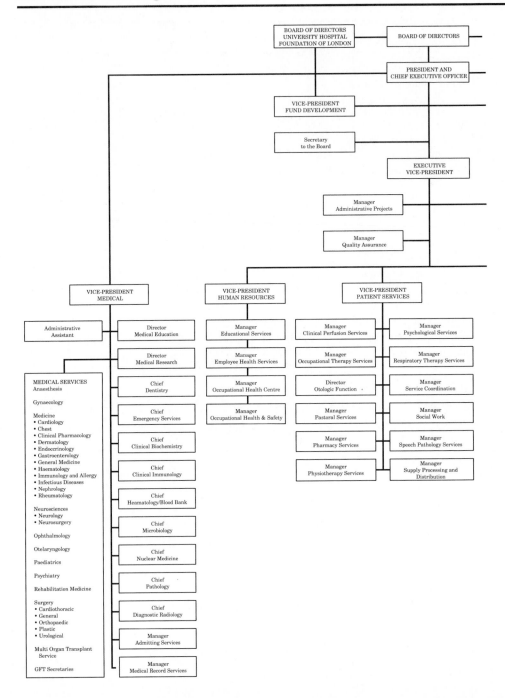

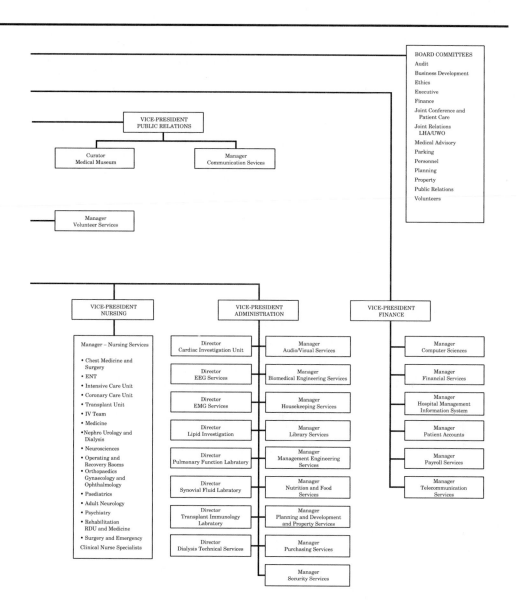

APPENDIX A UH Profile of Premier Service Categories

The premier product lines fell under four categories: cardiology/cardiovascular surgery, clinical neurological sciences, multiple organ transplant, and reproductive biology. More detailed descriptions follow.

Cardiology/Cardiovascular Surgery

The two major programs in cardiology/cardiovascular surgery were Arrythmia Investigation and Surgery, and the Ventricular Assist Device (VAD). Arrythmia investigation received a major breakthrough when in 1981, the world's first heart operation was performed to correct life-threatening right ventricular dysplasia. In 1984, UH entered into a collaborative relationship with Biomedical Instrumentation Inc., a Canadian research and development firm based near Toronto, to produce a sophisticated heart mapping device, which greatly advanced the surgical treatment of patients suffering from life-threatening heart rhythm disorders. The computer-assisted mapping system, which fit over the heart like a sock, enabled doctors to almost instantaneously locate the "electric short circuit" in the hearts of patients afflicted with cardiac arrhythmias. Physicians were then able to more easily locate and destroy the tissue which caused the patient's heart to beat abnormally.

The ventricular assist device (VAD), which UH began using in 1987, was functionally no different from some life support machines, such as the heart-lung machine already in use. In assisting the heart to pump blood, the VAD was used for patients waiting for transplants, those needing help after open heart surgery, and hearts weakened after a severe heart attack. The VAD worked outside the patient's body, carrying out approximately 50% of the heart's work. When the patient's heart recovered sufficiently or when a donor organ became available for those who required a transplant, the pump could be disconnected without difficulty. Other than UH, there was only one other hospital in Canada using the VAD.

Clinical Neurological Sciences (CNS)

There were four major programs in CNS: The Epilepsy Unit; Stroke Investigation; Multiple Sclerosis; and Aneurysm Surgery.

The Epilepsy Unit, discussed at length in Appendix B, was one of only a few of its kind in North America. The demand for its services had extended the waiting time for a bed to over a year.

A four-bed Investigative Stroke Unit was established at UH in 1983 to improve the diagnosis and treatment of stroke. In 1986, UH and the University of Western Ontario collaborated in the development of the Robarts Research Institute, which focused its efforts on stroke research.

The Multiple Sclerosis (MS) clinic at UH conducted exploratory research to study the causes and incidence of MS, a chronic degenerative disease of the central nervous system. One study involved 200 MS patients in 10 centres, coordinated by UH, to determine whether cyclosporin[1] and prednisone, either alone or in combination with repeated plasma exchange treatments could prevent further deterioration in MS patients.

Aneurysm Surgery became a centre for excellence and internationally renowned early on, when in 1972, Dr. Charles Drake pioneered a technique for surgically treating a cerebral aneurysm. In October of 1979, vocalist Della Reese underwent neurosurgery at UH. She returned to London the following year to give a benefit concert to raise funds for UH.

Multiple Organ Transplant Centre

The first kidney transplant at UH was performed in 1973, followed by its first liver transplant in 1977. In 1979, UH was chosen as the first centre in North America to test the anti-rejection drug Cyclosporin A. In 1981, the first heart transplant at UH was performed. In that same year, UH became the site of the Canadian Centre for Transplant Studies. In 1984, Canada's first heart-lung transplant was performed at UH.

In 1984, the provincial government announced that they would partially fund a multi-organ transplant unit (MOTU) at UH. The 12-bed MOTU, which opened in 1987, was one of the first units of its kind in the world. With the help of leading-edge computer technology, transplant patients were closely monitored for the first signs of organ rejection. A highly specialized team of transplant experts including surgeons, physicians, nurses, technologists and physiotherapists joined together in the MOTU to care for transplant patients.

Reproductive Biology

The primary work in Reproductive Biology was the In-Vitro Fertilization (IVF) program. The program was launched in 1982, with the first birth occurring in 1985. By 1987, the 100th child was born to parents who previously had been incapable of conceiving a child. The pregnancy rate was 27% using this method, with a birth rate of 22%. These results were comparable to those of well-established clinics world-wide. It was anticipated that with the combination of continually increasing experience together with basic science and clinical research interests in IVF, the success rate in the program would continue to increase. There was a two-year waiting period to participate in the program.

---

[1] Cyclosporin was the drug originally used to minimize the bodies' rejection of transplanted organs. Because of its transplantation experience, UH had a considerable expertise with this drug and immunology in general.

APPENDIX B   The Process of Innovation at UH

The Epilepsy Unit

Research and service innovations had been important to UH. This appendix described how one of these came about.

The epilepsy unit probably had its genesis when Dr. Warren Blume, a neurologist, joined Dr. John Girvin, a neurosurgeon at UH in 1972. Girvin had trained under a founding father in epilepsy treatment at the Montreal Neurological Institute (MNI). Blume had done post graduate work in epilepsy and electroencephalography (EEG)[2] at the Mayo clinic. Girvin was unique among neurosurgeons in that he had also gone on to obtain a Ph.D. in neurophysiology.

In 1972, the primary treatment for epilepsy was through drug therapy. However, there were many patients whose epilepsy could not be effectively treated this way. For those patients, the only hope was a surgical procedure to remove that part of their brain which caused the epileptic seizure. This required an EEG recording of a patient's seizure to identify the focus of the problem. There were few individuals trained in the use of EEG to study epilepsy. However, Blume had this expertise. Furthermore, Girvin had the training in neurosurgery to carry out the surgical procedure. Neither physician, however, was recruited specifically to do work in epilepsy. It was an interest they both shared and developed over time.

There were a number of factors that united Blume and Girvin, providing the impetus for the dedicated Epilepsy Unit that was eventually opened in May of 1986. One factor was the integration within UH of neurosurgery and neurology under the umbrella of neurosciences. In most hospitals the two departments were separate, neurosurgery being part of surgery and neurology being its own service. At UH, they were integrated organizationally and located on the same floor. Many attribute this unique relationship to the leadership and friendship of Doctors Barnett and Drake, the original Chiefs of neurology and neurosurgery.

In 1974, a young Italian boy and his father arrived on the doorstep of UH seeking help to control the boy's epilepsy; the precipitating factor that brought Blume and Girvin together to work on their first case experience. It was a complex case, requiring the expertise of both Blume and Girvin. The surgery was successful, and Blume and Girvin realized that by pooling their expertise, they could make a significant contribution to the field. Prior to that time, Blume's efforts had been focused on providing EEG readings for epileptic patients that would either be treated with medication or referred to the MNI for possible surgical treatment. Girvin's efforts had been directed at neurosurgery in general, having no special contact with epileptic patients.

---

[2] The mapping of electrical activity in the brain.

Blume and Girvin began to draw together a team. The technique of removing part of the brain for the treatment of epilepsy was based on the fact that most human functions were duplicated in both temporal lobes of the brain. In the early days of surgical treatment of epilepsy at the MNI, there was no method of ensuring that both temporal lobes were functioning normally. As a result in some cases where a malfunctioning temporal lobe could not duplicate the function of the part of the brain that had been removed, patients were left with serious brain dysfunction like loss of memory capacity. Later, a procedure was developed, whereby neuropsychologists were able to assess the level of function of one temporal lobe, while the other temporal lobe was anaesthetized. It so happened that a neuropsychologist with this expertise was working at U.W.O.'s psychology department. She was asked to join the team. For Blume and Girvin, adding a neuropsychologist was essential to their ability to deal with more complex cases. The addition of full-time researchers also served to enhance the team's capability.

Capability was further enhanced, when in 1977, Blume and Girvin were successful in obtaining funding to purchase a computer that would facilitate the recording and reading of the EEG. This was a significant step, since to obtain funding, they positioned themselves as a Regional Epilepsy Unit. This was the first formal recognition of their efforts as an organized endeavour. The computerized monitoring could benefit from a dedicated unit; at the time, beds and staff were still borrowed from other departments as needed. Epileptic patients were scattered around the neurosciences floor.

As the volume of patients increased, it became increasingly apparent that a unit was needed. In order to identify the focus of the brain that triggered the epileptic seizure, it was necessary to record a seizure. As a result, EEG recording rooms were tied up for several hours in the hope that a patient would have a seizure. There were a number of problems with this approach. The patient had to have a seizure while in a recording room, and the patient or technologist had to activate the recorder. It was estimated that over 50% of seizures were missed using this method. Furthermore, leaving the patient unattended without the benefit of medication to control their seizures was dangerous. A unit that would provide full-time monitoring in order to get the vital EEG recordings, and ensure patient safety was needed.

Blume, Girvin and the manager of EEG, developed a proposal for a four bed epilepsy unit. The beds that they had been using on an ad hoc basis were the neurosciences overflow beds which "belonged" to Paediatrics. Paediatrics was located on the same floor as EEG, so when Blume, who was also a member of the department of paediatrics, heard that Paediatrics was downsizing, he had approached the chief of Paediatrics to negotiate for four beds. As well, the Paediatric nurses, who had been responsible for the overflow beds, had become comfortable with providing care for epileptic patients, and it was agreed that they would provide continued support for the unit. Blume and Girvin approached

Blewett with a plan requiring funding of $400 000 for equipment and renovations. There was no provision for an annual budget, since Paediatrics was prepared to cover the nursing salaries and supplies.

Blewett and his senior management group supported the plan, and it was submitted as a new program to the TVDHC for funding in February 1984. The proposal was ranked tenth, which meant it was not one of the top few submitted to the Ministry for consideration. A revised proposal was resubmitted the following February. In the meantime, Blewett, Girvin and Blume met with the Assistant Deputy Minister of Health to make a plea for funding; to no avail. They subsequently received news that the TVDHC had given the proposal a ranking of sixth. Blume and Girvin did not lose hope, and were persistent in their efforts to obtain funding. After exhausting all alternatives, Blewett decided to fund it out of the hospital's operating surplus. However, compromises were made in the plans by cutting the budget back as far as possible. The Board approved the allocation, and shortly thereafter, the unit was opened.

DOFASCO INC.

Gerald R. Higgins
with Robert Gordon and
Roderick E. White

"Our Product is Steel, Our Strength is People."[1]

In June 1982, the members of a special task force at Dofasco Inc. of Hamilton, Ontario were faced with the unpleasant task of deciding how the firm should react to a serious downturn in the economy, which had become evident six months earlier and showed no sign of abating. The company's first response had been to initiate a hiring freeze, which had resulted in a workforce reduction through attrition of approximately 400 people over the past six months. It was clear, however, that further action, and quick action, was called for. The task force, which consisted of Dofasco's executive vice president, Senior vice president of operations, vice president of personnel, and the director of communications and public affairs, was considering cutting the company's dividends and/or announcing extensive layoffs.

STEEL MAKING

The production of steel involves two basic steps: steel making and steel rolling. Steel making is accomplished by one of two alternative methods. Both require enormous amounts of capital for fixed assets. The first method involves the melting of scrap steel into slabs, billets or blooms with an electric arc furnace (Exhibit 1). The other method begins with iron ore. In this process, iron ore, limestone and coal are crushed and processed through huge blast furnaces to produce basic iron. The iron is refined in a basic oxygen furnace (BOF). The steel is then poured into ingot molds. Once solidified, the ingot is then reheated and rolled into a slab, billet or bloom.

The second step in steel production is rolling. No matter what its origin, scrap or ore, the steel is processed through a rolling mill to produce anything from rails for railroads, to wire for nails, to sheet steel for automobile bodies or appliances.

---

[1] Company motto.

The replacement cost of an efficient facility to produce sheets in coils, starting with iron ore and coal, would be approximately $1.5 billion exclusive of land. To be cost effective, such a mill would have to produce and sell 2 million tons per annum. The life of the mill would be approximately 50 years. Once running, the mill would undergo a constant program of maintenance and upgrading to meet original equipment specifications, requirements for new developments in technology for cost efficiency and new plant safety and pollution legislation.

The planning of a mill required attention to detail and accurate forecasting. For instance, in 1983 Dofasco was due to bring on-stream the first stage of its number two hot-strip mill. It would produce steel sheets in coils used in the manufacture of automobiles and major appliances. This project began in the mid-1970s and its final stage would not come on-stream until the year 2010. The new technology incorporated into the mill was a vitally important part of Dofasco's plans to remain competitive with Canadian and international steel producers.

Cost efficiency in the steel business hinged on two factors: mill design, and mill scheduling and operations. A mill was usually designed to produce a certain type of product, such as steel sheets in coils, or bars in straight lengths. Each mill also had a particular product size range, outside of which it was not cost effective. For example, Dofasco's products were steel sheets light enough to roll into coils, as opposed to heavier steel plates—which could theoretically, but not economically, be produced on the same equipment.

Scheduling provided the next opportunity for savings. If steel were allowed to cool in inventory before being rolled, it had to be reheated in a furnace called a "soaking pit" before it was malleable enough for rolling. The time for heating was approximately 16 hours. To avoid this cost and delay, steel makers moved steel in large, specially designed trucks directly from the steel-making stage to the soaking pit. By doing so, the soaking pit time was reduced to as little as eight hours and the energy cost per ton was also reduced.

PRODUCTION SCHEDULES AND SALES

The drive to reduce costs and achieve scale economies dictated how steel was sold. Typically, a steel mill would announce a rolling schedule three to six months in advance. Large customers then bought a certain percentage of the schedule. For example, a mill would announce in January that it would roll A-36 sheet, .250-inch thick the week of April 5 and that it expected to produce 100 000 tons. Customers then had the opportunity to commit to buying a percentage of the rolling for delivery in the second week of April. This approach allowed the steel producer to set an efficient schedule and to keep costs down.

If a customer erred in their production/scheduling/purchasing, they either waited until the next rolling or they purchased the required incremental amounts of steel at a considerable premium from steel warehouses.

In this regard, Dofasco was considered unique. While Dofasco produced to a traditional cost-effective rolling schedule, the company had also developed the ability to adapt to variations in overall customer requirements. This was translated into an ongoing "float" of speculative steel inventory moving through the process. However, in order to realize the "float" and meet unanticipated demand, employees would often be asked to work overtime, or be called in on short notice. There were many legendary tales of Dofasco employees making heroic efforts to keep the plant open, no matter what the conditions. For example, one crane operator drove 32 km through a blinding snowstorm on his tractor to show up for the afternoon shift. Other employees worked double shifts for fellow employees who could not make it through the storm.

Management took great pride in pointing out that internal flexibility allowed Dofasco to help out a "good customer" in an emergency by having a special order on a truck within 48 hours of receipt of the request. This was accomplished without serious disruption to the regular rolling schedule: not a simple task! Sales reps felt that this ability gave them an edge in getting and holding prime accounts.

WORLD STEEL PRODUCTION

In the 1955-1970 period world steel capacity soared from 270 million tons to 747 million tons, far outstripping demand. Much of the increase came from Japan, which raised capacity by 180% during the period, and countries in Third World areas such as Africa, South America and Asia. Many small countries deliberately installed much greater steel-making capacity than the local market could absorb, in part because the economics of steel making necessitated large plant sizes and in part to earn foreign currency through exporting. This excess capacity, combined with the high fixed-costs of steel making and the cyclical nature of steel demand meant that price cutting was severe in periods of low demand. The response of many American companies had been to reduce their dependence on the steel business, with the result that U.S. steel production fell by 12% between 1964 and 1980.

THE HISTORY OF DOFASCO

In 1912 Miss Edna Aldridge answered a newspaper ad for a "typist and office clerk" and became the first employee of Dominion Steel Foundry, which had just been founded by two American immigrants, Clifton and Frank Sherman.

Production in the first year was 3 600 tons, and the workforce totalled 258. By 1980, Dofasco had grown to be Canada's second largest steel producer at 4 million tons per year with a total workforce exceeding 11 000 people.

Growth was not without its problems. In 1921, having grown rapidly to supply the war effort, Dofasco found itself over capacity and was placed in receivership. The firm was rescued by Canadian patent approval of a revolutionary method of producing the undercarriages of railway box cars. By 1927, Dofasco had recovered sufficiently to build Canada's first plate mill and in the mid-1930s the company introduced a 20-inch cold-rolling mill for the production of thinner sheet steels (used for such products as automobiles). This mill was eventually improved so that it could also produce tin plate for the food canning industry.

During the 1950s Dofasco became a fully integrated steel producer. In 1951, the company built the first of four blast furnaces and in 1954 Dofasco again broke new ground by starting up its basic oxygen furnace. Dofasco was the first company in the western hemisphere and second in the world to adopt this new technology. Over the next quarter century the firm spent over $1.9 billion dollars on capital equipment expansion and equipment replacement. While major technological changes were infrequent, small improvements to the process were almost continual. Dofasco's employees were adept at identifying and exploiting both major and minor innovations.

The results were a firm that in 1980 ranked 32nd in raw steel capacity in the world. More significantly, Dofasco ranked in the top 10 worldwide in critical areas such as efficiency and productivity: net income as a percentage of sales, net income as a percentage of shareholders' equity and output per employee (Exhibits 2 through 5). Dofasco was the only non-unionized integrated steel producer in North America. Much of its success was attributed to its people.

PEOPLE AND PROGRAMS

The Shermans felt there were three interdependent elements in the successful running of any firm; technology, systems and people. While Dofasco was clearly a technological innovator, the company also went to great lengths to develop a strong management team and a skilled cooperative workforce. Over time, this highly motivated, competent team developed very effective systems to control the firm.

The Dofasco management philosophy was summed up in the company's motto, on the cover of their annual report: "Our product is steel. Our strength is people." The founders of Dofasco had felt it was good business to create an environment of trust and collaboration between management and labour. This relationship was not static; rather, it was constantly being refined in an attempt to reflect the fairest possible treatment of all parties in a changing environment. John G. Sheppard, executive vice president of finance, stated:

> If a company chooses to regard its employees only as production units and time-clock numbers, it is unlikely to inspire very much loyalty and dedication. Human nature being what it is you can't ask for that kind of employee attitude (loyalty and dedication). You can't even buy it. It has been and must be earned.

The firm's "Golden Rule" approach of treating employees fairly in the expectation that they would perform well in return had its beginnings with the founders. Over the years, management at Dofasco had attempted to formalize this attitude by instituting a number of programs which, at the time of their introduction, were quite revolutionary. Some of the employee programs are outlined in the following sections.

Profit Sharing

Profit sharing was instituted in 1938 and was seen as just that, a sharing of the results of a years' hard work over and above but *not* in lieu of a fair, competitive wage and benefit package. Pretax funds available for profit sharing were broken into two accounts, one for retirement and the second for immediate profit sharing. In both plans, each member, whether a shop machinist or the company president, shared equally in the distribution of profits.

For the first three years, a new employee did not participate in the plan. Once the three-year probationary period was over and it was clear that the employee was going to stay at Dofasco and would fit in, he or she became a member in the plan. On the other hand, should anyone wish to leave after becoming a member of the profit-sharing plan, he or she received the full value of his or her contribution, plus a percentage of the company's contribution to the two accounts to date of departure. But the individual would *never be rehired* by Dofasco.

Supervisor Leadership Training

Since first-line supervisors were the key to productivity, Dofasco instituted a 16-session supervisory training course to ensure a consistent approach to the application of the firm's policies and practices. Every new supervisor was required to take the course, in addition to any other necessary technical courses, prior to assuming his or her first-line supervisory position. The company encouraged employees at all levels to improve their technical and supervisory skills by assistance with tuition and book costs.

Apprenticeship Program

In 1980, the apprenticeship program involved over 600 employees, allowing those who wished to improve their skills to do so while still on the job. People wishing to become machinists, electricians, mechanics, stationary engineers, etc. made use of a program set up by Dofasco in conjunction with the Ministry of Labour and the Hamilton Board of Education. The results were dramatic. Virtually all of the firm's trade requirements were filled from the program. The dropout rate was less than 2% and less than 2% of those graduating were lost to other firms.

Extra Curricular

In addition to programs for medical or occupational health and safety, retirement planning, open door policies and so on, perhaps the most visible employee programs were the recreational activities. These programs were administered by a full-time staff. Activities varied from model railroading to tennis, baseball, hockey or the Dofasco choir. In all, there were over 50 employee clubs. The company maintained a 100-acre recreational complex, which included floodlit baseball and tennis, an all-weather running track and a golf driving range, to name a few. Planned for the future were hockey, curling and a swimming pool and squash courts.

The Dofasco choir was known internationally. It had toured the U.S., had several record albums to its credit and sang each year on national television. Every December, Dofasco held its annual Christmas party where, for over 50 years, children of all the employees had received a gift from the company. The party, held under one roof, was reputed to be one of the largest in the world and had in recent years grown to over 35 000 people.

Suggestion System

The firm sponsored an employee suggestion program which brought in as many as 1 800 cost-saving suggestions annually. The top prize for the best suggestion was $30 000 in cash. In 1979, a total of $286 000 was awarded for suggestions that helped in reducing costs and increasing efficiency. The results of these and other programs were described to all employees in *News and Views*, the firm's monthly tabloid. The following excerpts are taken from the April 1982 edition.

THE DOWNTURN

Dofasco, like many other companies, is moving through a difficult period. Demand from customers for our products here in Canada is down significantly. the recession has hit nearly all major steel-consuming sectors, including automotive, appliances, farm equipment and construction. . . .

We must all do everything possible to reduce spending to maintain the company's cash flow. . . .

We must also look at, and question, every item that is a part of the cost of a ton of steel, and put a real effort into keeping these costs from going up, and where possible, reduce the costs.

Our performance so far this year in the amount of steel that has to be reapplied, or downgraded, or rejected, is not nearly as good as last year. This is an area where extra effort can produce real cost savings. . . . [2]

We have also reviewed all of our expansion programme expenditures planned for 1982. We will be proceeding with the installation of our second hot-strip mill scheduled for start-up in 1983. However, all expenditures for additional expansion projects have been deferred until the economy improves. . . .

World steel demand was lower at the end of 1981 than it had been in decades. Plants were idle or running at a fraction of capacity. Steel producers were dumping steel into other markets in an effort to maintain volume.

In March, General Motors, Detroit announced that it would be accepting bids for its steel requirements for the 1983 model year. Previously, GM had paid list prices for its steel from mainly U.S. sources. The move was obviously designed to lower costs in the face of record-low new-car sales. However, in an open competition for GM's substantial business, most Canadian producers felt that they would be in an excellent position, given the high quality of Canadian steel, the high efficiency of Canadian mills, plus the relative weakness of the Canadian dollar. A Stelco spokesperson commented that "GM is not going to put all its eggs in one basket . . . they want suppliers to sharpen their pencils." Algoma felt "if we are forced into a bidding system, I don't think we are going to come out the loser." Both Algoma and Stelco were optimistic about the GM move. Dofasco, while noncommittal, perhaps stood to benefit the most. Dofasco's main products, from its hot-strip mill, were flat rolled sheets. Dofasco was clearly the most efficient of the three large Canadian steel producers in this product area.

On the other hand, many market analysts were predicting that the worst was yet to come. Senior Dofasco management were, therefore, attempting to mobilize employees and management to prepare for even tighter market conditions.

In April, Dofasco's chairman noted:

As you know, many companies across the country have been forced to implement short-time or layoffs. We hope to avoid this happening at Dofasco. At the present time we are not planning any shutdowns or layoffs. We will keep you advised of any further changes in the situation.

---

[2] As steel proceeds through a mill it accumulates costs. The further it goes the more susceptible it is to technological or human error that would render it either scrap or seconds. Dofasco's operating employees had developed an enviable record of reducing these losses. Recently however, as mentioned by the chairman, their performance had deteriorated somewhat.

Also, in April, Statistics Canada reported that Canadian steel production for the first two months of the year was 2.8 million tons, or 10% down from 1981. Further, they reported that over 4000 steel workers who were employed in 1981 were now out of work. As far as relief was concerned, Mr. Gordon Bowlby, vice president of sales at Stelco commented:

> General economic conditions—interest rates in particular—are at the root of the industry's problems. Consumers are not buying cars or appliances that use large amounts of steel; companies have trimmed capital spending, including those in the energy resource field.

Investment analysts were cutting back their profit estimates for the publicly traded steel companies not only because of softening domestic demand but also because of the threat from off-shore competition. The flood of imports into the U.S. had sparked a sharp counterattack from domestic producers. The Canadian steel industry was nervous that, should an agreement be made between the U.S. government and the offending countries, or should the treasury department institute quotas or "trigger prices" as they did in 1976, Canada would become a dumping ground for low-priced steel that was originally headed for the U.S. This fear was very real because imports were already making themselves felt. Canadian imports doubled from 1980 to 1981 as world markets softened. For instance, plate prices fell 8% in the face of a 182% increase in import volume. Hot rolled sheet, Dofasco's main product, saw prices decline 10% with a 234% increase in foreign steel.

Other groups were also feeling the pressure. Wholesalers represented by the Canadian Steel Service Centre Institute reported a drop of 25% in orders received by its members. Further, they revised their estimates downwards for 1982 orders of structural steel from 430 000 tons to 325 000 tons. 1981 had been a weak year, but still shipments had been at least 418 000 tons.

As the first quarter of the year drew to a close Stelco announced its first quarterly dividend cut since 1933, from $.40 to $.25. Citing heavy capital commitment and "little indication of strengthening markets," management felt they had no alternatives.

1982 Second Quarter

During the second quarter of 1982 things went from bad to worse. Imports continued their assault on the Canadian market. For example, steel drilling tubes destined for the Alberta oil fields were increasingly being imported through the port of Vancouver at prices 40% below domestic producers' list. This prompted an exasperated Canadian producer to comment:

> There are tens of thousands of tons of imported products on the docks in B.C. that have yet to be sold . . . people are literally selling metal at prices below costs . . . everyone is laying off people and we're headed for the same thing.

Faced with such desperate market conditions Dofasco reminded its employees again that:

> With today's market prices it is impossible to recover our costs by increasing prices. It is therefore essential that we do everything to reduce costs and cut or defer both operating and capital expenditures. . . .
>
> We should look at everything; even the smallest items add up—for instance, reducing the use of consumable supplies for the plant, such as cotton gloves. They seem insignificant when they cost about $1.00 per pair, yet the company spends approximately $300 000 per year on gloves.
>
> Our suggestion system has always been an excellent vehicle through which improvements to our operations have been achieved—improvements originating from those who do the job. There has never been a time when the suggestion system could be put to better use. I encourage everyone to participate.

By June layoffs had become commonplace in the steel industry. Earlier in April, Stelco and Algoma had laid off literally thousands of steel and steel related workers. In one move alone Algoma laid off 1 500, then another 800. Stelco laid off 2300 people from one plant and for the first time layoffs were also affecting white collar workers. Despite hopes for a percentage of the GM contracts, Algoma continued to post layoffs and indicated that if things did not improve, up to three quarters of the tube division workforce and management could be laid off.

On June 9, Dofasco announced that it was deferring planned price increases because of "slowness in the economy." At the same time, management again revised their 1982 production forecast, from 4.1 down to 3.8 million tons. Dofasco's net income fell from $169 million in 1981 to $40 million for the first half of 1982. With falling income came a cash squeeze. If Dofasco broke even, during the remainder of 1982 cash problems might develop roughly as follows:

1982 Cash Flow (000 000s)

Sources	
Net earnings	40*
Depreciation and amortization	75
Cash available	115
Uses	
Common dividends	41
Preferred dividends	22
Normal plant repair	40
#2 hot strip mill	100
Cash needs	203
Cash shortage	88

---

* Any losses during the second half would reduce this figure. Predictions for 1983 were equally bleak.

OUTLOOK FOR THE FUTURE

Every industry analyst had a different prediction of how long the slump would last and how deep it would drop. However, looking further out, experts were predicting a complete reversal of current market conditions. For example, one analyst's exhaustive report examined current capacity and current expansion underway plus announced expansion due in the next few years, versus modest growth of world demand to the end of the century. The findings showed overall surplus capacity for 1982 at between 125 and 150 million tons worldwide (no news to industry participants) but predicted this margin dropping to only 30 million by 1985 and zero by 1986. Other industry observers argued with the timing of the shortage but no one contested the fact that it was coming.

With the shortage, of course, would come skyrocketing prices and profits, followed by rapid increases in capacity and surpluses. The roller coaster ride would begin again. The trick was to stay alive in the meanwhile.

Despite the bleak outlook, at least for the short term, Dofasco found itself committed to one of the most aggressive capital expenditure projects in the firm's history. The number two strip mill due to open in late 1983 was on schedule and on budget. It had an estimated final cost of $450 million. Because it was so far along, and such an important part of Dofasco's future competitive position, the firm felt it had no choice but to push forward with the project.

Cash Conserving Options

As indicated earlier, the task force was considering the following options: dividend cuts and/or extensive layoffs.

Cutting Dividends

This was certainly an option. Since management saw the firm as a contract between capital and labour it seemed only fair that the longtime suppliers of capital should help bear the burden of the poor market. However, Dofasco stocks were publicly traded on the Toronto Stock Exchange and a severe or prolonged cut in dividends could put downward pressure on the stock price. Management was aware that this could hurt their ability to raise capital for further expansion and annual equipment replacement. Dofasco's common stock was trading at $27–$30 in June 1982, down from $40 in January, and its lowest level since 1978.

Layoffs

Management was unclear about the long-term effects of this action. The finance department could attempt to quantify the effects of various dividend cuts on

Dofasco stock price. The vice president of operations could supply statistics on the incidence of breakdowns as related to the lack of preventative maintenance. He could also provide minimum personnel figures required to run the plant. However, no one could accurately forecast or quantify the long-term effects of layoffs on what was regarded as one of the most enthusiastic and efficient steel-work forces in North America.

Under consideration was the layoff of *all* employees (office and plant) with less than three years of service. These people would not as yet have been invested in the profit-sharing plan and could be rehired. Dofasco had 2 100 people (18% of its workforce) in this category, each with average annual earnings of $28 000 plus benefits of approximately 30% of base pay. Achieving the projected output of 2.8 million tons with a reduced workforce would require the cooperation and hard work of those remaining on the payroll.

A second question that management pondered in this regard was: if a layoff was chosen, how should it be handled? One idea considered was straight seniority: that is, last in, first out. However, certain talent was rare in the steel industry and personnel managers were constantly wooing scarce and talented people such as metallurgists, rollers, computer programmers and design engineers from competitors. Many new plant personnel were the best in their respective fields and had been secured at great expense to the firm. For example, just six months earlier the manager of the metallurgical department had succeeded in hiring two engineers from Japan. This manager had spent two years convincing these men to come to Canada. He would surely make a strong case to have them exempted from any layoff. In another case, Dofasco had hired a new company doctor who had worked out perfectly. These were only two examples. Undoubtedly, there were many more.

In fact, the task force knew that cases could and would be made for keeping 10 – 20% of those to be laid off on the grounds that these people were indispensable. Since the only other layoffs were in 1965, involving 71 200 and 500 people respectively, and they had been of very short durations, this would be the first major long-term layoff ever at Dofasco.

JUNE 1982

By the end of the first half of the year the rest of 1982 was becoming clearer and there was no relief in sight. Although interest rates had fallen from record highs of more than 20% in 1981 to the 12% range by June 1982, the economy was not responding, and demand for structural steel was at its lowest point in over 20 years. The chairman of the International Iron and Steel Institute told his annual conference that "my guess is that steel profit will be a global rarity if not actually extinct for the calendar year 1982." He went on to say "this year promises to go down in the books as the worst within the working memory of most, if not all senior steel executives." Other experts were also suggesting that all the major U.S. steel producers would show losses in 1982.

Finally, on June 23rd, bad news of particular interest to Dofasco hit. Despite hopeful signs to the contrary, General Motors U.S. announced that it would not accept quotations from Canadian steel producers for the next model year. Analysts and government officials suggested that GM was following a "buy American policy." With 100 000 U.S. steel workers laid off and only 42% of the country's steel capacity being used, GM felt that it would be "suicidal" to award large U.S. contracts to Canadian producers.

EXHIBIT 1 The Steel Production Process

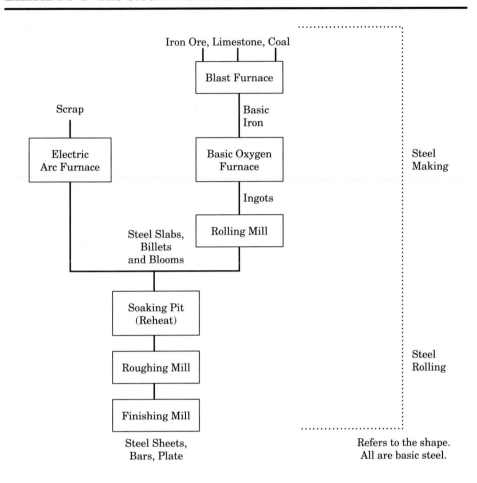

EXHIBIT 2   Dofasco's Position Among the Major World Steel Producers, 1981

Rank	Criteria	Data
30th	Raw steel production	4.3 million tons
31st	Sales	$1 767 509 000
11th	Net income	$169 274 000
2nd	Net income as % of sales	9.6%
8th	Net income as % of shareholders' equity	15.7%
14th	Assets per employee	$149 748
10th	Sales per employee	$129 01
57th	Output per employee	314 tons

EXHIBIT 3   Dofasco/Stelco/Algoma Comparison, 1981

	World Wide Rank		
Criteria	Dofasco	Stelco	Algoma
Raw steel production	30th	29th	35th
Sales	31st	29th	24th
Net income	11th	18th	12th
Net income as % of sales	2nd	11th	1st
Net income as % of shareholders' equity	8th	20th	6th
Assets per employee	14th	24th	18th
Sales per employee	10th	29th	20th
Output per employee	7th	21st	16th

Note: Financial data have been converted to Canadian dollars.

	Dofasco	Stelco	Algoma	Canada
Net income as % of shareholders' equity*	15.7	5.4	16.3	11.5
Net income as % of *average* shareholders' equity	16.6	5.3	17.5	11.8
Net income after preferred dividends as % of common shareholders' equity	17.3	3.4	17.4	12.1
Net income after preferred dividends as % of *average* common shareholders' equity	18.5**	3.4**	18.8**	12.6

*   Method used in this report.
** Method used in each company's annual report.

EXHIBIT 4 Dofasco Summary of Operational and Financial Data

Statistical Data	1981	1980	1979	1978	1977	1976	1975	1974
Production of ingots and castings—net tons[2]	4 258	3 681	4 060	3 588	3 333	3 335	3 053	3 060
Shipments of steel products—net tons[2]	3 223	2 914	3 099	2 830	2 596	2 652	2 348	2 475
Net income—percent of sales[1]	8.3%	7.0%	8.7%	7.6%	6.9%	7.3%	7.4%	10.2%
Net income after adding back interest on long-term debt (after taxes)—percent of average capital employed	11.3%	9.4%	11.5%	9.3%	8.7%	9.3%	8.7%	12.1%
Net income—percent of average common shareholders' equity[1]	18.5%	15.2%	20.2%	15.8%	12.9%	14.6%	13.2%	18.7%
Net worth per common share[3]	$ 17.45	$ 15.28	$ 13.95	$ 12.04	$ 10.77	$ 9.96	$ 9.06	$ 8.38
Income reinvested in the business[2]	$106 571	$ 68 283	$ 91 814	$ 59 317	$ 38 116	$ 42 615	$ 31 817	$ 49 577
Capital expenditures[2]								
—manufacturing	$238 259	$176 848	$ 61 257	$128 205	$152 168	$ 77 411	$100 722	$ 85 133
—mines and quarries	$ 10 985	$ 8 867	$ 10 732	$ 5 920	$ 7 906	$ 36 534	$ 36 419	$ 10 114
Total dividends declared[2]								
—preferred	$ 22 204	$ 14 940	$ 11 754	$ 9 485	$ 5 415	$ 971	$ 980	$ 987
—common	$ 40 499	$ 39 021	$ 33 377	$ 26 120	$ 24 414	$ 23 113	$ 22 676	$ 19 838
Average number of employees	13 700	14 100	13 700	12 300	11 300	11 500	11 700	11 500

[1] In thousands.
[2] After preferred dividends.
[3] Restated to include the effect of the 3 for 1 stock split.

EXHIBIT 5 Dofasco Financial Summary

	1981	1980	1979	1978	1977	1976	1975	1974
STATEMENT OF INCOME DATA								
Sales	$1 767 509	$1 541 914	$1 435 058	$1 120 383	$ 919 036	$ 904 958	$ 738 083	$ 681 636
Cost of sales (before the following items)	1 407 802	1 257 306	1 117 388	892 125	752 151	739 144	601 301	524 741
Depreciation and amortization	74 003	65 634	64 876	53 370	47 063	42 108	38 064	35 119
Employees' profit sharing	22 884	14 705	20 479	13 189	8 529	8 652	6 436	11 107
Interest on long-term debt	33 721	32 339	32 672	35 195	34 434	23 736	15 767	9 678
Income from investments	39 675	21 914	19 602	12 418	12 759	4 981	3 958	6 811
Income before income taxes	268 744	193 844	219 245	138 922	89 618	96 299	80 473	107 802
Income taxes	99 500	71 600	82 300	44 000	21 100	29 600	25 000	37 400
Net income for year	169 274	122 244	136 945	94 922	68 518	66 699	55 473	70 402
Net income attributable to common shares*	147 070	107 304	125 191	85 437	63 103	65 728	54 493	69 415
Net income per common share*+	3. 03	2.22	2.63	1.81	1.34	1.39	1.15	1.47
Number of holders of common shares	13 451	13 719	14 141	14 674	15 196	15 298	15 932	16 110
Percentage of common shares held in Canada	97.0%	96.6%	97.2%	97.1%	97.1%	97.1%	97.4%	96.9%
Dividends declared								
—per common share	.83	.81	.70	.55	.52	.49	.48	.42
—per Class A preferred share	4.75	4.75	4.75	4.75	4.75	4.75	4.75	4.75
—per Class B Series 1, 2 and 3 preferred share	2.629	2.108	1.808	1.427	.744	—	—	—
—per Class B, $2.35 preferred share	2.35	.5834	—	—	—	—	—	—
FINANCIAL POSITION DATA								
Working capital	$ 567 717	$ 600 070	$ 526 462	$ 429 983	$ 430 800	$ 260 666	$ 221 078	$ 167 258
Fixed assets								
—land buildings and equipment at cost	1 878 404	1 647 826	1 466 910	1 399 767	1 269 245	1 112 987	1 001 298	867 192
—accumulated depreciation	701 113	645 776	584 941	524 911	475 144	431 896	392 045	357 014
Total other assets	13 271	9 034	8 811	10 004	10 937	12 185	11 342	11 259
Capital employed	1 758 279	1 611 154	1 417 242	1 314 843	1 235 838	953 942	841 673	688 695
Long-term liabilities	372 760	371 291	333 869	368 996	379 277	297 665	242 598	140 979
Income tax allocations relating to future years	308 800	271 200	246 700	206 500	177 700	165 300	150 600	131 000
Total shareholders' equity	1 076 719	968 663	836 673	739 347	678 861	490 977	448 475	416 716

* After preferred dividends.

+ Restated to include the effect of the 3 for 1 stock split.

PART

7 MANAGING STRATEGIC CHANGE

WESTMILLS CARPETS LIMITED (Condensed)

Joseph N. Fry

"We are in quite a pickle with Westmills, and in dire need of a rescue program," said Derek Mather, senior vice-president of Canadian Enterprise Development Corporation Ltd. (CED), a venture capital company with a major equity position in the Calgary-based carpet manufacturer.

> Our losses are continuing and the prospects for early relief are poor since the market is soft and our operations disorganized. The banks are very nervous. Garry Morrison, whom we groomed for a year, has just resigned after two months as president. Harry Higson, his predecessor, is filling in on a stopgap basis, but neither Harry, the board, nor the banks want this to continue for more than a few weeks. The balance of the management team look promising but are as yet untested.
>
> As shareholders, we (CED) have to sort out our options and position on this investment, but the matter, for me, is a personal one as well. I've just been asked to step in as president, at least until we are in position to hire a new man. I'd appreciate your views on where to go from here.

THE CANADIAN CARPET INDUSTRY

The carpet industry in Canada, as it is presently known, had its beginnings in the later 1950s with the introduction of carpet tufting technology from the United States. Tufting was a low cost, flexible process for producing carpets of various qualities and styles. The new production capability coincided with expanding affluence in the Canadian marketplace and a prolonged boom in residential construction. Carpet sales grew dramatically in the 1960s and early 1970s, reaching a volume of 74 million square metres in 1975.

The growth of the Canadian market slowed in 1976 and 1977 with total sales of 76.5 million and 78.6 million square metres respectively. Nevertheless, Canadian consumption of 3.4 metres per capita was approaching that of the United States.

Between 85% and 90% of Canadian sales were domestically produced. Imports were limited to the less price-sensitive segments of the market by a tariff of 20% plus $.375 per square metre.

Carpet Manufacture

A tufted carpet was made in three principal sequential production steps: the tufting itself, dyeing and finishing. Equipment and process flexibilities were such that in each step there were a number of design options (Figure 1). By pursuing combinations of these options, carpet mills, within the constraints of their particular equipment configuration, could produce a variety of carpet lines. A major mill might produce over 25 different products and each of these would be produced in 10 to 15 different colours. This capacity for diversity had the effect of complicating both manufacturing operations and the nature of competition in the industry.

FIGURE 1   Main Steps in Tufted Carpet Manufacture

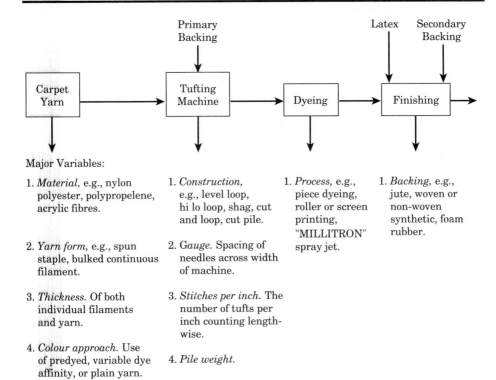

As noted in Figure 1, there was a variety of construction possibilities open for the design of carpets for particular functional and/or aesthetic purposes. A level loop pile design made with relatively coarse nylon yarn might be developed for a heavy-traffic commercial application, for example, or a plush, cut pile design of fine yarn might be produced for a high fashion location. Different carpet designs implied different materials costs and processing efficiency. The actual design decision was thus a mixture of craft, science and economics, as aim was taken at a particular target product market and a balance was struck between fashion, function and production costs.

The value added in carpet manufacture was relatively low in relation to the total value of the finished product. Purchased materials typically amounted to 75% or more of total costs, plant labour 5% and general overhead 20%. Production scheduling was a critical function in carpet mills—the challenge was to maintain customer service on the one hand and avoid excessive inventories, with their built-in working-capital demands and fashion risks, on the other hand.

Carpet Marketing

The Canadian carpet market was comprised of three major segments; retail, residential contract and commercial contract. An approximate division of the market into these categories is given in Table 1.

TABLE 1   The Canadian and Western Canadian Carpet Markets by Segment, 1977 (estimated volume in million square metres)

	Residential Retail	*Commercial Contract*	*Contract*	*Total*
Canadian market	51.0 (65%)	14.0 (17.8%)	13.4 (17.2%)	78.5
Western Canadian	8.8 (40.2%)	7.6 (34.7%)	5.5 (25.1%)	21.9

SOURCE: Canadian Carpet Institute, casewriter's estimates.

Retail Market

The typical retail customer was a homeowner purchasing a relatively small amount of carpet for first-time or replacement installation. The rough order of importance of purchase criteria in the retail market was generally cited as colour, style (texture), price, dealer service and guarantees. There was a very low awareness of brand names in the market, with perhaps only Harding (a carpet manufacturer) and DuPont (fibre supplier) having any significant recognition. Similarly, consumers had very little knowledge of the technical characteristics of carpets and the variables that would influence wear and care.

The retail market was serviced by a wide variety of outlets, including department stores, specialty floorcovering dealers, promotional carpet warehouses, furniture stores and home decoration centres. These outlets, depending upon their volume, their proximity to the mill and the manufacturer's distribution strategy, were in turn supplied directly from the mill, by mill-owned distributors or by independent distributors. The approximate proportions of the retail market serviced by mill-direct, mill-owned distributor and independent distributor were for Canada 35%, 45% and 20% respectively, and for western Canada 25%, 40% and 35%. The trend in the previous decade had been for the mills to seek greater control of their distribution by implementing mill-direct or mill-owned distribution programs.

Residential Contract

This market consisted of home/apartment/condominium builders and mobile home manufacturers. It was serviced directly or through contract dealer/installers. Builder preferences tended toward basic carpet styles at price points below those popular in the retail and commercial markets. Order sizes were quite large and price competition was severe, with orders switching on differentials as low as 5 to 10 cents a metre. Assuming price and style competitiveness, service elements—and particularly the dependability of delivery—were important in maintaining mill/account relationships (Table 2).

TABLE 2 Ranking of Channel Service Aspects by Segment

Service Item*	Retail	Residential Contract	Commercial contract
Speed of delivery	2	4	
Delivery when promised	1	1	1
Update of samples	4		3
Complaint handling	3	2	
Notification of price changes			4
Regular representative contact		3	2

* Original lists contained many additional items such as mill warranties, co-op advertising, salesperson personality, etc.

SOURCE: Westmills research files.

Commercial Contract

The commercial market consisted of new or replacement installations in offices, hotels, retail outlets, schools, etc. The majority of commercial business was controlled by specialty installation firms that purchased directly from the mills. Unlike residential contract sales, the product was usually specified for particular projects by architects and interior designers on the basis of information from many sources (building owner, project manager, architect, etc.). The most popular styles were patterned multi-colour carpets with specific wear characteristics for the intended use.

Competitive Structure

There were 28 firms engaged in the manufacture of tufted carpet in Canada in 1977. These firms could be divided into three categories on the basis of their scale, scope of activities and degree of integration in marketing and manufacturing.

Group 1

This group consisted of firms with sales of $20 million or more, wide product lines and, in most cases, yarn spinning and substantial captive distribution operations. Operating results for the five firms in this group are summarized in Table 3. Together these firms accounted for somewhat less than 50% of the carpet market.

TABLE 3   Summary Performance of Major Carpet Firms ($000 000s)

		1977	*1976*	*1975*
Harding Carpets	Sales	$73.0	$74.5	$58.7
(as of Oct. 31)	Profit before tax	(.2)	3.0	2.1
Celanese Canada	Sales	37.6	39.0	47.7
Carpet Division	Profit before tax	(5.5)	(4.1)	.9
(as of Dec. 31)				
Peerless Rug	Sales	40.0	37.8	32.4
(as of Feb. 28)	Profit before tax	.6	.9	(.7)
Peeters Carpets	Sales	22.0(est)	22.0 (est)	20.0
Westmills	Sales	21.7	23.1	21.7
(as of Aug. 31)	Profit before tax	(1.5)	(2.4)	(.7)

SOURCE: Corporate financial reports.

Group 2

This group consisted of approximately eight firms with sales ranging from $10 to $20 million. They were generally somewhat more specialized than the Group 1 firms in product line or geographic market coverage. Most were private firms or divisions of U.S. manufacturers, with the result that specific financial data are not available.

Group 3

The balance of the industry consisted of small firms specializing in particular product, channel or geographic markets. Firms with sales as low as $2 million were apparently viable operations. Such firms might use pre-dyed yarns exclusively in order to limit operations to tufting and minimal finishing.

As the total market grew in the 1960s and early 1970s, entry had been relatively easy. By 1977 there was substantially more capacity in the Canadian industry than was justified by current demand. Excess capacity, coupled with a fragmented industry structure and the dynamics of style obsolescence, had led to fierce competition, price cutting and a deterioration of industry profitability.

Style competition was a major aspect of rivalry in the industry, stemming from a heterogeneous and fashion-conscious market on the one side and flexible manufacturing on the other. The benefits of design innovations were frequently short-lived, however, as other manufacturers "knocked-off" the popular styles. The time lag before a new innovation could be imitated by competitors was as short as six to nine months. With lasting product advantages difficult to achieve, success in specific markets often turned on price and a mill's ability to deliver high quality and excellent service.

WESTMILLS' BACKGROUND

Westmills Carpets Limited was incorporated in February 1966 in Kelowna, British Columbia. The company was (and remained through 1977) the only carpet manufacturer in the west. The intention was to capitalize on the fast-growing mass housing markets in British Columbia and Alberta through the manufacture of a relatively narrow range of tufted carpet products. Westmills commenced production in September of 1966 and by 1969 had sales of $2.4 million.

Early Growth

After some start-up difficulties, Westmills capitalized on the emerging popularity of shag carpet to fully establish its operations. Growth accelerated and facilities were expanded. In 1970, a distribution centre was opened in Winnipeg. In 1971, the Kelowna distribution facility was enlarged and sales were commenced in Ontario. In 1972, the capacity of the Kelowna plant was almost doubled.

The pace of activity increased even further in 1973 as the company moved to become a national manufacturer and distributor. "We felt we were an awfully clever carpet company," Derek Mather recalled, "and that we might as well be clever on a national scale."

In January 1973, Westmills acquired Globe Mills of Meaford, Ontario in a move to reduce its dependence on outside yarn suppliers. In February, Westmills was converted to a public company. "This provided additional equity money for the company and an opportunity for the original investors to realize a profit," Mather explained. Financial statements for Westmills from 1973 onward are given in Exhibits 1 and 2.

Later in 1973, Westmills acquired the assets of Centennial Carpets in Trenton, Ontario. Further, to expand the company's marketing base, major exclusive distributors were appointed in Quebec and Ontario. By the end of 1973, Westmills had manufacturing plants in Kelowna, Meaford and Trenton and distribution facilities in Vancouver, Calgary, Winnipeg and Trenton.

"In retrospect it was overconfidence, but we felt awfully good about ourselves at that time," said Mather. Markets remained buoyant in early 1974. In Kelowna, however, the company was becoming entangled in changing political jurisdictions with different views and rules affecting plant effluent. Since this posed uncertainties and constraints on operation and expansion, a decision was made to move all dyeing operations to Calgary. This transfer to a purchased 13 000 square foot plant was initiated during the year. Distribution in Calgary continued to be handled through a separate 8000 square foot facility. The fiscal year (to August 31, 1974) closed strong, with the company booking record sales and profits.

Decline

In the last quarter of 1974, the carpet market across Canada turned soft and Westmills' fortunes started to sag. For the first time, the company faced significant price and style competition and found itself overextended.

In 1975, the Kelowna plant was completely closed and all manufacturing equipment was moved to Calgary for installation on an ongoing basis in 1975 and early 1976. The Trenton manufacturing facility and distribution centre were also closed. Sales volumes were maintained near $22 million but gross margins slipped from 23.4% in 1974 to 16.5% in 1975 and a before-tax loss of $715 000 was incurred (Exhibit 1).

Markets remained soft in 1976 and Westmills further consolidated facilities and attempted to reduce costs. The Winnipeg distribution centre was closed; now all carpet manufacturing and distribution was handled out of Calgary. Cost reductions were hampered by the need to re-establish production with an untrained labour force earning in most cases $1.50 more per hour than workers in eastern mills; quality declined, deliveries became erratic, inventory grew and market credibility slipped. In fiscal year 1976, the company experienced a before-tax loss of $2.4 million.

Mather explained,

> Through this period we (the board) were slow to realize that there was something fundamentally wrong with the company and the way it was being run. The market problem, withdrawing from carpet manufacture in the east, and the plant relocation from Kelowna to Calgary, all confused our perception of the real situation.

Management Changes

As poor operation results continued, the Westmills board moved to strengthen management. Mather commented,

> Harry's (Harry Higson, the president) difficulty was in building a team; he couldn't develop strong men around him. As a result, he was working under tremendous pressure and his health was beginning to suffer. The scale of operation wasn't for him and he realized it. But improving management meant going outside. There was no one in a functional job that was near strong enough to step up.

Mr. Garry W. Morrison was hired as executive vice president in late 1976. Morrison, aged 32, was an American citizen and now a Canadian landed immigrant. He held a B.Sc. in Textile Technology, an M.B.A. , and had had seven years of management experience with U.S.-based Riegel Textile Corporation. At Riegel, Morrison had moved quickly through management ranks. Just prior to moving to Westmills, he had been a significant figure in the turnaround of a Canadian division of Riegel. His initial job at Westmills was to back up Harry Higson, but it was generally assumed he would become president in the not too distant future.

Morrison set out to learn the business, address some of the more pressing issues and recruit a second echelon of management.

Operating Changes

From January through August 1977, steps were taken to improve Westmills' financial condition, to cut operating costs and to bolster the product line. The vacant Trenton and Kelowna plants were sold; the former for $915 000 cash and the latter for $200 000 cash plus mortgage receivable for $1 million. The cash proceeds were used to reduce Westmills' long-term indebtedness to its banks and the mortgage was assigned to the banks as additional security. Inventories were reduced by fiscal year-end to about $4.3 million in an attempt to reduce the pressure on interest costs and working-capital levels. Salaried and hourly personnel were cut and more stringent guidelines were introduced for administrative, travel and other expenses. Five new high-end commercial carpet lines and six new residential lines were designed and prepared for introduction in the fall selling season. This brought the total Westmills product range to 34 lines.

Management Additions

In August 1977, Mr. J. William Ford joined Westmills as secretary-treasurer and chief financial officer. Ford, aged 33, was an American citizen and a Canadian landed immigrant. He was also married to a Canadian. He had known and worked with Garry Morrison at Riegel's Canadian subsidiary. Bill Ford's background included undergraduate and graduate studies in management at Virginia Polytechnic and Clemson University; service with the U.S. Army including combat experience and decoration in Vietnam; and experience in senior financial positions in two Canadian-based textile companies. Ford explained his move to Westmills: "Garry didn't pull any punches in describing the situation, but we'd been through a difficult turnaround before and I knew I could work with him. It seemed like a great challenge and opportunity."

At the time, Higson and Morrison were also engaged in negotiations with David Hirst, which would lead to Hirst joining Westmills as vice president of manufacturing in January 1978. Hirst, aged 54, was born in Yorkshire and educated in the U.K. at Batley Technical College (Textile Engineering) and Bradford Technical College (Cloth Manufacture). He had moved to Canada in 1957 and worked in a variety of carpet-mill plant supervisory and general management positions. Hirst was well known in technical circles in the industry and highly regarded for his capability in carpet design and particularly for designing around equipment constraints. Prior to committing to Westmills, David Hirst had visited Calgary to review the operation and recalled, "It was clear to me that there were also significant opportunities to improve productivity and quality. I welcomed the challenge."

A third senior manager was also hired by Westmills in this period to assume the top marketing position. By the time of the case, however, it was apparent that this appointment was not working out and that the marketing/sales function would have to be covered by James W. Hamilton, the current general sales manager. Hamilton, aged 36, had 18 years' experience in sales and sales management in the floorcovering business. He had started with Westmills in 1971 as a contract sales representative in Vancouver and shortly thereafter had been moved to Toronto to "open up" the east for Westmills. This he had done very successfully and after a short sales management stint with another company had been persuaded by Harry Higson to come back to Calgary and address the now apparent sales problems in the west. He had been general sales manager since mid-1976. Jim Hamilton knew the grassroots workings of the carpet business and had a reputation as a top-flight sales rep and sales manager.

For fiscal year 1977, however, there were no miracle cures. The year closed with another significant loss having to be booked—this time about $1.5 million pretax. Working capital was at a perilous level and the banks were becoming increasingly uneasy about their position. Now the financial as well as operating foundations of the business were deteriorating and the very survival of the firm was coming into question.

THE RECOVERY PLAN

Through the latter part of the 1976–77 fiscal year, Westmills had been working on a recovery plan, which took form at the beginning of the 1977–78 period.

The essence of the plan was to reduce the company's product/market base somewhat, but maintain or improve volume by achieving greater penetration in the commercial and retail markets in western Canada. At the same time, steps would be taken to relieve financial pressure through the sale and lease-back of the Calgary plant. Projections for the 1978 fiscal year, which management regarded as conservative, are given in Exhibits 3 and 4. Significant parts of the new plan follow.

Marketing

In late 1977, Westmills distributed carpets through nearly 3 000 accounts across Canada, but primarily in the west. Geographic, customer type and product type segments, and Westmills share therein, are given in Table 4.

TABLE 4 Westmills' Position in the Canadian Carpet Market, 1976
(volumes in millions of square metres)

	Western Market			Eastern Market	
	Retail	*Residential Contract*	*Commercial Contract*	*All Segments*	*Total*
All Product Volume	8.8	7.6	5.5	56.6	78.5
Westmills' Volume	.51	1.76	.25	.80	3.32
Share (%)	5.8	23.1	4.6	1.4	4.2
Solid Colour Volume	4.4	4.6	1.8	N/A	
Westmills' Volume	.40	1.41	.20	N/A	
Share (%)	9.1	30.6	11.1	N/A	

SOURCE: Company and casewriter's estimates.

Under the plan for 1977–78, sales in the west were to be emphasized. Representation would be maintained in Quebec, but at a minimum level. There was some anticipation of better results in Ontario through a new sales agency arranged by Garry Morrison. This latter activity had been debated in the company as not fully consistent with the western focus, but Morrison had prevailed, arguing that the incremental volume was essential.

Segment and Product Emphasis

Westmills' traditional market in the west had been residential contracts. The new carpet lines mentioned previously had been developed as part of a program to increase Westmills' retail and commercial market penetration. Most were multi-coloured lines developed from pre-dyed acrylic-nylon blends. The reasons for emphasis on pre-dyed yarns in the new products were market preferences and the limitations of Westmills' post-tufting colouring capabilities. It should be noted that many dealers in the west serviced more than one and perhaps all three segments, although most had a particular emphasis in their trade. It was also true that certain carpet styles could suitably be used by purchasers in one or more of the segments. The ultimate market mix of a mill could thus be only roughly estimated.

As a complement to the new product lines, Westmills was readying a foam backing application process in the Calgary plant. Foam-backed carpet accounted for about 20% of carpet sales by volume, and was particularly popular in lower-priced print and multicolour styles. Since foam-backed carpet was easier and less expensive to install than jute-backed carpet, it had a specific advantage in the "do-it-yourself" market and in certain residential contract applications. Westmills intended, at least initially, to put foam backing on selected current solid-colour lines to build volume at minimum incremental investment.

Promotion

Westmills' sales force numbered 23 representatives, each covering a specified geographic territory or, in the major cities, a specific account list. The sales reps were paid a guaranteed minimum of $16 000, plus a commission which varied from 1% to 3% of sales, depending on the carpet line. Each sales rep had a $200 per month car allowance and a travel and entertainment budget. The average gross earnings of the sales force were about $30 000. No changes were anticipated in the size or nature of the sales organization, although certain specific personnel adjustments were foreseen.

A major promotional expense was the cost of samples, sample kits, "waterfalls," etc., for use by the sales reps, in trade showrooms and in retail stores. While as much of the sample cost as possible was recovered from the trade, the net cost of sampling a new line was in the order of $50 000. Overall, sampling expense in 1976–77 was about $420 000. Only incidental amounts were spent on media advertising.

Delivery and Customer Service

Westmills' 8 000-square-foot Calgary distribution centre housed the majority of the finished goods inventory as well as the customer service and shipping departments. This facility had never operated to management's satisfaction and was believed to be the weak link responsible for mounting customer complaints about late or mistaken delivery. There were plans for 1977–78 to reduce the space used by half, to relocate personnel to the plant (making changes and reductions in the process) and to ship more goods directly from the plant. One objective of the move was to reduce finished goods inventory by $1 million.

Manufacturing

Westmills' manufacturing costs had recovered somewhat from the effects of relocation and the coincident plateauing of sales. Efficiency had improved through 1976–77, but costs were still about 20% higher than those incurred by similar mills in the U.S. (after adjustments for differences in input costs).

A consultant hired by Westmills noted that the high costs in the plant were due to production scheduling problems, low equipment utilization (in dyeing) and inappropriate equipment utilization (in finishing). The production process, in short, was not as yet running in a smooth and balanced fashion. Regarding quality, the consultant commented,

> Off quality in manufacturing is approximately double what one would expect . . . Part of this may be due to operational reasons . . . some must be attributed to attempts to utilize substandard fibres and blends in the carpet yarns (creating problems at Globe as well as Calgary) . . . some is due to the high personnel turnover in Calgary.

While identifying these problems, Wilson noted that if Westmills could achieve the "U.S. level" costs it would be competitive with any mill in Canada and could dominate the west in the demand segments which fit its yarn and carpet production capabilities.

The 1977–78 plan anticipated the following changes.

1. Reducing plant direct labour.
2. Shifting the product line to achieve greater utilization of Globe Mills' spinning capacity, and having Globe seek external contracts.
3. Implementing more stringent quality control, with the goal of reducing "second" yardage from 7% to 4.5%.
4. Changing certain dye and chemical formulations to cheaper equivalently effective materials.
5. Eliminating a 4 000-square-foot warehouse currently housing raw materials and off-quality or slow-selling goods.

The aggregate savings were forecast to be slightly more than $1 million on a volume base equivalent to 1976–77. Morrison wrote, "We are performing major surgery on our operations to reduce their size to conform with sales volumes dictated by the marketplace." Westmills would still retain the capacity, however, to produce about 4.6 million metres of carpet, provided there were no unusual product-mix demands.

Finance

As part of the recovery plan, Westmills was pursuing financial arrangements that would "reduce long-term debt, improve working capital and generally put us in a better situation financially." The main elements of this plan were the sale and lease-back of the Calgary plant and the discounting and sale of the Kelowna mortgage.

Discussions with potential purchasers of the Calgary plant indicated that a $3 million price might be acceptable, with a lease-back based on an 8-10% capitalization rate. It was probable that one year's lease cost in advance would have to be maintained in a trust account. Negotiations were underway, with an anticipated closing in January or February 1978. Other discussions regarding the mortgage on the Kelowna property indicated that the mortgage might be sold for something in the order of $900 000 cash. It was anticipated that this, too, would close early in the new year.

THE CRUNCH

As Westmills moved through January and February of 1978, it became increasingly apparent that events were not unfolding as anticipated. Sales were substantially below forecast and losses were accumulating at a distressing rate (Exhibits 3 and 4). Garry Morrison had left the company to be replaced on an interim basis by Harry Higson. The company's plight became well known in the industry and it was losing credibility as a continuing supplier. Management was working, as Jim Hamilton put it, somewhere between desperation and chaos.

Westmills, seen from outside, was on the verge of collapse. Within the company the difficulties were recognized, but there was a resilience in management's attitude that offered at least the possibility of continuity and survival. The question they were asking was not whether, but how. An assessment by various managers of their areas of operation follows.

Marketing—Jim Hamilton

The problems Jim Hamilton was facing in the marketplace were, in simple form, credibility, product and reliability in quality and delivery. "Right now," he said, "we have a terrible image in the market."

Credibility

Hamilton commented,

> Most of our accounts have been real good and have tried to support us; but they have heard rumours of us folding and they are really very concerned about

the availability of goods. Some have come to us saying they just have to protect themselves by adding other suppliers. Others just won't do business with us; they say we are too shaky. Naturally our competitors are taking as much as they can and have kept prices real keen.

Product

The new product programs had not met expectations. The foam-backed solid-colour carpets had encountered market and salesperson resistance and took an inordinate time to run in the plant. The new multi-colour retail lines had been based on yarn imported from the United States; the depreciation of the dollar had sharply increased materials costs, forcing Westmills into a noncompetitive situation. No Canadian supplier had the capacity to supply on a reliable basis. Further, there was resistance at the retail level to purchasing samples and inventories, at least in part because of Westmills' uncertain position. It was too early to evaluate the contract lines, as the selling cycle in this market was considerably longer.

In spite of these difficulties, as Hamilton notes, "We have a good basic line in solid-colour goods, particularly for residential contract. We make a good solid-colour fabric. What we don't have are reasonable upgrades to cover the higher price points."

Quality/Delivery Reliability

Good intentions to the contrary, Westmills was not living up to its promises to customers. The "mechanics" of order processing, commitment, scheduling, production and shipping were, in Hamilton's words, the "worst ever." He commented, "We are missing delivery dates and we are having quality problems; we have had to issue a pile of credit notes for problems we have created. I have a 4 000-square-foot warehouse full of seconds to dispose of. How do I do this without upsetting the market?"

As a result of the foregoing, Hamilton was having trouble with sales-force morale. "There has been a tendency in this company to treat salesmen as a necessary evil anyway," he noted, "and now we aren't giving them product and service. How am I supposed to keep good men?"

Manufacturing—David Hirst

In the plant, Hirst was confronted with problems of morale, production scheduling and control, and product quality. His first test was immediate: on the very day he arrived in Calgary for work (having moved his family across the country), Garry Morrison had announced his resignation as president, to the surprise of all.

Morale

There was a bad morale problem in the plant, David Hirst noted, stemming from inadequate direction and control of work and further instability rising from concerns that there was "every possibility ... (we) ... may not be there tomorrow."

In his first weeks at the plant, Hirst had had a chance to assess his supervisory staff and was quite pleased, with the exception of one or two areas where he anticipated making changes. But overall he felt he could build on the strengths and experience of these people and that the problems being experienced were more the result of the context they had been working in than of particular personal shortcomings. In light of this assessment, Hirst felt his first priority was to earn the respect of the plant personnel, establish that one person was in control and from this foundation isolate and address the operating problems.

Production Scheduling

The production scheduling of Westmills had fallen into progressive disarray as market pressures, new-product development, quality problems and financing difficulties had accumulated, driving operations into a vicious circle of deterioration. Hirst commented, "We are dealing in chaos...the tufters are being scheduled on the spot by telephone calls, slips of paper that people walk in with...there is no way we can operate efficiently like this...sales and customer service just don't see the costs...how can they make the promises they do?" Such were the difficulties of co-ordination between sales, customer service, manufacturing and delivery that one sales rep had recently verified that an order he had placed for 2500 square metres of carpet had, quite simply, been lost.

The key to manufacturing efficiency in a carpet plant, Hirst pointed out, was proper scheduling and integration of equipment loads through the entire production process. This was quite impossible in the current circumstances and it was essential, as he put it, "to reduce the interference factors."

Quality

The sources of product quality problems were not all known but there principal contributing factors: the quality of the incoming yarns from Globe Mills, certain product designs, and deficiencies in training and experience in Calgary.

The limitations of Globe Mills had not been fully appreciated or considered in some product designs, with the result that it was stretching its capabilities to make certain yarns. Hirst, among others, agreed that Globe did a good job on yarns within its range and that the core problem was one of not balancing capabilities and efficiency in Globe and Calgary when designing fabrics.

Certain product designs, as well, were ill-fitted to the Calgary plant. An internal memo commented that one of the new multi-colour lines "makes our inadequacy in the multi-coloured area only too evident."

On training an experience, Hirst noted that "Calgary is not exactly a textile centre and there is little access to trained workers." Westmills was thus forced to hire in a booming, resource-based economy with the attendant high wage-rates and worker mobility. Substantial progress had been made in developing a stable workforce, but it was clear from the kind of problems arising from the plant floor that a great deal of training and experience were yet necessary.

Hirst weighed the circumstances:

> Sure we have problems. We have limitations in our equipment in Meaford and Calgary. But, with the exception of multi-colour, we can produce volume and quality and make carpets that sell. We can do more than has been done with what we have now. I guess, coming from Yorkshire, if that's all you have, use it well. The job can be done...I have no reservations.

Control and Finance—Bill Ford

In early 1978, Bill Ford was working to improve the quality and use of the company's information systems and at the same time doing battle day-to-day for cash to meet immediate obligations.

Information Systems

On arriving at Westmills, Ford had reviewed the control and financial systems and found that "a lot of good things had been started, but they were still in a half-finished state." The computer facility had been applied to the financial side of the business for such tasks as payroll and receivables accounting and financial reporting. These areas, he felt, were in pretty good shape.

The problems lay more in the lack of development and use of operating and cost accounting systems. Here there were shortcomings in most areas, from order entry through manufacturing cost control to inventory control. The general frame-work for a workable system was in place but the actual work being done was not up to a reasonable standard in either effectiveness or efficiency. The matter was further complicated by a lack of understanding and communication between accounting and the line managers and supervision. "There was a problem of attitude and capabilities both inside and outside the accounting department," Ford noted, "and it has been necessary to change some personnel and segment the general and management accounting functions." Work was proceeding to improve the control system, but in the prevailing circumstances progress had been fairly slow.

Cash Flow

Westmills' cash position in early 1978 was so tight that Bill Ford was personally monitoring all receipts and approving all disbursements. The noose was drawing tighter every day.

On the receipts side, sales were down and collections were becoming more difficult. The prop up sales, credit had been granted in questionable circumstances. Difficulties with deliveries and quality claims had led to a flurry of credit notes being granted in the field, which meant a very complicated reconciliation of accounts. Some accounts were deferring payment until such matters were clarified; others, sensing weakness, were simply being very slow to pay. On the payables side, suppliers were getting tougher about terms and some had put Westmills in COD for orders incremental to existing balances.

Ford described the situation: "I'm in daily discussions with the banks. They are very skeptical and very close to pulling the plug. If they did now, my guess is that they might end up 10–15% out of pocket. They have asked for a meeting within the next few days."

Derek Mather and CED

Derek Mather, aged 45, had started his business career as an investment analyst for Sun Life Assurance Co. In 1962 he had joined CED as an investment officer and was currently senior vice president. In his time at CED, Mather had been involved in recruiting and screening of new corporate ventures and the monitoring of venture investments. He had been a member of Westmills' board of directors since 1967. These jobs, he pointed out, had not brought him into direct operating management.

> I see my own involvement as a dubious solution...a solution with many flaws. Although I've been on the board for many years, I don't know the industry from a technical standpoint, nor do I know the market particularly well. I don't have the high level of skills in the business which I think financial people, considering and investment, would demand.

The countervailing problem at the moment was the expected difficulty of finding an experienced and credible presidential candidate. Mather commented, "I don't think we've got a hope of finding a guy like that in this present environment. I think whatever solution we are able to work out at this time...and by that I mean the next few days...will be a patchwork solution...if we were to go out and try to hire a new man we'd just be wasting out time." He continued, "It may be, from a banker's point of view, that if CED is prepared to supply additional equity capital and personnel, then that degree of shareholder commitment would be impressive."

CED was currently Westmills' major shareholder, holding approximately 40% of the 1 100 984 common shares issued and $402 000 worth of the $1.144 million in unsecured convertible debentures (convertible to common shares at $2.50). Westmills common stock was currently trading on the Toronto Stock Exchange at from $.70 to $.90.

On CED's future involvement, Mather and Gerald Sutton, CED's president, were of one mind: within reason, CED must stick with the investment and do what was necessary to revive the company. Sutton explained, "We took Westmills public and in so doing reduced our holdings, recaptured our initial investment and made a profit. Under the circumstances we can't just withdraw from this situation; we have a moral responsibility to the public. Mather added, "The business community in the west knows we started this company...we can't have them say we walked away when times got tough."

EXHIBIT 1   Westmills' Consolidated Operating Results for Fiscal Years Ending August 31 ($000s)

	1977	1976	1975	1974	1973
Net sales	$21 678	$23 056	$21 725	$22 823	$14 407
Cost of sales					
Costs	17 886	19 594	17 506	17 098	10 622
Depreciation	712	660	638	347	188
Total	18 598	20 254	18 144	17 445	10 810
Gross margin	3 080	2 802	3 581	5 378	3 597
%	14.2%	12.1%	16.5%	23.4%	25.0%
Marketing expenses	2 625	2 478	2 141	3 063	1 933
Administration	876	900	610	—	—
Financing:					
Long-term	756	681	597	309	133
Short-term	308	514	333	156	37
Extraordinary costs	—	635	615	—	—
Total	4 565	5 208	4 296	3 528	2 103
Net income before tax	(1 485)	(2 406)	(715)	1 849	1 494
Income tax	(305)	(361)	(309)	798	651
Net income	(1 180)	(2 045)	(405)	1 051	842
Extraordinary items	314	—	96	96	—
Net profit	(866)	(2 045)	(309)	1 147	842

SOURCE: Company documents.

EXHIBIT 2 **Westmills' Consolidated Balance Sheets for Fiscal Years Ending August 31** ($000s)

	1977	1976	1975	1974	1973
Current Assets					
Cash	$	$	$	$ 77	$ 169
Accounts receivable	3 880	3 874	4 506	3 480	2 337
Inventories	4 584	6 198	5 316	6 033	3 857
Prepaid expenses	253	227	169	168	173
Income taxes recoverable	—	—	354	—	—
	8 717	10 296	10 345	9 757	6 536
Current Liabilities					
Short-term borrowings	4 497	4 230	2 576	2 463	421
Accounts payable, accrued liabilities	2 458	2 796	3 421	3 279	2 164
Income and other taxes	195	255	236	231	519
Current portion, LT debt	470	402	397	653	442
	7 620	7 683	6 630	6 626	3 546
Working capital	1 097	2 613	3 715	3 131	2 990
Net fixed assets	6 644[1]	7 811	8 075	7 841	3 887
	$ 7 741	$10 424	$11 790	$10 972	$ 6 877
Long-term debt[2]	4 989	6 500	5 461	4 459	4 873
Deferred income taxes	408	713	1 074	948	586
Shareholders' equity:					
Common stock	3 362	3 362	3 362	3 362	3 362
Retained earnings	(1 018)	(151)	1 893	2 203	1 056
	$ 7 741	$10 424	$11 790	$10 972	$ 6 877

[1] Includes mortgage receivable of $1 000 000 on sale of Kelowna plant.

[2] The structure of the long-term debt as of August 31, 1977 was as follows:

9.5% First mortgage on land and buildings; payments $9 000 per month, including interest	$1 017 950
Term bank loans at 1.5% over prime; payments $30 000 per month plus interest. Secured by assignment of mortgage receivable plus a charge on land, buildings and equipment	$1 556 000
12% Series A debentures, due 1980; payments $22 000 per month including interest. Secured by charge on land, buildings and equipment ranking with bank term loan	$1 444 775
12% Convertible, redeemable unsecured debentures. Series A and B Semi-annual interest	$1 441 000
	$5 459 725
Less current portion of long-term debt	$ 470 705
	$4 989 020

SOURCE: Company documents.

EXHIBIT 3 Westmills' Forecast Profit and Actual Experience, 1977–78 ($000s)

	Recovery Plan Pds. 1–6	Forecast FY 1978	Estimated Actual Pds. 1–6
Square metres (000)	1 550	3 340	1 230
Net sales	$10 217	$22 138	$7 966
Cost of sales	8 712	18 611	6 888
Gross margin	1 505	3 527	1 078
Percent net sales	14.7%	15.9%	13.6%
Marketing	968	2 029	893
Administration	412	871	432
Finance-interest	415	777	461
Total	1 795	3 677	1 786
Operating income (loss)	(290)	(150)	(708)
Taxes recoverable	(96)	(201)	(106)
Income (loss before extraordinary items)	(194)	51	(602)
Extraordinary Items:			
Sale of mortgage (net)	(48)	(48)	—
Sale of plant (net)	892	892	—
Income tax recovery	356	356	—
Net profit (loss)	$1 006	$1 251	$(602)

EXHIBIT 4 Westmills' Balance Sheet Forecasts and Actual Experience, 1977–78 ($000s)

	Recovery Plan Forecast		Estimated Actual
	End Period 6	End 1978 FY	End Period 6
Current Assets			
Accounts receivable	$4 750	$4 500	$4 191
Trust account	300	300	—
Inventories:			
Raw material	1 600	1 600	1 355
Work in process	650	650	1 087
Finished goods	1 425	1 176	1 947
Total inventory	3 675	3 426	4 389
Prepaid expenses	225	316	156
Total current assets	8 950	8 632	8 736
Mortgage	—	—	1 000
Net fixed assets	3 691	3 495	5 427
Total	$12 641	$12 127	$15 163
Liabilities & Shareholders' Equity			
Bank indebtedness	5 501	4 507	5 701
Accounts payable	1 847	2 198	1 943
Taxes payable	225	214	220
Current portion:			
Long-term debt	—	—	470
Current Liabilities	7 573	6 919	8 334
Long-term debt	1 441	1 441	4 785
Deferred taxes	278	173	302
Shareholders' Equity:			
Common shares	3 362	3 362	3 362
Retained earnings	(13)	232	(1 620)
Total	$12 641	$12 127	$15 163

WHITBREAD MERSEYSIDE

J. Peter Killing

In December 1981, Mr. Bernard King, Managing Director of Whitbread West Pennines, met with Len Oliver, the newly appointed general manager of Whitbread Merseyside, to discuss the troubled state of affairs in the company's Merseyside operations. Plagued by strikes, a history of poor brewery management, and a recent rapid decline in sales volume and market share, the Merseyside company was considered to be one of Whitbread's most serious problem areas. Mr. King presented his view of the situation to Len Oliver:

> We can't just throw up our hands and say "Liverpool is unmanageable." We earn a lot of money there and we could be earning a lot more. What you've got to do, Len, is break the mould. Business as usual is not good enough. I'll support you—but how you do it is up to you.

THE COMPANY

Whitbread and Company was established in 1742 when Samuel Whitbread founded a brewery bearing his name in London. The company gradually expanded to become a national brewer, and by the 1980s, it operated twenty breweries and forty-one distribution depots in the U.K., as well as 7 000 pubs and more than 100 Beefeater steak houses. The company also played a role in the wine, spirits and soft drinks industries in the U.K. Sales in the year ending February 28, 1981 were £782 million, and net profits were £60 million. Since 1978 growth in sales had been approximately 11% per year, while profits had increased an average of 16% per annum.

Whitbread West Pennines was one of nine regional Whitbread companies in the U.K. It consisted of three sites, Liverpool, Salford and Blackburn (Shadsworth), which combined distribution and production operations, and five separate distribution depots. Whitbread Merseyside (Liverpool-based) was a sub-unit of Whitbread West Pennines, comprising Whitbread's Liverpool operation and depots in Birkenhead (across the Mersey River from the Liverpool brewery) and in Llandudno, North Wales.

Bernard King became Managing Director of Whitbread West Pennines in June 1981, having spent the previous six years running the company's soft drink operations. He inherited a situation which was considered by many observers to be an industrial relations nightmare, with profit performance significantly below standard. Peter Watkins, the general manager of Whitbread Merseyside when Bernard arrived, explained some of the origins of the company's industrial relations problems to his new boss:

When you realize that not so long ago Liverpool dock workers were kept in cages, with a chosen few allowed out to unload ships for the day, you begin to understand why the Liverpool workers and their unions are so militant. They are tough, smart (often smarter than the managers who are trying to control them), and a number of them are waging an ideological war to overthrow the capitalist system. The result of this has been that many major British union disputes, particularly dock and transport disputes, have begun in Liverpool and then spread to the rest of the country.

Whitbread's history of labour problems here is a long one. Our employees belong to the Merseyside branch of the Transport and General Worker's Union (the "T and G"), which is reputed to be the toughest branch of a tough union. The full-time union official who runs Merseyside is a strong character who more than once has forced a firm out of business. In the late 1960s, we went through a major struggle with him and the T and G to have the third man eliminated from our delivery fleet. In the early 1970s, the issue was our use of hired transport. We wanted to maintain a fleet of trucks and employees capable of meeting our base monthly load, and use hired transport to meet our seasonal peaks. The union felt we should staff to meet our peak loads on a year round basis. These are just two of the struggles we've had over the years, and both were long acrimonious disputes involving intermittent work stoppages and slowdowns, and demanding a hugh amount of management time.

We have also added to our own problems. In 1972, for instance, senior Whitbread management announced that over the next several years a number of regional breweries, including Liverpool, would be closed. The result was that many of our older, stable employees left the company and were replaced by younger, more transient people. However, one year later, the order was rescinded. The growth of lager beer had significantly exceeded market projections which meant that the breweries would stay open after all. Then in quick succession in 1973 and 1974, it was again announced that the breweries would be closed, and then that they would stay open.

This vacillation was the result of differences of opinion concerning the appropriate size of a new brewery which the company was planning to build at Samlesbury, near Blackburn. Production planners wanted this to be a very large, efficient brewery which would absorb the capacity of small local breweries like Liverpool, Blackburn and Salford, and it was their intentions which led to the second closure announcement. However, the marketers in Whitbread believed that the existence of these local breweries were very important to British beer drinkers who didn't want to drink a standardized product, but something which had been brewed locally, to local tastes. In the end it appears to have been a draw, as the Blackburn brewery was closed in 1978 after

Samlesbury opened, but Liverpool and Salford are still in operation. The uncertainty generated by the whole exercise definitely hurt our relationship with the unions.

More recently, Bernard, we have tried to put in place wealth creation schemes which would result in profit sharing for hourly paid workers. Unfortunately, your predecessor put a plan in place in 1978, the region's peak year, and most workers gained nothing because profits have never recovered to 1978 levels. The unions wasted no time in convincing them that it was just another management ploy to get more work for no extra pay. To make matters worse, the workers in the Samlesbury plant, which exports 50% of its volume to healthier regions, have benefitted, so now the workers we were most interested in, like those in Liverpool, have an extra grudge against us.

After six months as Managing Director—which included two major strikes in Liverpool and a temporary brewery closure because of quality problems—Bernard King concluded that management changes were needed if the region were to progress. He decided to place Peter Watkins in charge of the Blackburn operations, where he had spent much of his early career, and to look for a new man to run Whitbread Merseyside. What he wanted, he said, was someone "big, strong, and dumb enough to accept the job."

LEN OLIVER

Len Oliver was recommended to Bernard King by a Whitbread manager who knew Len and thought he could do the job in Liverpool. Len had joined Whitbread in 1976 in a senior distribution post after spending 17 years with a major British food products company, where he was primarily involved in distribution and industrial relations issues. After a few years as Distribution Manager, a job which involved solving a number of serious industrial relations issues, Len had been appointed general manager of Whitbread's Sheffield operations. He commented:

> When I arrived in Sheffield in 1978, the business had been growing nicely and a new management structure had just been put into place. I was told not to make any major changes for 12 months, to let everyone get used to the new structure and to me. Unfortunately, volumes started to fall in 1979—it wasn't just our problem, it was the whole industry—and I couldn't just sit still. I started cutting people, and in the end I reduced the original level of 400 employees to approximately 300.

Before taking over Whitbread Merseyside, Len Oliver met separately with Bernard King to learn more about the recent industrial relations situation in Liverpool. Bernard described the situation as follows:

> I had not been in my job two days when the Shadsworth brewery went on strike. I did not get good advice from my local managers on this issue, but in the end, after a two-week walk-out, the T and G came back to work without gaining

anything. I learned a lot about the union from that strike, and they learned that I don't back down. Then there was the Liverpool strike. Although the brewery had only 20 employees, the strike spread to the 40 workers in the packaging operation, and they jointly picketed our distribution centres, effectively shutting down all of Whitbread Merseyside. At one point, it appeared that our Samlesbury plant would also be picketed, which would have been a disaster of major proportions.

This strike, and the second one which followed it (a total of six weeks), were a major test of will between ourselves, the union, and Whitbread senior management in London. They were precipitated by two new managers that Peter Watkins had hired to try to restore order and supervisory morale in the brewery. We suspended five hard-core trouble makers who the new managers had seen, in spite of repeated warnings, in a pub during working hours. The suspension was followed by an investigation that ultimately led to their dismissal. During the investigation, the union officials said to us, "Are you really sure you want to go through with this?" We could have backed down, as we had so many times before, but we decided that the time had come to take a stand, to support our first line managers.

At one point during the second strike, I was called to London to meet senior Whitbread managers, who told me that I should give the union officials whatever they wanted, so the strike could be ended. I replied that if they forced me to do that, I would have to resign. It was a rather tense meeting, but I did not concede. As the strike dragged into November, however, we decided that perhaps we should permanently close the brewery. When I announced this to Merseyside management, they objected and said that they felt the union would yield, as they now finally understood that we were serious. They were right, and two days later the workers returned to work, minus the infamous five.

LEN OLIVER'S FIRST WEEK

Len Oliver began his new job in Liverpool on January 5, 1982. From the first day he made a point of being very visible and accessible, talking formally and informally to his managers, union officials and hourly paid workers. He explained to everyone that he came with no preconceived notions about what should be done at Liverpool, but when he did decide they would be told, openly and clearly. This message was received with scepticism by the union leaders, who were convinced that Oliver had been sent to Merseyside to close the brewery, and intended to give both him and Whitbread a very hard time if he tried to do so.

During the first week, Len's focus was twofold: to gain an understanding of the business situation facing Whitbread Merseyside, and to make an assessment of the individuals he would be working with. (An organization chart is presented in Exhibit 1.) A recently completed report (see Appendix) suggested that the company's market share decline was the result of high prices, underinvestment in pubs, not taking advantage of a trend to cask beer,[1] and stiff competition from local brewers. The market share decline was apparent in both the free trade business (sales to pubs not allied to any brewer) and the tied trade business (pubs owned by Whitbread). In spite of the fact that he had no personal experience at developing or managing pubs, Len was somewhat disturbed after discussing the report with the free trade and tied trade managers. He commented:

> The free trade manager does not believe that we have a problem. He seems to think that we have a God given right to survive. Unfortunately, he's been here a long time and his attitudes will be difficult to change. I think he sees himself as the number two manager in Merseyside, but he does not appear to me to be a good manager of people.
>
> The tied trade manager, on the other hand, has only been here about eight months and is new to the brewing business. In spite of this, he's a very independent character, and his position seems to be "I've got pubs to run and I know what I'm doing." However, I hear that the pub managers dislike and distrust him as he is very aggressive, openly runs checks on their honesty, and insists they are in their pubs virtually all the time. His drive is to reduce costs in general and overheads in particular.

Len also examined volume and profit figures during his first week in Liverpool, and these confirmed his belief that the Merseyside operation was earning approximately 50% less than it should have been. Volume sold in the Merseyside region had fallen from 356 000 barrels to approximately 250 000 barrels in a two-year period (Table 1). Part of this decline was due to a transfer of business to Whitbread's take home division, but most of it was due to declining trading conditions and the 1981 strikes. The Liverpool brewery was operating at approximately 60% of its 300 000-barrel per year capacity, and beers which it could not produce were shipped in from other Whitbread breweries.

TABLE 1   Whitbread Merseyside Performance February 28 Year End

	*Volume** (000 barrels)	*Profit* (£000)
1977–78	365	N/A
1978–79	355	4 824
1979–80	356	5 524
1980–81	308	6 000
1981–82 (est.)	250	4 800

* There are 288 pints in a barrel of beer.

[1] Cask beer was made the "old fashioned way", which meant that it was conditioned in the cask rather that the brewery, and dispensed in the pub with a hand pump.

Further probing revealed the employment figures presented in Table 2.

TABLE 2 Whitbread Merseyside 1981 Year End Employment

	Weekly Paid	*Monthly Paid*	*Total*
Production*	68	20	88
Cellar Service	—	36	36
Tied Trade	19	38	57
Free Trade	—	16	16
Distribution	161	62	223
Administration	9	18	27
	257	190	447

* Brewery and packaging.

After examining these figures, Len commented:

> In spite of the fact that they have laid off 157 people here since the volume decline began in 1979, there are still far too many. Based on my Sheffield experience, I would say that this operation should be run with about 300 people. I am not just talking about a reduction in weekly paid employees, there are about 70 middle level managers in this operation, and that's about 30 too many! One of the most blatant offenders is the distribution operation.
>
> We initially grew into this area by acquisition, and we still have too many depots, too many trucks, too many people. Naturally, I have talked with the distribution manager. He is very apprehensive, he knows he has problems. He strikes me as an honest man, he's genuinely concerned about Whitbread Merseyside and Liverpool's severe problems, but he's not getting the job done. I was told before I came here that I'd probably have to replace him, but I'm not sure if that's the best move. The problem is complex because we can't simply combine our various depots. The union has negotiated different restrictive practices in each location, which means such things as manning levels, overtime rules, and the organization of work, are different in Birkenhead than they are in Liverpool, even though one is just across the river from the other.
>
> The one area that clearly is *not* overstaffed is the brewery. It was reduced from 30 to 20 hourly employees in the last round of cuts, and that is the minimum they can get by with. Due to a quality problem prior to my arrival, the brewery was shut for a time, and a head brewer and number two brewer were brought in. Although new to the job, the head brewer has worked in this brewery before and appears competent. He reports to Samlesbury in terms of the quality of product he makes, cleanliness standards, and so on, but to me with respect to issues relating to his workforce.

The problem with the brewery is the incredible resentment that resides there. They hate every manager up to and including Bernard King for firing their five ringleaders, and they hate me because I'm the new boss and because I was put in here by Bernard King. They could start another strike at any time, on the slightest pretext.

I should also mention that when quality problems temporarily closed the Liverpool brewery, we shipped in beer from other Whitbread breweries, and our local customers didn't notice the difference. Another marketing myth destroyed! And there is certainly enough excess capacity at Samlesbury to absorb the total Liverpool production. We don't need this Liverpool brewery!

At the end of his first week in Liverpool, Len took a few minutes to talk about his personal situation, and the need for change at Merseyside:

It's a good thing I'm here without my family, because I'm spending 15 hours a day on the job, and it looks like it will continue that way for some time. I am eating with managers every night, and then we usually go out for a few drinks. Although the managers are being quite protective of one another, I don't detect any jealousy of me—I don't think any of them wanted this job! In fact, the personnel manager, who appears competent, had already arranged a transfer to Samlesbury before my arrival. It takes effect in about a month's time, but I could probably stop it if I wanted to....

I have talked directly with the union leaders. There are two key guys. The full-time union official is the incredibly tough character that Bernard first met in the Shadsworth dispute, and then again in the Liverpool battles. He is 62 years old, and has lost his last two fights with Bernard—I wonder if he's getting tired. It could be expensive to find out, of course. The other man is the full-time union convenor, a company employee, who is 57. He is reputed to have been a firebrand in his youth, but has settled a little now. Of course the young shop stewards below him are as tough and militant now as he was in earlier years.

My style is not to sit around. Bernard is expecting me to create changes, so is the union, so are my managers. I don't think next week is too early to begin.

EXHIBIT 1 Whitbread Merseyside Organization Chart

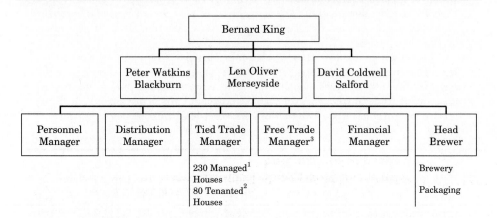

[1] Managed Houses were owned by Whitbread and managed by Whitbread employees.

[2] Tenanted Houses were owned by Whitbread and managed by entrepreneurs who leased the pubs from the company.

[3] Free Houses were pubs not owned by a brewer, and free to buy from whatever supplier they wished.

APPENDIX Whitbread Merseyside Analysis of Market Share Loss

Between 1978 and 1981, our share in the North West has declined from 18.26% to 16.36%, representing a 21% volume decline.

Whitbread Market Share—North West

	1978	1979*	1980	1981
Total Beer	18.26%	19.08%	17.86%	16.36%
Tied Trade	20.36	21.48	19.94	18.60
Free Trade	14.71	16.19	15.29	13.73

* Increased share due to Tetley strike.

The decline is due to a number of factors working together rather than any single factor.

A. Tied Trade

1. House Location

In West Pennines, 41% of the volume loss is accounted for the Liverpool Managed Houses. Sixty-six of these houses (0.25 of the Estate) represented 50% of the managed loss. The principal reasons for the decline in these houses were: 32 due to non-trading factors such as urban redevelopment, recession, and industrial decline; 18 due to high prices; and 16 due to miscellaneous factors. In addition, the recent growth of unemployment on Merseyside is concentrated in areas of Whitbread strengths, e.g., Ellesmere Port where we have 44% share. Whitbread also had above average presence in the inner city area (19% of the total), which has experienced above average growth in unemployment.

2. Investment

Compared with our major competitors, Whitbread have underinvested in the tied estate. For example, between 1976 and 1980, Allied spent 64% more on their pubs, and Bass 48% more on theirs. As a consequence, a large proportion of our estate is untidy and unattractive.

Tied Trade Investment 1976-80

	Per Tied House
Allied	£3 500
Courage	2 300
Bass	2 200
Whitbread	1 300

3. Pricing

Whitbread has been one of the price leaders in the North West for 1.5–2 years. At retail prices we have been up to 8p per pint more expensive than the local brewers. For example, in 1979, the difference between Whitbread and Boddingtons was 1p per pint. In the two years of recession since then, the difference has been 5p per pint. Combined with the underinvestment the Whitbread pub will be perceived as offering a lower value for money package. (The price of a pint of bitter in a Liverpool pub in early 1982 was approximately 56p.)

4. Cask Beer

Between 1969 and 1979, the cask beer market grew by 26%. By 1980, cask beer has grown to 20.7% of the market at a time when the total beer market was declining. Whitbread West Pennines' share of the draught market in 1979–80 was 13.4%, but our share of cask beer was estimated at only 1.3%, representing 1.7% of our draught volume. Cask beer represented about 75% of the local brewer volumes, and amongst the nationals, Bass had 25% of their volume in cask and Allied 15% of their volume in cask.

5. Local Brewer's Performance

We estimate that our share loss has been gained by the local brewers in the North West, e.g., Local 1.4% down, Nationals 5.6% down 1980 v. 1981. The major reasons why the locals have performed better are covered previously, but in addition, we feel that the locals have achieved a better image partly as a result of price, signage, etc., and partly because the consumer has developed a "small and local is best" philosophy. Local brewery brands consistently out-perform national brands in terms of product preference.

B. Free Trade

1. Small Accounts

In order to improve our Free Trade profitability we have closed our 0–20 barrel per year accounts. As a result, we have shed 12 000 barrels from the business, most of which we planned to transfer to wholesalers.

However, we would estimate that more than 50% of the transferred volume has been lost from the business. Our current intention is to evaluate the closure of 20–50 barrel accounts which would put at risk a further 22 000 barrels. There is evidence that other brewers, notably Bass, are accepting small accounts closed by Whitbread.

2. Price

Price is playing an increasing part in consumer choice. Up to 1980, Free Trade accounts would equalize their retail prices regardless of the Wholesale price. More recently, however, the retail prices now reflect the wholesale price and consequently, as Whitbread have been price leaders, the consumer has decided on the lower-priced alternative on the same bar. The Wholesale price differences, especially against the local brewers, has been significant.

HIRAM WALKER-GOODERHAM & WORTS (A)

Joseph N. Fry

In 1985, Hiram Walker-Gooderham & Worts (Hiram Walker) was one of the world's largest and most profitable producers of distilled spirits. Hiram Walker's five key brands—Canadian Club Canadian whisky, Ballantine's Scotch whisky, Courvoisier cognac, and Kahlua and Tia Maria coffee liqueurs—were sold internationally and held strong positions in their individual categories. Revenues were steady at about $1.5 billion, yielding consistent after tax returns of between 15% and 16% on invested capital. Hiram Walker's recently appointed President and Chief Executive Officer, H. Clifford Hatch Jr., was pleased with the company's performance and impatient to build on its prosperity: "We have done a great job with profitability ... but we want to grow, and we have yet to show results in this area ... we have to work this out, how are we going to grow?"

THE WORLD DISTILLED SPIRITS BUSINESS

Achieving growth would not be easy. World consumption of distilled spirits had peaked in recent years, and was now in slow decline. Shifting consumer tastes and aggressive competitive activity were threatening traditional product and brand positions. Market share had become a major source of growth and power, triggering a consolidation of producer and distributor structures. Observers expected these trends to continue, and to create unprecedented opportunities and risks for industry participants.

Demand

From a global perspective, the demand for spirit products and brands was highly fragmented. Product preferences varied widely by country market in relation to local traditions, tastes and pricing. And within markets these same factors often led to a broad distribution of brand preferences across local brands and global brands, which may or may not be locally produced (e.g., Smirnoff vodka, Baccardi rum), and global brands with unique national sources (e.g., Scotch whisky, cognac). Statistics for selected spirits product categories and country markets are presented in Exhibit 1.

In most country markets, domestic demand was served largely by local production. The reasons for this, which varied in importance by market, included unique national tastes, production and distribution economics, and government protection. The residual import volumes, which amounted to about 15% of world demand, were still significant, however, and crucial to the exporters of unique source products.

The United States was widely regarded as the most attractive of the world's spirits markets. The U.S. market accounted for about 22% of total world spirits demand and about 46% of world imports, and it was relatively open to competitive innovation. Thereafter the opportunities represented by specific markets dropped rapidly in magnitude, and became dependent on a wide variety of specific local conditions.

Competition

In spite of on-going consolidation, competitive concentration in the spirits industry was still quite low. In the U.S., for example, 30 brands sold over 1 000 000 cases per year, and the top 60 brands, sold by 24 different firms, held only 60% of the market. There were very large firms in the industry, of course. Table 1 lists the sales, profits and growth rates of the top 18 companies. In spite of their scale, however, these firms probably accounted for less than 40% of world spirit sales. The balance of business was done by virtually dozens of smaller competitors.

The emergence of intense competition had been an unsettling development for many participants in the spirits business. They were used to dealing in what was historically known as a gentlemans' trade. Now they were engaged in an all-out battle, in which the major weapons were aggressive new product and brand marketing, forward integration to control distribution, and acquisitions to balance and expand product portfolios.

Marketing

The great strength of the multinational firms was in their ability to build and support global brands. Their established premium brands provided very attractive returns and were protected from attack to some degree by traditional tastes and habits, and, in most countries, government regulations that limited advertising, sampling, price promotion and so on. Even when a traditional brand was affected by new developments, its decline was more a matter of erosion than critical failure. There was another side to this, of course. It was very dif-

TABLE 1 Top 18 International Spirits Firms[1], 1985 (US$000 000)

	Sales	Operating Income	Sales Growth (%)	
Distillers Co. (U.K.)	$1 600	$293	5.2	(81–85)
Seagram (Canada, U.S.)	2 821	246	0.4	(81–85)
Hiram Walker (Canada)	1 102	213	0.9	(81–85)
Grand Metropolitan (U.K.)	1 319	181	18.7	(80–84)
Brown-Forman (U.S.)	905	167	4.1	(81–85)
Heublein (U.S.)	N/A	152	N/A	
Bacardi (Bahamas)	950	150	8.0	(80–84)
Moet-Hennessy (France)	597	120	25.2	(80–84)
Allied-Lyons (U.K.)	1 334[2]	85	7.1	(81–85)
Pernod-Ricard (France)	581	78	–2.1	(80–84)
Schenley (U.S.)	416	48	–11.7	(80–84)
Arthur Bell (U.K.)	305	48	5.0	(80–84)
Martell (France)	236	38	18.0	(80–84)
Whitbread (U.K.)	672	34	N/A	
National (U.S.)	648	28	–2.8	(81–83)
Wm. Grant (U.K.)	101	19	7.9	(81–83)
Remy Martin (France)	110	16	11.4	(80–84)
Suntory (Japan)	2 191	N/A	–7.4	(83–85)

[1] Estimates for spirits and wine divisions where possible.
[2] Includes wines, spirits and soft drinks.
SOURCE: Hiram Walker records.

ficult to grow in these mature, competitive markets. New product launches were expensive, time-consuming and risky. Similarly, campaigns to capture market share by the further penetration of current markets or geographic expansion required long-term thinking and a willingness to make risky investments.

Competitive innovation in the industry was focused on three fronts. The first was the introduction, often by local producers or distributors, of low-priced brands into traditional categories. The second was the search and exploitation of niches as demand in the mature categories fragmented—such as in the promotion of single-malt Scotch whiskies. The third was in the pursuit of "new" categories, like those in the liqueurs business in the U.S., where there was a constant parade of new formulas and flavours—from peach, to kiwi, to root beer. Collectively these efforts created considerable turmoil in the industry, and chipped away at the traditional brand leaders.

Forward Integration

There were two basic channels of distribution for distilled spirits. In the monopoly markets, which included 18 American states, Canada and the northern European countries, spirits products were sold by a producer or import agency directly to government distribution organizations. In the open markets, which accounted for the majority of industry revenue, two- and three-tier channel structures were common—involving producer sales companies and/or import agencies, distributors, and retailers.

In the open markets the proportion of sales through retail chain organizations was increasing. This had stimulated the development of fewer and larger distributors. Producers were facing increasing demands for marketing support, price concessions and private brands, and were finding it more difficult to keep channel attention on marginal brands.

One of the producer responses to increasing channel power was forward integration through the purchase of channel units. There was by no means a consensus in the industry that this was a wise move. It was expensive, took distillers beyond their traditional expertise, and could result in channel conflict. Nevertheless, many of the major firms were moving in this direction.

Horizontal Diversificaiton

A number of major firms were pursuing acquisitions to diversify and to achieve greater market power. These included steps to diversify (1) outside the alcoholic beverage industry, such as with Seagram's purchase of a major position in DuPont; (2) across the major product classes within the alcoholic beverage industry, such as with Guinness' (a brewer) acquisition of Bell's (whisky) and takeover bid for Distillers (mainly spirits); and (3) across product categories within distilled spirits, such as with Hiram Walker's acquisition of Tia Maria. There was agreement throughout the industry that acquisition activity would accelerate in the coming years.

HIRAM WALKER BACKGROUND

In 1856, Hiram Walker crossed the Detroit river from Michigan, and built a distillery in the raw timberland on the Canadian side. The company grew, and a small community called Walkerville developed around the distillery. In the 1870s, Walker was the first to brand a Canadian whisky, calling his premium product Canadian Club.

Hiram Walker died in 1899, and his family managed the firm for the next quarter century. In 1926, Harry C. Hatch organized the purchase of Hiram Walker from the family, and merged its operations with those of the Toronto-based Gooderham & Worts distillery. The new company was in an ideal position to benefit from the prohibition laws in force at the time in the U.S. Spirits could not legally be produced or sold in America, but if products made and sold in Canada found their way south, well, so be it.

By the end of prohibition in 1934, Canadian whisky in the U.S. market had become a preferred drink beyond all previous measure. Canadian distillers such as Hiram Walker and Seagram moved quickly to consolidate their gains, and to establish new and now legal distribution and sales organizations.

Over time Hiram Walker added to its key brand portfolio, and broadened its geographic sales coverage. The major brand acquisitions were Ballantine's (1935), Tia Maria (49% in 1954, increased to 100% in 1984), Courvoisier (1964), and Kahlua (1964). Under Harry Hatch's son, H. Clifford Hatch, who became president in 1964, Hiram Walker developed the potential of these brands, grew profitably, and became a truly multinational operation.

Hiram Walker Resources

In response to the threat of a takeover, Hiram Walker was merged in 1980 with Consumers Gas and its subsidiary Home Oil to form what was ultimately known as Hiram Walker Resources (HWR). The new company encountered some early and serious difficulties with a major resource investment, but by 1985 it had recovered and was regarded as a healthy management company with holdings, as outlined in Table 2.

TABLE 2 Hiram Walker Resources Holdings, 1985
($000 000)

	Identifiable Assets	Revenue	Operating Earnings
Distilled spirits	$ 1 511	$ 1 516	$ 282
Natural resources	2 052	482	167
Gas utility	1 634	1 767	216
Other investment	551		
Total	$ 5 748	$ 3 765	$ 665

SOURCE: Hiram Walker Resources Ltd. annual report, 1985.

Hiram Walker's Role in HWR

Hiram Walker was a significant contributor to HWR earnings. Hiram Walker's revenue and profit trends were essentially flat, however, as shown in Table 3. Up to very recently the company had not been encouraged to grow by acquisi-

TABLE 3 Hiram Walker Five-Year Performance Summary
(Cdn. $ 000 000)

Fiscal Year Ending August 31	1985	1984	1983	1982	1981
Sales:					
Cases (000)	20 780	20 616	20 575	21 899	22 975
Revenue	$ 1 504.8	$ 1 437.4	$ 1 394.5	$ 1 435.8	$ 1 435.9
Gross Margin	695.6	659.2	623.6	623.7	624.1
%	46.2	45.9	44.7	43.4	43.5
Operating income	291.2	294.5	290.3	320.8	294.0
Net (after tax)					
operating income	176.4	169.1	175.1	189.6	N/A
Invested capital*	1 171.5	1 089.1	1 059.4	1 199.2	N/A
Return on average					
invested capital (%)	15.6	15.7	15.5	15.6	N/A

* Invested capital was comprised of current, net fixed and other assets less non-bank current obligations and deferred income taxes. This is a different concept than "identifiable assets" as used in Table 2. Other smaller accounting differences explain the discrepancies in revenues and income numbers between Tables 2 and 3.

SOURCE: Company records.

tion. A new and provisional role statement had opened the acquisition avenue, although Cliff Hatch Jr. noted that there was no particular pressure from HWR's board to pursue it because "they are more interested in the energy business." HWR's position was that:

> Hiram Walker is responsible for all HWR's distilled spirits and wine business. Requiring only small capital expenditures, Hiram Walker provides HWR with high levels of cash flow that can be used for additional investment. Hiram Walker is expected to maintain its relative industry strength with high steady return on invested capital of 16–18% from its current brands and assets. In addition, Hiram Walker is expected to capitalize on industry rationalization and propose profitable beverage alcohol acquisitions of at least $250 million within the next five years.

HIRAM WALKER'S STRATEGIC POSITION

In 1985, Hiram Walker operations encompassed production plants, marketing units and investments throughout the world. The company's key brands accounted for over 60% of Hiram Walker's revenues, and over 70% of profit contribution after direct selling expenses. Geographically, the U.S. accounted for about 60% of corporate revenues. The strategic positions of the key brands are outlined below. A summary of sales trends is presented in Exhibit 2.

Canadian Club

Canadian Club was Hiram Walker's historic flagship brand. It was produced and bottled in Canada for domestic and international sale. The brand's primary market was in the U.S. There, for years, Canadian Club and its arch rival, Seagram's V.O., had dominated the Canadian whisky business. Of late, however, both brands had been losing ground to lower priced entries, such as Canadian Mist and Windsor Supreme, that were imported in bulk from Canada. The loss of nearly a million cases of volume each over the past five years had left Hiram Walker and Seagram with significant problems of balancing current production levels and maturing stock inventories. Seagram had to some extent buffered its V.O. sales decline by the successful promotion of its super premium Crown Royal brand. Until 1985, however, there was no Hiram Walker entry in this category.

The strength of Canadian Club was with older, traditional whisky drinkers who, unfortunately, represented a declining market base. To revitalize the brand, Hiram Walker was shifting its marketing focus toward younger, upscale adults. The total advertising approach was being changed, and spending levels were being increased somewhat. Furthermore, a super premium brand, Canadian Club Classic, was being introduced to support and extend the brand range.

Ballantine's

Ballantine's was the world's fourth largest selling brand of Scotch whisky, after Johnny Walker, J&B, and Bell's. Ballantine's was strong in continental Europe and selected markets throughout the world. It was weak, however, in the U.K. and U.S., which together represented about 50% of the world's Scotch whisky consumption.

Hiram Walker expected Ballantine's to show volume increases of a little less than 2% per year through 1990. To this point Hiram Walker had not attacked the U.K. because of a very competitive and relatively low- profit market environment there. Further, in the U.S., Hiram Walker was unhappy with its current distribution arrangements. These were in the hands of an independent distributor who had been under contract since 1938. The company had yet to find a satisfactory resolution for this situation.

Courvoisier

Courvoisier's share of the cognac market had varied over time from a low of 12% in 1965 to a high of 21% in 1975, at which point it was the leading brand in the industry. Courvoisier's position had fallen more recently to 15.3%, placing it third behind Hennessy and Martell. Geographically, Courvoisier was strong in the U.K. and U.S., but relatively weak in continental Europe and the Far East.

The drop in Courvoisier's share was attributed to product development and marketing spending problems. Courvoisier had been late with new super premium qualities and package formats. This problem was now being addressed. There was a continuing issue, however, with respect to the unprecedentedly high marketing spending of Hennessy and Martell, which Courvoisier, to this point, had been reluctant to match. Striking a trade-off between profit and market share was a key strategic issue for the brand.

Kahlua

Kahlua was Hiram Walker's most profitable brand. It was a premium priced coffee liqueur produced in Mexico and sold primarily in the U.S. and Canada.

Hiram Walker's Los Angeles-based Maidstone Wine & Spirits organization had capitalized on Kahlua's versatility to build a strong position in the liqueur market. Kahlua was marketed variously as a traditional liqueur, as a spirit to be used in a mixed drink (e.g., with milk in the "Brown Cow" or vodka in the "Black Russian"), or as a flavouring in a host of cooking applications. Kahlua's position was now being challenged directly by low-price imitators, and indirectly by the emergence of rapidly changing taste fads for liqueurs and liqueur-based drinks.

In Hiram Walker's view, the major growth opportunities for Kahlua were outside the U.S. and Canada. Here there were two as yet unresolved positioning issues: whether Kahlua would be sold as a traditional liqueur or as a multiple-use product, and how the potential positioning and distribution overlap with Tia Maria should be handled.

Tia Maria

Tia Maria was a coffee-based liqueur produced in Jamaica. Tia Maria's traditional positioning was as an upscale, imported, classic liqueur product. Its prime market's were the U.S., Canada and the U.K. The brand was faltering in all of these markets, however, as a result, it was thought, of inadequate focus and effort, shifts in liqueur market tastes, and the ambiguity (in the U.S. and Canada) of positioning and emphasis relative to Kahlua.

The strategic issues facing Tia Maria were those of revitalizing the brand in its key markets, and developing distribution in other markets, particularly in western Europe. The latter efforts would be particularly complicated since Tia Maria, by itself, was in a relatively weak bargaining position in seeking distribution. It needed to be allied with other brands, but such natural allies as Ballantine's might not be available if, for example, Ballantine's and Kahlua were combined together in another distribution portfolio.

HIRAM WALKER'S ORGANIZATION

Hiram Walker was run through a functional management structure of production, marketing, financial and administrative units (Exhibit 3). This structure reflected a long standing management philosophy of engaging top management in critical strategic and operating issues. Decisions involving brand strategy, price, image, packaging and labelling, distributor representation, trade practices production levels, quality assurance, and so on, were made at Walkerville.

The top management group at Hiram Walker's consisted of Cliff Hatch Jr., Jim Ferguson, Jim Ford, John Giffen, Steve McCann and Ian Wilson-Smith. Short biographies of each are given in Table 4. Ferguson, Giffen and Wilson-Smith each headed up functional units as outlined in Exhibit 3. At the time of the case there was no corporate level marketing head. This role was being covered by Cliff Hatch Jr. Ford and McCann, both company veterans, were responsible, respectively, for the Courvoisier and Ballantine's supplier companies.

TABLE 4   Hiram Walker Senior Management

H. Clifford Hatch Jr., 44, was a native of Windsor, Ontario, and a graduate of McGill University and the Harvard Business School. He joined Hiram Walker in 1970, and in 1976 was appointed CEO of Corby Distilleries Ltd. (a Canadian firm in which Hiram Walker held a majority interest). In 1979, he became corporate vice-president for marketing of Hiram Walker, and became president and CEO in 1983.

James P. Ferguson, 49, was born in Landis, Saskatchewan, and earned a degree from McGill University. He worked for several years with the accountancy firm of Price Waterhouse, and joined Hiram Walker in 1974. He was currently corporate vice-president for finance and treasurer of the company.

James D.N. Ford, 49, was raised in Glasgow, Scotland, and was a graduate of the University of Glasgow and a chartered accountant. He joined Courvoisier in 1965, and moved to Canada in 1968 as comptroller of Hiram Walker and later vice-president. He returned to Courvoisier in 1980, and presently was head of French operations.

John A. Giffen, 47, came from Ingersoll, Ontario, and held B.Sc. (Engineering) and M.B.A. degrees from the University of Windsor. He became Hiram Walker's corporate vice-president for production in 1980.

W. Steve McCann, 64, was a native of Edinburgh, Scotland, where he received his education and became a chartered accountant. He joined Hiram Walker in the Ballantine's organization, and became managing director of the Scottish operations in 1971.

Ian M. Wilson-Smith, 52, was born in Middlesex, England, and was a graduate of Cambridge University. His early experience was in production with Harveys of Bristol England, and later in production and general management positions with other firms in the beverage alcohol business in England and Canada. He joined Hiram Walker in 1980, and was currently corporate vice-president for administration.

The Marketing Units

Hiram Walker International and the American and Canadian sales companies were the primary marketing units. They were responsible, within their territories and for assigned brands, for proposing marketing strategies and budgets, building distributor relationships and achieving sales targets. Special marketing services for legal, packaging, research and other needs were provided by Walkerville staff groups. Revenues and direct marketing expenses were directly attributable to each of the line marketing units, and further analysis of profitability was possible after allocating product and other costs.

The Supply Units

The supplier units, such as Courvoisier, were responsible for product availability, quality and cost and, depending on the situation, performed local accounting and administrative functions. The supply unit heads in North America, with the exception of wine operations, reported to John Giffen. Those in Europe reported directly to Cliff Hatch Jr., although the European units drew on technical assistance from John Giffen's groups. Wine operations, which were relatively small by Hiram Walker standards, reported to Ian Wilson-Smith, who had a special interest and expertise in this area. The supplier units were essentially cost centres, although profitability could be assessed by the attribution of revenues and marketing costs.

Formal Integration

The annual budgeting process was the primary vehicle for tieing the marketing and supply units together. Budgets were initiated by the marketing units, reviewed and extended by the supplier units, and approved at the corporate level. In practice this was a complicated process. Hiram Walker International, for example, had to deal with forecasts and marketing budgets for a number of brands across a range of countries, distributors and currencies. Further, as the planning process progressed, Hiram Walker International had to strike agreements with the supplier units, whose interests—in brand progress, capacity utilization, operational stability, and so on—were not always consistent with the marketing view. Finally all of this had to be assembled by marketing units across suppliers, and by supplier units across sales entities for corporate review.

Over the years the budget process had become increasingly complicated and time-consuming. This was the result of more complex operations and the tendencies of senior managers to micro-manage the operating units. John Harcarufka, head of W.A. Taylor in the U.S., would note, for example, that he had more autonomy in pricing and promoting Drambuie, an agency brand, than he did for Courvoisier. With the latter, he had to negotiate detailed approvals two ways, as he put it, with both Courvoisier in France and corporate marketing in Walkerville. There was also a strong feeling within the operating units that "Walkerville's" requests for information were too frequent, too detailed, occasionally unrealistic, and often unnecessary.

At the corporate level, the primary formal groups for coordinating the functional units were the management and strategic planning committees. The management committee consisted of Hatch, Giffen, Ferguson and Wilson-Smith; it met formally on a regular basis to consider corporate issues, and to review the proposals and performance of the marketing and supply units.

Informal Integration

A great deal of the burden of coordinating Hiram Walker activities was accomplished informally, by old hands working together. Hiram Walker took pride in the long service of its people, and in their development and advancement. The company promoted from within whenever possible; most of the top and middle management positions were filled by individuals who had worked their way up from entry level positions.

The management committee members worked together very closely. Their working relationships were strengthened by their long experience in the industry, the traditions of the company, and even by the relatively small size and isolation of corporate headquarters. Formal systems and meetings aside, it was perhaps more important for the running of the company that these managers met casually and frequently in the course of the day, in their offices, at lunch in the executive dining room, and in business and social entertaining.

The members of the management committee comprised the first circle of internal influence on corporate affairs. The second level included Jim Ford and Steve McCann who, in spite of distance, maintained a fairly high level of interaction with the Walkerville group through membership on the strategic planning committee, phone, correspondence and travel. The second circle might also have included David Evans, head of Hiram Walker International, except that he had only recently (1981) joined the company from Nestlé, and had not had the same opportunity to work with the Walkerville executives. The third circle of influence consisted of perhaps eight to ten executives, most of whom were marketing unit heads in North America and Europe.

Strategic Planning

Formal strategic planning at Hiram Walker was coordinated by a strategic planning committee consisting of the members of the management committee plus Ford and McCann. This committee met annually for two or three days to consider issues of corporate direction and priority, and to review progress in specific project areas such as acquisitions. On an informal basis, it served as a sounding board for most corporate initiatives.

For years Hiram Walker had based its forward planning on five-year rolling forecasts submitted by the operating units. These were discussed with Walkerville, adjusted where necessary, and used as the based for corporate financial and production forecasts. This forecast system was still in use, although top management was concerned that it placed too much reliance on a projection of the status quo. The February 1985, corporate forecast submitted to HWR projected 1989 revenues from continuing operations of $1 925 million and operating income of $350 million.

To remedy the limitations of existing procedures, the strategic planning committee started in 1982 to introduce a new strategic planning process. The aim was to push strategic thinking as far down the organization as possible—corporate management would be responsible for developing strategic guidelines and conducting reviews, while the unit managers would be responsible for proposing and implementing strategy for their operations. The process was tied to the existing organizational units, but strategy reviews were separated from forecast/budget activities.

The new process was slow to take hold. In spite of adjustments to provide headquarters coordination for new products and "brand champions" to coordinate information on existing brands, the system was not generating clear-cut priorities, commitment and action. Many of the business possibilities that had been identified remained just that. The terminology that came into use was that "more bite" was needed in the planning process, meaning more definitive guidelines and choices, more resources to back approved programs, and more delegation of authority and responsibility to get ideas implemented.

THE BIG ISSUES

As fiscal 1985 closed, very profitably but still without tangible progress on growth, Cliff Hatch Jr. was growing increasingly concerned. He had recently asked Ian Wilson-Smith to survey 35 to 40 unit managers to seek their ideas about what the company could do to become more aggressive in the market. Virtually all of the managers polled had responded in writing, often after consulting their colleagues and subordinates, and cumulatively they had offered literally dozens of suggestions. There was a focus, however, on three broad issues: (1) acquisitions, (2) new product development, and (3) organizational refinement. A summary of the views together with comments by members of the top management group follows.

Acquisitions

It was generally agreed that acquisitions were necessary to improve Hiram Walker's growth and competitive position. The sheer volume of suggestions from the management ranks on potential acquisitions and new ventures outnumbered the rest by a wide margin. The major themes were the need to think big rather than small, the desirability of acquiring a few significant "white goods" brands (vodka, gin, etc.), the need to increase Walker's involvement in the wine industry, and a strong interest in beer (especially high-image imports) soft drinks and mineral waters. The general opinion would have squared with John Giffen's remark that "the pluses and minuses of the existing brand areas add up to really slow growth ... our only avenue for real progress is through acquisition."

The problem in acquisitions, as expressed by several managers, was that Hiram Walker was simply not moving aggressively enough. Jim Ferguson put it bluntly: "Our strategic planning hasn't accomplished very much ... we haven't done anything yet!" While this was not strictly true— since the company had made three small acquisitions, it captured the prevailing view that significant action was needed.

Although the formal position of the strategic planning committee was to focus on acquisitions within the spirits industry, there was informal disagreement about this focus within the group. The arguments were classic. Several managers felt that acquisitions should be limited to the business Hiram Walker knew, and within this were concerned about availability, cost, synergy and returns. Other managers cast a wider net, suggesting the spirits industry was in decline, and that diversification was necessary, at least into allied fields of prestige products such as perfumes and cosmetics.

There was some feeling that the procedures for screening and pursuing acquisitions were delaying the acquisition process. Currently, various members of the strategic planning committee were asked to follow up on possibilities under the general coordination of Cliff Hatch Jr. and Ian Wilson-Smith. A count of the assigned projects indicated that most managers on the committee had upwards of five leads to pursue. The formation of a dedicated headquarters unit to screen and analyze acquisitions had been discussed by the committee, but no action had been taken on this matter.

New Product Development

There was an ongoing controversy in the company over what were perceived to be unnecessary delays in bringing new product initiatives—including types, flavours, packaging, labels, etc.—to market. On the one hand, some managers, primarily from marketing positions, argued that more resources and more discretion were necessary to speed up the pace of development. They saw a newly formed product development committee as a dubious solution, as just another corporate hurdle of which there were already too many. Gerry Gianni, who had joined Hiram Walker in 1981 from a large spirits import house and now ran Hiram Walker Incorporated in the U.S., commented on the four years that it had taken to bring Canadian Club Classic to market: "A disaster ... the project was mandated from the top, but after that nothing seemed to happen ... the very first thing you should not do is appoint a committee, nor set set up a coordinator that will not be around to see the project through ... politics and bureaucracy set in and the coordinator was forced into a referee's position deciding who should win instead of thinking about benefits for the consumer ... we are still trying to come to grips with packaging."

Other executives argued that checks and balances were necessary to avoid expensive product proliferation, to provide for the orderly development of production facilities, and to ensure that new initiatives were consistent with corporate policy. As one production executive pointed out, "Some of the marketing units seem to change their priorities with the weather ... one moment it's miniatures in plastic for the airlines, the next it's 1.75 litre bottles ... they don't seem to appreciate the supply, inventory and equipment complications." Furthermore, at the corporate level, the traditional position was reiterated: "We rely on just a few brands and we operate in markets where brand and corporate reputations are crucial factors ... we can't afford to have someone going off half-cocked and creating a quality or public relations problem."

The Organization

Organizational suggestions were abundant in the manager responses. The recurring themes were the need to decentralize decision-making, adopt a profit centre approach, and set up separate and properly staffed units to handle acquisitions and new products. These comments were echoed by Jim Ford and Ian Wilson-

Smith. Ford noted that "Hiram Walker's highly centralized functional management structure is inappropriate for an increasingly competitive environment ... it creates confusion and conflict between the functions and between field and geographical management...further, under the present structure, I cannot see us developing the well rounded businessmen we will need in the future ... we will always have to go outside in the crunch." Ian Wilson-Smith was of a similar mind: "We have no adequate framework for the integrated management of our key brands on a world-wide basis or, indeed, of our key markets on a geographical basis; we have succeeded in getting the worst of both worlds and the end result is a further reinforcement of the centralized decision-making process ... we need major structural changes to combine production and marketing activities into manageable business units, integrate the responsibility for our key brands on a world-wide basis and redefine the role of corporate headquarters."

Other top managers disagreed. They admitted that the organization was not working as well as it should but argued that the current structure was essentially sound. All that was needed were refinements in staffing, policy and procedures. Jim Ferguson's position was, as he put it: "You have to understand that our big problem is not in operations ... we have strong brands and we are doing well ... it is that we haven't gotten on with acquisitions ... (Insofar as current operations are concerned) ... what we need to do is get a marketing vice-president into place and get Cliff out of that role ... and then use our budgeting and accounting procedures to hold the sales companies more clearly responsible for results ... we haven't pushed hard enough." Steve McCann spoke of international operations, "I was involved (in 1965) in the initial conception of HWI and my position then was that the brand owning companies (e.g., Hiram Walker Scotland) should be complete entities entirely responsible for success and failure ... this view was not accepted and HWI was made responsible to Walkerville. While I continue to prefer my original position in principle, I cannot see how HWI can now be unscrambled (whether by returning its functions to the brandowner—in whole or part—or in in some other way) without great disruption. And the likely benefits are insufficient to compensate for the disruption ... HWI should be allowed to get on with its job without interference from Walkerville, which, in my view, should confine itself to decisions on ... (elements of brand, strategy, operating policy) ... the approval of the annual budget and rigorous ex post facto examination of HWI's performance." Another top manager put the point bluntly in an informal conversation: "There is *no* way that we are going to reorganize this company."

ACTION CONSIDERATIONS

Cliff Hatch Jr. was quite prepared to act, subject to two broad conditions. First, he ruled out major strategic or organizational gambles. As he noted: "I have no mandate to wreck this company." Change could and should proceed, but the steps would have to be carefully developed. He was particularly concerned that the disagreements among managers demonstrated that the obstacles to growth were not well understood. As a result, he had tried to this point to keep the options for change open, and to avoid the endorsement of specific "solutions." One of this reasons for postponing the appointment of a corporate vice-president for marketing, for example, was that this would tend to reinforce past structure and practices.

Second, change would have to respect the corporate values that had helped to build Hiram Walker. "As a company", Hatch said, "we have tried to take the long-term view, to build lasting relationships, and to respect individuals and individual contributions. We have tried to avoid short-term and temporary solutions. I believe these principles will serve us as well in the future as they have in the past."

EXHIBIT 1 Demand for Alcoholic Beverages in Selected Categories and Countries, 1984
(9 litre case equivalents, 000)

	Canadian Whisky	Scotch Whisky	Bourbon	Cognac	Brandy	Gin	Vodka	Rum	Cordials	Other Popular Liqueurs	Spirits	TOTAL Wine	Beer
United States	23 800	19 200	36 700[1]	1 800	5 200	14 300	31 200	12 200	16 300		179 400	232 900	2 385 300
Growth rate (80/84)	-0.5	-5.7	-4.3	10.0	-1.0	-2.0	.0	1.9	4.7		-1.3	4.1	0.7
Canada	6 700	1 200	LV	300	700	1 600	2 500	3 100	2 000		18 800	25 200	212 000
Growth rate (80/84)	-6.2	-3.9		3.5	-1.4	-7.6	-1.0	-2.9	1.7		-3.8	4.0	-1.4
United Kingdom	LV	12 000	LV	1 000	1 000	3 400	3 700	2 100	1 700		25 500	68 700	691 200
Growth rate (79/84)		-3.8		-5.3	3.4	-3.0	1.5	-5.3	3.6		-2.9	4.6	-1.8
West Germany	LV	1 900	500	900	10 600	400	900	5 800	4 000	9 500[4]	44 000	178 000	985 700
Growth rate (79/84)		-3.7	-7.7	-1.8	-0.8	-2.0	1.8	-3.5	-7.5	.0	-3.7	0.7	-0.1
France	LV	5 300	200	800	1 000	300	300	2 100	N/A	12 700[2]	30 000	522 000	250 000
Growth rate (79/84)		6.2	6.8	-8.0	-4.6	14.8	9.9	-7.4		-1.4	-0.6	-1.9	-1.6
Italy	LV	3 100	100	200	6 900	300	200	100	3 400		24 800	525 400	119 700
Growth rate (80/84)		2.4	20.0	-1.7	-3.5	15.0	-8.3	-13.0	-3.0		-3.6	-1.9	2.7
Spain	LV	2 000	LV	LV	11 200	6 700	500	2 400	5 200	1 600[3]	332 800	200 800	251 000
Growth rate (80/84)		1.9			-3.9	1.0	3.4	0.4	-0.3	10.4	-1.2	-2.4	2.9
Japan	LV	2 200	LV	500	2 000	200	N/A	300	LV	31 700[6]	50 800[5]	10 300	516 200
Growth rate (79/84)		-4.1		10.7	10.6	-2.7	3.4	4.8		-0.3	4.0	6.5	0.7
Australia	LV	1 900	LV	LV	800	200	300	800	400		4 900	35 000	204 700
Growth rate (79/84)		3.7			1.5	-2.0	1.3	3.4	-0.5		2.9	5.9	-0.8
World consumption (1982)	65 000			8 900	43 000	59 400	51 800						

[1] Includes straight bourbon and blends
[2] Anis, ougo
[3] Spanish whisky
[4] Korn, aquavit
[5] Totals include sake consumption of 186 million cases
[6] Japanese whisky
LV: Low volumes

EXHIBIT 2 Sales of Selected Hiram Walker Brands in Selected Areas
(9 litre case equivalents, 000)[1]

	Canadian Club	Ballantine's	Kahlua	Courvoisier	Tia Maria
United States, 1984 case sales (000)	2 900	380	1 570	540	130
Market share, point change (84/80)	12.1, −4.9	2.0, 0.3	26.1, −7.4	29.8, −3.3	2.1, −2.7
Canada, 1984 case sales (000)	650	130	210	60	130
Market share, point change (84/80)	9.7, −2.3	10.5, −0.2	18.6, −1.6	21.6, −5.0	11.5, −10.4
United Kingdom, 1983 case sales	LV	90	LV	320	120
Market share, point change (83/79)		1.0, N/A		30.0, 2.2	6.8, −3.2
Selected European,[2] 1983 case sales	LV	1 401	LV	160	LV
Market share, point change (83/79)		13.5, −1.1		8.2, 1.0	
Japan and Hong Kong	LV	130	LV	100	LV
Market share		10.0, N/A			
Company shipments, 1985 fiscal year	3 300	3 500	2 200	1 350	683
% Change (85/84)	−5.6	−10.3	3.0	1.8	N/A

[1] Individual brand/market data based on commercial estimates of wholesalers depletions known to somewhat overstate actual volumes. Market share based on category totals, e.g., Canadian Club share of Canadian Whisky sales.
[2] France, Italy, West Germany. Excludes duty free sales.
LV: low volume

**EXHIBIT 3 Hiram Walker-Gooderham & Worts (A)
Simplified Organization Structure**

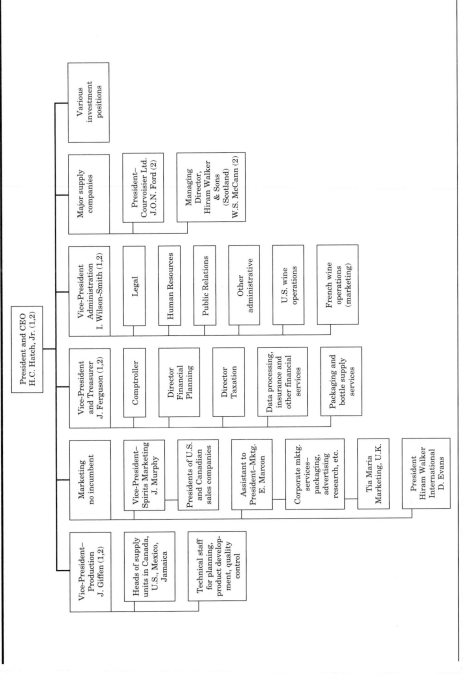

1 Member, Management Committee.
2 Member, Strategic Planning Committee.

SOURCE: Derived from company documents.

JAPANESE-AMERICAN SEATING INC. (A)

J. Michael Geringer and Joyce Miller

In mid-January 1991, Jim Needham was facing one of the first challenges of his new position as general manager at Japanese-American Seating Inc. (JASI). Located in southwestern Ontario, JASI was a joint venture between a Japanese seat manufacturer and a Michigan-based seat assembler. When Needham arrived at the beginning of the year, the JASI plant had been through 20 months of commercial production under his predecessor, Bill Stanton. After several hours of discussion in a recent meeting about how to strengthen project management, Needham's Japanese managers had finally gotten his agreement to hire a project coordinator who would report to the materials manager and schedule and control engineering projects. But the more he considered the situation, the more uneasy Needham felt about enlarging the role of the materials department. Could he renege on his earlier decision, or should he just let this one go?

THE NORTH AMERICAN AUTOMOTIVE INDUSTRY

The automotive industry accounted for a large part of manufacturing activity in both Canada and the United States, and contributed significantly to the expansion and recession of these economies. In the past decade, the "Big Three" U.S. automakers had experienced an unprecedented decline in market share and profitability, and they continued to battle against foreign car companies (Exhibit 1). A recent study noted that sales of vehicles made by North American manufacturers had dropped dramatically as the popularity of overseas models increased, particularly those from Japan, Taiwan, and South Korea. In the 1984–89 period, annual North American vehicle production was relatively flat at about 13 million units, roughly 30% of global production. Captive imports represented a growing phenomenon, and accounted for nearly 5% of North American motor vehicle sales in 1990. Pure imports accounted for an additional 24% of 1990 sales. Captive imports were vehicles imported by American companies. For instance, Chevrolet marketed the Isuzu I-Mark as the Spectrum,

General Motors' LeMans and Optima were manufactured in Korea by Daewoo, and Chrysler imported several products made in Thailand by Mitsubishi.

Overall, foreign name-plates had captured about a third of the North American automobile market, despite trade barriers designed to keep them at bay. Honda now claimed 10% of the North American passenger vehicle market, and Toyota had a 7.5% share. These companies beat the quotas by agreeing to voluntary restraints, and building plants in North America, sometimes in conjunction with domestic producers. These operations were called "transplants." The total transplant production in Canada for 1991–92 was forecast at 460 000 units or 16% of Canadian capacity, an explosive increase since 1988, when transplants represented only 3% and 9.5% respectively of total Canadian and U.S. production capacity. Under the Auto Pact, vehicles manufactured in Canada and having at least 50% Canadian or U.S. content could be exported duty-free to the U.S. This also applied to vehicles built by transplant operations.

In response to the challenge posed by foreign manufacturers, the Big Three had invested over US$8 billion in the past five years to upgrade capacity, and launch quality programs aimed at matching the Japanese. As well, they were streamlining the manufacturing process by using just-in-time (JIT) principles, and contracting out subassemblies. Outsourcing was part of an industry-wide effort to reduce costs. Where car makers used to retool and redesign components almost annually, they were now pushing the burden of design and engineering down to parts suppliers.

These developments had a dramatic impact on organizations supplying seats to the automotive manufacturers. Until the early 1980s, the seat industry was highly fragmented, and could be described as a series of hand-offs, from engineering through to marketing. Each supplier concentrated on one or two areas, such as headrests or suspension systems. The auto-makers handled most of the "cut-and-sew" activities in-house. By 1991, however, 40% of seat production was being outsourced to suppliers who designed and manufactured complete seating systems. A complete system included the frame, foam pads, cover, seat tracks, lumbar support, recliner, headrest, and trim. At this time, to cut overhead and increase quality control, the auto-makers were reducing the number of suppliers, and the seat industry was becoming more competitive.

JAPANESE-AMERICAN SEATING INC. (JASI)

In 1987, Kasai Kogyo Ltd., a seat manufacturer based in Tokyo, and Banting Seat Corporation, a seat assembler headquartered in a Detroit suburb, formed a 65-35 joint venture to exclusively supply seats on a JIT basis to Orion Manufacturing Corporation. JASI was one of several companies established in southwestern Ontario as dedicated suppliers to Orion. Located 15 km away,

Orion was a recently negotiated Japanese-American joint venture which expected to begin producing four cylinder subcompact cars in early 1989. The Orion plant would have the capacity to produce 200 000 vehicles annually, most of which would be shipped to the U.S. Actual production volumes would depend on the market's acceptance of these vehicles as well as cyclical movements of the industry.

Banting and Kasai were leaders in automotive seating in their respective countries. Banting employed about 5 000 people in their North American operations and another 2 000 abroad. They were an established supplier to the Big Three with over $1 billion in annual revenues. After several years of reorganization, Banting had shed all of their non-automotive businesses, and were focused exclusively on seating (approximately 70% of revenues) and other automotive interior parts. Their objective was to attain a position of leadership in the automobile seating industry. During the late 1980s, they had invested heavily in R&D and manufacturing facilities in the U.S., as well as acquiring several smaller European producers of automotive seating and interior components.

Kasai employed about 4 200 people, and had $1.5 billion in annual sales. Nearly 80% of Kasai's revenues were from the automotive industry, with the remainder coming from office and communications equipment, chemical products, building materials, and miscellaneous machinery. Overall, while heavily involved in their traditional business of automobile parts, Kasai's objective was to achieve greater growth and stability through product diversification and overseas market expansion.

While Banting relied on a myriad of raw materials suppliers to assemble their seating systems, Kasai had a more vertically integrated operation. Kasai owned 12 plants and 26 affiliated companies in Japan, most of them involved in auto-related activities. By applying just-in-time principles to seat production, Kasai had gained a strong reputation within the Japanese auto parts industry. In an effort to follow their customers and to increase penetration of international markets, Kasai had in the 1980s aggressively expanded their sales network throughout the world, including regional sales headquarters in the U.S., Canada, Spain, Brazil, Taiwan, and Thailand. Although they had also pursued international manufacturing through 11 joint ventures worldwide, the JASI venture marked Kasai's entry into North American production. The JASI venture was initiated, in part, to help Kasai maintain its supplier relationship with the Japanese firm which was the majority partner in Orion.

The venture was to be run as a profit centre. Banting held the minority participation, and JASI would supply Orion on an exclusive basis for a five-year period. The contract called for 3–5% annual price cuts. Construction on the 120 000-square foot facility began in mid-1988, and was completed in early 1989. An investment of $20 million was required, and break-even was expected within four years. The plant had the capacity to produce 245 000 seats annually, and would eventually employ 220 people on two shifts.

JASI's Start-up

Under the terms of the joint venture agreement, Banting would design the plant, contribute a general manager, and negotiate the purchase of major raw materials and components. Kasai would contribute their expertise in production and process technology and provide a President to head the venture. Orion placed great value on having an important representative from Japan on-site.

The start-up team was composed of Sumio Imai, President, Bill Stanton, General Manager, Akira Hoshino, Finance, Tadashi Abe, Robotics, Katsuhiko Ito, Engineering, and Yuji Yamanaka, Manufacturing/Quality Director (see Exhibit 2 for organization charts for mid-1989 and January 1991). This was the first time any of the Japanese managers had worked in North America. The Japanese who went abroad were typically on a five-year rotation. Rotating people to gain a cross-section of experience within a company was a widely accepted practice, and was, in fact, the foundation of management training and development in Japan. Lifetime employment was still the common practice in Kasai.

Except for Imai, all the Japanese managers brought their families to Canada. Imai chose to return to Tokyo three to four times a year for three-week periods. Imai commented through an interpreter:

> My children have finished university and are working; it made sense to do it this way. I go back regularly to spend time with my family and to maintain business connections. The biggest challenge of going on rotation is actually returning. I mean this in a couple of ways. First, companies are dynamic, always changing, and it is important to know the organization. This takes time. It is not uncommon for people to spend many evenings after work socializing with colleagues, building up networks. Second, those who relocate their families to another country often find returning quite an adjustment. They get used to the lower cost of living and the bigger houses. Some people have difficulty getting their children back on track for the best universities. There is a sense that they have gained "bad habits" abroad.

JASI adopted the principles of the JIT production system known as *kanban*, which was considered to be Toyota's invention. As one manager remarked, "Toyota has been doing it for 30 years and is seen as the master of the *kanban* system. In Japan, everybody likes and lives under *kanban*." Where the conventional production system was built on an earlier process continuously forwarding products to a later process regardless of its requirements, the *kanban* system was built on reversing this conception. To supply parts used in assembly under this system, the later process traced back to an earlier process, and withdrew materials only when they were needed. In this way, wasteful inventory could be eliminated. Imai was an early champion in applying the *kanban* system to the production of seats at Kasai.

In JASI's case, the *kanban* referred to a triangular vinyl envelope which accompanied parts and products as they moved through the plant. The *kanban* provided information about picking up or receiving an order so that only what was needed would be produced. The *kanban* controlled the flow of goods by serving as a withdrawal order, a work order, and an order for conveyance. Associates picked and replaced parts in small batches according to the *kanban*.

Work cells contained several machines designed for quick, easy changes and short set-up times so that a single operator could do a series of tasks. At any one time, there were no more than 4–8 hours of inventory in the plant, from parts through to the seats waiting on the rack for shipping. Seat storage and shipping were geared to the "live broadcast" of cars coming out of Orion's paint section which fixed the order through final trim and assembly. To meet JIT requirements, units were shipped sequentially based on material and other options according to Orion's production schedule. JASI typically had a 3.5–4 hour window to deliver a particular seat set to Orion. There was a substantial financial penalty for late or incorrect delivery. Incoming seats were transferred directly to the final assembly line in the correct position without having to sort through an entire truckload to locate a specific unit. An industry analyst observed:

> *Kanban* systems require a lot of training: training workers to monitor inventory levels and training suppliers to operate under just-in-time principles. Suppliers have to understand the concept of delivering 50 pieces at 10 a.m.—not before, not after, and not 49. It's about supplying the right quantities of the right product at the right time. It's changing the philosophy away from protecting business behind the delivery door; it's about partnerships.

JASI had approximately 100 suppliers of small stampings, nuts and bolts, cloth, foam, frame, recliners, and other raw materials. At some point, certain activities like manufacturing foam might be brought in-house in a separate facility.

In September 1988, Kazuo Nomura joined the company as materials manager. Following the Japanese model, Nomura had both purchasing and sales responsibilities, and oversaw all aspects of cost, material, and production control. In addition to being a liaison with Orion, handling suppliers, and scheduling incoming materials, he controlled engineering projects. However, expediting materials was taking up an extraordinary amount of his time. Nomura explained:

> North American suppliers don't give us the kind of support we're used to in Japan. I'd end up having regular quarrels with suppliers just trying to explain the *kanban* process. I was getting frustrated. It was taking longer than I expected to get them to buy in, to get them to deliver small quantity shipments on a JIT basis. It was hard to handle everything. Our reputation with Orion was key, and I wanted to be dedicated to building this relationship. In January

1990, I became the sales manager and JASI hired a Canadian, George Kirkpatrick, to take over the materials area. By this time, many of my responsibilities had been parcelled out to other departments. Kirkpatrick would schedule parts in and products out, keep suppliers onstream, ensure manufacturing had the materials to keep the plant going, and interact with Orion regarding product sequencing and shipping.

During the start-up phase, the management team generally worked well together despite some differences in management style. Stanton had designed the plant—knowing nothing about the Japanese management and production principles that would be used to operate it. Over a six-month period beginning in November 1988, three groups of two to three salaried managers and technicians went to Japan to learn about Kasai's production system, and see the same seats they would be making being built at the Tokyo facility. Throughout this time, JASI was producing pilot seats, programming and debugging the numerically controlled metal benders and robot welders, and training people how to properly fit seat covers.

Overall, there were few technical problems or difficulties with the nonunionized workforce. The area had an abundant labour pool, particularly with the recent influx of East European and Southeast Asian immigrants. Stanton's policy was to recruit young people without industry experience, and have them work in teams and cross-train. With a monthly absenteeism rate of 3%, where the industry average was 5%, JASI was considered a highly successful venture, especially on the interpersonal side.

JASI began commercial production in April 1989, coinciding with Orion's start-up. Over the next 20 months, the company made steady progress in training their workforce and suppliers, containing costs, and meeting the price cuts scheduled into their contract with Orion. From the start, JASI had adopted the Japanese concept of *kaizen*. Literally translated, this meant continuous improvement. This philosophy encouraged associates to submit ideas for new methods, rationalized setups, more efficient ways of operating machinery, and so on.

The Japanese managers considered that JASI operated relatively autonomously from both parent companies, particularly Kasai. Their communications with Kasai were principally about issues of product quality; major problems with customers, especially regarding product quality issues; engineering changes, and the development and testing of prototypes; and proposed investments. For example, in response to model changes at Orion, they would send samples of parts prototypes for testing in Kasai's labs, since JASI lacked the required capabilities. Interactions with Banting often involved operational details such as purchasing materials, changing suppliers, and introducing new products. They also communicated with Banting regarding cultural issues which the Japanese managers were unfamiliar with, such as donations to a local charity, or staging a company party for employees and their families.

On a monthly basis, both parent companies received a statement outlining the venture's general financial status. While Kasai had never requested additional detailed financial data, Banting had occasionally asked for figures on overtime, production costs and output, particularly during the venture's start-up. JASI's managers were strictly required to consult with both parents, including detailed documentation, whenever funding was required for new investments. One Japanese manager noted that requests for investment funds had never been rejected, and parent inquiries associated with these requests had diminished substantially as the venture became more established. However, he noted that where Kasai would allow the venture to have a negative cash flow for five years, Banting had a significantly shorter horizon and seemed to require stricter budgetary control.

As a sole supplier of a major component, quality or delivery problems on JASI's part could shut down Orion's plant. Of all of Orion's suppliers, JASI believed it faced the greatest potential for problems; the fabric, foam, and weave of the knit all affected the final product. Most returns were because of variances within tolerances. Nomura was the key liaison between the two companies, and he met daily with Imai to report current issues. He travelled frequently to the Orion site, and was in daily contact with the purchasing, engineering, and quality departments to feed information back into the JASI plant. Nomura explained:

> For minor problems, Orion's quality department talks directly with our quality area. When the problems are deeper, I get involved. I'll set up a meeting with people from both sides to analyze the current system and get at the root cause, then I report back to Orion about how we're implementing improvements. Everyone has their mind on corrective action and there's a lot of informal communication. We're still small enough to respond fast. When significant new investment is required, I'll get the president and general manager involved, but otherwise, it's up to me.

Showing a high degree of responsiveness and taking quick action to correct returns had enabled JASI to build an excellent reputation to the extent that the company had recently been taken off Orion's regular quality audit list, which meant that performance reviews would only be conducted every six months. By this time, a strongly knit culture had developed, in both management and on the plant floor.

When Orion geared up production in September 1990, JASI brought on a second shift which added 100 people to the payroll. Work groups had to be split up to train the new associates. Defects increased and productivity deteriorated significantly during this period. At this time, the Canadian Auto Workers (CAW) made a successful bid to unionize the workforce. In October, the CAW was certified as the official bargaining unit and began negotiations with JASI management.

JIM NEEDHAM'S ARRIVAL

In fall 1990, Banting finalized a deal to acquire a German seat assembler, giving the firm entry into the country which represented about one-third of the automotive manufacturing market in Europe. European seat makers had traditionally sold foam and metal components, but there was increasing pressure from the car makers to deliver complete seating systems on a JIT basis. Stanton was asked to take over the management of the plant in Germany, and Jim Needham was offered the general manager position at JASI, a promotion from his current position managing a seat assembly plant in Michigan. Needham, age 41, expected to spend at least three years at JASI. He reflected:

> Bill took the job in Germany because he felt he couldn't do much more here; he was ready to take on a new challenge. I accepted the job in mid-November and started commuting back and forth several times a week. A lot of my time was taken up with paperwork and immigration matters. I had to buy a house, move my family here at the beginning of the year, and get my two kids settled into new schools. My wife and 12-year-old son seemed to make the transition okay. But my 16-year-old daughter wasn't exactly thrilled about moving to a small rural town in another country. At first, it seemed like there was just one brick on my back after another.

Needham had worked for Banting for the past six years, coming up through the ranks from manufacturing manager. He continued:

> I'm an old factory nut, and I was really impressed with the JASI plant—how well it was laid out, the robotics and metal bending capabilities, the high tech product testing. JASI was making all their own frames whereas the plants I'd worked in before were building seats with purchased parts. I'd been through some consensus training but I had limited experience working with the Japanese. In Michigan, we were doing JIT, we had cards on the seats and were scheduling the replacement of batches. We thought we were doing a lot, but I've never seen *kanban* worked as thoroughly through the production process as here. It's hard to learn how to make *kanban* work, and making it work right is a real trick.
>
> Right now, I'm concerned about the union negotiations. I'd worked with the United Auto Workers in the past but the CAW has the reputation of being a more militant organization. I hope that we won't get into the typical adversarial relationship. JASI's wage structure is good and the benefits package is solid. We have a progressive-thinking union rep who seems open to a different approach. I'm not anticipating a lot of restrictions; the union knows our relationship with Orion, that the company will be growing.
>
> I think Bill took the decision to unionize quite personally. Bill put everything he had into this plant, and he had a strong feeling of personal ownership here. He was into all the details. Once he was convinced of something, he went all out to make it happen. He has quite a forceful personality with a decisive, direct style, even authoritarian at times.

Needham did not have a lot of preparation before taking on his new position. He remarked:

I only had three to four days with Bill, and I spent that time trying to get down the mechanics of the organization. I knew that I was coming into a tightly knit group. And I was coming into a situation where I couldn't even speak directly with my own boss and some of my key managers. Nomura and Hoshino had a working knowledge of English, but I'm not sure how much the other Japanese comprehend. They spend a lot of time together interpreting for each other. I suspect that Imai understands more than what he can express in English. Whenever Imai has a meeting with an Anglo, he'll always have someone else there, usually Nomura, to interpret. Still, I have to be careful. What gets said may be just the best way someone knew how to say it and not necessarily their intent.

It's hard to figure out the dynamics of the management group. Imai is gregarious and outgoing while Yamanaka gravitates towards the role of the "keeper"; he keeps situations in control, he's more grounded. Nomura seems to be the linking pin in the whole operation. Bill tried not to tell me too much; he didn't want to predispose me to certain individuals. One thing Bill emphasized was the need to maintain operational control, especially in order to achieve better cost/benefit ratios. He gave the example that the Japanese continually look for improvements and might request that eight people be assigned to the task of rearranging a work cell. They'll justify it as being for the good of the company, but the benefit might not come until four or five years later. Bill noted that this could generate problems at Banting, since Begar and the other executives at headquarters would expect him to regularly report key production data as Stanton had done, and they would not be pleased if the figures varied substantially from budget.

I'm mostly learning as I go along. I realize that I can't do things the same way as I did before. I didn't think people could tolerate an American coming in swinging. The last thing I want anyone to think is that I'm a dictator; I've worked for those types before, and it never works. I want to take the long view; changes will come over time. At the beginning, the important thing is to not make too many quick judgments or life-threatening decisions, to just get involved where you really need to.

I'm starting to have some interaction with Hoshino on the budget, and it's possible that he could be a window into the Japanese group, someone who I can put the sticky questions to and find out about personalities and political ramifications in Japan. At the moment, I'm very much the new guy. I have a sense that people might be looking for changes in the way things get done. I bring a new set of ears, and ideas that didn't get through before will be resubmitted. People are redefining relationships, and this isn't necessarily a bad thing. There are good reasons for making changes at this level—there's the saying that you can't change the players but you can sometimes change the coach. Maybe I'll have a chance to make the improvements my predecessor couldn't crack.

Shortly after Needham's arrival, the media reported that early January 1991 sales of North American vehicles had plunged as worries about the faltering economy and the Persian Gulf crisis continued to erode consumer confidence.

MANAGING IN A CROSS-CULTURAL ENVIRONMENT

Needham knew that his job at JASI would be more difficult, at least initially, than those he had gone into previously. He recounted:

> I'm used to reading a situation quicker. I come from a system where a good boss listens to his managers, then makes a decision; his people understand it and follow it. The Japanese look for consensus, and this is hard to get to. Management meetings are long. Recently, we spent an hour only to find that we had two versions of the same vacation policy, one for the Japanese and one for the North Americans. We spent another two hours trying to hammer out a single policy. There's always a risk that everyone will nod their heads, and then the Japanese will go off and run the business their way and the North Americans will go off and do things differently. People forget that they're supposed to be learning from each other; there's always some tension and sometimes it's hard to get over the humps. The North Americans aren't familiar with the *kanban* system and sometimes they don't go far enough; they had something that worked before. Put that against the Japanese guys who know and believe in their system.
>
> I see my role as bringing up issues for discussion. If I walked in with the solution to a problem, there would be immediate resistance. We need the extra step here, and I'm patient enough to go through it.

Through a series of conversations, Needham discovered that the Japanese were used to relying heavily on their technicians. In Japan, once these people were told the rules, there was apparently little need to follow up. However, he noticed that JASI's floor technicians were not consistently enforcing such simple things as wearing safety glasses. Shop rules and discipline seemed to be foreign ideas to his Japanese managers. Needham elaborated:

> The Japanese don't seem to recognize that the workforce might slip; they aren't trained to look for such problems. Even if they become aware of something, they appear to overlook it. I don't know if it's just a cultural difference, a case of not feeling comfortable dealing with the situation. For instance, it recently happened that someone was stealing and my Japanese guys didn't seem to realize that a person who behaved this way would have to be fired.

Another difference between the Japanese and North American systems was the role of the materials department. In Japan, this department was a large, central hub which ran new engineering and information programs, and scheduled and controlled all aspects of projects. In North America, these activities were typically handled by engineering or manufacturing. As a whole, JASI's Japanese management group felt strongly that the company needed to get better at project management to achieve continuing quality improvements and cost reductions.

THE JANUARY MEETING

On January 11, 1991, Jim Needham convened a two-hour meeting with virtually the entire management team, including Imai, to discuss the project management situation. Project management was intimately linked with costs. The decisions made in this meeting would affect everyone. The Japanese managers felt strongly that the materials department should enlarge its role and regain its original status. As the venture had moved toward commercial production, many of the responsibilities Nomura originally had as materials manager had been dispersed across departments as he dedicated more of his time to building JASI's relationship with Orion. The Japanese felt that the key to better project management was to centralize this function back in materials. They argued adamantly that a project coordinator needed to be hired in.

Reporting to the materials manager, the project coordinator would launch projects and follow them through to completion. For example, if an engineering study proposed joining three pieces to bolt onto a seat, the project coordinator would find parts suppliers and obtain quotes to facilitate a make or buy decision. This person would also interact with engineering, quality, and manufacturing to ensure each department carried out its responsibilities on the project. The Japanese contended that creating such a position would mean that everyone was informed of the status of ongoing projects. Starting up new projects would be smoother, less costly, and of better quality. Needham responded:

> I kept telling people I wasn't convinced that we needed to add an extra person. This hadn't been slotted in and I didn't want to bastardize the budget within the first month. I thought that the job could be handled by someone else already in the organization. I had recently talked to the quality manager, Paul Wells, and he was willing to schedule and follow up projects. This wouldn't make for as big a role for the materials department as the Japanese wanted— the real responsibility would still be with the pieces—but I didn't feel comfortable giving up some of my own authority when I still didn't completely understand the operation. My Japanese managers persisted. One even remarked that when I went to Japan in April, I'd learn why project management should be done in materials. After several hours of discussion, I finally relented.
>
> I suspected that Imai and the others were pleased with the outcome. They were comfortable that I went after consensus, and I had a feeling they would like JASI to operate even more like a Japanese organization.

A few days after agreeing to hire a project coordinator, Needham was having serious second thoughts. Besides concerns that the company was still too small to warrant this additional person and the accompanying costs, he did not feel that the materials department was ready to take on this level of responsibility, and ultimately, he was not comfortable defining the department as largely as it was in Japanese operations. Delegating this additional authority to lower-level managers before he was comfortable in his new position might also limit his own decision-making authority in the future. But what could he do now?

Needham was to meet with Imai at 8 a.m. tomorrow for their weekly meeting, and the agenda which Imai had sent to him was quite full. In addition to addressing several important strategic and operational issues, such as improving integration of local suppliers within JASI's *kanban* system, production planning and quality control issues, and finalizing a strategy for upcoming negotiations with union representatives, Needham and Imai has been asked by the materials manager to formally approve the proposal to hire a project coordinator, including funding to retain a personnel recruiting firm and placement of position advertisements. In fact, this latter issue was the first item on their agenda, along with review of the quality control report for the prior two weeks, which showed a continuing decline in production defects. Could he change his mind? And how would he even go about doing it?

EXHIBIT 1 The Big Three Auto-makers and the North American
Automotive Industry

	1973	*1978*	*1987*	*1988*	*1989*
General Motors Corporation					
Quality (defects per 100 cars)	–	–	176	165	158
Productivity (cars per person per year)	11.4	12.1	11.3	12.9	12.6
Inventory turns	5.4	6.7	18.0	18.8	20.0
Profit per unit ($)	490	684	435	692	645
Return on sales (%)	6.7	5.5	3.5	4.4	3.8
Market share (%)	51.5	47.3	34.7	34.9	35.0
Ford Motor Company					
Quality (defects per 100 cars)	–	–	156	169	143
Productivity (cars per person per year)	13.7	13.8	18.7	19.9	20.9
Inventory turns	5.3	6.5	15.6	17.3	18.0
Profit per unit ($)	260	360	1 023	1 014	663
Return on sales (%)	3.9	3.7	6.4	5.7	3.9
Market share (%)	29.8	26.5	23.1	23.7	24.6
Chrysler Corporation					
Quality (defects per 100 cars)	–	–	178	202	169
Productivity (cars per person per year)	13.0	13.1	16.2	18.0	19.5
Inventory turns	5.6	6.3	16.8	21.6	26.3
Profit per unit ($)	127	(129)	853	649	649
Return on sales (%)	2.1	(1.5)	4.5	3.0	1.0
Market share (%)	15.6	11.2	12.3	13.9	13.7

SOURCE: Annual reports and industry sources.

EXHIBIT 2   JASI Organization Chart

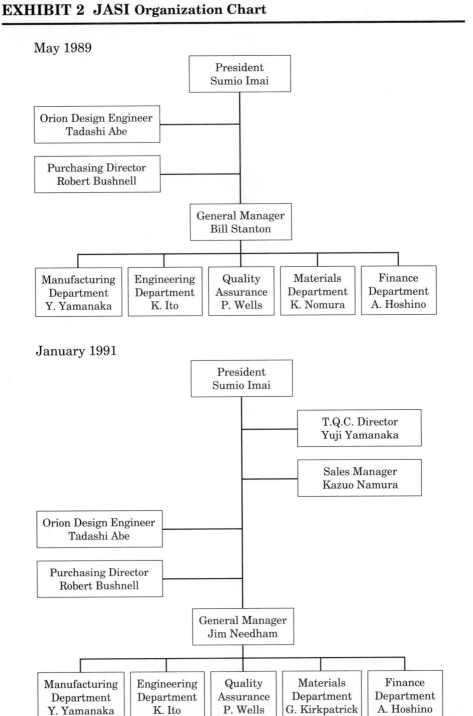

May 1989

January 1991

PART

8 COMPREHENSIVE SERIES

NESTLÉ–ROWNTREE (A)

James C. Ellert, J. Peter Killing and
Dana G. Hyde

Wednesday, April 13, 1988, 10.30a.m.

"Our offer to help remains open, Mr. Dixon, and I urge you to reconsider our proposals. Please keep in touch." Mr. Helmut Maucher, Managing Director of Nestlé S.A., replaced the receiver and shook his head regretfully as he looked out from his office over Lake Geneva. On receiving the news of Jacobs Suchard's dawn raid on Rowntree plc, Mr. Maucher had called Mr. Kenneth Dixon, Rowntree's Chairman, to offer Nestlé's help and renew Nestlé's earlier proposal to purchase a stake in Rowntree.

Rowntree had been an attractive takeover target for some time, and Mr. Maucher and his colleagues had often discussed the possibility of making a bid. However, it was clear that Rowntree would aggressively contest any takeover attempt and, as Nestlé had never engaged in a hostile takeover, Mr. Maucher had done nothing more than initiate talks with the British-based confectioner. But as he prepared for the meeting with his Comité du Conseil that afternoon, Mr. Maucher worried about Rowntree falling into the hands of one of Nestlé's major competitors.

THE CHOCOLATE INDUSTRY

"Confectionery" was conventionally divided into "chocolate" confectionery and "sugar" confectionery. "Chocolate" confectionery included products made with chocolate; "sugar" confectionery included boiled sweets, toffees, chewing gum, and other gums and jellies. Chocolate consumption represented a stable 54% of the total volume of confectionery consumption in the major world markets between 1982 and 1987.

Markets

In value terms, more chocolate was consumed than any other manufactured food product in the world. In 1987 the population of the world's eight major markets consumed more than 2.7 million tonnes of chocolate (the equivalent of over 100 billion Kit Kats), with a retail value of over $19.5 billion (Exhibit 1). In volume terms, chocolate consumption in the eight major markets represented 61% of total world chocolate consumption in 1987. Average per capita consumption in these markets was 4.3 kg per annum, with an annual per capital expenditure of $31. Between 1982 and 1987, volume growth averaged 2.8% per annum in the eight major markets. Future growth was estimated at 2.2% per annum for the next five years, with some variations across individual markets (Exhibit 2).

Product Types

Within chocolate confectionery there were three major product types:[1]

Blocks: generally molded blocks of chocolate, with or without additional ingredients (Hershey's Chocolate Bar, Nestlé Cailler, Suchard's Toblerone);

Countlines: generally chocolate-covered products, sold by count rather than weight (Mars' Mars Bar and Snickers, Rowntree's Kit Kat and Smarties);

Boxed chocolates: included assortments (Cadbury's Milk Tray, Rowntree's Black Magic) and also products such as Rowntree's After Eights.

A few manufacturers had succeeded in branding *block chocolate*, but in many markets block chocolate was considered a commodity product. Each manufacturer's range included a standard variety of block chocolate (milk, dark, white, etc.), and additional ingredients (nuts, fruit, etc.) sold in standard sizes (usually 100g and 200g). Block chocolate was sold mainly through grocery outlets, where it was displayed by manufacturer's range; all of the Nestlé block chocolate products would be grouped on one section of the store shelf, with the other manufacturers' ranges displayed in adjacent sections.

In constrast to block chocolate, *countlines* comprised a wide range of branded products, which were physically distinct from each other in size, shape, weight, and composition. Countlines had wider distribution than the other two product types, with a higher proportion sold through non-grocery outlets including confectioneries, news agents, and kiosks.

Boxed chocolates comprised a wide range of individually branded products, although in some markets boxed chocolates were marketed under the manufacturer's name, and displayed by manufacturer's range. Because boxed chocolates were regarded as a "gift/occasion" purchase, sales were very sea-

---

[1] Product definitions varied widely by country. For the purposes of this case, British product definitions have been used.

sonal. Approximately 80% of sales took place at Christmas and Easter, a high proportion through grocery outlets; steady sales through the remainder of the year were made through non-grocery outlets.

The popularity of the three product types varied by market. In 1987, for example, Europe consumed approximately twice as much block chocolate and four times as many boxed chocolates as North America. The British and French together accounted for about 70% of European boxed chocolate consumption; North Americans consumed 44% of the world's countline consumption, followed by the British at 20%.

At 7% average annual growth between 1982 and 1987, countlines was the fastest growing segment of the world chocolate market. Block chocolate sales showed an average annual volume increase of 1% over the same period, while sales of boxed chocolates had declined by an average of 1% per year. By 1987 countlines represented 46% of the world chocolate market by volume, up from 38% in 1982; block chocolate had declined to 30% from 33%, and boxed chocolates to 24% from 29%. In addition to growing demand for countline products, future growth was expected from "indulgence" products such as chocolate truffles, and from specialist branded chocolate retailing.

Industry Structure and Performance

In 1987, there were six major producers in the world chocolate industry: Mars, Hershey, Cadbury-Schweppes, Jacobs Suchard, Rowntree, and Nestlé. With individual world market shares ranging from 18% (Mars) to 4% (Nestlé), these six companies accounted for 50% of the total world volume of chocolate confectionery. With the exception of Jacobs Suchard and Nestlé, countline production represented the largest proportion of the chocolate confectionery portfolios of the major confectionery producers (Exhibit 3; additional detail on the product segment and geographic positioning of each company is outlined in Exhibits 4, 5 and 6).

The next tier of competitors included Ferrero, George Weston Ltd., Nabisco, and United Biscuits, each of which sold 2% or less of the total world volume of chocolate confectionery. The remainder of the market was supplied by a large number of smaller (largely national) companies.

The major industry competitors had healthy rates of profitability. Because Mars was a privately held U.S. company, it did not publish sales and profit figures. For the other major competitors, trading profit on sales averaged 9.3% over the five-year period ending in 1987; trading profit on assets averaged 16.1%, and the rate of return on stockholders' equity averaged 16.1% (Exhibit 7; Exhibits 8–12 provide additional financial information for these companies).

Over the past five years, several major producers had acquired a number of smaller, national chocolate companies. Between 1986 and 1988 Jacobs Suchard acquired six confectioners, including E.J. Brach (the third largest confectioner in the U.S., behind Mars and Hersey), Van Houten (Holland), and Cote d'Or (a famous Belgian chocolatier which Nestlé had also considered acquiring). In 1987 Hersey purchased the Canadian confectionery assets of RJR Nabisco. In early 1988 Cadbury acquired Chocolats Poulain, a famous French chocolatier, and Nestlé was negotiating the purchase of Buitoni, an Italian food group which included the leading chocolatier Perugina.

Business System

Chocolate was made from kernels of fermented and roasted cocoa beans. The kernels were roasted and ground to form a paste, which was hardened in molds to make bitter (baking) chocolate, pressed to reduce the cocoa butter content, and then pulverized to make cocoa powder, or mixed with sugar and additional cocoa butter to make sweet (eating) chocolate. Sweet chocolate was the basic semi-finished product used in the manufacture of block, countline, and boxed chocolate products.

Average costs for a representative portfolio of all three product types of sweet chocolate could be broken down as follows:

Raw material	35%
Packaging	10
Production	20
Distribution	5
Marketing/sales	20
Trading profit	10
Total	100% (of manufacturer's selling price)

For countline products, raw material costs were proportionately lower because a smaller amount of cocoa was used. For boxed chocolates, packaging costs were proportionately higher.

Research and Development

Research and development (R&D) generally focused on making a better chocolate, and on developing new products, although one executive related, "there is never really anything brand new in the confectionery market, just different ways of presenting combinations of the same ingredients." There were minor differences in R&D across the product types, although R&D in the countline segment tended to emphasize applied technology.

Raw Materials

The major ingredient in chocolate confectionery was cocoa, followed by sugar and milk. Although Jacobs Suchard claimed to benefit from large purchase hedging, some manufacturers purchased cocoa supplies as needed at the spot price quoted on the major cocoa exchanges, while others purchased cocoa a year or two in advance to obtain the "best price" and to ensure long-term supplies. Between 1977 and 1988, the international cartel of cocoa producers had fallen into disarray; the price of cocoa had fallen by 50% ($US terms), and surplus cocoa stocks continued to accumulate.

Industry practice was for manufacturers to absorb raw material price changes internally to smooth extreme changes in consumer prices. However, Mars had made an unprecedented move in taking advantage of the falling cocoa price to stimulate volume demand. The company held the price of its Mars Bar and increased the product weight in the late 1970s by 10%, and then by another 15% in the early 1980s, enabling Mars to gain market share.

Production

In general, it was difficult to sustain a competitive advantage based on manufacturing process, or on product features due to the lack of proprietary technology. However, some manufacturers had developed countline products which were difficult to duplicate (e.g., Rowntree's After Eights and Kit Kat). The major manufacturers tried to be low-cost producers through increased scale economies. Scale economies were more easily achieved in the production of block chocolate and countlines (both relatively capital intensive), and less easily in the production of boxed chocolates (which was more labour intensive). While minimum efficient scale varied by product, most major producers were moving toward fewer and more concentrated production plants, some dedicated to one or two products.

Distribution

Confectionery had the widest distribution of any consumer product. In the U.K., for example, wholesalers serving thousands of small "Confectionery-Tobacco-Newsagent" (CTN) outlets accounted for 50% of total confectionery sales, with multiple grocery stores accounting for 30%, and department stores and multiple confectionery stores the remainder. While distribution patterns and the balance of power between manufacturers and distributors varied across markets, retail concentration was on the increase. Canada and Western Europe (in particular the U.K., France, and West Germany) were noted for high levels of retail concentration. Manufacturers' trading margins in these countries averaged 8–12%, compared to U.S. averages of 14–16%.

In general, European multiple retailers tended to stock narrower ranges of competing products than their U.S. counterparts. As one industry executive commented, "In Europe you pay more of a premium to get shelf space in a store. In addition, many of the (multiple) retailers stock only the leading brand and the Number Two. If you are third, you lose visibility, and this damages brand reputation."

Marketing

Consumers displayed considerable brand loyalty. As one industry executive explained, "Most people have a 'menu' of products they like and know. They will buy a new product perhaps once or twice, but the tendency is to go back to the 'old familiars', the popular established brands." The most popular brands of chocolate were over 50 years old; Mars Bar, for example, was introduced in 1932, and Kit Kat in 1935.

In 1987 the six largest producers spent over $750 million per year on chocolate advertising. In recent years, manufacturers had dramatically increased their overall level of marketing spending, particularly with respect to launching new products. By 1988 one manufacturer estimated that new products, which generally had a much shorter life span than established brands, would have to generate at least $25 million in sales over the first two years to cover product development and marketing costs. Manufacturers therefore tended to focus on brand extensions into new product segments and particularly into new geographic markets.

MAJOR COMPETITORS

Mars

With the world's best selling chocolate bar, and other famous global brands such as Snickers, M&Ms, Twix, and Milky Way, Mars was the world leader in chocolate confectionery. In 1987 confectionery was estimated to account for $4 billion of Mars' $7 billion total turnover of confectionery, pet food, and electronics products.

With 38% market share, Mars dominated the world countline sector, with particular strength in North America and Europe (Exhibit 4). In 1987, Mars held the largest share of the European chocolate market, and was a close third to Cadbury Rowntree in the U.K. (Exhibit 5). Like Rowntree and Cadbury, Mars spent approximately £25 million annually on advertising in the U.K. In 1987 Mars was one of the top 30 U.S. advertisers ($300 million), and had five of the top ten best-selling chocolate bars in the U.S.

The 1986 introduction of Kudos, a chocolate-covered granola bar, was Mars' first new product in over ten years. Since 1986, however, Mars had mounted a major effort to acquire and develop new products, particularly those which would capitalize on the Mars brand name. Recent product launches included a Mars milk drink and Mars ice cream.

Mars' strategy was consistent across all brands: produce high quality, technologically simple products at very high volumes on automated equipment dedicated to the production of either "layered" (Mars, Snickers) or "planned" (M&Ms, Maltesers) products; and support the brands with heavy marketing spending and aggressive sales organizations and retailing policies. The company's future strategy focused on building and strengthening Mars' global brands. In 1987, for example, Mars had dropped Treets, a £15 million U.K. brand, and repositioned Minstrels under the Galaxy label, both in order to strengthen the 1988 launch of M&Ms into the U.K. market.

Hershey Foods

Founded as chocolate company in 1893, by 1987 Hershey was a diversified food group with total turnover of $2.4 billion. More than 90% of that turnover was in the U.S. (Exhibit 6); confectionery accounted for 66% of total turnover and 80% of trading profit. Although Hershey was a quoted company, it could not be taken over easily because 77% of the company's voting stock was owned by a charitable trust.

Hershey's strength was in block chocolate in North America, where it held a 62% market share. With Hershey's Chocolate Bar, Reese's Peanut Butter Cup, and Hershey's Kisses all in the 1987 U.S. "top ten", Hershey was second only to Mars in the U.S. chocolate market. Hershey also produced major Rowntree brands under licence in the U.S.

Between 1981 and 1987, Hershey had increased its advertising and promotion spending from 8.5% to 11.5% of total turnover to "consolidate market share". Hershey's chocolate production was concentrated in Hershey, Pennsylvania, which supplied export markets in Japan, South Korea, and Australia. The company also licenced some production in the Far East, Sweden, and Mexico, normally under joint venture agreements.

Hershey's corporate strategy was to reduce exposure to cocoa price volatility by diversifying within the confectionery and snack businesses. The company had expanded into branded sugar confectionery, pasta products, and ice cream restaurants, largely through acquisitions. By 1987, only 45% of Hershey's sales came from products composed of at least 70% chocolate, down from 80% in 1963.

Cadbury Schweppes

Cadbury Schweppes plc was founded in 1969 with the merger of the Cadbury Group plc and Schweppes Ltd. In 1987, confectionery represented 43% of Cadbury's total turnover of £2,031 million.

With 7% of the world chocolate market and brands such as Dairy Milk, Creme Eggs, Crunchie, Flake, and Milk Tray, Cadbury was a major world name in chocolate. Cadbury was the market leader in Australia, and three Cadbury brands (Mounds, Almond Joy, and Peppermint Patties) were in the U.S. "Top 20." However, Cadbury's main business was in the U.K., where it held 30% of the market, and had five of the top ten best-selling chocolate products. In 1986 and 1987, Cadbury had launched nine new U.K. brands.

During the late 1970s, Cadbury expanded overseas, and diversified within and beyond the food sector. However, with the appointment of Mr. Dominic Cadbury as Chief Executive in 1983, Cadbury Schweppes embarked on a more focused product and market strategy. Mr. Cadbury announced a restructuring of the Group "to concentrate resources behind (our) leading beverage and confectionery brands in those markets which offer the best opportunities for their development."

Major divestments were made, involving secondary activities in the food and nonfood sectors, and the assets of some under-performing core businesses. Acquisitions were made to strengthen the mainstream branded product lines, and to gain access to new geographic markets. The acquisition of Chocolats Poulain, for example, provided Cadbury's first manufacturing facility in Europe. In January 1987, General Cinema Corporation (which controlled the largest U.S. Pepsi bottling operation) announced the acquisition of an 8.5% shareholding in Cadbury Schweppes and, in November 1987, increased that holding to 18.2%. While General Cinema was less than half the size of Cadbury in market capitalization, industry observers speculated that the company was planning a leveraged buyout of Cadbury Schweppes.

Jacobs Suchard

Controlled by the Jacobs family and based in Zurich, the Jacobs Suchard Group was formed in 1982 in a reverse takeover by Jacobs (a West German coffee company) of Interfood, the parent company of the Suchard and Tobler chocolate firms. In 1987, Suchard's principal businesses were still coffee and confectionery, which accounted for 57% and 43% respectively of Suchard's 1987 turnover of SF6.1 billion.

Europe was Suchard's largest market, accounting for 83% of 1987 turnover. However, Jacobs Suchard operated in more than 20 countries, represented by subsidiaries and licensees, and exported its products to over 100 countries. The Group also had substantial operations in the trading of raw materials for coffee and chocolate production.

Jacobs Suchard held 23% of the European block chocolate market. Leading brands included Toblerone, Suchard, Milka, and Cote d'Or. Developing and expanding its portfolio of global brands was of primary importance to the Group; as Mr. Klaus Jacobs, the entrepreneurial Chairman of the Board, stated, "We firmly believe that global brands are the wave of the future." An increasing number of Jacobs Suchard's brands were marketed globally, under the sponsorship of global brand managers.

Since 1984 Suchard had been concentrating production of individual brands in fewer and larger plants in an effort to gain absolute cost leadership. In 1987, European production of chocolate and confectionery took place in 17 plants; Suchard planned to reduce this number to 7 by 1991, as improvements were made in its cross-border distribution system.

Rowntree

Rowntree was founded in York in 1725 by a cocoa and chocolate vendor who sold the business to the Rowntree family in 1862. In 1970, Rowntree merged with John Mackintosh & Sons, Ltd., a British confectioner nearly half the size of Rowntree. In 1988, Rowntree's headquarters were still in York and, with 5 500 workers, the company was by far York's largest employer. Many of the traditions of the Rowntree family, including a strong concern for employee and community welfare, had been preserved; many of the current employees' parents and grandparents had also worked for Rowntree.

In 1987, Rowntree was primarily a confectionery company (Exhibit 13), with major strengths in the countline and boxed chocolate segments. Rowntree's major market was the U.K. where, with a 26% market share, it was second only to Cadbury. Rowntree's Kit Kat was the best-selling confectionery brand in the U.K. (where 40 Kit Kats were consumed per second), and number five in both the U.S. and Japan. Kit Kat was part of a portfolio of leading global brands; many of these brands—Kit Kat, Quality Street, Smarties, Rolo, Aero, Black Magic—were launched in the 1930s; After Eights in 1962; and Yorkie and Lion in 1976. Since 1981 Rowntree had launched seven new brands in the U.K., including Novo, a chocolate cereal bar.

In 1987 Rowntree operated 25 factories in nine countries and employed 33 000 people around the world, including close to 16 000 in its eight U.K. operations. Group turnover was £1.4 billion, with the U.K. and Ireland accounting for 40% of total turnover (Exhibit 14).

Rowntree was headed by Mr. Kenneth Dixon, age 58, who had been with Rowntree for 32 years, and was appointed as Chairman and Chief Executive in 1981. In the words of a long-time senior Rowntree executive, "Mr. Dixon fostered a real sense of positive change in the company."

During the late 1970s, Rowntree's operating performance had shown significant deterioration (Exhibit 15). To reverse this trend, Mr. Dixon initiated a long-term program to improve the efficiency of the U.K. core business, and led diversifications into related businesses, principally through the acquisition and development of brand names. Mr. Dixon also delegated more responsibility to the operating levels of the company, while maintaining a central brand and product strategy.

Branding was the essence of Rowntree's strategy. According to Mr. Dixon, "The fundamental idea which drives Rowntree is branding, the creation of distinct, differentiated, positively identifiable and market-positioned goods. Rowntree seeks to build brands by marketing products and services at competitive prices, positioning them accurately in the markets they serve, and giving them clear identity and character."

In the 1960s, Rowntree granted Hershey a long-term license to manufacture and sell Rowntree products in the U.S. With its expansion into continental Europe underway at the time, Rowntree believed that it lacked the resources to develop an effective marketing presence in both continental Europe and the U.S. In 1978 the agreement with Hershey was renegotiated, giving Hershey rights in perpetuity to the Kit Kat and Rolo brand names in the U.S., which would be retained by Hershey in the event of a change in Rowntree ownership. Rowntree was still free to enter the U.S. market with its other brand names. In 1987 royalties from this agreement contributed about £2 million toward Rowntree Group profits.

Between 1982 and 1987, Rowntree invested nearly £400 million to upgrade manufacturing facilities, and develop high-volume, product-dedicated equipment for several of the company's leading global brands, including Kit Kat, After Eights, and Smarties. Products produced on this equipment had a consistent formulation, and were sold all over the world; the Hamburg After Eights plant, for example, shipped to 16 countries. By 1987 Rowntree's investment program for rationalizing capacity was well underway. The associated productivity gains were expected to continue to accumulate over the next few years.

In 1987 Rowntree's £100 million investment in continental Europe was still showing modest financial returns. Rowntree had entered the continental European market in the 1960s, establishing production facilities at Hamburg, Dijon, Elst (Holland) and Noisiel (France). Although advertising and promotion spending (as a percentage of sales) was double that of the U.K., volume growth had not met Rowntree's expectations; as one manager explained, "Kit Kats go well with a cup of tea, but not with wine and beer!"

The trading margin on the Continental European business had inched up very slowly, from 1.0% in 1985 to 3.7% in 1987. However, in early 1988 Rowntree believed that the long-term brand building strategy was finally beginning to pay off, with Lion Bar the second-best selling chocolate bar in France and with more After Eights sold in West Germany than in the U.K. Between 1983 and 1987, Rowntree spent nearly £400 million on acquisitions (Exhibit 16). The acquired companies expanded the company's presence in some traditional businesses, and also provided new activities, particularly in the area of branded retailing of specialist confectionery products. The retail shops acquired by Rowntree were viewed not as outlets for Rowntree brands, but rather as acquisitions of brands in their own right. Because of these acquisitions, a significant stream of Rowntree's profits were being earned in North America. While Rowntree had hedged its foreign exchange risk exposure on the balance sheet, it took a long-term view with respect to foreign exchange risk exposure on the income statement. The resulting transactions exposure concerned some financial analysts.

By 1987 Rowntree's capital investments were beginning to pay off. Over the past five years, the number of U.K. personnel had been reduced from 19 700 to 15 600, and productivity improvements were running at 9% per annum. Trading margins had nearly recovered to the high level previously achieved in 1977, and Rowntree executives were confident that 1988 trading margins would continue to show improvement.

In a highly competitive U.S. market, Rowntree's snack food acquisitions were not generating trading margins consistent with other company activities (Exhibit 13). In January of 1988, Rowntree announced its intention to divest its major snack food businesses to concentrate on confectionery, retailing, and U.K. grocery activities where the potential to develop distinct consumer brands was considered more promising.

Although Rowntree's overall operating performance continued to improve, the company's common share price performance between 1986 and early 1988 was weaker than that achieved by the Financial Times "All Share" and Food Manufacturing Indexes on the London Stock Exchange (Exhibit 17). In early 1988, London's financial analysts published mixed opinions regarding Rowntree's immediate prospects (Exhibit 18). Mr. Nightingale, Rowntree's Company Secretary, recalled, "For years we have been trying to get the value of our brands reflected in our share prive, but without much success. As a consequence, there have always been takeover rumours."

Nestlé

The Nestlé Group grew from the 1905 merger of the Anglo-Swiss condensed Milk Co., a milk processing firm founded in 1866, and Henri Nestlé, a Swiss infant food company founded in 1867 in Vevey. In 1988 the Nestlé headquarters were still in Vevey, and the Group operated 383 factories in 59 countries. In 1988 Nestlé employed 163 000 people, 10 000 in the U.K.

Nestlé was the world's largest food company, and the world's largest producer of coffee, powdered milk, and frozen dinners. In 1987, drinks, dairy products, culinary products, frozen foods, and confectionery products accounted for 79% of Nestlé turnover of SF35.2 billion; other food products accounted for 18%, and non-food products 3%. Only 2% of the Group's turnover came from sales within Switzerland. The 20 companies acquired between 1983 and 1985 (at a total purchase price of $5 billion) added new brands of coffee, chocolates and fruit juice to Nestlé's lineup of strong world brands such as Nescafé, Stouffer's, Maggi, and Findus, In 1985 Nestlé increased its U.S. presence through the $2.9 billion purchase of Carnation and, in early April 1988, was finalizing the $1.3 billion purchase of Buitoni-Perugina.

This series of acquisitions had been spurred by Mr. Helmut Maucher, age 60, who joined Nestlé as an apprentice in 1948, and who was appointed Managing Director of Nestlé S.A. in 1981. Under Mr. Maucher's direction, Nestlé had cut costs and divested less profitable operations, including the $180 million Libby's U.S. canned food business.

Mr. Maucher explained Nestlés approach to acquisitions. "At Nestlé we are not portfolio managers. Acquisitions must fit into our corporate and marketing policy. In other words, they must strengthen our position in individual countries or product groups, or enable us to enter new fields where we have not so far been represented. Acquisitions are part of an overall development strategy. That's why we cannot leave acquisition decisions purely to financial considerations. Of course, you must have some figures to evaluate an acquisition, but more important is the feel you have about why you can do with the brands."

Mr. Maucher was a strong believer in the importance of a long-term outlook. On his appointment as Managing Director, he had banned monthly 25-page reports and quarterly profit and loss statements in favour of a monthly one-page report which highlighted key numbers such as turnover, working capital, and inventories. As Mr. Maucher explained, "With quarterly reports all managers care about is the next three months, and they manage for the next quarter instead of for the next five years." For this reason, Mr. Maucher was reluctant to list Nestlé's shares on any stock exchange which required the disclosure of quarterly reports.

Nestlé entered the chocolate market in 1929 with the purchase of Peter-Cailler-Kohler, a Swiss chocolate group originally founded in 1819. Since 1981, confectionery sales had represented approximately 8% of annual turnover, and in 1987 confectionery was Nestlé's fifth largest business. Nestlé's main product strength was in block chocolate, where it held 15% and 14% respectively of the European and American markets (Exhibit 4). Nestlé's leading brands included Milkybar in the U.S. and Crunch in the U.K. Recent research into the new generation of chocolate and confectionery products had produced "Yes," a pastry snack product, and "Sundy," a cereal bar.

As a result of Nestlé's market-oriented organization structure, Nestlé's block chocolate products were generally produced and positioned according to the tastes of local markets. For example, Nestlé's white block chocolate products, often produced in the same plants as coffee and other food products, were made from several recipes and marketed under several brand names. In the U.K., Nestlé's white chocolate brand, "Milkybar", was positioned as a children's chocolate, whereas in the U.S., it was called "Alpine White" and was oriented toward the "female indulgence" market. "Block chocolate is a traditional product with traditional tastes," Mr. Maucher explained. "A local market orientation is particularly important, because this kind of chocolate must taste the way you got it as a child from your grandmother, whether you are French or Italian or German, and so on. This is true for the traditional chocolate products, not so much for the new generation of products such as countlines."

During the 1970s, Nestlé's confectionery operations had been among the smaller and often relatively less profitable businesses in the company. However, Mr. Maucher saw opportunities in the confectionery business: "The key success factors in confectionery are technology, quality, creativity, and marketing skills, and Nestlé has all of those. If Nestlé cannot be successful at this business, then there is something wrong with Nestlé!".

NESTLÉ–ROWNTREE

In the early 1980s, Mr. Maucher made confectionery a strategic priority. Nestlé increased investment in research and development, and acquired two small U.S. confectionery companies. Nestlé then began to analyze the possibilities for significant expansion in the world confectionery market. "It will take 25 years to develop a major stake in this industry," Mr. Maucher said, "so we are looking at acquisitions to accelerate that development." According to Mr. Ramon Masip, Executive Vice President in charge of the European market, "For some time we have discussed making a 'big move' into the confectionery business, and Rowntree has always been the number one choice."

"We have always seen Rowntree as a 'perfect fit'," Mr. Masip continued, "because its strengths would complement Nestlé's." Rowntree's strong position in the growing countlines segment would complement Nestlé's strength in block chocolate. In addition, Rowntree's strong position in the non-grocery outlets such as CTNs would complement Nestlé's strong contacts with the multiple grocery retailers. Rowntree also held a stronger position in the U.K. and in some markets in continental Europe.

Although Nestlé was interested in Rowntree's recent success in launching new products such as the Lion bar. "We are much more concerned with the brands that Rowntree already has in the market!" Mr. Masip exclaimed. Rowntree's strong, well-established world brands were the key reason for Nestlé's interest. "There are very, very few companies in the world with their brands and with their skills in this particular business," Mr. Masip concluded.

Nestlé believed that, should the opportunity to acquire Rowntree arise, additional operating synergies could be achieved in research and development, administration, and the sales force. With the potential acquisition, it was estimated that substantial savings—perhaps 5–15% of Rowntree's fixed overhead expenses—could be realized from combining the two companies' operations.

November 1987

In November of 1987, Mr. Maucher and Mr. Masip met in Paris with Mr. Dixon and Mr. Masip's counterpart in Rowntree, Mr. Guerin. The proposal for this meeting had stemmed from quiet discussions between Messrs. Masip and Guerin regarding possible Nestlé-Rowntree cooperation in continental Europe. For over a year, Mr. Maucher had wanted to arrange a meeting with Mr. Dixon to discuss possible forms of cooperation between Nestlé and Rowntree. In fact, some of Mr. Maucher's external financial advisors had advised him to take a position in Rowntree stock, but Mr. Maucher had always replied, "That is not our policy. We do not do anything behind any company's back and, as I have told Mr. Dixon, we will not do anything that would be perceived as unfriendly to Rowntree."

The Paris meeting in November 1987 began with Mr. Dixon advising Mr. Maucher, "Nestlé does not appear to be interested in confectionery, and Rowntree is prepared to buy Nestlé's confectionery business on a worldwide basis." Mr. Maucher exclaimed, "We propose just the opposite!" The ensuing discussion explored possibilities for cooperation in production, marketing, distribution, or in various geographic markets, in order to optimize the situation for both companies. To facilitate development of long-term commitment and cooperation, Mr. Maucher suggested purchasing a 10–25% stake in Rowntree.

After a lengthy and amicable discussion, Mr. Dixon promised to examine Nestlé's suggestions and take them to the Rowntree Board for consideration. According to Mr. Dixon, Rowntree had already considered cooperation with several parties as a basis for market development, particularly in Europe, but "we felt at Rowntree that we could proceed on our own and would prefer to do so." After making this reply to Mr. Maucher in February 1988, he added, "Unfortunately, any sort of association with a company of your size can only have one ending, and at this time we don't feel we need to make that kind of commitment to anyone." Mr. Dixon, responding to Mr. Maucher's grave concerns regarding the persistent takeover rumours, admitted, "This does not mean that we do not recognize there is a risk."

April 13, 1988

At 8:30 on the morning of Wednesday, April 13, 1988, Rowntree was advised that there was significant activity in the trading of Rowntree shares. By 9:15 a.m., Jacobs Suchard held 14.9% of Rowntree plc. While the firm had made no contact with Rowntree, Suchard had begun acquiring Rowntree stock in mid-March, and by April 12th held just under 5% of Rowntree shares. At the start of trading on the London Stock Exchange on April 13th, Suchard's intermediary telephoned major institutional holders of Rowntree shares, offering a 30% premium on the opening share price of 477p[2] if they sold immediately. The shareholders did not know to whom they were selling their shares, but in less than 45 minutes Suchard increased its holding to 14.9%, the maximum allowable under the City Code[3] for such a transaction. When the news of Suchard's raid reached the markets, Rowntree's share price jumped to over 700p.

In what was later described as a "tactical error" by some City observers, on the morning of April 13th, S.G. Warburg issued the following press release on behalf on its client, Jacob Suchard:

> We have acquired a 14.9% investment stake in Rowntree. The stake is a strategic investment in that Rowntree is a company with a great potential based on its excellent global brands. We intend to acquire not more than 25%, at a maximum price of 630p. As you know, we are only permitted to take our holding to 15% today. We hope to buy the remaining 10%, but at no more than the price we are currently offering. This is not a prelude to a full bid and there is no intention of increasing the holding beyond this 25%-figure for at least a year although we reserve the right to do so if there is a full bid from a third party in the meantime.

Exercising its interpretive responsibility, the City Takeover Panel swiftly ruled that Warburg's statement prevented Suchard from purchasing any further Rowntree shares for the next 12 months, provided that the Rowntree share price stayed above 630p, unless a full bid for control came in from another party during that time period.

Reaction from the City of London Financial Community

After years of persistent rumours of a Rowntree takeover, Suchard's move ignited speculation on potential counter-bidders. Hershey was identified by City analysts as a leading candidate; purchasing Rowntree would make it second only to Mars in world confectionery. Other rumoured candidates included RJR Nabisco, Philip Morris, Unilever, and United Biscuits.

---

[2] 1£ = 100 pence (p)

[3] Refer to Exhibit 19 for a description of the City Code rules which regulated takeover activity in the U.K.

As external financial advisor to Rowntree, Mr. David Challen, a Director of J. Henry Schroder Wagg, was encouraged by the Takeover Panel's ruling. As he explained, "The ruling puts Jacobs in a box. Provided that Rowntree's share price stays above 630p, he cannot purchase additional shares for at least a year. This gives Rowntree the necessary time to prepare an effective takeover defence." Mr. Challen argued that it would be "madness" for another bidder to enter the battle now, as the new bidder would be restricted to accumulating shares (beyond 15%) at the price of its initial offer. However, the entry of another bidder would free Suchard to bid above this price to accumulate more shares. In the scenario predicted by Mr. Challen, Suchard would ultimately emerge with 30% of the shares and be poised to make an offer for the remaining shares. The second bidder would be restricted by the City Code to accumulating 15% of the shares and would always be behind Suchard in share accumulation terms. Thus the second bidder would face a "mega disadvantage" in gaining effective control. Mr. Challen concluded that the situation facing Rowntree was not urgent: "The real challenge for Rowntree is to keep the stock price above 630p so that Suchard cannot accumulate more shares."

Mr. Peter St. George, a Director of County Natwest (Nestlé's financial advisor), recalled discussions with Nestlé in the summer of 1987 regarding a possible takeover bid for Rowntree: "We were in a raging bull market then; paper, not cash, was king; and the takeover bid premium required to purchase Rowntree could not be justified on the fundamentals. Besides, any takeover attempt would have been viewed as hostile by Rowntree."

County NatWest had approached Nestlé in early 1988, advising a raid on Rowntree. "Since the October 1987 crash, the world had changed," Mr. St. George explained. "Share prices had fallen to reasonable levels where one could justify paying takeover premiums. The market no longer wanted paper; cash was king now, and Nestlé had cash. However, Mr. Maucher demurred, stating that hostile raids were not in Nestlé's style."

"Suchard's raid put Rowntree 'in play'", Mr. St. George concluded. "We contacted Nestlé as soon as we heard the news and encouraged them to make a counter bid for Rowntree. We advised them to act quickly and go into the market with a credible price to test (the fundraising capability of) Jacobs Suchard. We cautioned Nestlé, however, that a successful bid would require a substantial premium on the current Rowntree share price." (See Exhibit 19 for a description of the size of recent takeover bid premiums; Exhibit 20 contains financial market reference data.)

Rowntree's Reaction

The dawn raid came as a complete surprise to Rowntree, and reaction was swift. Mr. Dixon stated in a press release that morning:

Rowntree does not need Jacobs. We regard the acquisition of a stake by Jacobs as wholly unwelcome and believe that the price at which Jacobs acquired its shares is wholly inadequate for obtaining a major stake in the Group. Rowntree has one of the best portfolios of brand names of any confectionery company in the world, far better known than Jacobs' own. We do not believe that it is in the interests of Rowntree, its shareholders, or its employees that a Swiss company with nothing like the breadth of Rowntree's brands should have a shareholding in the Group. Jacobs may need Rowntree, but Rowntree does not need Jacobs.

Nestlé's Reaction

Suchard's dawn raid also came as a surprise to Nestlé. Mr. Maucher's first reaction was to contact Mr. Dixon; in his telephone phone call that morning Mr. Maucher said, "I am sorry that what I warned you about has happened. I repeat our offer to help." He urged Mr. Dixon to reconsider Nestlé's earlier proposal to acquire a stake in Rowntree.

Mr. Dixon thanked Mr. Maucher for his offer of help, but replied that he did not expect Suchard to make any further moves in the short term. "According to the Takeover Panel, Jacobs cannot move for 12 months," he told Mr. Maucher, "and while I know that Suchard will try to become more involved with Rowntree, we have no intention of having any form of cooperation with Suchard. We fully intend to remain independent. It is our hope and belief that the situation will calm down and that nothing more will come of it." However, Mr. Dixon promised that he and his Board would nonetheless consider Mr. Maucher's proposal.

Mr. Maucher concluded the discussion by saying, "Our offer stands, and I hope you will reconsider and keep in touch. However, I fear that because of Suchard's move your independence is now an illusion. I must now feel free to act in Nestlé best interests."

Average Currency Equivalents, 1983–88

SF = Swiss Franc; $ = U.S. Dollar ; £ = British Pound

	1 Swiss Franc equals		*1 British Pound equals*		*1 U.S. Dollar equals*	
1983	$0.48	£0.31	SF 3.23	$1.55	SF2.08	£0.65
1984	0.43	0.32	3.13	1.34	2.33	0.75
1985	0.41	0.32	3.13	1.28	2.44	0.78
1986	0.56	0.38	2.63	1.47	1.79	0.68
1987	0.67	0.41	2.44	1.63	1.49	0.61
1988*	0.71	0.39	2.57	1.83	1.41	0.55

* As of April 1, 1988.

SOURCE: Schweizerische Nationalbank.

EXHIBIT 1 Major Chocolate Confectionery Markets Consumption and Expenditure Per Capita, 1987

	*Chocolate Consumption (000 tonnes)**	*Chocolate Expenditure (US$ million)*	*Population Mid-1987 (millions)*	*Consumption Per Capita (kg / annum)*	*Expenditure Per Capita ($ / annum)*
U.S.	1 189	5 202	243.8	4.9	21
U.K.	455	3 480	56.9	8.0	61
W.Germany	409	3 387	61.2	6.7	55
France	233	2 750	55.6	4.2	49
Japan	157	1 867	122.1	1.3	15
Canada	101	464	25.9	3.9	18
Italy	106	1 813	57.4	1.8	32
Australia	80	576	16.2	4.9	36
Total	2 730	19 539	639.1	4.3	31

* One metric tonne = 1000 kilogrammes

SOURCE: *United Nations Industrial Statistics Yearbook*; World Bank; National Trade Associations; Trade Estimates.

EXHIBIT 2 Actual and Forecasted Chocolate Consumption in Major Markets

	Consumption (000 tonnes)			Compound Average Annual Growth Rate (%)	
	1982 Actual	*1987 Actual*	*1992 Forecast*	*1982-87*	*1987-92*
U.S.	1 003	1 189	1 364	3.5%	2.8%
U.K.	411	455	469	2.0	0.6
W. Germany	401	409	412	0.4	0.1
France	192	233	251	3.9	1.5
Japan	148	157	166	1.2	1.1
Italy	83	106	127	5.0	3.7
Canada	99	101	106	0.4	1.0
Australia	63	80	95	4.9	3.5
Above 8 Markets	2 400	2 730	2 990	2.6	1.8
Rest of World	1 495	1 740	1 990	3.1	2.7
Total	3 895	4 470	4 980	2.8%	2.2%

SOURCE: Joint International Statistics Committee of IOCCC; *Euromonitor; United Nations Industrial Statistics Yearbook*; IMEDE.

EXHIBIT 3 Chocolate Product Portfolios of Major Confectionery Companies, 1987

	Mars	*Hershey*	*Cadbury*	*Rowntree*	*Suchard*	*Nestlé*	*Others*
Tonnes (000)	800	400	320	300	220	190	2240
World Market Share	18%	9%	7%	7%	5%	4%	50%
Companies' Turnover by Product Type:*							
Block	1%	46%	46%	11%	81%	73%	29%
Countline	99	54	36	55	8	17	32
Boxed	—	—	18	34	11	10	39
Total	100%	100%	100%	100%	100%	100%	100%

* For example, countline sales represented 99% of Mars' total chocolate confectionery turnover in 1987; block chocolate sales represented 1% of Mars' total chocolate turnover.

SOURCES: International Chocolate Workshop, Vevey, 1988; Trade Estimates; IMEDE.

EXHIBIT 4 Market Shares of Major Competitors by Product Type and Region, 1987

	Total Market*	Percentage Market Shares						
		Mars	Hershey	Cadbury	Rowntree	Suchard	Nestlé	Others
North America:								
Block	280	—	62%	16%	2%	3%	14%	3%
Countline	898	53%	23	5	2	—	1	16
Boxed	112	—	—	11	17	1	5	66
Total	1 290	53%	29%	8%	2%	—	4%	18%
EEC:								
Block	541	1%	—	9%	4%	23%	14%	49%
Countline	611	49	—	8	19	2	1	21
Boxed	437	—	—	7	14	4	2	73
Total	1 589	19%	—	8%	12%	10%	6%	45%
Rest of World:								
Block	521	—	2%	10%	1%	9%	4%	74%
Countline	544	4%	1	4	6	1	3	80
Boxed	526	—	—	3	4	1	1	91
Total	1 591	1%	1%	6%	4%	4%	3%	81%
World:								
Block	1 342	1%	14%	11%	2%	13%	10%	49%
Countline	2 053	39	10	6	8	1	2	34
Boxed	1 075	—	—	6	9	2	2	81
Total	4 470	18%	9%	7%	7%	5%	4%	50%

* In tonnes (000).

SOURCES: International Chocolate Workshop, *Vevey*, 1988; Trade Estimates; IMEDE.

EXHIBIT 5 European Chocolate Market Shares by Major Competitor, 1988

	Mars	*Suchard*	*Rowntree*	*Ferrero*	*Cadbury*	*Nestlé*	*Others*
U.K.	24%	2%	26%	2%	30%	3%	13%
Austria	4	73	—	—	—	5	18
Belgium	6	82	2	5	—	3	2
France	11	13	17	6	8	10	35
Italy	1	—	—	4	—	5	60
Netherlands	23	—	13	—	—	—	64
Switzerland	9	17	—	—	—	17	57
W. Germany	22	15	3	6	—	8	36
Total	17%	13%	11%	10%	8%	9%	32%

SOURCE: Henderson Crossthwaite.

EXHIBIT 6 Percentage Breakdown of Total Turnover by Region for Major Confectionery Competitors, 1987

	Nestlé	*Rowntree*	*Jacobs Suchard*	*Cadbury Schweppes*	*Hershey*
Europe	43%	61%[1]	83%[2]	63%[3]	
N. America	29	29	17	18	> 90%
Asia	13				
Oceana	2	4		19	<10
Others	3	6	1		
Total	100%	100%	101%[4]	100%	100%

[1] U.K. and Ireland = 40% of total turnover.

[2] West Germany and France = 58% of total turnover.

[3] U.K. = 47% of total turnover.

[4] Does not add up to 100% due to rounding errors.

SOURCE: Company accounts.

EXHIBIT 7 Operating Financial Performance of Major Competitors, 1983–87

	Confectionery Turnover as % of Total Turnover[1]	Total Trading Profit[2] as % of Total Turnover	Total Trading Profit[2] as % of Average[3] Assets	Net Income as % of Average[3] Shareholders' Equity
	1987	*Average 1983–87*		
Hershey Foods	76%	14.7%	15.8%	17.2%
Cadbury-Schweppes	43	7.5	20.5	17.1
Rowntree	76	8.3	25.5	16.8
Jacobs Suchard	57	5.9	12.3	16.3
Nestlé	8	10.2	14.3	13.1

Note: As a measure of relative risk, the 'beta' values for the common stocks of publicly-traded confectionery companies generally clustered around a value of 1.0.

[1] Turnover = Net sales.

[2] Trading profit = Operating profit before interest and taxes.

[3] Average of beginning and end of year.

SOURCE: Company accounts.

EXHIBIT 8 Hershey Foods Corp.—Selected Financial Data, 1984–87

A. Financial Statement Data ($ millions)		*1984*	*1985*	*1986*	*1987*
1	Turnover (Sales)	1 848.5	1 996.2	2 169.6	2 433.8
2	Gross Profit	578.7	640.4	716.2	821.7
3	Trading Profit	222.8	244.8	270.6	294.1
4	Net Income	108.7	120.7	132.8	148.2
5	Depreciation	45.2	52.4	59.0	70.6
6	Liquid Assets	87.9	110.6	27.6	15.0
7	Current Assets	385.3	412.3	393.4	484.9
8	Fixed Assets	727.3	785.1	962.9	1 160.3
9	Total Assets	1 122.6	1 197.4	1 356.3	1 645.2
10	Current Liabilities	203.0	195.3	222.2	299.8
11	Long-term Liabilities	258.7	274.2	406.2	513.0
12	Stockholders' Equity	660.9	727.9	727.9	832.4
B. Per Share Data ($)					
13	Earnings	1.16	1.19	1.42	1.64
14	Dividends	0.41	0.48	0.52	0.58
15	Stock Price (Average)	11.60	15.00	22.80	29.30
16	Price-Earnings (Average)	10.00	9.70	16.10	17.90
17	Equity Book Value	7.00	7.70	8.10	9.20

SOURCE: Company accounts.

EXHIBIT 9 Cadbury Schweppes PLC—Selected Financial Data, 1984–87

A. Financial Statement Data (£ millions)		1984	1985	1986	1987
1	Turnover (Sales)	2 016.2	1 873.8	1 839.9	2 031.0
2	Gross Profit	746.8	683.0	739.9	853.8
3	Trading Profit	154.4	113.0	140.4	180.6
4a	Net Income[1]	72.5	47.8	76.1	112.1
4b	Net Income[2]	65.1	41.9	102.0	110.7
5	Depreciation	55.9	54.7	60.4	63.3
6	Liquid Assets	36.6	47.1	177.4	139.9
7	Current Assets	710.7	618.9	723.4	795.5
8	Fixed Assets	627.5	594.0	555.4	603.5
9	Total Assets	1 338.2	1 212.9	1 278.8	1 399.0
10	Current Liabilities	531.2	479.3	536.7	688.7
11	Long-term Liabilities	288.3	262.6	278.9	233.6
12	Share Capital & Reserves	518.7	417.0	463.2	476.7

B. Per Share Data (pence)					
13	Earnings[1]	15.7	9.3	14.3	19.1
14	Dividends	5.9	5.9	6.7	8.0
15	Stock Price (Average)	137.0	153.0	170.0	238.0
16	Price-Earnings1 (Average)	8.7	16.5	11.9	12.5
	Equity Book Value	112.0	92.0	87.0	83.0
18	Employees (000)	35.5	33.8	27.7	27.5

[1] Earnings before Extraordinary Items.
[2] Earnings after Extraordinary Items.

SOURCE: Company accounts.

EXHIBIT 10 Jacobs Suchard Group—Selected Financial Data, 1984–87

A. Financial Statement Data (SF millions)		1984	1985	1986	1987
1	Turnover (Sales)	5 111	5 382	5 236	6 104
2	Gross Profit	1 104	1 156	1 304	1 955
3	Trading Profit	244	265	338	471
4	Net Income	120	150	191	265
5	Depreciation	84	092	103	128
6	Liquid Assets	230	788	1470	705
7	Current Assets	1 390	2 008	2 920	2 206
8	Fixed Assets	666	674	832	886
9	Total Assets	2 056	2 682	3 752	3 092
10	Current Liabilities	796	843	1 417	1 120
11	Long-term Liabilities	483	487	885	829
12	Shareholders' Equity	777	1 352	1 450	1 143*

B. Per Share Data (SF per bearer share)					
13	Earnings	351.0	353.0	414.0	19.1
14	Dividends	150.0	155.0	160.0	8.0
15	Stock Price (Average)	5 028.0	6 101.0	7 324.0	238.0
16	Price-Earnings (Average)	14.3	17.3	17.7	12.5
18	Employees (000)	10.6	9.3	10.0	27.5

* It is normal accounting practice for Swiss companies to write off "goodwill" when acquiring businesses. Nestlé wrote off SF3.2 million of shareholders' equity on its purchase of Carnation in 1985. Jacobs Suchard reduced equity by SF1.1 million in 1987 due to depreciation of goodwill.

SOURCE: Company accounts.

EXHIBIT 11   Nestlé S.A.—Selected Financial Data, 1984–87

A. Financial Statement Data (SF millions)		1984	1985	1986	1987
1	Turnover (Sales)	31 141	42 225	38 050	35 241
2	Gross Profit	11 301	14 926	13 603	13 616
3	Trading Profit	3 206	4 315	3 671	3 651
4	Net Income	1 487	1 750	1 789	1 827
5	Depreciation	1 004	1 331	1 157	1 184
6	Liquid Assets	6 168	3 853	5 619	6 961
7	Current Assets	16 407	15 236	15 820	16 241
8	Fixed Assets	8 067	9 952	9 275	8 902
9	Total Assets	24 474	25 188	25 095	25 143
10	Current Liabilities	7 651	8 858	8 119	7 547
11	Long-term Liabilities	3 834	5 092	4 775	4 939
12	Shareholders' Equity	12 989	11 238*	12 201	12 657

B. Per Share Data (SF per bearer share)					
13	Earnings	480.0	515.0	526.0	537.0
14	Dividends	136.0	145.0	145.0	150.0
15	Stock Price (Average)	5 062.0	7 400.0	8 600.0	9 325.0
16	Price-Earnings (Average)	10.5	14.4	16.4	17.4
18	Employees (000)	138.0	154.8	162.1	163.0

* It is normal accounting practice for Swiss companies to write off "goodwill" when acquiring businesses. Nestlé wrote off SF3.2 million of shareholders' equity on its purchase of Carnation in 1985. Jacobs Suchard reduced equity by SF1.1 million in 1987 due to depreciation of goodwill.

SOURCE: Company accounts.

Exhibit 12   Rowntree PLC—Selected Financial Data, 1983–87

A. Income Statement Data (£ millions)		1983	1984	1985	1986	1987
1	Turnover (Sales)	951.9	1 156.5	1 205.2	1 290.4	1 427.6
1a	Cost Of Sales	617.9	739.0	759.4	790.2	837.1
2	Gross Profit (1-1a)	334.0	417.5	445.8	500.2	590.5
2a	Fixed Overhead Expenses	265.6	328.3	350	400.5	465.8
2b	Other Operating Income	4.2	4.6	6.0	6.0	5.4
3	Trading Profit (2-2a+2b)	72.6	93.8	101.3	105.7	130.1
3a	Interest	12.2	19.3	22.0	21.7	18.0
4a	Profit After Tax	46.3	58.0	60.7	66.2	87.9
4b	Extraordinary Items	13.5	11.5	16.5	11.3	0.0
4c	Net Profit After Tax	32.8	46.5	44.2	54.9	87.9
5	Depreciation (£m)	28.6	36.2	39.1	43.7	51.0

B. Balance Sheet Data (£ millions)						
6	Liquid Assets	25.1	55.7	41.8	69.2	96.7
6a	Debtors (Receivables)	145.9	171.1	178.7	208.5	214.9
6b	Stocks (Inventories)	159.1	172.9	170.2	176.9	163.2
7	Current Assets	330.1	399.7	390.7	454.6	475.1
8	Fixed Assets	359.7	408.5	403.1	475.1	463.2
9	Total Assets	689.8	808.2	793.8	929.7	938.3
10	Current Liabilities	217.8	229.3	242.4	310.2	270.1
11	Long-term Liabilities	123.0	186.3	177.0	228.1	259.6
12a	Preferred Stock	2.7	2.7	2.7	2.7	2.7
12b	Share Capital & Reserves	346.3	389.9	371.7	388.7	405.9

C. Per Share Data (pence)						
13	Earnings*	31.0	36.0	34.8	35.0	40.8
14	Dividends	9.8	11.0	12.2	13.6	15.5
15a	Common Stock Price (High)	258.0	392.0	450.0	545.0	590.0
15b	Common Stock Price (Low)	200.0	212.0	337.0	363.0	367.0
16	Average Price-Earnings*	7.4	8.4	11.3	13.0	11.7
17	Equity Book Value (12b/19)	233.0	243.0	214.0	206.0	189.0

D. Other Data						
18a	Employees, U.K. (000)	19.7	18.9	17.7	16.4	15.6
18b	Employees, World (000)	31.2	32.4	32.0	32.5	33.1
19	Ordinary Shares (000'000)	149.5	160.6	173.9	188.7	215.0
20	Cash Flow (4a + 5)	74.9	94.2	99.8	109.9	138.9
21	Capital Expenditures (£m)	59.9	59.9	71.5	76.2	82.5
22	Business Acquisitions (£m)	159.6	3.3	34.2	189.9	14.2
23	Asset Divestitures (£m)	4.0	3.1	4.5	4.2	5.2

* Earnings based on line 4a (net profit after tax but before extra-ordinatry items) minus preferred dividends. Average of high and low stock prices.

SOURCE: Company accounts.

EXHIBIT 13 Rowntree PLC—Breakdown by Activity, 1987 (£ million)

Activity	Turnover	% of Total Turnover	Trading Profit	% of Total Trading Profit	Trading Margin
Confectionery	1 088.5	76.2%	101.0	77.6%	9.3%
Snack Foods	191.8	13.4	14.5	11.1	7.6
Retailing	97.3	6.8	8.1	6.2	8.3
Grocery (U.K.)	50.0	3.5	6.5	5.0	13.0
Total	1 427.6	100.0%	130.1	100.0%	9.1%

SOURCE: Company accounts.

EXHIBIT 14 Rowntree PLC—Breakdown by Region, 1987

Activity	Turnover	% of Total Turnover	Trading Profit	% of Total Trading Profit	Trading Margin
U.K. & Ireland	566.4	40%	61.7	47%	10.9%
Cont'l Europe	300.4	21	11.0	8	3.7
North America	416.1	29	41.0	31	9.8
Australasia	57.1	4	4.7	4	8.2
Rest of World	87.6	6	11.7	9	13.4
Total	1 427.6	100%	130.1	100%	9.1%

SOURCE: Company accounts.

EXHIBIT 15 Rowntree PLC—Operating and Financial Performance, 1976–81 (£ millions)

	1976	1977	1978	1979	1980	1981
Turnover	340.90	469.20	562.70	601.30	629.80	688.00
Trading Profit	36.80	46.90	51.70	46.60	44.80	48.00
Net Profit[1]	16.90	30.40	34.40	27.20	17.50	29.10
Average[2]	194.90	246.80	332.50	396.60	412.50	448.60
Average Owner's[2] Equity	77.30	120.60	182.30	218.40	231.80	278.90
Trading Margin %	9.60	10.00	9.20	7.80	7.10	7.20
Trading Profit/Assets %	18.90	19.00	15.60	11.80	10.90	10.70
Turnover/Assets	1.83	1.66	1.47	1.46	1.52	1.38
Net Profit/Equity %	21.80	25.20	18.90	12.50	7.60	10.30

[1] Net after-tax profit attributable to ordinary common shares.
[2] Average of beginning and end of year.

SOURCE: Company accounts.

EXHIBIT 16 Rowntree PLC—Major Business Acquisitions, 1983–87

Company	Location	Primary Area of Business Activity	Year of Purchase	Purchase Price (£m)
Tom's Foods	U.S.	Snack foods	1983	£138
Laura Secord	Canada	Branded retailing	1983	19
Original Cookie Co.	U.S.	Branded retailing	1985	32
Hot Sam	U.S.	Branded retailing	1986	14
Sunmark	U.S.	Branded confectionery	1986	154
Gales	U.S.	Honey products	1986	1
Smaller Acquisitions	U.S., U.K., France, Australia	Snack foods, Confectionery, Branded retailing	1983-87	29
				£399

SOURCE: Company Accounts.

EXHIBIT 17 Rowntree PLC—Share Price Performance, 1980–87
Rowntree Share Price Performance compared to the *Financial Times'* Market and Food Manufacturer's Price Indexes on the London Stock Exchange (01/01/80 to 31/21/87, weekly).

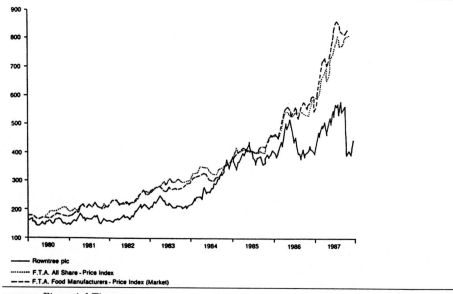

——— Rowntree plc
·········· F.T.A. All Share - Price Index
— — — F.T.A. Food Manufacturers - Price Index (Market)

SOURCE: *Financial Times.*

EXHIBIT 18 Stockbroker's Comments on Rowntree

Name of Broker	Date of Report	Forecast of 1988	Summary of Major Comments and Recommendations
County Natwest	01/21/88	125	Sell — Dollar weakness limits prospects for 1988.
BZW	01/25/88	127	Decision to sell snack food business correct but unable to give final verdict until consideration is known.
County Natwest	01/26/88	125	Surprise disposals, but good move.
BZW	02/24/88	127	Buy — Current rating of shares is not expensive with absence of bid premium.
Warburg Securities	03/17/88	128	Hold — Core business performed well but reversal in snacks and slowdown in retailing leaves strategy looking threadbare.
Hoare Govett	03/17/88	127	Over-valued in short term. Longer term outlook remaining clouded by current divestment/acquisition plans.
BZW	03/17/88	129	Hold — Lower consideration for disposals than expected would lead to downgrading of forecast. Share price will be susceptible to strengthening of sterling.
County Natwest	03/18/88	125	Good results. Disposal of snack business an excellent move.
Kleinwart Grievson	03/18/88	129	Hold — Fully valued.

SOURCE: Stock brokerage reports.

EXHIBIT 19 The City Code and the U.K. Takeover Climate

Takeover bids for public companies in the U.K. were conducted according to a complex set of formal rules contained in the City Code on Takeovers and Mergers. The City Code was designed to ensure fair and similar treatment for all shareholders of the same class, mainly through responsible, detailed disclosure and the absence of stock price manipulation. The City Code was administered by the Takeover Panel, a self-regulatory body whose members included Bank of England appointees and representatives of participants in the U.K. securities markets. The Panel was authorized to make rulings and interpretations on novel points arising during the course of a takeover attempt.

The City Code identified consequences associated with the acquisition of certain benchmark percentages of the equity of a takeover target. For example, within 5 days of acquiring 5% of more of the capital of a company, the purchaser was required to inform the target company of its interest; the target company was then required to make an immediate announcement of this fact to the London Stock Exchange.

A purchaser could not acquire 10% or more of the capital of the target within any period of 7 days if these purchases would bring its total interest above 15% of the voting rights in the target company. Between 15% and 30% interest, the purchaser could accumulate shares by tender offer or by a series of share purchases; however, each series of share purchases could not result in the acquisition of more than 10% of the total equity of the target during any 7-day period. Once acquiring an interest totalling 30%, the bidder was obliged to make a general offer for the remaining 70% of the voting capital (at the highest price previously paid by the bidder). After a bidder had obtained 90% ownership of a class of shares, it could compulsorily acquire the outstanding shares from the minority shareholders; similarly, any remaining minority shareholders could require the bidder to purchase their shares at the highest price previously paid by the bidder.

Proposed acquisitions could also be reviewed by the Office of Fair Trading (OFT), a sub-section of the Department of Trade and Industry. The OFT had responsibility for deciding whether the competitive implications of the merger warranted investigation. The OFT could refer merger cases to the Mergers and Monopolies Commission (MMC), an independent tribunal which ruled on whether the merger should be blocked in the interests of national competition policy. Referral to the MMC was often prized by managements of takeover targets. Aside from allowing the possibility of a referral decision favouring the target, the referral process gave the takeover target additional time (3–7 months) to mount a more effective takeover defence.

Takeovers of U.K. public companies were either recommended by the Board of the target company or contested. Action by the Board of a target to frustrate an offer for the target company or contested. Action by the Board of a target to frustrate an offer for the target company was prohibited without the approval, in a General Meeting, of the shareholders. Recommended offers in the U.K. were generally restricted to smaller companies; they were relatively rare for companies with market capitalization in excess of £200 million.

Between 1985 and 1987, takeover bids were initiated for 14 large U.K. companies, each with individual market capitalizations in excess of £1 billion. Only one of these bids was recommended; the rest were contested. Ultimately, 4 of these bids were successful while 10 failed. For the three successful cash bids, the average share price premium1 paid was 60%; the individual premiums paid ranged from 40% to 80%.*

More recent acquisition activity in France and the U.K. provided reference points for the value of brand names. During 1987 and 1988, Seagram (a Canadian drinks group) and Grand Metropolitan (a U.K. drinks and hotel group) waged a fierce takeover battle to acquire Martell (the second largest French cognac house). In February 1988, Seagrams emerged the victor, but only after bidding an estimated 40x the 1987 earnings of Martell. In March 1988, United Biscuits paid a price-earnings multiple of 25x to purchase the frozen and chilled foods division of Hanson Trust. At that time, the average price-earnings ratio for 5 comparable U.K. food companies was 11.9x.

---

* Share price premiums were calculated by comparing final bid offer prices against the share prices of the target companies two months prior to the date of the final offer.

EXHIBIT 20 Selected Financial Market Rates, 1984–87

	1984	1985	1986	1987	1988 (1st Quart. Annualized)
Inflation*(%):					
Switzerland	3.0	1.0	0.8	1.4	3.5
U.K.	5.0	6.0	3.4	4.3	1.8
U.S.	4.3	3.5	2.0	3.6	2.6
Long-Term Government Bond Yield (%):					
Switzerland	4.7	4.8	4.3	4.1	4.1
U.K.	10.7	10.6	9.9	9.5	9.4
U.S.	12.5	10.6	7.7	8.4	8.4

* Based on the Consumer Price Index.

SOURCE: International Monetary Fund.